Decline and Fall of Hollywood

BY EZRA GOODMAN

ALL RIGHTS RESERVED, INCLUDING THE RIGHT OF REPRODUCTION IN WHOLE OR IN
PART IN ANY FORM. COPYRIGHT © 1961 BY EZRA GOODMAN. PUBLISHED BY SIMON
AND SCHUSTER, INC. ROCKEFELLER CENTER, 630 FIFTH AVENUE, NEW YORK 20, N.Y.

FIRST PRINTING
LIBRARY OF CONGRESS CATALOG CARD NUMBER: 61-5833
MANUFACTURED IN THE UNITED STATES OF AMERICA BY GEORGE MCKIBBIN & SONS,
NEW YORK, N.Y.

ACKNOWLEDGMENTS

The author wishes to thank the following persons, newspapers and corporations for granting permission to quote material included in the text of this book:

Jimmy McHugh, Harold Adamson and Diana Music, Inc., for use of the lyrics from the song "Louella," © 1957 by Diana Music, Inc.

Abe Burrows and Frank Music Corp. for use of the song title "The Girl with the Three Blue Eyes," © 1945 by Frank Music Corp.

Dore Schary and *Daily Variety* for use of the poem "The Trades" from the 22nd anniversary issue of *Daily Variety*, 1955.

Robert Strauss and *Daily Variety* for use of the poem "Thanks" from the March 8, 1954, issue of *Daily Variety*.

In addition the author wishes to note the following books from which he has quoted brief excerpts or drawn information:

The Gay Illiterate, by Louella Parsons. Doubleday & Co., Inc., New York, © 1944.
From Under My Hat, by Hedda Hopper. Doubleday & Co., Inc., New York, © 1952.
Seen Any Good Movies Lately?, by William K. Zinsser. Doubleday & Co., Inc., New York, © 1958.
Habit, by Darryl Francis Zanuck. Times-Mirror Press, Los Angeles, © 1923.
A Tree Is a Tree, by King Vidor. Harcourt, Brace & Co., New York, © 1952, 1953.
The Fervent Years, by Harold Clurman. Alfred A. Knopf, New York, © 1945.
The Film Till Now, by Paul Rotha. Funk & Wagnalls Co., New York, © 1949.
Not So Long Ago, by Lloyd Morris. Random House, New York, © 1949.
Prater Violet, by Christopher Isherwood. Random House, New York, © 1945.
Hollywood Saga, by William C. deMille. E. P. Dutton & Co., Inc., New York, © 1939.
A History of the Movies, by Benjamin B. Hampton. Covici-Friede, New York, © 1931.
Theory of the Film, by Béla Balázs. Roy Publishers, New York, © 1953.
The Diary and Sundry Observations of Thomas Alva Edison, edited by Dagobert D. Runes. Philosophical Library, New York, © 1948.
Selected Writings of Dylan Thomas. New Directions, New York, © 1946.
Selected Poems, by W. H. Auden. Faber and Faber, London, © 1938.
Poems 1936-43, by C. Day Lewis. Oxford University Press, New York, © 1945.

CONTENTS

	Foreword	ix
I	Flashback	1
II	Tom Swift and His Flying Typewriter	16
III	Dreams of a Rarebit Fiend	100
IV	Through a Ground Glass, Darkly	121
V	The Great Brain Robbery	160
VI	The Girl with the Three Blue Eyes	217
VII	In the Order of Their Appearance	243
VIII	The Little People	297
IX	The Snows of Yesteryear	335
X	The Night Life of the Gods	375
XI	Fade-out	414
	Index	453

"... It's not a business. It's a racket! ..."

HARRY COHN

FOREWORD

What—another book about the movies? Why?

On my bookshelves are well over a thousand books about the movies, ranging from the zoetrope to Zanuck, from the camera obscura to the obscure camera—an odd hobby, particularly in Hollywood, where books are collected by the interior-decorating yard rather than by the intellectual yardstick. Most of these books are as flat as their titles—*Filmland in Ferment, The Truth about the Movies, Romance of the Talkies, Let's Go to the Pictures*. Occasionally, at least, I can recall a spry title, like the unpublished *Peasants in Ermine*, by the late Douglas Churchill, Hollywood correspondent of the New York Times; and *The Story of Cuddles—My Life under the Emperor Francis Joseph, Adolf Hitler and the Warner Brothers*, by S. Z. Sakall.

Very few books about the movies are either readable or reliable and hardly any are both. Most of them have been inadequately researched and are the result of second- and third-hand reporting. There are too few books like Terry Ramsaye's *A Million and One Nights*, with its solid, grass-roots reporting, and the more modest but authoritative and sprucely written *Hollywood Saga* by William C. deMille.

One theory recently put forth has it that what often passes for news and fact is really pretty much hearsay and gossip. If so, then there is a good deal of "news" coming out of Hollywood. Personally, I prefer the clearly labeled fictional variety, such as the gilt-edged thrillers of Raymond Chandler, with their Los Angeles settings, which are more accurate in a make-believe way. Too many volumes about the movies are composed by dilettantes, weak-wrist aficionados, ghostwriters and assorted rewrite men. Perhaps the people in the movie business who are in a position to know are too busy to write or find it impolitic to note down what they know. As even that old publicity hound Samuel Goldwyn once told me: "I'm never going to write my autobiography as long as I live."

This volume—largely as its reason for being—is a reporter's book. These notes are based on twenty or so years as a publicist, free-lance writer, columnist, correspondent and critic on the western front. This book was written on the journalistic firing line, so to speak. There is little here about abstract theory or the rehashed history of the movies. I have limited myself to matters I experienced at first hand. A good deal of this material never saw print, sometimes as the result of editorial restrictions or suppressions, sometimes because it might have been imprudent or actually even dangerous to have aired it at the time. In the following pages there are no willful restrictions or suppressions. I hope that these notes have some value if only because of their reportorial validity.

Today, in the television ice age, the motion picture has already taken on an archaeological tinge. It was only in 1872 that a bearded codger with the flavorful name of Eadweard Muybridge helped put motion into motion pictures with crude "movies," shot at Palo Alto, California, of horses trotting. From there the movies ultimately went east and later west again, to Southern California. In the process the awkward but vigorous horse in motion of Muybridge became a fat, spavined old Metro-Goldwyn-Mare. The great art of light and shadow that had its origin in the primitive magic lantern was clouded over and lost much of its magic. The bright dream faded.

The pioneers of the screen stumbled on a vivid new world of make-believe to which many millions were instinctively drawn. But this artistic bonanza was systematically debased and devaluated by a lot of shoddy merchants. These shysters of the silver screen accomplished the far from negligible feat of killing off the goose that laid the golden egg. They had a good thing all to themselves but managed to run it into the ground anyway. Then television came along to help derail Hollywood's gravy train and give the movie monopolists competition to which they were unaccustomed. The movies countered with larger screens and aspect ratios; during this technical upheaval a reporter in Hollywood was likely to feel that he should be equipped with a slide rule instead of a typewriter. Movies got wider and bigger and, in most cases, lousier. They laid on more production dollars but less artistic sense. And so television inexorably marched on.

In these pages I have tried, within the bounds of fairness and fact, to name names wherever possible. Any resemblance between these paragraphs and actual personalities and events is calculated.

E. G.

CHAPTER I

Flashback

THE FATHER of the American film sat in an easy chair in a hotel room in the heart of Hollywood guzzling gin out of a water glass and periodically grabbing at the blonde sitting on the sofa opposite him. It was David Wark Griffith, the maker of *The Birth of a Nation, Intolerance, Broken Blossoms,* and *Way Down East,* not only the father of the American film but the stepfather of the Russian film and of countless other films as well. Had not the great directors all over the world borrowed from him the luminous close-ups, the incandescent images, the dynamic editing, the very syntax of the screen? It was Griffith, all right, his lordly, arrogant, aquiline features surmounted by sparse white hair, attired in pajamas and a patterned maroon dressing gown, and, at the age of seventy-two, sitting alone, drunk and almost forgotten in a hotel room in the town he had been instrumental in putting on the map.

Standing about the room were several trunks. On one of them reposed Griffith's floppy felt hat; against it leaned his cane. In the kitchen were two large cans of film containing a rare, good print of the twelve reels of *Orphans of the Storm,* his successful silent film of the French revolution, made in 1922 with Lillian and Dorothy Gish and Joseph Schildkraut.

This was 1947. Griffith's last picture, made in 1931, was *The Struggle,* a groping, moving, violently realistic film about the evils of liquor in a slum setting that made *The Lost Weekend* look like cinematic near-beer. I saw the movie recently and it stands up very well; it would do credit to the reputations of some highly touted directors today. In spite of its occasional hamminess and bad sentiment, it possesses the virtue of brilliant realism in its settings, dress and incidental detail. A slum in *The Struggle* looks like a slum and not like a slum designed by

Cedric Gibbons. And, most important of all, the picture has compassion for its characters. It has a love of life, not a love of the box office.

Art and life are supposed to progress all the time. Very often they do not. Hollywood, in particular, has not. Movies today have a glossier finish and a bigger bag of technical tricks, but the mirror they hold up to the world is not necessarily a brighter one. Even technically a picture like *The Struggle* has some of the finest realistic photography ever seen on celluloid, and its cameraman, Joseph Ruttenberg, who later won an Academy Award for lensing *Mrs. Miniver*, has not improved on that accomplishment.

The Struggle, however, received poor critical notices and Griffith had not worked in the movies since then. Hollywood is a place where reputations fade fast. A man can have one box-office flop and be out of business—if he has individuality and integrity. And a man can make all kinds of flat, fraudulent, unprofitable films, artistically and economically, and continue to muddle along in Hollywood as long as he makes obeisance to the proper idols.

The roster of film famous who have exited from the Hollywood limelight is a long one. There was, for instance, Gregory La Cava, the febrile director of *My Man Godfrey* and *Stage Door*, who before his death in 1952 was sitting on the beach at Malibu shooting at sea gulls with a BB gun with only director George Stevens and a few other close friends bothering to visit him. E. A. Dupont, director of the classic silent film *Variety*, was, until he died in 1956, an agent in Hollywood, peddling the talents of less talented men than himself because he could not get a job directing at any of the studios. The directorial titans of the Thirties in Hollywood—Frank Capra, Leo McCarey and the late Preston Sturges—worked only sporadically in the last decade. Their talents were too rich and individualistic for the studio assembly lines.

Writing of Griffith's "alleged decline," Peter John Dyer commented in *Sight and Sound* under the heading "The Decline of a Mandarin": "Did he decline? Well of course . . . in certain respects. No director can be expected to go on creating monuments to mankind as patently sincere and exhausting as *The Birth of a Nation* and *Intolerance*." Dyer attributed Griffith's fall less to "artistic decline" than to his "megalomania" and "loss of influence"—he was overtaken by younger talent like Erich von Stroheim and Henry King. Dyer pointed out that *Broken Blossoms*, Griffith's "third masterpiece," made in 1919, was his 415th film. "In the circumstances," wrote Dyer, "it is both unreal and unreasonable to blame Griffith for failing to maintain, in the Twenties, the same innovatory influence that he had throughout the previous decade." Of Griffith's first talking picture, *Abraham Lincoln*, for which he was voted director of the year in 1930, Dyer found that it has many "good things," including "Walter Huston's unique impersonation of Lincoln, the impeccable playing of briefly seen historical figures" and "magnificent" crowd scenes. Dyer concluded that Griffith "has had a rather raw deal" in having "a prolonged, steady and uncomplicated" decline attributed to him.

In his later years, Griffith was a familiar figure as he wandered about Hollywood, lost and passé, dropping in at bars and ogling the girls, while the men who had been his office boys and assistants and had not one iota of his ability sat in big offices in the big studios doing hack work. They could not find a place for Griffith in the big, rich movie business. Columnist Sidney Skolsky tried for several years to sell a movie biography of Griffith, but finally gave up after it was rejected by all the studios.

I was in Griffith's apartment in the Hollywood Knickerbocker Hotel by accident. I was visiting Hollywood as a free-lance magazine writer and had run into Seymour Stern, movie critic and encyclopedic historian of Griffith, and at that time story editor for Preston Sturges. Stern told me that he was worried about D.W., as he called him, that Griffith had been holed up in his hotel room drinking for days and refusing to answer telephone calls. His mailbox was crammed with three weeks' letters. Occasionally he would have food and liquor left at his door and, after making sure that there was no one around, would whisk it inside.

I had interviewed Griffith a few years earlier—I had always been specially interested in the old-timers of the screen. At that time I had talked with Griffith in the lobby of the Hollywood Roosevelt Hotel at the other end of Hollywood Boulevard. He sported a jaunty Panama hat just as in the old days when he used to boss the big silents, and a cigarette was cocked under his hawklike nose as he discoursed on many subjects in his courtly, Southern speech. He was then visiting Hollywood for the first time in several years, one of the reasons being to discuss a screenplay about his career written by Lillian Gish, who became a star in his pictures.

His conversation at that time was in a rather satirical vein. "All life is a comedy, more or less," he said. He told me that he was living in Nevada and doing a great deal of traveling. He said he was an avid moviegoer and, at random, he mentioned *Mrs. Miniver*, *My Friend Flicka* and *Heaven Can Wait* as a few pictures he had liked recently. "I liked the way Lubitsch used color in *Heaven Can Wait*," he said. "And the way he used sound, too. Do you know that I made use of sound in a picture called *Dream Street*, which was exhibited on Broadway six and one half years before *The Jazz Singer* was released? I used the Kellum process in which the sound was recorded on records." Griffith's interest in technical matters was intense and he spoke a good deal of what he believed to be the next great development in motion pictures, the "broad" or "wide-angle" film, which would do away with distortion and lend to the screen the depth and reality of the stage.

"The first pictures," he said, "were made like stage plays, with the actors walking on and off screen. Then came the cut-in, the flashback and the principle of editing. Now the broad-angle screen will combine the best qualities of both the theater and the movies."

Griffith recalled that his very first contact with motion pictures was when he arrived in New York and wrote an article for a daily newspaper about the possibilities of talking and singing motion pictures. "That was before I ever made a picture," he said. "I always believed in talking pictures." He thought *Intolerance* was probably the best of his pictures, in the sense that it introduced the greatest number of technical ideas. Erich von Stroheim, Elmer Clifton and W. S. Van Dyke, all celebrated directors since, were assistant directors on that picture.

I asked him what he thought of the current Hollywood product. "It is all right," he said noncommittally. He held that good pictures were made by good directors working without interference. He said he was amused by some of the over-reverent things that had been written about him. "I've made some lemons, too," he pointed out.

Griffith told me that he was working on his autobiography as well as some plays, stories and verse. His motion pictures and his writings often reflected his sentimentality. "The simple things, the human things are important in pictures," he said. "There are supposed to be only seven or eight plots. They are relatively unimportant. The most important thing is humanity." He spoke with enthusiasm of Molly Picon, the Yiddish actress, as one of the great contemporary performers, and said he had tried, unsuccessfully, to sell her to Hollywood years ago.

Griffith described his visit to Hollywood then as "just a vacation." He was a well-mannered gentleman, both in his actions and his speech, as he sat in the lobby of the Roosevelt Hotel on Hollywood Boulevard in the community he had helped make famous.

That had been several years ago. On my present trip to Hollywood, I was busy with other assignments. However, Seymour Stern and I went to the hotel where Griffith was staying in another effort to get to him. We were unsuccessful. Stern finally had an idea: the best way to get to D.W. would be through a girl. I offered to introduce one to him. I called a young Hollywood secretary I knew and told her that we needed her for a gag. She was willing. It was a gray day in Hollywood and a good one for a gag. She did not know D. W. Griffith from Sonny Tufts, but she enthusiastically agreed to go along with the plan.

Stern wrote a note to D.W., saying that he wanted to introduce him to a girl and would he please answer his phone in five minutes? We slipped the note under Griffith's door. We rang his room from the lobby and Griffith answered. We put the girl on the phone and she gave him the come-on. Griffith asked her to come up to his room immediately.

We trailed along. Griffith opened the door warily, saw the young lady and grabbed her by the arm, pulling her into the room and quickly trying to slam the door shut. But we moved quickly, too, elbowing our way in after the girl. Griffith was tremendously displeased. He asked us to get the hell out. We stayed put. Griffith finally plunked himself down in the easy chair and continued drinking, from time to time lunging at the girl, who kept deftly maneuvering out of his reach. I sat in a corner, absorbing this fantastic scene, while Stern solicitously tried to talk to D.W.

Suddenly, somewhere along the line, Griffith started talking about the movies, about the old days, the silent films. It was partly incoherent, but partly it was eloquent, compounded of gin, wisdom and long years. I suddenly realized that I was witnessing an extraordinary event. Almost instinctively I reached for paper and pencil to scribble down what Griffith was saying. But I had no paper with me except for a long, white envelope on one side of which were scrawled other notes. I propped the envelope on my knee and started writing down what Griffith was saying as fast as I could. The verbatim notes cascaded all over the envelope, running up and down the sides.

Griffith saw me writing. "I am seventy-two years of age," he said in his rhythmical, resounding speech. "I can say anything I want about Hollywood. You can print anything you please. What's the difference? I don't give a hoot what anyone says about me.

"I was a reporter once myself. You know, they will not print any of this. But I don't care. I am seventy-two years old and I can say anything I like about this movie business."

Griffith set his glass down on an end table. The room faced out on a shadowy driveway in the late afternoon. The hotel was one block from the crossroads of the movie capital at Hollywood and Vine.

"It's all nostalgia," Griffith said. "I would love to be again at Forty-fourth and Broadway and love again to see George M. Cohan walking down the street. I would love again to see that. But most of all I would love to see John and Lionel Barrymore crossing the street as they used to be, when they were young and full of youth and vitality, going to a Broadway theater. They'd stop traffic, arm in arm, when they were young, in the blessed days when they were young."

He paused.

"There is a dreadful sameness in the sunshine out here. I love the rain and the sun. I love the change of seasons. I would love to be in New York again. The most brainless people in all the world live in Southern California. No one here has any brains except he comes from the East. But, for certain financial reasons, I am exiled from New York." (Griffith was referring to litigation over his motion pictures and other business affairs pending against him in New York City.)

"When I first went to New York—I was spoiled in my youth. I had my first poem—better say 'verse'—and my first play and story published at the same time. . . . I thought I was a great genius. That was a lot of baloney. Today nobody is interested in D. W. Griffith. I don't kid myself. They don't know who I am.

" 'D. W. Griffith and the Wolf'—that's my autobiography. It's lousy. I stopped writing it after eighty or ninety pages and I don't know where it is now. The Wolf is poverty. Nothing is so sad as poverty. My story would be the story of a fellow who is very poor, whose family lost all its money. In Louisville, Kentucky. Now, that's a story—how the young fellow becomes a cheap ham actor and makes a fortune which he loses. That's what they might be interested in, but not in D. W. Griffith, who once made movies."

Griffith, a titan of the screen in his time, earned big money as well as world-wide artistic prestige. *The Birth of a Nation*, made in 1915, is being shown in theaters today and is probably the most famous as well as the biggest grossing picture of all time. It helped establish the super-spectacle on the world's screens and it left its mark on moviemakers in other countries. His best pictures, like the epic *Intolerance*, embodied a boldness of technique and a moral fervor almost entirely absent from the screen today.

Some of the power of those pictures came from the fact that in those days Griffith was able to put on the screen things that would never have met with the approval of the Hollywood censors in later years.

Death, violence and the more sordid side of life came within the camera's ken in those beautiful, early, carefree days of the screen. Philip K. Scheuer of the Los Angeles *Times* once analyzed Griffith's *Intolerance*, made in 1916, in this light and found that it had a vitality and a knowingness which were overwhelmingly lacking in the contemporary Hollywood film.

"*Intolerance*," wrote Scheuer, "breaks practically every law in the Hays moral code book, except miscegenation—and Griffith had already taken care of that in *The Birth of a Nation*.

"*Intolerance* runs the gamut of 'don'ts.' It contains seduction and the more violent crimes of passion. Murder by every conceivable method takes place before your eyes—even dismemberment and decapitation. Soldiers are seen firing on strikers. A Bacchanalian revel in ancient Babylon is characterized by nudity and frankness. Vice conditions in a big city are freely exposed, and the evils of prohibition, with its bootleggers and home brew, are actually prophesied (this was in 1916!). Two of the principals elaborately commit suicide. There is even the pointed inference that somewhere along the line Judaism, Catholicism and Protestantism, respectively, have been less than perfect. The existence of the subnormal and abnormal in sex psychology is acknowledged. And practically all the villains go unpunished for their misdeeds!

"I recount these juicy tidbits not to send you rushing posthaste to see *Intolerance* (which is no longer playing, anyway) but to hold them up wonderingly for your inspection in the light of present-day cinema.

"In the first place, none of these incidents is introduced obviously with an eye to sensationalism or an ear to a snicker—like a Mae West line. They're all just part of what's happening up there in Belshazzar's court or Jerusalem or sixteenth-century France or the America of a little while ago. Griffith conceived of them as taking place that way, and that was the way he filmed them. He wasn't trying to corrupt people's morals, certainly—since neither he nor we had yet been told that people's morals were that easily corruptible. It took the reformers to dope that out.

"Now that our weaknesses are known to us we corrupt at the mere raising of Melvyn Douglas' right eyebrow."

Intolerance had profound world-wide ramifications. When Lenin saw *Intolerance* during the Russian revolution of 1917, according to Seymour Stern in *The Griffith Index*, "he found in the screen's supreme super-spectacle a prime example of the type of motion picture he felt best suited to the needs of the new Soviet society; and he issued the oft-quoted pronouncement: 'The cinema must, and shall, become the foremost cultural weapon of the proletariat.' Eight years later, as though in fulfillment of this injunction, Eisenstein's *Potemkin* (1925) launched the 'golden age' of the Soviet film.

"Eight years after *Potemkin* appeared, Hitler and the Nazi Party took power in Germany. Joseph Goebbels, Nazi Minister of Propaganda, named *Potemkin*, in turn, as the type of film useful more than any other for projecting on the screen the campaign of psychological terror waged by the Fascist counter-revolution. *Potemkin* was shown on his orders to the Nazi film-makers. Among them was a young woman, Leni Riefenstahl, who had earlier starred in and directed *The Blue Light*, based on a German legend. Eisenstein's semi-documentary, semi-historical techniques impressed her, and since she also enjoyed Hitler's special favors, she won the assignment to make the first important Nazi propaganda film. *Triumph of the Will* combines cinematic elements of both *Intolerance* and *Potemkin*, although its cutting pace and its internal tempo are considerably slower than those of its forerunners. It is not a true documentary, for its scenes were planned and staged, under the supervision of Hitler and Goebbels, as in any fiction film. It was designed to awe the German public, who had already acclaimed Hitler and Fascism with hysterical enthusiasm, and, at the same time, terrorize the rest of the world. . . . Two years after the film was released, Fascist Germany attacked the West. . . ."

Griffith's work has been called the greatest single contribution to the development of the motion picture. He took the rudimentary storytelling line Edwin S. Porter employed in *The Great Train Robbery* and gave it humanity, realism and cinematic technique. Griffith was the first to exploit the close-up, the flashback and cross-cutting extensively. He did not hesitate (in *Intolerance*) to cut from a contemporary scene to ancient times and back again to tell his story. This, plus his sense of dynamic spectacle, his use of thousands of extras to re-create history in dramatic grandeur, broadened the movie medium and influenced other directors. And in more modest movies like *Broken Blossoms*, he evolved an authentic kind of screen poetry.

Griffith is also credited with having been probably the first to recognize the possibilities of the semi-documentary screen technique that came into widespread use in later years. All the outdoor sequences of his 1914 film, *The Escape*, dealing with eugenics, were shot in a real slum section of New York City. For *Isn't Life Wonderful*, a story of post-World War I Germany, he took a troupe of Hollywood actors to actual German locations in 1924. His *Dream Street*, made in 1921, was one of the first talking pictures, with a phonograph behind the screen synchronizing dialogue with the action to give the illusion of Ralph Graves and Carol Dempster singing.

Director Frank Capra, who was given the D. W. Griffith Award by the Screen Directors Guild in 1959 "for creative achievement in the film industry," was quoted as saying at the time: "Since D. W. Griffith, there's been no major improvement in the art of film direction. Of course, there have been the strictly technical improvements—many. But as far as sheer creative direction is concerned, no one really has advanced beyond the achievements of Griffith. Run down the whole gamut—starting with his introduction of suspense, editing, the flashback, close-ups. You name it, and I can show you where he employed it." Capra conceded that there have been new "styles" of direction. "But," he added, "no one matches Griffith. He was, indeed, the poor man's Shakespeare."

Griffith was a tough directorial taskmaster—as just about all the best directors were. He once slapped Mabel Normand hard to make her crying-mad for a scene in *The Mender of Nets* (1912). After he shot the scene, Griffith put his arms around her and said, "There, darling, that's what I wanted. I knew you could do it." Lillian and Dorothy Gish recalled that when they first came to be interviewed by Griffith at the old Biograph studio in New York, he chased them all over the studio with a pistol to get their "emotional" reactions.

The money he made in the movies was always a bother to Griffith. He lost the fortune he made from *The Birth of a Nation* on *Intolerance* because he believed in the latter's message of good will toward men. *Intolerance* was a box-office failure, but is today recognized as one of the milestones in the history of motion pictures. When the Alexandria Hotel in Los Angeles, where Griffith had lived when he first came to Hollywood, went bankrupt in the early Thirties and was gone over by auditors, a packet marked "D. W. Griffith—Personal" was found in one of the vaults with $20,000 in cash that he had completely forgotten. Griffith retained a financial interest in some of his old movies. Not long before he died, his lawyer brought him a check for $3,000 representing certain income. The check was never deposited and was apparently thrown out with the wastepaper. The approximately 448 movies Griffith made took in a conservatively estimated eighty million dollars, some twenty-five million of it profit for Griffith and his associates. Griffith held on to almost none of his share. However, he never actually lacked for money and lived comfortably enough in his declining years. He rented his apartment at the Hollywood Knickerbocker, one of Hollywood's two first-class hotels, on a monthly basis.

"I never read a letter or answer a telephone," Griffith continued. "If it's important, they get to you. I go out sometimes to see movies. I haven't seen a picture in some time now. The best pictures I did were not popular. The lousy ones, like *The Birth of a Nation*, only a cheap melodrama, were popular, and *Way Down East*—they got five dollars for that one in New York, about a girl floating over Niagara Falls and being rescued." (This was typical of Griffith. He liked to run down his best work with an expression on his face egotistically inviting his listener to contradict him.)

Movie-chase expert Alfred Hitchcock once declared that the best screen chase he ever saw was the ice-floe scene in *Way Down East*. "There was the heroine on a block of ice," said Hitchcock, "and the hero leaping to her from block to block and then back again with her in his arms while all the time the camera was cutting to a big waterfall beyond. Griffith was the first to exploit the possibilities of the physical chase."

"I think," said Griffith, "*The Miracle of Morgan's Creek* is the greatest comedy I have seen in a long time. I saw *Gone with the Wind* twice and thought it better than *The Birth of a Nation*—not really of course. I saw *The Seventh Veil* four times. That Mason is the greatest actor. *It's a Wonderful Life* was a piece of cheese, *Duel in the Sun* a good melodrama, *The Best Years of Our Lives* just okay, *My Darling Clementine* lovely. The best directors today are Leo McCarey, Frank Capra and Preston Sturges, the best actors Spencer Tracy and Lionel Barrymore, and the daintiest, sultry-eyed beauty that Russell girl—not Jane, but Gail.

"I loved *Citizen Kane* and particularly loved the ideas he [Orson Welles] took from me. The various cycles, the goddam German pictures, I loved them all. I could see all the stuff they stole from me, because being very modest—George Bernard Shaw said any man who pretends to be modest is a darn fool. No one is modest. I am the only producer on stage and screen who knew Plato and the Vedic hymns, the first religioso published, and the Talmud, too."

Griffith leaned back. He took a long swig. Then he continued: "You can print anything you please. What's the difference? I'm 72 years old. This Washington business, the investigation—that's a lot of baloney. I was called a Communist myself in my youth when *Intolerance* was branded radical and dangerous. It's an old idea. All this stuff gives me a pain in the neck. I wrote *The Rise and Fall of Free Speech in America* to answer my critics. The movies should have the same freedom of speech as the press. There should be no censorship. According to the Constitution, you are allowed to say anything you please, but you are responsible for your speech and conversation by law and may be so punished. No one is really allowed to say what he pleases."

He contemplated his glass. "It is my ambition to see *The Treadmill* produced," he said. "It's a play that I have been writing over the years. It is so beautiful, it is too good for anyone to see. It is a story of the beginning of life to the ending of life. It is a play about the earth and solar system, with the idea of eternal recurrence. I began it when I was eighteen or nineteen. It says that the universe is nothing but foredoomed to annihilation, of the essence of dust. It is the greatest dream any man has had—ah, the superb egotism of this old man in a cheap hotel!

"It says that not man is God, but woman, the poor mother of the skies, and she has an ugly duckling running around her back yard and she is worried because the great son, Orsus, is streaming through the skies, streaming fecundity for twice three thousand trillion miles. And then all the little planets are drinking up the fecundity and each little planet is revolving and re-revolving through the great heavens. And then the poor mother wonders and says: 'Where is my great son lost in the depth of eternity?' And then she finds one of the little planets, a trio of little ducklings, lost, a little duckling—his name was Earth—the ugliest duckling of them all—Earth, an atom on the tail part of a louse."

He paused. "There has been no improvement in movies since the old days," said D. W. Griffith from his easy chair. "We did Browning and Keats then, *Pippa Passes*. Today you don't dare do those things. Imagine anyone doing Browning today. They have not improved in stories. I don't know that they've improved in anything.

"What the modern movie lacks is beauty—the beauty of moving wind in the trees, the little movement in a beautiful blowing on the blossoms in the trees. That they have forgotten entirely. They have forgotten that no still painting—not the greatest ever—was anything but a still picture. But the moving picture! Today they have forgotten movement in the moving picture—it is all still and stale. The moving picture is beautiful; the moving of wind on beautiful trees is more beautiful than a painting. Too much today depends on the voice. I love pictures properly done. Sometimes the talk is good, often very bad. We have taken beauty and exchanged it for stilted voices.

"In my arrogant belief," said D. W. Griffith, "we have lost beauty."

Finally, Griffith just sat there. The three of us took the occasion to leave. Griffith grumbled at our taking the girl with us. I said goodbye to Stern and our amused companion and left to keep some appointments. Later that night I returned to my hotel room, tired, but with the Griffith session still milling around in the back of my mind. I was sorting out my papers and tearing up the ones I did not need. Among them was the envelope on the back of which were the Griffith notes. Inadvertently, I destroyed that, too—was I unconsciously trying to get rid of the memento of a troubling event? The Griffith notes lay in a pile of tiny pieces in the wastepaper basket. There was only one way to retrieve the situation—to reassemble the bits of paper. At first I thought "the hell with it"—it was too much trouble and I was very tired. But then I thought better of it. I emptied the wastepaper basket and sorted out what appeared to be the Griffith scraps. Then slowly, laboriously and carefully I pieced them together like a crazy jigsaw puzzle. Hours later, I was finished. I pasted the pieces to the desk blotter and then typed out the notes on another sheet of paper.

I did not see Griffith or Stern again during the rest of my stay in Hollywood. On my return east I completed my magazine assignments, but my heart was not really in them; there was one article about producer Jerry Wald for *Harper's*, another entitled "Are the Movies a Menace?" for *Coronet*. I kept thinking of the Griffith interview that had not been commissioned by any magazine and that had cropped up so strangely and unexpectedly. One day I wrote it up in intelligible form, though leaving out some of the more colorful, circumstantial details.

The interview was repeatedly rejected by one editor after another, from *Harper's* to the New York *Times*, as being too "rough" for these publications. The editors objected to Griffith's drinking and to his broken sentences. I always make it a journalistic practice to note and quote a person's speech verbatim, with all its crudities and grammatical loose ends, a technique that runs counter to the usual, slick, pat method of interviewing but which I consider the only authentic method, as well as the one yielding the most dynamic, colorful results. One problem with Hollywood reporting—as with most so-called reporting—is that not enough precise and detailed notes are taken and that hardly anyone is accurately quoted. It is precisely because people are misquoted and sometimes not quoted at all—for reasons of diplomacy and "playing it safe"—that so much mediocrity and malfeasance, particularly in Hollywood, is perpetuated.

Finally, after a number of rejections, I got fed up with the whole thing and put the Griffith story in my files. I returned to Hollywood not long afterward to stay, more or less permanently. One day, the Griffith piece still on my mind, I mailed it, pretty much in desperation, to Ed McCarthy, Sunday editor of *PM*, the since defunct New York daily. I had done some pieces for McCarthy and knew him as an enterprising ex-Hearst editor. McCarthy was no student of Hollywood or Griffith, but, as an old pro unencumbered by the rarefied reservations of the egghead editors, he saw in the story a juicy piece of Sunday copy—a yarn about a great man down on his uppers. He printed it as the lead story in *PM*'s Sunday edition of March 28, 1948.

The Griffith story met with unusually enthusiastic reader and editor response. It was excerpted in weekly news magazines and the Hollywood trade papers, later referred to by the *American Mercury* (which had originally rejected it) as "the now famous interview with Ezra Goodman," reprinted at some length in Lloyd Morris' book *Not So Long Ago*, commented on in Homer Croy's book about Griffith, *Star Maker*, and otherwise noted in a variety of publications. I was criticized in some quarters for writing a story that invaded the privacy of an unhappy old man. Others, including Seymour Stern, thought that I had brought a deplorable situation realistically to light and thereby done a public service.

Some four months after the story appeared in print, on July 23, 1948, Griffith died at the Knickerbocker Hotel, at the age of seventy-three, of a cerebral hemorrhage. I had had the last interview with him. It was the best story I ever got in all my years of interviewing, and it was entirely accidental.

At Griffith's funeral, the sacred cows of Hollywood gathered to pay him homage. A week before that he probably could not have gotten any of them on the telephone. The official list of honorary pallbearers included Cecil B. DeMille, Samuel Goldwyn and Will Hays, as well as Mack Sennett, Jesse Lasky and Charlie Chaplin. The services were held on July 27 at the Hollywood Masonic Temple, whose 600-odd seats were only half filled, with the result that the doors were opened to tourists. Pious words were uttered. Actor Donald Crisp, who appeared in such Griffith movies as *The Birth of a Nation* and *Broken Blossoms*, delivered one of the main tributes, paying respects to "a man who has long since become a legend in the history of motion pictures. . . . It was, I believe, inevitable that the very momentum which he generated carried the industry ahead at a pace which finally left him behind. It was the tragedy of his later years that his active, brilliant mind was given no chance to participate in the advancement of the industry. . . . I cannot help feeling that there should always have been a place for him and his talents in the motion-picture field. It is hard to believe that the industry could not have found some use for his great gifts in his later years."

(Crisp, one of Hollywood's wealthiest citizens, was, according to an official biography issued by Paramount studios in 1947 ". . . also a director of the Bank of America, and most of the loans by that bank to would-be film producers are passed by him. The situation has occasionally been embarrassing to his career as an actor because he has had to turn down prospective employers.")

Producer Charles (*Sunset Boulevard*) Brackett, then vice-president of the Academy of Motion Picture Arts and Sciences, went on the record with "It was the fate of David Wark Griffith to have a success unknown in the entertainment world until his day, and to suffer the agonies which only a success of that magnitude can engender when it is past.

"I am proud to say that in 1936, when days were dark for him, the motion-picture industry, through the Academy, presented Mr. Griffith with its highest honor, an Academy Oscar for his outstanding contribution to the art of the motion picture.

"I'm afraid it didn't ease his heartache much. When you've had what he'd had, what you want is the chance to make more pictures, unlimited budgets to play with, complete confidence behind you. What does a man full of vitality care for the honors of the past? It's the present he wants, and the future.

"There was no solution for Griffith but a kind of frenzied beating on the barred doors. . . ."

And Charlie Chaplin put it simply at the time: "The whole industry owes its experience to Mr. Griffith."

On April 22, 1959, distribution rights to thirty-odd Griffith silent films and more than a dozen scenarios from Griffith's estate were acquired in Los Angeles by the Killiam Company of New York—the sole bidder—for the total price of $21,000. Included in the package were *The Birth of a Nation, Intolerance, Way Down East* and *Broken Blossoms.*

On December 13, 1959, a California State Highway "Historical Marker" roadside plaque was unveiled to Griffith at his old ranch—where he had shot a number of his movies—in San Fernando Valley. The event was sponsored by Fritz B. Burns, a commercial builder, who announced that he had "purchased the ranch from D. W. Griffith and is perpetuating the Griffith name in respect to the memory of the great film pioneer." The plaque had several errors in it, such as that

Custer's Last Stand was filmed on the site. Actually, Griffith had never made a film with that title and the reference should have been to *The Massacre*, which was based on *Custer's Last Stand*. Seymour Stern made the main speech of the occasion, stressing Griffith's constant struggle against screen censorship. Participating in the ceremonies were the Native Sons and Daughters of the Golden West, and Boy Scout Troop No. 424, sponsored by the Optimists Club of San Fernando. On hand also for the event was a delegation of two dozen students, boys and girls, and several faculty members from the D. W. Griffith Junior High School of East Los Angeles. The students wore special sweaters and jackets emblazoned with Griffith's name and a motion-picture camera. The only film folk present were Mae Marsh and Blanche Sweet, two of Griffith's stars. The Hollywood movie press did not even see fit to cover the historical event.

In April 1960 the King Brothers, Hollywood producers of low-budget and even lower artistry films, announced plans to remake Griffith's *The Birth of a Nation*. As a Hollywood wag put it, "the only thing left now is for the Marx Brothers to do it."

I sometimes think of my strange interview with Griffith. It seems to me to sum up the worst and the best of Hollywood, the worst in the callousness of the community, the best in that Griffith represented, far and away, the artistic peak of the American screen, that, for all his occasional moments of shallow screen poetry and mawkish movie sentiment, his best pictures were lyrical and fiercely lovely explorations in a fascinating new artistic medium. When I came to put together the notes for this book, the Griffith story loomed above everything else, and so it is that this accidental meeting with a fallen genius is the opener here.

CHAPTER II

Tom Swift and His Flying Typewriter

A MUCH-TRAVELED HOLLYWOOD MOVIEMAKER, emerging from an opium den in Calcutta's Chinatown not long ago, observed to his companion, also from Hollywood: "Wouldn't Hedda Hopper love to know about this!"

The long arm of Hollywood—and of the powerful Hollywood press—was reaching out even to the dark alleyways of India. Hedda Hopper had been taking cracks at this particular director in her column and he could not forget about it even thousands of miles from Hollywood and after several soothing opium pipes.

One afternoon I was lounging by the pool of a well-known Hollywood producer. The sun was shining on a gathering of rich and renowned film folk. The producer's swimming hole was almost large enough to accommodate an atomic submarine. Hamburgers of ground filet were being dished up by servitors in full regalia. And, in the midst of all this actinic splendor, the aforesaid producer sat moaning over a snide comment about his latest movie by some columnist who would not know Boris from Joe Pasternak. This columnist's crack was spoiling his afternoon by the pool.

The Hollywood press, it is evident, is an overwhelming power in the tight little egocentric movietown community. When you are unsuccessful and are trying to get ahead, or when you are successful and making money, and you have a big house and not too much to think about, what do you think about? Your press notices, of course, or the press notices of the producer or profile next door. One word, as some sage from East Hollywood once said, is worth a thousand pictures. Money is the life blood of the community, and publicity—or the lack of the right kind of publicity—goes right along with it.

Hollywood is narcissistically sensitive about the printed word. A good many film folk who make a great deal of money and have an appreciable reputation are frequently concerned about why they have been so rewarded. When pinned down to it, they would probably confess that they do not deserve what they have gotten. They are, therefore, excessively touchy about what is written about them.

You never know what will get a rise out of the local citizens. In the course of writing about the movies, I have run into some odd reactions. Restaurateur Dave Chasen once became incensed at me for casually referring in print to his establishment as a "hash-house." Director George Cukor resented a passing reference in an interview to his palatial swimming pool. Producer Darryl Zanuck harbored a grievance against me for years for alluding to his "fuzzy mustache" in an article about him.

The journalistic word in Hollywood can affect ego, box office, health, happiness and the frequency of visits to one's psychoanalyst. In fact, some local psychoanalysts court publicity themselves. And so anyone with a column or a piece of white space to fill in some publication, and with the power to praise or damn, is someone to be reckoned with in Hollywood. It does not matter if the author has no predicates in his sentences or no shine on his shoes. He is still a sort of Hemingway and a kind of Lucius Beebe.

As a result, the Hollywood press has become something more than just a press corps. It is an integral part of the social and business life of the community. The Hollywood press does not merely chronicle the show. It is part of the show itself. And, as the movie business has become more of a business and less of an art, and as Hollywood has become more subdued with advancing age and the gray-flannel impact of television, the press is one of the last strongholds of oddballism and high spirits still flourishing in the Southern California sunshine.

Some of the press have been covering the Hollywood characters so long that they are now among the characters who get covered in Hollywood. For instance, red-haired, horse-faced Florabel ("I'm not a lady—I'm a columnist") Muir, Hollywood correspondent for the New York *Daily News*, has made copy as well as written it on a number of occasions. While trailing mobster Mickey Cohen, she was once nicked in the posterior by a bullet during a gangland shooting on the Sunset

Strip. The *Daily News* rewarded her with a bulletproof corset. On another occasion actor Franchot Tone expectorated squarely in her face in Ciro's night club. She had him arrested and jailed and he was subsequently fined $500, although he never did apologize.

The Hollywood press is unlike any journalistic group anywhere. It consists of approximately 500 working (?) press, including about 150 representatives of foreign publications and 50 photographers. This contingent compares favorably—statistically speaking—with the press covering Washington, D.C., and the United Nations. The Hollywood press corps could undoubtedly be cut in half and still be top-heavy. And this press aggregation is as bad as it is big. It is strictly a second-rate fourth estate subsisting—with negligible exceptions—on press-agent handouts of mostly trumped-up tales, freeloading (another name for payola) and general incompetence. The professional standard of journalism, as it is known in Washington, D.C., New York or London, is almost nonexistent.

The Hollywood press is little more than a convenient transmission belt for the Hollywood press agents. It is shaky on grammar and shakier on facts. Some of the Hollywood press have been known to complain that every time they check a story, they lose it. "Inaccuracy," it has been said, "seems to be an occupational disease of gossipists, like silicosis among miners." There is probably more nonsense written about Hollywood than about the Abominable Snowman and the Loch Ness Monster combined. A remarkable instance of fanciful reporting occurred on January 8, 1959, when the Los Angeles *Mirror-News* ran a front-page banner headline—"LIZ TAYLOR IS A PATIENT IN THE MENNINGER CLINIC"—with a story that the actress was under observation at the famed Topeka, Kansas, clinic for the emotionally disturbed. When the newspapers hit the streets, Taylor happened to be in Los Angeles. She had never been at the Menninger Clinic. With the assistance of her press agents, she decided to call a press conference at Chasen's restaurant. She also announced that she was instituting suit against the *Mirror-News* for printing untrue and defamatory statements. In its January 9 editions, the *Mirror-News* ran a six-column front-page headline—"LIZ TAYLOR HERE, NOT IN CLINIC"—and offered its "sincere regrets" for printing the erroneous story, adding: "The mistake resulted from a misunderstanding during a telephone call direct to the Topeka clinic." The suit against the *Mirror-News* was subsequently dropped. As one of Miss Taylor's press agents put it, all agog: "But one never sues a newspaper!"

It is difficult to pin down the most elementary facts in Hollywood.

Sometimes it seems as if everything is apocryphal. Hollywood is the realm of elusive gossip. There isn't a fact in a starlet-load. You can't even necessarily believe what you see and hear. Hortense Powdermaker, a practiced anthropologist, came to Hollywood to conduct a survey of the community which appeared in book form as *Hollywood, the Dream Factory* in 1950. The Powdermaker study was a bit of a pipe dream itself. She had made the mistake of believing what the glib and persuasive local residents had told her. This might work with natives in Samoa, but not with the tricky and conniving denizens of darkest Southern California.

It is also advisable to take the printed word with a grain or three of salt. In his slickly written book *Hollywood*, of 1941, Leo Rosten quotes Hollywood trade-paper sources pretty much as gospel, a dangerous form of documentation indeed. Army Archerd's column in the March 8, 1960, *Daily Variety* gives a pointed and extreme illustration of the pitfalls of taking such material at print value. According to Archerd: "During our vacation, scripter Hal Kanter wrote a hilarious guest column, parodying this pillar, in which he item'd on Feb. 23: 'Happy birthday to Ikimima Yokahijimarika, prima ballerina of Tokyo's Yiddish Art Ballet, rumored to be Dinah Shore's summer TV replacement.' And on March 3 Walter Winchell duly reported: 'They say Dinah's summer replacement may be Ikimima Yokahijimarika, Tokyo ballerina.' Tsk, tsk." Trying to distill facts from the Hollywood trade papers is not dissimilar to deciphering the Dead Sea Scrolls.

It would be interesting to see how the shining stars of journalism would make out in Hollywood if they were given a trial run in the town. They probably would not survive for all their game efforts. Hollywood may well be the one news beat where sheer ability and enterprise can fail to pay off. In Hollywood, it is not so much what you know as who you know, and not how hard and well you work but what circulation you have and how kind you are in print to all concerned. News or what passes for news—and there obviously cannot be enough real news in Hollywood for 500 journalists—is funneled out by the studios and publicists via an ironclad reportorial pipeline which finds the most powerful syndicated columnists at the top and the correspondent of the Podunk *Gazette* at the bottom. The studios, strangely, often value a minor paragraph in an unimportant Hollywood outlet more than they do a major story in an important out-of-town publication, apparently on the ground that it is impressive local window dressing and that a word in the hand is worth two in the bush leagues.

One of the prime causes of this lamentable situation is that the editors who run the newspapers and magazines are mostly uninformed about Hollywood and not particularly concerned with Hollywood coverage except as inconsequential glamour filler about the nipups of the profiles. Some of the so-called hard-boiled editors in New York and elsewhere are the most easily taken in by fraudulent Hollywood stories fomented by the press agents. The conception many of these editors have of Hollywood harks back to the Mack Sennett–Rudolph Valentino legend and they persist in running the same old stereotyped movie material today. "Any deviation from the pattern," one Hollywood columnist once told me, "brings a complaint from my editors in New York. They just don't want anything different." A case in point of this editorial disinterest and incompetence was my D. W. Griffith interview.

Some editors who know better simply do not want to be bothered by Hollywood news. They have other and more important things on their minds. I was once called into the office of Lee Payne, editor-in-chief of the late Los Angeles *Daily News* and a tabloid-type, fire-breathing editor of the old school. There had been the standard number of movie-industry complaints about my irreverence as columnist and critic—mostly through the advertising department—and Payne wanted to have a talk with me.

Unlike most editors, Payne knew Hollywood well and was unimpressed with it. He had a firsthand knowledge of the movie business, which he did not particularly love. His strictures, if such, were indulgent and brief. "Look," he said, "I don't care what you write as long as it doesn't create any problems. We're trying to get out a newspaper here and I'm busy with the front page."

Payne had a point. There are obviously many things of greater consequence in the world than Hollywood—epidemics, floods, nuclear developments and wars, hot and cold, to mention just a few. As an editor, Payne was preoccupied with the major news problems of the paper. And Payne was a specially knowledgeable case. I once saw him chase a Hollywood press agent, who had come in with a complaint, the length of the city room and right out the front door.

Since most of the editors themselves are, for one reason or another, generally uninterested in Hollywood or uninformed about it—or both—it is small wonder that most writers and reporters who cover the movies for these publications are below par. Some of these gentlemen of depress are moved into these positions because they could not qualify for other jobs, or they may have even been given these assignments as a reward for long service on the police beat, the society section, or in some other department of the paper. Whether they had the proper qualifications for the job was apparently beside the point.

There was a period in Hollywood when two of the leading lights of the press were a former hairdresser and a physical-education instructor, both of whom had no experience whatsoever in writing, reporting or show business. The beautician, Joe Russell, was the close friend and collaborator of Mike Connolly, effusive gossipist of the influential trade paper, the *Hollywood Reporter*. The muscle man, Wojciechowicz Stanislaus Wotjkiewicz, who was known as Bow Wow for short, was husband–leg man (or work horse) of syndicated columnist Sheilah Graham—until he was muscled out of both jobs in 1957. Since both Connolly and Graham were high-ranking members of the Hollywood press, it automatically followed that their assistants also ranked high in the journalistic hierarchy. Bow Wow had worked with juvenile delinquents and as a prison athletic director—admittedly a good training for covering Hollywood. Upon his advent in the cinema city, he told reporters: "I've been to three movies in my life. I wouldn't know Mickey Mouse from Gary Cooper." In short order, he became a social and journalistic lion. For a time he was a familiar figure in the executive dining rooms, steam rooms and other spots where the Hollywood great gathered, and he hobnobbed with them on an equal footing, inveighing eloquently against the evils of nicotine and alcohol.

Like the movie business, the movie press is thoroughly stratified in a caste system that makes the one in India seem anarchic. For almost as long as anyone can remember, the Hollywood hive has been presided over by roly-poly queen bee Louella Parsons, with the rest of the scriveners holding down their ordained spots, from Hedda Hopper in descending order to the lowest reaches of cow-town journalism. There have been some minor shifts and some ameliorating of power, but each member of the press gang knows where he or she belongs and has no particular desire to get out of line. After all, the journalists are comfortable in the sunshine, too, and quite a few of them have swimming pools of their own. They enjoy the social whirl and being chummy with the Hollywood elite. They do not want to disturb the status quo.

As Sheilah Graham, who ranks third in the Parsons–Hopper distaff axis, once screamed at me when I was interviewing her for a press story for *Time* Magazine: "For Godsakes, don't make out that I'm trying to move into Louella's spot! I'm not trying to do anything of the kind! I love Louella!"

In Hollywood, where fear can be more potent than respect, just about everybody loves Louella and her toothy smile or gives a good imitation of it. Since the death of her boss, William Randolph Hearst, and the advent of powerful television publicity outlets, Parsons' stranglehold on Hollywood has loosened somewhat. But she still has her lifelong contacts with the movie tycoons, many of whom were pressing pants and making buttonholes when she was already writing a column, and this counts for a great deal in Hollywood. Parsons also comes through in print for people she knows and they are inclined to play ball with her.

As Samuel Goldwyn (or Samuel Goldwyn's press agent) said of Parsons: "Louella is stronger than Samson. He needed two columns to bring the house down. Louella can do it with one." Walter Winchell once suggested it ought to be retagged "Lollywood."

Parsons, who is now nudging eighty, still gets around with almost girlish agility. Since the death of her husband, Dr. Harry W. ("Docky") Martin, who was sometimes known as "Lolly's Pop," she has often been accompanied by songwriter Jimmy ("I Can't Give You Anything but Love, Baby") McHugh. Parsons is almost always kindly —and dull—in print. Bob Hope said that Parsons "turned the whole world into a sewing circle without too much needle." But when crossed she can become real nasty, in type or otherwise. At a 1951 *Photoplay* Magazine awards dinner at the Beverly Hills Hotel, she arrived late to find that she had been seated in what she considered not a choice place. She became loud and demanding about it and was quickly moved to a better table. Several years ago Parsons and her crony, columnist Cobina Wright, showed up late at a movie lunch at the California Racquet Club. A number of movie stars, among them June Allyson, Ann Sheridan and Joan Collins, had put on a show with special material for the event. They offered to redo the entire show for Parsons—and they would have, too. Fortunately for everyone present, Parsons graciously declined.

Those who have written things that have displeased Parsons have had occasion to regret it. Thomas Wood, a Hollywood press agent, with an anonymous and deft assist from movie producer and writer Nunnally Johnson, wrote a biting article about her in the *Saturday Evening Post* of July 15, 1939. Wood says that he sold the story to the magazine and that "without my knowledge, they sent it to Johnson for checking. He contributed some things to it." It was entitled "The First

Lady of Hollywood" and contained such literary nuggets as "Even in her own field, where bad writing is as natural and as common as breathing, Louella's stands out like an asthmatic's gasps." (Parsons later disarmingly and appropriately enough entitled her autobiography—which she wrote with an anonymous assist from the late Richard English—*The Gay Illiterate*, a phrase borrowed from the *Saturday Evening Post* piece.) For many years, says Wood, he found it difficult to get a publicity job in Hollywood because Parsons let it be known that she frowned on him. He describes it as "a kind of blacklisting." He says that he worked sporadically until 1954, when the ice was broken, fifteen years after the *Saturday Evening Post* piece. "When I was up for the unit press-agent job on the movie version of *Oklahoma!* then," says Wood, "Arthur Hornblow [the producer] called the columnists about me and he checked Parsons and she denounced me. But afterwards Rodgers and Hammerstein, who were from New York and who wanted me in the first place, said 'We're taking Wood anyway.' Since then I've worked fairly steadily." The obvious inference is that it took two strong men from the East and of the stature of Rodgers and Hammerstein to get Wood out of his jam with Parsons.

In *The Gay Illiterate*, Parsons fumed: "A name that will never fail to bring me to the boiling point is that of one Thomas Wood. . . . He sailed under colors too false for my stomach." She also kept riding Mrs. Wood, actress Lee Patrick, in movie reviews. In her review of *Over 21* in the Los Angeles *Examiner* in 1945, Parsons wrote of the character played by Mrs. Wood: "In the stage play, she was terribly silly, a young girl; on the screen she looks as old, if not older, than her mother. Lee Patrick, cast as the girl, overdoes the scene." Since it was not easy for Parsons to strike back at the well-entrenched Nunnally Johnson, she took journalistic jibes at Mrs. Johnson with items like "I ran into Dorris Bowdon last night. She used to be such a pretty girl before she married." When Johnson and Parsons finally made up—she showed up at one of his parties—Dorris Bowdon suddenly became pretty again in her column. By some peculiar process of reasoning, Parsons later tended to exonerate Johnson of most of the responsibility for the *Saturday Evening Post* article and to fasten it irrefutably on Wood. In *The Gay Illiterate* she wrote that "Nunnally Johnson, a top Hollywood writer and producer, actually authored the article, completely revamping a very botched-up job of Wood's. I still think Johnson is a good writer. What I think about Wood isn't to be printed."

Nor was Wood quite as put upon and blameless as he has made out to be. When I was writing a movie column for the Los Angeles *Independent*, Wood was features editor and he took occasion to cavalierly, maliciously and unethically insert in my column, without my knowledge, some digs against Parsons that ran under my by-line. He wanted to use someone else as a front in retaliating against Parsons. One such item, which Wood slipped into the Los Angeles *Independent* of May 23, 1949, under my name and unbeknownst to me, was a fanged reference to the fact that Parsons was trying to "muscle" her way into the wedding reception of Rita Hayworth and Aly Khan at Cannes, France, "but as yet, at this writing anyway, has failed to wangle an invitation to the wedding ceremony." Wood added: "Flash! A late communiqué from Cannes says, 'No reporters will be allowed to see the actual wedding.' Allah help Rita when Louella reviews her next picture."

Parsons never forgave Dwight Whitney, who, as Hollywood correspondent for *Time* Magazine, had gathered the original material for a cover story on rival Hedda Hopper in 1947 and had had a hand in a *Time* report about Parsons in which it was observed that she spouted gossip over Hollywood's back fence "like a ruptured water main." When Whitney left *Time* and was temporarily unemployed, Parsons' "Borgia vengeance" came to the forefront. Parsons kept snubbing him at parties and taking personal cracks at him in her column, even going so far, according to Whitney, as to intimate that his children were suffering from malnutrition. "Parsons hasn't spoken to me since," says Whitney. "She's never relented."

On the other hand, Parsons could lend some helpful assists when she wanted to. Her late husband, Dr. Harry Martin, was medical director of the Twentieth Century-Fox studio for many years. Her daughter, Harriet Parsons, has held down a number of lucrative movie-producing jobs. And her cousin, Margaret Ettinger, has long been one of Hollywood's most prosperous press agents.

Parsons works out of a second-floor office in her Beverly Hills home, complete with three telephones and a teletype connection direct to the Los Angeles *Examiner*. She has two secretaries, an assistant and a leg man, as well as a staff of four on the *Examiner*. Her entourage funnels news and gossip, under Parsons' name, not only into her newspaper syndicate but into movie fan magazines and other publications. In effect, Parsons is running a Hollywood word factory that reaches many millions of readers.

The so-called news that Parsons—and also Hedda Hopper—run

would seem to be of interest primarily to the people in the movie business. It is mainly movie production "news"—i.e., who is being cast in what film and what pictures are being planned. A typical example ran as the lead story in Parsons' column in the Los Angeles *Examiner* recently: "I cornered Ross Hunter at a recent party, and was happy to hear him say that when he produces *Back Street*, he'll make it in its entirety in the U.S.A. . . . Ross wants Efrem Zimbalist for the male lead, and he's hoping Jack Warner will give his consent because, Ross said, U-I loaned Warner's Sandra Dee for the highly successful *Summer Place*. Ross hopes to start *Back Street* in July. . . ."

This is the sort of "news" that might more appropriately run in the Hollywood trade papers. It is dished up in rather chatty, informal style, but that still does not disguise its essentially dull, trady and outdated nature. It is hard to believe that the great mass of readers are particularly interested in this type of reporting. And, what with production and production "news" on the skimpy side in Hollywood today, there would seem to be little to retail along these lines.

Parsons—and Hopper—like to give the impression in their columns that Hollywood celebrities just love to drop in at their homes to chat with them cozily, when actually the personalities in question have usually been escorted there, under duress, by platoons of anxious press agents. Another gambit of Parsons, as well as of other columnists, is to make it appear that the profiles regularly drop everything just to telephone each of them exclusively with some momentous morsel of information. The way Hollywood stars are supposed to be constantly telephoning columnists, it is a wonder that they have any time left to act. In my Los Angeles *Daily News* column in 1949, I documented the telephonic doings of some of the columnists under the heading "Temple on the Telephone Department":

"From Louella O. Parsons, Los Angeles *Examiner*, Oct. 14: 'Early yesterday morning, before I even had my breakfast, Shirley Temple telephoned to tell me she was going to divorce John Agar and would file suit immediately.'

"From Florabel Muir's column, *Daily Variety*, Oct. 14: 'I wasn't surprised when Shirley Temple called me yesterday to announce that she and John Agar had called it a day and she was filing her divorce suit, charging cruelty.'

"From Edith Gwynn's column, Los Angeles *Mirror-News*, Oct. 17: 'When Shirley Temple called to tell us (as she did a few scribes) that she was divorcing John Agar, we said: "Gee—hope you don't feel too low about it—it's such a shame." ' "

I concluded with this comment: "No wonder Shirley and her spouse phfft. She must have been spending all her time on the telephone."

One of the major problems of Hollywood press agents down the years has been how to keep both Parsons and Hopper happy. If one of them is given an exclusive bit of "news," the other may get mad. If both of them are given the same tidbit, they may both sulk. So press agents usually try to alternate equally between the two and keep them content from one day to the next, although Parsons will usually be given the slight edge over Hopper. Some of the more enlightened and daredevil press agents will give a sufficiently important story not to Parsons or Hopper, but to the wire services—the Associated Press and United Press International—which reach more newspapers and are patently the outlets for more legitimate news.

According to one veteran Hollywood publicist: "Parsons and Hopper are through and they don't know it. They think they are still important, but they are nowhere what they once were. It's just the ridiculous press agents who cater to them and keep the myth alive." This publicist pointed out that a columnist like Erskine Johnson, of the Newspaper Enterprise Association, with his approximately 786 daily newspapers and whopping circulation, "probably has more outlets than anyone, but he is not catered to by the press agents because he does not have a strong enough outlet in Hollywood. This points up the lack of logic here. It's a lack of actually doing a job. The press is supposed to be used to reach the biggest public for a picture. It doesn't make any sense. Eyewash is more important than the job you're supposed to be doing."

He added sadly: "It's tough for a publicist to break through the circle of the press. Parsons and Hopper have connections upstairs. The heads of the studios cater to them. Parsons came in through Hearst, Hopper through M-G-M. Hopper and Parsons could get people fired. It's a preposterous situation."

Some years ago, when Parsons had the field pretty much to herself, it was considered standard procedure to notify her before getting married or divorced. Hollywood legend had it that a glamour boy and girl, ready to elope, forgot Parsons' phone number and had to call the whole thing off. *Time* Magazine even noted that, according to some Hollywood reports, "the great stars consult her before conceiving a child. . . ." Bob Hope, before leaving on a World War II bomber flight, was asked who should be notified in case of his injury or death. He named Parsons as his next of kin. "She'd be mad," he explained, "if she wasn't the first one to know." At a Masquers Club testimonial dinner to Parsons on her thirtieth anniversary as a Hollywood columnist in 1953, comedian George Burns recalled that Hedda Hopper had once columned that one of Burns's movies—and his performance in it—were the worst she had ever seen. "The next morning," Burns said, "Louella called me. 'George,' she said, 'we've been friends for a long time. Next time you have an item like that, give it to me.'"

In 1959, when the Screen Directors Guild for the first time decided to give its annual award for "outstanding critical appraisal in the field of motion pictures" to a Hollywood critic, Philip K. Scheuer of the Los Angeles *Times*, the guild was confronted with a great problem. How, the guild officers were concerned, would Louella Parsons take it, since she also reviewed movies, for the rival Los Angeles *Examiner*? It was, obviously, out of the question to honor Louella for "outstanding critical appraisal," but the inventive guild executives rose—or descended—to the occasion. Convened in an emergency board meeting, they voted a special citation to Parsons "In recognition of her loyalty, devotion and many valued contributions to the motion picture industry through the years." It was presented to her, in the form of a miniature movie director's chair mounted on an inscribed trophy base, at the annual Screen Directors Guild dinner that year. Even the august Screen Directors Guild, it seemed, had to be wary of incurring the wrath of Parsons.

Testimonial dinners to Parsons are par for the Hollywood course. At the Masquers Club dinner for her, she was crowned "Queen of Hollywood" and a lollipop to which had been affixed a picture of Lolly was attached to each program. It was at this testimonial event that Eddie Cantor made the following eloquent statement: "I am here for the same reason everyone else is: they were afraid not to come."

The biggest testimonial to Parsons took place in 1948 when the Who's Who of Hollywood gathered at the Ambassador Hotel to pay her homage as Hollywood's Hearst Lady. Dwight Whitney, being exceptionally gallant about Louella's age, led off his report in *Time* as follows: "For fear or favor of a gushy, 55-year-old woman who frequently misspells their names, some 800 of Hollywood's most powerful personages sat meekly among the papier-maché monkeys and silver-lamé palm trees of Hollywood's Coconut Grove. Such well-established stars as Clark Gable and Cary Grant allowed themselves the liberty of not attending."

Parsons was flanked by industry leaders on a garland-strewn dais.

Darryl Zanuck paid tribute to her with "Louella, whether or not you spell names correctly is very unimportant. . . . You have a heart as big as the church itself." Parsons was presented with a gold plaque engraved with a testimonial to her "courage, accuracy, fairness and curiosity." Betty Garrett led a song, "Louella," composed for the occasion by Jimmy McHugh and Harold Adamson:

> "Louella, Louella, Louella,
> Everyone loves you;
> Louella, Louella, Louella,
> And Dr. Martin, too . . .
>
> "Press agents live for your column,
> Everyone's hustling you.
> Oh, how we love you, Louella,
> And your 900 newspapers, too."

In a Hollywood that is constantly in desperate need of reassurance, the evening was a stirring testament to the fact that Parsons can not only spank but that she can also cozily reassure in the best Lolly-palooza style. And that, perhaps, even worse than being unflatteringly mentioned in Parsons' column, is not being mentioned at all.

An instance of Parsons' journalistic persuasion took place in 1951 when, at my columnar suggestion in the Los Angeles *Daily News*, a great number of the Hollywood press got together, in one of their infrequent mergers, to stage something known as the Mickey Awards, a spoof of Academy Awards and the spate of many other movietown awards. In Hollywood just about everybody gets awards, from the people who are in charge of the placement of ash trays on movie sets, to the four-footed thespians in jungle epics. Dalton Trumbo (who was one of the original Hollywood Ten, excommunicated for assertedly subversive movie activities) once had the fairly final words to say on Hollywood's multifarious awards: "The man doesn't live who can spend a decade in motion pictures without accumulating at least one diplomat-size brief case full of kudos. I've got three gold certificates with blue ribbon, two medals, a bronze plaque and $736,000 in the bank. . . . I recommend certificates and citations above hollowware (bronze can cost you your life) because they're easy to lift, they pack flat, and you can always run faster with them."

The Mickey Awards were in the shape of Mickey Finn martini glasses with skull and crossbones painted on them, and they were held at Barney's Beanery, a one-arm Hollywood hash-house. In the noblest tradition of the Academy Awards, there were bleachers for bystanders, a velvet carpet and klieg lights. It was all in reasonably good fun, with such awards being handed out as "To the Actor Who Received the Most Phone Calls at the Brown Derby" and "To the Actor Who Gave the Best Performance in Schwab's Drugstore." The motto in Latin for the Mickeys was "Life Is Short, the Double Feature Is Long."

But Hollywood is a place of tender sensibilities. George Jessel, Hollywood's "toastmaster general," was selected to preside at the Mickeys. However, Harry Brand, the wily and devious publicity boss at Twentieth Century-Fox, construed the Mickey Awards to be derogatory to the Academy Awards. Since Fox's Darryl Zanuck was a strong contender for the coveted Irving Thalberg Oscar that year (he got it, too), Brand forbade Jessel, who was then a Fox producer, to officiate at the event. Jessel, embarrassed, bowed out. Dean Martin and Jerry Lewis were substituted. Brand—backed up by the publicity directors of the major studios—got in touch with the venerable Y. (for Young) Frank Freeman, head of Paramount, where Martin and Lewis were under contract, and before you could say "Oscar," Freeman ordered Martin and Lewis to desist from the Mickeys. The Freeman ban was issued the day of the Mickey Awards and so an emergency meeting of the Hollywood press was called at the office of Martin and Lewis's press agent, Jack Keller.

What were the hapless journalists to do? Army Archerd, then a leg man for columnist Harrison Carroll, had an idea: get in touch with Parsons. She was the only one who could straighten out the entire thing. Parsons, herself one of the sponsors of the Mickeys, was reached at her weekly staff meeting at the Brown Derby. Informed of this low blow to the Hollywood press, she promptly went into action. She called Freeman and told him that if he did not allow Martin and Lewis to officiate at the Mickey Awards, he would never hear the end of it. Freeman, a cagey gent who knows when to give in, quickly capitulated. That night, Martin and Lewis emceed the Mickey Awards and a crisis was averted. Probably only Parsons could have done it. A down-front chair for her was zealously guarded in the rush-hour throng by a couple of stalwart reporters. Parsons arrived late, was ushered in with ceremony and seated in the chair of honor.

But Brand still was not licked. He got a local columnist on an afternoon daily, who had been in cahoots with the studio for years, to pen a nasty piece about the Mickey Awards in his newspaper. So blatantly poisonous was this reporter's report that the newspaper yanked it after the first edition and substituted an entirely different and laudatory story by another writer.

The unimportance of the Mickey Awards cannot be overemphasized. But the Mickeys will do to illustrate the intrigue, skulduggery and general insanity that prevails on the journalistic and publicistic fronts in Hollywood.

An even more pungent example of the power of the press concerned a highly publicized screenwriter who was drummed out of Hollywood some years ago on un-American charges. This writer was doing well abroad ghosting screenplays, and attempts were meanwhile being made by his Hollywood producers and attorneys to clear him in Washington, D.C., so that his name could appear on the screen again. But one of the gadflies in his comeback was a Hollywood lady columnist who periodically went after him in print and who was a serious block to his getting cleared politically. When the lady columnist was visiting abroad, mutual friends got her and the writer together in an attempt to reconcile them. The meeting was not a pleasant one. The writer and journalist met in her hotel room. They minced no words with each other. Finally, having run out of insults, they decided to declare a temporary truce. The columnist brought out a bottle of booze. They had a few drinks. Then they had a few more. As the writer, a rather earthy fellow, told me later: "We finished the bottle. It was getting dark. I looked at the old bag and she looked almost good enough to crawl into the sack with. I didn't do anything about it [at least that is what he said] but she must have seen the expression on my face. It was the greatest compliment I could have paid her. Soon afterwards, she not only dropped all uncomplimentary references to me in her column, but she started running favorable comments. That, combined with efforts my lawyers were making in Washington, finally got me cleared of the un-American rap." The writer is not only doing very well now, but his name is emblazoned in sky-high letters on the screen, an indirect but eloquent tribute to the power of the Hollywood press.

Another example of the impact of the press—or, rather, in this instance, of the ex-press—and one of my favorite Hollywood reportorial stories, has to do with a movie columnist who was dropped by his newspaper in an economy move. He found it difficult to get a job. On top of that, hardly any of the film folk would talk to him as an ex-Hollywood columnist. For a time the going was tough. He worked as a salesman and did other odd jobs. One day, several years later, while lunching at Romanoff's (on *Time* Magazine business), I saw this ex-columnist at the bar. He was expensively attired and buying drinks for everyone in sight. We hoisted one together. "What are you doing?" I inquired. "I'm doing just great," he said. "I'm with a big collection agency. I'm in charge of handling the Hollywood deadbeats. The town is full of them. I know them all personally, of course, and it's my job to track them down and make them pay up on their delinquent bills. I'm cut in on the take and I make a pile of dough every week." He took a swig of liquor. "I've gone from deadlines to deadbeats," he continued, "and I'm happy about it." He added: "But I wouldn't like to have it appear as if I'm using it as a hate thing to go after people. There's no retribution. I'm just collecting bills." But the Hollywood press, as you can see, is to be reckoned with even when not behind a typewriter.

After another interval of several years, I again talked to this ex-columnist—this time on the telephone. He was no longer in the collection business. "I'm working now as a warehouseman in a hospital supply outfit," he said. "I fill orders for sutures, needles, bandages, compresses. I find it very fascinating. On the job they say, 'What are you doing here?' I say, 'I'm on the lam.' They think it's a joke and drop it. I'm known as———there. I get along perfectly beautifully with all my fellow slaves. You should see me. I have no stomach and I'm down to my fighting weight of 165 pounds. I feel good. I'm learning a new trade. I'm broke, but I'm paying my bills and I'm having a ball being out with people who just love to drink and make love and no crap."

Runner-up in the archaic-lady-columnist contest is Hedda Hopper, originally Elda Furry, a washed-up actress who became a columnist pretty much by chance. Louis B. Mayer, for whom she had worked in movies, helped set her up as a gossipist in 1938 with a command-performance party that, according to Hopper, put "the stamp of approval" on her. Mayer was reportedly irked with Parsons' domination of the Hollywood scene and wanted to give Louella some competition. Ironically, Hopper later had a serious falling-out with M-G-M and Mayer, who went after her well-hatted scalp, until matters were finally patched up.

At first Hopper almost flopped until she learned to be unladylike in print and to "uncover" the Hollywood scene. Like Parsons, Hopper goes in for trashy paragraphs. A recent lead story in her column in the Los Angeles *Times* was this shattering communiqué: "Dick Zanuck of 20th will star Lee Remick as Temple Drake in *Sanctuary*, which he hopes to have in the works by June for Darryl Zanuck Productions. He's close to a deal with Richard Brooks to direct."

Hopper hops up her column with clarion comments on politics and catty remarks about fashions, morals and what-have-you. Hopper is not as good a reporter as Parsons, or perhaps it would be more accurate to say that Hopper is a worse reporter than Parsons. Parsons also gets first call on the studio production "news" most of the time. In addition, Parsons has a larger staff working for her than Hopper does. However, Hopper has the advantages of comparative youth—she is about a decade younger than Parsons—and the fact that her column appears in two powerful outlets, the New York *Daily News* and the Los Angeles *Times*, where it is conspicuously spotted.

Hopper works with one secretary, one leg man and a girl "in charge of accounting and finances" out of a Hollywood office building. She has boasted that "I'm the only columnist with an office on Hollywood Boulevard and a listed phone number." At one time Hopper's leg man was King Kennedy, ex-son-in-law of Parsons. Hopper, who does not type, dictates her column. In her autobiography, *From Under My Hat*, she noted: "Louella Parsons is a reporter trying to be a ham; Hedda Hopper is a ham trying to be a reporter."

Hopper's trademark, aside from inaccuracy, is her extensive collection of "screwy" hats, with most everything from windmills and clocks to birds and an Eiffel Tower on them. She once wore two hats, one on top of the other, in the best mad-hatter style.

But the vitriolic Hopper doffs her hat to no one in Hollywood and she has her goodly share of enemies. In 1950 Joan Bennett, angered by an item Hopper ran about her, had her chauffeur deliver a live, deodorized skunk to Hopper's home. Hopper promptly announced to reporters that the skunk was "beautifully behaved. I christened it Joan."

In 1959 Ed Sullivan, the columnist and television master of ceremonies, got into a hassle with Hopper over the issue of payment for TV guests stars. Sullivan said that Hopper was "using plugs" in her column "to get performers free" on her short-lived television show. Hopper screamed back: "Liar." Sullivan, who had once been a Hollywood columnist himself and whose column appears in the New York *Daily News* along with Hopper's, countered with "This woman used to hang around the fringes of show business. She's no actress. She's certainly no newspaperwoman. She's downright illiterate. She can't even spell. She serves no higher function than playing housemother on Conrad Hilton junkets. And yet she's established a reign of terror out there in Hollywood." The storm soon subsided. But, as one longtime Hollywood observer said at the time: "It took Ed Sullivan, as a newspaperman and columnist, to challenge Hopper. Otherwise she would have murdered him if he had no column, no matter how big he was on TV. But Sullivan could fight her because he had recourse to his column."

In case anyone should presume to question Hopper's journalistic credentials, she has it on the legal record that she is a real, for-sure, honest-to-goodness columnist. In November 1948 Hopper appeared as a witness in a civil suit filed in Los Angeles Superior Court by Hollywood press agent Jack Proctor against boat distributor Wade Miller for collection of $52,000 fees for publicistic services rendered. Proctor claimed that he worked for Miller from May 1945 to May 1947 and that among his professional activities during that period was furnishing certain material to Hopper as well as helping her write a column about Andrew J. Higgins, a boat builder, whose crafts were distributed by Miller on the West Coast. Hopper, questioned by the attorney for Miller as to whether Proctor had had anything to do with the writing of the column in which she gave an account of the Higgins interview, replied smartly: "Nobody writes Hedda Hopper's column but Hedda Hopper." So there.

The overpublicized rivalry between Hopper and Parsons has never quite abated. In 1955 *Life* Magazine wanted to photograph the two bumptious broads together for a special Hollywood layout. Hopper, as lady-in-waiting to Parsons, was perfectly willing. Parsons declined. She was still the queen. *Life* never got the picture.

Sheilah Graham is unique among Hollywood's female columnists in that she is relatively youthful and attractive. A blond, green-eyed ex-chorus girl from London who was born Lily Sheil, she was the model for the Hollywood girl in F. Scott Fitzgerald's *The Last Tycoon*, and she recently retailed her real-life romance with Fitzgerald in book form in *Beloved Infidel*, which she composed, naturally, with the help of a ghostwriter. With the proceeds from the movie sale of her book, Graham, having sold her home in Beverly Hills, left Hollywood and has been doing a good deal of traveling. She operates mostly out of New York today and manages to write a Hollywood-datelined column from there and from other points, with the help of a leg man who feeds her information from Hollywood. Anyway, maintains Graham, "Hollywood is no longer a place, it's a condition." This may be the beginning of a new trend in Hollywood columns—namely writing them from anywhere but Hollywood. And, to tell the truth, there doesn't seem to be any noticeable difference in the final product no matter from where it is filed.

Graham is sometimes mentioned as a dark-horse possibility in the Parsons-Hopper dominated columnar sweepstakes, if anyone is still interested in the contest, and she could conceivably forge ahead in the final stretch. She used to live on the same street as Parsons, and, when Louella was critically ill some years ago, Graham was able to keep a strategic watch on developments from her windows. As a columnist, Sheilah Graham has the vital knack of the knock; for instance: "Errol Flynn says he doesn't worry about money just as long as he can reconcile his net income with his gross habits." Actress Constance Bennett once said to Graham: "It's hard to believe that a girl as pretty as you could be the biggest bitch in Hollywood." "Not the biggest," Graham retorted, "the second biggest."

One of the prerogatives of the pampered Hollywood press is freeloading. Since reporters are not exactly overpaid—the ego professions of journalism, law enforcement and teaching are traditionally undersalaried—it is customary for the fourth estate to be showered with all sorts of blandishments by the well-heeled film folk. There is a great deal of wining and dining. It has been observed that if you just slap a cold cut between two slices of pumpernickel and send out the word to the Hollywood press, a reportorial stampede will ensue. Many press interviews take place at lunch. The Hollywood press's appetite for news and gossip is proverbially exceeded only by its appetite. A local gastronome once noted that there are some of the best interview-eaters in the world in Hollywood. This is freeloading on the rudimentary—or should one say alimentary?—level. But it is also not unusual for some of the Hollywood press to be on the regular payrolls of Hollywood press agents for services rendered in print.

One veteran, exceedingly social columnist, who is renowned as the dean of freeloading, has a home in which most everything, from the washing machine and the refrigerator to the television set and grand piano, were supplied, and willingly, by press agents, profiles and producers. This journalist is not resented in Hollywood. He has his price and the community is more than willing to meet it. The film folk feel that they know where they stand with him, that for a few hundred dollars or so they can buy his columnar friendship. Besides, it is a justifiable, tax-deductible business expense. What the Hollywood operatives are wary of is the occasional journalist who may gum up the works with a misplaced sense of integrity.

Another standard form of freeloading is the free press trip or junket.

This was brought to almost classic perfection in 1951 by Howard Hughes's press agents. Hughes, who then owned the RKO studios, released a movie entitled *Hard, Fast and Beautiful*. To publicize this forgettable film, the Hughes drumbeaters arranged, for no special reason, for the Hollywood press to journey to San Francisco to see the picture. There, of course, they were put up at the best hotel and plied with the finest of everything. The cost of the junket was reputed to have almost equaled the cost of the low-budget picture. But meanwhile a knotty situation arose. The Los Angeles press was being brought to San Francisco to see the picture. But how would the San Francisco press feel about having to see the film in its own back yard without benefit of a junket? Would the San Francisco newspapermen not resent this? The problem was solved quite simply. While the Los Angeles press was en route to San Francisco to see *Hard, Fast and Beautiful*, the San Francisco press was flown to Los Angeles to see the same picture. Everyone was happy, including the press agents, who got a great deal of free newspaper space from the grateful journalists.

Junketing journalists are often overwhelmed by the spirit of the occasion. One Hollywood columnist boarded an airplane for the cinema city at Tucson, Arizona, during a movietown trip, looking decidedly bulky. It turned out that he had pulled a chewing-gum machine loose from its moorings and was transporting it back with him to Hollywood for his well-stocked trophy room. This same journalist once scurried up the steps to a waiting airplane at a remote, hick-town airport, precariously balancing a Moscow Mule (a drink, not an animal). Where he had managed to obtain this libation in the surrounding wilderness and how he contrived to keep it constantly replenished in the course of the flight was a source of wonderment and envy to his less ingenious journalistic confreres.

A bus load of Hollywood press, heading back to the film capital from a publicity trip, was kept waiting in Tijuana, Mexico, some years ago until one of the group—a devil-may-care trade-paper columnist who had been missing—was found. He was finally located, after a long search, at a Tijuana bordello. On the return voyage to Hollywood, he never stopped complaining about how rude it was for the rest of the press to have interrupted him in his journalistic labors in Tijuana.

One New York–Hollywood columnist, a most obnoxiously determined dame, is such a dedicated freeloader and party-crasher that there is seemingly no stopping her. Even her freeloading fellow members of the press frown on her. When the New York film critics were holding their annual awards several years ago, one of the main points on the journalistic agenda was how to prevent this particular columnist from invading the premises. Two members of the press were stationed at the door with explicit orders to keep her out at all costs. But the lady columnist won out anyway. Since she had not been invited to the event and had also gotten wind that she would be rebuffed if she tried to crash, she was momentarily stymied, but not for long. She showed up at the awards insolubly linked arm in arm with the actress who was being honored for the best performance of the year. There was nothing the film critics could do to detach her from the actress without precipitating a scene, and so the lady columnist had her way, as usual.

Another and less blatant form of freeloading is the casting of Hollywood reporters in movies dealing with the press in order to "lend authenticity" and to help give "technical advice." The journalists are handsomely reimbursed for playing themselves, and they also somehow manage to give the movie some helpful publicity in their columns. Almost invariably, however, they are cut out of the picture before it reaches the screen.

Freeloading in Hollywood, as most elsewhere, reaches its peak during the Christmas season. Since there are so many press representatives in Hollywood, the studios, through the Advertising and Publicity Directors' Committee of the Association of Motion Picture Producers, long ago worked out a co-operative plan—which they prefer not to discuss in public—to handle Christmas gifts for the avid recipients. There are some downtrodden individuals who get no gifts at all, but these untouchables one does not even talk about in Hollywood. For the great majority of the press there is an A, B and C list. The bulk of the press gets a C gift, which is usually limited to a ten-dollar or so ceiling, and may consist of anything from a rhinestoned antimacassar to a Technicolored doily. The B list, somewhat more important, gets gifts of a slightly higher value. And, finally, there is the A list, consisting of a handful of key columnists, who may get a gift as expensive as the studio wishes to make it. The publicists like to pretend that these latter gifts are given on a "personal" rather than on a "business" basis, not because the recipient is in the journalistic profession but because he or she is such an admirable individual.

In the exclusive A list, some of the tokens run into the many hundreds of dollars. Holiday freeloading on this plane can be Olympian. At Christmas, truckloads of studio gifts have been known to be sent to hospitals and institutions by one or two favored columnists. One Christmas, in the long ago, according to Hollywood legend, Parsons had an automobile load of gifts stolen. She supposedly went to the studios and picked up duplicate gifts. One version had her denying the story with "Why, I never would do a thing like that. I would have made them send the presents to my house!"

The story is told of one Hollywood producer who had the rare knack of being able to juggle both Hopper and Parsons and being chummy with both of them. One Christmas, in the mid-Forties, the producer bought expensive handbags for both of the columnists and enclosed personal cards to each of them. In the course of delivery, the cards accidentally got switched. Hopper, as the story went, telephoned the producer and made rather light of it. But Parsons didn't. According to an inside source, "the producer never got it straightened out, particularly with Parsons, who thought he had given Hopper a better gift than she got." This informant added philosophically, "This could happen anywhere, but it was a major disaster here and the worst thing that could have happened to the producer."

Naturally, there is much vying and jealousy among the press over the Christmas-gift caste system. But it took one very minor columnist to blow the matter up into a major public issue. This scrivener, who writes for a small string of West Coast newspapers as well as running a real-estate and insurance business, let his acquisitive nature get the better of him and sent an unprecedented, mimeographed letter to the studio publicity directors on December 26, 1951, deploring the inequities of their gift-giving. He protested that for a long time he had "felt the impact of the studio's caste system toward Hollywood writers. If you're in the top drawer, you're in. If you're lukewarm, you're on the fringe. If you're cold, you're out. This *modus operandi* applies to the routine of giving Christmas gifts." The man continued that "if a Christmas gift is sent to the few preferred columnists, it strikes a jarring note when a few hundred are completely ignored. It smacks too much of an intent to do great mental harm. It's a slap in the face. It's embarrassing. It slugs below the belt." Moreover, he complained, the small-circulation columnist "has his place in the newspaper trenches just as well as the Cliveden set columnists. This type of columnist has earned his E for effort at Christmas. He certainly does not deserve a kick in the pants at Christmas time." And finally: "Most of us know we're not as important as Walter [Winchell] and Louella, but not one of us will admit we're unimportant." And, still sobbing at his typewriter, he concluded: "It's not a pleasant feeling to feel low on Christmas Day when a man's spirits should be at their highest. . . . I feel uncomfortable when I'm ignored. . . . Give us a break next Christ-

mas, publicity directors.... Don't leave us with a dark brown taste....
We like our Christmas cheer as well as the next columnist, so why
make any of us weep in our beer?"

The Hollywood press aired this tender plaint in the most reverent
Christmas tradition. Daily Variety ran it under a special two-column
boxed head: "Santa, How Could You?" The story was picked up by
the national news magazines—in Newsweek it rated almost a column
and a half of space under the title "Loot Song." Newsweek noted that
most studio gift lists didn't include the writer. The studio publicists
were irked. This letter had opened up a big can of Hollywood beans
—and "has-beens." To this day, the whole matter is a sore point with
the studio flacks and they refuse to talk about it. Chastened, the writer
admittted: "Maybe I've made a mistake." He tried to rectify his error
in an abject letter to Daily Variety on December 31, 1951: "... it was
not my purpose to offend any of my motion picture or television
contacts who have always conducted our relationship with dignity."
He added: "After reconsidering my original plan for Christmas remembrances for all, I now believe that even a better idea would be the
abolishment of all gifts by all publicity departments so that nobody
would be offended."

In the old, pre-television Hollywood era, freeloading was a good
deal better than it is today. Even a relatively minor studio like Republic would send out whopping basketfuls of the finest imported liquor
to the major press. The avaricious journalists could stock their larders
for the year from just one good Christmas haul. To publicize Gone
with the Wind, the picture's press agents gifted the press with special
foreign-made typewriters on which the initials of the movie were spot-
lighted with colored keys. Some of these typewriters are still in use in
Hollywood today; they have even had more staying power than the
picture's producer, David O. Selznick, who is "gone with the wind" as
far as Hollywood is concerned.

In Hollywood, where mass authorship has been brought to fine frui-
tion, it is not surprising that most of the journalists do not write their
copy alone. In fact, many of them do not write their copy at all. They
have assistants and ghostwriters who do it for them. This, too, is considered perfectly normal procedure, like having someone hose down
your convertible or black your boots for you. The less important and
underprivileged journalists, who cannot afford their own writers, usually fall back on stories written for them by the more than co-operative
press agents. One long-time syndicated columnist, who almost never
writes his own copy, was heard upbraiding a press agent about a story

that the publicist had submitted to him: "This is not up to my usual standard."

So conditioned are the local citizens to a docile, pussyfooting press that they are quite easily thrown for a dead loss by a fairly independent reporter. In 1950 *The New Yorker* Magazine sent a young lady named Lillian Ross to Hollywood to do a story about John Huston and the making of *The Red Badge of Courage*. Now, Hollywood hates and fears no publication more than it does *The New Yorker*, which it considers as being inimical to the finest ideals that prevail in Southern California. But Miss Ross allayed their misgivings. In their estimation she was square, both literally and figuratively. She did not wear open-toed shoes, was seemingly not conversant with the latest Hollywood witticisms and merely asked many questions, often busily taking down notes (the latter in itself a novelty in Hollywood press circles). The Hollywood wiseacres figured they would just humor her along. She returned to New York with several crateloads of notes and wrote a rather lethal story about what she had seen and heard in Hollywood—some of it accurate, too. The screams in the film capital have not yet subsided. Hollywood's parochial attitude toward Miss Ross was reflected in the comment of one local citizen: "You take a chance when you let a stranger in and tell family jokes in front of them."

Apparently what Miss Ross had done was not live up—or down—to the Hollywood typecasting concept of a fast-talking, Glenda Farrell-style girl reporter. Since typecasting in Hollywood often extends into real life, a number of journalists have found this helpful professionally. The veteran Jimmy Starr of the Los Angeles *Herald-Express* is a fast-gabbing, mildly dashing columnist in the Pat O'Brien–Lee Tracy mold who has authored whodunits featuring a Hollywood gossipist not unlike himself. Joe Hyams, Hollywood correspondent of the New York *Herald Tribune*, is a journalist with a profile and a predilection for the use of recording machines. When Hyams was doing a story about Ava Gardner, who was averse to being interviewed, he rigged up batteries of miniature recorders on his person, in the glove compartment of his car, in a briefcase and under the table she always occupied at her favorite restaurant on La Cienega Boulevard to document the reluctant Miss Gardner's dialogue. Both Starr and Hyams are popular with the cinema citizens. In Hollywood, you do not necessarily have to be a good reporter as long as you conform to Hollywood's concept of a reporter.

In 1959 Hyams wrote a series of articles about Cary Grant in which he quoted the actor as having been under psychiatric treatment. Grant, labeling the series "completely erroneous," denied ever having had any psychiatric attention—a rather unusual statement for an actor to make, since most of the performers in Hollywood seem to relish publicity about their psychiatric experiences. Furthermore, said Grant, he had never even talked to Hyams, although he admitted talking to Lionel Crane, of the London *Daily Mirror*, with whom Hyams had had working arrangements on stories in the past. Grant alleged that Hyams had lifted the material from Crane's articles. Hyams countered that he had actually talked to Grant and that Grant had also given him permission to quote from Crane's story in the London newspaper. The Los Angeles *Times* ran Hyams' story as a three-part news series, starting April 20, 1959, and described it as a "purported interview," interspersing Hyams' statements about Grant with the actor's denial of them. The series also ran in the New York *Herald Tribune* and other newspapers. On July 2, 1959, Hyams filed a $500,000 slander suit in Los Angeles Superior Court against Grant, stating that the actor's denials had caused him "great humiliation, shame and mental anxiety" and were injurious to his "personal and professional reputation." Hyams retained as his attorney Arthur Crowley, who had helped represent the scandal magazine *Confidential* in court in 1957. Grant subsequently admitted that he had talked to Hyams but not on the subject of psychiatry. The Hyams suit is still pending. In the interim, interviews with Grant have appeared in other publications, such as *Look* Magazine, in which the actor spoke candidly about his psychotherapy. *Look* Magazine even named Grant's psychotherapist. (In the Hyams series, Grant had, ironically, been quoted as saying that, because of his psychiatric treatment, "I've just been born again. . . . I've had my ego stripped away. A man is a better actor without ego, because he has truth in him. Now I cannot behave untruthfully toward anyone, and certainly not to myself.")

Hyams recently observed: "I have no intention of dropping the suit. We are going to court unless he apologizes. He hasn't apologized. He's a proud and stubborn man. He's gonna have to apologize publicly." Hyams added, rather proudly: "This is the first time a newspaperman has ever sued an actor for slander. Usually newspapermen slander actors. It's quite unprecedented." Until things hopefully get cleared away—did Grant really have the psychotherapy? did Hyams really interview him on the subject or just lift the quotes from Crane?—this is where the matter stands, with plenty of publicity for both Grant, who doesn't really need it, and for Hyams, too, who could conceivably be in greater need of it.

The Hyams suit may have triggered a new, litiginous trend among the Hollywood press. On November 6, 1959, Jaik Rosenstein, proprietor of a little scandal sheet, *Hollywood Close-Up*, which was weekly slandering a good segment of the screen colony, also sued a film figure for maliciously slandering him—which may well have been the neatest journalistic trick of the year. The object of Rosenstein's disaffection was, of all people, producer Jerry Wald, a publicity-seeker who normally values his diplomatic relationships with the press above most everything else. There were fusillades and counter-fusillades. Supposedly Wald had alleged during the period of August 18-21, 1959, that Rosenstein had a penal record. Rosenstein kept referring to Wald in his rag as "Fat Sam" and making other even less complimentary remarks. In any case, Wald must have maligned Rosenstein more than Grant did Hyams, or maybe Rosenstein just put a higher premium on his reputation, because he asked for damages of three million dollars in Los Angeles Superior Court. Hollywood, however, seemed rather apathetic about the entire thing, with the general feeling being, in the words of one of the film folk, that "it's just a case of the pot calling the kettle black."

The studios and the press agents have never favored an independent press. All they want from the journalists is paeans of praise and a constant quota of sweetness and light. "Is it a knock or a boost?" is about the only thing the press agents are interested in. If it is a "knock," they attempt to make the journalist see that he should not be "bitter" —another word for honest—about Hollywood. (Actually, real rancor may well be one of the few legitimate approaches to much of what happens in Hollywood, in the sense that malfeasance can breed honest anger.) I have also had movie publicists argue with me that anyone who has "made it" in Hollywood more than deserves his success because it is so tough to survive in the Hollywood jungle—so why "knock" him? The Hollywood press agents want a handout press and nothing else. The resultant blackout on fact and truth has made the celluloid curtain as impenetrable as any supposed iron curtain.

If a journalist is recalcitrant, the publicists try to butter him up and then freeload him and buy him off, one way or another. If he persists in being "difficult," he will start getting double-talk, the slow stall and the freeze. The press agents will try to make him see the error of his ways in biting the "industry" hand that purportedly feeds him, warning him, in the words of one publicist, that "when the goose is cooked, there will be no more golden eggs." (This is another fallacy fomented by the Hollywood flacks, since it is the journalist's employer and not

Hollywood that pays his salary, and should he lose his job, Hollywood will give him its blunt boot instead of any glad hand.) Finally, if worse comes to worst, there will be concerted attempts to get him fired.

The studio press agents have a punitive weapon in the official "accreditation" they hand out through their committee on the AMPP, whose administrative "secretary" is Clarke (Duke) Wales, a specialist in the slow, smooth shuffle. (The AMPP—or the Association of Motion Picture Producers—is the West Coast branch of the Motion Picture Association of America, which is headquartered in New York City. Although the two "heads" have different names, they are both attached to the same monster.) If a journalist steps out of bounds, he may be barred by the AMPP publicity boys from studios and press showings. He could even starve to death as a result of being denied access to freeloading cocktail parties. For years, the AMPP publicity committee was dominated by Howard Strickling and Harry Brand, publicity directors of the two biggest Hollywood studios, M-G-M and Twentieth Century-Fox, and they were able to call the turn in disciplining untractable correspondents. M-G-M and Fox were then under the control of Nicholas Schenck and his brother Joseph, respectively, so that Hollywood's monopoly methods extended even to press agentry and the press.

Confronted by internal press pressures and external press-agent pressures, it is not surprising that the Hollywood journalists, as a group, are cynical, tired and corrupt and that even the most elementary facts about the movies rarely get into print. Hollywood press coverage is compounded almost entirely of apathy, ignorance, imagination, wishful thinking, press agentry and soft soaping. A journalist can even start off with fairly elevated ideals, but, as Simon Bourgin, ex-chief of Newsweek Magazine's Hollywood bureau, put it: "You need layers of exposure and, by the time you know something, you are corrupted and debilitated." The average journalist sent from New York or elsewhere to cover Hollywood may hate and despise it at first, but, before long, he finds that he is on the merry-go-round and is part of the local picture, and, after a while, you couldn't pry him loose with an atomic crowbar. It is easy for a reporter to be in cahoots with the mob, to play the game and to hand out the right kind of publicity where the powers that be want it, or to hush things up in "off-the-record" fashion. As a result, the pushers and promoters, the sacred cows and the tycoons usually get the publicity. The talented people, the little people, those who do not push, those who do not have press agents are generally lost in the publicistic and journalistic jostling.

This holds true of some of the most esteemed and venerable publications, as well as the lowly movie fan magazines and Hollywood tradepapers. There is today hardly any publication where it is possible to write freely and frankly about Hollywood for one reason or another, whether of commission or omission. It may be the publisher's policy, advertising persuasion or other pressures. Since the movies are a relatively unimportant part of press coverage, it is only possible to conjecture the pressures that exist in other, more meaningful areas of the news.

One of the few publications where I was permitted to express myself candidly about Hollywood was the New York *Morning Telegraph*, for which I wrote a daily movie column for several years in the early Forties, and that was largely because the *Telegraph* was a racing paper and was concerned not with Hollywood ham but with horseflesh. Literally not a word of my copy was ever touched by the editors—although some of it would undoubtedly have benefited by retouching. The sole exception to the *laissez-faire* editorial policy occurred when an entire column I had written about Lena Horne and anti-Negro discrimination in Hollywood was not run by the paper, undoubtedly because it touched on a rather touchy subject for some of its horse-racing readers. Although I probably got away with some slipshod prose as a result of this hands-off editorial arrangement, at the same time I also managed to get away with some pointed and pertinent paragraphs that might never have gotten past a less liberal copy desk. All in all, I can honestly say that my *Morning Telegraph* columns were, generally speaking, the most incisive pieces I ever wrote about the movies, primarily because I was allowed to make my own mistakes—as well as to speak my own mind to the best of my ability; to do my worst—as well as my best. But this rather Utopian state of affairs was bound not to last indefinitely. It came to an end when the New York *Morning Telegraph* established, temporarily, as it soon turned out, a Hollywood edition of the newspaper and put a man named Carl Schroeder in charge of it. Schroeder, at various times a movie fan magazine editor and Hollywood press agent, quickly started tampering with my copy in the most flagrant, high-handed and obtuse fashion (there is, apparently, no other fashion for Hollywood-style editors). It was the end of a just about once-in-a-lifetime, perfect—or near perfect—journalistic experience for me.

Actually, what is there about the movies, exactly, that is so journalistically sacrosanct and puts them beyond the pale of any remotely free and rational comment? Today one is allowed to express oneself with relative impunity even about Ike and Nikita and to intimate that they might have just a few human failings and foibles. But if one so much as presumes to utter a single word against Jayne Mansfield and Tuesday Weld—or George Stevens and William Wyler—one is given the bum's rush from all corners of the ball park. Perhaps the motion picture, as the last, desperately held myth of our times, with its mythological gods and goddesses, the movie stars, is considered, in this sense, to be above criticism, somewhat like Mother Love (although that has come in for plenty of harsh words in recent years, and the word "mother" has taken on overtones that are not indicated in the unabridged dictionary).

The myth of the movies—and a myth assuredly it is—has been enhanced and perpetuated by the Hollywood press. Since little or no journalistic light is cast on the motion-picture community and its works, this has enabled much mediocrity and misunderstanding to flourish. The press is at the root of much of the trouble of Hollywood. Mired in its narrow vision and venality, it has failed to act on behalf of either the original creator or the ultimate consumer. The so-called intellectual press is the most culpable in this respect. Out of its high-toned ignorance and illusions, it has played into the publicistic hands of the shrewd motion-picture operators. At least most of the lowbrow Hollywood journalists know what the screen score is—although they calculatedly do not transmit it to their readers. The vast majority of the highbrow commentators have hardly ever bothered to tote up the score at all and write in utter illusion and self-delusion of their subject matter.

In the opinion of one thoughtful and outspoken Hollywood observer: "The press is at the hub of the whole racket. Without the press, the entire thing would collapse. If, by some hypothetical stroke of magic, the Hollywood press were eliminated, the whole damn thing would vanish. There would just be pictures, with no hullaballoo or anything. The press has actually overwhelmed the product. They have had it to themselves for too long.

"If it weren't for the press, the Louis B. Mayers and the Harry Cohns wouldn't have been half of what they were. They simply wouldn't have been able to get away with it."

And he added: "The Hollywood press reflects the larger community press of Los Angeles. The unfree press of Los Angeles is the worst in the country."

The Hollywood press hacks have been doing the dirty work for the big boys for years and, as the scavengers and jackals of Hollywood, have been happy to feed on the leavings. In a multi-million dollar racket, the pathetic press has been content to be purchased for pennies. The journalists are the despicable little people who, as the pliant tools of the overlords, have participated actively in the colossal crimes. By its acquiescence and toadying, truckling tactics, the Hollywood press has not only heralded the clay gods but actually helped mold them. In this light, the press is Hollywood's single worst excrescence, the very crux of the movietown corruption.

Any attempt to break through this journalistic bottleneck is a hazardous one. The press is malicious, treacherous, vindictive and almost impossible to cope with in any honest, reasonable way. There are more prima donnas among the Hollywood press than among the Hollywood profiles. And the press discourages any revelations about itself. As a result there has, for instance, been almost nothing of relevance written about such vital and revealing areas of Hollywood journalism as the trade papers and the fan magazines. And if one attempts to tangle with the press, it will strike out with every dirty printed tool at its command and, without similar weapons with which to retaliate, it is a decidedly one-sided combat.

There have been a few, brave exceptions to this restrictive reportorial rule. Among them was the late Douglas Churchill, the Hollywood correspondent for the New York *Times*, who was repeatedly barred from studios for his forthright reporting. In the trade publication *Editor and Publisher* of August 10, 1935, Churchill wrote an illuminating story headlined "Hollywood . . . Gags Candid Press Critics. Studios Threaten Withdrawal of Advertising Unless Newspaper Correspondents Write Kindly—Crisis Seen Near in Press Relations." Churchill led off his piece with "Newsmen covering the motion-picture industry are engaged in a critical battle. Victims of a persistent and vicious campaign to impose censorship on them and the papers and press associations they represent, they are attempting to preserve their livelihood and their integrity.

"In the face of a united onslaught of the picture industry, many feel that they are regarded with apathy by their papers and services—and there seems to be evidence to justify the belief. Certainly but a few enjoy the militant backing of their employers."

Churchill added that "the determination of the industry to impose censorship on news emanating from Hollywood came into the open a year ago. Under threat of an advertising boycott, the lid was clamped on fan magazines and since then no stories have appeared without submission to and approval by studios. Heartened by the success of this, many of the studios have become brazen in threatening correspondents and through the theatres they control bringing advertising pressure on individual papers."

One of the objects of the studios' ire was columnist Sidney Skolsky, who, the studios averred, "destroyed the illusion of the screen" by writing revealing "facts about the industry." These are some of the facts that Skolsky revealed:

"A plate of glass protected the baby in *Sequoia* from the snake."

"In spite of studio publicity declaring Jean Harlow sang and danced in *Reckless*, doubles were employed."

"Scenes in *Les Miserables* between Charles Laughton and Fredric March were actually shot a month apart although they were supposedly looking at each other."

"A night shot in *The Glass Key* was made at noon and the door seen in the background was that of Marlene Dietrich's dressing room."

"Although appearing in a film as an aviator, James Cagney is afraid to look off a high building."

Churchill observed that "from a newspaper standpoint the charges against Skolsky's copy are too flimsy to dignify. . . . While the charges were unimportant, they are significant in one respect. They indicate the true frenzy to which the industry would be aroused should an attempt be made to report more serious derelictions. And there is not a reporter in Hollywood who could not rock the country by sitting down to his typewriter and recording merely a portion of the things he knows. In a business reeking with incompetence and corruption, the excitement of the lads at having an uncensored press is understandable. . . . Reporters are in good standing on some of the lots only when they act as unpaid press agents for the studios, a status the industry has attempted to foster."

Since those days, the major studios have lost much of their power to push the press around. But otherwise the basic situation Churchill described still applies: Hollywood news consists mostly of what is print to fit rather than what is fit to print.

The diminutive Skolsky, besides being a movie producer (*The Jolson Story*), is one of the more colorful members of the Hollywood press. For one thing, he is the only reporter on record who operates out of a drugstore, Schwab's, on Sunset Boulevard. Schwab's several years ago underwent an expensive façade-lifting and emerged looking like a Taj Mahal with pills. In the new Schwab's, Skolsky has a comfortable, balcony office with a sweeping picture window from which he can command a dramatic view of the action in the store below, somewhat like Ziegfeld looking down on the stage from his theater office.

Schwab's offers Skolsky a profusion of pills, to which he is addicted, and it serves as a jumping-off point for his getting automobile rides to wherever he wants to go. Skolsky does not drive a car; he is afraid of automobiles as well as of cats, dogs and children. But this has not hindered him from getting around in the vast wilderness of greater Los Angeles—an estimable achievement in itself. Skolsky knows, through long experience, who will be at any given place at a certain time and in what direction they are driving, and so he manages to make connections. At various times Skolsky has been chauffeured by most everyone from Marlene Dietrich to Marilyn Monroe.

Aside from his hitchhiking accomplishments, Skolsky will be remembered in Hollywood for at least three reasons. He once stood under Greta Garbo. It happened while she was making *Anna Karenina* at M-G-M in 1935, and Skolsky crashed her set, strictly closed to the press and outsiders when, as he tells it, the gateman thought he was Freddie Bartholemew, the child actor. Since he was not supposed to be there, Skolsky hid under a railroad platform while a scene was in progress. From this vantage point, he was able to make some unusual observations about Garbo's acting technique while standing under her —until discovered and evicted.

Skolsky spanked Shirley Temple when she was the junior queen and financial mainstay of Twentieth Century-Fox in the mid-Thirties. While he was visiting the studio one day, the movie moppet playfully tossed his new chapeau about until she damaged it. Incensed, Skolsky slung her over his knee—she was about the only one on the lot smaller than he was—and smote her. Shirley screamed and peacemakers separated the two contestants.

But probably Skolsky's greatest feat was biting Louella Parsons in the arm. Skolsky had been working for Hearst in the late Thirties and had gotten into a professional squabble with Parsons. According to Skolsky, she got him fired. Parsons denies it. In *The Gay Illiterate* she writes: "I like pint-sized Sidney and his Hollywood writings, and I had nothing to do with his dismissal. . . . His main trouble came from editors who insisted on cutting his copy to the bone. . . ." Skolsky, minus a job, was in Chasen's restaurant one night when he ran into Parsons and some of her friends. She gave him a big hello and said toothily, "My, you're a nice fellow. I'm sorry that we had a misunderstanding." Infuriated by her politeness, Skolsky leaned over and sank his molars into her arm, almost to the bone. It was an historic gastronomic moment.

When Skolsky is not at Schwab's, he can often be found at Twentieth Century-Fox. He just drives on the lot (in somebody else's car) and makes himself at home in whatever office is vacant (and there are plenty of vacant offices at Fox these days). So familiar has Skolsky become around the studio—he also likes to get shaved there—that most of the people on the lot think he works there. This is a nice arrangement for Skolsky. He is able to make use of all the studio facilities, and since he is not employed at the studio he cannot be fired. As a result, he has outlasted all sorts of "geniuses" at the studio, including Darryl Zanuck. And the way things are going in Hollywood today, with so many of the film factories closing up shop, he may even outlast the studio itself.

The representatives of the foreign press in Hollywood, comprising almost a third of the entire press corps, like to think of themselves as "the outside world's accredited ambassadors to Hollywood." But most of the foreign press are not professional journalists in the strict sense. A good many of the correspondents do little but carry a courtesy card from some foreign publication. They like to socialize and attend parties where they are very much in evidence. Since most of them get little remuneration from their publications in terms of American dollar exchange, they practice journalism as a sideline. Many of them work in other businesses—one is a pharmacist, another a baker, for instance— and a good many of them get payola-type acting jobs in movies. In a survey of seventy foreign correspondents printed in the spring 1952 issue of the *Quarterly of Film, Radio and Television*, it was found that "only 17% fully support themselves as foreign correspondents" and that the rest had some other form of income to supplement their none too-lucrative journalistic labors. The same survey concluded that the foreign correspondents did no better a job than their domestic colleagues in reporting motion-picture developments and that "on the whole the foreign readers are getting the same star-dusted image of the Hollywood scene as does the American public."

Although the foreign correspondents write for the all-important foreign market, which today accounts for an estimated 50 per cent at least of Hollywood's box-office receipts, they are, with a handful of important exceptions, not catered to by the studios. The *Quarterly of Film, Radio and Television* noted that 26 per cent of the foreign correspondents questioned in the poll commented on "a lack of co-operation on the part of the studios." One foreign department publicist at a major studio explained it as follows: "The local press gets the preferential treatment. Hollywood can read what the local press writes tomorrow. But not with the foreign press. It's as simple as that. The local press has the impact."

There are quite a few exotic characters among the foreign correspondents. Conspicuous among them for sheer local—or foreign—color are the Unger twins, Bertil and Gustav, a natty duo who correspond for Scandinavian publications, dabble in acting and wear monocles, Bertil in the left eye and Gustav in the right eye. Bertil also works in the credit department of the Los Angeles *Times* and Gustav is engaged in television production. In the words of one droll young Hollywood damsel: "Every girl should meet the Unger twins at least once."

At a 1954 Golden Globe Awards dinner given by the foreign correspondents in Hollywood, the Unger twins got into a set-to with another set of twins, Aly and Amad Sadick, cotton brokers and importers. Fists began flying and it was impossible for bystanders to tell which twin threw which punch. When it was all over, Bertil was sporting a black eye as well as a monocle eye.

Most of the foreign correspondents belong to the Hollywood Foreign Press Association, which bestows the Golden Globe Awards annually in open-handed style. The Golden Globe was inaugurated in 1951 by Henry Gris, who covers Hollywood for foreign subscribers of United Press International and who named them Henriettas at the time, after himself, prompting a local oracle to observe: "That's something a shrinking violet does not dream up." The foreign correspondents like to make tie-ins with the studios and with leading publicity firms which will deliver movie stars in person at the Golden Globes in the sure foreknowledge that each of them will get an award. Says the foreign department publicist: "The Golden Globes are a good advance event for the Academy Awards. They are a press agent's field day. People know pretty well who will get the awards in advance. The press agents just love this stuff. It's not like the Academy Awards where you don't know who wins until the envelope is opened. The foreign correspondents give out a helluva lot of awards. They try to cover practically everything. They give out International Star of the Future awards and let each studio make their own suggestions." One columnist cracked that "about the only thing they don't give an award to is the newspapermen who have to sit and suffer through the awards." At the 1960 Golden Globes, the foreign correspondents excelled themselves. They gave awards for "journalistic achievement" to both Louella Parsons and Hedda Hopper, simultaneously. Parsons' award was "for outstanding journalistic reporting throughout the world." Hopper's was "for news coverage and travels that have brought international prestige to Hollywood." Noted a gossipist: "They're not taking any chances!"

In the words of another film-colony quipster: "The only distinction one or two actors have in Hollywood is that they didn't get Golden Globe Awards."

According to a Hollywood press scribe of long standing: "The foreign press itself can out-ham Hollywood's finest. There's a tradition in the domestic press: you never see a picture of a reporter in a story in an accompanying photograph. But with the foreign press, wherever you go, the first thing that happens is that the still man runs up and says, 'We can take your picture now with Lizzie Glutz, the star.' It's par for the course. The correspondents send it back to their cousin, the mayor, who appointed them foreign correspondent in Hollywood. Everybody is famous together. The foreign press is something wonderful and the performances there have no peer except in the ballet.

"The foreign press are still back in the Menjou–Lubitsch era, spiritually speaking. So many of them can hardly speak English and also the ones who speak English, largely the British press, have a rather naïve outlook. And they do do a lot of throat cutting among themselves, like getting papers away from each other. We could consider it naïve, but they are writing for their particular readership. They are giving them pretty much what they want. It's pretty much stars-in-the-eyes."

The impact of the scandal magazines on Hollywood was an appreciable one until the leading publication in the field, *Confidential*, with a circulation of more than five million, eliminated most of its movie exposés and was later sold to new owners after being hauled into court by the Attorney General's office of the State of California on charges of publishing obscene and criminally libelous material. The case came to an anticlimactic close in Los Angeles in October 1957 after two months of blaring headlines, more than 2,000 pages of lurid testimony and a record fourteen days of jury deadlock. Afterward, the major charges against *Confidential* were dropped and the magazine announced that it would adopt a new editorial format minus stories about the private lives of celebrities.

In a community where collusion between press and press agents predominates and where hardly anyone ever gets out of line journalistically, the scandal magazines were feared—and also held a horrible fascination for most everyone. For a while, Confidential replaced even television as the favorite subject of conversation at Hollywood bars, cocktail parties and Schwab's drugstore. As Humphrey Bogart observed: "Everyone reads Confidential. But they deny it. They say the cook brought it into the house." It was simple for the scandal magazines to dig up the Hollywood dirt, which constituted the bulk of their editorial contents. Scandals were everywhere in evidence and, in Hollywood particularly, nothing is confidential. Confidential, for instance, would get tips from starlets, party girls, night-club hatcheck girls, cynical press agents with a meat cleaver to grind and any one of that great army of disgruntled movie people who hate somebody or other for once doing them wrong. Some of the tipsters were even among the press. One of the leading "male" gossipists in Hollywood was a source for Confidential—the magazine used an unpublished story about this columnist's amorous activities as a journalistic sword over his head.

Working from a tip, the magazine then put a private investigator on the story, tailing the subject over a period of time. When a sufficiently detailed and documented dossier had been compiled, complete with vouchers from witnesses, the magazines would run a portion of the story, holding the rest of the evidence in abeyance should there be any kickback. That was why, for all of Hollywood's indignant protestations about the magazine, there was almost no legal action taken against it until the major court case, which, technically, Confidential won (but, in effect, lost, since it was put out of business as is). Humphrey Bogart summed it up with "you've got to have guts or your skirts have to be awfully clean before you mess around with those s.o.b.'s."

One Hollywood producer, who had been the object of attacks by another scandal magazine, put "private eyes" on the trail of the editor-publisher to see what he could unearth about him. The investigators found out a good deal that was damaging about the editor, but they also found out that he was in possession of information that was even more damaging to the producer. From then on, the producer was scared to death—the scandal-magazine editor knew too much about him—and he quickly dropped his little private investigation.

During this period, particularly, Hollywood was a beehive of "private eyes," tapped telephones and recording machines. It sometimes seemed as if every telephone had a tape recorder attached to it—you never knew whether your conversation was being recorded or not. Miniature recording machines that could be concealed on one's person were big sellers at the leading recording concerns to everyone from members of the vice squad to vice-presidents in charge of production, and from agents to secret agents. The latest in listening devices, photographic equipment and electronic instruments were utilized to get the lowdown on the other fellow. Heinrich Himmler would have drooled over the whole set-up.

At the *Confidential* trial, the magazine's lawyers presented exhibits to prove that other publications had printed material even racier than *Confidential*. They also subpoenaed many members of the Hollywood press to try to prove their argument that *Confidential* operated along the reportorial lines of other publications, only better. Fortunately— or perhaps unfortunately for *Confidential*—the reporters were never called to the stand. Actually *Confidential*'s contention that in its reportorial methods—i.e., using private detectives to track down factual information—it was doing a more accurate and professional job than most of the so-called reputable publications had a certain amount of validity. For all of the magazine's sleazy journalism, lack of style and lapses of taste, when it came to fact-gathering, its "private eyes" were technically more observant and exact than the usually dim-sighted, press agent-brainwashed Hollywood reporters.

There was a great deal of hypocrisy about *Confidential*. During the trial, the press editor of a weekly news magazine, who was writing moralistic reports about *Confidential*, was discovered to be secretly editing another national scandal magazine. Hollywood itself was far from blameless. *Confidential*'s West Coast representatives, Fred and Marjorie Meade, lived conspicuously in a lavish Beverly Hills home and were *persona grata* at many a movietown gathering. What is more, some of the stories that *Confidential* and other scandal magazines ran stemmed from the studios themselves—to discipline or punish recalcitrant performers or to kill off another story that the studios did not want run. Twentieth Century-Fox funneled a yarn about Marilyn Monroe, with whom it was then at odds, to *Rave* in order to get that magazine to drop a story about a sensational triangle involving one of the studio's top executives. *Confidential* ran a story about Universal-International actor Rory Calhoun's jail record for robbery, conveniently provided by the studio, in exchange for the magazine's eliminating a story about the homosexual activities of a more important U-I star. Kim Novak was sold down the river journalistically by Columbia to get *Confidential* to kill a story about studio boss Harry Cohn.

But there were some film folk who did not mind being written up in the scandal magazines at all. When one press agent asked his newly acquired client for a biography that he could give to the press, the client, a Hollywood singer, blithely handed him an issue of *Confidential* which carried an article about him. Some Hollywood press agents even solicited *Confidential* to run stories about their clients. And after Sammy Davis, Jr., was the subject of an article in *Confidential*, he gave publisher Robert Harrison a pair of solid gold cuff links. At the *Confidential* trial, producer Mike Todd was said by the magazine's attorneys to have provided *Confidential* with photographs and data about himself in order to help publicize his movie *Around the World in 80 Days*. Todd denied it.

Since the demise of *Confidential* in its original form, the Hollywood exposé scandal-magazine formula has been absorbed into the movie fan magazines, the slick national periodicals (*Time* Magazine, particularly, goes in for this approach) and even seemingly elevated tomes like *Hollywood Rajah*, the story of Louis B. Mayer, by Bosley Crowther, motion-picture critic of the *New York Times*. The latter is an extraordinarily candid and clinical study, portions of which might even have given *Confidential* pause for editorial thought. The *Confidential* scandal formula is far from dead. It has just taken different forms.

I have always been of the opinion that *Confidential* was decidedly underrated. It was easy to indict the magazine for its sensationalism and for its sloppy writing. But what *Confidential* proved was that there was too much pallid, punches-pulled reporting elsewhere and that the average, untutored reader was probably wise to it and instinctively knew that he was being hornswoggled. He undoubtedly realized that *Confidential*, in its own way, was giving him a glimmer of the truth. True, *Confidential* operated primarily in the sexual-peccadillo department. But its editorial formula, applied to other areas, might have some interesting and worthwhile results.

Hollywood is a factory town (the factories turn out film instead of automobiles or steel) and *Daily Variety* and the *Hollywood Reporter*, the two daily trade papers, are like factory-town newspapers. They are read almost entirely by people in the business, usually with the morning Miltowns, and they are vitally important to them. They have been called the bibles of Hollywood, although "babble" might be a more appropriate word.

The trade papers claim to have between 8,000 and 9,000 circulation each. However, they supposedly wield influence quite out of proportion to their small readership. They are perused with a good deal of avidity in Hollywood by the people who want jobs and, assertedly, by the people who have the power to give jobs. Many of these people do not like to read anything but the trade papers since they do not want to disturb their precariously achieved and sustained sense of astigmatic security.

Since Hollywood is so deeply absorbed in itself and its problems and since the trade papers dish up this self-absorption in fairly concise, in-the-know style, they play a bigger role in Hollywood's closed community life than do any of the local newspapers or, for that matter, any other publications. The trade papers are also reportedly read by some newspaper editors and other so-called opinion makers around the country, who sometimes pick up items and ideas from them.

When Dore Schary was production chief at M-G-M, he took time out from making prosaic movies to pen a long, free-verse poem to the trade papers. Entitled simply "The Trades," it ran as an introduction to the twenty-second anniversary issue of *Daily Variety* in 1955. Here is Schary's poem in its pristine entirety:

> You can't possibly know what's going on
> Unless you read the trades—
> The trades.
> The daily trades.
> What's new? What's cooking?
> It's all in the trades—
> The trades.
> Things are bad, but TEN COMMANDMENTS is going to gross a hundred million dollars.
>
> Things are good, but boxoffice is off.
> Taub is buying M-G-M for Hope Hampton
> And Zanuck is leaving Fox.
> Irving Lazar planes to the Riviera and Charlie Feldman returns.
> "NEW FACES ALL THE RAGE"
> "STUDIOS LOADING VEHICLES WITH ALL-STAR CASTS"
> It's all in the trades—
> The trades.
> "EXHIBS DEMANDING MORE FILM FROM STUDIOS"
> "EXHIBS COMPLAIN STUDIOS TURNING OUT TOO MUCH PRODUCT"
>
> "BOXOFFICE OFF"
> "GROSSES UP ALL OVER THE COUNTRY"

It's all in the trades—
The trades.
Bill Taub is arranging purchase of M-G-M for Hope Hampton—
And Brando really sings.
So does Susan Hayward.
So does Jean Simmons.
And Kirk Douglas.
It's in the trades.
Every WORD is in the trades.
Mike Todd is making WAR AND PEACE—
And so is Ponti DeLaurentiis.
And studios are going all out—
All out, you understand—
For Todd-AO, VistaVision, Cinerama, CinemaScope, 65, 55, 35 and 75 millimeter—

Film, that is—
And all pictures are going to be made in color—
All pictures, that is—
In Eastman, Ansco, Technicolor—
Except for those that will not be in color, but in beautiful black and white.

It's in the trades—
All of it's in the trades.
Frankie Sinatra is scheduled for seven pictures—
And so is Jimmy Stewart—
And Humphrey Bogart—
And Gary Cooper—
And of course Grace Kelly—
And Bill Taub is buying M-G-M for Hope Hampton.
MOBY DICK is going to cost three million—no, four million—no, five million.

It's in the trades—
Variety liked it, but The Reporter didn't—
And The Reporter loved it, but Variety hated it.
And did you read?
And have you heard?
And is it true?

And did you see?
And Greg Bautzer stagged it at Ciro's.
It's all in the trades—
The trades.
"MOVIE NETS ARE UP"
"MOVIE DIVS ARE DOWN"
"MOVIE NETS ARE DOWN"
"MOVIE DIVS GO UP"
"STUDIOS SHUN TV"
"ALL MAJOR STUDIOS NOW MAKING TV FLICKS"
It's in the trades.
Every word is in the trades.
And there's a new era—
With Rock Hudson and Tab Hunter.
And soon Sock Johnson, Boff Murphy, Bang Jennings and Royal Crown.

And Taub is buying M-G-M for Hope Hampton.
It's in the trades.
It's all in the trades.
Every WORD is in the trades.
The trades.

Not too long after that, Schary's name was in the trades, too—he had been bounced out of M-G-M. But Taub never did buy the studio for Hope Hampton.

The trade papers would undoubtedly be deadly dull to anyone who does not have a special knowledge of Hollywood—and a personal stake in it. Here are some sample items. From a recent *Hollywood Reporter*: "New York—Natalie Wood reports to director Elia Kazan today for initial wardrobe fittings for her co-starring role in *Splendor in the Grass*, Warners release rolling in May." From a recent *Daily Variety*: "Ronald Stein was signed yesterday by producer Jack H. Harris to compose and conduct the score for *Dinosaurus*, which Universal-International will release in July." These are fascinating items—to Natalie Wood, Elia Kazan, Ronald Stein and Jack H. Harris.

A seasoned Hollywood press agent once told me in his distinctive patois: "If you got a group of scientists to find what is the fastest thing in the world—a greyhound running after an electric rabbit, a cheating husband leaving a room when his wife is coming in—they'd probably find that the most active thing in the world is the gland of an actor.

If he died and you put it in alcohol, it would keep aiming for Variety and the Hollywood Reporter. It doesn't need a body around it."

Of the two trade papers, the Hollywood Reporter is the more readable and colorful. It lays no claims to culture or noble journalistic ideals. Daily Variety, which purports to be more reasoned and restrained, is not substantially more elevated. It is just more reserved in its typography and makeup. As one moviemaker observed: "Maybe Daily Variety is five per cent more accurate than the Hollywood Reporter, but it is a helluva lot duller."

The Hollywood Reporter was founded in September 1930 by W. R. (Billy) Wilkerson, dapper trade-paper backer, restaurateur and nightclub impresario, who will undoubtedly go down in Hollywood history for reputedly having discovered Lana Turner, then AWOL from Hollywood High School, sitting on a drugstore stool, thereby setting in motion an endless cycle of young Hollywood hopefuls perched on stools in filmtown pharmacies. Wilkerson had been operating a plush haberdashery and barbershop on Sunset Boulevard and, when they flopped, he installed the Hollywood Reporter on the premises. The going was rough at first. The Hollywood Reporter made the mistake of being moderately candid. At the outset, it was fairly snappy and scrappy and avowedly on the side of "the creative genius and the creative and artistic brains in back of the motion picture industry." Known then as the Hollywood Daily Reporter, it ran a regular roundup of pro and con reviews on the new pictures from New York and elsewhere under the heading "Cream Puffs and Slams"—"cream puffs" is a good description of most movie reviews, but the Reporter then also excerpted the occasional "slams." The Hollywood Reporter's own reviews, Wilkerson promised in an editorial in his issue of November 5, 1930, ". . . will be impartial and written by men who, from their past association with the business, should know what they are talking about." And the reviews were, more or less, freewheeling.

Wilkerson wrote such rambunctious editorials as this one: "There are too many $1000 and $2000 and $3000 a week executives whose ignorance retards every effort that means anything; men who don't know what it is all about and never will; men who have been kept on the payroll through family relationship, friends or politics. They have to go. Waste will have to go."

As a result of this sort of editorial policy, the Hollywood Reporter found itself barred from a good many studios and much studio advertising. When Columbia's Harry Cohn banned the Hollywood Reporter from his lot little more than a month after the trade paper had been in existence, Wilkerson ran a front-page box headlined "Thanks, Mr. Cohn" with the following note: "The Hollywood Reporter has finally become important enough to be barred off the Columbia lot. Thanks, Mr. Cohn, for making the boast possible."

As Wilkerson recalled recently: "We couldn't get into the studios. We couldn't get anyone on the phone. They didn't want a paper like ours and they didn't want anyone printing factual news about the business. Finally, one by one, they reversed the ban."

And there was a simple reason for the reversal: Wilkerson before long started to massage the Hollywood egos even better than his barbers had massaged the Hollywood profiles. The Hollywood Reporter began to flourish. Today Wilkerson, pooh-poohing the oft-voiced and printed rumor that Joe Schenck and other tycoons helped finance the Reporter in order to use it as a mouthpiece, denies that any studios "were supporting the paper under the table at any time to gain favors."

The Hollywood Reporter's gossip column, "The Rambling Reporter," has usually been the best-read in town, and its present occupant, the frothy Mike Connolly, is considered, within the trade, as the most influential columnist in Hollywood, outranking even Parsons and Hopper. However, this is less a tribute to Connolly—who writes a chic and soignée column awash in lush lingo and untrammeled by plebeian facts—than to the breezy gossip tradition established by Wilkerson, a tradition that has sometimes made the scandal magazines seem almost tame by comparison. Some typical Connolly chatter: "Stan Kubrick's curiosity got the best of him. . . . Stan sent for Tuesday Weld. . . . Too bad—Tuesday's 'too Monday's-child-ish' for Lolita" (April 11, 1960). "Tuesday Weld is in love with Richard Beymer. . . . Or at least Tuesday was Saturday" (April 12, 1960). "Du bist a nudnick if you don't plunge pronto into your pet paperback pusher's emporium to pick up Jake Trussell's After Hours Poetry. Has crazy beat, will send hipsters into tribal snake dances" (April 14, 1960).

When former occupants of the "Rambling Reporter" did the column in past years, they were powers in Hollywood, too, like Connolly, but when they lost the column they lost their standing with it. Perhaps the liveliest—or at least the bitchiest—columnist the Hollywood Reporter ever had was Edith Gwynn, one of the much-married Wilkerson's ex-wives, who is supposed to have conducted the "Rambling Reporter" for several years as part of her divorce settlement and was given to such uninhibited items as "A starlet is worried that her husband has been untrue. Her baby doesn't look like him."

Another mercurial "Rambling Reporter" columnist was Jim Henaghan. He recalls this incident out of his columnar past: "I was drinking at Mocambo one night with a bunch of the guys. 'Fuck Hollywood,' I kept saying, 'screw Hollywood.' 'Why don't you leave?' they asked me. I woke up the next morning with a terrible headache and with a buzzing in my ears. 'Where am I?' I wondered. 'We are just landing at Kansas City,' a voice said. I was on an airplane. The guys had dumped me on there while I was out cold. I was writing a daily column then for the Hollywood Reporter. The field was closed in. I was in Kansas City five days and couldn't get out. I kept sending in stuff about who's at the Muehlbach bar. Gwen Verdon (the then Mrs. Henaghan) was writing the column in Hollywood. I filed columns for five days from Kansas City. Then I went to New York and wrote a Hollywood column from there. I wouldn't come back to Hollywood. Then I heard that Wilkerson was coming east and I went west."

Daily Variety was started in 1933 by weekly Variety to combat the upstart Hollywood Reporter and it basks in the reputation for supposedly hard-hitting, fair-and-square reporting that was cultivated by the weekly's founder, the late Sime Silverman, a reputation which has not always been in evidence in latter years. Like its parent publication, Daily Variety goes in for Variety-ese, a rather hackneyed blend of show-business "slanguage"—expressions like "beaucoup," "tempus fugits" and "sapolio"—and such archaic, lumbering circumlocutions as the following from a recent issue of weekly Variety: "In the not too distant future exposed for all to see will be the results of what might be the start of a new trend in theatrical film production. The actor, having eschewed the guidance of another individual through the various stages of his pretended emotionality, has taken unto himself the role of director. Kid Thespian never had such power." There is also a regular quota of trumped-up "dope" stories, which are really little more than hypoed publicity pitches.

Except possibly for a brief spell in the late Thirties and early Forties, when the late Arthur Ungar, who liked to think of himself as a "fighting editor," helped expose gangster Willie Bioff's hold on Hollywood unionism—a hold maintained with the submissive co-operation of the major movie studios—Daily Variety has not been overly freighted with journalistic principle. For a stretch Ungar even had a police bodyguard and his premises and person were protected against any possible bombings. Today, about the only thing Daily Variety—

and weekly *Variety*—are in danger of being bombed with is a flurry of press-agent handouts. In the words of one Hollywood columnist: "The one big thing that lifted *Daily Variety* out of the mudpile where the *Hollywood Reporter* is was when Ungar went after Bioff. That was the only thing."

During the Fifties, *Daily Variety* was erratically and acrimoniously edited by Joe Schoenfeld, a former Hearst reporter and Hollywood agent, who finally returned to the flesh-peddling business and was succeeded, in 1959, by Thomas Pryor, former movie editor and Hollywood correspondent of the New York *Times*. Under Schoenfeld's regime, according to Viola Swisher, who was the gossip columnist on *Daily Variety* in 1951–1952, the trade paper frowned on certain names being mentioned in its pages. Among them was Greg Bautzer, attorney for the *Hollywood Reporter*, who also figured importantly in many major news developments. On the other hand, according to Viola Swisher, such names as Joe Schenck and George Jessel were almost hallowed and could not be mentioned in anything but a favorable light.

Another "holy" name at *Daily Variety* was that of producer Stanley Kramer. Viola Swisher tells of an incident involving an item she wrote about Kramer—and its repercussions:

"Stanley Kramer," she says, "was a sacred cow on *Variety*. I had an item on January 23, 1952, that 'More 'n' more, it looks less 'n' less likely that Mary Pickford will make *The Library*.' [*The Library* was a projected Kramer production.] Apparently, Joe [Schoenfeld] was playing golf or sick. For some reason, he didn't eagle-eye the column before printing. The next morning, I came into the office and Joe greeted me with a shrill scream. People don't talk to me that way. I didn't know what struck him. Where did I get that item, he wanted to know. He was apopleptic with rage. 'You can't do this,' he said. 'You're sabotaging a man of great integrity and his picture.' He said that Kramer was such a liberal and was trying to do such great things. I didn't realize what a heinous crime I'd committed running this item, which I thought perfectly legitimate. He said: 'I've been on the phone all morning with Kramer about it.' He demanded to know where I'd gotten the item. I told him that I'd call my source to see if he minded my releasing his name to Joe. At this point, I called the Kramer office and Kramer wasn't there, but one of his assistants, Barbara Best, told me that the item wasn't that bad. I said that I'd been castigated for it and that it was bad. Kramer called me later that morning and he also said that it was not that bad. Joe again wanted to know where I'd gotten the item. I said, 'I'll check my source and let you know.' The guy who had given me the item was Walter Compton, a good friend of Mary Pickford's for many years. Compton said: 'Tell Joe it's true.' Compton had worked on Variety once. I told Joe and I told him who gave it [the item] to me and he said, 'Who's Walter Compton?' Joe said he never worked on Variety. Of course, the denouement was that Mary Pickford didn't make The Library and Mr. Kramer didn't make The Library. Julian Blaustein made The Library with Bette Davis. But Joe's attitude was 'Don't let facts interfere with my friendship with the producer.' That blow-off led to a parting of the ways for us."

"And it's such a sad little item," Viola Swisher ruminated. She added: "Did Walter Compton die? . . ." (He did, in 1960.)

An editorial staple of both Daily Variety and the Hollywood Reporter is to condemn "art" movies and hail "box-office" films, whatever they are exactly. In Hollywood and in its trade-paper estimation, "art" is, ipso facto, not "box-office," and vice versa. This spurious semanticism is further faulted by the bogus box-office figures that the trade papers regularly run. When I was publicity and advertising director for the 55th Street Playhouse in New York City in the late Thirties, we would regularly release exaggerated box-office compilations to the trade papers—such as that the current attraction had done the biggest business for a hot Sunday in July in the last ten years at our theater. These phony figures would automatically be published as trade-paper gospel—the trades, in any case, had no way of checking them unless they had access to the theater's books, which they did not have. Box-office figures from other theaters were similarly contrived. Like all movie-industry statistics, attendance figures are extremely suspect. They are little more than hopeful "guesstimates" and highly colored ones at that, put forth in pretentiously authoritative style. They are almost impossible to evaluate meaningfully and are not worth a bag of yesterday's popcorn.

Today, weekly Variety takes the precaution of qualifying its box-office "estimates" with the euphemistic disclaimer that they are "not, of course, fully 'definitive.'" In its April 13, 1960, issue, weekly Variety ran this revealing story headlined "How's Biz?—Try to Find Out," with the subhead "But Exhibitors Need Checking":

"How goes the box-office?

"Contradictions and other inconsistencies in reports on business by 'reliable sources' are becoming so widespread that it's almost just impossible to tell with reasonable accuracy how the film industry is going in terms of trends. . . .

"Certain . . . showmen, while trying to convey an atmosphere of good fiscal health in the picture business, abandon reality in their size-ups of conditions."

That same story carried these interesting paragraphs:

"Fitting punchline comes from the head man at a national circuit who was questioned about his b.o. ups and downs.

"He said: 'We make money when we have good pictures.'

"He thereupon was asked: 'What are good pictures?'

"His retort: 'Those which make money.'"

Both trade papers operate on vindictive and predatory hard-cash principles. If you are a friend of the paper's—primarily through advertising—you get a favorable notice. If you are not a friend—largely through not advertising—you get an unfavorable notice, or, what may be even more hurtful in Hollywood, no notice whatsoever.

On April 22, 1949, the Hollywood Reporter panned Columbia's *We Were Strangers*, a movie about the Cuban revolution with Jennifer Jones and John Garfield, as "the heaviest dish of Red theory ever served to an audience outside the Soviet. . . . It's party line all the way through." (Ironically, the Daily Worker of April 28, 1949, blasted *We Were Strangers* as "capitalistic propaganda." John Huston, the director of the picture, was understandably confused by it all at the time, but commented: "I'm proud and delighted to have both of these lunatic ends converging on me. I think it is a very hopeful thing that the Daily Worker and the Hollywood Reporter find themselves in agreement. It looks to me like Stalin and Wall Street can get together, an encouraging manifestation.")

As a result of the Hollywood Reporter review, the late Harry Cohn, terrible-tempered boss of Columbia Pictures, withdrew all his ads from the trade paper for the umpteenth time and barred the publication from his lot. The Reporter retaliated by slamming Columbia movies and went after Cohn personally, hook, line and typewriter, for years until the feud was settled in 1956—naturally, by Cohn resuming his advertising.

On January 8, 1940—a rather historic Hollywood day—the Screen Writers Guild adopted a resolution forbidding its members to advertise in any and all trade papers. This was tantamount, in the cinema city, to banning breathing. As a result, the Hollywood Reporter promptly dropped all writing credits from its movie reviews for extended stretches (although *Daily Variety* magnanimously continued to run them during the period of the advertising freeze).

The Screen Writers Guild edict had been inspired by the continued heckling of the *Hollywood Reporter*, which envisioned, in the words of a guild spokesman, "a Commie behind every typewriter in Hollywood." However, *Daily Variety* also suffered as a result. And it was, unexpectedly, *Daily Variety* and not the *Hollywood Reporter* which took action against the Screen Writers Guild because of the ban, suing the guild on April 12, 1949, in Los Angeles Federal Court on the grounds of conspiracy and as being in "restraint of trade." The ensuing legal proceedings dragged out over a period of several years and had some educational—and entertaining—sidelights.

"An important part of the revenue of both Variety, Inc., and Daily Variety, Ltd.," the complaint set forth, "is derived from the publication of paid advertising...

"Daily Variety . . . solicits and publishes advertising from all branches of the motion picture industry . . . [and] depends thereon for much of its revenue. . . .

"Prior to the 8th day of January, 1940, many individuals who were members of the said Guild used both of said publications as advertising media, with excellent results to the advertisers and profit to the publications and the said publications enjoyed the trust and confidence of said writers."

According to *Variety*'s battery of attorneys, the Screen Writers Guild "in violation of the rights of the plaintiffs, and in violation of the Sherman and Clayton Acts . . . entered into an unlawful combination and conspiracy" when the Guild adopted the rule "that no individual who is a member of the Screen Writers Guild, Inc., can use any paid advertising space in any trade publication whatever; setting forth as a reason therefor that such advertising was contrary to the ethics and beneath the dignity of the writing profession. . . .

"As a result of said illegal acts plaintiffs have lost a large amount of advertising and the revenue therefrom and have sustained and continue to sustain irreparable damage."

No money damages were asked, but the complaint petitioned for "relief" from these "unlawful practices."

In the report of this story in its issue of April 13, 1949, *Daily Variety* noted: "In bringing suit, *Variety* is aware that if it wins it will be only a symbolic victory, for obviously no lawsuit can force anybody to advertise. But *Variety* wants to preserve the freedom and privilege of the turndown by whomsoever it solicits, or with whomsoever it tries to do business.

"Variety doesn't want to be restrained from doing business by the directorial mandate of any organization."

At the time, George Seaton, president of the Screen Writers Guild, issued a statement that the Guild ban on trade-paper advertising had been "presented to its membership for reconsideration on several occasions recently" and had been "reaffirmed virtually without dissent. Writers believe that opportunities for employment should not be made to depend on the purchase of white space. Because the Guild values its good relations with the trade papers, it welcomes the opportunity to settle the question of the legality of the rule, and it is confident it will be upheld."

On May 27, 1949, the Screen Writers Guild, moving for dismissal, argued, in perhaps more polished legal style than Variety had, that the Guild's rule against trade-paper advertising "simply stated . . . is an agreement by consumer to refrain from using a particular service.

"This the plaintiffs contend violates the Sherman Act.

"If the plaintiffs' contention is good, then the nationwide members of the Legion of Decency commit a crime when they pledge themselves not to see a movie; the members of Alcoholics Anonymous restrain trade by agreeing to abstain from out-of-state liquor as well as from the local product; California vegetarians are criminals in refusing to eat Kansas (and other) steaks; because the raw products of the motion picture, whisky and beef are assembled from many states, and the finished products are distributed through the country.

"Nothing in the Sherman Act suggests such a conclusion."

By September 27, 1949, the legal contest had waxed quite eloquent. On that day, the Guild, denying that any of its practices restrained trade or commerce or were illegal, offered this illuminating observation:

"The motion picture and entertainment industries in Los Angeles County are served by approximately fifty (50) trade papers, all of which sell advertising space and most of which publish reviews of motion pictures, including critical comment purporting to appraise the work of the writers, directors, performers, musicians, and other persons employed in the motion picture industry. For many years past the practice has prevailed, and still prevails, among salesmen of advertising space for such trade papers to endeavor to sell advertising space by promising favorable reviews in exchange for purchase of such space and threatening unfavorable reviews if no purchase is made. It has become the practice for persons employed in the motion picture industry to purchase advertising space for display concurrently with completion or first showing of motion pictures. The value of reviews and critical comment in many of such trade papers has become debased; the purchase of advertising space by persons who offer themselves for employment in the motion picture industry has become known to the trade as a means of buying peace with the trade paper. Such advertisements are believed by the defendant to be not advantageous to the advertiser."

Brave legal words! The Screen Writers Guild had probably put the matter more bluntly than anyone had ever dared to before. Undoubtedly carried away by judicial fervor, the Guild had forgotten that things just aren't done that crudely in Hollywood and that diplomatic protocol must be observed at all costs.

And observed it ultimately was. Like almost all Hollywood contests, this one was called off before the final decision. It never came to trial. Why? Today both factions are reluctant to discuss the subject. Perhaps they find it embarrassing all around. Even attorney Martin Gang, who represented Variety in the long drawn-out case, blandly shrugs it all off today when queried with "My memory is not accurate."

At a special membership meeting of the Guild on April 22, 1953, the trade-paper ad ban was lifted. (Earlier, in defiance of the edict, according to Al Scharper, managing editor of Daily Variety, writer Borden Chase took out an ad in the trade papers and was fined $500 by the Screen Writers Guild. "He had little conviction," says Scharper, "that Variety and the Reporter would stand back of him. I don't think Variety and the Reporter ever got together in concert on anything.") On May 25, 1953, the court's stipulation for dismissal noted that "that controversy between Daily Variety, Ltd., plaintiff, and Screen Writers Guild, Inc., defendant, which is the subject of the above entitled action and is more particularly described in the complaint and answer on file herein, having been amicably settled; and all claims of every kind on the part of the said plaintiff against the defendant arising from said controversy having been fully discharged;

"It is now stipulated between the parties, each through its respective counsel of record, that the said action may be dismissed, and that the Court may make its Order directing the Clerk to enter the Dismissal of the said action."

Legalistic lingo for what obviously amounted to a little private deal between the two contestants. What had happened to the vigorous contention on the part of the Guild that "such advertisements are believed by the defendant to be not advantageous to the advertiser"? No matter. The Guild had not really welcomed, in George Seaton's words, "the opportunity to settle the question of the legality of the rule" precisely because it valued "its good relations with the trade papers" too much, even though declaredly "the value of reviews and critical comment in many of such trade papers has become debased." The issue had never really been fought through to its crucial conclusion. The trades, and their phony reviews, were too important to the Guild, and the Guild's advertising was too important to the trades—and so they decided to be buddies again.

Henceforth, Screen Writers Guild members were permitted to advertise again in the trade papers at their personal discretion, or, in the words of the Guild, "to resume their ads as individuals." *Daily Variety* was presumably no longer being restrained in its trade. And the *Hollywood Reporter* graciously started running screenplay credits again in its reviews.

Everybody advertises in the trade papers (or at least everybody who wants to remain on good terms with them). Although the trade papers do not actually come out and say to the film folk, "If you do not advertise, you will not get a good review of a movie," the pressure is there. Both of the trade papers have advertising staffs which cover the studios and personalities. It is an unspoken understanding between the trades and the movie industry. According to *Time* Magazine, "the tone of a review in the trade papers bears a remarkable relationship to advertising volume." A local quipster put it this way: "Maybe they call them trade papers because you can trade an ad for a nice notice."

It is customary for a producer who knows that he has a poor movie coming out to assemble a half dozen or so pages of advertisements from the various people connected with the picture and insert them as a package in the trade papers. This usually helps avoid a negative review. And, what is more, when the favorable, ad-conditioned review comes out in the trade paper, this self-same producer is likely to go around proudly showing it off to his friends. By this time he has talked himself into believing that his picture really received a good review without his having maneuvered it.

Among the biggest sources of revenue for the trade papers are the fat annual and anniversary editions bulging with ads. In 1955, Cecil B. DeMille bought the front cover of the *Hollywood Reporter* annual as an ad for his *Ten Commandments*. Still recalled at the *Hollywood Reporter* is a telephone conversation between Milton Epstein, an advertising solicitor for the *Reporter*, and DeMille. DeMille was apparently complaining that the engraving of Moses that was scheduled to run in the *Hollywood Reporter's* cover ad was not sufficiently forceful. "All right," finally shouted Epstein on the telephone, "we'll put more silver in Moses' hair!" and hung up.

Sometimes the trade ads are quite colorful. For a long while the *Hollywood Reporter* carried a series of ads about McDaniel's market, "grocery store of the stars." Sample ads: "Van Johnson bought a head of lettuce at McDaniel's market"; "Brian Donlevy bought Kleenex at McDaniel's market," all in the best small-town gazette style. When actor Sonny Tufts figured in the news headlines in 1954 after biting a couple of young ladies in the thigh, a supermarket advertised leg of lamb as "the Sonny Tufts special."

In July 1954 Dick Hanley, who had been secretary to Louis B. Mayer when Mayer was the head of M-G-M and the most powerful figure in filmdom, took out a small ad in *Daily Variety* reading: "Available, Dick Hanley, executive secretary ten years to Louis B. Mayer, Box 465, *Daily Variety*." Shortly thereafter, Hanley was hired by Mike Todd.

Real-estate ads in the trades are likely to be unique. The late Errol Flynn in 1954 advertised his hilltop, ten-acre estate, complete with caretaker, tennis court, "gorgeous pool," projection room and pony ring. This was the residence where Flynn once had a fancy-dress party featuring white-mice races emceed by George Jessel. The trade-paper ads cautioned: "Qualified prospects by appointment."

One trade ad read: "For rent. One brilliant mind with gear ratio suitable for any job. This great mind is fused into a body that is physically attractive but with the strength of Gibraltar. Nowhere in the world could you find anything to compare with such performance. Nor could you find any investment nearly as profitable. Box S-13, *Daily Variety*."

Another trade ad: "Disgusted young actor seeks employment abroad. Knows damn little else other than acting, but will do or try anything. Box 46, *Daily Variety*."

Congratulatory ads in the trade papers are standard procedure. Famed are what have come to be known as "The Dear Dore Letters." During Dore Schary's tenure as production chief at RKO in 1947, he was constantly being saluted by trade ads in the form of letters from admiring actors and associates. One ad, signed by producer Don Hartman, thanked "Dear Dore" for his contributions to the movie *Every Girl Should Be Married*. Actor Pat O'Brien took out an ad toasting "Dear Dore" for *The Boy with Green Hair*. And producer Stephen Ames followed with additional ads for the same picture. The "Dear

Dore" ads were so constant and conspicuous that they became a standing Hollywood joke and were finally discontinued.

When David Selznick had *Duel in the Sun* in production in 1944, the trade papers carried innumerable ads saluting Selznick and the picture in advance of release. Director Billy Wilder, an inveterate ribber, took out an ad for one of his own pictures, *Double Indemnity*, reading "*Double Indemnity* is the greatest picture I have ever seen," and signed George Oblath. Oblath ran a small beanery near the Paramount studio, where Wilder was then employed. Selznick was so infuriated by the Oblath ad that he threatened to withdraw all of his ads from the trade papers.

In March 1954, prior to Academy Award time, actor Robert Strauss took out a full-page ad in *Daily Variety* in which he thanked everyone in verse for helping him do so well as the hairy, underwear-clad character in *Stalag 17*, for which he was nominated for an Oscar. The poem was entitled "Thanks" and was minus punctuation:

> Thank you mother thank you dad
> Deciding to have me makes me glad
> Thank you sisters one two and three
> For your continued faith in me
> Thank you teachers back in school
> Including those who called me fool
> Thank you bosses one and all
> For all those jobs both big and small
> Thank you stagehands grips and props
> For your support that is the tops
> Thank you dear public just because
> You've let me hear that sweet applause
> Thank you friends so tried and true
> I haven't forgotten I still owe a few
> Thank you Paramount for the chance
> To show my stuff in them baggy pants
> Thank you Billy Wilder mine gracious host
> For your direction that I dig the most
> Thank you fourth estate you wonderful scribes
> For all those writeups including the jibes
> Thank you Mr. Banker for your friendly loan
> At six percent it's my house you own
> Thank you Sid most greatest gent
> Even in my will you'll get ten percent

> And last but not least my heart and life
> Thanks to my ever lovin' wife
> Thanks for everything especially our babies
> And for lovin' our hounds who don't dig rabies
> Thanks for your understanding and affection
> I hope I measure up when I stand inspection
> Thank you Audrey—thank you friends
> > Thank God
> Currently available
> Have underwear—will travel!

That same issue of *Daily Variety* carried a half-page ad with a picture of a personable chimpanzee sporting underwear and a hat and admiring herself in a hand mirror. The ad was signed "Peggy" and read to this effect:

My sincere thanks to all the wonderful people who nominated me for the PATSY best actor award for my portrayal of Tamba in Columbia's *Jungle Jim* series. Thanks also to the entire cast and crew, especially my co-star Johnny Weissmuller, without whose help this would not have been possible. Currently in release, *Bonzo* series (Universal-International) and *Bomba* (Allied Artists). Personal management, World Jungle Compound, Thousand Oaks.

Everybody felicitates everybody else in trade paper ads. In 1959 Dore Schary took out a full-page ad, in the form of a letter to producer Jack L. Warner, thanking him "for letting me see *The Nun's Story*." (Warner later reciprocated in a similar trade ad, thanking Schary for his upcoming production at that studio of *Sunrise at Campobello* which, although it had not yet even gone into production, was already being touted as "a motion picture long to be remembered.") Subsequently, Jack Benny also thanked Warner in a letter ad that lauded *The Nun's Story* as "one of the most beautiful motion pictures I have ever seen." The ads carried the headline: "GREAT TALENT MAKES GREAT PICTURES!" Assuming, for the sake of argument, that *The Nun's Story* is a "great" picture and that Dore Schary and Jack Benny are "great" talents, they still had nothing to do with its making. In 1960 director William Wyler addressed a page trade-paper ad, also in letter form, to "Chuck (Charlton) Heston for "an achievement of the highest order in the field of acting in *Ben-Hur*." Nor, as the director of the picture, did Wyler hesitate, by inference, to slap himself on the back in the ad, referring to the "... gratifying praise ... showered on the film...." and adding that "... the reception of the film, both critical and popular, is a tribute most highly deserved...."

During that same period Michael Todd, Jr., was the recipient of a full-page letter ad in the Hollywood trade papers as follows:

DEAR MICHAEL:

Have just come from a screening of your most recent effort, Scent of Mystery, and I must say I enjoyed it immeasurably. The children were fascinated by the beautiful background and vivid color. Our maid, Katherine—you remember her—was thoroughly delighted by Peter Lorre's droll performance. Her boys, Michael and Stuart, thought you made a real discovery in Denholm Elliott, who is charming in the leading role. Your use of the Smell-o-Vision! process was fun and in good taste.

We are all very proud of our association with you and look forward to your forthcoming musical comedy production of 80 Days which I understand is coming along wonderfully well.

Hope to see you soon.

YOUR LOVING WIFE,
SARAH

When it comes to trade-paper ads, the custom is for the same advertisement to run in both the *Hollywood Reporter* and *Daily Variety*. An ad usually runs in one trade one day and in the other trade the next day, making for economy in the use of the same advertising plate, which is "bicycled" between the two publications. Since both trades are presumably read by identical people, the ad gets a two-day "play" this way. And this alternating advertising policy also requires that if the *Hollywood Reporter* gets an ad first on one occasion, then *Daily Variety* is to be given top priority the next time around. If an advertiser favors only one trade paper, he is certain to hear from the other trade promptly, and he will be wheedled, cajoled and threatened until he comes around.

In the mid-Forties, producer Colin Miller took out an ad in both trade papers to announce the seasonal opening of the Lux Radio Theatre. The *Hollywood Reporter* made a mistake in the date and Miller insisted that the publication run a second ad with the correct copy. When the second advertisement appeared in the *Hollywood Reporter*, Miller received a telephone call from *Daily Variety* editor

Arthur Ungar demanding a second ad, too. Miller explained the circumstances of the repeat ad, but Ungar was adamant. "You can have the second ad on the same basis as the *Reporter* got it," Miller finally told Ungar, "for free." Ungar hit the ceiling. From then on he refused to talk to Miller, turned his back on him at parties and, as one witness to the incident recalled, "practically tried to run him out of town."

Says a sagacious Hollywood publicist: "The trades exist by fiat from the studios. They live on the ads from the studios. But the studios want them. And they want two trade papers. They're afraid that one trade would have a stranglehold on them. So they play one against the other. They need the trades for self-adulation. They know how the stuff is printed in the trades, but when they read about themselves, they forget."

There is no love lost between the two trade papers. "Weekly *Variety*," sneers Billy Wilkerson, "had to start *Daily Variety* as competition to me." Originally, weekly *Variety* had a Hollywood office and a four- to eight-page wrap-around known as *Variety's* "Hollywood Bulletin," containing the latest news and reviews, which was distributed in the Los Angeles area. When the *Hollywood Reporter* had been in existence little more than a year, weekly *Variety*, on December 31, 1931, filed a $46,500 suit against the *Reporter* in Los Angeles, charging "news lifting." Weekly *Variety* alleged that the *Hollywood Reporter's* correspondent in the East took items from *Variety* when that publication came out each Tuesday and wired them to the *Hollywood Reporter*, which was thus able to publish them several days before weekly *Variety* reached the West Coast. According to weekly *Variety*, it had deliberately planted phony stories in its columns, and the *Hollywood Reporter* had appropriated them. Weekly *Variety* headlined the story of its suit against the *Reporter*: "VARIETY CHARGES HOLLYWOOD DAILY WITH STEALING ITS NEWS EACH WEEK." The suit, as is habitual in Hollywood, was settled out of court and the supposed "news" stealing apparently subsided.

In the final analysis, the movie trade papers are the voice of Hollywood. They may rib and sometimes needle the community. They may run bouncy gossip items like this one from the *Hollywood Reporter*: "Juli Redding, the girl with the rhinestoned Isotta (that's a car—ed.), is selling her big Doheny shack because the swimming pool motor keeps her awake." Or they may run edgy gossip items like this one from *Daily Variety*: "A young starlet's lament: 'The trouble with Hollywood is that all the nice young boys are tied up—with all the nice young boys.'" The trade papers may give Hollywood an occasional

71

hotfoot. But when the chips are down, and when Hollywood is confronted, as it so often is, with a cruel, unloving world, the trade papers are there to console the moviemakers and to stand up for them. As one cynical student of the Hollywood scene once observed: "Can you think of any big Hollywood picture of the past year that got a bad review in the trade papers?"

He added: "The trades are important in Hollywood. But once you leave here and you're in New York, say, for three days you don't miss it at all and you start wondering why you ever looked at it. Actors and other movie people don't think about the trade papers. They just accept them like the smog.

"I've never been able to figure out why the movie industry needs the trades in Hollywood. If only there were a daily paper out here to give comprehensive news about the movie industry, it could be the voice of Hollywood instead of the trade papers."

But there is assuredly no such daily paper—in Hollywood or elsewhere.

The movie fan magazines are a wonderfully whacky world unto themselves. Reading a fan magazine has been described as similar to eating a banana under water. Sometimes it seems more like a triple-scoop banana split. There is more mush in a single fan magazine than in a ton of instant pablum. Fan-magazine stories usually deal in what has been described as "Cupidiocy" and have titles like "The Real Alice Faye," "The Astounding Story of Toby Wing" and "Happiness Comes Again to Fess Parker." All the stories are pretty much the same and the names are interchangeable. Fan magazines, as a reader once noted, "are dedicated almost entirely to the dress, diet and metabolism of film actors." This bon-bon bilge, written with a chummy air, is aimed primarily at youthful moviegoers of the female persuasion. In the words of a West Coast wit: "The fan mags are written for would-be nymphets about nymphets and pre-nymphets." And, one might add, by superannuated post-nymphets. Most of the contents are pure fancy with an occasional smidgen of fact.

For years the fan magazines have been peddling the vicissitudes of the profiles. These stories fall under the general heading of what may be termed "Hollywood Heartbreak." They have haunting titles like "The Strange Fears of Ava Gardner" and "Is Bob Hope Killing Himself?" In fan magazines the stars, deep down, are usually unhappy, and every actress, in spite of her swimming pool and new sable coat, is, in the words of one fan magazine, a mess of "personality maladjustments, inferiority complex, shyness and insecurity, buried low in the subconscious." One of the most evocative stories along these lines appeared in Modern Screen in 1950. It was entitled "Hollywood's Six Loneliest Stars" and went like this: "They can wrap their sorrows in mink, drown them in champagne, but they can't escape the haunting solitude." The stars, for your information, were such sad sacks as Rita Hayworth, Lizabeth Scott and Ronald Reagan. Then there was this tale in Motion Picture Magazine that same year with the title "Little Girl Blue": "Shelley Winters is a famous star, her name and phone number in the best looking little black books in town, autograph hunters following her constantly. For her there's adulation all day every day—but frustration, loneliness and unhappiness are her constant and intimate companions." And there was, in the early Forties, Modern Screen's heart-breaking ". . . story of a lad's fight through childhood, a spunky, tight-lipped kid who started life knee-deep in eight-balls." The lad? Alan Ladd.

Many stories are authored by that old fan-magazine writer Anonymous, such as this one, also from a 1950 Motion Picture, in which Anonymous is described as "a famous star who for obvious reasons prefers to remain anonymous." Writing under the title "Nobody Knows the Trouble I've Seen," Anonymous asserts that "there isn't a star in Hollywood who hasn't had to fight some seemingly fatal handicap. . . . Jane Wyman had to live down the stigma of being called 'plain Jane' . . . Ava Gardner felt insecure, Betsy Drake stammered and even the suave Bing Crosby experienced self doubts." And then Anonymous wound up for the finish on the usual fan-magazine note of hope and camaraderie: "If you think you have an inferiority complex or feel yourself an ugly duckling, don't envy us Hollywood stars. For we're all alike, all of us; knowing fear and doubt and a sense of inferiority. All of us die a thousand little deaths—all of us: the renowned and the unknown; the great, the small, the rich and the poor, the homely and the beautiful.

"Obstacles? Handicaps? What of them? If you know fear, you also can know courage. I, who have been there, know."

The people who write fan-magazine stories are a baroque lot. There are about seventy-five of them, with perhaps a third of that number working regularly. There was one fan-magazine authoress who rarely left her room in Hollywood for years. According to an in-the-know fan-magazine publicist: "She didn't come to the studios. She had a great, protruding abdomen. Maybe she was pregnant? Actually, it was some kind of tumor. She was a wino and she had a horrible apartment. We preferred to take people there if we had to rather than have her at the studios. We never took really important stars there, but usually someone on the way up." The material for most of this writer's articles was delivered to her by messengers from the various publicity departments, who handed it to her through a shuttered window, and she usually wrote her stories without even meeting her subjects.

This press agent also tells of another prominent fan-magazine writer who "was 8,000 years old. She had a bladder condition. She would come to the studio and bring her stinking, lousy little dog with her. If a star gave her a lovely story, she always cried. If a star refused to give her good copy, she always peed. You always had water on either occasion."

Fan-magazine writers are inclined to be smitten with Hollywood's make-believe and to be emotionally involved with their subjects. From this same publicistic source: "Almost all of them are undersexed, oversexed or no-sexed women and they get their kicks out this stuff."

In an article entitled "Vultures of Hollywood" in the *American Mercury* in 1943, our old friend Anonymous, who is identified as a fan-magazine writer in disguise, had a few informative things to say about fan-magazine writers and readers:

The fan publication customer (the fan-mag reader is almost always a "she") lives vicariously in a supercharged world, mostly invented by bored press agents, with its own synthetic romance, homey philosophy and diluted sinfulness.

Fan magazine writing is insidious. It is so simple, for the most part, that a dull high school boy could do it. The result is that we fan authors tend to take the easiest way: we manufacture drivel at so much a word. There are about a hundred of us, roughly three quarters of us women and the rest men, or at least people who wear trousers. Our "take" runs from nothing to eight hundred a month, with perhaps half a dozen touching the top figure and a majority hovering at the zero level on a freelance basis. This in the Hollywood of six-figure incomes! But most of us find consolation, if not compensation, in pretending that we are part of an exciting world, in calling a few stars by their first names, and in having the run of the studios when at work on a story.

We have no illusions about our readers. We dish out gossip just short of slander and sticky romance in great big gobs, even if we have to make it out of the most unromantic ingredients. We attribute lowbrow profundities to actors who have never been within hailing distance of an idea. We glorify clothes horses, most of whom we despise and all of whom we envy. . . . We pounce on every tragedy in Hollywood—a juicy divorce, the collapse of a career—like so many vultures. Sorrow is our meat and a malevolent glint comes to our eyes when we hear that someone with a boxoffice name is unhappy. . . .

Those of us who have at one time led a normal existence soon find ourselves soaked through and through in the phony emotions, tangled in the mixed-up "love lives" and confused by the moronic "opinions" with which we fill those five and a half million copies of fan magazines.

Everything is very mysterious—not to mention psychiatric—in fan-magazine stories, and the most successful fan writers are those who can sustain the mystery for several thousand vague words without ever really beginning to come to grips with it. Adela Rogers St. Johns wrote a masterful story of this type in *Photoplay* Magazine in 1944. It was called "Thank You, Irene Dunne" and it unfolded "the gentle mystery of a lovely lady." It took the author more than a page of type to get down to the first intimation of this mystery.

"All the time though," she wrote, "I was thinking and remembering and trying to put together what it is that Miss Dunne has that nobody else has." (Maybe it was an Adela Rogers St. Johns write-up in a fan magazine.)

"I thought it might be something you could never define, something nameless, but I kept on trying."

At this point, St. Johns gave the reader another chunk of verbiage and the impression that she was getting warm, that she was on the track of something or other, something big and gentle and mysterious.

". . . I became conscious of several things . . ." she wrote. "You can see high, hot temper in her, oh, yes, she'd really go to town, the serene and lovely Miss Dunne, if you got her good and mad. And a degree of steel-cut ruthlessness. An admirable sort of ruthlessness which manifests itself, for all her wit and humor, all her graciousness, in a finely tempered self control."

After many more words, St. Johns finally got to the climax of her story:

"All of a sudden I knew.

"Though I know myself, it's still not very easy to put into words"— you can say that again—"but I think it's important, so you must bear with me and probably add some of your own.

"Irene Dunne makes being good more fun. More dramatic. More beautiful. So many people don't. But when you sit and watch her . . . you get from her a feeling of real goodness, inner goodness. But there isn't anything stuffy about it, there isn't anything dull or sanctimonious or cold. You begin to think with all your heart that being really good is gay and bright and glorious.

"When she is being funny, which she can be so very well, you know she is good all the way through, the way a woman ought to be, and when she is being good you know she can be funny any time she wants to."

And that, finally, was the "mystery" of Irene Dunne. Miss Dunne was good, just plain good. And Adela Rogers St. Johns was even better to have been able to wring several thousand words out of this mysterious subject without saying anything in particular.

In the old days, before the movies were taken up by the daily press and the intelligentsia, the fan magazines had a near monopoly on movie comment. Some of the fan magazines were reasonably respectable, too. One of the better ones was *Photoplay*, which, under James R. Quirk's editorship, printed fairly uncontaminated movie reviews and commissioned such worthwhile features as Terry Ramsaye's *A Million and One Nights*, a carefully researched history of the American movie that ran in *Photoplay* in 36 installments in the early Twenties before appearing in book form. It still remains the best and most authentic study of the American film, although it deals only with its earlier phases. Ramsaye was one of the rare writers on the subject who went to original sources. Rupert Hughes, Burns Mantle and Robert Sherwood were among *Photoplay*'s contributors. Today, *Photoplay* is still one of the leading fan magazines, although its character has changed in the intervening years and it has lost any cultural pretensions it may once have had.

One of the factors that contributed to the editorial decline of the fan magazines from their unpretentious but rather decent beginnings was the censorship imposed on them by the movie studios in 1934. This crackdown coincided with Hollywood's implemented self-censoring of its own movies that occurred at the time as the result of church outcries against current films. There was also attempted censorship of the rest of the Hollywood press. In that year, the movie studios accused the fan magazines of running "hog wild" and printing "sensational and salacious material." Cited were such fan stories as "Unmarried Hollywood Husbands and Wives"; "How Jack Oakie Gets His Women"; "One Girl's True Hollywood Experiences," telling of an actress' efforts to remain "pure" while breaking into the movies; "If I Should Love Again," an interview with Miriam Hopkins beginning "Women Shouldn't Marry"; "Are You Sick of Hollywood Divorces?"; "She Ain't No Angel," in which Janet Gaynor was described as "a flirtatious little sex appealist"; and "How Long Will Hollywood Protect [Jean] Harlow?" A leading fan publication of the period even went so far as to run a story about a prominent female star with a headline to the effect that she was searching for the father of her child (who was supposedly an equally prominent male star).

The fan magazines were extremely important to the studios since they were read by the young people who comprised such a large part of the moviegoing audience. Pointing up the vital role the fan magazine played promotionally for Hollywood was the fact that, during 1933 and 1934, the *Hollywood Reporter* ran a regular department called "Reviewing the Fan Mags" in which was measured the free publicity space, in square inches, racked up by the various studios. And so the publicity directors of the major studios, through their committee in the AMPP (the then Hays Office), held a series of emergency meetings in which they went about "cleaning up" the fan magazines —at the same time that the studios were supposedly "cleaning up" the movies. The publicists declared that they were out to correct what was described as the "unholy story" of Hollywood and to "curb the inaccuracies, misrepresentations and exaggeration of facts by certain fan writers, which tend to create false impressions in the mind of the public in regard to motion picture personages, and which prompt much unfavorable public reaction." At a meeting of the publicity chiefs on August 9, 1934, one of the points of discussion, reported the *Hollywood Reporter*, was "that the fan magazines have been one of the major factors that brought about the church attack on films."

At another meeting of the publicity directors with the Western editors of fan magazines on August 15, 1934, it was decided to cut down the then list of approximately 300 fan-magazine writers to a list of approximately 50. This "white list" was to be made up, as the *Hollywood Reporter* stated, "of writers who are established and who are noted for their honest and clean writing. . . . The 'white list' will be the only one with which the studios will do business." The publicity directors were henceforth to examine the writing of each fan author and issue a sort of deportment card for well-behaved fan magazine writers who were "acceptable." Those who did not make the grade were denied credentials as well as access to stars and studios.

At that meeting, the fan-magazine editors signed a pledge that ". . . we shall endeavor . . . to cleave to a policy of clean, constructive and honest material . . ." and ". . . to divest our individual publications of false and otherwise salacious material, either directly stated or implied."

Since this "housecleaning" of the passion and profile publications, all fan-magazine stories that have been arranged through studios have had to be cleared by the studio publicity departments before publication As a result, the fan magazines, instead of taking raps, have been operating under wraps. M-G-M once forbade mentioning that Norma Shearer had two children and that Robert Montgomery was a father. With copy having to be authorized instead of authored, the resultant goody-goody-ism eventually weakened the fan magazines. The fan publications were also undercut by a noticeable trend in the national slick periodicals toward Hollywood coverage of the almost fan type. In recent years, fan circulation has fallen off and some fan magazines have died. Today, there are approximately a dozen movie fan magazines with a total estimated monthly circulation of about five million. Only two of them, *Photoplay* and *Motion Picture*, even bother to maintain full-fledged Hollywood offices. The fan magazines are all edited and written in New York. "They are out of touch with Hollywood," says one fan-magazine writer. "Once the fan editors went in for a great wooing of Hollywood. Now the editors are in a rut. One top fan magazine has an editor who has been to Hollywood just once."

The trend today is for more muscle and less mush in fan magazines. Fan editors try to bypass the studios and to arrange interviews outside of official channels without the stipulated publicity okay. They also try to steer as clear as possible of the powerful independent publicity firms which represent many movie stars today. As the aforesaid fan writer explains it: "There's been a great change in the Hollywood scene. The studios no longer have fan magazine contacts in their publicity departments and few of them have long contract lists. As a result, all the players who can afford it have hired personal press agents. Take Tony Curtis and Janet Leigh. Rogers and Cowan handle them. To do a story about them, you have to submit it to their office. And so you lose interest."

Today, much of the scandal eliminated from the fan magazines more than a quarter of a century ago is coming back and the fan publications hope this will accelerate sales. Hollywood movies today are less Pollyanna—and so are the fan magazines. The scandal magazines have left their mark on the fan magazines, too. When a magazine like *Confidential* ran a story about Melody Myopic, the Hollywood personality, shacking up with every male in sight, the fan magazines were left out on a journalistic limb. They could not very well keep running articles about how sweet, snow-white, wholesome—and unhappy—this same Melody Myopic was, because, after all, the youngsters who read the fan magazines also saw *Confidential*. So the fan magazines countered with articles like "Is Melody Myopic Really Shacking Up with Everybody in Town?" It was the scandal-magazine formula in reverse.

"The fans are a sort of watered-down, teaser-type *Confidential*," said a fan authoress. "They're no longer fan books really. They say some horrible, ugly thing to point a peachy, darling little moral. In the fan magazines, you have to have a situation, a struggle, a conquering. In the struggle you have to have some kind of conflict and some acute situation and the hero can look like a slob all the way through but has to come up smelling like a rose. You have to point a moral and usually some obscenely moralistic moral. The worst of this teaser-type thing is that it is distributed to the teen-age reader. This is who the fan magazines live on and they are just as bad as the peddlers who hang around selling dope at high schools." She added that she never used her real name when writing for fan magazines. "I'm ashamed to," she said. "I despise myself for doing this."

Confidential also pointed another moral for the fan magazines. A fan-magazine editor recently remarked that "the fan books submit their material to the studios. They felt they had to be in line to maintain their sources of material. *Confidential* gave the lie to this story that you could not get out a book dealing with the studios and personalities unless you played ball. Not only did they get out a book, but it had the biggest circulation in the country. They didn't have to go to the studios for art, for stories, for anything."

A rundown of some 1960 fan-magazine contents indicates that the trend is decidedly toward the scurrilous, or at least the teaser-type scurrilous. "For One Glorious Afternoon, I Was Rock's Mate," rhapsodizes Jane Wilkie in *Motion Picture*, telling about her experiences on Rock Hudson's forty-foot ketch ("I not only had a glorious afternoon as his mate—but I also got my interview!"). "I Was a Weekend Wife" in that same issue of *Motion Picture* is actually actress Dolores Michael's story of how "I lived with my husband only on weekends." *Photoplay* has "What I Learned About Men Since Last Monday" by teen-age actress Annette Funicello (". . . they're really just human and so often they feel just the same way girls do. Honest!"). In *Photoplay*, too, is "Please Stop Those Whispers About Me," authored by William Tusher, about sixteen-year-old Tuesday Weld, who is described as "a beatnik with too much cheek who dated older men, smoked, took an after-dinner cocktail and said just about anything that came into her head." (Tusher concludes that Tuesday is really "a little girl" with a "mask of aloof worldliness behind which lay hidden hurts.") Actress Gale Storm writes about "My Baby's Four Fathers" in *Screenland Plus TV-Land* ("When Susanna Jo was born to Gale," the subhead explains, "her three big brothers were so elated that they practically took over raising her"). *Modern Screen* smears "Doris Day's Secret Child" all over the cover. ("Doris' most ardent fans," informs *Modern Screen*, "are not aware she's a mother, few know that her son Terry is eighteen years old, and none of us have seen any pictures of Terry in the last few years"). *Hollywood Screen Parade* reveals "The One Man Kim [Novak] Can't Get." (". . . a man whose love Kim has always sought and never won," elaborates the magazine. "That man is her father" and goes on to quote Novak that "I don't think he ever forgave me for being a girl instead of a boy. No matter how successful I am, I can never feel that he really loves me.") "Love Triangle! Who's Gonna Get Bobby [Darin]—Jo-Ann Campbell or Connie Francis?" asks *Motion Picture*. " 'I'm afraid to love him!' says Connie Francis." " 'I do love him!' says Jo-Ann Campbell.". " 'The trouble is—I love them both!' says Bobby Darin."

But not all of the fan-magazine articles are on the teaser side. *Movies Illustrated* has a piece entitled "If You Were Ava Gardner's Husband" with the information that "Ava is a passionate woman. She will love you as you have never been loved before. . . . One also must get used to some very outspoken language, and a problem which Ava has yet to conquer: her heavy drinking." But author Robert Peer adds encouragingly: "There are, however, no instances when Ava has become violent because of her excesses."

Motion Picture carries "I Was a Lolita," in which Robert Peer passes along some candid revelations by actress Linda Cristal. "Until her wedding night," the article leads off, "Linda Cristal had never been alone with a man in her life. Schooled by nuns and guarded by the rigid customs of Argentina, she knew less—much less about everything—than gum-chewing, sex-conscious, American Lolita, the 12-year-old heroine in Vladimir Nabokov's novel."

The article goes on to speak of "the terrors" of her marriage. According to Linda, when she was sixteen, she married a man much older than she was, who "had known me all of my life." After the wedding reception in Buenos Aires, "I felt a little uneasy about sharing a room with a man, but my husband merely took me to our bedroom, helped me get ready for bed, and tucked me in, just as he had done when I was five years old. I remember thinking, before I fell asleep, how sweet and safe marriage was.

"I changed my mind the next night.

"He started by telling me the rights a husband had. And then . . . I can still see myself trying to elude him. I can still feel my skin cold with fright. I can still see him chasing me around the bedroom—around and around the bedroom—until he finally caught me, brutally, in his arms. Did I faint then? I don't know. I don't remember what happened next. Maybe I just don't want to remember. Later I started hitting him with my fists. I hit him and hit him and hit him, but he was too strong to be hurt by me. . . ."

Peer wraps it up with a Hollywood postscript: "When the make-up has been scrubbed off with cold cream and the arc lights have been turned off, her memories take over, 'memories of two nights of marriage which have left me a fear and apprehension which I may never be able to overcome completely.' As she leaves her dressing room, a young actor and actress walk by, hands folded around each other, voices thick with laughter. They disappear into the night and she walks to her bright new American car. As she walks, she realizes that she is invisibly scarred, forever scarred, and her eyes are sad."

Bringing up the tag end of the article right after the foregoing paragraph is the line "Linda Cristal co-stars in UA's *The Alamo*." (Fan magazines usually run helpful current movie credits after each heartbreaking story.) Incidentally, the press agents for *The Alamo* sent out a publicity release about Linda in which she was described as "the pepper pot of the pampas" and as a "tempestuous, sloe-eyed looker with eye-filling proportions—bust 36½, waist 22, hips, 36." The publicity release also noted that "Linda projects that rare combination of tenderness, tumultuous animal vitality that makes strong men weak and weak women envious." Linda figured in the gossip columns recently when a rather unclothed picture of her appeared in *Playboy* Magazine.

"Today," says a voluble but retiring fan-magazine writer whom we might as well call Mr. Anonymous, "the fan magazines have completely adopted the *True Confession–Confidential* Magazine style. It goes way beyond *True Confession* and that sort of thing. What they have now is fiction writers back in New York who have not been to Hollywood and know nothing about Hollywood. Most of the time, anyway, they're written from newspapers. Sometimes they have someone in Hollywood to send them 'notes.' The fan magazines say 'we go on the assumption and contention that we cannot write the truth about most of the people in Hollywood because it is so sordid and horrible. So we make them look better.' But they make them look like assholes. They just make it all up. It's 100 per cent fictionalized. When Jimmy Dean died, a fan book decided they'd make money out of the Jimmy Dean thing. 'Jimmy Dean Fights Back from the Grave' was a cover line story. They did everything they could to keep Jimmy Dean alive and make a fortune out of it.

"Today only a small number of people get in fan magazines, the younger, untalented slobs mostly. The teen-agers have taken over. Joan Crawford you can hardly get into a fan mag or Cary Grant although they have color. The fan mags have polls about who is the most popular. Everyone is sick of Debbie Reynolds, but she ups circulation. They're running out of stills of Debbie. They are taking old black-and-white pictures and tinting them for color. Debbie sells books. It's a horrible thing they call reader identification. Debbie's press agent crucified Liz Taylor in the fans. He made up quotes about Liz and put them in Debbie's mouth. . . . And there's also Elvis Presley and Ricky Nelson."

The elliptic references were to the Debbie Reynolds–Elizabeth Taylor–Eddie Fisher triangle, the greatest and most cataclysmic story that has hit the fan magazines in years—in fact since Alan Ladd had a record run in the fans in the early Forties. At that time, desperate fan-magazine editors tried to scrounge up every minute facet of the actor's life, finally getting down to such fine points as how Alan Ladd took a shower, how Alan Ladd tended the petunias in his garden and what his old grade-school teacher, who was tracked down after a nation-wide search, thought of him. Ladd, like Debbie Reynolds latterly, was then constantly being voted tops in fan-magazine reader-popularity polls and the editors had no recourse but to keep chronicling him, month after month.

Explains the all-knowing Mr. A.: "They call it the fan magazines' self-perpetuating poll. Some fan magazines do it formally and others in an informal sort of way. They base the personalities who appear in their publications on popularity polls. For example, you can have the most wonderful interview in the world with Bette Davis or Cary Grant and I can assure you, you can't put it into a fan magazine because they're not on the poll. The polls are interesting because of the people who are on them from one month to the next. Joan Evans, for instance, never amounted to much. She was a teen-age-type star in whom there was some interest at one time. If a Joan Evans story was in last month's magazine, the readers would choose her on the popularity poll because she was there. They wouldn't dream of Bette Davis who went so far back because they could not see her in the fan magazine. They choose one who is already there and this can go on and on. I suppose people like Alan Ladd and June Allyson practically had to quit making pictures before they got off the polls. The trick is to get on. You start with a series of maneuvers known as layouts of the youngsters who are coming up. This is where they get their box-office from a lot, from the teen-agers. The studios service the fan magazines free with picture layouts and after there have been enough layouts and the kids begin to notice them, then finally a writer is assigned to the story."

If all this seems highly technical and involved, it still bears documentation and study, for the fan magazines are emblematic of the font from which much of Hollywood, journalistically and otherwise, flows.

The Debbie-Liz-Eddie yarn was dubbed "the most explosive triangle of the past decade." Debbie was nudging twenty-six when she divorced Eddie Fisher in February 1959. The breakup of their supposedly "ideal" marriage—in Hollywood, all marriages are "ideal" until they are suddenly splattered all over the front pages—was attributed to Liz, who married Eddie several months later in Las Vegas, Nevada, in a religious ceremony of the Jewish faith, which she adopted. The wedding was attended by a small army of press and press agents. It was Liz's fourth marriage. She and Eddie spent their wedding night in the cocktail lounge of a jet en route to New York. Debbie got custody of the two children and embarked on an accelerated acting, social and fan-magazine career. "Trouble Put Debbie at Top," commented Hedda Hopper at the time. And Louella Parsons observed: "Debbie's career has become big business." Parsons attributed it to the publicity engendered by the "almost hysterical sympathy" following her divorce.

The Debbie-Liz-Eddie story sent the fan magazines off on the greatest binge of marathon mush in at least a couple of decades. A purely random rundown of fan magazines over a period of just a few months in 1960 will give you a rough idea. At first, Debbie was cast in the role of the wronged wife and the stories were all in her favor. "The Terrible Fear of a Divorced Woman," in the April *Motion Picture*, indicated that "Debbie is afraid she'll not find love." But this theme did not prevail for long. The May issue of that magazine had what it termed a "scoop" about "Debbie's Secret Suitor," namely Harry Karl, a wealthy, publicity-minded shoe manufacturer. "The incredible story," *Motion Picture* gasped, "of the romance Hollywood said couldn't happen, wouldn't happen, mustn't happen. Here's why Debbie went from Glenn Ford to Harry Karl." Actually, *Motion Picture's* story was far from a "scoop." The April *Modern Screen*, billing its story as an "insider's report on the biggest, most surprising romantic news of the year," had inquired: "Wedding Bells for Debbie and Harry?" "Has Debbie come to the second dangerous crossroad of her life?" *Modern Screen* wanted to know. "Have the expensive gifts of a millionaire turned her head?" *Movieland and TV Time* came up with "How Debbie Grew Up Faster Than She Planned!" ("Debbie hasn't let gossip about her 'romances' upset her. She's faced the hard breaks in her life and emerged with new maturity.") *Screen Stories* was on hand with "Debbie, Are You Sure Now Is the Time to Marry?" ("Included in Debbie's Romantic Sweepstake Is Texas oil tycoon Robert Neal, who helped make her Miami vacation a lively one.") And *TV and Movie Screen* discussed "Why Debbie May Lose at Love Again"— because "every time Debbie starts clowning, her pals want to cry—for her . . . the clown in Debbie [outwits] the dream girl."

Debbie meanwhile found time to pose for a comic valentine (*Photoplay*) and went yacht shopping (*Movieland and TV Time*)— "That recent trip to Florida put Debbie in a buying mood. After almost closing a deal to buy a house there, she changed her mind at the last minute and went shopping for a 50-foot yacht." She also threw a party, with the help of the L. A. Debbie Reynolds Fan Club, for Susan Sturies, "Debbie's first official fan-club president," from Spirit Lake, Iowa. *Photoplay* carefully noted that the menu consisted of cream cheese and chives sandwichettes, a cracker dip of onion soup mix and sour cream, eggs chartreuse stuffed with mashed yolk and avocado, and ginger ale with cherry and mint leaf.

The fan magazines ganged up on Liz and Eddie. Liz, who had denied breaking up Debbie's marriage ("I don't go around breaking up homes. You can't break up a happy home. Theirs was never happy") was made out to be a kind of junior Theda Bara in the fan books. "Does God Always Punish?" *Photoplay* asked pointedly about Liz and answered it with "You've got to pay for everything. Nothing's free." In another issue, *Photoplay* gave Liz the biz in why "Liz Had to Leave the Party Before It was Over." According to author Mark Adams, Liz had precipitously walked out of a going-away party in her honor before her departure for England. The reason, he explained, was that Liz was "trying to be a *real* lady" and had "failed" at it. Liz, wrote Adams, was the only one at the party "who had so much jewelry on" and "unlike the rest of the women, she had not been able to talk about all the subjects an aristocratic, well-educated lady usually knows about. Liz has just never had this kind of education. And I think she's very conscious of it. . . . Liz would give almost anything to be considered a lady."

As the mere man in this ring-around-the-fan magazines, Eddie didn't get quite as much attention. But he was not exactly overlooked either. In "Eddie Fisher's Secret Fear," *Hollywood Screen Parade* vouchsafed that although Eddie is "married to one of the world's reigning beauties, he worries lest she outshine him, lest the public be more concerned with the wife than the husband in the Fisher family, lest he become 'Mr. Taylor.' " "Two of Eddie's stratagems in his fight to keep from being outstripped by Elizabeth Taylor," the article noted, are to "talk her into retiring" and to "work in the same movies" with her.

Before long, it was time to take long-range stock. The May 1960 *Movie Life* put it this way: "At the End of the First Year with Eddie— Does Liz Have More Than Debbie Had?" The magazine methodically analyzed both marriages in a number of departments. In the "Honeymoon" category, it found that Debbie and Eddie "got married on Monday, flew to Washington on Tuesday," while Liz and Eddie took a "jet flight to Europe May 13," the day after their marriage. As to "Homes," Debbie had "a rambling ranch-style home in the Pacific Palisades outside of Beverly Hills" and Liz occupied "a mansion, Crown House, outside of London" during the shooting of *Suddenly, Last Summer* as well as "hotel rooms in New York and other parts of the world." "No home of their own to settle in," observed *Movie Life*. When it came to "Way of Living," Debbie "made Eddie's breakfast" and "shopped at local supermarkets personally to get the best buys in food. Made old clothes do. Lived the life of a middle-class housewife." For Liz, life outside of movies consisted of "night clubs, parties, late to bed, late to rise. Breakfast usually served in bed by hotel staff." "Problems"? With Debbie it was "Eddie's stomach trouble" and her "dislike of Eddie's friends." With Liz it was "coping with public censure . . . Liz's ill health . . . lack of privacy." In the "Gifts from Eddie" division, Debbie got "two dozen roses a day when she was working, a beautiful Breath of Spring mink coat, scores of cashmere sweaters, a diamond pendant, toy poodle worth $1,500." Liz got "a blue velvet coat lined with white beaver, a mink sweater, $800 worth worth of sweaters and bathing suits, a small $1,000 watch."

Movie Life was far from through. Under the heading "Things in Common," Debbie had "strong family ties and a deep love of home." With Liz, it was "a liking for fancy restaurants, night clubs, partying, traveling, witty people. Both share an interest in the Jewish faith and have a deep devotion to the late Mike Todd." (Liz had been Mrs.

Todd, Eddie had been a Todd protégé.) In the "Children" classification, "at the end of the first year, Debbie was eight months pregnant," while "as of this writing, Liz is not expecting a baby." "Career Shared" listed Debbie as being "together with Eddie" in the picture *Bundle of Joy*, which, *Movie Life* added, "was not a hit!" In Liz's case, she was "together with Eddie in *Butterfield 8*—at her insistence." And what about "Own Career"? Debbie was "under contract to M-G-M, her stock was sky-high, her popularity zooming, her salary a weekly one of a good but far from spectacular amount." Liz, on the other hand, "became the highest paid actress in motion picture history by being able to demand and get $1,000,000 for one film." In the case of "Eddie's Career," with Debbie he had "no hit records for the first time since he shot to fame," but with Liz he had "a smash engagement at the Waldorf-Astoria. Critics said he never sang better." And finally, documenting "Press Reaction," *Movie Life* noted that Debbie and Eddie were "referred to in the press as America's Sweethearts, voted 'the cutest couple in the world.' 100% favorable public and press approval." With Liz and Eddie, there were "wild stories, snide items, rumors of splits, editorials by such leading world columnists as Max Lerner and George Sokolsky criticizing their actions and hoping it doesn't end with their being bored with one another. A 98% bad press."

And, having provided this excruciatingly exhaustive list of comparisons, *Movie Life* threw the whole thing at the poor, exhausted reader with "Who do you think has the stuff of which lasting marriages are made?"

But, in due course, things started going into reverse. Liz began to come off better in some fan-magazine stories. "Is Liz Taylor Living a Lie?" *TV and Movie Screen* wanted to know (the fan magazines have a habit of asking shattering questions—and then neatly sidestepping them). "In public," the magazine amplified, "Liz Taylor is an adoring mother to her three beautiful children. Some people call this just another performance. Are they right?" The answer: "What the whole world is surely discovering for itself is—as a mother Elizabeth Taylor is one of the best." *Screen Stories* analyzed "The Secret Reasons Why Liz Taylor Is Always Sick." ("The many illnesses that have plagued lovely Liz through her young lifetime have only made her all the more beautiful!") There was "Liz Taylor's Private War" in which *Movie Mirror* revealed that Liz wants "to be loved for 'the real me'—not for beauty, talent, wealth or prestige. . . ." *Screen World and TV* depicted "Liz Taylor as a Suburban Housewife." ("Who would have thought that America's most glamorous actress would give up all for a rambling house in the suburbs? . . . Well, it's about to happen. Liz is on the brink of a new life. . . ."

The fan magazines were warming up to Liz again. *Movie Stars TV Close-Ups* asked: "You've Forgiven Liz—But Can She Forgive You?" ("The true love that exists between Liz and Eddie is the only thing that can make her find forgiveness in her heart for the fans who didn't stick by her when she needed them most.") That same issue of the magazine spoke reverently of her conversion to Judaism and quoted her as saying, "It gives life more meaning. As old a religion as Judaism gives a foundation and direction to me." The magazine added: ". . . she has found a faith in which she is happy." And *Popular Screen* posed the question "Isn't Love Enough?" "Condemned by many," the editors sobbed, "understood by few, Ed and Liz stand alone, asking, beseeching . . ." Sara Hamilton wrote in *Photoplay*: "In My Opinion: It's about time to leave off those slambang attacks against Liz Taylor. The constant rumors suggesting growing friction between her and Eddie Fisher must be awfully hard to bear. So let's give the two a chance to live their own lives and mind our own stores, shall we?"

Meanwhile, things were looking up for Eddie, too, at least fan magazine-wise. *Motion Picture* featured a homey layout entitled: "Children, Eddie Is Your Father Now," described as "the most exclusive pictures, the most intimate story, ever published on Liz and Eddie and the children." *Movies Illustrated* inquired: "One Year Later: Is Eddie Losing Liz?" The magazine quoted a "friend of the Fishers" in reply: "Perhaps Eddie and all of us have lost the Liz we once knew. The insecure, the restless, the capricious, the impulsive Liz who thought she would never succeed in her search for happiness. Maybe that Liz *is* lost forever. But if she *is*, you can bet that in her place is a warm, wonderful, understanding woman and wife. Yes, I guess that Liz of old is no more. And I suspect it's the kind of losing that has made Eddie Fisher the winner." *Movie Mirror* posed this one: "Is Eddie Stopping Debbie's Wedding to Glenn [Ford]?" "Certainly" was the ringing reply. "Eddie Fisher will do nothing that would stand in the way of Debbie's happiness."

And what about Debbie? She was not faring so well any longer. "I think Debbie Reynolds is letting herself be overpublicized," shrilled Hedda Hopper in *Motion Picture*. "Dear Debbie: Please Don't Be a Sex-Pot!" advised *Hollywood Screen Parade*. The magazine printed a letter purporting to be from one of Debbie's fans:

I know you must receive just about a thousand letters a week telling you how great you are.

All of us kids think you're pretty terrific, and I guess you know that our thoughts and our hearts were with you when you and Eddie Fisher broke up. It's because we know how tough that must have been for you that I'm writing you this letter, and I hope you'll take it in the spirit in which it's written.

Gosh, Debbie, you just don't realize what a blow it's been for us to read about how maybe you were the "other woman" in the break-up of the Glenn Ford–Eleanor Powell marriage. Mind you, we don't know whether you were or not. But we read all those stories about how you and Glenn were having a lot of fun together in Spain making those two movies. And right after that, bang! the Glenn Fords split up. And then there was that TV program with Jack Paar.

We know you're a cut-up Debbie, and we're sure you didn't mean that to look the way it did look. You meant to be gay and cute, but that bit about unbuttoning his shirt and all just didn't go over with your teen-age fans. I mean, it's not you. To us, you're still the girl next door.

You're the cute teen-ager who became the lovely bride and the loving mother. And you've also turned into a pretty fine actress, if you ask me. But you're changing too much, Debbie, too fast, and we're not sure we like all the changes. Some of them even make us wonder whether Eddie was right when he insisted that "Sympathy would be on my side if people knew the whole story of our marriage." Because when you say things like, "Of course I have to make lots of money to support my children—Eddie will probably have children of Liz's to take care of—" it sounds a little unfair. After all, it seems to us that Eddie was pretty generous in the matter of alimony and settlement and letting you have custody of the children.

Sure, the whole situation was a heart-breaker. That's why you had practically everyone in your corner. And having lost your husband to a woman who's practically the national symbol of sex, maybe you have to prove you're sexy, too. But please don't. Stay as sweet as you are. We like you that way.

And we hope that this will be your year to marry again and find the happiness you deserve!

Movie Stars TV Close-Ups nailed "Debbie's Latest Phony Romance" ("The whispers concern Debbie Reynolds and Tab Hunter"). "No girl in Hollywood," the article led off, "is as well loved and as much hated as Debbie Reynolds. Loved because she's an old-fashioned 'good girl.' Hated because there are those who delight in thinking that someone beyond reproach is actually cheap and common. In some circles, rumors that Debbie had broken up Glenn Ford's marriage to Eleanor Powell were propagated with relish."

The fan-magazine circle had come complete. And it was beginning to spin even further. Now voices were again being raised on Debbie's behalf. *Movie Illustrated* protested: "Why Don't They Stop Kicking Debbie Around?" ("It's about time someone spoke out and told the truth about those vicious Debbie Reynolds rumors.") In time, Liz and Eddie would probably come in for a fan-magazine drubbing again.

Meanwhile, however, business was going on at the fan-magazine stand as usual. There was still money to be made out of Debbie, Liz and Eddie. One issue of *Photoplay* carried a cover shot of Tony Curtis whispering to Janet Leigh, and the legend: "Inside Stuff: Did You Know—Liz Phones Debbie 4 Times a Day." Inside the magazine Sara Hamilton noted in what was labeled "Exclusive Interview with Debbie": "I couldn't figure out what Janet and Tony were whispering about. But just as I was going to ask them, someone asked me, in a whisper, 'Did you know Liz calls Debbie 4 times a day?' Debbie wasn't at the party. She'd told me she'd be working late that night, so she'd finish her new record, the theme song from *Suddenly, Last Summer*, in time. But see what happened when I checked with her." Illustrating all this patter was a shot of Debbie staring at the camera in open-mouthed amazement. It was all an April Fool gag, but it undoubtedly helped sell many copies of *Photoplay*—with the help of a phony cover line about Debbie and Liz.

"Yes," continued Mr. A., "Debbie is number one. There were three of them in the fan-book-cover league—Liz Taylor, Natalie Wood and Debbie. They were the big three. There have been no newcomers in that league. Wood conked out. Debbie slipped into the number-one spot. It was the sympathy for her that did it.

"The big audiences for the fan books are girls. Girls are supposed to be interested in men, but men don't sell books. It's identification primarily. At least ninety per cent of the readers are girls, from twelve to twenty-four.

"We base our cover choices on the book that sells more than others. Our sales go up and we get a pattern that way. Debbie is number one.

"The teen-agers are the bulk of the buyers. The teen-agers are number one circulation-wise. But the beauty-parlor audience is very important. It ranks second to the teen-agers. A couple of issues in beauty parlors, you figure many readers. It's a more mature group. We run some stuff for the other people—Crawford, Cary Grant, John Wayne.

"The minute the readers get beyond the age of pimples and puberty they know what crap they [the fan magazines] are. Every few years we get a new batch of readers. But we do a great business under the beauty-parlor hair dryers, too. . . .

"A fan mag writer I know had to do a Shirley MacLaine interview. She had 45 minutes at lunch. Her editor told her: 'I want you to get into the very heart of this woman.' All she had was 45 minutes. I'm sure she didn't get into the 'very heart' in 45 minutes.

"The fan magazines want a story in depth with a deep, emotional narrative hook like 'Tuesday Weld stood in front of her mirror sobbing deeply: "Why have I done this? Why have I done this?" she cried.' It really doesn't matter too much what you write about. The important thing is who, not what. One editor recently told me: '. . . and, of course, anything you want to do about Debbie Reynolds, anything you can get from Debbie.' He didn't care if she would talk about her divorce or her boy friends."

The fan magazines are afflicted with some rather special editorial problems. One of these has to do with the appreciable number of gaudy young movie actors who are quite disinterested in girls. How are the fan magazines to keep presenting these profiles to their swooning, girlish readers as ardent, romantic personalities, and how are they to explain the fact that these movie idols seem to be so oblivious of the opposite sex? The fan magazines turn themselves inside out trying to drum up romances for these unsusceptible swains, and they trot out such tricky and evasive verbiage as "Trying to escape from any romantic involvement"; "He wants a free life"; and "Few women have been able to get really close to him."

Because most of their subjects are in the teen-age classification, the fan magazines have to try to resolve their youthfulness with a supposedly vast, worldly sophistication. Here are some samples: "The New Rick Nelson" finds its debonair and rather jaded hero "sipping a bottle of low-calorie root beer." The article finds that the "new Rick" is "not a confirmed bachelor but an uncommitted teenager who isn't planning a plunge prematurely into the most important event of his life." Then there is "Dear God . . . How Do You Handle a Marriage When You're Only 15 and Your Husband Is Only 18?" ("Tommy Rettig of 'Lassie' fame and his Darlene are both still so very young, and yet they are married. Did they do the right thing? Read their story.") "Exclusive Confessions: Secrets of My Past" proclaims one fan magazine. ("Hear the rattle of skeletons in closets? We're not going to tell the stars' secrets. . . . Instead, let them tell on themselves!") Among the stars who spill all is teen-ager Annette Funicello ("I seldom talk about it. My fear of hospitals and doctors, I mean," and she goes on to tell about her "tonsillectomy" and its aftermath when "I almost died"). And there is also teen-ager Molly Bee ("I was going steady with Tommy Sands and I didn't want to hurt his feelings. Still, I knew that Elvis Presley was making a movie at Paramount Studios and I was dying to meet him. No romantic ideas—I just admired the guy"). That same issue of the magazine announces that "June's Exciting Issue of Screen Stars" will carry an "intimate, exclusive" story about "Tuesday Weld and the 'secrets' of her past." Tuesday Weld, of course, is a comparative *femme fatale* among the teen-agers. "Make the Man Love Me" in another fan magazine offers "the story of Tuesday Weld's hopeless love affair with a man three times her age. . . ." The man, in case you are concerned, is actor John Ireland, who, the magazine marvels, shaking its editorial head sadly, is all of forty-five.

Since fan magazines are printed well in advance of newsstand sales, they are often caught with their deadlines—and their romances—down. By the time a fan magazine reaches the reader, the profile who is being profiled in its pages is quite likely to have ditched the dame with whom the publication has him pitching ardent woo and gone back to his fourth frau. This has been a perennial occupational hazard of fan magazines.

A brave attempt to surmount this problem occurred in 1933. In the words of an authority on the subject, who perforce has to go unidentified: "Fan mags print thirty to sixty days in advance. Joan Crawford was married to Douglas Fairbanks, Jr., and she was about to divorce her husband and, naturally, he was the last one to know about it. Joan was phoning a very close friend of hers, Katherine Albert, a fan magazine writer, in New York, and gave the story to her exclusive for her fan book, *Modern Screen*. This meant giving a news story thirty to sixty days in advance. Plans were carefully carried out. Albert came out from New York and was Joan's house guest. Knowing that Joan would divorce Doug, she took notes in the house. The day before *Modern Screen* would hit the stands, Joan would give the story to the newspapers and *Modern Screen* would come out one day later and beat all the other fan magazines. This was a well-conceived plan and a big scoop for *Modern Screen*. Joan was being loyal to a dear friend.

"But not long before this monumental story was to appear in *Modern Screen*—which was already on the press—a man in Hollywood sued Doug, charging alienation of affection of his wife. It made such banner lines, it put Joan in a horrible, horrible spot. This was her dear husband and should she be a bitch and leave him after this? It would put Joan in lousy with her fans as a lousy, stinking wife with no understanding. A woman does not do this. A woman stands by her man. Joan called *Modern Screen* and said she was not leaving Doug. *Modern Screen* said, 'You can't do this to us. It will cost us a fortune.' She wanted to play the role of the forgiving wife. Was she to let down her husband or her friend on the fan book? She finally decided to let down her husband. The fans were up in arms for months. The upshot today is that Joan and Katherine Albert are the bitterest of enemies, over something else."

Katherine Albert recalls today: "I was a free-lancer for *Modern Screen*. She [Joan] was at that time a very good friend of mine. She is no longer. She called me. I was living in New York and she called me and asked me to come out and visit her, which I did. Then she told me that she was leaving Doug. Nobody knew it but me. He didn't know it. I don't know how I conned her into letting me do this, but I did. It was the first time in history that a magazine has beat the dailies. The day the magazine was coming out, the dailies did simultaneously. Ernest V. Heyn, editor of *Modern Screen*, knew it was coming and he saved space. It was at least thirty days in advance. It was a big scoop."

It was on March 16, 1933, that Douglas Fairbanks, Jr., was sued in Los Angeles by Jorgen Dietz, who was said to be a Danish baron and sometimes called Von Dietz, on charges of stealing the "love and affection, comfort and assistance" of his wife, Mrs. Solveig Dietz. Dietz also filed a second suit for false imprisonment, charging that several months earlier Douglas Fairbanks, Jr., and Michael Levee, who was described as "a motion picture producer and business manager for Mary Pickford and others," had "compelled him to go to a room at a hotel where he was imprisoned for four hours without authority," as the newspapers reported. Dietz said that Fairbanks, Jr., and Levee threatened him with imprisonment to make him drop any claim against Fairbanks, Jr. He asked for $50,000 damages on the first charge, $10,000 on the second.

On the day the story of the Dietz suit broke, Joan Crawford announced that she and her husband had "discussed these flagrant charges together. It is an outrage and there is no truth whatever in the charges." The following day, Crawford left her husband, declaring that the Dietz accusation had nothing to do with her separation. "It is merely a case of two people being unable to get along together," she said. "It is the only brave thing for us to do." She denied any divorce plans.

On April 29, 1933, Joan Crawford sued Douglas Fairbanks, Jr., for divorce in Los Angeles, charging "grievous cruelty." Simultaneously, the May 1933 issue of *Modern Screen* came out with "The Exclusive Inside Story of the Joan-Doug Separation" billed on the cover. It was one of the most extraordinary instances of journalistic jiu-jitsu on record.

Joan got her divorce from Doug several weeks later, thereby dissolving another one of Hollywood's "perfect marriages." And, as a rather poignant postscript, when Doug was confined to Doctors Hospital in New York in June with an attack of lobar pneumonia, Joan was publicized as gallantly "ready to hasten to his bedside."

Even Louella Parsons got into the act. In *The Gay Illiterate* she claims that SHE "scooped" *Modern Screen* with the story of the Joan-Doug divorce. After the Dietz suit against Doug, writes Parsons, "knowing nothing of the strained relations between the junior Fairbankses, I whipped up a whale of a sob story. I had Joan standing shoulder to shoulder with Doug through his troubles, staunchly defending their home, their happiness, and their marriage.

"The story, written editorially, was a beauty. But it needed 'quotes' to give it the right punch—so, as innocent as a newborn babe, I called Joan and told her I needed some devoted, little-woman quotes direct for headquarters.

"Her reply was not enthusiastic. 'I wish you would not print anything like that right now,' she said. 'If you will wait I will have another story for you.'

"I had been a newshound too long not to recognize the scent of a scoop. 'I'll be right down,' I said, and pretended not to hear her protestation that 'this was hardly the time for a visit.'

"Two seconds later I was on my horse galloping to Joan's Brentwood home. She was distraught and upset—but not exactly 'beside herself,' as the saying goes. She had known as far back as when she gave Katherine Albert the scoop of her impending divorce for the magazine that she was leaving Doug. Now her big problem was that she was torn between loyalty to her friend and her canny knowledge that there would be 'hell poppin'' if my sweetness-and-light yarn broke in a newspaper just five days before Katherine's magazine, with the divorce exclusive, reached the newsstands.

"To her everlasting credit and my deep gratitude, Joan gave me the true story—that she had made up her mind to divorce Doug long before he got into any difficulty.

"I've never been a backward girl where a good story is concerned. This was one—and how! Right under my surprised hostess's eyes I grabbed her portable typewriter and started writing my yarn before the competition could arrive! Maybe I can only brag about beating the other newspapers by one bare edition—but that was enough! I did have the 'beat,' and the many stories written that I dislike Joan because she gave a magazine the first story of her separation are just so much sauerkraut. If the whole thing wasn't just plain old luck, however, I'll give my next scoop to Hedda Hopper."

In some ways, though, the fan-magazine deadline problem is not as deadly as it might seem to be. The Hollywood personalities who are written about in the fan magazines are perfectly well aware of the deadline factor and that there is an interval of from at least one to several months between the time an interview or photographic layout is finished and its appearance in print. As a result, they are more than likely to take this into account in making any moves that might affect an upcoming story. Debbie Reynolds and Harry Karl, for instance, would be cutting their own publicistic throats if they decided to split up, knowing that a slew of fan-magazine stories about their "romance" was soon due off the press.

You can find out all sorts of strange and contradictory things from the fan magazines—as well as make an unfounded reputation for yourself as a wit merely by quoting from them at random. For example, *Movie Life* of May 1960 tells about "The Brutal Loneliness of [Marlon] Brando." On the other hand, the May 1960 *Modern Screen*, in "Memoirs Beautiful and Bitter of Casanova's Ladies," which is described as "a psychoanalyst's intimate report on the strange love-life of Marlon Brando," indicates that he has not much time to be lonely, what with Anna Kashfi, France Nuyen and Barbara Luna among the ladies in his life.

The May 1960 issue of *Motion Picture* grimly warns: "Jerry, Stop Before You Kill Yourself" ("The full story of Jerry Lewis' heart condition—what his doctor says, what his wife fears"). But in the March *Photoplay* of the same year, in "The Day the Undertaker Called—for Me," Jerry Lewis himself has some fun with the erroneous report that he had passed away suddenly on the set of his Paramount picture,

Cinderfella (naturally, one always gets in the picture credit). Describing himself as "a talking corpse," Lewis says that "If I were going to die, I'd die with a bigger audience" than he had on the movie set.

The fan magazines yield an amazing assortment of abstruse items. In her Hollywood diary in *Popular Screen*, May Mann chronicles, in a paragraph of complexity that beggars Marcel Proust: "TUESDAY: Honestly, Troy Donahue has me confused. He introduced Nan Morris, a twenty-two-year old secretary, to me at a big party and before I could item it, Warners told me it was all off for good. Nan started dating John Ireland since he and Tuesday Weld are splito. So I caddy out to Warners to lunch with Troy and he says he is dating Diane McBain, a contract pretty at Warners. Then I go to this big party for Connie Francis last night—and there's Troy and Nan again!"

No slouch at this sort of thing either is Hedda Hopper, who, in a column entitled "Under Hedda's Hat" (and it's usually old-hat), writes in *Motion Picture*: "Al Hedison who escorted Jill St. John when Lance Reventlow was out of town is really serious about Ruth Rigler, a production assistant." Incidentally, Hopper writes a monthly column for *Motion Picture*, Parsons is featured in *Modern Screen* (Sara Hamilton, of Parsons' staff, contributes to *Photoplay*), and Sheilah Graham does a column for *Silver Screen*. Most of the established columnists are regularly represented in the fan magazines. The ramifications of the journalistic comintern in Hollywood are seemingly endless.

A standard feature of fan magazines is the letters-to-the-editor department. The February 1959 *Modern Screen* offers these tidbits— "Q: Does Elvis Presley really prefer German frauleins to American girls? A: Only so long as he is stationed in Germany. Q: Are Nick Adams and Kathy Nolan on or off? I keep reading different versions. A: On and off—daily. Q: Who was Pier Angeli's first love? Natalie Wood's? A: Kirk Douglas—for both. Q: Why does Montgomery Clift go for older women like Libby Holman and Myrna Loy? A: A noted psychiatrist says Monty is looking for a mother. Q: Has Kim Novak got a private pact with her secret love never to marry so long as it is impossible for them to marry each other? A: No, but both prefer being single for the time being." (It might be helpful if the unenlightened reader were let in on who Kim Novak's "secret love" is exactly, but then, I guess, he would no longer be "secret.")

One of my favorite morsels of fan-magazine information appeared in *Motion Picture*'s "The Answer Man" department—"Q: Are Loretta Young and Marie Windsor the same person? If not, who is Marie

Windsor? A: Marie Windsor is Marie Windsor and Loretta Young is Loretta Young. What more can I say?"

But, for all its venality and incompetence, it is considered politic in Hollywood to be at peace with the press, from the fan magazines to the more refined publications. Journalists are regarded as a necessary evil, somewhat like the carbon-monoxide fallout, the freeway traffic or the man in the white smock who administers a high colonic. A good many film folk have largely built their careers on a well-developed ability to get along with the press. One of those who had a tiptop talent at making the trained press seals jump through their hoops was the late Mike Todd. Todd's technique was primarily one of con and payola on various levels—at one time, he even disbursed a small "piece" of the profits of his *Around the World in 80 Days* to some of the editors of a leading national magazine. In return, he got more than his money's worth in the form of several highly valuable layouts in the publication.

Still recounted in the cinema city is the time the high-ranking editor of a weekly news magazine came to Hollywood for a visit with his wife, who had acting aspirations. The late Louis B. Mayer, then head of M-G-M, benignly arranged for a screen test for the editor's wife. It was elaborately shot, and the editor and his spouse returned east happy in the thought that they had gotten such magnanimous attention from the mighty Mayer. The test, unfortunately, came to nothing. It could not have had any other result. The film was never developed. There was even some doubt as to whether there was any film in the camera.

A former *Time* Magazine cinema editor, now engaged in television, tells this apropos story: "Many years ago, a *Time* senior editor was going out to Hollywood and called the Time-Life bureau chief there and said he wanted to meet a starlet at his bungalow at the Beverly Hills Hotel. The bureau chief called Harry Brand at Fox and Brand said he'd get a $100-a-night girl and he'd pick up the tab. Brand kept getting a $100 tab every day, three of them. Brand called the bureau chief. The bureau chief called the senior editor at the Beverly Hills Hotel and the editor said, 'It looks, the way things are going, I think in another day or two I'm gonna be able to lay her.' "

The moviemakers are expert at what has been described as "taming the journalistic beast" and "seducing the despised reporter." And many of the press, hobnobbing cozily with the Hollywood great, sometimes get the idea that they are loved for themselves alone. Lulled by the fawning flattery of the press agents and the moviemakers, they delude themselves into thinking, as one ex-movie commentator, Theodore Strauss, once put it, that they are "gods of the lightning able to pulverize Louis B. Mayer's gate with a single bolt. They are the victims of delusions of grandeur dispelled only by the discovery—if and when they should lose their office—that the film industry has difficulty remembering their names."

"The press," says one of its lesser members who has thought about the subject a good deal, "is a group always vacillating between arrogance and belly crawling. The Hollywood press—what they find so difficult to understand, and maybe don't want to understand it, they are not people who have established abilities that can carry them into any other world. They're just so many outlets. They're not people—they're outlets. They're desks. It depends on which desk you sit behind as to how important you are. There are so many euphemisms they have for their belly crawling—'co-operation' is a favorite excuse. There is always this ambivalence—tremendous arrogance and nauseating belly crawling.

"The press is so dependent on the press agents—that's one reason for their pathetic crawling. There is no such thing as going out and digging up a story. It's all releases and private press agents. It's the evil of the free item. Some columnists have it down to a system: three free items allows the press agent to get one plug. And usually the plug is so deadly. You'd think that if the people lavished half that ingenuity on the plug item, it would be wonderful."

The *Saturday Evening Post*'s Hollywood specialist, Pete Martin, has occasionally toyed with the thought of getting his magazine to let it be known that he has been dropped and then coming out to Hollywood to see how he is received by his erstwhile film friends. But Martin has never gone through with his plan. He undoubtedly suspects that, minus his press credentials, he would get a cold shoulder instead of a warm welcome from the moviemakers.

In my own personal experience, I have found that, when I was between journalistic jobs, the moviemakers, with almost no exception, invariably cut me deader than if I were Khrushchev at a meeting of the D.A.R. But as soon as I was accredited as a correspondent again, my phone would start ringing with the perennial Hollywood endearment of "Darling!" from the selfsame people whom I could not have reached on the phone, had I wanted to, a few hours earlier. The pattern is predictable—and overwhelmingly tedious.

Several years ago Edwin Schallert, who had been motion-picture editor of the Los Angeles *Times* since the early Twenties, retired from his job. Schallert had never been a particularly distinguished Hollywood journalist, but, as one correspondent put it, "he was a factor in this town." Schallert was well liked by the movie colony—for the simple reason that he did his best to like the motion-picture people and their product. Schallert was also known for making an appearance at just about every social event in Hollywood, usually quite late. "If he promised to show up, he did," says a local newspaperwoman. "He was conscientious and he had always had stars in his eyes." She recalls that one night some years ago she and her husband "were invited to a cocktail party given by a press agent. We dropped in on the way to the Pasadena Playhouse. We had to cover a show. We came back to the party later—I had covered the show and written a story—and we looked in again for a night cap. The doorbell rings. It's around two A.M. It was Schallert. He was just arriving—for a five-to-seven cocktail party.

"The Schallerts," she adds, "still get around. But now they have to fight for their seats at previews. They try—but it isn't the same."

Perhaps the most notable instance of the journalistic fall from Hollywood grace was that of Harry Crocker, for many years a movie columnist on the Los Angeles *Examiner*. Crocker, a personable, well-heeled scion of the wealthy San Francisco banking family, had been an actor in Chaplin movies (*The Circus*) and a production assistant to Chaplin (*City Lights*). Later he became William Randolph Hearst's *aide-de-camp* and finally a Hearst movie columnist. Crocker's column was entitled "Behind the Makeup"; one day, before he took it over, it accidentally appeared as "Makeup the Behind," "the only time the column came out with the right name," according to a Hollywood gagster. Amiable and innocuous in the extreme, "Behind the Makeup" was rather dull to read. However, as Crocker once told me, he thought of himself not as a writer but as a "mosaicist." He was unique among movie columnists in that he never penned an unkind word about anyone. He resided in a munificent home in Beverly Hills, drove to work in a Lincoln Continental and was *persona grata* just about everywhere. The studios always welcomed him. He squired many of the "great ladies" of Hollywood, from Joan Crawford to Garbo, to places where the rest of the press was strictly barred. Crocker attended so many ultra-exclusive social functions that he would even tip off Louella Parsons occasionally about what was going on. Everyone liked him. "I go out mostly as a friend, not as a columnist," he once told me. "I've heard and seen all kinds of things. People talk in front of me. I never break a confidence."

After Hearst's death in 1951, Crocker lost his column, or "retired," as they say in Hollywood. He soon disappeared almost entirely from the Hollywood social scene. I would sometimes see him walking alone in Beverly Hills, a rather sad, philosophic and ailing man. He died, at the age of sixty-four, on May 24, 1958, practically forgotten by his onetime Hollywood cronies. They simply had no use for him any longer as a former columnist.

The obituary in the Los Angeles *Examiner*—Crocker's onetime newspaper—grandiosely stated that "leaders of the world of motion pictures and journalism" were present at the funeral services for Crocker at the All Saints Episcopal Church in Beverly Hills. Actually, there were only a handful of oldtime stars like Marion Davies and Mary Pickford and a scattering of press agents, to whom Crocker had been so kind as a columnist.

"There was a shocking lack of turnout of Hollywood people at Crocker's funeral," said press agent Nat James, who knew him well. He added: "The loss of his column was a terrible blow to him. By the nature of not having a column, he was not so active. He just withdrew from activity. His friends called him, but not the studios."

In Hollywood, there is nothing deader than yesterday's newspaper —unless it is yesterday's newspaperman.

CHAPTER III

Dreams of a Rarebit Fiend

IN HOLLYWOOD, press and press agents go together, like the two sides of a counterfeit coin, like Romulus and Remus suckling from the same fiendish teat. Many of the press agents are former newspapermen who gave up journalism for more lucrative publicity pay and now spend the better part of their professional time ghosting fanciful essays for their less well-paid confreres. The journalist gets the credit (?) and the anonymous press agent gets the cash. The press agents at least have the saving grace of being honest whores.

There is at least one press agent—and perhaps more—per press representative in Hollywood. Between the two of them they manage to grind out an estimated half million words daily, pipelined to Karachi, Brazzaville and Pleasantville, New York. From the press-agent standpoint, anything that mentions the picture or personality he is ballyhooing in a fairly favorable light is usually considered a job accomplished. In Hollywood, the theory is mostly that as long as you spell the name right and do not identify the person in question as an agent of Lucifer himself, all is well. The emphasis is on press agentry rather than public relations.

Everybody in Hollywood, it has been said, is a press agent, whether labeled so or not. And just about everybody who can afford it hires a press agent. Even some of the press agents have press agents. At one time the United Nations had a press agent in Hollywood and he explained his presence there with "The United Nations has come to Hollywood because when Bing Crosby speaks many more people listen than would listen to a United Nations spokesman." Hollywood itself has a press agent, in its AMPP publicity committee, which is supposedly dedicated to seeing to it that reason and enlightenment about the movies are disseminated to the press. Actually, the AMPP publicists are mealy mouthpieces for the movie business. Their main job is suppress agentry and the squelching of any disinterested and objective comment about Hollywood.

With the decline of the major studios, there has been an increase in the number of independent press agents who represent the many profiles and moviemakers no longer under contract to a particular picture plant. One of the biggest independent Hollywood publicity offices, whose size is exceeded only by its incompetence, has more employees than *Life*, *Time* and *Newsweek* combined have in their Los Angeles offices. These particular publicists operate on the two-fisted theory that, since they represent so many big Hollywood names, the press needs them more than they need the press—and they may be right.

The only thing that is super-colossal about most of Hollywood is the adjectives of its press agents. The "ballyhooligans" have done their work well—it sometimes seems almost too well—in promulgating the myth of the movies, in selling Hollywood to a palpitating world. The press agents may actually be the only ones in Hollywood who have so excelled themselves professionally.

A press agent, it has been said, is one who takes in lying for a living. Fib and fantasy are the stock-in-trade of the tub thumpers. Since most of the cinema citizens are not really very colorful, the motion-picture pitchmen have to work overtime to dream up interesting things about them. Most publicity stories fall into one of several familar categories. There is the story about the studio gateman who did not recognize an eminent star in costume (actually, gatemen are most efficient and their jobs are rather uneventful). There is the calamity story about how a light fell off a catwalk, narrowly missing the leading man (this story would come to life if the light only hit the profile instead of missing him). And there is the yarn about how Edward G. Cagney, who plays tough guys on the screen and beats up his leading ladies with his bare fists, is really a softie away from the camera and likes to putter among his petunias and collect Grandma Moses canvases. There are other overworked publicity gags, like announcing a sequel to a current movie hit (which is never made), instituting a search for an unknown to star in a big production (a star usually gets the role) and letting the gossip columnists in on the momentous news that Ronald Devil-May-Care is running around with Mamie Maunciple, his new leading lady (actually, in narcissistic Hollywood, where the old proverb has been amended to "an I for an I," Ronald

Devil-May-Care is going steady with—Ronald Devil-May-Care). All these stories add up to the same old Hollywood hoopla.

Once in a great while the pattern is broken. Director George Stevens, for instance, actually cast an unknown, Millie Perkins, in the title role of *The Diary of Anne Frank*, as he had promised—in this case, it might have been better if he had not. One of Stevens' press agents enthused about the casting as follows: "We had a big campaign for the search for a girl to play Anne Frank. We got more than 10,000 letters from all over the world, including like Japanese girls and that sort of thing. Hollywood had its usual skepticism—he was searching for an unknown girl. And she was an unknown and not even experienced as an actress. But not Jewish, but Irish-Catholic. Everyone was skeptical. You announce you're looking for an unknown girl and you end up with Natalie Wood. Stevens has given a new integrity to the 'unknown girl.' Should he announce an unknown man to play Jesus in his next production, that's what he would mean."

One of my first contacts with Hollywood-style press agentry occurred in New York in the late Thirties when I was employed by an independent publicist named Irving Hoffman. Hoffman was retained by Warner Brothers as a special public-relations consultant. Hal Wallis, now an independent producer, was then production chief at Warners. In the course of a Florida fishing trip, Wallis brought in a marlin that weighed around 300 pounds, and a photograph of the film executive standing proudly beside the outsize fish duly arrived in New York. The Warner Brothers publicity department was electrified. There were urgent, high-level consultations. It was imperative that the picture of Wallis and the fish should appear in every New York newspaper the following day. Although this may not have been directly related to moviemaking, it became a top priority matter.

All sorts of drumbeating experts, among them Hoffman, were called in. Hoffman had a pow-wow with his own staff of flacks. Publicists, specializing in individual editors, were assigned to various newspapers as go-betweens. Other operatives were commandeered where deemed necessary. No expense was spared. The platoon of publicity specialists fanned out on the job. Inevitably, the Wallis fish photograph appeared in every New York newspaper the following day, and everyone, including Wallis, presumably, went on to make better movies. (Wallis still has the head of the marlin mounted in his home, undoubtedly as a memento of his fishing prowess—and the prowess of the publicity boys.)

Some time thereafter I was engaged in independent publicity work with a press agent named Leo Guild, who specialized in ingenious stunt ideas. To promote a Warner movie entitled *Luck of the Irish*, Guild planted a four-leaf clover in a crack in the sidewalk in front of the Strand Theater on Broadway where the picture was playing and saw to it that it was "accidentally" discovered, with a good deal of resultant publicity. For a Paramount picture, *Seventeen*, he had a bill introduced in the New York State legislature to lower the legal age of consent for marriage from eighteen to seventeen. Naturally, the news of this legislative measure coincided with the premiere of *Seventeen*. (Neither of these stunts, I am afraid, helped the movies, which were beyond any publicistic succor.)

It was during this period that I began to realize more fully how it was possible to utilize the channels of the press and press agentry to maneuver most anything—a knowledge that the movie manipulators have in heaping measure. At one point Guild and I did some publicity work for an affable but quite inconsequential fellow named Michael Mordkin, Jr. Mordkin was a printing salesman, but he liked to kick around show-business circles socially and he asked us to promote him as a sort of Broadway personality for that purpose. Since Mordkin had nothing to do with show business aside from his social activities, this was not a particularly easy assignment. We finally came up with an idea. We simply threw a party every month at Mordkin's lavish penthouse apartment, inviting the Broadway press, press agents and assorted show-business personalities. The parties were an instantaneous hit. Mordkin was an excellent host and, since he apparently did not want anything of his guests, he got a flood of publicity from the press, who found him thoroughly likable and ingratiating. (As insurance, we had made up an imposing display book to indicate that Mordkin did some work as an industrial designer, specializing in night clubs, but hardly anyone was interested in looking at it.)

The first such party we threw was in honor of humorist H. Allen Smith and his book, *Low Man on a Totem Pole*. We invited all the subjects of the book, from former Columbia University president Nicholas Murray Butler to Broadway Rose. Butler sent a wire saying that he unfortunately could not make it, but Broadway Rose and a host of other characters showed up. Some people flew clear across the country for the event, which ran on and on over a period of several days and was a smashing success. As a result of these parties, Mordkin soon became a Broadway character in his own right. No one ever bothered to ask anything much about him. It was sufficient that he was such an open-handed and magnanimous host.

Spurred on by our success with Mordkin, Guild and I figured that if we could accomplish this sort of publicistic feat with so little material to work with, we would go the Mordkin publicity campaign one better and see what we could achieve with a completely non-existent subject. Accordingly, we invented a mythical playboy from Chicago—whom we shall call X—and had him flying to New York and indulging in all kinds of playful activities. In due course, gossip-column items about this non-existent playboy began to appear in all sorts of journalistic pillars, documenting his colorful accomplishments. We had X escorting young ladies from the stage and screen to El Morocco, the Stork Club and "21." He was supposedly very much in evidence at the most distinguished social events. We even had him spiritedly dunking himself in the fountain in front of the Plaza Hotel.

X was the ideal publicity client. Since he did not exist, he could not impede our inventful publicity campaign about him in any way. He was the best kind of clay for a creative press agent since he could be molded any way we wanted to. As time went by and as X began to get more and more publicity—no one ever asked for proof whether he existed or not—we even began to get some requests from the press to interview him in person, which we managed to forestall. However, ultimately we decided to drop X and let him die a natural (or unnatural) death. We figured we had proved our publicistic point and that there might be complications if we pursued this gambit any further. So X was laid to rest, just when he was on the brink of a notable Broadway–Hollywood type career.

In later years, when I had extensive dealings with the motion-picture people in Hollywood, I occasionally thought of the non-existent X and how simple it had been to build him up via contrived publicity. Although the motion-picture personalities actually existed, they were similar in many respects to X. Much of their fame and their personalities was pure press agentry and invention.

Another Broadway press agent, an unorthodox fellow named Jack Tirman, surpassed Guild and myself in this respect. Tirman was publicizing a small Manhattan night club and, since there were no noteworthy acts at this spot, he fabricated an exotic dance team which was supposedly starring at this establishment. Tirman was able to get quite a bit of publicity for this fictional terpsichorean duo. But the entire thing blew up in his typewriter one day. A Broadway columnist reviewed this dance team at the night club and gave it a poor notice. The columnist, of course, had never set foot in the club and his review was compounded, as was par for many Broadway gossip columnists, of ignorance, apathy and spite. Tirman was tremendously upset about the adverse notice that his mythical dance team had received. After some deliberation, Tirman decided to drop the dancers from the club—if they were that poor, they did not deserve to be there in the first place. And so the non-existent dance duo was given its walking papers and Tirman booked another and better act—also non-existent—into the night club.

In due course, partly as a result of these formative experiences, I came to Hollywood as an employee of the Warner Brothers publicity department. My boss was Charles Einfeld, one of the more renowned names in Hollywood's Ballyhoo's Who. Einfeld, a shrewd fellow, was noted for developing the Hollywood press junket to its high estate. It was Einfeld who, in 1933, sent a train labeled "The 42nd Street Special," bulging with stars and starlets, cross-country to promote a Warner musical, coincidentally entitled *42nd Street*, and who later dispatched mammoth contingents of press and press agents to Virginia City and Dodge City in connection with the opening of the films of the same names. Under Einfeld's regime, a rather colorless motion picture entitled *Juarez* became enshrined in publicistic annals. Ben Cohn, the press agent who dreamed up the *Juarez* stunt, tells it as follows: "A guy jumped into a cab in New York City. 'Take me to *Juarez*,' he said. He was a night worker and he fell asleep. When he woke up, the cab driver told him, 'We're in Philadelphia. We ought to make Juarez, Mexico, in four days.' There was an argument. Two cops jailed them both. It hit page one of every paper. It got tremendous space."

Among my initial assignments at Warners was to ghost articles and speeches under the by-line of studio boss Jack Warner. Einfeld would carefully outline what he wanted in the piece and I would then write it. One day, sitting in Einfeld's office, while he was telling me what I should write under Warner's name, I asked him if it would not be helpful for me to talk to Warner personally in order to make the article more persuasive. Einfeld looked at me as if I had taken leave of my senses. Swiveling around in his chair, he transfixed me with his piercing eyes and said, pointing his finger at me: "*I* can tell it to you better." I left Einfeld's office chastened, feeling as if I had committed an unpardonable social error by alluding to the idiot grandfather in the attic.

The World War II years were profitable ones at Warners—and at every other studio. Almost every movie released made money. The atmosphere at Warners was pleasantly informal. At one time, one of the offices in the writers' building was occupied by William Faulkner, who was working on the dialogue of an aviation movie. In the adjoining office sat Mary Dowell, a six-foot-tall Broadway showgirl who was known as Stuttering Sam because of her speech impediment. Stuttering Sam expressed herself best on the typewriter, in the form of letters to her friends, and, as a result, had been hired to work on the script of a movie about Broadway chorus girls. While the reserved Faulkner pored over his writing in his office, Stuttering Sam sat in the next cubicle at her typewriter, attired in a petticoat and a sky-high turban and taking an occasional nip from a bottle of spirits which was strategically at hand for inspiration and to help her overcome her stuttering. Neither Faulkner's nor Stuttering Sam's literary output, incidentally, ever reached the screen.

During those years Warners was preoccupied with its slogan of "good citizenship and good picture making." The movies the studio turned out were mostly of the mass persuasion. However, one day a front-office memo was circulated in the publicity department to the effect that movies were henceforth no longer to be referred to as "movies" but as "motion pictures." "Movies," the Warner high command felt, was too undignified and did not have a sufficiently aristocratic sound, particularly for the proletarian epics they were producing in a time of crisis. Jack Warner himself held the rank of colonel in the Army, and, according to studio legend, had had a treatment of the U.S. Army manual for recruits prepared for him by his diligent story department so that he could study it with a minimum of effort.

Einfeld was more enterprising than the average studio publicity director. When Warners made *Mission to Moscow* during World War II, Einfeld detached me from regular publicity duty for several weeks to write a special article for *The Nation* about Hollywood war films, with some mention, naturally, of *Mission to Moscow* and other combat pictures. When the piece appeared, Einfeld saw to it that it was reprinted and commented upon in other publications, thereby garnering a goodly amount of publicity for the movies mentioned. This sort of tactic differed from the attitude at, say, Paramount, where I had at one time tried to get some information for another article I was writing for *The Nation*. The Paramount publicity director said that he had never heard of *The Nation*. When I informed him that the magazine had been in existence before Paramount and even Hollywood came into being, he seemed somewhat nettled. But after ascertaining that *The Nation* actually did exist, he informed me brusquely that the studio's policy was not to accommodate publications with as small a circulation as it had.

For some strange reason I became a sort of contact man in the publicity department with Errol Flynn, at that time one of the biggest box-office—and biggest problem—stars the studio had under contract. Flynn was constantly at odds with Jack Warner and the studio brass and, by indirection, with the publicity department. He would not speak to anyone from publicity and would not co-operate with the unit press agents assigned to his pictures. Flynn, who was then being sued in a paternity suit, was also writing a novel (he was really writing it himself) and we somehow got into a discussion of it. He offered me the manuscript to read and I made some constructive criticisms. This seemed to please Flynn and we became quite friendly.

Flynn's novel, *Charlie Bow-Tie Proceeds*, was on the autobiographical side. Its leading character was an Irish adventurer, Shaun O'Flagherty, nicknamed Charlie Bow-Tie, who was transported from the South Seas to Hollywood. In the cinema city, he became involved with an actress named Ciro Charnel. Also figuring in the plot were two movie directors, Kurtiss and Krapper (two of the Warner directors at the time were Michael Curtiz and Irving Rapper). The entire thing was told in swashbuckling prose. The book was published in 1946 under the title of *Showdown*.

As a result of my literary relationship with Flynn, whenever a member of the press wanted to get to him, I was usually asked to see if I could arrange it, and most of the time I was able to do so. But Flynn continued to feud with the publicity department. He once gave me a graphic explanation of why he was so antagonistic toward the studio press agents. He showed me the official studio biography of himself and then, carefully and in detail, penciled the actual facts of his life in the margins of the mimeographed story. This fascinating paper has, unfortunately, disappeared or it would have made a classic Hollywood document. Actually, the real facts of Flynn's life, it seemed to me, were even more colorful than the ones invented by the press agents.

To strike back at Flynn, the studio placed under contract a young actor named Paul Brinkman, who was almost a double for Flynn. Brinkman's main function seemed to be to sit in the Warner Brothers Green Room, where the stars and directors lunched, and thereby irritate Flynn. Brinkman finally got to appear before the camera in minor roles in several pictures, but his major acting was reserved for the Green Room during the lunch hour. Flynn retaliated in his own characteristic way. Whenever a group of tourists, shepherded by a press agent, arrived on one of his sets and stood there gawking at him, Flynn would ostentatiously and with great relish start picking his long and classic nose.

Flynn, according to Jerry Asher, who was a publicist at the studio then, "had a perverse, sardonic, degenerate sense of humor and he hated that studio. Every time the studio put him on a spot, he always got sick when on salary and held up production and cost them lots of money and trouble. Flynn had a pain in the ass once and the doctor told him to have a hemorrhoidectomy. But he went through the pain for weeks so that he could have the operation when his next picture started. That cost Warner Brothers a fortune."

One of Flynn's sidekicks was a stunt man named Buster Wiles. At one time Flynn took Wiles to New York with him and introduced him to everyone as a Count who was his house guest. Wiles became all the rage on the high-society circuit and, for a time, even eclipsed Flynn himself socially. Flynn got a great kick out of it.

Flynn was a Lothario off screen as well as on. He had a custom-made Darrin Packard with seats that, at the push of a button, became horizontal. Flynn did not allow his work to interfere with his amorous pursuits. While on location at Monterey, California, for a picture entitled *Edge of Darkness*, Flynn disappeared at a crucial moment during the filming. A cast and crew of several hundred had been waiting on the Monterey pier for some time for the sun to come out so that they could continue shooting. When the sun finally materialized, Flynn had unaccountably vanished. A manhunt uncovered him with a young local lady in the loft of a fish house on the pier. The Warner operatives, through long experience, knew how to deal with such emergencies. Flynn was rushed in a fast car in one direction. The girl was rushed in another fast car in another direction. Bills of large denomination were handed to various interested parties. And shooting on *Edge of Darkness* finally continued.

Flynn was one of the most urbane and amusing actors I ever met. He was also a good performer. I recall actor Morris Carnovsky, during the shooting of *Edge of Darkness*, telling me that Flynn was a better actor, for the sort of thing he did, than most movie actors, for the simple reason that he didn't "act." He lived his role—on and off screen. As a result, Flynn in *Edge of Darkness* was more believable than Carnovsky himself.

Flynn was also well liked by the "little people" at the studio. He always treated them with courtesy. His battles were reserved for the studio bosses where the contest was not a one-sided one.

John Garfield was another actor who didn't "act" in the customary sense, and his performances were the better for it. Garfield was the most democratic actor, in his personal relationships with people, that I encountered in all my years in Hollywood. His forte was the "socially conscious" films that Warners turned out so regularly during the Thirties and into the Forties. John Bright, the scenarist who authored quite a few of them, once explained how Warners came to make these movies. According to Bright, it was because they were, quite simply, good, money-making "action formula" films and not because the Warner brothers were particularly "socially conscious" in any way.

Dane Clark was a sort of junior John Garfield. He was originally Bernard Zanville from Brooklyn and he hated the new name Warners had given him. One day some gagster at the studio, an actor, told Clark that his name was being changed to Bernard Zanville. "It's my name," Clark screamed. "They can't do that to me!"

George Tobias was also part of the standard proletarian cast in Warner pictures. One of the phony names the studio press agents used was that of Mary Doss, a supposed sugar heiress. The flacks had this mythical Mary Doss going out with the bachelor actors at the studio for publicity purposes. One day the publicity boys planted an item in one of the gossip columns that Mary Doss had been dancing cheek to cheek with George Tobias. Tobias stormed into the publicity department angrily waving the clipping and shouted, "Don't tie me up with that dame! She's a tramp! She goes out with everybody!"

While doing publicity for Warner, I also became friendly with Ida Lupino, an imaginative actress. On one occasion, she danced, sang, read parts of a musical comedy aloud and told me, in all seriousness, about the ghost of her late father Stanley who came back one time and hit her then husband, Louis Hayward, over the head with a cocktail shaker.

Another young actor at the studio, Gig Young, owed some of his success to the ministrations of the press agents. Young, a promising performer, was also a most affable fellow. The studio publicists liked to take him to lunch because they enjoyed his company and also because they could have a free meal when they signed for it in the company of a profile. When the press agents had no one to take to lunch in the Green Room, they would still sign Gig Young's name to the bill. The arrangement with Young was that he would at all times confirm that he had been in the Green Room even if he had not been there. This gastronomic collusion generated much good will on both sides, and Young was the recipient of special publicistic attentions that other actors did not get. When Young was drafted and had to leave for the service, the assembled Warner press agents threw him a lavish and tearful farewell party. After Young was gone, the publicists did not eat as well as they once had.

Publicity for performers was ardently desired at the studio, but at the executive level publicity for producers was discouraged. Such publicity was supposed to be reserved for Jack Warner, from whom all accomplishments theoretically flowed. When I wrote a lengthy treatise about Henry Blanke, talented producer of *The Life of Emile Zola*, *The Maltese Falcon* and *Treasure of the Sierra Madre*, and turned it in to the publicity director, this piece of prose quickly disappeared. However, the studio had a hard time holding down Jerry Wald, who had been a writer and had recently become a producer. Wald, a fast-talking operator, had a natural affinity for publicity and he knew all the ins and outs of the press-agent business. He would telephone Hollywood columnists on his own and give each of them the same "exclusive" story—about Jerry Wald. Wald became a gadfly in the publicity department's operation since he was probably a more enterprising and energetic press agent than any publicist at the studio. He always gave the press top priority even though he might be in the midst of a fire, flood or story conference. This talent ultimately helped carry him far in Hollywood.

I first met Jim Moran, the press agent's press agent, when I went to work at Warners. The rotund, easygoing Moran was employed in the publicity department fresh from his promotional triumphs in selling an icebox to an Eskimo, looking for a needle in a haystack, leading a bull into a china shop and other contemplative pursuits. Moran, in fact, was as much philosopher as publicist and that may have been his undoing in Hollywood, where philosophy was not much in demand. At Warners, after much deliberation, Moran came up with a publicity stunt that seemed to have just about everything in it. It was during the wartime meat shortage and it was Moran's idea to cross a turkey with a centipede in order to obtain an unprecedented number of turkey legs. The studio made up a plaster turkey with dozens of legs sticking out from it, and a number of photogenic starlets were photographed cutting this hybrid prop.

Soon afterward, Moran left the studio and it was during this period that he evolved some of his more ingenious ideas. For a movie entitled *The Egg and I*, Moran sat on an ostrich egg—by means of a specially rigged-up harness—and, after 23 days, hatched a baby ostrich which was named Ossip Moran. Moran was then residing in a small Hollywood cottage that was badly in need of a paint job. The landlady, however, declined to paint the place. One morning Moran telephoned her breathlessly to please hurry over and see what some slob had done to the house. The landlady arrived to find a four letter word, in ten-foot-high letters, painted on the side of the domicile. The place was quickly repainted, thereby erasing forever Moran's fine lettering.

Moran occupied himself haphazardly during this period. Spurred on by his house-painting accomplishment, he entered a modern-art contest in Hollywood by submitting an "elaborate doodle that took me two or three months to do." He signed it Naromji, which was, more or less, Jim Moran spelled backward. "I just did it to see what they thought of the work I did," says Moran. "I felt if I entered it under my own name everybody would think it was a gag. It was a legitimate entry in a legitimate show." The doodle was selected among the top five entries in the show and Moran later sold it to Madman Muntz, an automobile dealer, for $750. "It was the best work of my non-objective painting period," says Moran solemnly.

While en route from Hollywood to New York during this time, Moran sat in the lounge car of the Super Chief industriously reading a publisher's dummy book with nothing printed on its pages. He perused this book for the duration of the trip until the rest of the passengers were beside themselves with incomprehension. Moran's explanation: "When I'm exhausted and have a hangover and wanna be left alone, I have to do something to discourage others. I was really beat—that was why I took the train. I wanted no one to talk to me. The book was a sort of way to amuse oneself in a mild way without having to do anything in particular. It had a signal effect on the people in the train."

Back in Hollywood, Moran stashed coins of various denominations over restaurant, night club and other door sills throughout the film capital, and whenever he was out with a group of people, he would casually reach up here and there over a doorway and bring down a fistful of silver. "Just to astound people," says Moran.

Since houses were constantly being moved in Los Angeles, Moran threw a different kind of party. He invited a large number of convivial souls to his home for what he called "a moving party." Moran plied his guests with alcohol. "They actually knew it was a moving party," he says. "There was the house coming down Wilshire Boulevard with a whole group of people drinking. I did it to astound the outsiders. It was just for fun—a lot of these things are just for pure fun." Moran adds: "No one jumped out of the windows."

It was at this time that Moran announced that he planned to build a needle with an eye big enough for a camel to go through, and that he intended to bite Sidney Skolsky in the arm so that he could go around boasting that he bit the arm of the man who bit the arm of Louella Parsons.

Moran is a specialist in what is known as the double reverse publicity stunt. A choice example of this occurred in 1947 when Saud El Saud, the then crown prince of Saudi Arabia, was visiting Hollywood with much attendant publicity. Moran called in some of his friends of the Hollywood press and briefed them on his latest project. It was Moran's contention that Hollywood was a community of fakes and pretenders and that one had to be a fake and pretender to get ahead there. To prove his point, he was going to outfit himself as the crown prince, go to Ciro's night club with a retinue of retainers and there perpetrate a vast rib on the night club, its customers and Hollywood in general.

With the delighted press tagging along, Moran drew up in front of Ciro's in a long, rented limousine and was ushered, with his staff (a number of unemployed profiles), to a ringside table, where he was waited on ceremoniously. Moran was dressed in an elaborate Arab outfit from Western Costume Company. "I had on dark glasses which corrected my blue eyes," says Moran. "I had a great stain job—not the ordinary Hollywood make-up job. It lasted for three to four months afterwards. I really looked like Saud El Saud. I had three retainers. My men all had jeweled scimitars and all the paraphernalia, like knives and guns. And I had a real Arab, an actor, in American business clothes with me to throw them off the trail. He looked like an American businessman of Arab descent."

The band played the Arabian national anthem and there was no end of fuss and commotion made over the bogus suzerain. Moran explains what happened next: "The way I got attention was I sent a note to the bandleader requesting him to play a number, 'Begin the Beguine,' and afterwards I sent him a gift, one amethyst, beautifully cut. It cost thirty dollars. And I left a few minutes after I sent it. No one there was clever enough to appraise the stone. I pre-fed it by that device. That was what made the jewel thing so successful."

"The jewel thing" consisted of Moran's "accidentally" dropping a chamois bag of gems (actually "very clever imitations of rubies and diamonds and emeralds") as Moran and his staff swept out in style. One of Moran's retainers made as if to retrieve the jewels, but Moran grandiosely waved him on. It simply would not do for a crown prince to stoop for mere gems. As Moran and his retinue exited, Ciro's became a scene of bedlam. Waiters, busboys, musicians and customers were all scrambling and slithering over the dance floor for the phony gems. As Moran put it: "That flipped the whole fucking place." The press meanwhile avidly noted how Ciro's and its clientele were being played for suckers by the inventive Moran. The story ran in all the newspapers the following day as a prime example of how the Hollywood weisenheimers can be taken. Actually, it was the press that had been taken. What the reporters did not know—and still do not know to this date—was that Moran was secretly in the employ of Ciro's all the while and that this was a highly involved publicity stunt for the night club.

"Nobody was in on the stunt except Herman Hover [then boss of Ciro's]," says Moran. "The management didn't know whether to charge cover charges for the guys standing up behind me. It was such confusion. Finally, they decided not to charge anything. The whole thing was on the house."

Moran's most masterful Hollywood achievement, though, was one that did not receive much publicity because it was of a rather delicate and touchy nature. Moran says it was "for fun." Like the Mickey Awards, it took place in 1945 during the season when Hollywood is plagued with a profusion of awards. Moran, like a good many other local citizens, was fed up with this multiplicity of awards and decided to add another to the roster, namely the Moran Awards of the Year. He obtained the anal portions of some slaughtered pigs from a wholesale butcher and placed them on the roof of his house to dry in the sun. He then placed each of these anatomical segments on a velvet cushion in a beautiful gold jewel box, had them elegantly wrapped and ribboned and dispatched, by special messenger, to every studio head in Hollywood, from Louis B. Mayer to Jack Warner, as Moran's Asshole Awards of the Year. Most of the recipients did not find this amusing, and the press, at somewhat of a loss as to how to handle this story in print, did not do much with it. But it remains one of Moran's noblest efforts.

Moran ultimately left Hollywood and now operates in the East. When recently heard from, he was engaged in such projects as raising a "furtle," or giant turtle, with a coat of possum fur glued to its shell, for no readily discernible reason. "Just for fun," insists Moran. "Just to sort of screw people up." For an eyeglass defogger known as X-M, Moran fitted out 200 homing pigeons with eyeglasses, treating some of them with X-M and others not. The pigeons were turned loose from the Shoreham Hotel in Washington, D.C. "About 90 per cent of the X-M ones came home all right," says Moran. "The rest—well, some of them were picked up in Omaha and Nebraska and only a couple got in."

In 1959 Moran was retained to do some publicity for a British movie, *The Mouse That Roared*, which he describes as being "a story about the smallest country in the world involved with the U.S. in war by a fluke." Moran, or Viscount James Sterling Moran in this instance, says that he "opened an official embassy in Washington, D.C. I was the ambassador to the U.S. from the Duchy of Grand Fenwick. I did it up bright. I had beautiful uniforms. I had them made. I had four different uniforms, one naval, one military and two nondescript. One was white, one pale blue, one dark and one black. They were elaborate and exquisitely done. I headquartered at the Shoreham. I drove around in a Mercedes Benz. I was there for two weeks. It ended up with a party for 250 people at the Shoreham and we showed the picture. It was not a hoax as such, but everyone went along with it. It got a lot of space. I was retained by Columbia Pictures and they think it made this picture."

Moran's attainments as a press agent are indicated in a newspaper headline which he had, at one time, framed in his bathroom. Moran had arrived in Amarillo, Texas, some years ago with no specific publicistic objective. He was merely passing through town. The local newspaper thought this important news. "JIM MORAN IN TOWN. NO PUBLICITY," it headlined on its front page. "I got publicity for not doing any publicity, which is an ingrown toenail of some sort," says Moran.

In his spare time, Moran writes children's books. He has published *Sophocles, the Hyena* and *Miserable*, the latter described as "a fable about a dinosaur." Asked why he writes children's books, Moran stroked his beard and replied, "I'll be goddamned if I know why I write them."

"Indications are," says Moran, "that I perhaps have gone square. I have a legitimate business going handling various activities with offices in various big cities in the country. I wear a Homburg hat and carry the proper type of briefcase. But you never know when I'm gonna break out."

Publicity work at a movie studio was not all fun. At times it generated some nerve-wracking and suspenseful moments. A Hollywood classic along these lines has to do with an ingenious publicist at Paramount who, in 1934, devised an unusual publicity stunt for a Mae West movie, *It Ain't No Sin*. He put a platoon of parrots in a room with a phonograph record that kept playing the name of the picture over and over. After a while, the publicist had fifty or so parrots who would say *It Ain't No Sin* on cue. There was just one hitch. At the last minute the studio retitled the picture *I'm No Angel*.

In the mid-Forties, press agent Herb Sterne whipped up a Dr. Fraime Serterodos, who supposedly held the chair of demonology at Lzrun University in Transylvania, to help publicize a minor Columbia horror picture entitled *The Cry of the Werewolf*. The good—or the bad—doctor became the technical expert on the movie. He announced that he had a certain type of poltergeist-omatic film with which to shoot in the dark and capture spiritual emanations. He also had special wolfbane flown in from Transylvania because the movie was so authentic.

As Sterne says, "It printed like crazy. But then on a bad day—and this is the payoff—we had no news at the studio. I suggested we send out a story that Dr. Serterodos had been signed to a three-way deal at the studio as a producer-writer-director. The story wound up running as a banner headline in Ed Schallert's column in the *Los Angeles Times*. We had thought he would just give it a few lines, but he was hard up for news and it got the banner. That was the boomerang. I was afraid Harry Cohn would see the story and I would be fired. So I put out a story that Dr. Serterodos had been burned to death in a circus fire in the South. There had actually been a circus fire that had hit the news and I got in on it. That took care of Dr. Serterodos." Sterne adds: "Schallert was never let in on the gag."

There was a time, in the early Forties, when Warner Brothers was embarked on an all-out campaign to make Bette Davis "sexy." The studio publicists were stymied. Finally, they came up with the hoary idea of getting Bette Davis voted as the girl somebody or other most wanted to be marooned with on a desert island. But they were far from hopeful of getting anyone to come through with this unlikely accolade. In desperation, one of the publicists got in touch with an undergraduate he knew at New York University who was editing the college magazine. The student editor refused even to consider the suggestion "on the basis of principle." But the publicist kept wiring and phoning. After much maneuvering, one fraternity at N.Y.U., which was anxious for publicity, agreed to vote Bette Davis as the girl they were desirous of being marooned with. The vote was rigged, the fraternity got its publicity, Bette Davis got the citation—and the harried Warner publicists got off the hook.

Harrison Carroll, gossipist for the *Los Angeles Herald-Express*, likes to run accident-type stories. Sometimes these are dreamed up by inventive press agents. Carroll, however, also likes to check all his stories, so that this involves elaborate and careful arrangements on the part of the plotting publicists. When a Warner press agent sent Carroll a contrived story that an old Indian grave had been discovered on the studio back lot, Carroll was delighted with it and wanted to come out immediately to examine the burial place. The harried publicist had a phony grave hurriedly rigged up by the plaster and prop department, just in time for Carroll's arrival.

On another occasion, a Warner actress, an uninhibited sort, had had a gay all-night party. Some of the participants had pursued other participants of the opposite sex or even of the same sex up and down the mountainside where the actress' house was located. When morning arrived, all the celebrants were out cold. Some had passed out in beds, some on the floor, and a couple, with glazed eyes, were propped up in front of the fireplace clutching armfuls of foliage. At this unpropitious juncture, the doorbell rang. The maid, who was the only one up and about, answered. A publicity girl from Warner Brothers was at the door with a reporter and photographer from *Look* Magazine to shoot a pictorial layout on a day with the aforementioned profile. The maid hurriedly roused her employer, and between the two of them they dragged all the supine bodies into one room and locked the door. Meanwhile, the publicity girl was stalling the reporter and photographer. Some excuse was finally made and the layout was postponed until the next day, but the publicity girl aged visibly in the process.

Studio publicity departments in former years were quite expert in covering up the peccadillos of their stars. But as the influence of the big studios waned and with fewer stars under term contract, such tactics became less in evidence. Several years ago one major studio managed to cover up with the press when one of its directors was caught at a sex orgy in downtown Los Angeles. But *Confidential* Magazine ran the story subsequently anyway.

Publicists are called upon to make all sorts of sacrifices in the course of their work. An M-G-M press agent, George Nichols, once served his studio beyond the call of duty. *Time* Magazine was doing a cover story about Ava Gardner, then an M-G-M contract star, and had dispatched one of its editors, Henry Anatole Grunwald, from New York to Hollywood to meet Gardner personally. Although this editor was fairly adept with words, he was not quite at ease with glamour girls, and the studio was concerned that he might run into some complications with the volatile Gardner. Nichols was assigned by the publicity department to keep a close watch on Gardner and the visiting editor, not to let them out of his sight and see to it that no social errors were committed.

All went well for a while, but one night when the inseparable threesome, this time accompanied by a *Time* Hollywood correspondent, were out on the town, Gardner and the editor, who were quite cozy by this time, put their heads together and decided to shake the ever-vigilant Nichols. They plied him with liquor and finally got him so drunk that he passed out, at which point Gardner and the editor, together with the *Time* correspondent, hot-footed it to her hacienda, where they began to indulge in gay pastimes like dancing barefoot on table tops.

Just as their merriment was reaching almost epic proportions, the doorbell rang. When they opened the door, a strange sight greeted them. Nichols, stiff as a board, was leaning on the doorbell. True to his publicistic duty, he had somehow managed to get to Gardner's home and had summoned up his last bit of strength and consciousness to ring the doorbell. He staggered into the house, trying, in the words of the *Time* correspondent, "to protect his client from the demons of the press. But he was so goddam stoned." Having done his duty, like a good little M-G-M press agent, he fell down and passed out again. Gardner, the editor and the correspondent went into a laughing fit.

But the ultimate sacrifice was made by another M-G-M press agent. During the regime of Dore (née Isadore) Schary at M-G-M, this publicist, Isadore Freeman, patriotically changed his name to Dore Freeman. Not long afterward, Dore Schary left M-G-M. The studio is now being run by a producer named Sol Siegel. Thus far, Dore Freeman is still Dore Freeman.

As a movie press agent you can get to see some of the eminent film figures close up. When I was publicizing a French film, *Personal Column*, in New York in 1941, Erich von Stroheim, who played the role of a mad fashion designer in the picture, arrived from France for promotional purposes. I arranged a series of press interviews with him, all of them characterized by many and frequent libations. These sessions were climaxed by an interview von Stroheim had with a girl reporter from the United Press. Obviously fairly new to the job and not particularly conversant with the movies or von Stroheim, she asked a number of far from perceptive questions which kept increasingly irritating von Stroheim. Finally she came up with "What is your hobby, Mr. von Stroheim?" The great man, who had by then knocked off a dozen or more slugs of Scotch neat, looked at her menacingly and replied in one brief, pungent, Anglo-Saxon verb. The young lady was so taken aback that she ran out of von Stroheim's apartment, leaving her notebook and purse behind her, and von Stroheim was out one wire-service interview.

Not all press agents are of the buttering-up persuasion. Some can be quite aggressive. Such a one was a Hollywood publicist and former prizefighter named Dave Epstein, who is now more or less subdued but who was in former years one of the most forceful and flourishing of independent press agents, specializing in producers, directors and writers. Among his clients were eminent studio heads, producers, producer-directors and directors. A few of his clients were less eminent. At that time Epstein was the publicity representative for the famed director Leo McCarey. When I asked him one day to arrange an interview for me with McCarey, he replied; "Okay, kiddo, but you'll also have to interview Lucky Humberstone." H. Bruce (Lucky) Humberstone was a nice and talented director who was not quite so famous as McCarey, and Epstein was making a publicity package deal. In order to get to the illustrious McCarey, I first had to interview the less illustrious Humberstone, who was also an Epstein client. I wound up interviewing neither of them.

Since some of Epstein's clients were rather artistic personalities who, from time to time, became embroiled in complications with the law, like drunk driving while directing a religious movie, Epstein kept a large pile of ready cash in a strongbox in his home for last-minute contingencies. Epstein was also known to meet visiting press representatives at the plane or train on their arrival in Hollywood, give them a big hello and greet them with "Need any dough, pal?" while flourishing a stout roll of bills.

One of Epstein's publicity plays to get space for producers and directors, who are not the most easily publicized personalities, was to send out rigged-up stories that a certain mythical Broadway producer, Ned Farrington by name, had bought a property by such and such a writer (who happened to be an Epstein client). This communiqué would subsequently be followed by another to the effect that such and such a director (also an Epstein client) would direct this property for Farrington on Broadway. And so on. Farrington, in due course, became quite famous. In 1942 the New York *Times* reported that Ned Farrington was "an elusive Broadway producer who is forever reported to be holding conversations with Hollywood writers, producers and directors, among whom are some of the following: William LeBaron, Lou Pollock, Sam Wood, Arthur Hornblow, Jr., and others. Several correspondents have tried to check Farrington stories without success. He's usually traveling between New York and Hollywood."

After a while, Jim Henaghan, the mischievous Hollywood chronicler, sated with the stream of stories about the illusory Farrington, decided to kill him off. Here is Henaghan's version of the event: "It was a very simple thing. Epstein had invented this guy Ned Farrington. Epstein keeps a file of publicity stories and runs it every five years and doesn't even change the names. He just uses the same stories. If he wanted items about Sam Wood, it was always good to have a Broadway producer come out to talk to Sam Wood about doing a musical version of one of his pictures. It got printed. Epstein used Farrington over the years. He became a very well-known Broadway producer. This sort of stuff went on for over ten years, but nothing ever got on the boards. I was with Gene Fowler one night and we were talking about Epstein's gimmick. The next morning, I ran an item in my column in the *Hollywood Reporter* that Ned Farrington, Jr., the Broadway producer, died in his sleep last night. Epstein called me and wanted to know where I got it. Epstein said, 'He's alive and he's in very good health. I just talked to his son.' I said, 'To hell with you.' The next day I ran another item that Farrington's will was up for immediate probate and that he had left no heirs. I killed off the son, too."

Henaghan's *Hollywood Reporter* items were picked up by *Daily Variety*, which ran a front-page story about Farrington's funeral, itemizing a long list of pallbearers. All the pallbearers were Epstein clients, and Epstein was listed among them, too. That was the end of Farrington, but not of Epstein. Following Farrington's demise, Epstein in the mid-Forties came up with another mythical character named Choteau Fresnay, who was identified as European representative of Sam Wood. Vance King, then on the desk at the *Hollywood Reporter*, got a release one day from Epstein saying that Fresnay had arrived in Hollywood from Europe "to discuss the filming of Wood's *Tatiana* overseas." According to King: "I knew it was a phony. I called Dave and said, 'This could be a good story and I want a reporter to interview Fresnay.' Epstein said that it would be okay for three P.M. the next day and he said, 'But I don't ever want to talk to you again,' because I questioned the existence of Choteau Fresnay. I assigned Henaghan to the story. While Henaghan was out, I wrote a story that the European representative of Sam Wood, Choteau Fresnay, died in the producer's arms at M-G-M yesterday, etc., etc., and that the funeral arrangements were in charge of Dave Epstein. Henaghan came back saying he met Fresnay and had the story. We wound up using an innocuous interview, a phony. Later, I heard that Henaghan was indebted to Dave Epstein. Henaghan was not only killing off Epstein clients, but creating them. . . . The next day, there was a release from Epstein that Fresnay was going back to Europe."

CHAPTER IV

Through

a Ground Glass, Darkly

MOVIE REVIEWING has been described as "yawning as a profession." It is one of the more thankless forms of journalism. The reviewer finds life complicated. Just plain folk will ask him, "You mean you get paid to see movies? What else do you do?" The moviemaker will say, "Why don't you try seeing a movie first sometime before reviewing it?" And his journalistic colleagues are likely to look on him as something of a misfit farmed out to rear-line operations.

Down the years I have reviewed movies for daily newspapers, movie trade papers and weekly, monthly and quarterly magazines. This has not endeared me to anyone, from the people who make the movies to the people who put out the publications. And I sometimes wonder whether what I have written has been of any particular value in guiding and enlightening the reader.

Part of the problem has to do with the intrinsic vagueness of words and the difficulty of verbally pinning down attitudes and insights. It has been said that there are sometimes more clichés in movie reviews than in the movies they are discussing. Sample review phrases: "surefire," "stunning," "taut with suspense," "lavish and exciting," "sumptuous," "captures the imagination," "moving," "significant drama," "sheer screen artistry," "uncommonly good performance," "dramatic urgency," "enormous compulsion," "spectacular finish" and, once in a while, "ineptly directed," "singularly dull." I did not make up any of these. I just lifted them at random from a cross-section of movie reviews.

The semantic problem, of course, is one that is not peculiar to movie reviewing. But writing about movies does pose some special prose problems. The late Wolcott Gibbs, who once reviewed movies and finally gave up when he found that "the cinema resists rational criticism almost as firmly as a six-day bicycle race, or perhaps love," held that "ninety per cent of the moving pictures exhibited in America are so vulgar, witless and dull that it is preposterous to write about them in any publication not intended to be read while chewing gum." The conscientious reviewer writing about these million-dollar parodies on life, Gibbs observed, "gets an uneasy feeling that such massive vulgarity somehow requires massive treatment," with the result that his discussion of them is "on the grand scale . . . and takes on a very peculiar accent, enormous, educated and fuzzy. He writes, you might say, rather the way Henry Wadsworth Longfellow used to look." The reviewer's language, Gibbs noted, consists of a special vocabulary in which "words come to transcend their exact and customary meanings. 'Luminous' is such a word. Coming from the typewriter of a skillful operator, it means that the performance given by a young woman who has probably gone through each scene from ten to twenty times with her director and still has only the vaguest idea what it is all about is strong, beautiful, humorous, tragic and lit with something of the same strange, ineluctable fire that once burned bright in Duse and Bernhardt."

Among other problems confronting the motion-picture critic is the perennial plaint of many movie producers that movie reviewers are massacring their pictures with destructive criticism. But this lament is usually a reflection on the weakness of the movies rather than on the strength of the movie reviewers. It is doubtful whether many moviegoers bother to read movie reviews at all and, if they do, whether they are particularly influenced by them. (One unusually philosophical moviemaker said, after getting a poor review of his latest picture: "Half of the people who read that paper never saw the review. Half of those who did failed to read it. Half of those who read it didn't understand it. Half of those who understood it didn't believe it. And half of those who believed it were of no consequence anyway.") Darryl Zanuck recently stated that "I don't believe that the vast majority of theatergoers follow the critics. I don't believe a critic can make them go to a movie or keep them away." In Zanuck's estimation, it is "ego more than anything else that can upset a producer." Zanuck ought to know. But since most moviemakers are touchy about having their works criticized and since movies are normally backed up by much advertising, the movie producers can put pressure on the reviewer where he is often most vulnerable—through the advertising and publishing offices of his publication.

In an article entitled "Some of My Best Friends Are Critics" in the *American Mercury* in 1945, Arthur Mayer wrote: ". . . I can discern no correlation between critical approval and box-office success." He added that "Condemnation is apparently no more effective than praise." Although when the Rivoli Theater in New York City played a picture called *White Zombie* that had been massacred by the critics and was a big hit, the theater took out ads quoting the negative reviews with the caption "When the critics' noses went up, the box-office receipts went up as well."

There is, finally, a disinclination on the part of editors to run any particularly serious and informed movie comment. Theodore Strauss, a former New York *Times* motion-picture critic, in an analysis of reviewers entitled "No Jacks, No Giant Killers" in the *Screen Writer Magazine* in 1945, wrote that critics are selected by editors "on the basis that they write English in the style to which the particular newspaper is committed, that they are reasonably intelligent and that they are more or less adequate reporters—but not necessarily that they are greatly or sometimes at all experienced in the craft on which they sit in judgment."

All this is rather generalized. Here are some specific examples:

No less a newspaper than the New York *Times* in 1939 yanked a negative movie review from print and replaced it with a less astringent review by another critic. Benjamin R. Crisler, a perceptive and highly able reviewer for the New York *Times*, had penned a deftly slighting review of *They Shall Have Music*, a Samuel Goldwyn production starring the unlikely combination of Jascha Heifetz and some Dead End-type kids; the crack at the time went that "Heifetz fiddled while Goldwyn burned." Crisler's review ran in the first edition of the *Times* of July 26. Publisher Arthur Sulzberger, a close friend of Heifetz's (they had attended the premiere of the picture together), was displeased with the review and high-handedly ordered it pulled out of the paper—an extraordinary move for the good gray *Times*. Bosley Crowther, now the *Times's* film critic but then a third-string reviewer, who had happened to see the picture at the premiere and was at the newspaper at the time, was commandeered by Sulzberger to write a more reverent review, which ran in the final editions of the paper.

Crisler recalls today that "Sulzberger and Heifetz in their tuxes came back to the paper after the premiere. Sulzberger wanted to be able to show Heifetz a glowing review in the *Times*. They went up to see it in the composing room. The first edition was already gone. They tried to get me to rewrite it, but they couldn't find me. They couldn't get me in Long Island. They found Bos some place around there so he was elected. I wouldn't have been able to do it anyway. I couldn't write anything unless I felt it. I'm glad I didn't get the job. It was not for me. I have to write what I think."

All this seems like a pipe dream today—*They Shall Have Music* was a crashing bore that has long been forgotten—but it can be checked, by anyone who is sufficiently interested, in the files of the New York *Times* editions of that date. But precisely because *They Shall Have Music* is such a preposterously minor cause célèbre, I think it is educational to survey the chronology of this review discord in detail. This was Crisler's review (signed "B.R.C."):

Carnegie Hall occasions are so rare in the cinema that when a great virtuoso arrives on the screen it is not easy for the uninitiated film critic to know what to wear, intellectually speaking. Is it the proper thing to write eloquently about the music, as would a James Gibbons Huneker, and forget the film? Or would it be in better taste to go ahead and modestly review the picture as usual, in one's customary simple, cinematic style?

In the case of They Shall Have Music (at the Rivoli) which marks the screen debut of Jascha Heifetz, and has been announced as Opus I in the musical works of Mr. Samuel Goldwyn, the temptation is to write about the music (which is, of course, superb) and to skip lightly over the movie with some graceful side remark, such as "All is not Goldwyn that glisters." It might even be a tactful thing to combine the two methods and, while writing about the music like Lawrence Gilman, to express polite regret that the precision and authority of the violin passages are not matched by similar qualities in the plot department.

But, while emphasizing one's delight with the Rondo Capriccioso of Saint-Saens, the Hora Staccato (Dinicu-Heifetz), the Ponce-Heifetz Estrellita, and the last movement of the Mendelssohn Concerto, should one go on to mention casually that the dramatic accompaniment is purely synthetic? When one can obtain such music for the price of a movie admission, would it not be rude to insist that the char-

acters—young Gene Reynolds, who is saved from the streets when he crashes a Heifetz concert; Andrea Leeds, daughter of a poor musical idealist, who teaches the neighborhood children for love alone; and Joel McCrea, who foils the dastardly plot of Walter Brennan, the villainous instrument dealer—are even more fictitious than the foreword would lead one to believe?

Those announcements from the Goldwyn organization, during the filming of They Shall Have Music, to the effect that Mr. Heifetz refused to act, were strictly true. But he does permit himself to be utilized as a dramatic prop for the proceedings, especially as the last-minute saviour of the big concert being staged by the youngsters (ably represented by the California Junior Symphony Orchestra) when Walter Brennan is coldly confiscating their 'cellos and woodwinds with a Sheriff's order. Mr. Heifetz had no need to act, though; his fiddle speaks for itself.

Certainly it can be said, more than twenty years after the event, that this was a reasoned—and most readable—review. Crisler had really let the picture down quite easily. But although the review was sane, it was not sufficiently safe—at least from the New York *Times* standpoint. After all, this was an expensive Samuel Goldwyn production starring the great Heifetz, and it had to be treated more expansively and respectfully, no matter how bad it was. As Crisler told me recently: "I didn't make the review very long. I didn't treat it in important fashion. Perhaps that was a mistake." It was not a mistake from the readers' viewpoint—but the readers be damned.

Crisler added: "The boss never liked a man so stupid that he had to tell him what to do. He was supposed to divine when to praise and how to do it. I didn't know Heifetz was a personal friend of Sulzberger's—and it wouldn't have made much difference. I'm not a padding-type critic. If I had, I might have added a few paragraphs. Maybe journalistically my judgment was wrong. They overwrite everything at the *Times*. I wrote down to the bone. That was my judgment of what it deserved."

Crowther's review, which replaced Crisler's in the later editions of the *Times*, in effect "blew up" the first review and, stringing a lot of words end to end, let the picture down even more gently, though less readably. Crowther was much more polite but his writing was less pointed and his reasoning perhaps less to the point. This is Crowther's review (signed "B.C."):

The evening of October 27, 1917, is gloriously memorable in the annals of American music, for it was on that evening that Jascha Heifetz, a 17-year-old violinist from Russia, made his American debut at Carnegie Hall. No such breathless excitement as marked that historic occasion may have been perceptible last evening in the Rivoli Theatre, where Mr. Heifetz made his screen debut, by courtesy of Samuel Goldwyn, in They Shall Have Music. It was a hot night (for everybody) and Mr. Heifetz is past being "discovered." But the occasion had its historic aspects and was the source of considerable delight.

When Mr. Goldwyn announced two years ago that he had obtained the consent of the great violinist to appear in a motion picture, the obvious question asked by everyone was "What will Heifetz do?" That problem was likewise of some apparent annoyance to Mr. Goldwyn, too, for he was more than a year finding a story to suit the talents of his renowned artist. The question was answered last evening: Mr. Heifetz plays the violin, that's all. He plays it rapturously, and with surpassing brilliance—such a quality and abundance of magnificent fiddling as has never before been heard from a screen.

Perhaps a critic of music might better remark upon its excellence. Suffice it for a journeyman of the films to comment enthusiastically that the crystal purity of Mr. Heifetz's playing, the eloquent flow of melody from his violin and the dramatic presentation of the artist commanding his instrument—closeups of his graceful fingers upon the strings, of the majestic sweep of his bowing arm and brilliant angle shots of the man before an orchestra—create an effect of transcendent beauty which is close to unique in this medium.

The story? It is sufficient to support the ethereal grace of the music and little more. It is a sentimental tale of an underprivileged boy who falls in love with music, is driven from his squalid home because of it, lands in a modest musical foundation where a lovable old maestro enkindles the souls of youngsters with the magic of melody and eventually saves the school from evil creditors by persuading Heifetz to come there and give a concert. It is the sort of story which is known as a "tear-jerker"—a direct assault upon the soft spots in all doting parents and elder folk. It is made more so by music, and will probably be very popular.

A good cast of actors supports Mr. Heifetz, who is woefully deficient in the few brief excursions he makes in that department. (Just enough to keep the story together.) Gene Reynolds, as the boy who makes good, carries the heaviest role commendably, if one excuses the tearful moments. And especial mention must be made of the Peter Meremblum California Junior Symphony Orchestra, which accompanies Mr. Heifetz in one number. It is the grandest appeal for musical education in the picture. It—and, of course, Mr. Heifetz.

By the time the Sunday, July 30, edition of the *Times* came out, Crisler had also somewhat tempered his original review. In the lead movie column, under the title "Music and the Movies," subtitled "Wherein Is Noted the Screen's Curious Unadaptability to Cultured Company," Crisler wrote, with the proper genuflections to Goldwyn:

> Snobbish and superior as the attitude of the arts has always been toward the movies, the movies have made repeated rather wistful efforts to scrape a back-slapping acquaintance with the arts. And of all Hollywood producers, Samuel Goldwyn has had the greatest yearnings in this direction. Mr. Goldwyn loves art; it was he who brought Maurice Maeterlinck, the Belgian poet, to America and tried to break him in as a screen writer; who started the big-name system of talent hiring in Hollywood, and who, finally, with adoring reverence, and the worthiest production money could buy, has brought Mr. Heifetz to the screen in the Rivoli's current They Shall Have Music.
>
> For Mr. Heifetz, the infallible virtuoso, the man whom George Bernard Shaw once accused of being too perfect, the occasion is a grand success; his five solos, generously provided by the script, are turned off with the precision and clarity and tonal loveliness for which he is famous on the concert stage. Incidentally, these particular sequences are even more satisfactory than they would be on the concert stage; the closeups of the artist's fingers, working like inspired machinery, are lessons in bowmanship. Mr. Heifetz never played more brilliantly, but for Mr. Goldwyn, also a master in his line, the occasion was less triumphant, less, that is, than one feels entitled to expect from the producer of Dodsworth, Dead End and Wuthering Heights. If one was disappointed in They Shall Have Music as a motion picture, it is Mr. Goldwyn's own fault for having done so much better in previous attempts. But none of these successful efforts was achieved by Mr. Goldwyn in his culture-club mood; that mood, for some reason, always seems a little precious for such an ephemeral medium as celluloid.

That same Sunday, July 30, edition of the *Times* carried a column in the music section by Olin Downes which lambasted *They Shall Have Music* much more mercilessly than Crisler had in his original

July 26 review. Downes wrote that "we fancy that no one will dispute the unanimous verdict of the moving picture critics of this city that the story of Jascha Heifetz's film, *They Shall Have Music*, is a poor one. It is unnecessarily poor. In fact, it misses patent opportunities for a significant story which would have given Mr. Heifetz's glorious performance its proper setting and not left it almost entirely to his reputation and genius to carry the show." But then Downes was not a mere movie reviewer, but the distinguished music critic of the *Times*, and so he could get away with it.

And, finally, in that *Times* Sunday edition, Goldwyn took out a two-column ad for *They Shall Have Music* which was bannerlined: "An event—when capacity audiences, and the nation's severest critics, unite in praising a motion picture." The lead-off quote was from Bosley Crowther's review: "Heifetz plays rapturously . . . with surpassing brilliance." (Movie ads always manage to find quotes, even in the most unfavorable reviews. A reviewer may write of a movie "A new high in boredom," and the ad will read "A new high . . .")

Looking back down the years, one can only marvel at all this solemn hogwash about a movie that has long since mercifully vanished. If *They Shall Have Music* is ever remembered at all, it may, ironically, well be recalled not for Goldwyn, not even for Heifetz, but for this fantastic critical crisis at the great New York *Times*, which might appropriately be entitled "They Shall Not Have an Honest Review." If this sort of thing goes on at a newspaper like the *Times*, one can only begin to imagine what transpires at other, lesser publications.

Walter Winchell summarized the matter in his column: "Newspaper circles are amazed over the manner the N.Y. *Times* cinema page covered the Heifetz film. A sour notice lasted one edition, and a better one replaced it. Publisher Sulzberger, it appears, so ordered."

That year Crisler was running into some strange problems in trying to write movie reviews for the New York *Times*. On February 10 a documentary feature film entitled *Spain Fights On* opened at the Belmont Theater. The ads for it proclaimed: "See Why the Spanish People Will Never Surrender." (The Spanish Loyalists were still desperately defending Madrid—although the headlines at that time were already sounding the Loyalist death knell with "FRANCE AND BRITAIN PREPARE TO RECOGNIZE FRANCO REGIME".) The day *Spain Fights On* opened in New York City, *Tail Spin*, a Twentieth Century-Fox glorification of women in aviation, with Alice Faye, Constance Bennett and Nancy Kelly, opened at the Roxy Theater, and . . . *One-Third of a Nation*. . . , a Paramount picture about slum clearance, with Sylvia Sidney, opened at the Rivoli. Naturally, the two American movies got the preferred critical attention—they were playing at bigger theaters and were taking out more advertising. Crisler covered Spain Fights On and turned in the following review:

Now, when the terms of surrender are being discussed, the very title no less than the contents of the picture, Spain Fights On, at the Belmont, takes on an unintentionally tragic significance. Obviously yet not obtrusively designed as an appeal to the conscience of the world (it seems the line is busy: there have been so many calls of late) it reminds us with unbearable poignance that these people who ask for so little—only the lifting of an unequal embargo—are, after all, dying among the ancient olive trees and the crumbling masonry. The bewildered children of an antique world—herded in the roads like cattle—are being slaughtered by the very latest devices of modern warfare.

In libraries and learned discussions, war is an abstraction; at bottom, in fact, it is always the abstractionists who wage war, but it is the people who die. In Spain Fights On, we learn some of the unbeautiful aspects of dying suddenly, without warning, in the midst of what has always been one's home and country. We discover that the dead lie in uncomfortable positions, that the dead are without eyes, lower jaws, noses, entire faces; that the dead cannot stand up and deliver speeches, but that the mouths of the dead are eloquent.

We discover a few of the ghastly realities behind all this fine abstractionist talk of "conflicting ideologies": in the historical sense, perhaps, it may not especially matter that around the brave broken institutions and the unpicturesquely dead heroes of Republican Spain has already begun to gather the pathos and the graveyard mold of lost causes. But right or wrong, these people are dying, and regardless of where one's sympathies lie in the struggle, it should be impossible for any member of the human race (excepting abstractionists, of course) to look at Spain Fights On without some measure of heartbreak.

The Times copy desk had deleted from the review the following words: "who ask for so little—only the lifting of an unequal embargo—"; "—herded in the roads like cattle—"; "we discover that the dead lie in uncomfortable positions, that the dead are without eyes, lower jaws, noses, entire faces; that the dead cannot stand up and deliver speeches, but that the mouths of the dead are eloquent."

According to Crisler, "the Spanish item is the original galley [proof] on which some parochial punk first feebly endeavored to make my poor copy presentable, before giving it up as a hopeless job." Crisler's review —a plain, eloquent, humanitarian statement—never ran. In its place, on February 13, was the following Bosley Crowther review:

By all reports, the desperate civil war in Spain is fast drawing to its close—a fact which lends ironic emphasis to the new documentary, Spain Fights On, now showing at the Belmont. For here, in an excellent job of photographic synthesis, is compressed the tragic story of human suffering and death which has been visited upon so many pitiful victims in that unhappy country within the past three years.

To be sure, the nature of the Spanish struggle has been such that thinking people outside have found it difficult to avoid taking sides. And the fact that this present picture has been made by Loyalist sympathizers and is circulated as an appeal for Loyalist aid is certain to predispose many persons either for or against it on political grounds.

But the nature of the picture is such that the superimposed voice of its commentator is the only truly definitive thing about it. Basically this is the graphic story, made up from actual shots taken in and behind the firing lines, of a people's war and a people's ruin—of cities destroyed, of homes laid waste, of simple, innocent people killed. The picture begins with a composite representation of Spain as it was before the war—a land of hard-working peasants, cultivated citizens, beautiful cities and thriving industries. It passes swiftly over the outbreak of hostilities, the rise of the people's armies and the stubborn tightening of the battle lines. It is devoted mainly to the grim, unresisting business of war and the suffering which it brings.

Joris Ivens, in his film, The Spanish Earth, gave us an eloquent picture of the Spanish peasant's stoicism and perseverance in spite of war and destruction. Spain Fights On may not possess the poetic eloquence and detachment of that other, but it accumulates much more convincing and heartbreaking evidence. The successive glimpses which it gives of terrified mothers clutching their children in doorways as the camera fairly reels with the concussion of bursting shells, the sight of soldiers mowed down by machine-gun fire before your very eyes, of orphaned children crowded into refuges; of the badly wounded and the hideous dead—these are nightmare images which transcend all political appeals. They are an invocation to man's shame and pity.

No one who has a decent regard for humanity can possibly view Spain Fights On without a sense of deepest tragedy and despair.

On September 26, 1939, the New York *Times* reviewed a British war picture entitled *Torpedoed* that had opened at the Globe Theater. The front page of the New York *Times* that day proclaimed: "French Shell Reich Forts on Rhine as Nazi Troops Mass Near Basle; Soviet Army at Estonian Frontier." The weather was "mostly cloudy and much cooler today; rain tonight or tomorrow morning and continued cool."

Crisler wrote the following review of *Torpedoed*, which was killed:

Mr. Herbert Wilcox, producer of the anti-militarist film Nurse Edith Cavell, appears in a different mold this week at the Globe Theatre (the un-Shakespearean Globe)—a mood which might be described as the British-colonial, or don't-be-the-aggressor-at-any-cost mood. Mr. Wilcox is a former service man himself, and consequently Torpedoed has about it a loftily uncounterfeit ring of conviction, a sincere faith in the divine right of the British Navy to protect the lives and trading prerogatives of British nationals wherever domiciled—even to the extent of sinking the entire, one-battleship fleet of the offending nation if necessary.

The result is a stirring piece of strictly-for-defense militaristic cinema: an eloquent reminder that one perfectly groomed and cool-headed Briton in a ketch is worth a furious flotilla manned by ill-dressed and badly disciplined natives. Actually, the contest this time is between a light cruiser, captained by the handsomely capable Robert Douglas, and a revolutionary super-dreadnought (commanded by Esme Percy and Henry Victor in soiled tropicals). And the deciding factor is a brace of torpedoes launched overside—only after great provocation, mind you!—by the marvelously restrained Captain Douglas.

As the gourmet-Presidente of the country (which is evidently of Caribbean persuasion) Noah Beery is a pure joy, especially in his fondness for gamey dishes, when it is a well-known fact that there is no fairer game in a Caribbean country than a Presidente. We repeat that Mr. Wilcox's Globe Theatre antidote to his current Music Hall mood is swell cinema, but we protest that it's going to be hard to convince the Broadway trade that a picture entitled Torpedoed, and frankly advertised as "made with the cooperation of the British Navy," hasn't in it something in the nature of a gag.

As a replacement for Crisler's review was one by Frank Nugent, then the first-string movie critic of the New York *Times*:

Torpedoed—and we'll wager it had another title until the Globe got hold of it—is an amiably understated overstatement of the invincibility of the English fleet, of the relentless rightness of His Majesty's consular corps. Although it is a service film, made with the acknowledged cooperation of the British Navy, it is completely free from the self-consciousness which is the common, and the most annoying, trait of comparable Hollywood ventures. For Torpedoed is never aware of glorifying its subject; its attitude is unmistakably that it is dealing reticently, even shyly, with a glorious subject. If that is conceit, and we're afraid it is, at least it is thoroughly likeable. So is the film.

Without bothering to offer more than passing introduction to its characters and to hint at a triangular love affair, Torpedoed is the simply-told yarn of a British cruiser's handling of a messy job in the Caribbean. There has been a revolution in one of the more implausible republics. Its president has been sheltered in the British consulate—for purely humanitarian reasons, nothing political or economic of course. The rebel warship has threatened to open fire unless he is surrendered. In its path, 6-inch guns against the enemy's 16 and strict orders not to take the offensive, even though the enemy's first broadside may blow it out of the water, rides the British cruiser. Who wins, matey? Didn't we mention that the cruiser was the Audacious?

Hebert Wilcox, who directed it, has worked in some exciting shots of action on the battle wagons, of a cruiser slipping through a smoke screen, of men leaping from a stricken ship. Nothing the cast can do touch these for melodrama and, frankly, the cast hasn't bothered to try. The performances, except those of Richard Cromwell and Noah Beery from Hollywood, are in the British tradition: stiff upper lip including the forehead. Mr. Beery's caricature of the republic's presidente is as bad as his Spanish, and Mr. Cromwell's gayety rings like a cracked chime amid the generally dour thespic proceedings. But the film as a whole is sound, mannish entertainment.

Observes Crisler of these two items "which were totally censored by the Roman Catholic bloc (*Spain Fights On*) and by the pro-British bloc (*Torpedoed*)" "please note how impartially I offend all the pressure groups, but you see I could afford to be disinterested, since I never made more than $75 per week at the *Times*."

Crisler left the *Times* in 1940. He says today: "The *They Shall Have Music* business more than anything else destroyed my confidence in my future there. One has a tendency to stay with a stable organization. But I'd have been kind of stupid to have stayed around."

The foregoing were choice instances of internal newspaper pressure. There were other internal pressures at the New York *Times*. All movies with Grace Moore were treated gently by the reviewers because she was a favorite of the late publisher Adolph Ochs. Even after Ochs died, says Frank Nugent, "Grace Moore movies still got rave reviews." When Madeleine Carroll was a Paramount star and appearing in a series of innocuous film fables, she was a Technicolor nightmare for the *Times* reviewers. The actress was then the close friend of a highly placed *Times* executive. Whenever a Madeleine Carroll vehicle had to be reviewed—and the dictates of taste usually decreed that it be reviewed badly—the critics would scramble to get out of the assignment. Some of them even tried to jockey their vacation schedules so that they would not be around when a Carroll picture was released.

There were external pressures, too. On August 17, 1938, Crisler reviewed M-G-M's gimcrack, multimillion-dollar spectacle *Marie Antoinette*, starring Norma Shearer and Tyrone Power, which was then, as he put it, "in imperial, two-a-day residence" at the Astor Theater. Crisler, trying to look at the brighter side of things, charitably noted that the picture's "expensiveness in itself is impressive" and that "the splendors of the French monarchy in its dying days have not simply been equaled, they have been surpassed." According to Crisler, Louis B. Mayer and his publicity director, Howard Dietz, paid a personal call on Sulzberger to complain about Crisler's review and to try to get him fired. Observes Crisler with a wry smile today: "L. B. Mayer was complaining about me, a man with the biggest income in the nation, over one million dollars. Dietz was making over $100,000. How much was I making? Seventy-five dollars a week."

As Crisler says, it is difficult for a critic to dismiss an "important" picture that opens with great advertising and publicity fanfare. "With any M-G-M picture that bought big ads," he says, "you'd start off your review by saying it was 'sumptuous,' even if it was lousy. That's the way to do it."

A more recent example of such critical double-talking and pussyfooting occurred with M-G-M's new behemoth, *Ben-Hur*, in 1959. The reviewers were apparently so browbeaten and brainwashed in advance by the picture's religious theme, its outsize budget and its thundering publicity campaign that they trotted out all the adjectives in the critical lexicon. According to Dwight MacDonald in *Esquire*, "*Ben-Hur*, as everyone knows, cost $15,000,000 to make, runs for almost four hours, has a cast variously estimated at 50,000 (by Metro-Goldwyn-Mayer) and at 10,400 (by *Time*), was directed by William Wyler, and has had the biggest advance sale ($500,000) in film history. But what no one knows who hasn't seen it is that it is lousy. The secret was well kept by the New York newspaper critics." After quoting some of the "bellows of approval, which might have been emitted by the M-G-M lion himself," MacDonald added that "I can only pipe that I found *Ben-Hur* bloody in every way—bloody bloody and bloody boring. Watching it was like waiting at a railroad crossing while an interminable freight train lumbers past, often stopping completely for a while."

Crisler hammered at this point on many occasions in his writings in the *Times*. He once defined "Investment" as a Hollywood word that denoted "that part of a picture which the producer naïvely expects a critic to be impressed by when the picture has nothing else about it to inspire respect. Too often the be-glamoured critic forgets that the investment theory, if sound, must work two ways: that the public's money is at least as important to the public as the producer's money is to the producer."

In one of his Sunday columns entitled "A Theory of Criticism" in 1939, Crisler had this to say about movie reviewers:

It is true that our judgments are too depressingly average in the main, that we lack the scholarship and the fine intellectual fire of a Huneker. It is true what our best enemies say of us, that we are still too much impressed by the cost of a picture as distinguished from its value—its value, that is, to the customer who pays the admission price. Even when we cannot praise a million-dollar spectacle we are sheepishly inclined to write at least two more paragraphs about it than we would waste on less pompous, possibly superior efforts. We call this "production value" in our trade jargon: the stage reviewer is similarly awed by the theatrical fleshpots, as well as by the reputation value of the people concerned. But these are essentially false values, by which the critic should not allow himself to be blackmailed.

So much for the critic's first duty, which is, or at least should be, to the picture-going public. In his relations with the industry itself, on the other hand, there are several obvious pitfalls against which he would do well to arm himself. Probably the most persistent of these is the fallacy of economic self-pity, which at times—not very often, let us hasten to add—publicly motivates the producing fraternity. This odd neurosis is usually expressed in the simple phrase: "I've got a lot of money tied up in that picture." Now, if money is indeed as sacred as this statement implies, it must also be important to the customer at the box office. But the basic fallacy of such a position, we think, lies in the fact that no producer who wants us to worry about his investment has ever showed the slightest inclination to worry about ours—some of which are conspicuously bad, too. It is strange that anybody should expect universal sympathy just because his money is in movies instead of oils or public utilities.

Every opinion is personal and every screen review is necessarily an opinion. The critical absolute has not yet been achieved, not even by Variety or the most cold-bloodedly utilitarian of the trade journals. If it ever is, we want to be the first to congratulate everybody on finally being able to dispense with a human critic in favor of some robot mechanism like stars (including that astranomaly, the fractional star), movie clocks or meters, but until the dawn of that unlikely era the critic will remain—an evil, no doubt, but a necessary evil, possibly even a lesser one than the film advertisers, with their stables of superlatives, or the press agents, from the most restrained and dignified of whom flow the most amazing blurbs. And whatever you may say of the film critic, his function is not that of another barker to confuse and entice the wavering public into every passing sideshow; let this one shred of dignity at least cling to his diffident form.

Was Crisler too "flip" about the movies he reviewed? Not at all. He was writing his reviews in the best interests of the readers and not in an attempt to truckle to the moviemakers. He was not burying the point of his opinions in a lot of puffed-up, glucosey prose. And that is precisely why he is not reviewing movies any longer today. There is no place for him to do so. As he says—and he is right—newspapers today have become downright dull.

External pressures at the New York Times were in evidence in earlier years, too. Frederick Mordaunt Hall, who reviewed movies for the paper in the Twenties and Thirties, was the subject of displeasure of several of the motion-picture companies. Hall wrote rather prosaic, even plodding—but never weasely—reviews. Recently, Hall recalled in Editor and Publisher that, when he became the Times screen critic, William Fox, head of the powerful Fox Films, "did not welcome me as motion picture critic of the Times. But Mr. Ochs's comment to some derogatory remark by Mr. Fox soon ended objections of the producer."

One day, Hall had a telephone call summoning him to the office of Harry Warner, president of Warner Brothers, who was unhappy with Hall's reviews. "I listened to Warner for some time," Hall recollects, "and then asked when I was going to be permitted to say something.

" 'You are taking the bread and butter out of my mouth,' he declared. 'You like Ernst Lubitsch's pictures, but they don't make money. You pan pictures that do pay.'

" 'When am I going to be permitted to answer you?' I asked again. 'Not for a long time yet' was his reply.

" 'Then talk to yourself.'

"With that I got up and left. From then on I was constantly the target of Warner Brothers' publicity men. They made things as uncomfortable as possible for me when I covered a Warner film premiere. A policeman's lot may be hard, but his existence is enviable compared to that of a critic in the last days of silent films."

An unusual clash between a critic and a movie company involved Frank Nugent, reviewer for the New York *Times* in the late Thirties, and Twentieth Century-Fox, which had been at loggerheads with Nugent for some time over his "sneering" reviews. Fox, which has always adopted an aggressive attitude toward the press, withdrew all its advertising from the *Times* for almost a year after Nugent's review of *The Story of Alexander Graham Bell* on April 1, 1939. The *Times*, however, stood its ground and, despite an estimated loss of $50,000 in advertising, backed up its reviewer. As Nugent says: "I was subjected to no pressure from management [at the *Times*] at any time. I never had anyone tell me what to write or how to write it. The paper, even in the Fox business, closed ranks. There was never any backing down."

According to Nugent, "in the opinion of Darryl Zanuck [at that time production chief of Twentieth Century-Fox], I was being rough then on Fox products. That was the period of the Ritz Brothers, Shirley Temple and phony biographies with Tyrone Power and with Don Ameche inventing things all over the place. It was a period of extravagant bad taste. Fox was complaining constantly to the business department about my reviews."

The "payoff," as Nugent puts it, came when he reviewed *The Story of Alexander Graham Bell*, which has since gone down in gag—if not in movie—annals as the picture in which Don Ameche invented the telephone. Nugent, oddly, rather liked the picture, but led off his review with "If only because of the omission of Tyrone Power, Twentieth Century-Fox's *Bell* must be considered one of that company's more sober and meritorious contributions to the historical drama. . . . It is interesting, even when it is not exciting. . . ." "Fox," recalls Nugent today, "said it was bad enough to criticize a performer while in a picture, but when he was not in it, it was hitting under the belt."

In the April 9, 1939, Sunday edition of the *Times*, Nugent saw fit to take note:

> The Story of Alexander Graham Bell *subjected us to some bombardment through an unfortunate misinterpretation of a line in the original review. It read: "If only, etc., etc., etc." It was not our intention to take a gratuitous swing at Mr. Power, who, poor chap, has suffered enough in these columns, but to point out the advantage accruing to a picture through the casting of a player—in this case, Don Ameche—in a part which called for a greater degree of maturity than, in our judgment, Mr. Power possesses. The mention of Mr. Power at all was purely a reflex action, inspired by the many historical roles he has played at Twentieth Century-Fox.*
>
> *The picture is quiet in tone and leisurely in its narrative development. Somehow we found both qualities effective, tending to create a more sincere and persuasive treatment of fact than the screen generally provides. It was a great relief, for example, to find that Mr. Ameche's Mr. Bell invented the telephone for its own sake and not to restore hearing to his deaf sweetheart, played by Loretta Young. If Twentieth Century truly has reformed in its approach to the historical drama, we must insist on being among the first—and, we hope, not the last—to congratulate it.*

But Fox, unmollified, withdrew its ads anyway. "Fox," says Nugent, "claimed that, if my reviews were accurate, the New York *Times* readers were not going to Fox movies and so I was not reviewing for an audience for Fox pictures. . . ." While the Fox ad ban was on, Nugent reviewed that studio's *The Grapes of Wrath*. "I hailed it," he says, "and the next thing I knew, Zanuck sent Joe Moskowitz [Fox's Eastern representative] to sign me as a writer." Weekly Variety documented this paradoxical situation on February 7, 1940, with the following headline: "20TH FOX NO LIKE NY TIMES CRITIC BUT WANTS NUGENT AS SCRIPTER" and noted that "at the time the offer from Fox came, Nugent had belted Fox's *Little Old New York* at the Roxy, shortly after his rave on *Grapes of Wrath*." Nugent went to work for Fox in April 1940 as a writer on a one-year contract. "The Fox ads," he says, "were reinstated in the *Times* shortly after I left."

The inference in Fox's signing of Nugent was that "if you can't fire 'em, hire 'em." With Nugent on the studio payroll, he obviously was no longer in a position to criticize Fox movies, at least publicly. Nugent says today: "I want to make it clear that I wasn't bribed off the paper and if I was bribed I didn't know about it." He adds, "When the offer from Joe Moskowitz came out of the blue, I was puzzled and skeptical, frankly. The offer was financially flattering and was for a solid year, and beyond the purely financial thing it was very flatteringly worded. I would be on the creative end of the business and not as a critic. I was only thirty at the time, not even thirty.

"I asked Nunnally Johnson if this was an attempt by Zanuck to get me off the *Times* and lure me away. Nunnally Johnson said he couldn't see it that way, that this was characteristic of Zanuck. In spite of that assurance, I further wanted to protect myself against being knifed and went to Sulzberger and asked for a year's leave of absence from the *Times* and he agreed."

Nugent never returned to the *Times*, staying on at Fox. At the studio, he was given little opportunity to function as a writer, for which he had been signed. "Shortly after I went to work there as a writer," says Nugent, "Zanuck began sending me scripts to read and criticize in advance of production. I was functioning as a critic, as a reviewer in advance. I did become in effect a story doctor under Zanuck's plan. He was using me to send him confidential expressions of opinion on scripts being done. Invariably, I stepped on everyone's toes and most writers avoided me like the plague. I was there for four years until I could take no more of it and resigned because they did not give me a chance to write. They kept telling me that 'We feel you're a good critic but you're not a creative writer.'"

When Nugent left Fox in 1944 he got "a fancy letter" from Zanuck:

DEAR FRANK:
Now that you are leaving the studio, I want you to know that I regret exceedingly the fact that you were never able to properly display your writing talents. I mean this sincerely.

When you first came with us you were of great service to me. Your critical opinions and reviews of scenarios contributed more than once to the success of some of our finest films. I have told you personally that this resulted in an unfortunate break for you as an individual. Very frequently sincere criticism is not appreciated, especially in a business like ours where there are many creative but temperamental elements to deal with. Had you been less honest in your attempts to criticize, I regret to say that perhaps you might have fared better. On the other hand, probably the trouble lies in the fact that you got in a rut and by rut I mean you were looked upon as a critic more than as a creator.

Your last option was exercised when I was overseas. If I had been here at that time, the option would not have been exercised because I would have frankly told you that I believe that you could do better elsewhere. You are not the type of man who wants to hang around doing nothing, and I want you to know that in the whole situation I feel personally responsible. I have been so devoted to the production of Wilson in the past eleven months that I have had to neglect many things that should have called for my personal attention. Nevertheless, I still believe, as I told you the other day, that there is no reason in the world why you cannot continue your writing career, but I urge you in your next assignment to go on the lot as a writer and not as a critic. Unfortunately, a brand burns deeply and sticks. In your case I am sure this is not true if in your new work you start out definitely as a writer.

Good luck to you.

Kindest regards,
DARRYL

Nugent replied:

DEAR DARRYL,

Many thanks for your friendly note, as for the many other courtesies you have shown me in the last four years.

It has, of course, disappointed me that none of my writing has reached the screen, except indirectly, but it is some satisfaction to know that you, at least, recognize that I have contributed to many of the studio's more successful pictures. If I have done that, then my time here has not been wasted.

It is my intention now to knuckle back to writing and I hope someday to submit a story here that will make even the producers whose feet I've stepped on forget their aching corns.

With all good wishes.

Cordially,
FRANK

Adds Nugent: "About one and one half years later it gave me a great deal of satisfaction to sell Fox an original for $35,000." Nugent also made good as a screenwriter for director John Ford and others, and now he has to worry about those darn movie reviewers himself. He says today that he could never be a motion-picture critic again after knowing the blood and sweat and tears of moviemaking, and he scoffs at the average reviewer's Olympian handing out of credit on a movie without really knowing whose touch is whose.

When one rereads the reviews of Frederick Mordaunt Hall, Frank Nugent and Ben Crisler in the New York *Times* today, they seem rather mild, and it is difficult to see what all the ruckus was once about. It was not so much that the movie reviews were deadly, but that most of the movies were deadly dull—and the moviemakers were hypersensitive about any form of reasonably lively and detached critical comment. It is a situation that still exists today. In 1956, for instance, United Artists withdrew its ads from the New York *Times* after Bosley Crowther gave *Trapeze* a poor review. The *Times* stood fast and the ads were reinstated after five days.

The New York *Herald Tribune*, more vulnerable economically than the New York *Times*, has also been the subject of some strange shuffles in the movie department. First, the outspoken and forthright movie critic Otis Guernsey was removed from his job and made drama editor instead. There was some talk at the time about Hollywood pressures. Then William Zinsser, his successor, left the movie-reviewing job to become an editorial writer on the *Tribune*. *Time* Magazine at the time inquired: "Was Bill Zinsser kicked upstairs because of pressure from advertisers?" In 1958 Zinsser authored a book, *Seen Any Good Movies Lately?*, in which he discussed the subject of movie reviewing and its pitfalls. "I often heard it rumored about town," wrote Zinsser, "that a certain company was 'out to get' me. . . ." But, he declared, he reviewed movies "regardless of outside pressures" and "held my ground." However, he added, "as the fortunes of the movie industry began to sag alarmingly, I could see that the sands were shifting, and I asked for my release." Zinsser's successor, Paul V. Beckley, is a more easygoing critic than he was. Zinsser concluded in his book: "I regret that movie criticism is losing its fiber."

Today both Guernsey and Zinsser have left the *Herald Tribune*. According to Archer Winsten, movie critic of the New York *Post*: "Zinsser and Guernsey were fired for being too tough and the pressure came from Einfeld." (Einfeld had long left Warner Brothers and was now vice-president in charge of advertising and publicity at Twentieth Century-Fox, the movie company with the most actively vindictive and vengeful policy toward the press.) "They were upped in the organization," says Winsten, "and didn't feel like biting the hand that fed them. Both were personal and social friends of the Reids [the *Herald Tribune* publisher]. I urged them to. I wanted to write this at the time."

In his book Zinsser noted that "by all the rules of journalism, there should be no relation between advertising linage and editorial content. And yet it is generally assumed in New York motion-picture circles that a movie studio can soften an adverse review—in advance—by bringing pressure on a newspaper. Unhappily, there is some truth in this belief."

In 1956 the New York *Daily Mirror* reviewed a Paramount picture, *That Certain Feeling*, starring Bob Hope. The review was captioned: "Some Mild Humor in *Certain Feeling*." In subsequent editions the caption was changed to read: "Hope Rates a Rave in *Certain Feeling*" although the body of the review remained unaltered. Paramount was able to quote the revised caption in its ads.

In 1958 Justin Gilbert, the *Mirror* reviewer, failed to evince enthusiasm for *The Hunters*, a Twentieth Century-Fox movie about jet bombers. Einfeld cabled the *Mirror* publisher, who was then abroad, expressing "shocked regret shabby dismissal of our very important ambitious costly above all sincere patriotic film." Einfeld added that the review took no regard of "extensive advertising campaign in *Mirror* including two full three-quarter pages over and above regular space."

Archer Winsten was the most vocal of the New York film critics in decrying some of these events. At the time he said: "If critics cannot express their own opinions, right or wrong, alone or in a crowd, there is no such thing as freedom of expression." The New York Film Critics Circle was exercised about some of these happenings, particularly about *The Hunters* incident, and got together in emergency session. But nothing came of it. Says Winsten: "It darn near broke up the critics circle. The critics didn't want to do anything about it. Bosley [Crowther] was loath to pull anyone else's chestnuts out of the fire. And one of the girls was a good friend of Einfeld's."

In 1959 publisher William Randolph Hearst, Jr., dispatched a memo to the *Mirror* and other Hearst newspapers cautioning the movie critics—as well as reviewers in other departments—"not to be biting or sarcastic or bitter toward personalities in their comments. . . . I don't believe our readers are interested in reading the personal likes and dislikes of our critics and I don't intend to waste our valuable space printing them."

Winsten was involved in an unusual review incident in 1944 when he was the only one of the New York movie critics not to like Darryl Zanuck's personal production of *Wilson* (the years have borne out Winsten). Winsten's original review was followed two days later by a favorable review. This prompted *Motion Picture Herald*, a trade paper, to carry a story headlined "FAST CROW EATING." The story read in part: "Archer Winsten of the New York *Post* last week became the first motion-picture critic in the memory of living men to eat his own words within the brief space of 48 hours." *Motion Picture Herald* gleefully compared Winsten's two reviews. The first review carried such wordage as "*Wilson* does not dig deeply into the conflict involved"; "the accomplishments fall far short of any high goal"; and "As entertainment, *Wilson*, the mammoth biographical picture at the Roxy, settles down massively into the worthwhile category. It does not, as its producer, Darryl F. Zanuck, seems fondly to have hoped, mark a point of departure in the development of the motion picture medium." Winsten's second review carried such lines as "When the surfaces recede to their proper focus, the essential climax, the Wilsonian idea, remains and finds a noble expression"; and "The goal attained is an extraordinarily high one."

Winsten explains this today as follows: "The *Post* was strongly anti-isolationist. I felt that the picture was ineffective and not in agreement with its purpose. Wilson was a strong man in the picture and he had nothing but straw men to fight. There was a lack of real conflict. The picture falsified history and was not a good picture. When I saw the other reviews in the isolationist papers—the picture was given a big play—I went back and checked to see if the people coming out of the theater got the idea. I interviewed twenty to thirty people coming out. Almost to a man they reversed what I had said. I modified my feelings about the picture. I have a policy of taking a second look at a picture and writing second thoughts on it. There was no pressure in this case. Actually, Zanuck had dispatched an irate wire to the editor of the *Post* after my review and he'd later felt the wire had been effective. But I didn't even know about this until much later."

When I was press agent for the 55th Street Playhouse and other movie theaters in New York years ago, it was generally known and accepted in screen circles that one could get the movie meter, which rated films Excellent, Good, Fair and Poor in the New York *Post*, adjusted through the newspaper's advertising department. Winsten was far from buyable or pressurable, but even if he wrote, say, just a fair review of a movie, the meter could be adjusted via the advertising department to read "Good." Since many readers never got beyond glancing at the meter, this was a tactic often used by movie press agents and advertisers to tone down the effect of a negative review. According to Arthur Mayer, the plethora of stars, bells, clocks, orchids, etc., that run as critical symbols in connection with many movie reviews are used so as not to burden the "prospective patron with the effort of reading." "Most picture audiences," says Mayer, "are by their nature less addicted than drama audiences to the written word."

Winsten says that the *Post* movie meter was "created by Irene Thirer [of the *Post* movie section], who created the star system on the [New York *Daily*] *News*. It was not my idea and I felt it burdensome rather than convenient. I ran the meter about fifteen minutes fast—it was then like a clock. There was a difference between the meter and the body of the review. I felt that for a person too illiterate to read, a different standard should be applied. I had to make a bad picture better for the person who was unable or unwilling to read. I was serving two publics, one with the meter and one with the review. If I didn't adjust the meter ahead, there would have been too many damnings on the meter." The meter was discontinued, says Winsten, "about three or four years ago."

Winsten has expressed himself on the predicament of the movie reviewer this way to Zinsser:

"During the past twenty-two years of movie reviewing for the New York *Post*, there isn't a major movie company that has not tried, as a result of unfavorable reviews, or reviews not favorable enough, to have me fired. Obviously they have not tried to work this kind of maneuver through me. Various bosses, at various times, have told me what was happening. On one occasion I actually read a flattering letter stating that, in the opinion of the writer—head of publicity, advertising and exploitation of a very major company—my reviews were much too good for a daily paper. They should be in *The New Republic* or *The Nation*.

"It is my firm belief that there are many ways of neutralizing, softening and counteracting the opinions of movie critics, and the movie companies know them all, and use them whenever it seems advantageous to do so."

Winsten added philosophically: "After all, there is a good reason why fighting papers expend their heaviest blasts on matters of international debate, the United Nations, politics, traffic problems, Southern bias and Northern housing. It's not going to cost a penny of advertising, and it brings back a dollar of public esteem. But bravery in the face of movie companies can be very expensive, and it is hardly appreciated at all by the general public."

In 1960 I asked Winsten, as one of the more articulate and outspoken of film critics on the problems of movie reviewing, if he would not like to set forth some of his views in these pages. Winsten promised to do so. And then he sent me this letter, dated April 11:

DEAR EZRA:

A thousand apologies if I've held you up only to disappoint you. The trouble is quite simple, too much work, not enough time or personal force, and there you have it: no further diatribe on what is wrong with the movies, and movie reviewing.

Besides, as you say, it's a dead horse, or, at any rate, I am today, having skied myself into oblivion Sat. & Sun. Use what you want from what I gave Zinsser. More power to you. Fight the good fight, and all that sort of thing. I'm stubborn and I'm going to keep on in the future exactly as in the past, but without illusions. It won't change a damned thing, and gradually some other corruption of taste and integrity will take the place of the corruptions that now prevail.

Yrs. on the sidelines,
A. WINSTEN

A rather sad letter, but then it is possible for a movie reviewer to become rather sad with the passage of time.

However, another long-time New York movie critic, Jesse Zunser of *Cue Magazine*, is of the opinion that movie-company pressures on reviewers are just "a fact of life. Moviemen are surely entitled to make their views known and felt, just as newspapers and magazines do. All that is necessary is for the critic—and his publisher—to give the companies a fair hearing and then tell them where to get off. It's as simple as that."

Or is it?

These, mind you, are the New York newspapers, generally considered among the best and most powerful in the country. The situation is worse in other cities where newspapers are even less independent and usually have lower journalistic and critical standards.

One of the few relatively unshackled reviewers Los Angeles has ever had, Philip K. Scheuer of the *Los Angeles Times*, has been subjected to unremitting pressure from studios over the years in an effort to tame him or get him fired. The moviemakers have not taken kindly to such Scheuer comments as "The overly romantic leading man played his role with his part on his sleeve" and "After the first few reels, there seemed to be less on the screen than met the eye." But Scheuer is still there. Since a time-honored tactic of Hollywood press agents is to confront a critic after a movie showing and press him for his opinion, Scheuer developed a neat dodge of his own. He would utter some conventional reply, like "You've done it again," and shake his interrogator's hand warmly, leaving in his palm a round metallic slug on which had been imprinted "It stinks. Scheuer—*Times*." After a while, Scheuer ran out of slugs—there was such a run of stinkers—and dropped the device. But recently, emerging from the showing of a current "epic," he said reflectively, "I think I'll do it again."

When I was movie columnist and critic for the Los Angeles *Daily News* from 1949 to 1952, the newspaper was extremely shaky economically (it finally folded and was absorbed by the Los Angeles *Mirror*). I had a kindly editor-in-chief, Lee Payne, and an even kindlier drama editor, Mildred Norton. But pressure was brought to bear on me in other directions.

Touchy movicmakers would often come back at me after a review. Occasionally their complaints were rather suavely handled, such as this letter I received in 1951 from that veteran complainer, producer Hal Wallis, after I reviewed his *That's My Boy*, a Dean Martin–Jerry Lewis movie. "Dear Ezra," Wallis (or his press agent) wrote, "I just read your review on *That's My Boy* and I am convinced that you wandered into the wrong theater and saw another picture by mistake. That's the only excuse I can find for your review, for had you seen the picture with the audiences that are literally falling in the aisles from laughter I don't think you could raise the question whether or not this picture has funny moments. I am enclosing a pass for the Paramount Hollywood theater and wish you would go to see *That's My Boy* for real enjoyment and to see the reaction of an audience to this comedy."

I printed the letter in my column in the *News* and added: "I saw *That's My Boy* at the Westwood Village Theater, but I'll have to take another look at it at the Paramount Hollywood Theater. Maybe the aisles at the Paramount are more conducive to falling into than those at the Westwood Village." (They were not.)

Usually the complaints were less adroitly couched. Al Horwits, then publicity director of Universal-International, barred me from the studio and from all press showings for several months after a critical review I wrote of a U-I movie. In my euphoric state I didn't even know for a long time that I was barred from U-I until I wanted to go out there one day and found I was not welcome. In any case, this did not matter particularly since I preferred to see the pictures at the theaters anyway.

The powerful Fox West Coast movie-theater chain, displeased with my reviews, demanded, through the Daily News's advertising department, that I be barred from reviewing their movies or they would discontinue their ads. As a result, Darr Smith, with whom I shared the movie-reviewing assignments and who also did a movie column, was from then on assigned to review Fox West Coast films. When drama editor Mildred Norton attempted to ascertain what the complaint against me was, the Fox West Coast publicity boys told her that it was not their idea but that pressure had been brought to bear on them by Twentieth Century-Fox publicity boss Harry Brand. Since Charles Skouras, head of Fox West Coast, was the brother of Twentieth Century-Fox chief Spyros Skouras, Brand's request, of course, had been immediately acted upon.

And, finally, I was called into the office of Daily News publisher Robert L. Smith and bluntly told to modulate what I wrote about the movies. Smith hobnobbed with the Hollywood brass and might have found any critical comment about the moviemakers in his newspaper a damper on his social life.

The pressures on the financially wobbly Daily News were, for the most part, simple economic ones. When I became cinema reviewer for Time Magazine in 1952—they call it "cinema" at Time, not "movies" or even "motion pictures"—the pressures were more insidious. There was, obviously, no advertising problem on Time. The magazine carried little movie advertising and did not need any such advertising. Furthermore, movie—oops, cinema—reviews were run as a sort of social service to the reader. The magazine operated on the theory—based on a number of subscriber surveys—that the typical Time reader was too high-toned and intellectually elevated to go to the movies anyway except on very infrequent occasions. However, should the subject of the cinema come up at, say, a cocktail party or in the course of chit-chat at the country club, it would not do, of course, for the typical Time reader not to know what the hell it was all about. So the magazine ran the Cinema department as it might run a report from Red China. The editors did not expect the reader to go there, but just to read about it quickly in capsule form and get the hang of the damn thing. The emphasis in the cinema reviews, therefore, was on form at least as much as on content. The reviews had to be entertaining at all costs so as not to tax the non-moviegoing subscriber, and the writing, accordingly, tended to be of the English trifle variety, with a large number of fruity and very unfunny puns imbedded in the fluffy prose.

In the course of functioning as *Time*'s cinema critic for two years, I had some educational experiences, even for a movie reviewer. When producer Stanley Kramer's faltering film fantasy *The 5000 Fingers of Dr. T.* came out, I wrote an adverse review of it—the picture got poor notices almost everywhere. I was called in by my immediate editor and informed that he was not running my review because he felt that I had misjudged the movie. He said that he was not going to ask me to rewrite the review, but was assigning Henry Darrach, from the book department (and now cinema critic), to review the film. Darrach filed an even more negative review. This was also scrapped. The editor, by this time having just about run out of writers whom he might call upon to give him a favorable review of the film, sat down at his typewriter and, with his own ten fingers, composed a carefully doctored, highly complimentary review of *The 5000 Fingers of Dr. T.* This was the review that appeared in the magazine, and it was one of the very few favorable reviews that the picture got anywhere. The editor in question was, coincidentally, a close personal friend of George Glass, Stanley Kramer's industrious press agent.

Charlie Chaplin's movie *Limelight* posed a problem, particularly at *Time*, since Chaplin was then a sensitive subject politically. I wrote a lengthy, what I considered to be a balanced, pro-and-con review of the film, and, after a good deal of editorial deliberation, it was finally cleared—even by my immediate superior. In due course the review, having been duly researched, checked and double checked by everyone up to the managing editor, was sent through for actual publication. But at the very last minute T. S. Matthews, then editor-in-chief of *Time* and a notorious tamperer with copy, stepped in, shelved the review and, going over everyone's head, including the managing editor's, took it upon himself to write a blistering notice of the picture. Not long afterward, Matthews himself was shelved by Henry Luce.

One may justifiably ask if all this is not beside the point at a publication like *Time*, where reviews and all copy are unsigned and anonymous and where what is known as "group journalism" is the thing. But such tactics still constitute censorious meddling with fact and opinion that puts the writer behind a psychological eight ball—and leaves the poor, unaware reader behind an even bigger, invisible one.

Most of the *Time* problems were interior ones. But there were also some external pressures. Roy Alexander, then managing editor, indignantly told me of the time Dore Schary, then production chief of M-G-M, flanked by his press agents (Howard Dietz and Howard

Strickling), marched into the magazine's offices on the twenty-ninth floor of the Time-Life Building to protest the *Time* review of Schary's personal production, *Battleground*. Schary's argument was that Manny Farber, then the cinema critic, was not qualified to review a war film since Farber had been a 4F during World War II. This enraged Alexander, who was a military buff and who had personally passed Farber's review, and, in the words of one spectator to the scene, "he pissed all over the idea." From then on it was almost impossible to mention Schary in *Time* except unfavorably. Soon afterward, Farber left *Time*, not because of the *Battleground* review, but Schary's press agent, George Nichols, boasted for a long time that Schary and he had gotten Farber fired. (Schary subsequently had the gall to sound off on the "Open End" television show about what he termed "shocking" and "reprehensible" squeeze plays on critics by movie studios. He termed such tactics "bad manners and very bad public relations" and stated that it was "absolutely necessary for critics to resist" these "pressures.")

As cinema critic for *Time*, I was subjected to the usual Hollywood sniping to which a reviewer soon becomes accustomed. Director Billy Wilder complained to my editor, in rich, Teutonic phraseology, that I was "the beast of Belsen" because of a negative review I had given one of his movies. But when I penned a positive review of another Wilder film, I was promptly de-Nazified in his estimation. The moviemaking team of Norman Panama and Melvin Frank, seeing red after a review of one of their films, wrote a long letter to the publisher intimating that I was some sort of subversive. Since the Panama–Frank picture had nothing to do with Communism, this seemed immaterial, even had it been true. Producer Albert Zugsmith, a less intellectual type, simply threatened to assault me. Temperamental producer Stanley Kramer paid me a personal visit at my office, seriously demanding to know why I did not, *ipso facto*, give the critical nod to all his movies because of their high-minded aims. When I tried to reason with him that good intentions did not automatically make for a good movie, Kramer became even more indignant. Although Kramer professed to be a liberal and an intellectual, he strangely seemed to draw the line at any free, rational discussion of his own work.

Kramer and his press agent, George Glass, kept trying to undermine me at *Time*, as they had at the Los Angeles *Daily News*. This heckling came to a head one day when I was called in by the senior editor in charge of Cinema, Hillis Mills, who told me that he had a report from the Kramer camp that I had been overheard, somewhere or other, at some time or other, making some remark or other that was not complimentary to Kramer. I had supposedly been overheard in this alleged criminal statement by a man named Hall Bartlett, a Hollywood producer of sorts and a friend of Kramer's, who had reported it to him. Since the charge was so vague, I was at a loss as to how to reply to it except to state to Mills that, if I had made any such remark, it was my constitutional right to do so and that I had been hired by *Time* to write movie reviews and nothing else. Apparently, as far as Kramer and his publicity gang were concerned, not only was it unlawful to write anything critical about Kramer but even to speak it.

But the Kramer faction finally had its comeuppance at *Time*. Riled by a slightly slighting review of one of the Kramer movies, the Kramer troops came storming into the magazine all set to prove that I had, once and for all, overstepped the bounds of free speech. They had to slink out with their publicity releases between their legs. It seemed that I had not even written the review at all. I was abroad on vacation at the time and a relief reviewer had done it. I didn't even know about the matter until I returned to the magazine several weeks later. From then on, there was a period of relative quiet on the Kramer front.

Hollywood's reaction to movie reviews and movie reviewers has always been extreme. The movie reviewer, in the words of Theodore Strauss, appears to the average moviemaker as "some monstrous abortion, the illegitimate offspring of a Coney Island cretin, a cynical sycophant whose palm is regularly crossed with silver in return for laudatory reviews, a talentless man who compensates for his sense of inferiority by attacking the work of others, a corrupt idiot who—by some whimsical wand of fortune—has been given the power to influence millions of moviegoers."

Even in the primeval days of Hollywood, the movie people were already in a dither about the movie reviewers. Grace Kingsley, who was drama and movie editor of the Los Angeles *Times* starting in 1913 and who retired recently as Hollywood's original lady columnist, remembered that theater managers in the old days "used to take it hard when you roasted a picture." One manager tried to get her fired for a sour review. Failing that, he had a sign flashed on the screen of his theater: "Grace Kingsley thinks this is a bad picture. What do you think?" A college friend of Kingsley's and some of his chums came to the theater and, when the slide was flashed on the screen, they got up and chanted in a chorus, "We think Grace Kingsley is right" and walked out.

Response to movie reviews sometimes verges on the pathological. Director William Wyler once cornered me at a cocktail party at the

Beverly Hills Hotel and, in the presence of onlookers, spent the better part of an hour bemoaning the unfairness of a *Time* Magazine review of his movie *Friendly Persuasion*. Renowned as one of the toughest directors in Hollywood and a multi-take terror on the set, the illustrious Wyler was quite broken up over the review. I was then Hollywood correspondent for *Time* and had nothing to do with the reviews, which were written in New York, and so I could serve as a sounding board for Wyler's lament. I tried to reason with him, telling him that I personally disagreed with the review, that it was basically only one man's opinion, even though unfortunately broadcast in an influential magazine, and that this same publication had not long before that blithely dismissed Vittorio De Sica's great Italian movie *Umberto D.* with a few rather slighting paragraphs. But Wyler was not to be consoled. The situation finally became downright embarrassing, and Mrs. Wyler had to step in to try to calm her husband down.

Reaction in Hollywood to not entirely complimentary reviews often seems to be predicated on the belief that the reviewer, for some unfathomable reason, does not like the moviemaker personally. George Pal, a most affable movie producer, once telephoned me after I had written a slightly less than ecstatic notice of one of his films and inquired plaintively, "Ezra, what is wrong? Are you mad at me?" The implication was that there was some trouble between us, entirely unrelated to the movie.

Some moviemakers can get quite virulent. Director Herman Shumlin became incensed at me for a remark I made in an article which I wrote for the *American Cinematographer* Magazine about James Wong Howe. Howe had photographed Shumlin's movie version of Graham Greene's brilliant political thriller *Confidential Agent*, starring Charles Boyer and Lauren Bacall, and in the course of the story I made the very much in order comment that the picture had turned out to be not particularly political or particularly thrilling. Shumlin called me at my home and reviled me on the telephone.

Walter Wanger was notoriously vindictive with the press. While pretending to be a harbinger of the brave new world on celluloid, Wanger was regularly grinding out old-hat Technicolor trash. He did not like to be reminded of this contradiction in print. When critic Herb Sterne observed in *Script* Magazine in 1944, apropos a Wanger movie, "*Ladies Courageous* is still another addition to the long line of cinematic duds sponsored by Walter Wanger and things have definitely arrived at a pass where one wonders how much longer the president of the Academy of Motion Picture Arts and Sciences will have the audacity to make public and frequent harangues on what he terms 'the art of the motion picture,' " Wanger went after Sterne with a vengeance, persistently trying to get him fired.

Presumably nettled by some criticism of his film fables, Wanger took out after me too in 1943. I was then doing a movie department for *Common Ground*, a quarterly periodical of limited circulation, now defunct, which was published by the Common Council for American Unity in New York and was devoted to minority-group problems. On its editorial board were Pearl Buck, Thomas Mann, Louis Adamic and Lin Yutang. I was paid, as I recall, approximately twenty-five dollars for my contribution as film critic every three months. Wanger made an uncommon effort to get me fired at *Common Ground*. He embarked on a letter-writing campaign to discredit me with the editors, who were good enough to keep forwarding to me copies of his vitriolic communications. Finally, after some time, realizing that he was making no headway, Wanger gave up.

The reviewer is frequently tempted with blandishments. These may range from a benign Samuel Goldwyn personally telephoning him, just prior to the release of a Goldwyn production, and indulging in some chummy, flattering chitchat with him, to the offer I once had from a Walt Disney publicity representative in New York, before the opening of a Disney animated-cartoon feature which I was reviewing for *Time*, of the company of a real, live young lady for the evening. According to Arthur Mayer, gigolos have even been imported to woo female reviewers on occasion. Press showings of movies are often preceded by a good deal of wining and dining in the hope that the best way to a reviewer's typewriter, if not his non-existent heart, is through his stomach.

In Hollywood's estimation, the best kind of movie reviewing is that of the trade papers. Almost every picture with a big budget and big stars is acclaimed in the trades as a "smash" and a "block-busting bonanza at the box office." At worst, the enthusiasm of a trade-paper review may be slightly tempered, usually in the case of a low-budget movie minus stars—and also minus much trade-paper advertising. In such an instance, the review will read something like this: "*The Great St. Louis Bank Robbery* isn't great."

From reading the trade papers you might understandably infer that Hollywood is turning out masterpieces daily. (In Hollywood, a "masterpiece" is usually a movie made by someone without talent but with a talented press agent.) Then the pictures arrive in New York and, presumably having spoiled in transit, are less ardently received by the

Eastern reviewers. For a while the *Hollywood Reporter* ran periodic digests of the New York movie reviews, which were decidedly at variance with the Hollywood reviews. Some producers even tried to get the *Hollywood Reporter*'s New York operatives strategically to edit these digests of reviews of their own pictures on the theory that what you did not read in the Hollywood trade papers you did not know. The *Hollywood Reporter* finally discontinued the Eastern review digests entirely.

The Hollywood trade papers look with suspicion upon the New York reviewers. The *Hollywood Reporter* once led off its compendium of Eastern reviews with "The authors of the criticisms capsuled below are given the widest possible latitude. Their opinions do not necessarily reflect anything but the state of their digestion, the location of their seat, the holes in their bobby-socks, the tenacity of their hangover, the efficacy of their sleeping pills, the promptness of their laundry, the angle of their political leanings, and the number of their prejudices."

The New York critics, the trade papers claim, ignore the box-office value of a movie. When both the New York *Times* and the New York *Herald Tribune* panned *Love Is a Many Splendored Thing* in 1955, the *Hollywood Reporter* declared in editorial outrage: "Yet this film, despite a heavy downpour at one of the peak hours, grossed a phenomenal $90,000 in the first three days of its New York run." *Daily Variety*, in 1955, ran an appraisal of New York reviewers as viewed by the movie companies. It was found that the *Herald Tribune*'s William Zinsser "writes a readable piece but has a penchant for biting sarcasm. Also likes foreign films. Cares nothing for b.o." (signifying box-office, not body odor). On the other hand, Kate Cameron of the *Daily News* "knows what her readers like and don't like. A friend of the industry. Goes by popular appeal rather than 'art.'" And Frank Quinn, of the *Mirror*, was hailed with "Likes most pictures and therefore is a great favorite with the companies." As Loew's president Joseph Vogel said in accepting the New York Film Critics Award for *Ben-Hur* as the best picture of 1959: "This is the first time I have ever been in complete agreement with the critics."

Once in a while, though, some movies leave Hollywood unacclaimed and are "discovered" by reviewers in New York. These are usually "sleepers" that the studio has overlooked because they cost little and have no big names in them. A case in point was *Narrow Margin*, a low-budget, high-caliber thriller which RKO quietly released in 1952. On the strength of my review in *Time* and its favorable reception in some other publications, the film was saved from a fate worse than scrapping—namely the bottom half of a double bill in neighborhood theaters. Instead, it was booked, at the last minute, into a small, first-run Manhattan movie house and given, at least, a fighting chance to be seen and appreciated.

Hollywood trade-paper review jargon is about as amorphous as the Los Angeles smog. In reviewing Jean Renoir's India-made movie *The River*, in 1951, *Daily Variety* pilloried it as being "too slow." At the time, I commented in the Los Angeles *Daily News*:

> There now arises a question of semantics: what, exactly, does "too slow" mean? I happen to have seen The River and think it is one of the better films that have come along recently. The point of the picture, in Daily Variety's own words, is "that life flows on just as the river." The movie, therefore, has a leisurely pace because that is the tempo of its subject.
>
> At the same time, The River has intellectual and emotional movement that is much more stimulating than most of the slambang action epics to which Daily Variety would probably give the nod.
>
> So I say that the word "slow" is a meaningless word, except in relation to the purpose of a picture. And, used as a derogatory label in a movie review, it reveals an extraordinary lack of understanding on the part of the typewriter-tapper.

Joe Schoenfeld, then editor of *Daily Variety*, infuriated by this critique of his critic, screamed at me over the telephone, "How dare you criticize *Daily Variety*?" He accused me of being an egghead and strongly suggested that he would knock same off the next time he saw me. From then on my name was anathema in *Daily Variety*. Even reviewers and editors are ultra-sensitive in Hollywood.

The field of movie reviewing runs the gamut from fan-magazine lowbrow, where there may not be any predicates in the sentences, all the way to the effete, dilettante effusions of a publication like *Films in Review*, where each sentence may have two predicates. But perhaps the apogee of tortured writing was achieved by the late James Agee, functioning variously as reviewer for *Time* and *The Nation*. Agee was an over-meticulous stylist. When I moved into the cinema reviewer's office at *Time* Magazine, I found in one of the desk drawers a massive pile of writing paper on which Agee, as *Time*'s reviewer, had endlessly written and rewritten the opening paragraph of a review of a Sir Laurence Olivier Shakespearean movie. This paragraph had gone through perhaps thirty-odd drafts, with a single word or punctuation mark being changed from one version to the next. The words were all written in a small, neat and painstaking longhand. It was an extraordinary series of documents, almost blood-chilling in their near microscopic intensity, and all the more forbidding because all this labor had been lavished on a product for a weekly news magazine.

But if Agee's style was meticulous, his thought processes were chaotic. He often seemed to be writing about something other than the movie under consideration. As Theodore Strauss observed, if reviewing at the ordinary newspaper level was "hardly reviewing at all," the Agee style of reviewing was "at least as deadly to healthy criticism." "Agee," Strauss found, "seems to believe that a sentence should be the longest distance between two points. In his hands the English language is a poor thing. He finds it necessary to stitch its inadequate and makeshift word meanings with a hyphen." Strauss quoted a passage from a review of *National Velvet* in which Agee described the qualities of the early Elizabeth Taylor: ". . . [They] are most conspicuously a mock-pastoral kind of simplicity, and two or three speeds of semihysterical emotion, such as ecstasy, an odd sort of pre-specific erotic sentience, and the anguish of overstrained hope, imagination and faith." Labeling Agee a "self-conscious connoisseur of exquisite trivia," Strauss concluded that, with all his "anguished, hair-splitting English," he still missed "the point entirely as to a film's vitality or lack of it."

There is no movie reviewing today of the caliber of the Twenties and early Thirties when such perceptive, pioneering critics as Richard Watts of the New York *Herald Tribune*, John S. Cohen of the New York *Sun* and André Sennwald of the New York *Times* served, in the words of one commentator, "as the excited prophets for a new and exciting medium." There were good movies in that period, and to have good critics you ultimately have to have good movies, and vice versa. Neither of them exists in a vacuum. The good critic needs channels to express himself and freedom to write—as well as something worth while to write about. The moviemaker needs informed and invigorating comment about his work. Forceful and healthy film comment goes hand in typewriter with forceful and healthy films. But Sennwald committed suicide and Cohen died in a sanitarium—was there some correlation between their own, personal decline and the decline of general screen standards?—and Watts forsook the screen for the stage. Since then the quality of movie reviewing in the United States seems to have deteriorated with the quality of movies—and is nowhere near the standard of the best film criticism in such countries as England and France.

Watts once explained why he gave up movie reviewing. In his estimation, "the old silent motion pictures had an excitement and a promise about them that the current talking product somehow lacks. Some of the early films were foolish, inept and primitive and a number of the present-day works are skillful and impressive, but, on the whole, it is my stubborn impression that there was a vitality, a freshness and a pioneering vigor in the cinema before the sound track overtook it that are absent from the slicker and smoother movies of today. . . . I must say I found films more fun in the earlier era. Certainly there was something very stimulating about writing of them in those days. Here was a new uncharted medium, without standards of criticism or written code of esthetics or any particular established values. A fresh and potentially tremendous form of expression was springing up, and there seemed no end to what it might achieve. We who were its pioneering critics may have had little prestige or recognition, but the opportunity we had to aid in the establishment of standards and values, to start a new code of criticism from scratch, as it were, was enormously exciting. I even think we did a pretty good job."

Watts added that his objection to the movies today "is far more to Hollywood than to the screen as a medium. . . . Hollywood, with its cheapness, phony values, ridiculous caste system, and the sense of fear that dominates it, seems to me a disgusting place, even though I confess I have always had fun visiting there. As long as the West Coast Babylon rules the films, I, for one, will be suspicious of them."

A movie reviewer soon becomes disenchanted with his work. Wolcott Gibbs, writing in the *Saturday Review of Literature* in 1945 under the title "The Kingdom of the Blind—An Ex-Moving Picture Reviewer Considers His Ex-Job," said he finally gave up movie reviewing for *The New Yorker* when he saw "the whole absurdity of what I was trying to do—to write, that is, for the information of my friends about something that was plainly designed for the entertainment of their cooks." A snobbish attitude, to be sure, but there is no denying that vast body of movie output which Hollywood likes to dignify with one of its favorite labels, "escapist." Jesse Zunser defined "escapist" otherwise. Reviewing a movie entitled *Sudan*, he observed: "It may be unkind to refer to *Sudan* as an 'escape' picture, because Mr. Webster's dictionary says escape means 'to flee from.' But this is the kind of film that Hollywood itself calls 'escapist'—so it is no choice of mine. To those who enjoy these Montez–Hall–Bey marshmallow movies, no plot explanation is necessary; to those who do not, no explanation is possible. For they are, in every sense, pure escapist movie fare—especially in that they flee from reason, logic and common sense, bearing no relation whatever to reality in story, plot, dialogue, development—or performance."

Bogged down in this movie morass, the reviewer, as Strauss put it, "is constantly subject to a dozen grinding pressures which tend, in time, to deaden his sensibilities and obscure his judgment, to slowly sap away any objective integrity and render him a more or less pliant tool of the Hollywood motion picture publicity departments." And this is the way Hollywood wants it. British movie critic Milton Shulman once commented that Hollywood confused "the whole conception of criticism" with "free publicity." Shulman himself was the object of Hollywood's ire in 1953 when M-G-M and eight other Hollywood movie companies withdrew all their ads from the London *Evening Standard* because of Shulman's reviews. The *Standard* backed up Shulman at the time. Today he is no longer reviewing movies for the paper.

The movie reviewer after a while takes the easy way out. Worn down by pressures from within and without, he soon learns to play the Hollywood game and roll with the punches. Movies critics are rarely honest with themselves or with their readers. Dishonesty, in movie reviewing, is the best policy for the critic who wants to keep his job.

In 1958 *Time* Magazine noted that "as a journalistic form, the movie review has descended to the level of the press agent's blurb. . . . Many papers leave the job [of reviewing] to worn-out deskmen, middle-aged ladies (the New York *Daily News* has three) or unqualified cubs, or else, like the Des Moines *Tribune*, spread it through the city room, at $3 a review." As *Time* put it: "In tireless pursuit of mediocrity and unreadability, the nation's run-of-the-film movie critics have transformed themselves into a group dispensary of tasteless, colorless and odorless treacle, ignored on a wholesale basis by the moviegoers, sampled only by the movie industry itself, which is merely vigilant for any sign of recalcitrant tartness."

And yet a movie reviewer who is not free to express his opinion is not really a movie reviewer. As Bosley Crowther observed: "A critic has to have certain moments of real enthusiasm, of real controversy. In other words, he has to allow himself to become vigorous and perhaps even violent on certain points. He has to be positive, perhaps to the point of what may be considered extreme, in order to make himself a forceful critic. I think a critic is no good at all if he isn't forceful."

It may be that James Agee stumbled upon a solution to the predicament of the movie reviewer—namely, to write about a movie without seeing it. In this way, the critic saves a good deal of time, and the critic's critics can dismiss his review as thoroughly disqualified.

Of course, some reviewers have been known to do just this, working from prepared studio publicity reviews. One Los Angeles reviewer once got his pressbook plots mixed up and ran the wrong synopsis with the wrong picture. But Agee went a step further. In commenting on *Mrs. Miniver* in *The Nation* in 1942, he wrote that "not having seen *Mrs. Miniver*, I have nothing to say, beyond mentioning that one look at the *Miniver* stills was enough to keep me away."

Subsequently Agee reviewed a show for the *Partisan Review* and panned it without having seen it on the grounds that some of his friends, whose opinions he held in high esteem, told him they did not like it. *The New Yorker* then panned Agee for such an illogical form of criticism. The *Partisan Review* in 1945 ran a lengthy article, "Mr. Agee and *The New Yorker*," in which Agee's critical procedure was defended in this wise:

> The real point of interest, and it is the subject of the present inquiry, is how any one, whether amusingly or unamusingly, could come to the conclusion that because a man had not seen certain plays he should not write about them.
>
> Mr. Agee's actual procedure was scientific in the extreme. He had heard the opinions of friends who had liked the plays and of friends who had not liked them. That is, although he had not been there he had seen his object from two separate and known points of view and had placed it accordingly. This is the precise method used in map making. How often we were told in trigonometry class that if ever we wanted to map an inaccessible point across a river, we had only to measure the angles made with the trans-river point by any two known points on our side, and then the trans-river point would be as well mapped as if we had been there. The river was used but as an instance; one might stay at home and measure the sun and the moon. It is discouraging on leaving the classroom to see the method literally applied by Mr. Agee and to a more modest project, and to find his use of the method authoritatively denounced. If Mr. Agee must go, trigonometry must go.

There are other ways of circumventing the problems of movie reviewing. At one time or another I have tried various dodges. I once took a twelve-year-old girl to see a movie (movies, it has been said, are aimed at the twelve-year-old mentality). In this case, it turned out, the picture must have been aimed even lower because the twelve-year-old's critical verdict was "It stinks." On another occasion I had my dentist review a movie about dentistry, *The Great Moment*, starring Joel McCrea. His critical conclusion was that it was a pain in the tooth.

Still another possibility in movie reviewing is to have the moviemaker review the movie himself. This can make for rather interesting results. From the returns that have come in thus far, it seems that the moviemakers are often tougher on their own pictures than any mere outside reviewers would be. Author Elliott Paul, who wrote the movie *Rhapsody in Blue*, commented on it in the *Atlantic Monthly* in 1945 in a sort of "Rhapsody in Boo." He observed that the picture was "the life of the late George Gershwin, as he would have lived it had he been obliged to live it with the Hays Office looking on." He added that "the somewhat stodgy story . . . does not spoil Gershwin's very gay and poignant music."

Even more lethal was writer Paul Gallico in a 1945 *Esquire* review of the M-G-M movie *The Clock*, which was based on his original story. The picture was generally liked, but Gallico called it "a thundering bit of cinematic sleeping potion" and added, "At the outset, I wish to absolve Mr. Louis B. Mayer from any blame in connection with this turkeroo. At the time it was being produced, filmed and edited, Mr. Mayer, who is the head of M-G-M, had the misfortune to fall off a horse and was laid up in the hospital. This was our tough luck. Once he was unavailable, the entire producing unit would have had to fall off horses daily and twice on Sundays to have made any real difference."

Gallico then confessed that he and his wife, Pauline, were to some extent to blame for the finished product. "We are ashamed of ourselves," he wrote, "for we could have prevented it. Yes, we could. Because, and I blush to admit it, one of the men who wrote the screen play from our original story, Mr. Robert Nathan, the poet, was in our house for dinner one evening before departing for Hollywood to keep his assignation to murder our piece, and we had a chance to kill him then and there. We didn't do it. We knew we should after listening to him talk for ten minutes. Now it's too late. We believe in cool-headed, cold-blooded assassination as a preventive, but not for vulgar revenge. Eventually Mr. Nathan will have to account to his Maker anyway, and there is little to be gained by hastening the day.

But it was nothing less than criminal on our part to let the opportunity slip when we had it."

Director Josef von Sternberg told me that the New York *Times* once offered him a column so that he could reply in rebuttal to a negative review of one of his pictures. "I told them," he said, "that nothing the writer said was half as bad as what I thought of the picture myself.

"In Hollywood, though," von Sternberg added, "it doesn't really matter what they write about you. The only thing that matters is what you say about a guy's picture. You can seduce a man's wife here, attack his daughter and wipe your hands on his canary bird, but if you don't like his movie, you're dead."

Von Sternberg made these statements in 1952 while he was directing an RKO movie, *Macao*, starring Jane Russell. I am afraid that I did not like *Macao*.

CHAPTER V

The Great Brain Robbery

"THE GREAT MOTION PICTURE is made by a director and cutter and a writer who alone make something live and struggling to be born. In the Hollywood studios, the mass attack of a mob of half-wits in sport shirts and fifty-dollar shoes stamps any real idea to death before it leaves the studio."

Thus veteran movie writer Stephen Longstreet on the crucial issue of why so many Hollywood movies are so bad. For the authority has been taken out of the cameras of the creators and put into the coffers of businessmen and bankers. The result has been artistic bankruptcy.

All the milestone movies, from Edwin S. Porter's *The Great Train Robbery* to Akira Kurosawa's *Rashomon*, from D. W. Griffith's *Intolerance* to Vittorio De Sica's *Umberto D.*, from Erich von Stroheim's *Greed* to Federico Fellini's *The Nights of Cabiria*, have been the work of a director, working closely with a writer and cameraman, and often combining some of these other functions in himself. The director is, historically, artistically and logically, the man who makes the movie.

The dictionary defines "director" as one who runs the show. But today the Hollywood director, with very few exceptions, is no longer in control. The director does not direct. He is directed instead. His authority has been usurped by someone called a producer, who has become the director's boss. This has led to a topsy-turvy situation, akin to a top sergeant giving orders to a general.

Once, in the past, Hollywood movies got made—and many of them made very well, too—without producers. Even abroad today the producer, for the most part, is just a business overseer. The director is free to direct. This is one important reason why foreign films so often have more excitement and individuality than the Hollywood product.

Old-time director Allan Dwan told me some years ago that "the movie business has gotten out of hand. Costs are much too high. In recent years the banks have taken over the studios and become authorities on making movies. They have fouled it up in good style. Money control and not artistic control should be in the hands of the money men. Years ago we had no supervision. We made pictures our own way. We pleased nobody but ourselves and the public. Hollywood has crept away from the public and is no longer in contact with it."

The Hollywood producer, who started out as a business representative of the studio front office, gradually jockeyed himself into creative control of moviemaking, with disastrous results. In the old Hollywood days, the only producers were the studio bosses, and they were primarily untutored businessmen and administrators who hired creative talent and pretty much let them do their work. It was under the Mayer–Thalberg film-factory regime at M-G-M that the system of supervisors, to keep tabs on directors, was given its greatest impetus. As moviemaking became more complex and expensive with the advent of sound, these business delegates were raised to more exalted positions with the titles of assistant producers, associate producers and producers (an assistant producer, it has been said, is a mouse studying to be a rat, and an associate producer is the only one who will associate with the producer). As time went by, the front office gradually made the director take a back seat and individual enterprise was supplanted by "production by committee."

Director Fred Zinnemann has said of the producer system at M-G-M, where he worked for some years: "M-G-M was a factory geared to put out fifty-two pictures a year. They were concerned with quantity, not quality, with being well oiled and functioning. That is great for sausages and automobiles, but a director with specific ideas inevitably got into trouble" (as Zinnemann himself did).

In 1927, prior to sound, there were only 34 producers in all of Hollywood to help make 743 pictures that year. By 1937, there were 220 producers to make 484 pictures. According to Ben Hecht, "there is absolutely no reason to make a picture in Hollywood any more. There is very little talent left and what there is is kept down by the bosses. Hollywood is the most boss-ridden town in the world. It's getting worse because although there is a decrease in the number of pictures, there is no decrease in the number of bosses. Where you used to have three bosses on a picture, now you have six bosses."

In 1939, director Frank Capra complained in the New York *Times* that "there are only half a dozen directors in Hollywood who are allowed to shoot as they please and have any supervision over the editing." Today the producers, in cahoots with the stars and their agents, are in firm control of Hollywood, with the result, as director King Vidor said, that "the final decisions are made by businessmen, not artists."

The producer has allocated to himself the fame, if not the function, that rightfully belongs to the artist. For what is a producer anyway if he is not a business supervisor or administrator? A producer has been defined as an executive who wears a worried look on his assistant's face. A producer does not write, he does not direct, he does not photograph, he does not even dress the sets or do the leading lady's hair. He may, at best, possibly advise, console, try to help and guide. He may be a father confessor. He may be a sympathetic and even intelligent organizer and editor. But he certainly does not *produce* anything. The late writer Sidney Howard said that there were only two kinds of producers—"those who produce pictures that the writers and directors create for them, and those who try to be directors and writers without competence as either."

The typical Hollywood-producer attitude toward the director and toward moviemaking is illustrated in the conflict that David Selznick had with John Huston in 1957 when Huston was relieved of his job as director of A *Farewell to Arms*. Selznick explained the issue at the time in these words: "In Mr. Huston, I asked for a first violinist and instead got a soloist. . . . When I am the producer, I must produce." In the case of A *Farewell to Arms*, Selznick, after appointing a new director, produced strictly a dud.

If a movie is presupposed to be a work of art, it must, in the final analysis, be the work of one creative artist. He may be helped by various people, but it is ultimately his vision that emerges on film. A movie cannot be made by an army of people. It has to be made by an individual. Nor can it be made behind a desk. Its creation must be filmic, not literary. The director, by the nature of the moviemaking process, is the film's central, crucial craftsman.

Director Jean Renoir, who is of the firm opinion that the director is not given enough creative authority in Hollywood and is merely a cog in the motion-picture assembly line, told me recently that "creation must be total for the director from the beginning to the end. I'm convinced that the present failure of Hollywood is because of this. To divide, in art, is not to conquer. There is a lack of passion in Hollywood pictures. How can they have passion if pictures are divided into little bits?" Renoir's own Hollywood movies are a testimonial to this indictment. They never came up to the standard of his French accomplishments like *Grand Illusion* and *The Lower Depths*.

Renoir had some thoughts on why Hollywood so often defeats the moviemaker and particularly the Continental moviemaker: "It is the American mania for organization which frustrates them. You go to work in a studio. You are on the floor, ready to begin work. And what do you find? You find you have to go by the schedules, and so many of them. Which means you are supposed to run on time like a railroad train.

"And then they begin to check. They check the sound and double-check it, so that you get perfect sound, which is good. Then they check and doublecheck the lighting, so you get perfect lighting, which is also good. But then they check and doublecheck the director's inspiration—which is not so good."

Hollywood's division and departmentalization is accentuated by the plethora of guilds, groups and assorted societies—such as the Directors Guild of America (formerly the Screen Directors Guild), the Screen Producers Guild, the Writers Guild of America, the American Cinema Editors, the American Society of Cinematographers, the Make-Up Artists and Hair Stylists—who are often more concerned with claiming billing and credit for their members than with making a creditable movie, and with financial principal rather than the larger principles of picture production. The guilds are preoccupied with their individual, parochial, promotional activities and not the wider, broader, over-all aspects of moviemaking.

The few fairly good pictures turned out in Hollywood today are the work of individualistic producer-directors who have some degree of control over their projects and are able to express themselves to the best of their ability. But most directors today are little more than stagers. They are handed a script by the producer, maneuver the cast in front of the cameras, and then step out of the picture while the producer takes over once more.

Director Josef von Sternberg, eccentric, stormy petrel and self-styled "genius" of the screen, told me on his return to Hollywood in 1949, after a "retirement" of eight years, that he was not questioning his comeback assignment, *Jet Pilot*, in any way and that "my job is to transfer the script to the screen. I have no freedom whatsoever beyond that. I don't see why I should have. At this point, they want to see if I can make an actor walk across the set."

And that is just about all that most Hollywood directors do today.

Very few directors cut their own pictures. The director, by the terms of today's contracts, is allowed to approve only the first rough cut of a picture, but this is usually nothing more than a tentative shape-up of what the final film will be like. It is the cutter who does the editing under the supervision of the producer. And still, as Griffith and his talented successors all over the world proved, a movie has to be put together, to be edited creatively in order to have impact and individuality. A critic once described this as the grammar of the film. Today's hyperthyroid big screens, furthermore, are not conducive to dynamic cutting and the telling closeup detail.

The best movies are the product of a continuing process from script through editing. The editing gives the picture tempo and character, arising from the way in which the separate shots are combined. Obviously, that is the director's job, for the man who shoots a picture should, artistically and morally, also edit his own shooting. Director Mark Robson, an ex-cutter, has said that "the average director in Hollywood doesn't work on a picture during the script and cutting stages. But if he is really to direct the picture, in the fullest sense of the word, he should. The editing of the picture, in the script and directing stages, is vital. If a director does not envision a picture as a pre-edited entity, he is not in control of the film. Then the film editor in the cutting room becomes the director of the picture by virtue of assembling it in his own way and imposing on it the character of his cutting."

This inattention to the grammar of the film is constantly evident. Most movies are little more than photographed stage plays without either physical or psychological action. Too many movie writers pile words one on top of another as if they were writing to be read and not writing for the camera. But in the movies, where the eyes have it, it is better to be right than to write. Good little movies, it has been said, should be seen rather than heard. In movies, in the beginning was the camera and not the word. Before talking pictures came along, movies spoke in what documentary-maker Robert Flaherty called "the language of the eye." As a result, many of the silents were truly golden.

Even the better moviemakers fail to use the tools of the trade sufficiently. In Fred Zinnemann's *The Men*, Marlon Brando, as a paraplegic paralyzed from the waist down, is shown building up his arm muscles by pulling himself up a rope with great difficulty. The scene was filmed in long and medium shots. One of Hollywood's foremost cameramen, later commenting on this sequence, wondered why there was no closeup of Brando's hands straining on the rope, which the scene obviously called for. Such a simple shot would have pointed up the scene tremendously and made it far more dynamic than it was.

William Wyler, another of Hollywood's more renowned directors, is known for such films as *The Best Years of Our Lives*. Probably the best sequence in that picture was a simple and wordless one in which Dana Andrews, as an ex-war flier, climbs into a junked bomber on a deserted air field. As Dana Andrews sits at his bombardier's post in the plexiglas nose of the B-17, there is a long shot of the exterior of the plane stripped of its engines and propellers. Then the camera moves in from a low angle toward the plane, giving the illusion of the B-17 coming toward the camera as if for a takeoff and there are sound effects of the engines starting. The film then cuts to Andrews inside the plane, reaching for the bomb release, as he relives his combat experiences. Here the director used the camera eye and the sound track —minus dialogue—to make his point powerfully. But Wyler's talent is essentially theatrical rather than cinematic. His movies usually talk too much. This is lazy moviemaking. Most picture makers do not sufficiently appreciate the eloquence of silence in a movie.

As a journalist, I early became aware that a good many of Hollywood's most touted names were more talented at publicity and promotion than at making movies. In Hollywood, whatever else they do or do not have, most of the celebrated citizens have one thing in common: they are promoters, pushers, press agents and operators of the first order, even if their moviemaking is of the second order. They may not always be motion-picture artists, but they are at all times public-relations artists, short on ken, long on con.

In Hollywood, where success is often equated with energy and larceny rather than ability, the best directors are not necessarily the most famous ones. Henry King, a long-time moviemaker who has to his credit such pictures as the early silent *Tol'able David* and the more recent western *The Gunfighter*, is one fairly creative director who has not had the acclaim he deserves. Michael Curtiz has a knack with the camera and a fluent way of mounting such films as *Casablanca* that many more publicized directors might well emulate.

Most of the leading directors today are keenly conscious of the importance of publicity. William Wyler, a former publicity man himself, has had a high-powered press agent on his personal payroll for more than twenty years. George Stevens is astute at public relations and has excellent contacts with the press. He had three different sets of publicity experts working for him on *Giant* and *The Diary of*

Anne Frank. For his next movie, *The Greatest Story Ever Told,* Stevens' contract provides that he have control over the allocation of a mammoth publicity and advertising budget. *The Diary of Anne Frank* was billed on many theater marquees and elsewhere as George Stevens' *The Diary of Anne Frank,* with Stevens' name above the title of the film and in letters as large as or larger than the name of the movie. This is a thoroughly unwarranted billing. The picture is, if anything, Frances Goodrich's and Albert Hackett's *The Diary of Anne Frank.* Goodrich and Hackett, an established screenwriting team, adapted the original diary into its successful Broadway stage version. They afterward transmuted the play into a screenplay, adhering almost word for word to the footlight original. Stevens' contribution to the movie, as he himself admitted to me, was decidedly secondary. But still the picture was billed as George Stevens' *The Diary of Anne Frank,* a tribute to Stevens' contractual and promotional acumen. The picture could even, just possibly, be Anne Frank's *The Diary of Anne Frank.*

Director John Huston is a colorful character whose peccadillos have been extensively documented in print. This does not necessarily have to do with his moviemaking aptitude. Huston sometimes puts on a better show behind the camera than in front of it. Billy Wilder, the Peck's bad boy of directors, is witty and highly quotable. His press interviews are often more memorable than his movies.

None of these directors has any real on-screen individuality or identity, although each has plenty of off-screen press agentry. When you come right down to it, the difference between the work of a William Wyler, a Billy Wilder—and even a W. Lee Wilder—is not much greater than the difference in their names. I defy anyone to spot a Fred Zinnemann or a John Huston movie without being tipped off as to its maker. And a film student would have astonishing difficulty, no matter how well versed in the medium, in ascertaining the style of any of George Stevens' movies because they are qualitatively indistinguishable from the mass of other rather mediocre films of the time. On the other hand, there is no mistaking an Eisenstein or a Griffith movie.

Many moviemakers today spend more time promoting their movies than making them. The extent to which publicity has taken over from picture-making is indicated in the promotion campaign for Otto Preminger's movie version of *Exodus.* The day the movie went before the cameras in Israel—March 28, 1960—simultaneous ads appeared in fifteen major newspapers in New York, Chicago and Los Angeles announcing that the picture would open in those cities in December and placing tickets on sale for the opening engagement.

Preminger is no laggard when it comes to publicity. Prior to the production of *Exodus*, he held a pow-wow with his press agents to discuss the presentation and billing of the picture. "I see it as Otto Preminger's *Exodus*," he told the assembled flacks, in a spirit of the highest dedication. "But, Otto," hazarded one drumbeater, "that's just what a lot of people are waiting for." Needless to say, the press agent is no longer with Preminger.

A choice instance of Hollywood's preoccupation with publicity was once in evidence on the wall of *Look* Magazine's Hollywood office. It was a framed photograph of Napoleonic producer David O. Selznick, his face not visible in the shot, walking away from the camera across his own studio lot. The picture had been taken by Selznick's press agents and sent out to the press as sufficiently newsworthy, even if the great man's back was toward the camera. The *Look* editors, in turn, thought this faceless photograph of a self-important Hollywood tycoon preposterously noteworthy enough to put on display.

In the course of my journalistic experiences, I came to find that it was easier and more satisfying all around to write about the offscreen, publicistic achievements and high jinks of my subjects. This eliminated the touchy and mostly unrewarding area of art, a matter that was usually of no particular interest anyway to either the reader or the subject.

A candid revelation of how publicity and promotion go into the making of a Hollywood "genius" was given in 1953 by Darryl Zanuck at a Screen Producers Guild testimonial dinner for him. Undoubtedly under the influence of this abnormal social stimulation, Zanuck made some exceptionally frank confessions. He told how he was a struggling writer of two-reel short subjects, *The Telephone Girl* series, in the silent era and, finally, barged into Jack Warner's office and sold himself as a feature film writer. Warner, related Zanuck, said he was too young, that he should grow a mustache and wear glasses. But he got the job. He wrote dog-eared scripts for Rin Tin Tin and other Warner stars, and his output was so vast that he functioned under three different names—Melville Crossman, Gregory Rogers and Mark Canfield.

"And then," said Zanuck, "I decided to become a genius. Hollywood was full of 'yes men,' so I decided to become a 'no man.' I knocked everything, even Warner pictures. One day Jack Warner said he bet I thought I could run the studio better than he did. I told him I was sure I could. The following Monday morning he made me executive producer.

"Now that I had the job of genius, I was going to make the greatest picture of all time. I picked a man who is now one of the finest directors in the business, Mike Curtiz. I got top stars and I made *Noah's Ark*, one of the biggest flops ever turned out. Now, Jack Warner and his brothers were certain that I was a genius.

"And being a genius, I had to live that way. I took up polo, big-game hunting and skiing. I owe everything to three wonderful men. First, Jack Warner. Second, Joseph M. Schenck. Third, Spyros Skouras. I've had thirty exciting years. It's great fun being a genius and I am going to continue playing the role."

Zanuck did not continue to play the role of genius for long. Spyros Skouras, Twentieth Century-Fox boss and one of the "three wonderful men" in Zanuck's career, gave him his exit cue in 1956.

Zanuck left out a few things in his "kidding on the square" confessional speech before the Screen Producers Guild. When he was first trying to become a movie writer, he thought that it would be helpful to have a published book to his credit since Hollywood was always impressed with literary lights. In 1923 Zanuck had a volume entitled *Habit* printed and announced to the studios with swanky, engraved cards. *Habit* consisted of three of Zanuck's rejected scenarios in narrative form and a disguised 100-page blurb for a hair tonic, Yuccatone, which had paid the printing costs.

Habit was written in what has been described as "cloth-of-gold style and the unbending grand manner of a half-educated adolescent." The opening sentence read: "Ling Foo Gow riveted his jet orbs on the burly figure that advanced on the narrow sidewalk of cracked asphalt, and with an excessive display of facial contortion, brought the aged lines of his poppy-hued countenance to an intensified scowl." But the book was sold to a studio anyway, for $11,000, and Zanuck was in business as a fledgling genius.

As a Hollywood genius, he, of course, needed an entourage of stooges, clowns and court jesters. Zanuck assembled one of the most notable entourages in the history of Hollywood. It was a sort of muscle-bound brain trust, consisting of Fidel La Barba, a former fisticuffer who doubled as a scenarist and bodyguard; Otto Lang, a ski instructor who was a director for a while; and Aidan Roark, a polo player. They helped advise Zanuck in his momentous moviemaking decisions.

The career of Zanuck is wonderful, goofy proof that, in order to be acclaimed in Hollywood, you should do everything in a big way, even if it is being lousy. Zanuck also proved that you can become a Hollywood genius and then hire real geniuses or at least near geniuses—Zanuck at one time or another retained the services of Aldous Huxley and Robert Sherwood—and order them around.

Hollywood's legendary producer was Irving Thalberg, production chief of M-G-M, who died in 1936 at the age of thirty-seven. He is today enshrined in screen circles as Hollywood's young, classic genius; the coveted Academy Award bestowed periodically on assertedly deserving producers was named after him. Partly, Thalberg's reputation came from some good movies, made for him by good directors and writers. Partly, it was a triumph of real-life type casting; he was pale, wan, successful, married to a glamorous movie star (Norma Shearer) and he died young. He looked rather like an artist and behaved consistently like a producer. Partly, it was that he was a powerful exponent of the buck, which is non-arguable in Hollywood. Thalberg may have been a genius at money-making, but not at moviemaking. His pictures simply do not bear it out.

Although he had a genteel façade, Thalberg was quite a callous customer. He had been trained in the movie business by Carl Laemmle, head of Universal. The story is told that Laemmle, upon returning to his studio from a trip east, was greeted at the entrance to the lot by a delegation of cowboy and cowgirl performers in picturesque garb who lined up to welcome him and shouted "Hail" to "Uncle Carl." Laemmle stood up in his car. It was a lovely, sunshiny morning, ideal for filming (that was Hollywood's pre-smog era when pictures were shot by sunshine instead of artificial light). "Look at all the sunshine!" Laemmle shouted. "Why ain't you people working?"

Director King Vidor's story, in his autobiography, *A Tree Is a Tree*, about how Thalberg coolly conducted a story conference during a funeral, is a hair-raising tip-off to the man's character. The funeral was Mabel Normand's, and the screen story under discussion was that of the homicidal Billy the Kid. The busy Thalberg did not have any time to waste. The conference between him and Vidor started in a limousine en route to the funeral parlor, continued intermittently through the services ("Too many murders," Thalberg whispered of the movie plot at one point), and was concluded by the time the car reached the studio again. Thalberg bounded up the steps to his office, told Vidor "I'll call you" and, as Vidor noted, "the story conference was at an end."

Thalberg's name supposedly never appeared on an M-G-M movie.

"If you have the power to put your name on the screen," he once said, "your name on the screen is meaningless." He probably would not have wanted his name on many of the movies he made anyway. For sheer bad taste and bad moviemaking, it would not have been easy to beat some of the pictures Thalberg turned out in the early Thirties, as television audiences, who can see many of them today, are painfully finding out.

But still Thalberg was known as "the wonder boy" and as Hollywood's original "white-haired boy"; today Hollywood is full of real, aging, white-haired "white-haired boys." By Hollywood's standards, Thalberg was a sort of Shakespeare of the screen and had intimations of immortality. What can be said with certainty today is that he knew how to turn a dollar.

Thalberg ran M-G-M with a steely hand. In his frequent battles with directors, he usually won out. Producer Carey Wilson offers evidence of how Thalberg operated. When the brilliant but nonconformist Erich von Stroheim was assigned to direct *The Merry Widow*, Thalberg kept a watchful eye on him. Von Stroheim did not like to be shackled by the usual moviemaking restrictions. Thalberg had an alternate director conspicuously sitting by on the set in case of complications. Even in comparison with the other products of those pre-Purity Code days of the screen, von Stroheim's celluloid was pretty sizzling. Thalberg went over every sequence carefully while von Stroheim constantly tried to get his own way. In one fiery seduction scene, von Stroheim had John Gilbert making love to Mae Murray while his suspenders dangled on the floor. Thalberg, who had given von Stroheim specific orders not to have any dangling suspenders, was momentarily stymied, but not for long. He had the suspenders blotted out in the laboratory with a trick traveling matte shot in an optical printer at a cost of $15,000. Thalberg edited most of *The Merry Widow* while he was ill in bed, lying flat on his back, with the picture being projected on the ceiling above him.

Thalberg was the model for the movie producer Monroe Stahr in F. Scott Fitzgerald's *The Last Tycoon*. It was a romanticized portrait. The late writer F. Hugh Herbert liked to tell of how, when he was unemployed at one time, he repeatedly tried to get an appointment with the inaccessible Thalberg without success. One night the doorbell of Herbert's home rang and, when he answered it, there was none other than the godlike Thalberg in person. Herbert, taken aback, did not know what to think. Thalberg seemed a little ill at ease himself. There was a moment's silence. "You are F. Hugh Herbert, aren't you?"

Thalberg said. After a pause he added: "Come in to see me at the studio tomorrow." Thalberg departed, leaving Herbert completely mystified. But the next day, sure enough, when Herbert reported to Thalberg's office, he was granted a prompt audience and signed to a lucrative long-term writing contract. It was not until some time later that Herbert discovered the real reason for Thalberg's mysterious nighttime visit. It seemed that Thalberg had a girl friend living nearby. In the dark he had accidentally rung the wrong doorbell. When he saw Herbert, he thought fast in an effort to cover up his error. And that, literary students, is how long-term writing contracts are sometimes negotiated in Hollywood.

Thalberg's successors never enjoyed the esteem he did. It has been said that the imposing M-G-M executive building, named after Thalberg, is air-conditioned and hermetically sealed "so that the ghost of Irving can't get in to see what they are doing." This building, prophetically perhaps, was built around a mortuary. The mortuary owners stubbornly refused to sell out to the studio and so the building went up right next to it. Judging from current Hollywood trends, the mortuary may yet outlive M-G-M.

In his time, Louis B. Mayer, Thalberg's boss, was the number-one tycoon in Hollywood. There were many years when he topped the income-tax lists with his annual million-dollar income. As Bob Hope once said of Mayer at one of Hollywood's perennial testimonial dinners: "Mayer came west in the early days with twenty-eight dollars, a box camera and an old lion. He built a monument to himself—the Bank of America."

Leo the Lion was the trademark of M-G-M movies when that studio was the most flourishing in Hollywood. M-G-M's slogan was "The Lion Roars." Emblazoned on every M-G-M movie were the Latin words "Ars Gratia Artis." This was a rather peculiar motto for a movie factory devoted to "art" for the sake of box office.

Mayer believed in the star system. M-G-M was known as the studio with "more stars than there are in the heavens." This was inaccurate numerically. Also, the M-G-M stars did not last as long as the celestial variety. At one time Nicholas Schenck, who was Mayer's boss, said that "there's nothing wrong with this business that a star worth $10,000 a week can't cure." This turned out to be a fatal diagnosis. The M-G-M star system often made for movies that were little more than vehicles for profiles whose expressions were limited to joy and indigestion.

Mayer also went in for four-footed as well as two-footed performers.

In less than three years after taking up horse racing in 1942 as a hobby for relaxation, he had the second best stable in the United States. "I'm going to run this stable the way I run my studio—build it on personalities," he said. In 1946, Nicholas Schenck laid down an ultimatum to Mayer to "produce horses or produce pictures."

Although, in Hope's words, "Mayer is one of the real pioneers of Hollywood. He's done more for movies than dark balconies," Mayer was never actually a maker of movies. As W. R. Wilkerson gushed in the *Hollywood Reporter* in 1951: " 'Louie' was never a picture maker, but he was and still is the maker of the men and women who did so much to bring our product up to the high plane that bounced our business up to the big ticket sales it has enjoyed. He always believed in getting the best, paying the best and giving them the best in order to come out with the best."

Mayer was an absolute czar at M-G-M. The studio was strictly run. It was hard to get in the gates and it was sometimes harder to get out. Located in drab Culver City, the studio, with its gray, grim sound stages and high walls, was sometimes compared to a penal institution (a number of prison pictures were shot right on the premises). When an actor signed an M-G-M contract years ago, a friend sent him a cake with a file in it.

In spite of its forbidding atmosphere, M-G-M was known as a citadel of screen glamour. Millions of dollars were lavished on the trappings of pictures. Often, extravagance rather than ideas prevailed. The ballroom in *Marie Antoinette*, for instance, was advertised as being considerably larger than the one at Versailles. This led *Time* Magazine to observe: "Historians may cavil at *Marie Antoinette* for ignoring facts whenever convenient, but ordinary cinemaddicts are likely to guess instead that the picture is far superior to the revolution from which it was derived, and that, if there are any disparities between them, they can be charged off to the latter as the mishaps of a dress rehearsal." This sort of thing helped finish off M-G-M movies in due course.

Mayer was a highly emotional man with histrionic abilities. He was sometimes called Lionel Barrymore Mayer. When it came to talking an actor or actress into a contract, Mayer could turn on more emotions than an Academy Award winner. He was known to plead, importune, threaten, advise and otherwise register every possible emotion during a business conference and, after achieving what he was after, to register still another emotion—crass contentment.

Although Mayer did not lead a precisely Spartan existence, he prided himself on his ability to commune with the common man. "The audience won't understand it," he said of one picture. "I don't understand it." In an editorial obituary, the Los Angeles *Times* hailed him for his "particular talent. That talent was an understanding of the so-called average man's yearning to look at life as he could never hope to live it."

Mayer's associates claimed that he had an instinctive comprehension of what was right or wrong in a movie. When a preview audience failed to laugh at a comedy scene in an Andy Hardy movie in which Andy, after a spat with his girl, refused to eat dinner, Mayer called in Carey Wilson, the producer, and instructed him to retake the sequence.

"No boy," pontificated Mayer, according to Wilson, "no matter what the reason, would say to his mother that a dinner is no good. The audience resents such a thing."

The sequence was assertedly filmed again, without the offending line, and the audience is said to have eaten it up.

After Mayer's death in 1957 at the age of seventy-two, the *Hollywood Reporter* reverently noted, "He was Mr. Motion Picture. He could drive home a deal involving millions, drop to his knees to show Andy Hardy how to pray for his mother, all in the same afternoon." And one of Mayer's associates solemnly told me after his death: "He revered the sanctity of the home, love of marriage and mother. He didn't believe in perverts, Communism and excessively problem-type pictures."

But a writer who had worked at M-G-M for many years once put it otherwise: "I'd rather have TB then L.B."

Mayer was a vengeful man. He never forgave Dore Schary, who succeeded him as M-G-M production boss, when Nicholas Schenck fired Mayer in 1951 after he had been with the studio for twenty-seven years. Of Joseph Vogel, who later stepped into Schenck's job, Mayer told a reporter: "Vogel is a fool. I don't think he is capable of filling the post, no more capable of it than you would be fighting the heavyweight championship."

In Hollywood, it has been observed, all a producer produces is relatives. Under the Mayer–Thalberg regime, M-G-M had its share of nepotism. Producer Jack Cummings, for instance, was Mayer's nephew. Producer Lawrence Weingarten was Irving Thalberg's brother-in-law. Douglas Shearer, head of the sound department, was the brother of Norma Shearer (Mrs. Thalberg). Clarence Brown, long one of M-G-M's leading directors, in discussing the plight of the director in Hollywood, said: "We were all right in the old days before the relatives got in as producers."

But Mayer's hold on the movie metropolis reached even beyond M-G-M. When Mayer's son-in-law (and later ex-son-in-law) David O. Selznick, who had been a producer at M-G-M, independently made *Gone with the Wind*, M-G-M distributed the picture. Since *Gone With the Wind* was the biggest box-office grosser of all time, M-G-M made a tremendous profit from the film. Another Mayer son-in-law, William Goetz, was for a while head of Twentieth Century-Fox and then of Universal-International. Since Joseph Schenck, chairman of the board of Twentieth Century-Fox, was the brother of Nicholas Schenck, president of Loew's Inc., the parent company of M-G-M, this also made for rather comfortable connections. The ramifications went even further. Spyros Skouras, president of Twentieth Century-Fox, was the brother of George Skouras, president of United Artists theaters, and of Charles Skouras, head of the Fox West Coast theater chain. It was a cozy and convenient setup all around.

But sometimes the relatives had falling-outs. Goetz and Selznick were involved in a parochial squabble because Selznick thought that Goetz's International Pictures sounded too much like his Selznick International. For a time Goetz was Mayer's favorite son-in-law. At the 1943 Academy Award dinner at the Coconut Grove, Mayer, in accepting an Oscar, occasioned raised eyebrows when he put his arm around Goetz and said; "Some day you may even be as great as I am." Hedda Hopper commented: "There was a something so naïve and fresh about that." (That was the Oscar event where two Spartan M-G-M press agents literally knelt attendance at the side of Mayer's chair throughout the entire dinner.) However, Mayer later came to think less of Goetz. This was attributed partly to the fact that the Goetzes were ardent Democrats while Mayer was a staunch Republican.

In any case, Mayer, in his will, disinherited Mrs. Edith Goetz with these words: "I make her no bequest nor to her children, nor to any other member of the Goetz family, as I have given them extremely substantial assistance during my lifetime through gifts and financial assistance to my daughter's husband, William Goetz, and through advancement of his career (as distinguished from that of my former son-in-law, David Selznick, who never requested or accepted assistance from me) in the motion picture industry."

A suggested title for a Hollywood epic was "The Son-in-Law Also Rises."

In 1950, Hollywood, already plagued by television and by architect Frank Lloyd Wright's going so far as to damn movietown swimming pools, was hit by another low blow. Warner Brothers and United States Pictures had a stockholders' suit filed against them in Los Angeles Federal Court charging "nepotism." Milton Sperling, head of United States Pictures, was the son-in-law of Harry Warner, president of Warner Brothers, which financed and distributed the United States Pictures productions. The suit demanded an airing of the profits in Sperling's company on the ground that the Sperling earnings were the property of Warner stockholders.

The year before that another stockholder suit against Warners, which was still pending, charged Harry Warner with "conspiracy to enrich his son-in-law."

At the time, son-in-law Sperling dismissed the suit with these words to me: "Nepotism is an ugly word. It stopped annoying me a long time ago. It's just like death and taxes. This is one of the hazards of being in this business."

Producer Jerry Wald commented: "If this sort of thing keeps up, the son-in-law business in Hollywood will be set back at least ten years."

The late Harry Cohn, like Louis B. Mayer and Jack Warner, studiously and wisely avoided the press. He left the publicity to his underlings. Cohn undoubtedly felt that he had too much to lose in an encounter with journalists. I had a rare interview with Cohn and he saw me, as representative of *Time*, not for himself but because the magazine was doing a cover story about Kim Novak, one of his stars at Columbia, with whom he was then at odds over salary. Cohn wanted to get in a few digs at Novak.

I was ushered into Cohn's office through a labyrinth of outer offices, most of them populated by snotty secretaries of the male persuasion. I was accompanied by Al Horwits, publicity director of Columbia, who had a slightly green, apprehensive look on his face. A buzzer sounded. A door swung open and I was in Cohn's mammoth office. Present was Lillian Burns, wife of George Sidney, then a favorite producer-director of Cohn's. Throughout the interview session Horwits maintained a strict silence. Miss Burns's dialogue consisted almost entirely of the phrase "Yes, boss." The scene seemed to be something out of an old George Abbott farce.

Cohn, a bald, beefy gent who had been a piano player in nickelodeons and who was then one of the last of the Hollywood tycoons, liked to cast himself in the role of a professional ogre. Actually, Cohn was a rather refreshing exhibit in the Hollywood zoo. His cage had a large sign on it plainly reading "Monster." He worked overtime at convincing the world what a mean, gruesome character he was. "If you print anything good about me, nobody will believe it anyway," he said. Undoubtedly, Cohn was monstrous. But his evil was forthright and quite exhilarating in a community where hypocrites are as numerous as starlets and where some of the foremost glorified gangsters have set themselves up as Albert Schweitzers.

Ben Hecht once dubbed Cohn "White Fang." When I saw him, Cohn, looking like the grandfather of Cro-Magnon man, was sitting in an oversized black leather chair enthroned behind a huge desk that had everything but a pinball machine built into it. Behind him loomed augustly two banks of gold-plated Academy Award statuettes that his pictures had won down the years. Cohn punctuated his dialogue with an oversized riding crop with which, from time to time, he beat the top of his desk. This riding crop, according to horse lovers, was too big to use on a horse. There was nothing, however, to prevent it from being used on human beings.

After some pungent remarks about the ingratitude of Kim Novak, Cohn sat back and began to reminisce. He told a story about his meeting with Mussolini. In 1933 Cohn had released a documentary feature, *Mussolini Speaks*, and while he was visiting Italy on a vacation trip a meeting was arranged between him and Il Duce. As Cohn described it, he entered a vast office (apparently not unlike Cohn's office) and, after walking a long distance, reached Mussolini's desk. Mussolini was comfortably seated, but there was no other chair in sight. Cohn had to stand. At this point in the story, Cohn looked at me and I had the feeling that he resented my sitting there while he was talking. After an exchange of conversation between Mussolini and Cohn, Mussolini got up, a door at one side of Mussolini's office opened without human help, and the meeting was over.

"The son of a bitch must have had a pedal under his desk," Cohn said, slamming the top of his desk with his riding crop.

At this point Cohn stood up and bade me goodbye. A door suddenly opened at one side of his office without human help. And I was back in the outside world.

Producer Alex Gottlieb told how he once went to work for Cohn. At first Gottlieb turned down Cohn's offer of a job. "Everyone says you are a son of a bitch," Gottlieb told him frankly. "That ain't so," Cohn assured him. "You'll see. Anything you want you can have. You'll get A-1 treatment. You won't have to worry about a thing.

You'll be responsible only to me and everything will be just the way you want it."

A contract was finally signed with all the stipulations Gottlieb demanded. Cohn pressed a buzzer and called in his number-one assistant. "Gottlieb is new here," he said. "I want him to have the best. See that he gets anything he wants."

Cohn's assistant took Gottlieb to his new office and asked him if it met with his approval. Gottlieb thought it was fine. Then the assistant said, "And you'll share a secretary with the producer next door." Gottlieb said that he needed a full-time secretary. Cohn's henchman told him that he could not do anything about it, that this was the way things had been arranged. Gottlieb protested, but to no avail.

An hour or so later, Gottlieb entered the executive dining room at Columbia for lunch. Cohn was already there with a retinue of yes-men. Cohn looked up, saw Gottlieb and shook his fist at him. "Troublemaker!" he shouted.

Within a week, Cohn had Gottlieb practically swabbing the latrines. Gottlieb never made a movie for Cohn. The contract was settled not long afterward and Gottlieb left Columbia, paid off in full on his agreement. Gottlieb thinks that Cohn just wanted to get him into the studio and teach him a lesson for calling him a son of a bitch and that money was immaterial.

In 1946 director Charles Vidor sued Cohn in an unusual legal action. In trying to break his $2,500 a week contract at Columbia, Vidor charged that Cohn had used vile and obscene language and insulted and humiliated him to the point where he became ill and had to consult a doctor. All sorts of Hollywood figures testified at the trial, which made headlines for a week.

In dismissing the case, after studying 900 pages of court transcript, Federal Judge Ben Harrison commented that both Vidor and Cohn "inhabit a fictitious, fabulous, topsy-turvy temperamental world that is peculiar to their own way of life.... Such language was a part of Mr. Cohn's speaking vocabulary, used by him as superlative adjectives, and not intended by him as insulting. Mr. Vidor knew the kind of language he and others in the employ of the defendant would have to encounter."

Cohn died in 1958. Funeral services were held on a sound stage at Columbia, with a crowd of 1,300 in attendance. Current at the time was a cruel, typically Hollywood wisecrack: "This proves that people will turn out for something they really want to see."

And still Cohn may not have been quite the monster he and others claimed he was. He had no intellectual pretensions. And at his studio such directors as Frank Capra, Rouben Mamoulian, Fred Zinnemann and others found that they were able to function without too much interference. Cohn, as an ex-nickelodeon piano thumper, probably had more respect for the creative artists than a lot of egghead pseudo-artists did. He did not have any particular illusions that he could make the movies.

Among Hollywood's producers Samuel Goldwyn is today the veteran, in many ways the toughest and the trickiest, and a wily infighter who has survived all his competitors. Tall, slim, erect, packed with anecdotal charm and foxy shrewdness, Goldwyn has today cast himself in the role of Hollywood's elder statesman, a sort of bald-headed Barney Baruch.

Goldwyn is renowned for his Goldwynisms, but he no longer likes to have them publicized. He pooh-poohs Alva Johnston's book *The Great Goldwyn*, which retails many of these malapropisms, as being inaccurate, and he has reportedly tried to buy up all the copies of his 1923 autobiography, *Behind the Screen*, as not being in character with the present-day legend of the avuncular Goldwyn.

Goldwyn claims that the Goldwynisms are the inventions of columnists, and says, "Some of them were very good and I wish I could take credit for them." And still I have personally heard him utter some rather choice ones. Speaking of the old days, he once said, "We have passed a lot of water since then."

Had Goldwyn not been a producer, he would have made probably Hollywood's greatest press agent. In a town full of press agents (some of the best of whom have sweated it out for Goldwyn) he is his own best press agent. Goldwyn's contacts with the press are primarily, and calculatedly, on the influential-publisher level—a fact known, and respected, by most reporters. Goldwyn has been known to arrive in New York and be met at the plane by New York *Times* cityside reporters who are usually assigned to cover straight news and not show-business events (New York *Times* publisher Arthur Sulzberger is a close friend of Goldwyn's).

Goldwyn can be controversial, and his controversial statements are usually well timed to coincide with the release of his latest production, thereby making for publicity for the picture. Goldwyn says: "People say that whenever I have a picture coming out I always start a controversy about something that gets into the papers. Well, in all sincerity, I want to assure you that as a general proposition—there's not a single word of untruth in that."

Goldwyn's name was originally Goldfish. The "wyn" was borrowed from producers Arch and Edgar Selwyn with whom he went into business in 1916 and combined the names to call the outfit Goldwyn. Two years later the company was bankrupt and Goldfish had legally changed his name to Goldwyn. The Selwyns later told him: "You not only broke us, but took half of our good name as well."

If Samuel Goldfish had not changed his name to Goldwyn, Metro-Goldwyn-Mayer might today be known as Metro-Goldfish-Mayer, which would be rather dissonant. At the time M-G-M was formed in 1924 by a merger of the facilities and manpower of the Metro, Samuel Goldwyn and Louis B. Mayer studios, Goldwyn had no interest in the new-founded film plant (he had sold out his own studio two years earlier). Goldwyn went on to make pictures independently under his own name as Goldwyn Productions. The new owners of the Goldwyn studio sued to prevent him from calling himself Goldwyn, and a compromise was reached when the producer agreed to label his films "Samuel Goldwyn Presents." Later, it was reported that negotiations for Goldwyn to join M-G-M fell through, one of the reasons supposedly being the producer's insistence on changing the name of the studio from Metro-Goldwyn-Mayer to Metro-Goldwyn-Mayer and Goldwyn.

Goldwyn is the center and showpiece of any picture he produces, and he always steals his own shows. When Goldwyn embarks on a project, the project is all Goldwyn. When he made the movie version of *Guys and Dolls*, it became Samuel Goldwyn's *Guys and Dolls*. Abe Burrows, Frank Loesser and the others involved in the original Broadway hit were relegated to the background. Now that he has filmed *Porgy and Bess*, it is no longer Gershwin's *Porgy and Bess* but Samuel Goldwyn's *Porgy and Bess*. It would be interesting to see what would happen if Goldwyn were to film Shakespeare's *Hamlet*.

Goldwyn has no partners, no board of directors and no bank financing for his films. He puts up the money for all his own pictures. Goldwyn is Hollywood's perennial independent. "I am a lone wolf," he once said. "I am a rebel. I make a picture to please me. If it pleases me, I feel there is a good chance it will please others. But it has to please me first."

Critic Lindsay Anderson put it in other words: "There are lucky ones whose great hearts, shallow and commonplace as bedpans, beat in instinctive tune with the great heart of the public, who laugh as it likes to laugh, weep the sweet and easy tears that it likes to weep.... [Goldwyn] is blessed with that divine confidence in the rightness (moral, esthetic, commercial) of his own intuition. . . . That, I suppose, is the chief reason for his success."

At the age of 78, Goldwyn keeps in excellent physical condition. He has the best personal chef in Hollywood at his studio. He is an inveterate walker. Goldwyn is always ready for a fight. As an ex-glove salesman, he has never used kid gloves in his Hollywood battles. Goldwyn drives everybody who works for him crazy. He states his philosophy thus: "Usually when people are happy making a picture, it's a flop." Goldwyn has produced many movies, some good, some bad, depending on who the directors and writers were. William Wyler directed most of his best movies for Goldwyn, even though, or perhaps because, they fought bitterly most of the time.

Playwright Sidney Kingsley once told of Goldwyn telephoning him in New York when the producer was about to film Kingsley's play, *Dead End*. Goldwyn told Kingsley that he had certain ideas about making the movie but that William Wyler and writer Lillian Hellman disagreed with him. Goldwyn wanted to know what Kingsley thought. Kingsley replied that he had no opinion and preferred to leave the entire matter in Goldwyn's hands as a professional moviemaker.

"Goldwyn," Kingsley told me, "got pretty sore about my attitude. He thought that I should take a stand on the subject. After all, unless I disagreed with him, how would he know he was right?"

Jack Warner is the playboy of producers. As Jack Benny said: "This is a man who would rather tell a bad joke than make a good movie—and he has proved it time and again."

Warner likes to gamble. In 1958 he was seriously injured when a car he was driving on the French Riviera collided with a truck. The Hollywood wiseacres came up with "Harry Warner must have been driving the truck." (The late Harry Warner, Jack's older brother, and he were enemies, and Jack did not attend Harry's funeral.)

Warner's studio down the years has made a number of well-remembered pictures, of what used to be called the socially conscious persuasions, such as *Little Caesar, The Public Enemy, I Am a Fugitive from a Chain Gang* and *They Won't Forget*. In spite of this preoccupation with social topics, Warner sometimes found it difficult to personally orient himself in relation to the great masses. During World War II he was addressing a large gathering of studio workers, including laborers, grips and technicians, on one of the sound stages, exhorting them to greater efforts on behalf of a Red Cross drive. Since most of the studio help had already made contributions and taken salary cuts, Warner did not have any ready answer as to how they should go about making further donations. Suddenly his face lit up. "You've just gotta do something," he told the assembled studio workers. "Tighten your belts even more than you have. And, when you leave here, call your business managers immediately. They'll help you find a way."

When Warners filmed A *Midsummer Night's Dream* in 1935, this momentous (and monotonous) cultural event was commemorated with an oblong medallion with a three-quarter, bas-relief profile of Shakespeare on the left, a three-quarter, bas-relief profile of producer Max Reinhardt on the right and a full, bas-relief profile of Harry, Jack and Albert Warner in the center. Shakespeare did not even manage to get top billing. A Hollywood newspaperman's wife took such a fancy to the medallion that she occasionally wears it around her neck at movie parties. It makes a thunderous conversation piece.

Henry Blanke was one of Warner Brothers' better producers during the Thirties and Forties, with such movies as *The Story of Louis Pasteur, The Life of Emile Zola, The Adventures of Robin Hood, The Maltese Falcon* and *Treasure of the Sierra Madre*. As a result, he was signed by the studio, in 1945, to an "unprecedented," air-tight, high-priced, fifteen-year contract. But when television came along to plague Hollywood and when the studios were divesting themselves of expensive contract help, Warners was stuck with Blanke. The studio tried to get rid of him by the time-honored Hollywood tactic of assigning him inferior properties and otherwise pushing him around. But Blanke held out. The gag in Hollywood at the time was that Blanke was afraid to eat in the executive dining room at Warners for fear he'd be poisoned. After his contract had run its course, he left Warners for Paramount in 1960.

When John Huston graduated from writing to directing at Warners, it was Blanke who worked with the tyro director on his first picture, *The Maltese Falcon*. What is probably Huston's best movie, *Treasure of the Sierra Madre*, was made under Blanke's production aegis. The picture was shot on location in Mexico, and while Huston, Humphrey Bogart and the rest of the company were south of the border, Blanke ran interference at the studio. Jack Warner was not pleased with the rushes that were coming back from Mexico. He expected singing, dancing and cucaracha-type color, but instead he was getting a bunch of unshaven slobs moping around in the mountains. In one sequence that kept shooting four days, Bogart was looking for water. Warner looked at the four days of rushes at the studio and said, "If that son of a bitch doesn't find water soon, I'll go broke." Warner also wanted Bogart to live instead of die at the end of the picture. Warner kept issuing clarion communiqués to the company, but Blanke stood fast at the studio and so did Huston, with the support of Bogart, in Mexico, and they won out. The picture was acclaimed and won a number of Academy Awards, which Jack Warner graciously accepted on behalf of the studio. "Blanke," said Huston, who has little respect for producers in general, "is a wonderful professor. He was always my buffer at the studio."

Blanke thinks that movies talk too much, that although talk is part of life, it should be integrated into a picture and not be used as a convenient way out of the problems of making a movie. His sensible concept of a producer's job was well summed up in these words: "I don't really like the title 'producer.' The word is tainted with commercialism. I have nothing to do with the money side except to live up to a fixed budget. I like to think of myself as an artist with business responsibilities.

"Actually, as a producer, I am not a creator in the customary sense of the word. I am a mediator and a friendly adviser. There has to be such a person on every film. The creative people, those who direct and act and write, sometimes get too involved in the pressure of events to retain any perspective on the film as a whole. They get lost and snowed under by detail work. They need someone to weld and rivet their loose ends. I feel that even if this function of judgment and mediation isn't creative it is essential to the efficiency of the creators."

Bryan (Brynie) Foy, an earthy, fast-talking producer, who was known as "The Keeper of the B's" at Warners for many years, once filled me in on some of the tricks of manufacturing low-budget movies. Foy laid no claims to art. His policy was to keep costs down by remaking a successful picture with a few plot twists.

"I don't want to do a script better," he said. "I want to do it like it was. In the old days at Warner Brothers, I made one picture eleven times. It started off with a picture called *Tiger Shark*, a fishing story, in which Edward G. Robinson lost his arm. I followed the script of *Tiger Shark* scene for scene and made the same thing as *Lumberjack*, only this time the guy lost his leg instead of his arm. Then I made it as *Bengal Tiger*, exactly the same, scene for scene, only now he was a lion tamer with a circus and lost his arm. The writers protested that he had lost his arm in *Tiger Shark* and I told them that he may have lost his arm in *Tiger Shark* too, but he's got two arms. Later I did *Tiger Shark* over again in Africa with a big-game hunter."

The Foy films, made at small cost, usually returned big profits. But some other pictures of other producers, generally conceded to be good, did not do so well. Whenever Hollywood producers are confronted with the criticism that they do not make better movies, they are likely to reply that the public simply does not want better movies, and cite a number of outstanding pictures—some of them debatable examples—to prove their point that art is synonymous with lack of success at the box office. Among such better-then-average movies, which assertedly lost money, are frequently mentioned The Informer and The Ox-Bow Incident. I once had occasion, on behalf of Coronet Magazine, to delve into the box-office returns of The Informer. After a good deal of detective work I found out that, far from losing money, The Informer had made and was still making money in reissues, not a vast amount of money, to be sure, but enough to put it decidedly in the black.

On another occasion I had a long talk on this subject with William Goetz, who was then in charge of Twentieth Century-Fox during Darryl Zanuck's absence at the wars. Fox had recently released The Ox-Bow Incident, which was hailed by the reviewers but supposedly shunned by moviegoers. When pinned down to it, Goetz confessed that the outcries about The Ox-Bow Incident not making money were coming from those who did not want meaningful and meritorious movies to be made. The Ox-Bow Incident, Goetz told me, had made some money, again not a good deal, but sufficient for it not to be a losing proposition. Goetz also admitted that the movie would have done far better commercially if its grim story of a lynching had been embellished with more popular box-office names, if the budget had been held to a reasonable level for this sort of picture, and if the film had been more enthusiastically promoted by the studio, where it was, more or less fatalistically, dismissed in advance as a lost cause. In sum, it seemed as if just about everyone concerned actually wanted The Ox-Bow Incident to be a flop so as to bear out their contention that such movies should not be made.

Goetz later went into independent production with International Films and, to set himself up all the better for the making of meritorious movies, signed as his first contract employee a chef. He was a good chef, too, and it was too bad that he was not also in charge of Goetz's celluloid recipes, because International Films soon went out of business.

When you think of a Walt Disney cartoon you think of bunnies peeking out from behind bushes, baby elephants, rambunctious rodents, dear little deer and a host of other anthropomorphological animals. Well, as they say in Hollywood, the real is a lot different from the reel. The Walt Disney studio may be Grimm, but it is also grim. The fifty-one-acre, multi-million-dollar, modernistic, air-conditioned Disney plant in Burbank, next door to a hospital and in the shadow of Forest Lawn Cemetery, has an antiseptic atmosphere. It has been called the Donald Dachau plant. The myriad animators, illustrators and artists—some with such Disneyesque names as Ub Iwerks, Ham Luske, Amby Paliwada, Gerry Geronimi and Toby Tobelmann—labor in their various cells, toiling away at the difficult, painstakingly plodding job of bringing small drawings of mice, ducks and other such critters bouncingly to life on the big movie screens. On behalf of *Time* Magazine I once spent several months looking into Disney's operation and interviewing many of his present and former employees. I found both apathy and fear at the prison-like Disney studio. When all this thoroughly documented information was transmitted to *Time*'s editors in New York, they tabled it, after some deliberation, and ran a Walt Disney cover story in the usual, cute, Disney–Mickey Mouse tradition. *Time*'s reason for this particular disregard of the facts was that the Disney yarn was a Christmas cover—and it would not do to print the truth during the holidays.

And the truth is that the Disney studio lives under the paternalistic pall of "Walt," as he is always called. It is a one-man operation. Nothing gets done without Walt's okay. There are many talented people employed at Disney's, but they are severely limited by Walt's say-so and by his basic taste, which has accurately been described as "cornball."

Disney has hardly ever given his many talented employees credit. Disney is the only name you hear about from the hard-working Disney drumbeaters. And Disney has exploited his help economically; his studio was the scene of one of the most bitter labor strikes in Hollywood. The strike was called in 1941 because of abominably low salaries, poor working conditions, a series of layoffs and Disney's adamant refusal to sit down and negotiate with his help. About half of his thousand or so employees went on strike. Disney hated the strike and fought it bitterly. But after nine weeks he finally gave in under pressure. The Disney strike helped establish minimum wages in the low-paying animated-cartoon field, but the wounds of it have never entirely healed.

Today Disney is occupied with television production, live-action features, nature films and his highly commercialized Disneyland amusement park, more than he is with animated cartoons. Cartooning has become increasingly expensive and unprofitable. But Disney still has a great sentimental attachment to Mickey Mouse, who got him started in the business. He once instantly fired an employee for referring to Mickey Mouse as "that little——." He still does Mickey's voice once in a while. Mickey has been described as Disney's alter ego, and Disney has been called "the old mousetro."

When he is not in his office, surrounded by a mammoth collection of award statues, statuettes, medallions, scrolls and certificates which he has garnered over the years, Disney likes to putter around with his model railroad train that runs on a half-mile track around his Holmby Hills estate. He also collects miniatures and has a fancy soda fountain in his home projection room, where he likes to mix ice-cream confections.

Disney's sweet and syrupy animated-cartoon concoctions, with their cute picture-postcard style—a style that has unfortunately carried over into his True-Life nature films, which are not particularly true or lifelike—has in recent years been superseded by the more ingenious and imaginative work of United Productions of America. UPA was formed in 1943 by some of Disney's best men, headed by John Hubley, who brought a fresh and vigorous approach to the medium with the "Mr. Magoo" series and other cartoons. In the belief that animated cartoons can be aimed at adults as well as children, UPA discarded Disney's elementary pratfall gags and evolved a simplified, more creative style of animated cartooning with greater emphasis on both animation and cartooning. Disney himself has had to take recognition of UPA's achievements and his cartooning has become somewhat crisper recently. On the other hand, since John Hubley left UPA several years ago, some of the bounce has gone out of that outfit.

The recent crop of producers is not quite as colorful as the oldtimers. There is a trend toward typecasting among producers. The late E. Maurice (Buddy) Adler, for instance, who was head of Twentieth Century-Fox (where but in Hollywood would a big executive be called Buddy?), looked more like a banker than an artist. He was suavely and conservatively turned out and had distinguished-looking white hair. And since bankers, in the final analysis, are the ones who put up the money for movie producers, Adler and his ilk always got jobs, even though they often made movies that did not make money. When a banker thinks of a movie producer, he thinks of someone who looks like a banker. That is human nature.

This trend toward the polite, smooth, businesslike brand of producers was blazed by Walter Wanger in the Thirties. Wanger, a distinguished-looking Dartmouth man, stood for respectability, culture with a capital C and what has been described as "the intellectual values at the crossroads of Sunset and Vine." When Wanger spoke of Anderson, he meant Sherwood, not Bronco Billy. Wanger talked a great movie, but his pictures were largely poor. He wrote about the cinema for high-brow periodicals while he ground out mostly low-brow celluloid on which these publications would never even have bothered to comment. But Wanger was an astute press agent for himself; he had on his payroll an expert magazine writer, the late Lupton Wilkinson, who ghosted slick by-lined articles for him in a variety of publications. Hollywood legends die hard, particularly among the double domes. These eggheads are strictly square when it comes to the movies and they are notoriously the greatest fall guys for the Hollywood flacks. So firmly was the myth of Wanger, as moviedom's male Joan of Arc, established by smart publicity that it took headlines, about his shooting agent Jennings Lang in the groin on a Beverly Hills parking lot in 1951 for alienating his wife's, Joan Bennett's, affections and "breaking up my home," to shatter this imaginary image once and for all.

The Wanger torch was later carried aloft by Dore Schary, an intellectual former necktie salesman, press agent, newspaperman and scenario writer, who stepped into Louis B. Mayer's custom-lasted shoes as M-G-M boss. Schary—with the help of his wily and militant press agent, George Nichols—was publicized as a progressive and as the first writer in Hollywood history to become a movie mogul. He declared that he wanted to make movies that he and his associates could be "proud of as picture people and as human beings." Schary was well cast for the role. He had a studious expression and he wore sincere horn-rimmed glasses. He was also active in any number of do-good causes. This prompted Groucho Marx to observe, "In the old days, to see the head of M-G-M [Mayer] you had to be dressed like a jockey. Today you have to be carrying a plaque for civil service."

But although Schary talked earnestly of movies with "messages," his pictures turned out to be otherwise. Under his M-G-M regime, Leo the Lion's onetime roar dwindled to a pathetic squeak. When Schary left M-G-M he had accomplished the not negligible feat of making Louis B. Mayer look quite impressive by comparison. Schary is now writing Broadway plays and producing pictures on his own. His first independent movie, *Lonelyhearts*, a picturization of Nathanael West's *Miss Lonelyhearts*, was the subject of a devastating analysis by Dwight MacDonald in *Esquire* Magazine in 1959. After microscopically examining the novel and movie, MacDonald found that

Schary had managed to convert West's "prose poem" into "just another soap opera." He concluded that Schary's achievement was double-barreled: "no art and no box office."

Stanley Kramer and company would make a good subject for a major novelist, providing a theme that is a more complex and intellectualized *What Makes Sammy Run?* of the Hollywood Forties and Fifties. Kramer, a promotion-minded ex-film cutter, script editor and production man, went into business in 1946 on a shoestring with writer Carl Foreman and press agent George Glass. Their aim was to make "A movies on B budgets." Their first picture *So This Is New York*, in 1947, was a critical and financial failure. But their next pictures were more successful. *Champion* was a hard-hitting prize-fight picture, in a well-grooved movie mold; *Home of the Brave* was an outspoken film about the Negro problem that had, for debatable showmanship purposes, been switcherooed from a play dealing with anti-Semitism. Neither of these movies was notable, but Hollywood, quick to praise, was enthusiastic about them.

Kramer played his part well. He had a clean-cut, collegiate look and he spoke intensely and intelligently. But his partners were even better at their roles. Foreman wrote some commercial, if wordy, scripts. But, most of all, the hard-knuckled Glass did such an inspired job of promotion that the fledgling company was soon hailed as a Hollywood phenomenon and Kramer was acclaimed as a "genius." Before long Kramer began to believe Glass's publicity. As Glass said later, "I found myself in the position of a Frankenstein who had nurtured a monster."

When I first interviewed Kramer, for the New York *Times*, in 1949, a sign above his desk in his unpretentious Motion Picture Center studio office proclaimed: "Please, God, make the pictures big and the heads small." But this sentiment did not prevail for very long. In 1950, when I wrote a few paragraphs in the Los Angeles *Daily News* about the creative limitations of the producer's role in moviemaking and cited Kramer's *The Men* as an example, I received a frantic letter from Glass: "Your piece about Stan really was most unfair. In every respect he is the creative head of the company. . . . This is one producer who is creatively gifted. . . . Why, Ezra, why? It's a shabby reward to hand a man who is elevating the whole damned business." In short order, Kramer and Glass were industriously trying to get me fired at the *Daily News*.

But had Kramer really "elevated" the "whole damned business," as Glass so pithily put it? Certainly not, as the passage of time has overwhelmingly borne out. The Kramers—and the Wangers and the

Scharys—far from being saviors of the screen, could not even salvage their own movies, artistically or economically. Their pictures were a "pot of messages." They had the gift of gab, but not moviemaking; they talked a better picture than they produced. If words were all that made a movie, they might really have been the geniuses they claimed to be. Actually, they were little more than press agents with a *rozhinke* (raisin), which is an old Yiddish saying for someone who puts on airs.

The Kramers—and the Wangers and the Scharys—discovered that if you dressed up a little picture with the big publicity lie you could make it seem important. They found that you did not have to make a good picture as long as you had good press relations. Unlike their forebears—the Mayers, Warners and Cohns, who avoided the press like the plague—the Kramers, Warners and Scharys courted the press assiduously. They were first publicists, next picture makers.

The Kramers—and the Wangers and the Scharys—said and did all the "right" things; they were liberals; they were respectable; their ideas seemed fresh. They had many a theme—but it always remained a theme in search of a movie.

The Kramers—and the Wangers and the Scharys—brought politeness and little else to the movies. They may have had college degrees, but they made the same old movies Hollywood had always made—with more pretension and less know-how.

If decency and good intentions were all that is required to make a good movie, then Grandma Moses would have been the logical successor to Louis B. Mayer. Kramer, Schary and Wanger did not beat their grandmothers, they read the *Reporter* Magazine, they could discourse about Kafka and F. Scott Fitzgerald, and they were against little people being pushed around. All this was commendable, but unfortunately it did not necessarily add up to a good picture. Many an old-line moviemaker who had matriculated only in the school of hard knocks and who was an unmitigated slob physically and intellectually turned out better and more honest movies than Kramer, Schary and Wanger did. It was under Louis B. Mayer's regime that King Vidor's *The Crowd* got made; Frank Capra's *It Happened One Night* was produced at Harry Cohn's Columbia; and William Wellman made *The Public Enemy* for Jack Warner. The Kramer–Schary efforts, at their best, were never half so good.

Kramer, spurred on by his initial success, in due course became dissatisfied with being just an independent producer making a limited number of select movies. He wanted to expand his operation. In 1951 Kramer, Glass and Foreman joined forces with one of the old Hollywood robber barons, movie-theater tycoon Sam Katz, and became part of the Columbia Pictures assembly line for, in Kramer's words, "a certain degree of potential security." But Kramer's pictures at Columbia—among them *The Juggler*, *The Happy Time*, *The Fourposter* and *The 5000 Fingers of Dr. T.*—were not as warmly received by the critics as his earlier efforts had been and, to make matters worse, they lost money. After three years of his five-year contract were up, Kramer left Columbia, having made only eleven of the thirty pictures he was scheduled to produce, and leaving behind him a whopping loss to the studio at the time of six million dollars.

Kramer told me then: "In the last few years I have made many mistakes, mistakes for which I take full responsibility." He said that "my particular talents gravitate to making one picture at a time and then going out and selling it."

The old harmonious Kramer–Foreman–Glass team was also plagued with internal dissensions. Foreman and Glass felt that Kramer's ego had gotten out of hand and that he was hogging the limelight. Foreman was cited by the House Un-American Activities Committee as a former Communist and left the combine in 1951. It was Foreman who, concededly, sparkplugged the scripts of Kramer's early successes as well as that of the later *High Noon*. Rumors of a rift between Kramer and Glass began to be heard, and, with the dissolution of the Kramer Company in 1953, they went their separate ways.

Today Foreman, having been "cleared" politically in 1956, produces and writes movies in England—for Columbia Pictures. Glass co-produces pictures for Marlon Brando's company in Hollywood. And Kramer directs as well as produces movies independently. None of them has set the world—or even Hollywood—on fire. And they cordially detest one another.

Kramer's recent hortatory film *On the Beach*, which has to do with the end of the world via atomic fallout, was modestly advertised by its producer with these words: "If You Never See Another Motion Picture in Your Life You Must See *On the Beach*." Dr. Linus Pauling, Nobel Prize winner in chemistry, was quoted as commending the film with "It may be that some day we can look back and say *On the Beach* is the picture that saved the world."

However, there were contrary opinions. C. A. Lejeune in the London *Observer* deplored the picture on several counts: "First, because the authorities responsible for the fate of nations are unlikely to be moved either by the arguments of Mr. [Fred] Astaire [as a nuclear scientist] or the plight of Miss [Ava] Gardner [as a doomed playgirl].

Second, because its effect on general audiences, who know they can't do much about it anyway, is so blisteringly miserable that it reduces one to a state of feeling 'What's the good of anything? Why, nothing.'" Captain William Schazman, Connecticut state director of civil defense, charged that the movie "misleads audiences" in that it ignored the fact that defense against radioactive fallout was not only possible but relatively simple. Captain Schazman termed *On the Beach* a mythological movie" and urged that "viewers should go to their local civil defense offices and get facts instead of fiction."

Dwight MacDonald in *Esquire* called the picture "a scandal . . . it is a scandal because Stanley Kramer, who enjoys, or did till now, some reputation in serious film circles, has taken the greatest theme of our day, the destruction of all human life by radiation, and has cut it down to size, Hollywood size, which is very small indeed." MacDonald labeled the picture "slick, vulgar, sentimental, phony" and "equipped with a plot of special banality." A good deal of the film footage had to do with an amour between Ava Gardner and American submarine commander Gregory Peck, prompting one Hollywood wit to comment: "In this case, the world doesn't end with a whimper—it ends with a bang."

The story of the rise and fall of the Kramer company is one of the most striking and dramatic in movie annals. As George Glass told me in 1953 when I was interviewing him for *Time* Magazine about the Kramer company crisis: "I'm sure you'll want to take notice of it—an independent company that got as much publicity as this one, folding."

Of the "younger" group of producers, Jerry Wald is a phenomenon, purely for his energy and his ability to talk anyone to death. Wald is a sort of small human dirigible who gives off about the same amount of gassy air as a blimp. On the slightest provocation he will readily discourse on anything from Aeschylus to the atom bomb to Elvis Presley, without being particularly informed about any of these subjects. As one of the foremost pursuers of publicity in Hollywood, Wald throws up a smoke screen of words that often disguises the fact that the movies he is making are something less than he is making them out to be. To help him grind out the constant barrage of publicity words he disseminates, he has a staff of ghostwriters who keep penning pieces under his name for any and all publications.

Wald always had a facile tongue. Before coming to Hollywood he wrote a radio column for the New York *Graphic* entitled "The Walds Have Ears." When he applied for the job at the *Graphic*, the only column the paper did not have was a radio column, so Wald informed the editor that he was an expert on radio. He was told to bring in some samples of his work and if they were good enough he would get the job. Wald, needless to say, knew next to nothing about radio or about writing a column. He went up to the Columbia Broadcasting System and located a co-operative office boy, who put together some special material for him. Wald handed in four sample columns and got the job, writing a column for the *Graphic* at twelve dollars a week. The office boy, whose name was Robert Taplinger, subsequently became a ranking genius in Hollywood publicity circles.

One of the many columnists on the *Graphic* was Walter Winchell, whom Wald asked what he should do to write a good column. Winchell advised him always to take cracks at higher-ups, so Wald promptly panned Winchell's own radio show in his next column.

It was inevitable that Wald would go to Hollywood. His meteoric rise there reportedly served as the inspiration for Budd Schulberg's *What Makes Sammy Run?*, a high-tension novel about a boy wonder who becomes a radio columnist on a New York paper before he is twenty and gets ahead in Hollywood largely through sheer gall. Wald today characterizes this rumor as "silly." Schulberg himself says that "it was not entirely fair of many Hollywood people to identify Sammy with Jerry to the exclusion of at least half a dozen other possibilities."

The other main prototype mentioned for Sammy was producer-writer Norman Krasna. In 1950 Wald and Krasna went into business together. At that time I noted in my column in the *Los Angeles Daily News* that the two halves of the fictional Sammy had finally gotten together in real life. It was not a particularly felicitous or tasteful remark and I soon regretted making it. Krasna, understandably, vowed eternal vengeance. Wald just telephoned me and asked, in a slightly hurt voice, "How could you do it, Ezra? Connie is so hurt." (Connie is Wald's wife.)

Wald, it is evident, is willing to take almost any kind of punishment professionally. He has worked, at various times, for Jack Warner, Howard Hughes and Harry Cohn—and survived. Also helpful to him in his Hollywood career has been his uncanny ability to take material wherever he finds it and make use of it. As a writer he once worked with such writers as Julius and Philip Epstein and Richard Macaulay, and it was said at the time that they did most of the writing while Wald did most of the talking and took most of the credit. But these writers fell by the Hollywood wayside and Wald went onward and upward.

When I was a publicist at Warner Brothers, I had occasion to see how masterfully Wald operated. Periodically I would drop into his office. He would ask me what I knew. I would tell him. He would make notes—Wald always makes notes. These notes were then filed and cross-filed in the monumental filing system that Wald maintains. Several days later I might encounter Wald again and ask him what *he* knew (in Hollywood, everyone asks everyone else what he knows all the time, and, as a result, everyone is uninformed about everything.) Wald would then blithely rattle off the very things that I had told him a day or two ago. By now Wald had appropriated them for himself and he had no thought but that they were his. This tactic was calculated to inspire only awe and wonderment in the beholder.

The production firm of Harold Hecht, James Hill and Burt Lancaster, before its recent breakup, was a unique one on several grounds. Hecht, a small, high-strung ex-Martha Graham dancer and Hollywood agent, who is known as "the Mole," merged his talents in 1947 with Burt Lancaster, a burly and belligerent ex-circus acrobat who is still given to trotting around the UCLA track for his morning constitutional. Later they brought in Hill, a dapper former NBC page boy and TV and movie writer, as a full-fledged partner. The trio were highly athletic, going in for conferences in steam rooms and otherwise combining mental and physical gymnastics. The firm was quite successful with lavish swashbuckling movies starring Lancaster and, once in a while, with a more modest intellectual effort like *Marty* ("At last," said Hecht of the latter, "here is a story where no one gets punched in the eye"). As a result, Hecht was able to acquire a Cadillac station wagon and an El Greco, which hung above his fireplace at home. His lesser paintings, and those of which Mrs. Hecht was not enamored—such as a Matisse, a Rouault and a Corot—hung in Hecht's office, which was done in bleached, antique, Beverly Hills Oriental, of what is known as the L. B. Ming dynasty. The collecting of paintings, incidentally, is fashionable in Hollywood, where Samuel Goldwyn, Jerry Wald and William Goetz are among the many who pride themselves on their oils. Goetz, in fact, is better known for his paintings than for his movies. It sometimes appears as if some of these producers are inclined to think that still pictures are better than motion pictures.

For a time Lancaster and Hecht had a personal and professional rapport. When Hill came along, things became a little complicated.

At first Hill functioned with Hecht. Then Lancaster and Hill began to collaborate. Lancaster and Hill wanted to make *Sweet Smell of Success*, a story of a ruthless Broadway columnist and a Broadway press agent, which had been written by Ernest Lehman, an ex-publicist. Lehman had originally written the tale as a magazine short story and it so angered a real columnist and press agent that they put the finger on him on Broadway and in Hollywood with the result that he found the going tough. Lehman finally made peace with the duo, the ban was lifted and he went to work as a writer in Hollywood. After some time Lehman sold his story to Hecht-Hill-Lancaster, with himself as screenwriter.

Hecht had certain ideas about making the movie but was overruled by the combined Lancaster and Hill. I had the opportunity to fly to San Francisco with the trio, their then press agent, David Golding, and a handful of technicians, for the sneak preview of the film. After the preview, Hecht asked me, in the theater lobby, what I thought of the picture. I told him that I thought it was poor. Hecht was overjoyed. His face broke out into a wide, CinemaScope-type smile and I became his buddy. *Sweet Smell of Success* was a flop and lost a great deal of money, but Hecht was happy. He had proved his point.

On the return flight from San Francisco to Los Angeles late that night I was suddenly and rudely shaken out of a sound sleep. I was sure we were cracking up. But it was only Jim Hill. He was standing over me and laughing. "You were asleep!" he said. "Ha! ha! ha!" And he returned to his seat.

Hecht, Hill and Lancaster maintained a luxurious apartment on Wilshire Boulevard to house visiting celebrities like Sir Laurence Olivier. The apartment was decorated by Mrs. Hecht. I once had occasion to browse through the establishment. There was a Utrillo hanging in the hallway near the toilet. The ash trays and antiques all had price tags affixed to them. One ash tray, I discovered, was valued at $125. There was gold-plated dinnerware in the kitchen. An elegant Italian desk with a leather top contained only one piece of paper in the drawer, with the telephone numbers of Nate 'n' Al's delicatessen and Schwab's drugstore. A massive antique breakfront was filled with authentic leather-bound sets of the works of Sir Walter Scott and other classic authors. Almost all the books were upside down. But it is possible that some of the occupants of the apartment read them upside down.

It was at this apartment one night that I again encountered Hill, this time with Rita Hayworth, whom he later married. The apartment was then temporarily occupied by a talented photographer, Sam Shaw, who had been ferried from New York to Hollywood by Hecht-Hill-Lancaster to shoot some still pictures for them. Shaw, a bohemian fellow, was wandering around the lavish premises clad in an old terry-cloth robe and munching on some salami (from Nate 'n' Al's?) from the gold-plated dinnerware. Hill and Hayworth dropped by casually and the conversation became rather animated. Before long Hill became quite tipsy. This seemed rather odd since he had seemingly been sober when he arrived and had only one drink in the course of his stay. Hill asked Shaw and me all sorts of strange, leading questions about Hollywood and H-H-L—which one might not exactly ask when sober—and made all sorts of strange, leading remarks about Hollywood and H-H-L—which one might not exactly make when sober. But this was overlooked since he was supposedly under the influence of alcohol. However, as Hayworth and he were leaving, Hill waved goodbye from the door and, suddenly and unaccountably, winked—quite soberly—at Shaw and myself, as if to say that the whole thing was a rib, that he was not really drunk and that he had been going through a make-believe routine for good, sober, diabolical reasons of his own. After he left, Shaw and I, somewhat baffled, discussed Hill's odd behavior. We came to the conclusion that he was not drunk at all and that, under the pretense of being high, had been trying to provoke from us any lowdown, classified information we had about Hollywood and H-H-L that might prove tactically helpful to him in his business operations.

The late Mike Todd was a one-shot Hollywood phenomenon. As one producer observed: "Todd walked through stone walls" to produce his hugely successful *Around the World in 80 Days*. The bombastic Todd—originally Avrom Hirsch Goldbogen from Minneapolis— bamboozled, conned, cajoled and prodded any number of stars, from Frank Sinatra to Marlene Dietrich, to appear in bit parts, or, as he called them, "cameos," in his picture. To some he gave automobiles, to others money, to still others paintings, and to almost all of them he applied massive massages to the ego to get what he wanted. It was said that most of the profiles really appeared in the picture for the love o' Mike.

Todd was essentially a promoter and gambler ("when he gambles, he loses race tracks," a friend said of him). He was addicted to foot-long cigars, multiple telephones (he liked to call someone in Los Angeles not from Los Angeles but, say, from New York—it was more exciting that way and ran up a bigger phone bill), taking planes at the drop of a propeller (in the course of making *Around the World in 80 Days*, he said he racked up enough air miles to take him around the world eleven times), and otherwise creating a commotion. He talked fast and many of his sentences did not have predicates or follow one another in any understandable continuity. "He talks and he talks," one acquaintance said, "and you think you know what he's talking about and then you start wondering."

A typical example of Todd's sales technique was how he got Fernandel, the famed French comic, to do a bit part as a hack driver in *Around the World in 80 Days*.

"Fernandel," Todd explained, brandishing a cigar, "is the number-one French movie star. He gets fifty per cent of the profits of a picture and the largest salary in France. I wanted him and Martine Carol [then France's top female film star] for the picture. I set Fernandel on a Saturday night at his broken-down hotel in Paris and he shot Sunday morning. He doesn't speak English and I don't speak French. But that didn't matter. I bullshit my way through Europe. I'm a great faker of languages. A couple of words, if you know how to, do the trick. Fernandel later told me, 'It's better you don't speak French—you express yourself better.'

"First I found out where he lives and who knows him good who I know, Georges Lourau, head of the motion picture society of French so and so and so and so. Lourau was amused about the idea of Fernandel playing a bit. 'Impossible,' he said. 'Just get me with him,' I told him. I could see that Lourau was thinking, 'the *chutzpah* [gall] of the guy.' But he humored me. We got to see Fernandel at 4:30 P.M. Saturday. Fernandel's agent was present. First Fernandel was staggered at the nerve, the audacity of me asking him to do a bit. I said 'a cameo.' He was intrigued how a guy could come to him and ask him to play a hack driver. 'Your pictures only play art theaters in other countries,' I told him. 'You should pay me for being in this picture, but you're a nice man. I'll pay you.' When we finished our first meeting, he was happy. He would have paid me. On the set, after the take, he said, 'Hey, Mike, is okay?' I paid him a token payment. I don't remember how much.

"Martine Carol was a pushover after Fernandel. 'The leading female star in France belongs with Fernandel,' I told her. She was very flattered I asked for her."

A spectator at this scene, Kevin McClory, Todd's assistant, filled in some additional details: "Todd gave Fernandel a big cigar and told him his face would be sixty-five feet long and twenty-five feet high in the greatest picture ever made and when people saw this face they'd know they were in France. Fernandel's agent started interpreting. 'Shut up, you,' Todd told the agent. He didn't need an interpreter. He makes himself understood. His cigar is more international than Esperanto. Fernandel, by this time, was agape with astonishment and could not understand Todd's English. At this stage he was trying to find an out. He said, 'I can't get the costume in time.' Todd says, 'You're right and if only I'd had the foresight you'd be the biggest thing in the world and I'll have to get someone else.' He strikes a cigar and starts talking to me about nothing at all. Fernandel sits there with egg on his face. Finally he says, 'If you had these things, I'd play the part.' We had three suits, a makeup man and a hairdresser in the car downstairs. It was eight P.M. On the way out, Todd strikes a cigar and says, 'Where is this Martine Carol?' He got Carol that night by telling her he had Fernandel. Fernandel he had told he had Noel Coward."

But Todd, the promoter and con man, also had artistic aspirations. He wanted more than anything else to be known as an artist. He was proud of having directed several sequences of *Around the World in 80 Days*. But the picture, for all its box-office success, was essentially a circus on celluloid with little film-making finesse. When I was doing a profile of Todd for *Life* Magazine, I was at his home in the Hollywood Hills one evening browsing through some of the books on his shelves. Todd seemed ill at ease. He took a book out of my hand, put it back on the shelf and said, "These are not my books. I just rent this joint. I have my books at my place in New York." A little later I took another book off a shelf (there is nothing like reading a good book when you are with a Hollywood producer). Todd was quite unhappy. "If you want to see my books, come to New York with me," he said. A few days later we flew to New York. At his duplex Park Avenue penthouse, Todd proudly showed me his art treasures and books (which were of a higher caliber than the books in his rented Hollywood home) and I gave him a book as a gift. That did the trick. He quieted down and I hardly saw him from then on. He had won me over, culturally speaking, and no longer had any particular use for me.

Todd liked to operate solo. He put up almost the entire $6,000,000 for *Around the World in 80 Days*. "I don't like investors," he said. "I'm too arrogant a guy. I don't like guys to kibitz me. I don't like partners.

"When setting something in motion, you can't have twelve or

fifteen voices. When you break the molds of existing methods of equipment, distribution, etc., you have to be on your own.

"Show business of the future is in special attractions. The strange, the unusual, the unique. Too many of the guys are thinking in terms of the nickelodeon, and the nickelodeon is dead. Going to the movies is a premeditated crime. There will be only one theater in a town and it will be the institution of that town. And there will be fifty such theaters in top cities in the world and out of these fifty theaters grows sixty per cent of the potential take. One installation is all. Strange and unusual. If there were twelve circuses called Ringling Brothers and Barnum and Bailey, that wouldn't be good. The one thing the circus has got going for it is it's the only joint in town.

"A producer's job," Todd continued, "doesn't end with making a picture. I made a four-wall deal on the Broadway theater for the opening of the movie. I leased the whole theater. I will furnish ushers, the whole ——— thing, so I don't have to worry about guys yelling about souvenir programs during the performance. I will even see to it that the ——— toilet paper is the right color.

"The revolution is going on. I got to teach these old guys, these goddam hillbilly sons of bitches. You can't re-educate and unlearn these guys, so you gotta show them and after you show them maybe they'll be all right. Meanwhile," he said, puffing away heartily at one of his stogies, "I'll be off and running."

And Todd indubitably did give Hollywood a showmanship shot in the arm. "It's fun working for Todd," said Marlene Dietrich. "He still has the enthusiasm that has gone out of Hollywood. The atmosphere here has become like a factory, General Motors."

And David Niven, who played one of the leads in *Around the World in 80 Days*, told me: "Todd's the best thing that's happened to Hollywood. I'm so sick of dreary bankers that call themselves producers. He's a man with vision and some guts and generosity."

But Todd's bulldozing tactics did not particularly endear him to Hollywood. "The whole industry tried to screw me," he said. "They don't like showmanship." When Todd and I flew to New York, Buddy Adler, the late production head of Twentieth Century-Fox, was on the plane. When Todd wandered away from his seat, Adler said to me, "What are you doing with Todd?" I informed him that *Life* Magazine had scheduled a story about the producer. "He has gigantic gall," Adler said. "He's a tremendous gambler. He's not Hollywood, but really Broadway, and they blame Hollywood for it. This is what I thought Hollywood was like before I came out here." When *Around the*

World in 80 Days was released and became a big success, Adler and Todd's other enemies changed their tune. Today, Fox even shoots some of its pictures in Todd-AO, the wide-screen process that Todd pioneered.

On that flight Todd's independence was strikingly contrasted with Adler's subservience. Spyros Skouras, the tough old boss of Twentieth Century-Fox and one of the original lions in the movie jungle, was on the plane with Adler. Skouras treated Adler like a flunky. When the flight was about to land in New York, Adler stood up to put on his coat. "Sit down," Skouras contemptuously said to him. Adler dutifully sat down.

It has been said that one trouble with Hollywood is that the old-line monopolistic movie pioneers, who started and ran the business for years, never bothered to build up successors. They were partly afraid of anyone muscling in on their profitable territory and partly they just did not care what happened to the business after they were gone. They surrounded themselves with pimps and polo players, sons-in-laws and sycophants, yes men and guess men. When they got on in years, they appointed mild stooges. Skouras, for instance, had had all sorts of trouble with the forceful and egomaniacal Darryl Zanuck. After getting rid of Zanuck, Skouras put in as production chief the more tractable Adler, who would respectfully execute his commands like a dutiful office boy.

During the time I was with Todd, he hardly ever stopped talking, running and smoking except on one occasion when he had no alternative. We were returning to New York from Baltimore in a small private plane, just the two of us and the pilot. There was no telephone on the plane. This alone was enough to make Todd miserable. He had run out of his omnipresent cigars—he had desperately tried to get some of his brand in Baltimore but without success. And he had also, for the moment, run out of dialogue. As the tiny plane headed into the sunset with its silent passengers, I never saw a gloomier man.

Curiously enough, though, when it comes to movie tycoons, the Hollywood variety are hayseeds compared to the powerful and shrewd Shaw brothers in Singapore. Runme and Run Run Shaw are a couple of cagey Chinese peasant boys who run the largest entertainment empire in southeast Asia. They control everything from movie studios and theaters to night clubs, restaurants and amusement parks. And, not to be outdone by any upstarts in Hollywood, they have two air-conditioned Rolls-Royces apiece. Runme's are blue, Run Run's silver.

I had an unconventional interview with Runme Shaw in his Singapore office recently. Runme spoke of everything but movies. He talked about yachting, horse racing, automobiles, even television (of which there is as yet little in Asia), and what-have-you. Whenever I tried to engage him in a discussion of movies, he would dismiss it with a remark like "I don't really know much about it. I hire people and pay them well to look after my movie interests for me." This was a pleasant change of pace from the compulsive conversation about motion pictures that characterizes the film folk in Hollywood. The closest competitor to the Shaw brothers, Loke Wan Tho, head of the giant Cathay organization, who has a mere fifty or sixty million dollars, also was loath to talk about the movies. When I saw him in Singapore, the British-educated Loke discoursed at length about his hobbies of ornithology and racing Lancias and looked at me as if I had committed a social error when I mentioned motion pictures.

Carol Reed, the British director, told me how the Shaw brothers conduct business. If you want to buy something from them or sell them something, they receive you in their dignified, wood-paneled office in the three-story Shaw Chambers on Robinson Road in Singapore, where they sit at opposite sides of a gigantic desk. They listen to your sales talk without uttering a word. You are then ushered outside to wait while they confer. Presently, you are again summoned into the presence of the brothers. They simply inform you "yes," they will, or "no," they will not. That is all. There is no amplification, comment or bargaining of any kind. And you are once more ushered out. That is the end of it. This sort of razor-sharp business procedure is calculated to put the petitioner in a defensive frame of mind and make him try to bend over backward to get a "yes" out of the smart Shaws.

There are very few directors whose names mean anything to the great mass of moviegoers. Alfred Hitchcock is well publicized, largely through his television appearances, and at one time the name Frank Capra meant something on a movie marquee. But the late Cecil B. DeMille was undeniably better known than any other moviemaker and, for that matter, than most movie stars.

DeMille was a masterful publicist, and his large flamboyant shows lent themselves to publicity. His theory of moviemaking was summed up with "I will trade you forty gorgeously beautiful Hawaiian sunsets for one good sock in the jaw." DeMille's Biblical spectacles were craftily compounded of sex, sin and salvation. "DeMille," another moviemaker paid tribute to him, "has proved that God is big box office." When DeMille made *The Ten Commandments* in 1955, a press agent suggested that the advertising pitch on the movie should be "You've read the best-selling book. Now see the picture."

The critics usually thought that DeMille's movies were run of DeMille. "Nobody likes DeMille's pictures except the public," one of his staff commented. Bob Hope, at another one of those endless Hollywood testimonial events, said that "Cecil B. DeMille is indeed 'Mr. Motion Picture.' His films have brought something new to theaters. They call them customers."

The late William C. deMille, Cecil's older brother, who was a well-known playwright and movie director, spelled his name with a small "d." Cecil spelled his with a large "D." He did everything large. In his case, it could accurately be said that nothing succeeds like excess. He put on as colorful a show on the set as he did on the screen. While directing a movie he was attired in a green corduroy suit and leather riding boots and was tailed by an entourage that might have made Genghis Khan envious. There was a mike boy to see to it that a microphone materialized in front of DeMille's mouth whenever the master wanted to make an utterance. There was a chair boy to see to it that a chair was in place beneath the DeMille posterior whenever he decided to sit down. There was his assistant director. There were two script girls. There was a dialogue director. There were a couple of press agents. There was his associate producer, Henry Wilcoxon. There was his personal female aide. And there was a field secretary who followed him around, as another DeMille assistant explained, "to make notes on his innermost thoughts." It was one of Hollywood's great performances.

DeMille started making movies in 1913 in the Lasky Feature Play Company, with Samuel Goldwyn (then Goldfish) and Jesse Lasky. Of the three, Lasky was the most intellectual and cultural, a raconteur and writer of sorts, and a man of some sense and sensibility. Ironically, and undoubtedly foreseeably, he was the only one of the three who did not survive professionally. Not long before his death in 1958 he was in income-tax trouble and turned to DeMille and Goldwyn for aid, which was not forthcoming. DeMille regularly employed Lasky's son, Jesse Lasky, Jr., as a screenwriter and browbeat him mercilessly, as he did all of his employees. I am sure a Freudian could make a snap analysis from this.

DeMille was such an eminent Hollywood figure that he was cast in the role of DeMille in *Sunset Boulevard*, a movie about the movies, in 1949. Billy Wilder directed DeMille in a scene in which the director was depicted shooting a scene for his own movie, *Samson and Delilah*.

At that time, DeMille told me, "I'm lost on the other side of the camera. It's a vast unknown land which I have to explore like a boy scout. I was an actor once, you know. In the first *Squaw Man*, which I directed thirty-six years ago, I played a western croupier. Before that, the public had had a look at me as an actor on Broadway before I came out here and I decided to let the matter rest. Discretion is the better part of valor."

Billy Wilder said that "it's easy to direct DeMille. He understands the camera moves and what is needed. Of course, he had to overcome a certain, shall we say, shyness at first, but he was fine after that. He takes to direction like a fish to water."

Had DeMille offered any suggestions on how the scene should be directed?

"No," replied Wilder. "I made a deal with him that I wouldn't make any suggestions as to how he should direct *Samson and Delilah* and he would not make any suggestions on this picture."

When it was all over, DeMille stepped into a portable dressing room to recover from the ordeal of portraying Cecil B. DeMille on the screen. "It's harder to play a director than to be a real one," he said. "Sometimes it's hard to do either."

He added: "I am thinking of retaliating by casting Wilder in my next picture."

The sardonic Wilder, an Austrian-born ex-newspaperman who looks like a stoutish, balding leprechaun, has been described by his friend, William Holden, as having "a mind full of Gillette blue blades." Wilder likes to talk, and his talk, with its Teutonic flavor, is razor-keen. His pictures are not always as fine-honed. Wilder's movies are mostly sensational melodramas, like *Double Indemnity*, *Stalag 17* and *Sunset Boulevard*, or wearing japes such as *Some Like It Hot*. Sometimes, in films like *Ace in the Hole*, a picture about a ruthless reporter, his movies become what one critic described as "sub-human. . . . a vicious caricature of human nature" that leaves the moviegoer "horrified, then sick, and finally incredulous."

When Wilder is talking, he paces about nervously, striking his leg with that familiar Hollywood implement, the riding crop, and keeping his head cocked to one side. He sometimes wears a Tyrolean hat with a feather in it. It is such a dynamic rendition that William Holden has even taken to imitating it himself, except that he substituted a long Dunhill cigarette lighter for the riding crop.

But no one can quite imitate Wilder's gift of gab. When Wilder was preparing *The Spirit of St. Louis*, he spent some time with Charles

Lindbergh. Lindbergh offered to teach Wilder how to fly. Wilder declined the offer. "I can just see the headlines," he said. "'Lone Eagle and Unknown Student Pilot Killed in Crash.' I don't like the billing."

When Wilder was shooting *Sunset Boulevard*, he told cameraman John Seitz: "Johnny, keep it out of focus. I want to win the foreign-picture award."

In the same picture, Gloria Swanson was lying in bed in one scene with slashed wrists. Seitz asked Wilder what kind of camera setup he wanted. "Johnny, it's the usual slashed-wrist shot," Wilder said.

There was a dead chimpanzee in *Sunset Boulevard*. Seitz again asked Wilder about the camera setup. "Johnny, it's the usual dead-chimpanzee setup," Wilder said.

Holden traveled with Wilder through Europe for several months in 1952. They were driving through the Austrian countryside with their wives in a big Cadillac when they ran into a washed-out bridge and were forced to make a detour. They proceeded to another bridge that was little more than a cattle crossing and that looked as if it might momentarily collapse. "We're gonna drive across it," Wilder decided. "Everybody out of the car. Billy, drive very slowly." "What?" Holden said. "I'm gonna drive?" "I'm the director! You're only the actor!" Wilder commanded. And Holden drove across, with Wilder, as he said, "giving me hand signals like he's bringing in an airliner."

Wilder recently summed up his moviemaking credo this way: "What I look for is whether the idea is true and entertaining. However, if I were ever forced to make the choice I would prefer that it be entertaining."

Among current directors, John Huston is one of the most conspicuously individualistic. Publicity comes to him easiest of all the directors—he is really a character. A tall, lean, gangling man, he likes to wear outlandish outfits, such as resplendently tailored blue denims, riding boots and a Shetland cap surmounting his small, bony, bespectacled face. Huston has been known to fly to remote movie locations with hundreds of pounds of excess wardrobe baggage. During the making of *Roots of Heaven* in the wilds of Africa and in France, members of the company were laying bets as to whether Huston would sport the same costume twice in the course of production. After almost six months of shooting, he had not repeated an outfit, in spite of the fact that the unit had been in highly uncomfortable and difficult locations much of the time. Huston was always fastidiously and fantastically turned out in a different getup daily.

A former reporter, boxer, actor, professional soldier and movie writer, Huston prefers to work away from Hollywood and to shoot his movies in all kinds of exotic locations. He makes his headquarters in a remodeled Irish castle, but he is rarely there. He has made movies in France, Italy, Mexico, Japan and Africa. No matter how rigorous the locations, Huston rarely gets ill, even when the rest of the company is laid up. He attributes this to a diet consisting of a minimum of solid food and a maximum of alcohol.

Huston is a restless sort. Two thirds of the way through a picture, he is likely to lose interest in it and start planning his next project. He is sometimes affectionately called "the monster" by his friends. Humphrey Bogart said that when Huston became bored he often took on a frightening resemblance to an ape or monkey. Once, Bogart recalled, Huston was sitting in the executive dining room at Warner Brothers in the company of other high-priced studio employees listening to Harry Warner expound on the international film situation. "Warner talked on and on," said Bogart, "and Huston's face gradually got to be just like an ape's, with his mouth wide open, as he sat there and listened."

Huston plays as hard as he works. Bogart and Huston once engaged in a football game at Huston's home in Tarzana, California, against movie executive Collier Young and writer Charles Grayson. The game was played in the mud, with a grapefruit and with Henry Blanke refereeing. Everyone was wearing tuxedos. The spirit of competition became so keen that two of Young's ribs were fractured, and Ida Lupino, who had decided to get into the proceedings, had her sacroiliac thrown out of joint.

Huston is also a confirmed practical joker. During World War II he mastered the art of hypnosis and he liked to put distinguished film folk into a trance. At a Hollywood party he hypnotized William Goetz and had him crowing like a rooster.

During World War II Huston enlisted in the Army while he was directing *Across the Pacific*, a melodrama with Bogart, Sidney Greenstreet and Peter Lorre. While he was still engaged in shooting the picture, he received an urgent communication from Washington, D.C., to report for duty the following day. The movie sequence he was filming at the time found Bogart trapped in a room, surrounded by hostile Japanese. Huston kept shooting this scene until late that night. He added extra guards and booby traps to the sequence and made sure, before leaving the studio, that Bogart was in a thoroughly impossible predicament. Director Vincent Sherman, called in to complete the picture the next day, looked at what Huston had already shot and exclaimed, "How the hell are we going to get Bogey out of here?" Production was suspended for two days while Sherman and a corps of writers tried to devise a way to extricate Bogart from the dilemma in which Huston had placed him. It was finally decided that someone in the room should go berserk and start shooting and that Bogart should escape in the ensuing confusion. "I'm not easily trapped, you know," Bogart observed.

Prior to departing for the wars, Huston had also been working on the script of another Warner thriller, *Background to Danger*, for George Raft. Several weeks after entering the service, Huston was passing through Hollywood and attended a script conference on *Background to Danger* with the producer, director and Raft. Raft, who had in the past been known to refuse to die in a picture and even to smoke a cigarette on the screen on the grounds that his film fans might not think him a wholly admirable and clean-cut chap, was insisting that his role in *Background to Danger*, as a U.S. government agent, be built up and that a scene be written into the movie showing the President of the United States personally thanking him for the job he was doing. Huston, sitting at the conference in his uniform, with his long legs propped up on a desk, his cap pushed back on his head, sketching and listening (he likes to sketch people during conversations), finally stood up, yawned, adjusted his cap and said, "Gentlemen, I am going to the Aleutians" and walked out.

The result of Huston's trip to the Aleutians was the first of his war documentaries, *Report from the Aleutians*, shot in that remote Northern combat zone. It was followed by the moving *San Pietro*, about the taking of one portion of the Liri Valley in Italy by Allied infantry. Perhaps the most powerful of Huston's wartime films was *Let There Be Light*, dealing with emotionally disturbed war veterans. Shot at Mason General Hospital in Long Island in 1946, it had some gripping sequences of "casualties of the spirit" undergoing treatment through hypnosis and narcosynthesis. Since the entire picture was filmed with real soldiers, it was never publicly released because of its invasion of privacy, although the U. S. Army Signal Corps later re-made it for public consumption under the title of *Shades of Gray*, with professional performers re-enacting the scenes from the original film.

Huston screened the classified *Let There Be Light* for me at his home one night and told me something about its filming. As many as three concealed cameras were used simultaneously to photograph patients reliving their battle experiences during psychiatric treatment. The results on the screen were often harrowing. One soldier, who stuttered badly, began to speak without impediment under narcosynthesis and became almost hysterical with joy when he found he had regained his power of speech. "Oh, God," he cried out repeatedly, "I can talk! Oh, God, listen, I can talk!" It was found that he stuttered because of the "s" sound a German high explosive shell made before it blew up near him. Other cases, involving men who had lost the power of walking and of talking entirely, were just as emotionally intense. Walter Huston, who narrated the commentary, commented on these scenes: "All actors should see them to see what acting can be."

Huston, like William Wyler, George Stevens, John Ford and Frank Capra, did some of his best movie work during the war away from the make-believe of the Hollywood studios. But he refused to take credit for these films. "I didn't make these pictures," he said. "I just put them together. The men who appear in them deserve the real credit."

Huston's best Hollywood movie was *Treasure of the Sierra Madre*, for which he and his father, the late Walter Huston, won Awards in 1949, as best director and best supporting actor. Shortly after the Oscars, I had a singular interview with father and son in a room at the Beverly Wilshire hotel. John Huston, who was once described as "a towering caricature of his father," said that "there was nothing coincidental about our getting the awards the same night. Someone said to me the morning after: 'Your father's performance made it the best writing job of the year and the best direction.' " Walter Huston commented that John "is the best director I ever worked for," and he added that his ambition was "to be known as John Huston's father."

Being as colorful as he is, it is apparently not absolutely necessary for Huston also to make colorful movies to sustain his reputation. The way Hollywood seems to look at it, it is mostly just enough that he is John Huston. And a number of Huston's movies, it is true, have failed to live up to their maker. One sometimes get the impression that Huston is more interested in just plain living and in living it up than in making movies and that his directing films is little more than an excuse to go places and have a rousing time in various parts of the world. Huston sometimes seems to cool on his own pictures before they are completed. And he is often not around for the vital editing of a film. He is usually off to some new cinematic adventure.

George Stevens is something of a riddle among directors. In terms of publicistically maneuvered prestige, he probably ranks near the peak of today's Hollywood moviemakers. Whether his repute is justified is thoroughly debatable.

A large, rugged, slow-spoken man, Stevens started out in silent movies as a cameraman. He photographed many Laurel and Hardy comedies for director Leo McCarey. He is one of the few cameramen who became directors (some others: Rudolph Mate, Ted Tetzlaff, the late Victor Fleming and George Hill).

As a former cameraman, Stevens is preoccupied with the technical end of a movie. He is a painstaking technician. He shoots endless thousands of feet of film and then spends months putting his picture together in the cutting room. Like most cameramen, who see things visually instead of verbally, Stevens is not easy to interview. Not a glib talker, he articulates his thoughts in rather involved fashion that is often more ponderous than profound. But he does have some fairly reasonable things to say about movies and moviemaking:

"I do believe that a movie serves its purpose well if you do not hear the sound track and are still well aware of the cause and effect of a story. . . .

"I shoot lots of angles on every scene. I have never yet seen a scene where the camera explored it as fully as it might, as a careful observer might. The camera has its limitations. It has one eye and no perspective. It has to grope around to observe, to see as much as it should. . . .

"In a general manner, I have the final editing of the picture in mind while I am shooting. I like to shoot a great deal of film so that I can play around with it in the editing.

"To get a given part of a scene at gamma in a particular closeup, you have to do a greater part of the scene over. You can't pick up the scene at one point. Excess film is no real expense. You figure against time and you find that film is something with which you charge and retain indefinite values that you pay much for.

"All you get from $2000 an hour is what you get on film. When the camera is whirring, you're mining your vein. When it isn't whirring —nothing.

"Today this whole movie thing is governed so much by economics, expenditures, and it is becoming more and more so. That is one reason why there is a terrific struggle between film that moves as a movie— an expensive mosaic of many shots—instead of a camera on a boom and talk it out for fifteen minutes."

In Hollywood's earlier, more carefree years, a director was often free to improvise on the set. This frequently made for exciting, off-the-camera-cuff results. "That technique," says Stevens, "verges on the impossible today because of the economic aspects of the business. In the old days, it was so simple. We just moved a camera, not the

Missouri, like today when you have to change a set. Then it took five to ten minutes to shift the camera. Now it takes one and one half hours or more."

Stevens shoots on the average of one picture every two or three years and he likes to take plenty of time to make his mosaic-like movies. Since time equals money, this has not endeared him to the studio financiers. Normally a dignified, soft-spoken man, Stevens can be a tough taskmaster on the set. I once saw him give a brisk dressing-down to child actor Brandon de Wilde, who was getting out of hand during the filming of *Shane*. As a producer-director, Stevens is also a fierce individualist. He will brook no interference while working. He had frequent fights with Y. Frank Freeman, head of Paramount, while working at that studio. At Columbia, he reportedly had it written into his contract that Harry Cohn was not to talk to him while he was making a movie.

Stevens says of the major studios: "I don't think the big companies see a motion picture for what it's worth. They see it only in terms of product. They don't consider what an attraction can be or should be, but keep looking for assurances of having seen it before. That alone eliminates the possibilities of a picture being interesting."

Recently, through his industrious publicity agents, Stevens has presumed to assume to himself the mantle of D. W. Griffith. He received the D. W. Griffith Award of the Directors Guild of America in 1960 for "outstanding directorial achievement." In bestowing this honor upon him, director George Sidney solemnly said of Stevens: "His initials reversed are SG—Screen Greatness." But the mantle of Griffith is a little large for Stevens, and none of his movies has evinced any particular "screen greatness."

As an ex-cameraman, Stevens knows how to get the right lens focus, but his characters and themes are often blurred. *Shane*, for all its surface sheen, was simply a big, glorified western. *A Place in the Sun* omitted the real tragic core of Theodore Dreiser's *An American Tragedy*. *Giant* was a diffuse, sprawling film that suffered from dramatic elephantiasis. And the recent *The Diary of Anne Frank* was a pretentiously plodding, offensively soft-focus film without any real cinematic technique or inner or outer reality. Stevens managed to turn a proven international stage success into a faltering Hollywood film and, in so doing, to accomplish what the murderers of Anne Frank had never been able to do—to destroy the spiritual testament she left behind her. The picture was a critical and commercial flop. Stevens arrogantly explained it with "They [the moviegoers] didn't want the experience." Or, at least, they didn't want the experience as Stevens dished it up to them.

Henry King's career has spanned almost the entire history of the screen. He was a leading man in early silents. Today, in his seventies, he is a tall, white-haired, good-looking man who is known as "the flying director" because he likes to scout movie locations in his own plane, which he pilots himself.

A modest, easygoing man, King is mainly interested in making movies and not in publicizing himself. As a result, he is not as well known as he might be. Among his pictures have been some smooth, rather undistinguished, commercial jobs: *In Old Chicago, Alexander's Ragtime Band, The Song of Bernadette* and *Twelve O'Clock High*. He also directed the silent *Stella Dallas, Romola* and *The White Sister*. His earthily lyrical *Tol'able David* of 1921, with Richard Barthelmess, is one of the finest films ever made in Hollywood, and *The Gunfighter*, with Gregory Peck, one of the best westerns.

In 1951, when I flew with King to Reno, where he was getting a Silver Spurs award for *The Gunfighter*, he told me that he still works at his craft just as he did many years ago. "I do all my preparation myself," he said. "In the old days, when I had my own company and was in business for myself, I was production manager, producer, head of the scenario department, director, just about everything. Today, at Twentieth Century-Fox, I have more equipment and more departments than I can call upon. The studio gives the director everything he can use. But I still work as I did in the old days—only I have more help."

King defined the producer's job as "executive work—reading and finding stories and passing opinions." As director, "every scene and every word in the story pass through my mind. I don't write the scenario myself, but it has to be adapted to the screen. No matter how good a script is, I usually have to adapt the script and get it in the camera groove.

"I believe that we are in the motion-picture business, not in the radio or theater. Motion pictures are founded on the basis of pictures. I try to tell a story in action rather than words, to eliminate everything in the script that can be told without words.

"You can't make motion pictures by making two people stand up and talk. That's just lack of ability, of know-how.

"You see, in pictures there's no use, if you can tell a thing with the camera, to do it with talk. I try to make the camera talk. The camera will tell the story with as few words as possible—that's the right medium of motion pictures."

And, King added, "I follow through on the cutting of a picture to the very end. A motion picture without cutting is like a writer without vocabulary. Your thought and your story can go astray in cutting by improper assembly."

After all these years, King thinks that the movies are "still a new and exciting business with a tremendous future. It is still a business of exciting possibilities, of challenge."

Some of veteran William Wellman's movies are *Wings, The Public Enemy, A Star is Born, Nothing Sacred* and *The Ox-Bow Incident,* an impressive inventory. Wellman is as flinty as his films. He is often called Wild Bill or Wild Willie. A lean, wiry man with rumpled, steel-gray hair, a thin mustache and a boyishly satanic expression, he is one of the last of the breed of individualistic directors harking back to the days before industry and respectability took over in Hollywood. His specialty is the fast-moving movie with muscle that Hollywood can occasionally do so well—and attractively.

Wellman has said of himself: "I'm a son of a bitch." He is tough on actors. "I like to keep them guessing," he says. "Never tell them anything." He addresses profiles as "Mr. Barrymore" and "Handsome." He peers through the camera finder at an actor, summons the cinematographer ("Rembrandt") and, shaking his head sadly, tells him to "look at that face." His approach is not always verbal. He has, at times, applied the pointed end of any handy object to the posteriors of performers, making them snap to attention—and, presumably, alerting them artistically. He once shot a gun at one of his assistant directors who had displeased him. Wellman missed, but no one is sure if it was intentional. He barred the producer of one of his pictures from the set. While the mogul fumed, Wellman explained that "after all, if you're the director, you've got to direct. You've got to be the boss. I'll make my own mistakes, not somebody else's."

"My contention has always been," said Wellman, "get a director and a writer together and let them alone. That's how the best pictures get made."

Like director John Ford, who had to battle to make *The Informer,* Wellman had to fight to film some of his better pictures, such as *The Ox-Bow Incident.* As King Vidor once told me: "You've got to take assignments sometimes to keep a commercial aura about your name so you can get the money for the things you want to do."

Wellman purchased the screen rights to *The Ox-Bow Incident* from another producer for $6,500 and peddled the property all over Hollywood. It was rejected by most every studio as not having sufficient box-office potential. In desperation, Wellman submitted the story to Darryl Zanuck at Twentieth Century-Fox. Zanuck and he were not talking to each other then as a result of one of their recurrent spats. Zanuck, though, agreed to make the picture if Wellman would, in turn, direct any two pictures he was handed by the studio. Wellman directed a couple of highly unmemorable productions for Zanuck, and that is how the more memorable *The Ox-Bow Incident* reached the screen.

Wellman co-authored the original story of *A Star Is Born*, starring Fredric March and Janet Gaynor, one of the best movies about Hollywood. The picture won an Academy Award for its screenplay in 1937. Wellman said that most of the material in that movie "was just a job of remembering things that have happened in the years I have been in Hollywood."

Wellman, no man to mince words, thinks that there are too many kibitzers in pictures today. "Stars are my pet peeve," he complained. "You can't get stars. They know too much about stories, or so they think. If they know as much as they do, I don't know why we have so many lousy pictures. Their agents don't help either, those————. They just sit around and count the money.

"Too many people rewrite pictures at the big studios. Suddenly whatever was going to get on the screen is gone. Someone has to be in control. In the big studios you have to be a soothsayer, magician and director and you have to know whose behind to kiss."

Wellman had a particularly unfortunate experience with Dore Schary when that producer was in charge of M-G-M. Wellman directed two of Schary's personal projects, *Battleground* and *The Next Voice You Hear*. When the smoke of the critics' blasts had cleared, the hard-boiled director, by now thoroughly disenchanted, observed of the egghead producer: "Schary gives the quietest and wickedest goose in town."

In the early Fifties, when I profiled Wellman for *Esquire*, he declared that "there are only twelve or so directors in Hollywood today who have control of their pictures—William Wyler, Billy Wilder, George Stevens, John Ford, Alfred Hitchcock, John Huston, Cecil B. DeMille, Elia Kazan, Howard Hawks. These are the guys responsible for seventy-five per cent of the good pictures. They make their own pictures and that's the way it is. They're the guys who yell 'camera' and 'cut.'"

Michael Curtiz has gotten a good deal of publicity for his Curtizisms, which are another form of Goldwynism. Some of the phrases attributed to the Hungarian Curtiz, often by inventive press agents, are "This scene will make your blood curl"; "Bring on the empty horses"; "The pinochle of his career"; "Boy cows" (for "cowboys"). Curtiz invariably addressed Errol Flynn, who did some of his finest feats of filmic derring-do under Curtiz's direction, as "Earl Flint," or what sounded very close to it.

But although Curtiz may mangle the English language, his movies are usually nicely articulated on the screen. He is a camera expert who can make a movie take form and rhythm through moving camera shots, movement before the camera and ingenious camera angles. Some of Curtiz's kinetic camera effects can be seen in the atmospheric *Casablanca*; *Black Fury*, with its raw bohunk realism; the swashbuckling *The Sea Hawk* and *The Adventures of Robin Hood*; the punchy fight film *Kid Galahad*; and the bouncy musical *Yankee Doodle Dandy*.

One of Curtiz' movies, *The Charge of the Light Brigade*, which he directed for Warners in 1936 and which has been seen extensively on television in recent years, is in my opinion one of the most dynamic Hollywood films ever made. It is a straightforward and strikingly carried-off exercise in motion, culminating in the final, head-on charge, and, as such, for camerawork, cutting and over-all pace, ranks with some of the best things done in this field. The entire picture is essentially one elongated spiral of slowly but surely intensifying movement, building up to the electrifying charge at the end. *The Charge of the Light Brigade* does not pretend to be anything but an action adventure story. It is not a great human document—and how many American movies are?—but for downright technical virtuosity it would be hard to find anything to remotely equal it in the work of a Wyler, Wilder, Stevens or Huston. Curtiz was assisted in this production by action expert B. Reeves Eason and cutter George Amy (more about them later) and they managed, between them, to achieve, fortuitously perhaps, a high mark in the American action movie.

While working at Warners I spent a good deal of time with Curtiz. The hawk-nosed director, a solid-as-a-rock six-footer, was a hard-driving perfectionist. He never ate lunch, on the theory that this would slow him up. For many years he was the work horse at the studio, averaging three big, back-breaking pictures annually. He left Warners in 1953, after twenty-six years at the studio, when he refused to take a salary cut, and today free-lances as a director.

Curtiz was not able to articulate his moviemaking methods in fancy words—or, perhaps, he just did not have anything much to say. I guess he reserved his instinctive expression for the screen. However, he did make it plain that he believed in action, not words. "I don't see black and white words in script when I read it," he once said. "I see action." On another occasion, he spoke of the director's job this way: "My theory is that when we start movie sequence, it is just like unfinished canvas—here the characters, there the background—and I just mix the paints right to finish the canvas properly."

The cherubic Alfred Hitchcock is fat and slow-moving in person, but his best movie thrillers are the reverse. They are lean and muscular and they move at an accelerated clip. Unlike George Stevens, Hitchcock shoots very little film. He pre-edits his movies in the script almost down to the last frame. In effect, he cuts his pictures on paper before shooting them. A onetime art director, he makes detailed diagrams of each camera setup. Everything is planned in advance and the editing later is largely a mechanical process.

Hitchcock's best movies were made in England, before he came to Hollywood, where his moviemaking became comparatively flabby. In my estimation—and in Hitchcock's—one of his lesser known British movies, the 1936 *Sabotage* (American title: *The Woman Alone*), is undoubtedly the most crackling melodrama he ever made. This thriller, about a gang of foreign saboteurs planning to destroy London, is practically a lexicon of the grammar of the film.

Hitchcock always hitched his talent firmly not to movie stars but to the camera, and in *Sabotage*, as in many of his other films, the best performances were given not by the actors but by the camera eye. Some of the shots and camera setups in this picture are among the most inventive ones ever seen on the screen. In one sequence two saboteurs are standing before a fish tank in an aquarium. Their backs are toward the camera, their faces cannot be seen and their conversation is inaudible. Suddenly Hitchcock's camera moves forward between the two conspirators into the tank as the floating fish slowly dissolve into Piccadilly crumbling under a bomb blast. Hitchcock's camera speaks more sharply than words.

Another dramatic scene in *Sabotage* finds a young boy unwittingly carrying a time bomb to the Piccadilly underground station. The audience knows when the bomb is supposed to go off. As the boy interminably dawdles and delays en route, the suspense becomes excruciating, and Hitchcock plays it for all it is worth.

The boy, finally, is killed when the bomb explodes in a bus. When his mother hears of his death, she frantically rushes into the street. As she hysterically runs down the avenue, she sees, for one heart-wrenching, hallucinatory moment, her son running toward her among a crowd of people. Hitchcock here used a lap dissolve for overpowering effect.

Another neglected, pre-Hollywood Hitchcock film, the 1937 *Young and Innocent* (American title: *The Girl Was Young*), has to do with a young couple tracking down a killer. The only clue to the murderer's identity is that he has a nervous eye twitch. After a long and hopeless chase, the boy and girl have just about given up. They are sitting forlornly at a tea dance at a seaside hotel when, without warning, the camera pulls suddenly up and back, encompassing the entire room. The camera starts moving over the heads of the dancers, down among them, in between them, toward the dance band, in among the musicians, toward the drummer (who is in minstrel blackface) and, relentlessly, up toward the drummer's face until the man's twitching eyes fill the entire screen for a knock-out screen climax.

Hitchcock knows how to begin and end a movie. *Young and Innocent* opens with a fast, startling close shot of a man and woman murderously shouting at each other in a dark room. The next shot is that of a body being washed up on a beach.

For *The Lady Vanishes*, Hitchcock contrived a superb ending. Dame May Whitty, portraying an apparently helpless old British lady, has been given up for dead by Margaret Lockwood and Michael Redgrave. Following a tense train ride, complete with spies, shootings and other suspenseful goings-on, they arrive at the British foreign office to report what has happened. There they unaccountably find the kindly old woman, who, as it turns out, is really a British secret agent. As the doors to her office slowly open, she is seen sitting at a piano, where she has been playing a theme song around which much of the action revolved, and she graciously extends her arms to the two surprised lovers for one of the most felicitous fadeouts ever filmed.

As Hitchcock puts it, "There's too much talk in pictures. Sound is important in pictures, not talk. Sound shouldn't make the same statement as the image. They should counterpoint each other."

Hitchcock has used the sound track imaginatively in his movies. In *The 39 Steps*, a woman, on discovering a dead body, opens her mouth to scream and out comes the sound of a train whistle as the camera cuts to a speeding train. In *The Man Who Knew Too Much* a cymbal crash ingeniously blots out a dramatic pistol shot during a symphony in Albert Hall. In *Sabotage*, Hitchcock staged a murderous chase after a spy in a movie theater while a Walt Disney cartoon sound track provided a contrapuntal note with *Who Killed Cock Robin?*

Hitchcock's thrillers of the Thirties had style, to be sure. They also had something more. At the time they were made, they were often labeled far-fetched melodramas. Today, upon re-examination, these pictures about saboteurs, spies and secret agents seem to have been prophetic of headlines to come (e.g., the Teutonic enemy agents blowing up London in *Sabotage*). Several decades after they were produced, they shape up as more realistic than most other pictures of that period. Now, as Hitchcock says, the newspaper headlines have outdistanced most movie plots.

In any case, thinks Hitchcock, there is an unfortunate demand for logic in movies today. "But logic can be a handicap," he says. "We lose some of our fantasy. In *Sabotage*, for instance, we didn't know who the agents were working for. That didn't prevent the picture from being convincing. But today we want the McGuffin."

Hitchcock defines the McGuffin as "an object in any chase or spy story that is being chased or spied on or sought after, the secret plans or the formula or the secret code." What it is, actually, is a matter of supreme unimportance.

And Hitchcock, who is also a master at the art of publicity and press quotes as well as being the acknowledged master of movie thrillers, solemnly offers this story as the derivation of the word McGuffin: Two men strike up a conversation on a train. "What do you have there in that funny little package?" asks the first man. "That?" replies the second man, "Why, that's a McGuffin." "What's a McGuffin?" "A McGuffin is something you use to kill lions in the Adirondacks." "But there aren't any lions in the Adirondacks." "Oh, well, in that case, it isn't a McGuffin."

And that, says Hitchcock, just about sums up the motivational essence of every one of his movies.

Hitchcock, a believer in what he describes as "pure cinema," laments the decline of "pictorial storytelling." "The lost art of the movies" he calls it.

Perhaps the only moviemakers doing any kind of fresh work in Hollywood today are Andrew Stone, a veteran screen writer and director, and his wife, Virginia. The Stones make spry thrillers that are produced for relatively small sums but yield a goodly measure of suspense.

Among their movies are *The Night Holds Terror*, a galvanic suspense story about a gang of desperados who move into a peaceful home; *Julie,* a no less chilling thriller about a wife who takes it on the lam from her psychotically murderous husband; *Cry Terror!* a headlong hair-raiser about a maniacal blackmailer; and *The Last Voyage,* a clangorous melodrama about a fire on a giant ocean liner.

All the Stone movies have highly ingenious, ultra-melodramatic plot twists and are made for relatively small budgets, particularly in these days of outsize epics (*The Night Holds Terror* cost only $75,000, *Julie* $300,000 and the spectacular *The Last Voyage* around $1,000,000 —the latter much less than it would normally have cost). The Stones shoot their pictures, sound and all, hot off the camera in actual locations (there is not one studio shot in any of them). They have no studio headquarters and cut their movies in their home. Instead of employing a highly departmentalized staff, they do most of the work themselves. Virginia Stone doubles as cutter and script girl. Andrew is producer, director and writer. They use a minimum of technical equipment.

Although the Stones deal in the most arrant kind of movie melodrama, there is nothing errant about their moviemaking. Their pictures have much of the vivid, on-the-spot effect of the primitive early silent films. They are a throwback to the lively, individualistic, old-time moviemaking of pie in the sky and camera smack in the eye. Shot mostly in black and white and on fairly standard-size screen, all scenes are filmed in actual, untouched-up settings (a police station, confined apartment, an airplane, an ocean liner, etc.). The technical results are often crude but always excitingly credible. There is bold, slashing cutting and drum-tight continuity. The Stones have gone back to the primer principles of moviemaking and, as a result, their pictures are all the better for it. They are among the very few moviemakers in Hollywood who are working with the tools of the trade. There is nothing involved or intellectualized about the Stones. They are simply solid craftsmen in a field where the elementary principles of film-making have been too long forgotten. Their thrillers are unique and acutely sustained suspense dramas, and they themselves are a couple of jack-in-the-box motion-picture producers who assuredly gather no movie moss.

When you go out to talk to a moviemaker, you never know exactly what you will come away with. Perhaps my most unorthodox interview with a movie director was with Mervyn LeRoy, who has made such pictures as *Little Caesar, I Am a Fugitive from a Chain Gang* and *They Won't Forget.* At the time I sought him out, he was preparing *The Robe* at RKO (another director finally made it at another studio). LeRoy received me in his resplendent office. He apologetically explained that he had a bad cold and had to go to the doctor and would I mind coming along with him? We drove off in a long, chauffeured limousine. LeRoy was worried about his health. There had been a few fatalities among movie tycoons recently, and whenever that happens scores of Hollywood hypochondriacs rush to their doctors.

I made a few attempts en route to discuss *The Robe* with LeRoy, but finally gave up and just listened to his strictures on his physical condition. Before long, as LeRoy discoursed eloquently on his health, I even began to think of doing an article about him for the *Medical Journal*. "And how do you feel?" he asked me after a while. "Okay," I said. "Have you had a checkup lately?" he asked. He inquired what pills, if any, I was taking and recommended some to me for any nonexistent affliction I might have. When we reached the doctor's office, LeRoy urged me to come in and join him and have a medical going-over as his guest. I politely declined. By the time we left the doctor's office and returned to RKO, several hours had elapsed. LeRoy had to go on elsewhere and so did I. I never did get to find out anything about *The Robe*, but I am more or less of an authority on Mervyn LeRoy's physical condition, and I am in an authoritative position to tell you that, whether his movies are ailing or not, LeRoy's health is better than ever.

CHAPTER VI

The Girl
with the Three Blue Eyes

As HOLLYWOOD CORRESPONDENT for *Time* Magazine for some four years, it was part of my job to assemble the material for the Hollywood covers. *Time*'s policy was to run approximately two Hollywood covers a year in order to step up newsstand circulation. The magazine preferred a glamour girl for decorative cover purposes, and a Kim Novak accordingly would get preference over a Cecil B. DeMille, Samuel Goldwyn, or John Huston, even though the latter might be better stories. As a matter of fact, although they were repeatedly suggested as cover stories, DeMille, Goldwyn and Huston never could make the grade at *Time*.

During the course of my tenure in *Time*'s Beverly Hills bureau (known as Bevedit), I worked on cover stories about Audrey Hepburn, Humphrey Bogart, Kim Novak, Walt Disney, Frank Sinatra, Gwen Verdon, William Holden and others. The most interesting and strenuous assignment was Marilyn Monroe. *Time* got around to the highly publicized blonde late in the journalistic game, as was usually the magazine's wont. The editors seemed to think that if a celebrity had been sufficiently documented in other publications, he or she ultimately rated *Time*'s Olympian attention and that *Time* would then say the last, august word on the subject.

When I worked on a cover story, I devoted my full time to it. In the case of Marilyn Monroe, this ran over a two-month period of intensive, almost detective-style research, during which I immersed

217

myself in the miasmic, emotional swamp world in which most movie actresses exist. I interviewed more than a hundred of Monroe's friends and enemies, spent a good deal of time with her and then transmitted my thoroughly documented findings—running to almost book length—to New York via the magazine's private teletype system. This material was then put into the editorial meat grinder and came out the other end, as it invariably did, couched in *Time*'s portentous and stentorian gobbledygook and without much resemblance to what had been fed in. As one of the writers at the magazine once pointed out, "*Time*" is "emit" spelled backward, and much that was fed into *Time*'s editorial, word-grinding maw came out facts backward. Once the editors had made up their minds about something, they did not like to have their opinions dislodged by mere facts.

Time has been called "the Hollywood of magazines" because of its addiction to mass authorship, its vast, well-oiled and frequently mysteriously operating machinery, the whims of its editors and the country-club atmosphere prevailing among its employees, who are among the best paid in the journalistic profession. When "the Hollywood of magazines" got around to writing about Hollywood, the results were not always felicitous. *Time* liked to maintain an attitude of indulgent contempt toward the movie business, perhaps because deep down there was a basic similarity between the whacky, extravagant, assembly-line way the magazine and, say, M-G-M operated. When the top editors of *Time* visited Hollywood at intervals, they rubbernecked and gawked like any yokel and were positively devastated at being admitted into the glittering presence of such Hollywood personalities as Zsa Zsa Gabor and Terry Moore.

In its Hollywood cover stories, as in all its reporting, *Time* insisted on only the best and most exhaustive. It was not enough to note that Frank Sinatra had a titanic collection of cuff links. The magazine wanted to know exactly how many, what kind, how much they cost and how they were housed. All this took an appreciable amount of time and effort to ascertain, and then—likely as not—it did not run in the magazine anyway or it ran in garbled form. *Time* tried to hire the most experienced reporters, paid them extremely well, gave them lavish expense accounts and, generally, sufficient time to file the facts. But it then persisted in slanting this material to its own desires, fancies and preconceptions. The avowed intention of the magazine was to entertain as much as to inform and, in its so-called "back of the book" sections like Cinema and Books, to entertain even more than to inform. Like Hollywood itself, *Time*'s policy was to divert its readers, and the contents be damned. As a result, the magazine regularly heaped large gobs of journalistic whipped cream on bare reportorial bread and turned non-fiction into fiction. This, naturally, made for chronic unhappiness and complaints among the staff. (One writer would throw up every morning before going to work.)

Much has been written down the years by a variety of disillusioned and jaundiced journalists about *Time*'s handling of the news, national and international, in its own peculiar way. Certainly, what happened to a Hollywood story at *Time* is of no cosmic significance in a world that is concerned with more important problems than getting a few glimmers of fact about a movie blonde. But it may be of interest and of some educational value to record the step-by-step events—naturally in much condensed form—leading up to the appearance in *Time* Magazine in 1956 of what purported to be a true story about such an inconsequential subject as Marilyn Monroe.

I came to the assignment with some knowledge of Monroe. I had read quite a bit about her and I had met her on a number of occasions earlier in her career. One of these meetings took place in 1951 when she was an ambitious starlet under contract to Twentieth Century-Fox, and columnist Sidney Skolsky, who had a professional eye for promising young actresses, introduced her to me at Schwab's drugstore. The three of us were having coffee when we were joined by a certain Hollywood producer of very minor movies. This producer, like most people at that time, had not yet heard of Monroe and did not know who she was. He gave Monroe the eye, thought she had "movie possibilities," handed her his card and asked her to get in touch with him for the proverbial screen test. Skolsky, getting the hang of the conversation, quickly introduced Monroe as Miss Barton, or something like that, and nudged her under the table to go along with the gag, which she did. I sat there and looked and listened.

It was a lark, of sorts, and the producer left, again urging Monroe—or Miss Barton—to phone him at the studio the next day. Of course, she never did. He subsequently called Skolsky to find out what had happened to the little blonde. Skolsky kept playing the producer along for the gag. I was the one who burst the bubble when I wrote a tongue-in-typewriter column in the Los Angeles *Daily News* about the incident, identifying Miss Barton as Marilyn Monroe. The producer was quite put out about the whole thing.

Later I met Monroe when she was somewhat better known and was escorted, by a studio publicist, to the Farmer's Market in Hollywood one evening for a party at Michael's cheesecake stand. Miss

Monroe, naturally, was Miss Cheesecake (of 1951). She wore a skimpy costume with a frilly chef's hat and was photographed cutting Michael's cheesecake with an old rapier. Monroe was of sufficient unimportance then for the studio to feel this publicity might be helpful to her career.

And, still later, when Monroe was already well known, I had dinner at Chasen's restaurant one night with her and Jane Russell simultaneously, through the mighty ministrations of Skolsky. Even the chef came out of the kitchen in his uniform to get a gander at the two glamour girls dining in the same booth.

Armed with this profound background, I embarked on the *Time* cover. My first stop was Phoenix, Arizona, where Monroe was starting the movie version of *Bus Stop*. But this time it was a different Monroe I encountered—or, rather, failed to encounter. Now she was Miss Marilyn Monroe, a sort of combination of Toby Wing and Garbo. She was starring in the picturization of a New York stage hit being directed by the eminent Joshua Logan; she had had imported as her dramatic coach Paula Strasberg, wife of the famed acting teacher Lee Strasberg; and she was holed up incommunicado in a penthouse suite at the Sahara Hotel in Phoenix while a passel of Fox press agents were themselves trying to keep an even bigger passel of press—some of whom had come to Phoenix from as far away as New York and London—at bay.

The story was that Monroe, the "new" Marilyn Monroe, was alternately sick and alternately studying her lines with Paula Strasberg (as it turned out later, Monroe may have been sick, but she was not doing much studying with Mrs. Strasberg). Anyway, Monroe, everyone was told, was out of commission as far as the press was concerned. This was a situation fraught with potential trouble, since you cannot keep journalists, particularly of the Hollywood variety, cooling their heels. And so a trio of resourceful Twentieth Century-Fox press agents tried diversionary tactics. A Gardena, California, strip-teaser named Stormy Lee Scott was commandeered to take the minds of the fourth-estaters off the absent Miss Monroe. While the representatives of the Beaverbrook papers of London, the New York *Herald Tribune*, *This Week* Magazine, *Collier's*, the Los Angeles *Times* and other illustrious publications studiously looked on, Miss Scott gradually divested herself of her attire, to a musical background of jazz records and the clicking of cameras, in the suite of Fox publicist Roy Craft. In addition, approximately $500 worth of bottled liquid was consumed on the premises. This reporter, like all the others, never got to see

Monroe except once, at a distance, when she came out for a breath of air on her penthouse veranda. She was unreachable, like some mythological goddess, and only the crassest of earthlings would have presumed to aspire to her.

After a breather back in Hollywood, the *Bus Stop* company took off for Sun Valley, Idaho, for a snowy change of scenery. This time the press was left behind. It would be too much trouble to transport Miss Scott and her ecdysiastic tactics to Sun Valley to keep the newspapermen preoccupied. But a seat was made available on the chartered flight for me. Monroe and her manager at the time, Milton Greene, were there, too, deep in conversation, and with no time for interviews. Monroe wore the regulation Hollywood disguise of a brown Venetian gondolier's straw hat, smoked glasses, no makeup whatsoever, and a floor-length mink coat over a man's long black sweater and gray striped pants. This getup, supposed to camouflage her from prying eyes, naturally—and calculatedly—got her more attention than if she were J. Edgar Hoover in OGPU headquarters.

It was a couple of days after we had arrived in Sun Valley (and after the consumption of several barrels of beer in the Sun Valley Lodge bar with press agent Roy Craft to fill in the time) that I finally got to the elusive Monroe. It was evening. She had been shooting most of the day out in the snow a few miles from the hotel. Now she was thawing out in her penthouse suite (movie stars always occupy penthouse suites, just as movie moguls always wield riding crops). This was our first meeting for interview purposes. Wearing a white terrycloth robe, she curled up on a sofa, sipped a glass of sherry and talked while I took notes. It was a rather movingly delivered story, but also a confusing, extraordinarily involved and often contradictory one.

In previous years, Monroe had declared that both her parents were dead and that she had been raised in foster homes as an orphan. Over a period of time it had come to light (from other sources) that Monroe was born out of wedlock, that her mother was alive and that her father probably was too (her reputed father, a man named Mortensen, or Mortenson, supposed to have been killed in an automobile accident, presumably never existed). At Sun Valley, Monroe told me that she was born Norma Jeane Baker on June 1, 1926, in Los Angeles General Hospital, the daughter of Gladys Baker, who was listed on the birth certificate as "Mexican" but was not. Monroe now averred that her mother was living. (It was later established that Monroe's mother is today in a private sanitarium in Los Angeles under a different name and that Monroe pays for her keep, as Twentieth Century-Fox urged her to do.) Monroe also told me that she was "illegitimate." She admitted that her father might still be alive, "but I don't know for sure." She added mysteriously: "I can't tell you who he is." (It turned out that Monroe knows who her father is, that he is very much alive and residing in Southern California. He was once connected with the movie business, although he no longer is today.)

Besides being, understandably, secretive about her parents, Monroe was also vague about her foster parents. According to Monroe, her mother, who had been a film cutter, had a nervous breakdown when Monroe was a baby and she had been brought up as a ward of the county in a dozen foster homes and had been cruelly mistreated. But according to other versions, her mother had taken good care of her until Marilyn was eight years old, when Monroe's mother had her nervous breakdown, and she had grown up in three foster homes, where she was well looked after. But it was impossible conclusively to confirm or deny these stories since the official records, at the Bureau of Public Assistance of the Los Angeles Department of Charities, were exceptionally rigidly classified and completely inaccessible (partially, the report went, through Monroe's intervention).

Monroe told me how she was particularly abused by one unidentified set of foster parents, "a very religious family." (I got to this supposed family later and most of what Monroe told me could not be corroborated.)

She told me that she was admitted to the Los Angeles Orphans' Home Society when she was nine. There, she said, she was forced to do all sorts of dirty work, like washing hundreds of dishes. (This, too, turned out to be an exaggeration.) After this, she lived with "Aunt" Ana Lower, a Christian Scientist, now dead, who was not really her aunt and who was "marvelous" to her, and then with Grace McKee Goddard, a friend of Monroe's mother, who was Marilyn's legal guardian and who has since passed away.

Monroe told me that she used to live in a world of "play acting." When she was twelve, she said, "I looked seventeen" and suddenly she acquired lots of boy friends. She said she was "sort of shy" then. She married Jim Dougherty, a twenty-one-year-old Lockheed worker, when she was sixteen. After four years of marriage, and while Dougherty was away during the war, she got a divorce. "We were never happily married," she said. She worked in a defense plant, modeled in Hollywood and was taken on by a small Hollywood agent, Harry Lipton, who got her a $125-a-week contract at Twentieth Century-Fox. She was cast in a bit part in *Scudda Hoo, Scudda Hay*, starring June

Haver, but was later cut out of the picture "because they said it was confusing with two blondes in the picture." However, her name was left on the screen, even though she did not appear in the movie. (Time marches on. During the making of Bus Stop, Marilyn Monroe, now a big star, objected to actress Hope Lange's blond hair in the picture because it conflicted with hers. When director Joshua Logan refused to have Lange's hair darkened, Monroe walked off the picture on location, causing an expensive delay. Lange's hair was finally darkened.)

At Fox, Norma Jeane Dougherty had her name changed to Marilyn Monroe—Marilyn for Marilyn Miller and Monroe because that was her mother's maiden name. After a year at Fox, she was dropped. Old movie tycoon Joe Schenck—"I used to go to dinner at his house. In those days, I was not eating so good"—helped her get a contract at Columbia.

She worked in a few unimportant pictures at Columbia. One studio executive invited her to spend a weekend on his boat with him. She refused. "What are you trying to do, be naïve?" he asked her, as she related it. Shortly afterward, she was dropped by Columbia. She went to live at the inexpensive Hollywood Studio Club for young girls. She also posed nude for photographer Tom Kelley for fifty dollars (this later became the much publicized nude Monroe calendar shot). She worked in some minor movies. There was publicity that she was an orphan—which, she later said, was disseminated by the studio publicity departments. But she did nothing to correct the orphan story until the news about her mother being alive accidentally broke several years later.

During this time there were two important people in her personal and professional lives. One was Natasha Lytess, a thin, intense Russian woman and then drama coach at Columbia, with whom Monroe lived and studied for years and on whom she relied in every way. Lytess left Columbia to devote all her time to Monroe. They are on the outs today. The other was the late Johnny Hyde, a pocket-sized man who was old enough to be Monroe's father and who was a bigwig in the William Morris talent agency. Hyde, according to Monroe, told her on their first meeting that "he sensed something in me that the masses would like." The William Morris agency bought her contract from agent Harry Lipton. Monroe started getting better roles, in John Huston's The Asphalt Jungle and Fox's All About Eve. Lytess would stand by on the set constantly when she was shooting to help coach her. As a result of her role in *All About Eve*, Fox signed her again.

After Johnny Hyde passed away—"I stayed with Johnny and just held him until they took me away. He was cold. It was dreadful"—she had a series of rather innocuous movie roles. But publicity, mostly photographic—still photographers always loved Monroe—was beginning to take hold. She switched from the William Morris agency to Charles Feldman's Famous Artists agency. Feldman got her better parts and more money—she went from $500 to $750 and then to $1,000 and finally to $1,500 weekly. During this period she married and divorced Joe DiMaggio with much attendant publicity. After the breakup, all she would say was "We are friends today—very distant friends." DiMaggio refused to say anything. She became dissatisfied with her roles at Fox; she said she wanted better things. She refused to do the musical *Pink Tights* and went on suspension—the first of a series of suspensions. She went to New York, studied acting with Lee Strasberg at the Actors Studio and lived with the Milton Greenes —Greene was a magazine photographer. She decided to go into business with Greene as manager and sent Feldman a letter of dismissal. Then she appointed the Music Corporation of America as her agent.

At the time *Time* did its story about Monroe, this was about where her personal and professional life stood. It was typical in most ways of the average Hollywood glamour-girl story. Jerry Wald, never at a loss for words, summed it up this way: "It's the same story with different names. First they say, 'If only I could get a part.' After they get the part, it's 'Gee, they like me! I wonder if I'm gonna get another part?' Then comes phase three: 'I should be getting bigger and more important parts.' After that: 'How can I get more money?' At this stage they start to become surrounded by sycophants and suckerfish who feed on the whale, who massage their ego. In the next stage, they're frightened: 'I have to make lots of money now. How long can I last?' Then comes the stage where they're like a Roman candle. They've reached the first plateau. Everybody wants interviews with them. They get to meet Aly Khan. They're invited everywhere. The stage after that is when they become a mature star and accept everything. They stop pushing. That may take two or three years. The next stage is to break from the friends who disagree with them. Then comes the phase when they need help from someone, so they change agents and boy friends. There's a feeling of constant insecurity. The final phase is where they get culture. It's the 'I was listening to Beethoven's

Ninth the other night.' They never heard the end of the record even. These are certain props that come in handy for interviews. The names may change, but the anxieties and pushing and disappointments are still the same. They're all reaching for the biggest jackpot in the world."

Director George Sidney, also a handy man with a quote, put it in these words: "These girls go through it all not for the money or the purple Jaguar but for the poison, the fire—they want to be an actress and nothing is going to get in the way of it. I say you take a normal person, your aunt Matilda, and put makeup on them and it affects their brain. I say to the makeup man: 'What have you got in that stuff?' When these girls get this ambition and drive, nothing stops them."

Monroe's version of things, of course, was only one version. And, at different times, she has given out varying versions. A good many of the people who had been involved with her—and most of whom had been dispensed with along the way—had different stories to tell. And their stories often checked out a good deal better than Monroe's.

The "religious family" who were supposed to have abused her as a child were presumably Mr. and Mrs. Albert Bolender of Hawthorne, a small suburb of Los Angeles. I got to the Bolenders more or less by accident and by putting together a number of stray interview clues. The Bolenders had never been interviewed before and hardly anyone knew of their connection with Marilyn Monroe. Albert Bolender was a retired postman. They lived in a neat, old-fashioned, six-room house on a quiet street. In the living room were an old piano, a red print rug, a wooden rocker and a copy of *The Letters of Edna St. Vincent Millay* on the coffee table. Ida Bolender, a gray-haired woman with horn-rimmed glasses who took in homeless children for boarding from time to time, told me that Gladys Baker, Marilyn's mother, had lived on the same street as they did and that they were friendly. Norma Jeane, or Marilyn, lived with the Bolenders from the time she was born until she was eight years old. Most of the time, Mrs. Bolender said, "Mrs. Baker was with me. She stayed in Hollywood when working nights, as a negative cutter, and stayed with me while working days."

Mrs. Bolender showed me a number of snapshots and documents to corroborate her story. She also showed me dated receipts to prove that Marilyn's mother had footed the bills for her daughter's upkeep. "She was never neglected and always nicely dressed," Mrs. Bolender said. "Her mother paid her board all the time until her breakdown from overwork, when she was put into Norwalk hospital and Norma Jeane went into the children's home. Before that her mother supported her all the time and bought all her clothes and she had beautiful clothes. She went to Washington school in Hawthorne until she was about eight. She always made good grades in school. Lots of folks here in Hawthorne remember her.

"After the orphan home," Mrs. Bolender said, "Norma Jeane stayed with Aunt Ana and with Grace McKee Goddard until she got married. We went to see her lots of times. I don't know where those stories come from about her staying in twelve foster homes.

"I've often thought of telling somebody this story before," she added, "but I didn't know whom to get in touch with."

Describing herself as "a churchgoer" and not "a moviegoer," Mrs. Bolender said that "I've never seen a picture of Norma Jeane's. I talked to Norma Jeane on the phone about two years ago when her mother was staying with me between times in hospitals. On the phone I said, 'Norma Jeane, why don't you come to see me?' She said, 'I always thought because I'm in the movies you might not like me any more.' 'Because you're in the movies don't make any difference,' I said. 'You come to see me.'

"But she didn't."

The reportorial trail next led to the Los Angeles Orphan Home Society, where Monroe stayed from the age of nine until she was eleven, when she went to live with her appointed guardian, Grace Goddard. "We recommended finally," said superintendent Margaret Ingram, "that she had had enough of group living and needed some family life." The Los Angeles Orphan Home Society is privately endowed and superior to the average orphan home. It consists of a group of rather attractive Colonial type red-brick two-story buildings near the old RKO studio in Hollywood. Recently, a half-million-dollar building program was completed. Inside, the dormitories, locker rooms and dining rooms were clean, neat and quite pleasant. Monroe had said that she had been "very unhappy" at the Orphan Home and had had to scrub floors and toilets and do other menial work for which she was recompensed five cents monthly. "A child disturbed and unhappy could get that impression," said Miss Ingram, but added that the children got twenty-five cents a week for juniors and fifty cents a week for seniors—as spending money—and were required only to make their own beds and help set tables.

Norma Jeane Baker had been the 3,463rd child in the orphan home since it opened its doors in 1911. According to the records in her case history, Norma Jeane was "normal . . . slept well . . . behavior normal . . . bright and smiling . . . considered normal child." The rest was classified and untouchable, particularly to reporters. There were a few newspaper and magazine clippings about Marilyn Monroe, the movie star, in her file. "This is her fame," Miss Ingram said. "We have been interested." Was Marilyn Monroe the most distinguished alumna of the Orphan Home? "Certainly our most glamorous child," said Miss Ingram. "She has had far more publicity than any of the judges or attorneys we have turned out. I'd hate you to think we were producing film stars here."

A blond, sad-eyed, twenty-five-year-old movie starlet named Jody Lawrance was the reporter's next contact. Lawrance was the stepdaughter of the late Grace McKee, who married Lawrance's father, "Doc" Ervin Sillaman Goddard. Jody Lawrance's relationship with Monroe had been kept secret, and this was the first time she had been interviewed on the subject. Lawrance and Monroe lived together for several years. "The first time I met Marilyn," said Lawrance, "I was about eleven. I remember she was a shy, introverted little girl. Marilyn and I were neurotic children. That's why we have taken this business as a way of life. Instead of accepting things as they were, we sort of clammed up. We were very sensitive toward our surroundings." She related how she and Monroe made a tree house with boards in a pepper tree in their front yard and "we used to crawl up there when we thought we'd get in trouble. We knew my father and stepmother could not climb up there. That tree house was our escape then." Lawrance added: "I've been in two dozen foster homes myself. But once you've been in a couple, you've had it. You become cagey, cynical, and you know how to get the most out of people. You can call your story 'The Girl from the Broken Home.' Marilyn is in this business not for money, fame or glory. It's a release for her. It's as necessary as becoming an alcoholic or dope addict. She's looking for a father, mother and family all rolled up into one."

Jim Dougherty, Monroe's first husband, was a cop on the night-felony detail in Van Nuys, California, when I interviewed him. At first he refused to talk, because, as he explained, he had remarried and his wife was touchy about the subject of Marilyn Monroe. We sat in the back of the Van Nuys police station drinking coffee. The rain was coming down by the bucketful. Dougherty, a good-looking, rather beefy, curly-haired man, told me that he had written an article several years ago for *Photoplay* about Monroe at the magazine's urging and that she had been entertaining harsh feelings about him on the grounds that he was "cashing in" on their former marriage. "She was easy to get along with," Dougherty said. "She was a very good cook. She used to gossip with the neighbors. She was very domestic. She loved kids. She never wanted to have any. She was scared to, scared of pain. Once she thought she was pregnant and she went psycho she was so scared." While Dougherty was in the Merchant Marine during World War II, Monroe sent him a "dear John" letter telling him that their marriage was over and that she was getting a divorce. "I got this letter from her attorney and it reached me in Yangtze. I was kinda shook up at that and then I got kinda P.O.'d and I sent a cablegram canceling my allotment to her and I went to Shanghai and had a ball." He blamed the marriage breakup on his being away so much and also "she married me not as a husband but more as a father."

"We live in two different worlds," he said. "I never have any contact with show business." The nearest he came to Monroe and the movies was long after their divorce when he "worked a premiere one night, *The Asphalt Jungle*, at Grauman's Chinese. I was out watching the crowd. That one she didn't show up for. I guess not. I couldn't look for her. I was too busy keeping watch on the stands."

I interviewed just about everyone who ever had anything much to do with Monroe, filling up dozens of stenographic books with notes. Sometimes the proceedings took on a resemblance to the biographical jigsaw of *Citizen Kane*. There was, for instance, Emmeline Snively, who ran the Blue Book School of Charm and Modeling in Hollywood, where Monroe had worked prior to her movie career. Snively recalled that when Monroe first came to her "she had a high, little-girl voice and an astonishing bust which made her size-twelve dress look too small." Monroe already had "that wiggly way of walking. I call it double-jointed knees. It gave her a little bounce." Snively taught her, among other things, to "bring her smile down and show her lower teeth." Monroe specialized in outdoor, bathing-suit shots then. "She was a good all-American type girl," said Snively. "She was the little-girl-next-door type when she was with us." She added: "People often ask me how she got there. I tell them not her wiggle or her sexy look or her mouth open, but a combination of that and luck and fortitude. I looked up fortitude in an old dictionary and right below it it says 'Fort Monroe' and then 'Fortress Monroe.' Fortitude is a real good word."

Was there a photographer anywhere—excepting one whose camera was out of commission at the time or who may have been in traction—

who did not photograph Marilyn Monroe? A reporter could make a career of just talking to photographers about Monroe. The first "name" photographer to shoot Monroe was André de Dienes, a swarthy glamour lensman who was born in Transylvania and now lived in a modernistic house hanging over Hollywood's Sunset Strip. Monroe was sent to him by Snively and he was impressed. "She was a go-getter," he said. "She had a terrific figure." Dienes took countless shots of her. "I photographed her a great deal from the rear—in fact, too much so. Her fanny was always sticking out." Dienes said that Monroe's present success would not have come about if she had not co-operated so wholeheartedly with many photographers. "In fact," he said, "no girl can succeed in this business unless she poses for any Tom, Dick and Harry photographer. She was always enthusiastic and appreciative with photographers. Anita Ekberg could be the greatest of them all if she posed for any photographers. She has the most beautiful breasts in the world, firm and large. She is strong and intelligent. But Anita loves to enjoy herself and stays up all night and sleeps all day and she does not have time for photographs." De Dienes added: "Marilyn is not sexy at all. She has very little feeling toward sex. She is not sensuous. Since she is not the slave of sex, her work comes first."

Natasha Lytess was once very much in with Monroe. And, according to the Monroe pattern, she suddenly found herself very much out. Twentieth Century-Fox fired her and she could not get Monroe on the phone. Lytess was not only Monroe's dramatic coach, but friend, adviser and general guide. They lived together. Monroe washed diapers for Lytess' baby. Lytess told me that Monroe put her on a spot with directors and studios in Hollywood by insisting that she be on the set with her and guide her, acting-wise, from behind the camera. This aroused resentment on the part of many directors and did not help Lytess professionally. The gray-haired Lytess said: "I worked with her on every line, every gesture, every breath, every movement of the eyes. I worked on all her dances and songs. Marilyn wouldn't move without me.

"I introduced her to books—Rilke's *Letters to a Young Poet* and others. I gave her the things I believe in myself as I would give them to my little daughter. She was like a child.

"She needed me like a dead man needs a casket. I have letters in my drawer saying she needs me much more than her life.

"She'll never be a star to me. She's Marilyn...."

Lytess told how some years ago Monroe and she drove out to a Southern California community because Monroe wanted to try to see her father, whom she had never met. "We went to this farm," said Lytess. "Marilyn tried to contact him from the area. She called him three times and finally got through to him. He refused to see her. His voice sounded cold and cruel. He said, 'I have a family and children.' He took her phone number and said he'd contact her in Los Angeles and never did." Lytess said Monroe had known about her father for a long time and had finally worked up the courage to try to see him. "Marilyn once told me that Grace McKee Goddard had told her that her father wanted to adopt Marilyn when she was a year or two old but that Marilyn's mother didn't let him because she hated him so. Grace also told Marilyn that she looks a lot like her father."

Sidney Skolsky plugged Monroe in his column. He helped get her her first starring role (in *Clash by Night*). She chauffeured him from Schwab's drugstore to Fox. She would telephone him at all hours, in tears, for his advice. He accompanied her to many a movietown event. Skolsky was set to produce *The Jean Harlow Story* with Monroe at Fox. And then Skolsky, like Lytess and others, was suddenly no longer in the picture. He could not get her on the telephone either. Skolsky never expressed himself on the subject. He found himself in a rather embarrassing position. After years of being Monroe's confidant, adviser and booster, he was on the outside.

If money matters were a consideration with others, they were less so with Charles Feldman, Monroe's ex-agent. As head of Famous Artists agency, Feldman is one of the three top Hollywood agents. Among his hundred-odd clients are William Holden, John Wayne, George Stevens, etc. Monroe gave him the exit with a snappy letter of dismissal and Feldman was still smarting from the whole thing. Monroe claimed to have been underpaid at Fox. But, largely through Feldman's ministrations, her total take had increased to $125,000 per picture, including collateral payments and "expenses," for the last two pictures she did at Fox before leaving Feldman. There was also a $250,000 Fox capital-gain payment to Monroe for a screenplayed novel, *Horns of the Devil*, which she had acquired from Feldman for $25,000 (this is how these matters are sometimes manipulated in Hollywood). Monroe had never bothered to divulge these figures. At the same time that Feldman was dismissed, Loyd Wright, Monroe's West Coast lawyer, also was given his notice.

The one who succeeded all of them in Monroe's affections at the time was Milton Greene, a slight, thirty-four-year-old magazine photographer. Greene met Monroe when he photographed her for *Look Magazine* wearing a black robe and holding a white coffee cup against a black background and also carrying a lutelike instrument. "I felt I didn't have to show her practically nude," said Greene. "I felt she was a tremendous person. Something about this girl was very different. She was very honest and sincere and sensitive about her work."

Monroe was enchanted with Greene's photographic approach and ultimately they set up in business corporately with Monroe as president and Greene as vice-president and treasurer. Greene has since been given the gate, too.

Drama coach Paula Strasberg, a short, plump woman, is the mother of actress Susan Strasberg. Whenever Monroe was unavailable or incommunicado, it was explained that she was studying her lines with Paula Strasberg. But Strasberg told me that the first two weeks she was in Hollywood on the *Bus Stop* assignment, she could hardly get to Monroe herself. Either Monroe was indisposed or she was with Milton Greene or perhaps just daydreaming.

One day in Sun Valley, when Monroe was in her suite, I was told I could not see her because she was studying with Strasberg. A few minutes later I met Mrs. Strasberg in the hotel ski shop. She told me that she was unable to get in touch with Monroe herself and had been told that Monroe was being interviewed.

In Strasberg's opinion, Monroe had great potential as an actress. But to help her study her lines in *Bus Stop* meanwhile, Strasberg had had Monroe's dialogue in the picture typed up separately in a small, neat, brown book, less bulky and daintier than the complete screenplay of the film. Strasberg described this as Monroe's "sides," in stage parlance. "If she has two lines in a long scene," said Strasberg, "she does not have to work from a cumbersome script this way." In *Bus Stop*, Monroe played a night-club singer who desperately wanted to get to Hollywood. "This longing for something is very real to Marilyn," said Strasberg. "For instance, she has a scene in the picture where she talks about this place she's going—her destination. What it means in the script can't possibly mean anything to Marilyn. In order to make it real for her, she will substitute in her mind a place that's real for her."

Billy Wilder, who directed Monroe in *Seven Year Itch* and who has since directed her in *Some Like It Hot*, was more restrained than Strasberg in his appraisal of her acting ability. Wilder once said that his task of extracting a performance from Monroe was "like pulling teeth."

"The question," Wilder said, "is whether Marilyn is a person at all or one of the greatest Dupont products ever invented. She has breasts like granite and a brain like Swiss cheese, full of holes. She defies gravity. She hasn't the vaguest conception of the time of the day. She arrives late and tells you she couldn't find the studio and she's been working there for years.

"You can take forty-two takes of her in one scene and then you take her aside and say, to calm her down, 'Don't worry, Marilyn,' and she'll look at you with wide-open eyes and say, 'Don't worry about what?'

"This girl is in a terrible predicament. She was brought up at Fox, the CinemaScope studio. In CinemaScope you have to remember more than one line because you cannot cut—the screen is too wide—and therefore you cannot cheat. You have to sustain a scene and have to learn the dialogue. She was completely unaware of her lack of training and inadequacies, at least B.A.S [Before Actors Studio period].

"You give her a one and one half page scene, one hundred twenty words, and once she gets past the second word—if she gets past the second word—she's fine. When you call for 'action' for a scene to start, with Monroe you have fifteen seconds of nothing. For instance, she may have to make an entrance through a closed door. A cue light is flashed on behind the door. Two guys are playing a scene on the other side of the door. The guys have twelve lines and to get her to come in at the right time, after they are done speaking, I press the light button for the cue before they even say the first line. It has to do with the slowness of her thinking process. But then she's *zaftig*, as the Germans say.

"There are certain wonderful rascals in this world, like Monroe, and one day they lie down on an analyst's couch and out comes a clenched, dreary thing. It is better for Monroe not to be straightened out. The charm of her is her two left feet. Otherwise, she may become a slightly inferior Eva Marie Saint."

Monroe was constantly late. Director Howard Hawks told of how she showed up at 10:00 P.M. for a 9:00 P.M. date and explained: "I was here mentally at 9:00 P.M." Most people were of the opinion that Monroe's tardiness stemmed from her fear of facing up to any given situation. Lee Strasberg once took her aside and said, "Obviously you can't be on time. But do you have to be late? Why not come early?" Monroe came early a few times and then reverted to coming late again. When writer Jim Henaghan drove her to a dramatic lesson at the home of Michael Chekhov, he waited in the car while she went to Chekhov's door. In a minute, she came running back. She was there on time, all right, but a day early. Roy Craft recalled that Monroe once got herself a daily diary and memo book to keep her time schedule on schedule. "But there was one thing wrong with it," said Craft. "She got a diary for the wrong year."

Nunnally Johnson, who directed Monroe in How to Marry a Millionaire, observed that Monroe's complaints about playing "daffy, wide-eyed dames and about being shackled by the studio reminds me of the Don Marquis story about the wild man shackled in a carnival with snakes, screaming and yelling. One day the chains broke and there was nothing but a bewildered old colored man standing there. There is nothing more beneficial to a rebel than chains. When he is released, he has to prove something. Marilyn should play exactly what nature made her for—a girl with a big bust."

In Johnson's estimation, Monroe was "an asset to the Strasbergs and that whole New York crowd. They're like most people in show business. They're not above showmanship."

Robert Mitchum, one of Hollywood's more authentic characters, who co-starred with Monroe in River of No Return, gave out an interview about her one morning in his modernistic office on the Sunset Strip. Mitchum was wearing a red leather cap and was drinking splits of Mumm's champagne. At intervals he patted his secretary's posterior.

I asked Mitchum if he believed Monroe really read the high-toned books she was so widely publicized as perusing, and Mitchum told this relevant incident that took place during the making of River of No Return:

"Marilyn was reading a dictionary of Freudian terms. I asked her why she was reading it and she said, 'I feel one should know how to discuss oneself.' I said: 'What chapter are you up to now?' She said: 'Anal eroticism.'" I said: 'That's charming and do you think that will come up in a discussion?' She went back to reading and looked up after a while and said, 'What's eroticism?' I explained. A minute or two later she looked up from the book again and said, 'What's anal?' My stand-in, Tim, who was working on a scratch sheet nearby, couldn't stand it any longer and butted in: 'That's the keester,' he said."

When I had asked Monroe some weeks earlier for suggested names of people to whom I should talk about her, she gave me Marlene Dietrich's name. I telephoned Dietrich in Hollywood and she seemed baffled by my request to talk to her about Monroe. "I only met her once at a party, I think," Dietrich said. "I just said hello to her. I don't know what to tell you." When I asked Paula Strasberg why Monroe had given me Dietrich's name, she replied, "You must understand that Marilyn never had any friends. She never had time to make friends.

So she probably gave you Dietrich's name more as someone she would like to have talk about her than as someone who knows her well."

Joe Schenck, at seventy-six a massive, bald, Beverly Hills Buddha, received me in his feudal manor off Sunset Boulevard. His eyes were half closed. He had been ill. He spoke slowly and laboriously.

Had Schenck been sort of a father to Monroe?

"She used to come here quite often for dinner," he said. "I think she liked to eat. We have good food here. No, I never had any romantic thoughts about Marilyn and she never had any such thoughts about me. But it makes me appear very old if you say I'm a father."

Schenck had some other thoughts about Monroe: "A girl doesn't have to be a great actress to be a success. A girl must be able to be herself, which she is capable of doing. She had a very good reputation around the studio. She didn't run around with a lot of boys, which is natural, but not worth while doing. She always wanted to learn something. If she came to dinner and a good smart man was at dinner, I'd always put her alongside that man. She always wanted to improve herself."

Brisk Lucille Ryman, who was head of M-G-M's talent department for fifteen years and who once put Monroe under personal management and paid her seventy-five dollars per week while she took dramatic lessons, told me: "Under Marilyn's baby-doll, kitten exterior, she is tough and shrewd and calculating or she wouldn't be where she is today."

Harry Lipton, Monroe's first agent, was out of show business and running a candy store in Hollywood when I spoke to him. The mild-mannered Lipton said, "Marilyn has a fantastic quality—it's an electricity she turns on. She brings out the desire in people to help her, to protect her, to mother and father her. It's not a sex thing at all. She's playing a role—this sex thing.

"Marilyn has played everything up to a point and then dropped it and gone on to something new. She has a gift for timing. She has milked people and things dry. She'll play Milton Greene to the point where it becomes a bore and then drop him," he added prophetically.

Fox's publicity boss, Harry Brand, with whom Monroe was always at odds, complimented her with "She's the biggest thing we've had at the studio since Shirley Temple and Betty Grable. With Temple, we had twenty rumors a year that she was kidnaped. With Grable, we had twenty rumors a year that she was raped. With Monroe, we have twenty rumors a year that she has been raped and kidnaped."

I talked to Hollywood gagwriters about Monroe. (Sample: "How did

Marilyn Monroe get those wonderful parts?" "By having all those wonderful parts.") I got a cross-section of her fan mail, which averaged 1,500 letters per week, including about a dozen marriage proposals. I talked to Roy Craft ("Marilyn is a crazy mixed-up kid. I handle her like I would a seven-year-old"). Craft denied that he wrote Monroe's wisecracks for her (sample: When asked what she wore to bed: "Chanel No. 5"), but there was good reason to believe that he had a hand in the witticisms. I examined the publicity questionnaire she filled out at Columbia in May 1948. I interviewed outspoken Fox photographer Leon Shamroy, who shot her first screen test and who said, "When you analyze Marilyn, she is not good-looking. She has a bad nose, bad posture and her figure is too obvious. She has a bad profile—hers is a phony sex. In order to be sexy, you don't have to shake your behind. Sex is not a physical thing. It is something inside you."

I interviewed Jim Henaghan, who told me a typical Hollywood story about Monroe. It was Henaghan, who knew her well, who originally got Monroe together with agent Hugh French at Famous Artists, and that was how Monroe joined that agency. When Monroe moved to a new apartment, Henaghan called French for her new phone number. French told him that he could not give out Monroe's phone number. (Subsequently, French could not get to Monroe himself.)

I interviewed a local movie critic about Monroe, the actress. He said: "Nobody ever accused Clark Gable, John Wayne or Betty Grable of being able to act. Acting can be a liability in the movies."

I interviewed Mme Renna, who lifted Monroe's profile, on the Sunset Strip. "We don't use instruments," she said. "We just lift up the muscles of the face to the natural position with the hands. We have taken care of her face muscles and neck. It's a beautiful piece of work."

I interviewed Mike Todd. "She's the greatest con artist of them all," he complimented her authoritatively.

I interviewed her lawyer, her former stand-in, her dress designer, actress Mamie Van Doren (who had been ballyhooed by Universal-International as "another Marilyn Monroe"), directors Joshua Logan, Henry Hathaway, Jean Negulesco, Fritz Lang and Walter Lang (the latter: "No comment. I just don't want to get into it"), photographers Earl Leaf and Earl Theisen, Fox studio manager Lew Schreiber, William Saroyan, Monroe's make-up man, Fox studio boss Buddy Adler, Jane Russell, Betty Grable and Lauren Bacall, Arthur O'Connell and Betty Field (who appeared with her in Bus Stop) and Groucho Marx. Other reporters, away from Hollywood, interviewed Marlon

Brando (Japan), Arthur Miller (Denver), Darryl Zanuck (Paris), Fleur Cowles (London), etc., etc., etc. All this material was transmitted to *Time* Magazine's New York nerve center. It made a pile of prose almost as high as an elephant's eye.

I summed up my findings about this Bernhardt-in-a-bikini for the editors as best I could, *Time*-style:

"Most of the highly publicized Marilyn Monroe legend about her family background and upbringing has been revealed as being nothing more than a legend. There are grounds for being skeptical about a good many other aspects of the Monroe story.

"The strange thing about the Monroe myth is that even the most seasoned reporters come away from her swearing by her candor and honesty. Mortal man is apparently unable to cope with Monroe. When she transfixes him with the wide, luminous eyes of a lost, very appealing little girl, no other man seems to exist for her. (The fact that she does the identical thing to the next man who comes along is conveniently overlooked.) As one bitchy Hollywood lady columnist put it: 'Marilyn gives a man the business and she is terrific at it.' The 'business,' oddly, is not primarily sexual. Underneath the highly publicized sexpot is a little girl who arouses the protective instinct in many people, both female and male. This lost little girl element in her emotional make-up may well be the vital thing that has endeared her to the world. In actuality, she is more child than siren.

"There are many movie stars and starlets with better bodies and faces and with more character and intelligence than Monroe. It has been pointed out by authorities that her legs are a little too heavy, her beam a little too broad, her jaw a little too hammer-like. She has reportedly had her hairline plucked, her teeth straightened, cartilage grafted into her chin, her face lifted and corrective work done on other portions of her anatomy. The Marilyn Monroe the world knows is, physically, the product of a great deal of artifice, including that of the make-up men, hairdressers and dress designers. She has done her best to alter her appearance—and to alter her background by repeatedly disassociating herself from people and places in her past. It may be, as has been psychiatrically observed about her, that she has such contempt for herself that she is trying to make peace with the world not by adjusting to reality, but by reconstructing herself and the world around her.

"Her sex appeal is an outer, not an inner, one. But there is in her some sort of enigmatic, almost magical, quotient, which no one has really been able to define, that has gotten her where she is today in spite of a background that might normally have found her ending up a schizophrenic in a state mental hospital or an alcoholic in the gutter. Perhaps the quality that many people find attractive in her is her very insecurity, her unhappiness, her sleep-walking through life.

"Monroe is, emotionally, a disturbed girl. And her emotions make her physically ill. She throws up often, breaks into rashes and sweats, is affected by motion sickness. She constantly gets colds and viruses. She arouses one's sympathy because of these things and she instinctively knows how to play upon people's pity. And, in spite of some years of psychoanalysis, she is not beyond self-pity herself.

"Marilyn Monroe exists on two contradictory levels. One is the baby-faced girl seeking shelter. Another is the cleavaged glamour girl of Amazonian proportions. On the one hand she shyly appeals to the father and mother in people. On the other hand, she shrewdly knows how to get the most out of everybody (probably as a result of her hand-to-mouth upbringing). She takes hours to get her hairdo and make-up just right for public appearances. Privately, she likes to scamper about without any make-up at all and with hair disheveled. She is at once a lost soul and the president of a corporation. She has been pictured in the past as the economic contractual victim of a ruthless movie studio. The fact of the matter is that last year, according to the most authoritative sources, she got a colossal collateral under-the-table payment of $450,000 (which hardly anyone knows about) from Twentieth Century-Fox to keep her happy and bring her back into the film fold. She had repeatedly stated that she is fed up with the dumb-blonde roles that Fox gave her. So what does she do? She stays away from the studio for more than a year in protest—and comes back to play a dumb blonde in *Bus Stop*. And she will follow that with her own independent production of *The Sleeping Prince*—in which she will play a dumb blonde. She seems to be candid to an exceptional degree. She may be candid about unimportant things and not quite so candid about important ones. She colors and even invents—sometimes about matters that don't make much sense.

"Monroe is habitually late. She is charmingly vague. She often seems to be off in a private world of her own and not hearing or seeing anyone else. She impresses many people who know her quite well as being an enigma, and among the many people to whom I have talked in the course of gathering this material, not one really claimed to have the answer to that enigma. The people at the Actors Studio in New York know the double-dome Monroe who is preoccupied with character motivation. They do not know about the Marilyn who attended the lush parties at the Holmby Hills estate of Joe Schenck. Her first husband, Jim Dougherty, speaks of Marilyn's right good housekeeping when they were married. Dougherty wouldn't know Edith Sitwell (who is a fan of Monroe's) from a mushroomburger. Norman Rosten, the poet and playwright, knows Marilyn as an intellectual. There are many citizens of Hollywood, eminent and not so eminent, who know her otherwise.

"Milton Greene saw her through his camera lens as a madonna type, while Tom Kelley photographed her sprawled naked and voluptuously on red velvet. Joshua Logan and Paula Strasberg earnestly speak of her as potentially a great actress. There are any number of top-notch Hollywood directors whom she has driven to professional distraction and who will tell you firmly that Monroe cannot act her way out of an old brassiere. (I myself can testify that her best acting is reserved for real life.) And through this crazy patchwork of characters, which ranges from Harry Cohn to Sir Laurence Olivier, Monroe herself runs like a violent red thread.

"In Hollywood you divide everything you hear by nine. With Marilyn Monroe you can divide by eighteen and still have enough left over to fill the next twelve issues of *Confidential* Magazine—or a psychoanalytic quarterly. The topography of Southern California is littered with the remains of people who have been involved with her and who are now hollering bloody murder at having been left in the lurch. For Monroe has a neat habit of latching onto people, of having them mother and father her, and then dumping them unceremoniously by the wayside when she has done with them. This goes for agents, drama coaches, columnists, lawyers, foster parents and just plain folk. She acquires them—and gets rid of them—in shifts. She likes to change people like other women change hats.

"She got rid of her last coterie, consisting of agent Charles Feldman, columnist-adviser Sidney Skolsky, drama coach Natasha Lytess and lawyer Frank Delaney, at one fell swoop and replaced them simultaneously with agent Lew Wasserman, photographer-adviser Milton Greene, drama coach Paula Strasberg and lawyer Irving Stein. As a result, Feldman is now screaming among his French impressionist paintings in Coldwater Canyon, Lytess is brooding among her volumes of Rilke and Dostoevsky on North Crescent Drive, and Skolsky is sulking at Schwab's drugstore.

"It is understandable, then, that putting together any sort of remotely searching story about Marilyn Monroe takes on all the aspects of a pathological detective story, a blend of Bertha the Sewing Machine

Girl and Raymond Chandler, with maybe a dash of Tennessee Williams. The difficulties in the way of ascertaining the facts about Monroe are many. For one thing, she herself is not very accessible now. She is sick (or maybe just scared at having to prove that she is an actress in *Bus Stop*) and, at this writing, is incommunicado in St. Vincent's Hospital with what is described as bronchitis while Joshua Logan is desperately trying to find scenes to shoot around her. (Monroe likes to hide out in hospitals—and in ladies' rooms.) And, when you get to Monroe, if you are lucky, she is disarmingly vague and uninformative. The people around her only complicate matters. There is a conspiracy of silence around her, perhaps because of the high publicity value of anything involving her and also because of the sensitive nature of much of her past (Monroe is reported as being scared to death about what *Time* Magazine will unearth about her). Since she is now big business, she is surrounded with intrigue and a coterie of advisers headed by Milton Greene, who run interference for her and do their best to gum up the works where a reporter is concerned. Greene, a suave fellow who looks like a thin Peter Lorre and wears tams with tassels, black silk shirts and trousers, and crimson kerchiefs at the neck, has been described as Monroe's Svengali. Greene assertedly owns fifty per cent of Marilyn Monroe Productions, Inc., and no one gets to Monroe without first clearing through him. Since Greene is a likely looking heavy who seems to have stepped out of the pages of an Eric Ambler novel, he is constantly being blamed for everything concerning Monroe. But there is some doubt as to whether Greene is the heavy he is reputed to be. It may well be that Monroe cagily typecast him in a role where he has to take the rap for whatever goes wrong. It is quite probable that Greene is an artistically inclined promoter who has gotten a bear by the tail and is rather unhappy about the situation, and that Monroe is really running the show. The smart movietown money is betting that the Milton Greene gang will, before long, go the way of its predecessors and be replaced by a new group of Monroe doters and advisers.

"Where do you start on a story like this? It might be helpful, to begin with, if the yarn were being co-authored by Sam Spade, Sigmund Freud and Paul Mantz. In the past two months, I have been subjected to more evasion, doubletalk and general film-flam than I have gotten in years of journalistic legwork. The far-flung trail has led from Phoenix, Arizona, to Sun Valley, Idaho, from the antique-decorated inner offices of the mighty Music Corporation of America in Beverly Hills to a simple home in Hawthorne on the fringes of Los Angeles, from the Van Nuys police station to the Los Angeles Orphans' Home Society in Hollywood. There have been sessions with Marilyn Monroe at her Beverly Glen home with swimming pool and unlisted phone— and also visits to crackerboxes, dumps and hovels in the far less glamorous parts of the city, places with names like Torrance, Norwalk, Verdugo. And, strangely enough, some of these places have hard-to-get telephone numbers, too. In the course of covering all this territory and talking to the many people involved, much of what Marilyn Monroe has told reporters in the past has been disproved and a good many other facts have been uncovered. But the riddle that is Marilyn Monroe has not been solved. It is doubtful whether a year of ambulance chasing, flagpole climbing and flatfooting would do the trick. That is probably one for the analyst's couch."

The foregoing gives you just a brief idea of what was transmitted to Time. The editors commended "the absolutely first-rate" research, and then, as usual, proceeded to ignore it. What appeared in Time can be read in the May 14, 1956, issue of the magazine. It bears little or no relationship to the laboriously assembled and documented material that was sent to New York. Of course, some things could not be printed in Time; there are even, as you might imagine, some things that cannot be printed in a book. But the final result in the magazine was more fictional than factual. It blithely disregarded the reporter's report and was compound mostly of hearsay, myth, old file clippings and just plain invention. Walter Winchell, no friend of Time's, had taunted the magazine in his column with "What can the Time cover say that's new about Monroe?" The story that appeared in the magazine did nothing to offer a rebuttal to Winchell.

If, as a Hollywood medical friend of mine maintains, "all actresses are made of steel," Monroe was cast in an even mightier mold than most of them. But what appeared in Time was a sort of high-toned, polysyllabic fan-magazine story about an innocent in the Hollywoods. As one relieved Twentieth Century-Fox press agent, who had been concerned about the Time cover, said to me when it was all over: "Well, it's just another version of the same old thing—Little Orphan Annie in Hollywood." He offered his condolences for the effort that had needlessly gone into the story.

The Bolenders, who were wrongfully described as "a family of religious zealots" living in a "semi-rural semi-slum" on the outskirts of Los Angeles, were mollified by Time with a cash payment. Monroe's mother, who was made out to be a sort of heavy, undoubtedly never got to read the story. The Los Angeles Orphans' Home Society was unfairly depicted as a kind of snake pit. All this by writers and editors in New York who had never been near any of these people and places. There was no mention whatsoever of Johnny Hyde, Natasha Lytess, Charles Feldman or Sidney Skolsky, to mention only a few of the main figures in Monroe's career. There were scores of omissions and errors. Monroe was quoted as saying she remembered someone trying to smother her with a pillow when she was two years old. Psychiatrists will tell you that clear memories at that age are rare and often distorted. Monroe said she was raped at the age of six. At other times, she had told reporters that she was raped when she was nine and eleven. And so on and so on.

The then Los Angeles bureau chief of *Time* sent a strongly worded protest to New York about this cavalier disregard for the transmitted research. He received a polite reply suggesting that Bevedit let the matter drop. And that was that.

Reader's Digest subsequently picked up *Time*'s Monroe story and I got $400 as my share of the reprint rights. And so the Marilyn Monroe myth was further disseminated.

The *Time* story ran in May 1956. On June 29 of that year, Monroe was married to playwright Arthur Miller in a civil ceremony (and on July 1 in a Jewish wedding). Monroe has been quoted as saying that she worships his "intelligence." She stood by him during a Congressional contempt hearing where he was acquitted on political charges. The Millers are still hoping for a child after two miscarriages.

Miller took over from the departed Milton Greene as Monroe's professional adviser. He has apparently not been writing any plays, but he has authored a screenplay, *The Misfits*, which was brought to the screen by John Huston, with Monroe playing a young divorcee in Reno. In the endless spate of photographs of Monroe—in the newspapers, the magazines, the movie fan magazines—Miller sometimes appears in the background, a gaunt, bespectacled man with a rather surprised and startled expression who looks as if he wants to be ducking for cover. As one Hollywood citizen who knows them well says, "Miller has gotten in way over his head. He doesn't know which way to move. In the next three or four years, if it lasts that long, she's gonna drive him nuts." Another irreverent observer remarks: "You might call this little drama *The Death of a Playwright*." Perhaps it was a choice between that or the death of a marriage, for in November 1960 Monroe and Miller separated and she announced that she was filing for divorce.

Monroe is still working with the Strasbergs on her "acting." Following *Bus Stop*, she made *The Prince and the Showgirl* in England with

Sir Laurence Olivier. She played a dumb blonde in that picture. After two years of idleness and four years away from Hollywood, she returned in 1959 to do *Some Like It Hot*, in which she played a dumb blonde. In 1960 she made *Let's Make Love*, in which she played a dumb blonde.

If you want to find out about Marilyn Monroe—or the Marilyn Monroes of Hollywood—go to see Paddy Chayefsky's movie, *The Goddess*. It is in the guise of fiction. But fiction is sometimes less strange—and more accurate—than so-called fact.

CHAPTER VII

In the Order

of Their Appearance

IN HOLLYWOOD, the player and not the play's the thing. No matter that the vast majority of stars can't act, or, as Dwight MacDonald put it, "are at no point in danger of impersonating real people." No matter that most starlets are addlepated doxies (in Hollywood, according to Ben Hecht, "starlet is the name for any woman under thirty not actively employed in a brothel"). They are still the very elite of the California kingdom. In Hollywood's scheme of things, Tuesday Weld ranks higher than Joan of Arc.

I believe that my first disillusionment with the Hollywood profiles took place more than twenty years ago. I was interviewing Norma Shearer, then the first lady of M-G-M, in New York. Miss Shearer occupied a ducal suite at Hampshire House and I was ushered into her gracious presence. We were to have lunch. My stomach—for both food and film stars—was stronger then than it is now and I was looking forward to the occasion. A procession of uniformed servitors wheeled in large silver trays. My boyish appetite was whetted. But when the gleaming tops were removed, all that was visible were a couple of truncated ham sandwiches, not much larger than hors d'oeuvres, and two glasses of milk. That was Miss Shearer's lunch, and I—a mere reporter who had not been consulted—found that it was mine, too.

In later years, as I met quite a few of the movie personalities, I found that not only was there not much food where I was concerned, but also not much food for thought. The typical interview with a profile took place at a restaurant frequented by show-business people. Such establishments may have been selected for interview purposes because they were so noisy that you could hardly hear what anyone was saying (and who wanted to hear?).

As such a conclave, the profile, his publicist and the reporter usually sat in a booth beaming moronically at one another.

"Mr. Profile," I would say—I never called the actor by his first name, on the theory that familiarity might breed contempt, or something worse—"what do you think of the difference between stage and screen acting?" (An alternate question would be: "What do you think of the difference between movie and television acting?")

The profile would ponder this and reply, "Yes, and then again no. But don't quote me on it, chum. Off the record. You know, I gotta watch out what I say. Things are tough all over."

So we would proceed to the next subject.

"Would you rather do comedy or tragedy in the pictures?" I would inquire.

"Well," the profile would come back smartly, "I feel that an actor should not be typecast. In my last 4,985 pictures, I did nothing but heavy stuff. I think the time has come for a fine fellow like me to switch to something lighter, don't you think, hah?"

During all this time, you understand, the profile might be eating like mad, shoveling the food into his photogenic maw, while neither the press agent nor I had any provender in front of us. This was because, in the above-mentioned restaurants, it was common practice for the waiter to serve only the celebrity, looking disdainfully on and otherwise giving the brush to the low-salaried no-goods.

And so it would go. The profile would eat and discuss fascinating subjects, such as how he wanted to go from heavies to lovable heroes or vice versa; how he would like to return to Broadway because Hollywood was frustrating his art, only nobody had offered him the lead in a contemplated production of *Hamlet*; and what he thought of the big movie screens compared to small television screens.

My most memorable interview along these lines was with a dwarf named Jerry Austin who acted in movies. When I interviewed him in 1943, after he had appeared in *Saratoga Trunk*, with Gary Cooper and Ingrid Bergman, Austin told me: "I feel that I am being typecast in pictures."

One of the most volatile characters I encountered was Frank Sinatra, the skinny crooner and actor whose well-tailored suits seemed to consist mostly of a padding of chips around the shoulders. Sinatra was constantly fighting all sorts of people and things—or, perhaps, as a friend of his observed, "just shadow boxing with himself." As was well known, he had a beef, some of it possibly justifiable, against the press. In Sinatra's opinion the press in general, and the Hollywood press in particular, were a bunch of lousy, freeloading, vicious crumbs. Sinatra once sent Hollywood columnist Kendis Rochlen a wire: "It is too bad you're such a lying, low, dishonest reporter." He also characterized her as a "beast." One night Sinatra even attempted to run down a group of reporters and photographers with his Cadillac when they tried to approach him at Los Angeles International Airport.

It was Sinatra's contention, and one that bears some looking into, that because a person was in the limelight it did not necessarily follow that his or her private life should be open to public scrutiny. Because someone was a celebrity, Sinatra argued, this "is no reason anyone should be inquisitive as to what goes on in his bedroom, which is practically what a lot of people want to know." (Oddly enough, Sinatra's long-time manager, Hank Sanicola, was a close friend and financial backer of Jimmie Tarantino, publisher of the late *Hollywood Night Life*, one of the most scandalous of all the Hollywood scandal sheets.)

Sinatra's attitude, therefore, put a slight strain on our relationship, which continued on and off for several months in 1955 while I was doing a *Time* cover story about him. Sinatra was touchy about being interviewed. He frequently showed up late for appointments or broke them entirely. He made any number of stipulations. He refused to discuss his private life in any way. He was extremely sensitive about his receding hairline (he wore a hairpiece) and refused to be photographed without his hat on.

When the *Time* story appeared, Sinatra screamed louder than ever. He felt that the story had definitely invaded his privacy (which, of course, it had). The last paragraph of the piece quoted Sinatra as saying, "I'm going to do as I please. I don't need anybody in the world. I did it all myself." Sinatra stated that he had never made that remark to me, to anyone from *Time* Magazine, or to anyone at any time. And, to tell the truth, he was right. Some creative writer or editor in *Time*'s New York office had helpfully put the words into Sinatra's mouth. I am afraid that *Time*'s story, for all its merit, did not do much to allay Sinatra's suspicions about journalists.

Sinatra, as a result, had a continuing grudge against *Time* and particularly against me as its West Coast operative. He would not speak to me. This antagonism came to a head one day when I was on the set of *Pal Joey* at Columbia to interview Kim Novak for a *Time* cover.

Novak was co-starring in this musical with Sinatra and Rita Hayworth. Sinatra saw me on the set and walked away from the camera. He informed director George Sidney that either Sinatra or Goodman was leaving the set, which was simply not big enough for the two of us. The fact that I was there to see Novak and not Sinatra was beside the point. Inevitably, I left the set.

Studio boss Harry Cohn received me in his office. He was sympathetic. "But what can I do?" he said helplessly. "We're doing a big musical number with all the stars and if Sinatra walks we'll be out a day's shooting." So I saw Novak away from the set of *Pal Joey*. The next day I found out that, although I had left the set, Sinatra had walked out anyway, thereby fouling up production for the day and costing Columbia a small fortune.

Sinatra can be a difficult and sometimes impossible person. He has been called "a middle-aged delinquent." He went from a cold-water flat in Hoboken to become one of the hottest attractions in show business, and he has said that if he had not made it as a show-business star, he would have wound up a hoodlum. He has a hair-trigger temper. His favorite phrase, whenever anyone tells him anything, is "Don't tell me. Suggest. But don't tell me." Sinatra fights with all kinds of people. He once even took on the redoubtable Samuel Goldwyn (Goldwyn, naturally, had the last word). Sinatra has been described as a "Dr. Jekyll and Mr. Hyde." He alternates between being utterly charming and being a snarling Dead End kid. He can hand you a bouquet of sweetness and light, but there is a pearl-handled revolver concealed in it that can go off at the drop of a feather.

To his friends, Sinatra dispenses flashy and expensive gifts like a gang overlord. There were years when he averaged $50,000 in gifts. One Christmas he gave out thirty-five solid-gold Dunhill lighters, valued at several hundred dollars apiece, to the entire personnel of his NBC "Hit Parade" band. Some years ago, during a national phone strike, he wanted to make a long-distance call from Los Angeles to New York. Although it was not an emergency, one of the phone girls put Sinatra through. He found out the girl's name and sent her a fancy console radio-phonograph worth almost $1,000.

Almost everyone has an extreme opinion about Sinatra. They either love him or hate him. He has many friends and enemies—and he has been called his own worst enemy. Humphrey Bogart described him as "a kind of Don Quixote, tilting at windmills, fighting people who don't wanna fight. He's a cop hater. If he doesn't know who you are and you ask him a question, he thinks you're a cop. Sinatra is terribly funny. He's just amusing. Because he's a skinny little bastard and his bones kind of rattle together."

One of the most balanced—and most candid—opinions about Sinatra was given to me by Bing Crosby, who is a close friend of his: "Sinatra is quite a fellow, a paradoxical cuss. Without taking any bows or making a big fuss about it, he goes quietly about doing many wonderful things for people who are in a bind, who need a little help. He can be generous, kind and completely selfless. And then he'll turn around and do something so inexplicably thoughtless, so unnecessary, that you wonder if it's the same fellow. I think, secretly, he's always nurtured a childish desire to be a 'hood.' But having too much class, too much sense to go that route, he gets his kicks barking at people—newsmen, photogs and so forth. Talent? He's loaded! It's no surprise to me that he's such a good actor. Any singer worthy of the name is acting when he sings a song—ergo, he's a good actor. Great host, this fellow. Pure hell with spaghetti, meat balls, and that two-day sauce. But you have to listen to Puccini records all night, which is all right with me."

One has to grant that Sinatra is a man of convictions—sometimes even the right ones—who acts on them. Anyone who will tangle with the Hollywood press is a brave and admirable soul indeed. It is too bad that Sinatra cannot pursue his differences with the journalists in a more reasoned and logical way, for there is merit to many of his arguments about the press. He might do much in that fashion to help clarify a problem that is of general concern to many thinking people in and out of show business.

When the research on the Sinatra cover was completed—I had interviewed the usual platoon of people, from bandleader Harry James and Judy Garland to Jo Stafford and Sinatra's ex-press agent, Jack Keller—the result was submitted to a psychoanalyst for a snap analysis. *Time's* editors originally wanted me to transmit the Sinatra research to Sinatra's own analyst—he was rumored to have had one at one time—for a professional rundown. This, of course, never came to pass. I was unable to locate Sinatra's alleged analyst, and, if I had, as I informed *Time's* editors, even a Beverly Hills psychoanalyst has to draw the line somewhere. And so an eminent New York analyst, a long-time friend of Time, Inc.'s, who often advised the editors on psychiatric matters, was called upon instead. The psychoanalyst read the research and came up with a few quick conclusions about Sinatra's formative years emotionally that were supposed to be helpful in putting together the final picture of the man in print.

This was the customary procedure at *Time*, particularly with show-business cover stories. At one time I seriously suggested to the editors that they put on a psychiatrist as a full-time member of the Hollywood staff. Sometimes the cover-story material was shown to a West Coast psychoanalyst, sometimes to an East Coast one. After a while *Time* was not only running out of Hollywood subjects but out of psychoanalysts to psychoanalyze them. The psychoanalytic approach, of course, is today par for the journalistic course. The subjects of most interviews, particularly if they are show-business folk, are rich, successful, famous—and miserable. Their misery goes back to some traumatic experience long ago. In the past, most everyone in Hollywood was happy and cheerful in print. Today the reverse is true. It is fashionable to be miserable. I suspect the trend will change again one of these days as readers and editors become sated with all this amateur psychiatry.

At *Time* the emphasis on two-bit psychiatry was particularly pronounced because most of the personnel at the magazine had been or were in analysis and were preoccupied with the subject. Often the stories in the magazine read more like psychiatric than journalistic reports. At one time the magazine seriously considered adding a new department entitled "Psychiatry." The section was put through a test run, but was finally tabled.

My work, therefore, brought me into extensive contact with Los Angeles psychoanalysts. Many analysts have flocked to the area for the movie money. John Huston, who is planning to do a movie about Sigmund Freud, holds that psychoanalysis to date has accomplished little that is worth while and that its application has been limited largely to people who indulge themselves in it and who are of no special value to society as a whole. As Huston put it, mentioning the name of an eminent show-business figure: "The main accomplishment of analysis up to now is that it has kept ——— from being a pederast."

Most of the analysts were located in Beverly Hills on Bedford Drive, known as "headshrinkers' row," right around the corner from the *Time* office, which made it rather convenient for me. I must confess that, after some of my experiences with these gentlemen, I was not a blind devotee of them as a professional group. Many of the headshrinkers suffered from swelled heads. One Beverly Hills analyst, who runs a gigantic, Technicolor-type psychiatric clinic backed by film funds, was an exceedingly social fellow who went to many of the Hollywood parties and courted publicity. He once wanted me to ghost, under his name, articles on psychiatric analyses of current events. Another analyst, who specialized in the children of the Hollywood notables, also was not averse to publicity. He was introduced to me by a press agent at a cocktail party and told me stories about some of his juvenile patients, mentioning names in the most flagrant, unprofessional way. One of this analyst's stories had to do with a movie star's child who had been sent to him for consultation. As he usually did, the analyst asked the kiddie who his favorite actor was. The child gave the name of a relatively minor performer who played bad men in pictures. It seemed that this thespian was his favorite, as he told the analyst, "because he knocked my father down four times in his last picture." "The boy," the analyst observed to me earnestly, "had an intense hatred of his father and projected himself into the other actor."

I ran the above story in my column in the Los Angeles *Daily News*, mentioning the analyst's name but, of course, not using the name of the patient involved. The analyst was most pleased with the publicity.

Another psychiatrist, who had his Hollywood patients draw free-association pictures as part of their therapy, showed me a sketch of a monstrous octopus drawn by a movie-writer patient. Upon investigation, the psychiatrist informed me, it was found that the octopus represented the writer's producer.

Psychoanalysts were everywhere in evidence. There was one occasion when a redheaded starlet was caught speeding in a foreign sports car with a gentleman friend. She informed the police that the gentleman in question was her psychiatrist and that she was traveling fast because she was emotionally disturbed. The cops, somewhat baffled, let the matter drop. I once had lunch in the executive dining room of Twentieth Century-Fox with Darryl Zanuck and his staff of high-priced producer-stooges. All of these wealthy and voluble gentlemen dummied up when Zanuck started talking and listened quietly and respectfully without once opening their mouths except to eat. The only ones at the table who said anything occasionally were I, seated at Zanuck's right, and a man identified as his psychoanalyst, seated on his left. Reporters and headshrinkers, at least, still have some freedom of speech in filmdom.

Beverly Hills psychoanalysts, it is said, have their own special neurosis. This is the fear that Oscar Levant, the professional show-business neurotic, who is mortally afraid that he will be taken well, will come in to see them. Levant, by now, has been a patient of a good many of the local analysts, without any beneficial results to himself but with apparently destructive ones to the medicos.

In my case, the psychiatric trend came to a head, so to speak, when

I interviewed a young and rather social psychoanalyst who was the subject of a goodly amount of publicity in the gossip columns as the escort of Kim Novak. The interview was not a particularly fruitful one. The two of us had coffee one afternoon at a Beverly Hills beanery and I queried him about Novak for a *Time* cover story. The analyst seemed ill at ease at having to do the talking instead of being the listener. And, besides that, he was not even getting paid for the session.

But the most preposterous psychiatric-type story *Time* ever embarked on concerned, of all people, Dinah Shore. The Television-Radio department of the magazine decided, after much pondering, that it wanted a story about the durable songstress. This was not to be a lengthy and exhaustive cover story, but a short piece running only a column or two of type. Accordingly, I went to Shore's beautiful home in Beverly Hills, where I met her handsome and successful actor husband, George Montgomery, and their bouncing offspring; she beamingly told me how happy she was personally and professionally, how great her television show was doing, how George and she were building a new and even more magnificent house in the hills, etc., etc. There was no alternative but to conclude, reasonably, that nothing could be finah for the contented Dinah.

This roseate material was dispatched to the *Time* editors in New York, and it did not meet with their approval. A communication came back, via a desk man named James Shepley, that the editors in New York knew that Dinah Shore was not really happy, that she was a miserable mess racked with neuroses and frustrations and that they, the fearless and perceptive editors of *Time* Magazine, intended to depict her that way in print.

So I ventured forth once more into the great wilderness of Southern California and talked to a number of people, both friendly and unfriendly, about Dinah Shore. I had difficulty in rounding up even a few moderately unfriendly ones. And I was unable to obtain any evidence that she was unhappy. If she was unhappy, she was doing a masterful job of keeping it from everyone.

These further findings were sent east. This time the editors were real mad. They were not going to be contradicted, in their lookouts on top of the Time-Life building in Manhattan, by any mere reporter on the ground in Los Angeles. No one was going to palm off a happy Dinah Shore on them. They knew, they snapped, that Miss Shore had tried to commit suicide in New York one Christmas night several decades ago and they wanted Miss Shore to cut out all the happy crap and tell them all about it.

I told my immediate bureau editor, Frank McCulloch, that I did not believe it either good taste or good journalism to confront Dinah Shore with this question. I made the point that if she had conceivably tried to commit suicide long ago, she would be foolish to admit it to *Time* Magazine. I added that if she was unhappy in any way, she might not want to admit it even to a Beverly Hills psychoanalyst, no less to *Time* Magazine. That, I argued, was her own business as long as she wanted to keep it her own business. But McCulloch, a faithful, two-fisted Time, Inc. employee, thought otherwise. If the editors in New York ordered it, it was good enough for him. So he got hold of Dinah Shore and boldly and dynamically threw the question at her: Had she or had she not, by God, tried to commit suicide in the long ago? She had not, Dinah Shore replied sweetly. To her credit, she handled herself like a lady in a trying situation. Her husband, a muscular fellow, had a less well-mannered reaction to the entire thing. He threatened to knock McCulloch's block off.

New York was informed, by the hard-driving McCulloch, that Dinah Shore denied the suicide story point-blank. This seemed to calm the editors down somewhat. Ultimately, the profile of Dinah Shore ran in the December 16, 1957, TV-Radio section of *Time* and it was a rather glowing and happy piece, as it had originally started out to be. It could have been entitled "She Lived Happily Ever After." Meanwhile, *Time* had put the scandal magazines, which it was then pillorying in print in its Press section, to shame with as boorish an invasion of privacy as I had ever run across journalistically.

William Holden was another subject—or victim—of *Time*'s psychiatric approach. Holden was a most unactorish actor. When *Time* did its cover story about Holden in 1956, he was thirty-seven years old, a tanned, muscular six-footer with an Arrow collar look who could easily have passed for a successful young business executive. "When you look at him," one of his directors said, "the map of the United States is right on his face." One Hollywood producer held forth that Holden, in his businesslike, clean-cut way, was representative of the Eisenhower era (Holden was a Republican) in the same sense that John Garfield, for instance, typified the turbulent, proletarian Thirties. Holden had been married for fifteen years to the same woman, former actress Brenda Marshall, and they lived with their two boys, twelve and nine, in a pleasant but unpretentious home in the unglamorous Toluca Lake section of North Hollywood.

Holden had been born William Beedle in O'Fallon, Illinois, the son of an industrial chemist and a schoolteacher. On his mother's side of the family, he said he was descended from George Washington, and in his office at Paramount studio hung a coat of arms of Washington presented to him by the National Society of the Sons of the American Revolution. When he was four the Beedles moved to California and Bill grew up in well-mannered, strait-laced Pasadena. Holden got into the movies by accident. He never intended to be an actor. Originally, he was going to go into business with his father. (Even after he became a movie actor, he would say, "My father is a success in the horse-manure business and I can always go back with him if I don't make it.") But as the result of a brief appearance at the Pasadena Playhouse, he was seen by a movie talent scout and, by luck, his first screen test propelled him into the starring role of *Golden Boy* in 1938. The studio publicists at that time dubbed him "a male Cinderella." After a slow and steady progress as a movie actor, he had wound up as one of the handful of top stars in Hollywood.

Holden handled his movie career without temperament, almost as if it were a business. He had a good business sense. One movie director said of him: "He is diplomatic. He knows how to handle himself very cleverly. He's more like an executive of his own career, of his own life, not so much in it. But he thinks how to handle it." Holden was not satisfied to be known as just an actor. He was active in professional and civic activities—he had served as an officer of the Screen Actors Guild, the Academy of Motion Picture Arts and Sciences and other movie organizations, and had been a member of the Los Angeles Park and Recreation Commission. He professed to have decidedly strict views, not only on his own deportment (he avoided Hollywood parties and night clubs) but on the deportment of the movie community in the world at large.

Holden liked to think of himself as a representative of the movies, and the movies as representative of national and international good. He traveled extensively abroad on behalf, he said, of his studio, Paramount, and of the movie industry in general, as "an ambassador of good will." He was particularly exercised at the time I was interviewing him by Humphrey Bogart's Holmby Hills rat pack, an aggregation of fun-loving profiles with Dead End kid inclinations. Holden sounded off on the subject eloquently. "It's terribly important for people to realize," he said, "that their conduct reflects on the way a nation is represented in the eyes of the world. That's why a rat-pack idea makes our job so tough. If you were to go to Japan or India or France and represent an industry which has made an artistic contribution to the whole world and were faced then with the problem of someone asking, 'Do they really have a rat pack in Holmby Hills?' what would you say? It makes your job doubly tough. In every barrel, there's bound to be a rotten apple. Not all actors are bad. It might sound stuffy and dull, but it is quite possible for people to have social intercourse without resorting to a rat pack and even to drink or do anything without resorting to a rat pack. It's so easy for the bad to be printed. People have worked for years to lend some dignity to our profession and it [the rat pack] reflects on the community and on my children and on their children and everybody's children.

"I consider that, as an actor," Holden continued, "I have a job to do. I consider acting a job. Like anybody, I go to work. Carole Lombard years ago went on a publicity trip to New York for Paramount. She went shopping down Fifth Avenue with a studio publicist. The publicist said, 'It's amazing. No one recognizes you.' 'That's simple,' she said. 'It's because I don't want them to.' Then she tossed her blond hair back and swung her mink coat and people started asking her for autographs. 'See what I mean?' she said to the publicist, and then she quietly went back to window shopping. If she could do it, I could do it. I've never been bothered by people or notoriety. I don't choose to be. I don't need to be."

Since Holden did not slug hatcheck girls in night clubs and engage in similar extroverted activities, he had a rather dispirited press, along the lines of "Behold a New Breed of Movie Idol—Who's Made Normality Pay Off"; and "Solid Citizen on Screen and Off, Holden Usually Plays the Role of the Good Fellow Who Lives Next Door." For years Holden went along without any particular screen identity. When he was already well established as a screen star, he was in a Toluca Lake market one day buying some hamburger. A woman in the market, who had been looking at him, came over and said, "You ought to get in pictures. You look so much like Alan Ladd." Holden was finally rescued from his "Smiling Jack" roles when Billy Wilder cast him as a Hollywood writer kept by an aging movie star in *Sunset Boulevard*.

Of course, in this Freudian era, nothing is quite what it seems to be on the surface. And, more or less predictably, Holden turned out to be a good deal more complex and colorful than he appeared and one of the most unconventional and paradoxical personalities in the movie business. Far from being a panty-waist, he was an exceptionally live-wire character, but he handled himself smartly and sensibly—with a resultant lack of publicity. Although, as an actor, he seemed to be one of the easiest performers in the movies, he was really tense and inhibited. He was not averse to a drink or two—the liquor helped loosen him up in front of the camera—and his standard saying to his stand-in, Sugar, in the morning, was "Warm up the ice cubes," signifying that he was ready to go back to his dressing room for a drink. At Paramount, where boss Y. Frank Freeman, a commercial proponent of Coca-Cola, was vehemently opposed to hard liquor on or off the screen, Holden had the only dressing room with a bar in it. He once playfully set fire to a dry martini and dubbed it a "hot martini."

"I would not paint him exactly as a sort of Jekyll and Hyde type," commented Billy Wilder, "but he's a very tense man and drinks to pull himself together and to go on the set in the next scene. His drinking is to overcome his natural inhibitions. Deep down in his heart he is an inhibited boy who feels very uncomfortable to act. It is not easy for him to act. He is the exact opposite of the ham. He was sort of pushed into acting. He drifted into the profession slightly against his own will. At heart he's a wonderful hot-rodder. He would rather have been a race driver. He's a goddam good driver." One of Holden's friends said that "Bill has to apologize to himself for being an actor. The only thing he is desperately frightened of in his professional life is acting. He finds it an endless challenge." Another friend observed: "He believes that being a movie actor is not a noble profession for a man."

Holden often did his own stunts in pictures. He liked to race around in hopped-up sports cars (which he occasionally cracked up) and, as an expert gymnast, to do handstands on ledges of upper-story hotel windows. In the middle of a cold winter night, Holden demonstrated his aqualung to Billy Wilder, staying at the bottom of a pool for thirty-five minutes. "He came out blue, with his teeth chattering and happy about the whole thing," said Wilder.

Wilder said that "Holden is in constant revolt against authority and his family and against everything." A close friend of his held that "Bill's living in a strait jacket manufactured in Pasadena. He is the typical American boy who wanted to become a slob—but never did." Arguing that Holden's proper Pasadena background was at war with his work as an actor and that he was in revolt against Pasadena itself, this acquaintance added that Holden would like to chuck both Hollywood and Pasadena and go off on his own to some remote place as an "intellectual beachcomber."

"He is the original displaced person," said this friend. "Bill would be the happiest person in the world as a fugitive from society. He has a deep yearning to be let alone and not have to prove anything. He detests the challenges and trappings of society. That's why he loves

Hong Kong. This is one reason why he travels abroad so much. Hong Kong is a long way from both the movies and his father's chemical analysis business."

Holden had some comments of his own. "I'm glad of the opportunity to get away," he said. "It is quite a relief to walk down the streets of Delhi and pass people who have never seen a motion picture and don't give a damn. They're just concerned with whether they will starve tomorrow." When Holden was on location in San Juan, Puerto Rico, for the *The Proud and Profane*, he had to dye his dark-brown hair black and grow a mustache for his role. He sat in the Caribe Hilton Hotel for several hours and no one recognized him. "This is great!" Holden said.

Jerry Wald, ready with a quote on anything, as usual, said that "Holden is a clean-cut guy, yet people sense that inwardly he has tremendous sex drive without being an obvious sex type." "Bill probably enjoys his vices more than his virtues," said a crony of his. "If you hear a phony ring in some of his speeches," commented Wilder, "that's because he wants to be proper at all times." Wilder was of the opinion that Holden made inflated pronouncements about the American way of life because "he probably thinks some form of major statement is required of him." Holden himself summed it all up in one of his favorite sayings: "Never crap a crapper," meaning "I'm fooling myself and don't try to fool me."

Billy Wilder, as usual, was on hand with more of his crackling quotes. He attributed Holden's success to his being "the kind of leading man who not only wears well, but he does not rub men the wrong way. Just because women like a man on the screen is not necessarily it. Men should approve of their wives and daughters carrying a torch for the guy."

Wilder remarked that "the refreshing thing about Holden is that, coming from Pasadena, he has never been exposed to the deep-dish acting seminars. When he comes to my office to discuss a part, he never sits in the middle of the rug, but on a chair. He does not wear moldy sweatshirts. And if a scene requires him to ask a girl if she wants two lumps of sugar in her coffee, he does not ask me if his grandmother on his father's side is supposed to be a screaming nymphomaniac. And he uses underarm deodorant.

"Normality is exactly his quality. The originality of the man is that he is normal. It's an odd quality these days. He does not bite women's thighs. He does not ride a motorcycle. He would like to. He is a hot-rodder at heart and physically courageous.

"Actors are a special breed between a human being and an amoeba. Only actors who are ashamed to act are worth their salt. Anybody who tears himself to shreds being hammy, I suspect. That's why I'm fond of Holden. He dies every time he has to act. If anybody offered him a job somewhere else, he'd quit the damn thing completely.

"He is the ideal motion-picture actor. He is beyond acting. He is there. It is as simple as that. You never doubt or question what he is. Jimmy Stewart is a prime example of that sort of canny actor. So is Gary Cooper. There is no crap about them."

I had the uncomfortable experience of being present when a visiting, psychiatrically obsessed editor from *Time*'s New York office third-degreed Holden's parents about what they thought was wrong with their son. Holden's well-bred mother and father comported themselves admirably under this questioning. The editor would not give up. He wanted Holden's mother to tell him for publication that her son was really a no-good and why. When the Holden cover story appeared in *Time*, there were several allusions to the fact that Holden "drinks to relax" and that he was "a man who in his time has admittedly fired off as many cannon crackers as the next man." There was also a profound reference to the moral "abyss" between Hollywood and Pasadena. These few rather innocuous remarks so riled Holden that he refused to have anything to do with *Time* Magazine from then on, and, as a result, some of us *Time* reporters lost one of the best drinking companions we ever had.

There was nothing goody-goody or hypocritical about the late Humphrey Bogart. He did not pretend to be raising civic and moral standards on the one hand while he was actually raising Cain on the other. One of the shibboleths of the plaster city, in a class with "They Lived Happily Ever After" and "Love Conquers All," is the legend that all movie heavies are really gentle souls at heart. Dear to movie fans and fan-magazine editors are the revelations that two-gun Jimmy Cagney is really an ex-chorus boy, that snarling Edward G. Robinson is dedicated to his Matisses and Renoirs, that Richard Widmark, with his hyena laugh, is actually a pleasant-looking, soft-spoken egghead, and that toweringly and frighteningly skeletal Jack Palance is really "withdrawn, highly sensitive, very cultural, reads omnivorously and writes poetry" (his press agent's very words).

Bogart was the most notable exception to this reverse-type casting rule. On the screen, Bogart was usually a tough, trench-coated character sporting a gat and a growl. He shoved everybody around, from the leading louse to the leading lady. Off the screen Bogart may not have been quite as tough, but he tried his darnedest to act so, tangling with a night-club hatcheck girl over an outsize toy panda, barging into the chi-chi premises of Romanoff's hashhouse in Beverly Hills unshaven and minus a cravat, spouting profanity, and in general behaving like a middle-aged Dead End kid leader of a high-society rat pack that boasted such members as John Huston, Judy Garland and Frank Sinatra.

Bogart looked his role on screen and off. Although nature gave him rather photogenic features to start with, he had, as a result of four marriages, innumerable bouts with the bottle and a paucity of food and sleep, developed what was described as a look of intelligent depravity that appeared to be the product of one of the most monumental hangovers in saloon annals. His wife, Lauren Bacall, said of his face that it looked "as if somebody'd stepped on it."

Actually, Bogart was not as hard-boiled as he pretended to be. When pressed, he admitted: "Physically, I'm not tough. I may think tough. I would say I'm kinda tough and calloused inside. I could use a foot more in height and fifty more pounds and fifteen years off my age and then God help all you bastards."

As Hollywood restaurateur Dave Chasen put it: "The trouble with Bogart is that he thinks he is Bogart."

Typical of Bogart was his reaction to the news, in January 1954, that *Time* was about to do a cover story about him. Normally, this information made strong Hollywood profiles lie down and cry. But not Bogart.

A telephone call to his home brought Lauren Bacall, a sort of Humphrey Bogart in skirts, to the phone. In her boozy, low-pitched voice she said: "Don't give up hope, old boy. He's on the way. He's coming from the other end of the room. He's combing his eyebrows, now he's lighting a cigarette, he's stretching, now he's here, tapping his toe."

Bogart got on the phone. He received the news that *Time* was about to profile him in surly silence. Since Bogart was about to leave for Rome in a few days to make a movie there, I asked him if he could spare me as much time as possible in the interim and whether I might even tag along after him if he was busy.

"Okay," replied Bogart in his saturnine lisp, "but you're such a —— bore."

We made an appointment for lunch at Romanoff's, where Bogart regularly spent his lunch hours when he was not making a movie. Bogart arrived there with an entourage, consisting of his press agent, Bill Blowitz, actor Peter Lorre and two free-lance magazine photographers. As a result, not much interviewing got done during the lunch session. Perhaps Bogart wanted it that way and brought in reinforcements because, deep down, he was not entirely sure of himself.

I asked him whom he would suggest that *Time* interview on the subject of Humphrey Bogart. Bogart immediately replied, "Check Mark Hellinger, Robert Benchley and Charlie Butterworth."

All three were deceased.

After that Bogart gave me a list of names, ranging from Louis Bromfield and John O'Hara to Nunnally Johnson and Robert Sherwood. At this point, Romanoff joined the table. Informed of *Time*'s intention to profile Bogart, Romanoff threw up his hands in mock horror. "Now I know *Time* is slipping," he said. "I'd be as infuriated if they did a cover on me as on him."

Dave Chasen's quote about the trouble with Bogart is that he thinks he's Bogart came up. Bogart admitted that "I think it's true at times. But," he cautioned, flashing a biliously charming smile, "I have other facets to my character, you punk. I want this to be a portrait of a dignified character, like Alfred Lunt."

When he was in front of the camera, Bogart was a real, hard-working old pro. But away from the camera, ribbing or "teasing," as Peter Lorre put it, was "his greatest entertainment." Lorre attributed this to Bogart's resentment of "stuffiness, pompousness and pretentiousness." Bogart summed it up with "I don't like placid things. I get bored if there isn't a little action going on. There should be a little more color in this town."

Bogart stirred up much of this "action" in the company of Lorre, a gnomelike, moon-faced fellow who was one of the charter members of Bogart, Inc., a sort of Hollywood offshoot of Murder, Inc. In the movies, Lorre usually played the evil little sidekick of the main heavy. In real life, Lorre played the sadistically funny crony of Humphrey the Horrible. "I like Bogey because he is one hundred per cent what he is," said Lorre. "That is very rich if you know him. So you take all the disadvantages with the advantages."

A good deal of the "action" had revolved around Bogart and his third wife, actress Mayo Methot, who were known as "the battling Bogarts." The story is told that Bogart and Mayo were emerging from "21" in Manhattan one night and were besieged by autograph hounds. Mayo snarlingly told them to scram. "Gee," commented one autograph hound, "she's tougher than he is."

Over a bucketful of martinis one afternoon, Lorre told me about some of the adventures of "the battling Bogarts" as he waxed lyrical about the manifold virtues of Humphrey Bogart.

"One night," Lorre said, "Bogey and Mayo had a terrific fight. They were hitting each other over the head with old whiskey bottles. Bogey finally got fed up and went tearing out of the house. He headed for a night club. As he was going into the club, the doorman told him that he was bleeding in the back. It turned out that Mayo had stabbed him in the back with a knife during the fight and he didn't even know it.

"Charlie Lederer [a writer] and I once made a bet of a hundred dollars. I swore I could make Mayo and Bogey have a tremendous fight within five minutes, starting from scratch. I invited Mayo, Bogey and Lederer to my house one night. As I was walking through the bar carrying some drinks, I said, more or less to myself. 'General MacArthur.' That was all I said. Within three minutes Bogey was hitting her over the head with a glass and she was biting and scratching him. She was for MacArthur and he was violently against.

"One night Mayo walked out on Bogey from my house and Bogey stayed with me. Finally, I got fed up with Bogey and threw him out. He disappeared into the night. He was making the rounds. At six A.M. I got a phone call. It was Bogey's voice or the remains of it. 'Pick me up and take me to the studio,' he said, and gave me a certain telephone number. I did not know the address. I finally phoned and got the address. The place was two blocks from me in the Hollywood Hills. It was a private house. After all the joints had closed, Bogey kept wandering in the Hills. We were then doing *Passage to Marseilles*. He was unshaven and dirty for the part. It's ugly enough, his face, without it. As he was wandering around in the hills, he smelled coffee from a house. He puts his face against the lit-up kitchen window, his horrible face. 'Could I get a cup of coffee?' he said. The woman inside let out a horrible shriek. But then she recognized him. She had just arrived in Hollywood and was a movie fan. 'Mr. Bogart, come in,' she said. So there he was, when I got there, sitting with four kids around him, drinking brandy and coffee, talking to the kids, a big story conference."

A good deal of the "action" had also centered on Jack Warner and Warner Brothers, where both Bogart and Lorre were at one time under contract. Bogart liked to battle with Warner. "I'd read a movie script that I'd think was not right for me," he said. "I'd be called for wardrobe and refuse to report. Jack Warner would phone and say, 'Be a good sport.' I'd argue and say, 'No.' Then I'd get a wire from the

Warner Brothers lawyers ordering me to report. I'd refuse. Then another wire from Warner saying that if I did not report he'd cut my throat. He'd sign it 'Love to Betty' [Lauren Bacall]. I took about ten or twelve suspensions at Warners. If I met Jack out some place we were the best of friends. I kind of miss the arguments I had with Warner. I used to love those feuds. It's like when you've fought with your wife and gotten a divorce, you kind of miss the fighting."

According to Lorre, "no matter how bad a hangover Bogey had, he'd always be there when it came to a shot on the set. One night we'd been out drinking all night. We hadn't been in bed. For Bogey's puss, it didn't matter. He'd go direct to the studio in the morning after a night out drinking. This particular morning Bogey said, 'I want to go to Jack [Warner] and explain.' A bad conscience prompted him to do this. He'd go to Warner and say he'd never do it again. But there was really nothing to explain or apologize for because he was always on time and always ready to step in front of the camera and do the scene right. But you couldn't hold him back when he got the idea in his head that he had to explain to Warner. Warner liked it very much. Naturally he liked it, a star coming to him and apologizing. Bogey did this many times. It was a funny facet of Bogey's.

"But then Bogey and I would go to New York and give out horrible interviews about Warner. Warner would complain about them with tears in his eyes. 'How can you do this to me?' he'd say. 'I love both of you.' Bogey would tell him: 'We do it to get publicity for the studio and you.'"

Once Bogart referred to Jack Warner in an interview as a "creep." "Warner called me at ten A.M.," Bogart said. "'How dare you call me that?' he demanded. 'The dictionary says that a creep is a loathsome, crawling thing.' 'But we spell it "Kreep," not "creep."' I explained to him."

Michael Curtiz was another object of the Bogart–Lorre "action." "Mike Curtiz does not have a sense of humor," Lorre said. "When he was directing *Passage to Marseilles*, in our drunken stupor we decided to blackmail Curtiz into a sense of humor. Curtiz has no sense of humor particularly when shooting. He eats pictures and excretes pictures. Bogey and I are one-take people. In addition to that, we were not supposed to waste any film during the war. We came in from a horrible night. Bogey apologized to Warner. Then we went on the deck of a big boat set. Bogey was in the first shot. Mike says to Bogey, 'You do this,' and Bogey says, 'I heard the most wonderful story' and tells some stupid, square joke, endless. Bogey gets through and Mike says 'Now we shoot.' He made nineteen takes and didn't get it. He almost went out of his mind. Then I started to tell a long story. It took him [Curtiz] about two days to find out whenever he laughed he got the scene in one take and whenever he didn't laugh he didn't get a take. Two mornings later, Bogey and I, two staggering little figures, arrived on the big set. Mike saw us a block away on the set and he started laughing like crazy in advance."

According to Lorre, Bogart "had great fun at it, liquidating a creep. He would do it to his best friends. Like a true general, he knew when to retreat and advance."

Mike Romanoff was another Bogart victim. "Mike Romanoff's pet hatred on earth," said Lorre, "was Preston Sturges [the movie director and writer]. One day Bogey was out drinking with Bob Coote, an English actor who was staying with Mike. Bogey and Coote picked up Sturges and got Sturges completely drunk and they deposited this monster in Mike's living room."

Lorre himself was not exempt from the "action." Lorre had a strange, compulsive quirk about where he sat. At Romanoff's he insisted on sitting only on the outer right side of the booth. If he sat anywhere else, he became vastly apprehensive. Bogart liked to arrange matters, before Lorre's arrival at the restaurant, so that some prominent personage would already be sitting on the outer right side of the table when Lorre showed up. Since Lorre could not very well ask this celebrity to move, he had to sit elsewhere, with resulting distress. This seemed to amuse Bogart.

On the other hand, as Lorre explained, "Bogey and I invented a gag that if somebody was very boring, we'd sit next to him and puff smoke in his face until he started coughing his lungs up. It's the smoking gag."

Restaurants and night clubs were often settings for the "action." "One night," said Lorre, "a lot of fans were waiting for Bogey outside '21.' Bogey came out with a napkin on his arm and said, 'Sorry, boys, I'm broke. No autographs.'

"Another night Bogey and I were bored at Chasen's. With two other guys, we dragged out the safe from Chasen's office and onto Beverly Boulevard, several blocks away from the restaurant. We were loaded at the time. It took twelve people to drag it back."

One night Bogart and producer Mark Hellinger were about to enter a Sunset Strip night club. The doorman barred Bogart because he had been involved in so many drunken brawls there. Hellinger said, "He's my guest. He's okay now. He has reformed." Just as Hellinger had convinced the doorman that he should admit Bogart, there was a tremendous ruckus from the direction of the taxicab in which Bogart and Hellinger had arrived. The well-lubricated Bogart was punching the cab driver.

Bogart had some rather unlikely cohorts in his activities. One of them was the elegant Clifton Webb, a long-time friend. Webb, who was of the opinion that Bogart "was a warm, friendly fellow," said that "he loved to pull your leg and sometimes people took it for an insult. He and I had a running gag. We insulted each other at every party. It was a regular act. People's eyebrows went up."

Bogart's evil appearance, which stood him in good stead before the camera, also helped get him into an assortment of scrapes. He was constantly being challenged by drunks. Director-writer Richard Brooks recalled an incident at a formal New Year's party given by director Lewis Milestone. "Bogey," said Brooks, "was having a good time looking under girls' dresses and stuff like that. Bogey creeps into many a heart that way. In walks this guy, Jeff Cassell, a French writer. Bogey is at the bar. There is a mass of people around. Cassell is at the bar, talking about lousy Hollywood writers. Cassell says, 'Hey, Bogart. You're a tough guy.' Bogey says, 'No, no. I'm not a tough guy. I just seem like a tough guy.' Cassell says, 'Bang, bang, do something tough' and grabs hold of Bogey. Bogey says, 'You're a tough guy? What do you do that's tough?' Cassell says, 'I eat glass.' Bogey says, 'Let's see.' So Cassell eats a piece of champagne glass and then wants Bogey to eat glass too. Bogey says no. Cassell then puts Scotch, bourbon, brandy and gin in one glass and drinks half of it and gives the rest to Bogey so Bogey can drink it. Bogey usually drinks a little Scotch and lots of water and likes to hold the glass a long time. So Bogey drinks it. Cassell then eats another piece of glass. Bogey then decides he will eat a piece of glass, too. He bites a piece of glass and starts bleeding from the mouth. Then he and Cassell became buddies."

Brooks held that "one reason Bogey needled people was that he was bored. It made for action. He also had an inner complex, especially when he got tight, hidden in him for the purpose of the confessional. He liked to get the truth out of people. Bogey had to get to the basic truth somehow. It was a constant drive. Perhaps that is so because part of his life was a lie. He hadn't realized his own potential as an actor in Hollywood.

"Bogey had a 16 mm. projector and liked to run pictures at home. He liked to run *A Star Is Born* [with Janet Gaynor and Fredric March] and cried bitterly every time. He associated himself with

March's character [March plays an alcoholic Hollywood star] and with his downfall and being unable to pull himself together. That was the only time I saw Bogey cry."

For many years Bogart played nothing but gangsters at Warner Brothers. He played them so effectively that many people thought he had been one himself and he would get fan letters from inmates at San Quentin and other prisons. When Bogart switched to playing detectives, he got irate communications from his prison fans wanting to know how he could go back on them.

Bogart, however, thought that "the gunmen I've played are all one-dimensional characters. They are all the same. You could almost make a card index of the lines they speak: 'Get over against the wall,' 'Get your hands up,' all the stock gangster lines. I played heavies in Hollywood for eight or nine years. I was a punching block for Cagney, Raft, Robinson, everybody. I wore a kind of uniform in those roles. It was the Warner uniform: a blue suit, blue shirt, black or red nondescript tie and snap-brim hat. I wore it in all the pictures, The Roaring Twenties, They Drive By Night, etc. I always wound up dead and never got the girl. A gangster is never allowed to have any sex life. The Breen office, you know, old boy."

As a gangster, Bogart wore "a dark, well-cut overcoat." When he began to play private-eye roles, he said, he simply changed to a trench coat. Otherwise, his clothing and characterizations were pretty much the same.

Jerry Wald, who produced a number of Bogart's pictures, said that "Bogart was always on the gangster team at Warners. I once suggested that we organize a Burbank-Bogart film festival [Burbank is the locale of the Warner studio]. This festival would feature seven interpretations of the same role, all gangsters, by Bogart. It would be something like the Salzburg Festival.

"We used to call the gangster lineup at the studio 'Murderers' Row.' The first team was headed by Jimmy Cagney, Paul Muni, John Garfield and George Raft. I once wanted to make a movie, Rogues' Gallery, with all the gangster types in it. It never got made. But then all the gangsters went artistic—Muni, Robinson and the rest of them.

"There was always somebody ahead of Bogart in the gangster pictures. He picked up the leavings. It was tough in those days for an outside gangster-type actor like Bogart to get in and come to bat. You had to carry a machine gun in your pocket to make the grade. To get on the gangster team was tough.

"Bogey had everything against him. He had a peculiar name, Humphrey, definitely not in keeping with the character he played. He had a slight lisp. He was not a pretty boy or the conventional leading man. He violated every rule of the movie business. But he was a good actor. He could project. He had tremendous force."

Bogart got his first big break as a movie gangster in *High Sierra*. George Raft was originally supposed to do the role, but as director Raoul Walsh said, "Raft wouldn't die in the picture. But the censors demanded that the character die since he had committed six killings. So Bogart got the role instead. It was the first picture where he got big billing.

"You couldn't kill Jimmy Stewart, Gary Cooper or Gregory Peck in a picture," Walsh added. "But you could kill off Bogart. The audience did not resent it."

According to Clifton Webb, Bogart's "toughness was an identification with his screen roles. In this particular business people think you are like what you play on the screen. That is sometimes completely erroneous. Everybody in the world thinks I hate children because of my screen appearance as Belvedere. If that's the way they want to think, let them go ahead.

"Humphrey was not a tough guy, not at all. He was about as tough as Little Lord Fauntleroy."

Jerry Wald thought that "Bogart was not tough. Despite his roles, he was quite the opposite. He was almost a Caspar Milquetoast. Bogart was liked by audiences because he had, in the toughest gangster roles, a pathetic quality which made the audience feel that the environment made the character, not Bogart. He always gained sympathy. The audience was frightened but did not hate him." Stanley Kramer, who produced *The Caine Mutiny*, with Bogart, said of him: "He had the damnedest façade of any man I ever met in my life. He was playing Bogart all the time, but he was really a big, sloppy bowl of mush. I believe that the façade was a defense mechanism."

"One fascinating thing about Bogey," said producer-writer Nunnally Johnson, "he was a Mellins food baby. Earlier in the century, Mellins was standard for babies. On the product was a picture of a beautiful baby, a dream baby. All children who ate Mellins food were supposed to look like this baby. That was Bogey. His mother painted it. She painted old Bogey when he was one or so years old. It was used on all cans of Mellins baby food. And then he grew up to look like this s.o.b."

Johnson hazarded that "his movie character had become his character and it could be pretty exasperating at times. Bogey thought of himself in the role of Scaramouche, the mischievous scamp who sets off the fireworks and then nips out. He never stopped thinking how he could stir things up here or there. I don't think it was an act. It was natural in Bogey. It was no act on Garbo's part to want to be alone. She really wanted to be alone. It was just Bogey's natural impulse to stir up things a little. He liked to deadpan his way into something. He was an ingrained mischief maker."

"Was he tough?" said Lauren Bacall. "In a word—no. Bogey was truly a gentle soul. . . . 'Humphrey'—well, it's long and rather-old fashioned, but this was a rather old-fashioned fellow. He really believed in the original concept of the home and a wife's place in the home. He was a turn-of-the-century boy. He was born in 1899. If that isn't turn-of-the-century, I don't know what is."

And Mike Romanoff sounded off that "Bogey conceived a character that he played. It was quite distinct from himself. He played it in public. . . . Bogey was probably the most generous and kindest man. He was anything but tough. He would like to think he was tough, but he wasn't."

There were some local citizens, though, who thought that Bogart not only was not tough but that there was nothing especially edifying about his pranks or personality. One publicist said that Bogart was "a bully. He liked to insult little people like waiters and make-up men. He was a ribber. But the rib always goes one way. He liked ribbing as long as he did it." Another publicist pointed out that "Bogart usually ribbed people at '21' and Romanoff's, where he was known and protected. He got away with a lot of things that way. If he had tried his routine at some average place, he might have been in for a lot of trouble." In this connection, Nunnally Johnson had told this story: "Bogey once needled Rock Hudson about his first name. I said to Bogey, 'Some day a guy like that will knock you flat on your behind.' Bogey replied, 'I keep seated when talking to a guy like that.' There's a careful strategy there."

One of those who was not enamored of Bogart at all was the omnipresent Billy Wilder. Wilder had directed Bogart in *Sabrina*, with William Holden and Audrey Hepburn, and they did not get along together. Bogart characterized the picture as "a crock of crap" and said that "Wilder is the kind of Prussian German with a riding crop. He's the type of director I don't like to work with. He works with the writer and excludes the actor. I didn't know what the end of the picture would be, as to who gets Sabrina [as Wilder put it, "Bogart gets the girl. Holden gets a beautiful sports roadster"]. It irritated me so I went to work on him. I came in one morning and he gave me a two-page scene. I was not too impressed.

" 'Billy,' I said, 'you got any kids?'

" 'I have a daughter two years old,' he said.

" 'Did she write this?' I said.

"One thing led to another . . ."

Wilder, granting that Bogart was "a tremendously competent actor," said that he "took tremendous joy in being a troublemaker. He liked to incite two people against each other and watch them have a fight. Bogart would come to me and say, '[John] Huston told me who he thought the ten greatest directors were and you were not on the list. Isn't that Huston a bum?' and try to promote a fight that way. He had a peculiar sense of humor. It was both impish and sadistic. But I learned from the master, Erich von Stroheim [whom Wilder directed in several pictures] and this [Bogart] was just child's play. I'm in the major leagues. Bogart was a bore. You have to be much wittier to be that mean."

Wilder also thought that Bogart, far from being tough, was a coward. "Charlie Lederer had a New Year's party a couple of years ago," he said. "Two eighteen-year-old pimply-faced Canadian Air Force cadets on leave crashed the party, which was loaded with stars. Lederer was aware that they had crashed the party, but let it go.

"The two guys got very boozed and started pinching the behinds of many a famous star. Suddenly, one of them pinched the behind of Bacall. Bogart saw it. He swung the guy around—the guy must have weighed 108 pounds—and, with the delivery that gets him $200,000 a picture, he bared his fanglike teeth and snarled, 'Now see here, sonny, what do you think you're trying to pull here?' No one in the world can read a line like this. The kid looked straight into the eyes of the big he-man and answered right back, 'Why don't you go—— yourself?' Bogart ran and locked himself in the toilet. When it comes to a fight, he's a big coward.

"After a while, Lederer finally called the police to get rid of the two cadets. Eight Beverly Hills police dragged them off. At this point, Bogart opened the toilet door and bravely shouted, 'Out!' He's a coward.

"Bogart was colorful and a character, but whatever made him colorful was deplorable."

Bogart was plentifully aware of the power of the press and publicity, but he liked to take a bravura offensive with the Hollywood reporters. He described them as "a bunch of creeps." He said, with a straight face, "Hell, newspapermen can drink and drink well and that's the best tribute I can pay them." A gossip columnist once asked Bogart why he was worth $200,000 a picture. "Because I can get it," he snapped. He particularly loathed movie-fan magazines. "They are the damnedest bilge," he said. "They distort everything. I can't stand them. They build up an audience of people who read fan magazines."

Once Bogart invited two lady columnists to lunch with him and Richard Brooks at Romanoff's He did not tell Brooks that the ladies were columnists. Bogart got the conversation around to lady columnists and Brooks started sounding off against them. "Bogey got a great kick out of it," said Brooks.

Unlike Sinatra, Bogart claimed not to be concerned either about his loss of hair or possible loss of standing with the press. "I don't resent criticism in the press," he maintained. "It's the opinion of one person. I don't resent prying into my private affairs as long as the newspaperman checks with me and prints the facts. I like publicity. I like to watch it operate. When I was bored, I used to drop into the publicity office at Warner Brothers and invent stories. I invented a story about Paul Muni's beard to the effect that Muni had a beard room and that he left the window open and all the beards flew into the ocean. The story got printed. I also invented a story that Pat O'Brien had a tattoo on his chest and his wife did not like it so she cut it off and made a lampshade out of it. The newspapers will print anything. We used to amuse ourselves with these things."

The press, however, generally had an affection for Bogart, and the more he abused them, the more they liked him. Bogart was usually good for uninhibited quotes and he did not care whom he took on. "I believe in speaking my mind," he contended. "I don't believe in hiding anything. If you're ashamed of anything, correct it. There's nothing I won't talk about. The power of the press doesn't frighten me a bit. There's nothing deader than a dead actor or yesterday's newspaper."

With *Time* Magazine, Bogart was even more belligerent. *Time's* legendary expense accounts intrigued the parsimonious Bogart, and the business of check-grabbing—or, rather, of non-check-grabbing—became a battle of wits between us. Bogart would have all sorts of people at his table at Romanoff's, eating and drinking to excess, and then strategically disappear when the check was brought around so that I would have to pick it up on behalf of the magazine. As a result, I became wary. One day Bogart asked me to join his table at Romanoff's after both of us had lunched separately. I saw no danger in this. Bogart and several of his friends finished off their drinks and left. I found that Bogart had left behind an unpaid check for several rounds of Drambuies that had been consumed prior to my arrival. I paid the bill—as a warranted business expense.

However, Mike Romanoff became irritated that a profile should so abuse the press, particularly on his premises, and, with Romanoff's collusion, I rigged things in Bogart's disfavor for a lunch session I had with him the following day. The agreement between us was that Bogart was to pay for that particular lunch. Accordingly, I rounded up a half dozen or so hungry journalists and invited them to have lunch at Romanoff's with Bogart. They responded with alacrity. By the time Bogart got to the restaurant, we were all already there, partaking voraciously of a colossal bowl of cracked crab, champagne and other Romanoff delicacies. Bogart had no recourse but to pay the astronomical tab.

Most of my interviews for the Bogart cover story took place at Romanoff's. There I interviewed Bogart, Mrs. Bogart and Romanoff himself, among many others. My interview with Lauren Bacall got off to a snappy start. Her first words were "I love myself better than Bogey, so why talk about him? I'd rather talk about myself." I assumed she was jesting.

Bogart was probably Romanoff's most steady, illustrious customer. "Why do I go to Romanoff's?" he said. "It's the only place to go. I like Mike very, very much. He is a very entertaining, interesting and kind man, a civilized citizen. I can meet my friends here. It's kind of like a club. There is no club out here."

When he was not working, Bogart invariably arrived at Romanoff's at 12:30 P.M. He always occupied the same booth, the second from the left corner as one enters the restaurant. His lunch usually consisted of bacon and eggs and toast with a beer or milk and coffee and Drambuie. "I don't like to eat at all," he said. "I only eat to keep alive."

Romanoff had a strict rule that all customers must wear ties, but Bogart insisted on coming in tieless. Romanoff finally had a showdown with Bogart and he agreed to don a cravat. The next day Bogart and Peter Lorre showed up sporting minute bow ties, about a half inch wide and an inch long, in protest. Technically, Romanoff conceded, they were in the clear.

My sessions with Bogart, continuing on and off over a period of several months at Romanoff's, made for an execptionally fat *Time* expense account. They also made for some exceptionally pungent Bogart quotes on a variety of subjects.

His looks: "I'm not good-looking. I used to be but not any more. Not like Robert Taylor. What I have got is I have character in my face. It's taken an awful lot of late nights and drinking to put it there. When I go to work in a picture, I say, 'Don't take the lines out of my face. Leave them there.'" Bogart quoted "an old saying that I remember since I was a kid: 'My face I don't mind it because I'm behind it. It's the people in front that I scare.'"

Movie stars: "Movie stars? I don't like the name. Was Edwin Booth called a star? The words 'movie stars' are so misused they have no meaning. Any little pinhead who does one picture is a star. Gable is a star. Cooper is a star, Joan Crawford, as much as I dislike the lady, is a star. But I don't think the so-called others are. To be a star you have to drag your weight into the box office and be recognized wherever you go."

Screen love: "I have absolutely no interest in who gets the girl. I don't care. I don't see any reason to spend two hours to see who gets the girl especially since you know who's going to get her from the beginning—usually the actor who gets the most money."

The movie industry: "I don't give a damn about the industry. If they go broke, I don't give a ———. I don't like the term 'industry.' I don't hurt the industry. The industry hurts itself by not taking positive stands on controversial matters like censorship, by not always trying to do the best, as if General Motors deliberately put out a bad car."

Movie heroics: "Anybody who sees me kill 200 Japs in a movie knows I couldn't possibly do it off screen. I laid away all those Japs in *Across the Pacific*. I almost exceeded Errol Flynn's record in that one. When I was making *Action in the North Atlantic*, Raymond Massey and I had big mock arguments as to whose double was the bravest."

Acting: "What is a good actor? To me Spencer Tracy is a good actor, almost the best. Because you don't see the mechanism working, the wheels turning. He covers up. He never overacts or is hammy. He makes you believe he is what he is playing. If you watch newsreels, for instance, you see that human beings do not react like actors. People are not running around gesticulating. Some are not doing anything at all. I try to give the impression I'm not acting. It's hard to do. You think it. If you think it, you'll look it. If you feel sorry, you'll look sorry. You just have to believe you're doing it. If I'm holding up a bank I imagine I'm doing it and this is the way I do it. This is for my kind of acting, not Shakespearean acting. I don't know anything about Shakespearean acting."

Publicity: "As long as they spell your name right and you are not accused of dope or rape, you are all right." And, judging from Hollywood history, there was probably no need for Bogart to have qualified his remark with "dope" and "rape." In motion-picture publicity, it seems, truly anything goes.

Few, if any, film folk were as outspoken and quotable as Bogart. Most of them were veritable volcanoes of clichés, and their opinions had all the resilience of a day-old chocolate éclair. When I interviewed Jack Benny and his wife Mary in 1953 for a *Time* cover story about Audrey Hepburn, who, they proudly said, was one of their closest friends, they were most effusive—and unenlightening—about her. This is a verbatim transcript of my exceptionally unfruitful session with the Bennys:

MARY: "Audrey's like a little pixie, like a little bird, fluttering around."

JACK: "She's a fine actress."

MARY: "The great thing about Audrey is that she enjoys people."

JACK: "She's crazy about show people."

MARY: "She's entirely different and unusual."

JACK: "And yet you can't put your finger on it."

MARY: "She's a very unspoiled and very natural girl."

JACK: "She's so easy to be with. But there's nothing obvious about her."

MARY: "She's a great beauty in an exotic way. She's always reminding me of Ingrid Bergman. She wears very little make-up. She has that natural thing, a great skin and great beauty."

JACK: "All our friends have seen *Roman Holiday* and rave about her."

MARY: "I've never heard anything like it."

JACK: "I've never heard such raves from the producers and directors."

MARY: "Her nationality is part French, part Dutch. She has a teeny bit of an English accent. It's very intriguing. She doesn't look like anybody."

JACK: "Except Leslie Caron."

MARY "Uh-uh. The closest thing to her is Jean Simmons. But she is entirely different."

JACK: "She is. In order to get an interview about someone you need not only nice things, but faults. But nobody here has been long enough with Audrey to know her faults."

MARY: "The trouble is that we, like everybody, have known her such a little time and she's been around such a little time."

And so on. About all that repeated prodding could extract from the Bennys about little Audrey was that (a) she liked chocolate cake, and (b) she once came over to see the Bennys' Beverly Hills home while the Bennys were at their Palm Springs home (this, apparently, was supposed to indicate how unconventional she was).

In sum, the Bennys rapturously agreed that Audrey Hepburn was lovely, gracious, talented, industrious, vital, vivacious, co-operative and did not kick her maiden aunt. But the foregoing will give you a general idea of why the press was so appreciative of Humphrey Bogart.

As usual, it took Billy Wilder to come up with some rip-snorting remarks about Audrey Hepburn. Wilder, who was about to direct her in *Sabrina*, said: "After so many drive-in waitresses in movies—it has been a real drought—here is class, somebody who went to school, can spell and possibly play the piano. The other class girl is Katharine Hepburn. There is nobody else. Just a lot of drive-in waitresses off to the races, wriggling their behinds at the 3D camera.

"She's like a salmon swimming upstream. She can do it with very small bozooms. Titism has taken over this country. This girl single-handed may make bozooms a thing of the past. The director will not have to invent shots where the girl leans way forward for a glass of Scotch and soda.

"She's a wispy, thin little thing, but you're really in the presence of somebody when you see that girl. Not since Garbo has there been anything like it, with the possible exception of Bergman. It's the kind of thing where the director plans sixteen closeups throughout the picture with that dame—that curious, beautiful, ugly face of that dame.

"Audrey," Wilder added, "is a tall girl. She's five feet seven, I think. She'll need tall leading men. Maybe she'll have to wear flat heels in *Sabrina* and Bogart will have to wear high heels. But if we can do it with Alan Ladd, we can do it with anybody."

Another patrician addition to Hollywood, before she abdicated to become Princess of Monaco, a country that was denigrated in the movie metropolis as being "not much larger than the M-G-M lot," was Grace Kelly. The cool Miss Kelly, at the time I saw her, was probably the hottest leading lady in Hollywood, but she was only a lukewarm interview.

She was then making a movie with the rather plebeian title of *The Country Girl* at Paramount, and we lunched in her dressing room. I attempted to elicit some information from her about her past with some mild biographical questions. She was quite uncommunicative. I decided to try a less personal and more theoretical tack with some inquiries about her movies and her directors. This also came to nothing.

The lunch ended in a total stalemate. I came away knowing, if possible, less about Kelly than when I had arrived.

Later, the *Saturday Evening Post*'s Pete Martin, a low-pressure reporter who had interviewed just about everyone in Hollywood and who seems to have a knack for getting along with the most reserved subjects, told me that he was also nonplussed by Kelly. He too had gotten nowhere with her. He had come to Hollywood in 1954 to do a two-part piece for the *Post* about her and finally had trouble eking out only one installment. Martin found her "an elusive subject" and added that "writing about her is like trying to wrap up 115 pounds of smoke."

Since every editor was screaming for a story about the aloof actress, the press kept butting its collective head against the cryptic Kelly façade. Her publicists contended that Kelly simply was not addicted to talk. One fan magazine, commenting on her flair for taciturnity, noted that "it was her long silences that Clark Gable fell in love with during the making of *Mogambo* in Africa. When he is hunting, he wants no talk and no talk comes naturally with her."

Since Kelly was so unapproachable, her moviemaking associates were pressed into journalistic service. Alfred Hitchcock, who directed her in several pictures, thought that "she is that rare thing in movies, a lady." One of her producers, William Perlberg, enthused that "we're glad to see a girl from the right side of the tracks—Philadelphia society and all that—make the grade in Hollywood for once. It's a new twist."

During this period it was already beginning to look as if Kelly might soon be lost forever to Hollywood, and the local saying went, "M-G-M's executives are worried that she will fly off to Monte Carlo and be seen henceforth only on postage stamps." When Kelly finally flew the Hollywood coop, the movietown comment was "Show business wonders how Grace will do at the palace."

And so the Kelly reportorial impasse was finally resolved by her migrating to Monaco. I sometimes wonder whether Kelly was reticent, snooty or just plain did not have anything to say. In any case, this journalistic ploy, if such it was, was a most effective one. It intrigued many people and helped get her more newspaper and magazine space in a short period of time than even the legendarily elusive Garbo.

In the period following Kelly's defection from Hollywood, Kim Novak ranked as the number-one female box-office star, with Audrey Hepburn as runner-up. After I had assembled my material about Novak for *Time*'s cover story in 1957, it was, as usual, submitted to a psychonanalyst, in Beverly Hills this time. His comments were:

"Girls like Kim Novak, Marilyn Monroe and Jayne Mansfield—

the most popular actresses in movies—all reflect the times we are living in. They are blobs, faceless wonders, poor lost souls that go well with an era that suffers from a loss of identity. They are part of the folk-hero image of the times. They reflect their times. Most people have suffered a diffusion of identity because of the complexity of society, atomic scares, imminent wars. They feel they have no tie to anything.

"In more stable times, there was the virginal Mary Pickford, America's Sweetheart. In the sensual Twenties, they went for Valentino, the Sheik. During the depression, in the Thirties, the movie heroines, like Katharine Hepburn and Rosalind Russell, were much stronger. And in the Fifties, with their pronounced loss of identity, the most popular movie stars are pudding-faced, undistinguished girls, not particularly talented—like Monroe, Mansfield and Novak. Their undistinguished background appeals to most people. These girls have no father or mother, figuratively speaking, and sometimes literally. They seem to come from nowhere."

Kim Novak filled this psychiatric bill as well as she filled a sheath gown at a Hollywood premiere. Novak, to be sure, had a face. It was almost alabaster. It was the face of a madonna, superimposed on the body of an ox. But the face was blank—except for the eyes, which were deep and haunted. One could call her faceless.

At the age of twenty-four, this silver platinum blonde, who came from a Czech immigrant background in Chicago, was rated the most popular distaff star in Hollywood by movie exhibitors, casting directors, producers and other pundits. She had skyrocketed to this position in the Hollywood heavens in less than four years and in eight pictures, in all of which she had star billing.

In many respects, her story was practically a paraphrase of Marilyn Monroe's. Like Monroe, Novak had no professional background whatsoever. She was a small-time model who got into the movies largely by accident. She had never had any acting experience and not much education. The pressures of her career led to nervous breakdowns. And, like Monroe, she was battling with her bosses for more money.

As a child, Novak related, she had been withdrawn and insecure because she was tall and skinny. She told of locking herself in a room when she was a little girl and of her mother taking her to a psychiatric clinic in Chicago for treatment. Novak liked to analyze herself, in pseudo-psychiatric style. She said: "I always think psychologically. I'm always aware of my problems. I'm always studying people and wondering why I'm so shy. I see it but am unable to master it. I always look at things and think 'Why are people doing it?' Anyone with a complex has to work at it all the time." A Beverly Hills psychoanalyst, with whom she was going out socially, observed, "She is inclined to be introspective, but there is some doubt as to how correct her conclusions about herself are."

On top of this history of pre-Hollywood insecurity came the stresses of her movie job. She was engaged to be married when she came to Hollywood as a model and decided to stay on, calling off her marriage. For a long while she vacillated between the idea of quitting the movies and marrying. Then her career took over entirely and everything else, including marriage, was pushed into the background. Her long-time boy friend, theater owner and builder Mac Krim, complained: "We started out four years ago seeing each other seven nights a week. Then, when she made *Pushover* [her first picture], we saw each other four nights a week. And now, while she is on a picture, she won't go out except on a Friday. I see her every Friday definitely and in between, if I'm lucky."

Hollywood forced her to change her name, from Marilyn Novak to Kim Novak. Her work also affected her otherwise. Since she could not act—the best compliment that I could get for her from veteran performers and directors was the polite remark the she was trying and learning—she felt uneasy in her star status. And she had come up so fast that she had lost most of her bearings.

The pressures on her were quite overwhelming. She was besieged by press, press agents, photographers. She took dancing lessons, singing lessons, acting lessons, gym exercises, stood still for costume fittings, spent hours getting her hair done and being made up. And, most of all, she studied, studied, studied her lines. Because she knew that she did not really know how to do things well, she kept working all the harder.

The resultant wear and tear led to crying fits and breakdowns. Because of working pretty much around the clock, she was hospitalized for a week after making *Jeanne Eagels* and before starting *Pal Joey*. She was up to her head in it and, most of the time, way over her head. One of her studio associates said, "The whole thing is a horrible strain on Kim. She knows she isn't an actress, but she's ambitious. She cracks up under pressure. She throws up, gets carsick and airsick. She throws tantrums and hysterical fits. She is now driving everyone at the studio nuts. She will go nuts herself in the next five years or at least wind up on a psychiatric couch."

Her psychoanalyst friend said of all this, "She is very young and this skyrocketing business is difficult for her to get used to. It is a difficult adjustment—from obscurity to international fame.

"I think she's doing a remarkable job of it. Anyone at that age who has had such a meteoric rise would be plagued by insecurity. If I were suddenly made head of state mental hygiene, it would be threatening to me, too."

Novak somehow suggested, in her own photogenic way, that hapless, rather pitiful and threatening monster in a Hollywood horror movie. As one local citizen put it: "She doesn't have a peg in the back of the neck, but there she is anyway."

Novak did not really ask to be created as a movie star. She was forged in the laboratory of the mad professor—in this case Harry Cohn—and finally, as in the classic scene of the Frankenstein films, Cohn's creation had taken on a life of its own, gotten off the laboratory table and was running amok, without anyone to stop it.

She was hired originally by Columbia at $100 a week. At the time I was documenting her story, she was earning $1,000 a week, which was chicken feed in the movie market. In other words, for making a movie like *Jeanne Eagels*, on which she worked some thirteen weeks, she got $13,000. Jeff Chandler, her co-star, obtained on a loanout from another studio, drew down $200,000. This was obviously economically inequitable. And yet the studio felt that it had a proprietary right in its creation and that it could call the salary turn. But the creation was beginning to feel otherwise.

Just at that time, Novak had gotten rid of her old agent and acquired a new one, the high-pressure William Morris agency. Conflict was in the air. Novak was making rather nasty sounds from her pretty throat. Harry Cohn was issuing two-fisted statements. Her agent at William Morris, the shrewd Bert Allenberg, pointed out that Novak was worth at least $300,000 per picture on the free-lance market and was the most valuable feminine property in Hollywood. A walkout on Columbia was imminent.

Ironically, Novak was originally nourished to movie life by Cohn and his associates as a threat to Rita Hayworth, Columbia's then number-one star, who was squabbling with the studio. The idea was to build up a girl in order to intimidate the intractable Hayworth and possibly even to step into some of her pictures in case Hayworth should get completely out of hand. Novak, indeed, did inherit Hayworth's regal status at the studio. And now she was doing a Hayworth herself and tangling with the bosses. In due course there would undoubtedly be another girl to take Novak's place.

As a result of all this tension, many people were suffering. Novak's temperament, or rather tantrums, were falling on the heads of the little people at the studio—the publicists, photographers, hairdressers, etc. Most of them despised her cordially, but were constrained from saying anything against her. As one publicist told me: "Why should I endanger my $210 a week by talking to you?" And one could not blame them.

Even illustrious directors and producers were hesitant to discuss Novak frankly. There was too much money at stake. Politeness was the order of the day. The twenty-four-year-old girl from Chicago, said one publicist, "thinks she is running the studio" and, in many ways, she actually was.

As a reporter, I myself got a taste of Novak's great ways. She arrived at her first interview one hour late and made no apology. She demanded at that session, quite seriously, that she be allowed to check *Time's* copy, so that she would not be misquoted. She parroted, almost word for word, Frank Sinatra's line about the press. Novak was an ex-flame and still great admirer of Sinatra's, and she had learned her lessons under him well.

Subsequently she broke several interviews without notifying the studio or me. She walked out in the middle of one interview session, saying that she was too busy to stay on. She was generally unco-operative and ungracious.

The studio's publicity department and even executives were thoroughly unable, at that point, to cope with her. They could only sit by and stew in silence. At that time, interestingly, while Novak was playing prima donna to *Time* Magazine, the Beverly Hills bureau of *Time* was preparing a cover story about Norman Chandler, publisher of the Los Angeles *Times* and probably the most powerful man in California. A reporter had numerous sessions with Chandler, who was pleasant, polite, co-operative and always on time. But then Chandler was not a Hollywood profile.

Tyrone Power, who had appeared with Novak in *The Eddy Duchin Story* and who had been a movie star for twenty-one years, had some pointed things to say about the nip-ups of a Novak. Power, who came from a theatrical background, said, "Temperament? Sometimes I can understand, if you happen to be in the middle of a particularly difficult scene and your concentration is distracted by trivia, there may be a momentary outburst. That's understandable in any business. But confusion between temperament and bad manners is unfortunate."

During the time I was working on the story, Novak excelled herself temperamentally, or whatever you may call it. It was one of the final days of shooting *Pal Joey*. Rita Hayworth and Frank Sinatra, her co-stars, both of them not exactly renowned for stability and punctuality, were ready and waiting on the set for the last scene of the big musical production number in the picture. Also waiting was a gigantic company of actors, extras, musicians, dancers, technicians, etc. They were all waiting for Kim Novak—who showed up on the set two hours late. The girl from Chicago had really arrived in Hollywood.

The Novak crisis became so critical that even Harry Cohn decided to talk. I was summoned to his office. The fact that Cohn even saw fit to see a reporter was a testament to Novak and her drawing power. Cohn did not give out interviews. He had, in the past, turned down the most influential publications, from the *Saturday Evening Post* to *Fortune*. In fact, according to students of the Hollywood scene, Cohn had never been interviewed at all. So this was an occasion.

Cohn, the prototype of the Hollywood monster, beat on his imposing desk with a riding crop and screamed about "ungrateful actresses." The reference, of course, was to Novak, who had come to the realization that maybe she should be getting more of a piece of the take than the lousy one grand a week Columbia was paying her. Cohn did not take kindly to the idea.

Cohn proceeded to charm the reporter.

"Why? Why is this girl a star? The public said that. It's a simple answer. Let's take the history of the girl. Everybody takes credit for her. Let 'em all have it. What difference does it make?

"Let's take Arnow [Max Arnow, Columbia's talent head, who discovered and nurtured Novak along on her career]. He drops in at an agent's office and sees the girl. And then the studio sees her and makes a test of her. The rest is history."

Cohn pointed his fearsome riding crop at me. "Great parts make great pictures!" he screamed. "Great pictures make great parts! This girl has had five hit pictures. If you wanna bring me your wife or your aunt, we'll do the same for them."

Cohn had a point there. Novak's career had been babied along carefully by the studio, particularly once Cohn was convinced that she had something on the celluloid ball. Novak had been given big parts in big pictures. She had had a goodly variety of pictures and an impressive lineup of leading men, from Tyrone Power to Frank Sinatra.

Cohn, according to many of his underlings, was an ornery fellow. Even if he himself wanted something and thought it was right, he would make his employees sweat it out to convince him that they wanted it badly, too. That way, it was figured, he could be sure that everybody wanted whatever it was strongly enough and that he could then proceed full steam ahead with the project. Novak had to be sold to Cohn hard at first by Arnow and others. But once he made up in his mind in her favor, Cohn backed her completely, even to forcing director Joshua Logan to use her in *Picnic*.

The story was told that, when Cohn decided to take over as Novak's mastermind, he called her in to his office and told her in a fatherly way how to behave at Columbia. "Don't go to bed with any of these s.o.b.'s at the studio!" Cohn cautioned her. "They can't help you a —— bit."

"Why is she a success?" Cohn continued. "They all give you different answers. They have to. Logan had to put her in *Picnic* or I'd have taken him off *Picnic*.

"The parts are what made her."

Again he aimed the riding crop in my direction. And again he said, "It's normal studio procedure. If your sister or your aunt got the same treatment, that would happen to them too!

"She was right for the parts."

What about Novak's future at the studio?

"We've got plans for her if we can keep a rein on her. You know anybody who isn't hard to control?"

What was Novak worth to Columbia?

"You can't put a figure on her. Star salaries are astronomic today. We've got twelve to fifteen million dollars invested in her. She's the number-one woman star in Hollywood. Audrey Hepburn is the only one else. The public has accepted this girl.

"But they [the stars] all believe that publicity after a while. There's nothing you can do about it.

"I have never met a grateful performer in the picture business.

"[Rita] Hayworth might be worth ten million dollars today easily! She owned twenty-five per cent of the profits of her own company and had hit after hit and she had to get married and had to get out of the business and took a suspension because she fell in love again! In five years, at two pictures a year, at twenty-five per cent! Think of what she could have made! But she didn't make pictures! She took two or three suspensions! She got mixed up with different characters! Unpredictable!"

Would this happen to Novak?

"Who knows? Who knows? Who knows? Here she's treated like a queen. I hope she doesn't fall into a trap. This is a girl you take out of Chicago. She works in one scene at RKO and goes to her agent. Fortunately, our casting director is there. The part [in *Pushover*] is perfect for her. She stepped right into it.

"Certainly she will ask for more money. And I think she'll get it. I'm only afraid she'll ask me to make Kim Novak pictures instead of Columbia pictures."

Cohn swung around in his big black leather swivel chair.

"I think she's a great personality. I can't hurt the girl. Remember, you're leaving here and I still have her under contract."

He went on: "The girl was a star in four pictures! They're all difficult! You can't help yourself with that. If the girl keeps her feet on the ground—you understand?"

Cohn pondered on the ingratitude of those who worked for him.

"I have one rule. When a picture is great, they can all take the credit for it. When it stinks, I take the credit.

"Tell me the names of those men who put her in any pictures— [Richard] Quine [a director], et cetera! Logan! Arnow! She was put into each picture from this desk!

"Logan tells you she's great and he picked her. What do I care? At the end I got *Picnic*."

So what was the trouble?

"The trouble with her? They're all alike!

"You see, it's not a business. It's a racket! . . .

"She will do the Hitchcock picture next and then *Bell, Book and Candle*. And then, I will tell you, who knows? She'd be perfect for Gladys Glad [in *The Mark Hellinger Story*]. Yes, it's definite.

"I won't loan her out. The only reason for the Hitchcock picture was that in return for doing Hitchcock, Stewart does two pictures for Columbia at his salary, ten per cent of the gross."

This was quite a testament to Novak, that in return for her starring in one Alfred Hitchcock picture, *Vertigo*, with James Stewart at Paramount, Stewart, who is practically unobtainable, was doing two pictures at Columbia, even at his usually appreciable percentage.

"You cannot get money with cheap pictures any more," Cohn continued. "That's past. You can only make money with important pictures. Her next three pictures will be blockbusters. For the cheap pictures, you sit at home and tune in that box, television. But when there's a big picture, the public will go into the theaters."

A big door, controlled from somewhere or other, swung open noiselessly. The interview was over.

And, undeniably, Kim Novak was created not so much by her own talent, which is debatable, but by her diligent application and what Harry Cohn rightly called the "studio." Novak put in mostly her own sweat—by the bucketful. A great many other people put in their own highly specialized talents, from Cohn's propensity for making use of the right people, to the lowliest technican who pitched in, as part of his or her job, to build up the glamorously monstrous creation that was Kim Novak.

There is a definite pattern to the careers of Hollywood glamour girls. Before anyone pays any particular attention to them and before the wheels of moviedom start turning for them, they are usually photographed by still photographers who get to them with their appreciative lenses. This was true of Novak, as it was of Monroe. One of the first to train his camera on her was a bearded, free-lance lensman named Earl Leaf, who savors photographic cheesecake. He took hundreds and hundreds of pictures of her when she was an unknown and these shots were helpful in furthering Novak's movie career. Leaf told me, "She's so busy now. Her old friends never get to see her any more. Only the people on her pictures get to see her. But she's still loyal. She still sends me notes and Christmas presents and birthday presents. And at a party she comes over and she whispers some little piece of ———. It makes you feel good all over."

During this interval Novak acquired an agent, Louis Shurr, a short, bald, stout gentleman who likes to step out socially with tall, beautiful girls. The Hollywood legend is that Shurr kindly provides his young charges with a mink coat for the evening—which is promptly returned to Shurr's closet after the festivities are over. Novak might conceivably have wound up as one of Shurr's mink-coated girls had not by chance Columbia's Max Arnow stopped in to see Shurr and run into her.

When Novak got to Columbia and the publicity department began to appreciate her potentialities, she fell into the hands of Bob Coburn, director of still photography at the studio. Coburn told me he simply could not keep up with the demand for Novak photographs. "No matter how you shoot her," he said ecstatically, "she's beautiful. She's like a female Gary Cooper. You shoot him from the back and you still know it's Cooper. She's perfect. All the angles are good."

Leonard McCombe, a *Life* photographer who traveled with Novak cross-country for a magazine layout, observed that her "face is her fortune. It it the sort of face that looks as if the rest of the body is making love. She just laps you up with her eyes and lips and tongue. Her face is like a sponge that can soak you up."

As queen of Columbia studio, Novak had an impressive and industrious retinue of ladies and gentlemen in waiting at her command. Not the least among these were the publicists who saw to it that her name and likeness were disseminated via practically every medium of communication to a palpitating world. George Lait, who was publicity director at Columbia when she arrived there, told me how Novak was ballyhooed into being. At first she was turned over to Coburn and to Benno Schneider, the drama coach (Schneider said he tried to "connect her heart with upstairs" or to develop "a thinking heart"). She also had her teeth straightened, and the studio worked on her "bum ear." She went on a rigid diet and was sent to the Terry Hunt gym to come down to "fighting weight." Her name was changed from Marilyn Novak—"Arnow and I felt one Marilyn [Monroe] was enough," said Lait. "She was named Kim because she said when she was a kid she was called Kim or Mickey and she liked Kim." Novak elaborated: "I like Kim. It's plain and simple and seems rather direct. A name influences you. If you gave me a name like Mamie, I'd be a different kind of person. Kim sounds like she has a clean face. I see a little boy or girl with a shining face looking you straight in the eye."

Most movie stars undergo a name change. The most industrious exponent of name-changing in Hollywood is an agent named Henry Willson (this is his real name, too, with two "l's"), who specializes in what is known as beefcake. It was Willson who named Tab Hunter (originally Arthur Gelien), Rock Hudson (originally Roy Fitzgerald) and Rory Calhoun (originally Francis Timothy McGowan). Willson finally outdid himself when, in a reverse twist, he began representing a profile with the rather individual name of Robert Van Orden. In a burst of inspiration, Willson came up with a new name for Van Orden: John Smith. At the time that such names as Tab and Rock were becoming Hollywood standbys, Humphrey Bogart volunteered his own suggestion for a name for one of these type profiles: Dungg Heap.

There was also a period in Hollywood when Sam Spiegel, a producer, changed his name to S. P. Eagle. This led to all sorts of patronymic speculations in the cinema city, and, along these lines, it was suggested that Darryl Zanuck should henceforth be known as Z. A. Nuck. Eagle finally changed his name back to Spiegel, putting an end to that particular titular trend.

A choice movie name-changing story concerned Elia Kazan when he first came to Hollywood. According to Harold Clurman in *The Fervent Years*, a studio executive advised him to change Kazan to the more euphonious Cézanne. When Kazan pointed out that this was the name of a rather well-known painter, he was told: "You make just one good picture and nobody will even remember the other guy."

Marilyn—or Kim—Novak lent herself helpfully to the publicity department's tactics. "Publicity-wise," said Lait, "the dame was just great. Coburn made a corny, sexy photo of her lying down on a tiger rug with her tits hanging out practically. The damn thing was an eyecatcher." Lait noted that "Kim has a cute habit of getting herself set for a still picture and at the last minute she unbuttons one more button in her cleavage."

The publicity department hit on a gimmick for her. "We dreamt up the story," said Lait, "that she was supposedly riding a bicycle down Rodeo Drive in Beverly Hills when Louis Shurr discovered her." (Actually, anyone riding down Rodeo Drive on a bike would probably be run down in two minutes by either a Jaguar, an Eldorado or a Beverly Hills cop bent on protecting the high transportation standards of the community.) "The bicycle thing caught on great. I got her a lavender bicycle and she'd wear lavender shoes, slacks and sweater and she'd drive the bicycle to the studio and park it in my office."

Lavender was Novak's favorite color because, as she explained, "it is always associated with happy things for me." Her hair had a lavender cast to it. Everything from her bathroom towels and soap to her sheets was lavender. She even had lavender frosting on her cookies. Her fans sometimes wore lavender bow ties or blouses. "They get such a kick out of pleasing me," she said, "and I get the biggest kick out of it."

Novak was stepping out socially with Mac Krim, but Lait felt that Krim did not fit into her life "publicity-wise." "He was no name to help her in the beginning," said Lait. "The press is not interested in a dame whose boy friend is an insurance man or a theater owner." So Novak would be sent out on dates with other actors for publicity purposes and, after the evening was over, would wind up with Krim. After a while, as a result of getting enough gossip-column mentions himself, Krim also "became good publicity fodder." Novak and Krim devised rubber stamps with "Kim and Krim were here" and "Mac and Novak are back," which they would imprint on restaurant menus and elsewhere. However, Novak never got around to marrying Mac. One columnist explained it this way: "Naturally, Kim Novak doesn't want to marry Mac Krim. Who'd want to be called Kim Krim?"

Lait sometimes got into arguments with Novak because she liked to wear sloppy-looking pants and sweater in public. "I'd tell her she was a peasant," said Lait. "There comes a point when she stops being Kim and becomes Miss Novak. The studio tries to make a movie star out of a girl. She's not supposed to wear slacks or eat at the corner drugstore any more. There comes a time when the waitresses at the studio call her not Kim but Miss Novak. And then you get the ass-kissers and the phony advisers. She gets mixed up and she becomes Miss Novak."

Another Columbia publicist had some additional slants on Novak, and he put them this way, in choice Hollywoodese: "When a new girl comes into a studio—and they come in like towels in a sporting house—each one heading for the big dipper, with stars in their eyes, the first thing that's done is to send them through the publicity department. Beautiful girls at a studio are as common as five fingers on a hand. Here was another new girl, a serial number. But Novak's eyes attracted. They had an almost tigerlike slant." Novak filled out a publicity questionnaire "and left most of the questions blank. She filled in her name, address, phone number, agent and the fact that she likes to ride a bike. This is not much clay for a sculptor, even with three hands. But from the bike came a spark."

The bike stunt "jelled" and it had all sorts of repercussions. One reporter conducted an interview with Novak on a bicycle built for two, and "Louis Shurr was besieged at his office by one hundred broads on bikes." But there was more to the publicity than just the idea of Novak pedaling a bicycle. "Lots of girls," said the press agent, "can ride on a camel or a tractor, but nobody cares. There has to be a meshing of gears. It has to be the proper subject—a Monroe, a Mansfield, a Novak. The bike was as good for her as the drugstore stool was for Lana Turner." He added: "Look, I'm in the publicity business. If you're a rug weaver, you like to see more carpet come out. From the beginning, we practically both rode the bike."

Novak soon went into her first picture, *Pushover*. Jerry Wald, who was then production chief at Columbia, had a script of the picture bound in leather and sent it to her with the following inscription: "This is the first in a line of hits and misses. Don't be disturbed about the misses and don't get worked up about the hits."

"At the beginning of their career," Wald commented, " an actor or actress is like a little chicken coming out of an eggshell. The feet are wobbly and they don't know which way they run. At the beginning you have to give them confidence, massage their egos. Later on, they have plenty of ego of their own."

As Novak's publicity took hold, producers and directors at the studio began to take notice of her. Richard Quine, who directed her in *Pushover*, observed that, like most female stars, Novak had the "proverbial quality of the lady in the parlor and the whore in the bedroom. Kim has a ladylike quality, but it goes a step further. She has a combination of that with sex appeal and a childlike quality. It is most unusual. Although she had no acting training—she had never even read the funnies out loud—she brought a childlike pathos to her first role. It was something inherent—the little girl-woman personality."

One of her producers, Fred Kohlmar, remarked that "whatever movie fans are left are young people and Novak's appeal apparently is in that direction. I imagine she's the dream at the moment of what every young man would like to take to the school prom and what every young girl would like to look like." And director George Sidney, describing her as "a talent machine—the way she knocks herself out to be better," noted that "basically this girl is two girls. She has the façade certainly, and the equipment of a bitch in the long shot. And yet when you look in Kim's eyes in a closeup, she's like a baby. She's a dual personality. You can't tell whether she's an angel or a bitch. Kids are starry-eyed about Kim, not about Monroe and Mansfield. Monroe is a kept woman for old men. The kids laugh at Mansfield. But Kim is many-faceted."

The press agent summed it up with "Novak's great appeal is to the male gland. Mansfield is whorey. With Mansfield you cheat on your wife. With Novak, you leave your wife to marry her."

During all this, the studio publicists were grinding out lush verbiage about her along the lines of "Curvaceous chassis, somnolent chrysoprase eyes and moonlight-blond hair." And there were endless publicity stunts and appearances. One of the early ones found Novak handing out the PATSY (Picture Animal Top Star of the Year) awards." You'd only ask a starlet to go there," said the press agent. "Shortly afterwards she was already a star and would never have been asked to go. She wore a tight skirt and sweater at Devonshire Downs [outside Los Angeles]. She even took the publicity play away from the animals. She posed with a chimp, a horse, dogs, parrots, etc. The chimp was gazing at her cleavage. Stealing a picture from a chimp is like stealing a gold piece from Fort Knox."

Novak also represented the studio at an automobile show at Pan-Pacific auditorium. She was photographed with actress Judy Holliday and some of the automobile people. Jerry Wald remembered that Novak "was holding a big pocketbook and she was very nervous. She handed her pocketbook to Judy Holliday while the picture was being taken. Holliday was left holding the bag. I said to Novak, 'You're learning fast.'"

It was soon obvious that the studio had a real box-office find in Novak. "It happens once in a blue moon," said the publicist. She was beginning to feel her oats a little. When the press agent in question told her that she would one day become a big star and that "she was bound to go the way of all Hollywood flesh, she told me that she would never change. But she was by now irrevocably committed to screen stardom. And she'll never chuck it—no more than a narcotic addict."

As a reward, the studio sent Novak to Europe. And by now movies and moviemaking were all that concerned her. While Novak and a studio publicity girl were being driven across the Swiss Alps, the chauffeur said to Novak, "Mees Keem, I have had the honor and privilege to drive some of the greatest dignitaries of our time—the Duke and Duchess of Windsor, Field Marshal Montgomery, and also your President." Novak replied, in all seriousness, "You mean Harry Cohn?"

And so it went, until the demands made on her and the rewards withheld from her erupted in the fireworks with Cohn.

"Today," said the press agent philosophically, "when she snaps at you, it's not really her, but what the pressure cooker of Hollywood has made of her."

Ultimately, as Cohn himself had prophesied, Novak won her battle with the studio. And, ultimately too, Cohn passed away. The studio truly became the Girl from Chicago's.

One of the more unlikely journalistic events I covered was in September 1953 when Lucille Ball, the red-haired, scatter-brained television and movie comedienne, was hauled up before an Un-American Activities Committee in Los Angeles on charges of being politically suspect. A platoon of reporters descended on the story and it made sky-high headlines for days.

Prior to this shattering revelation, the saucer-eyed Lucille's talent had been one for low-comedy mugging. With her Cuban-born husband, Desi Arnaz, she helped make the "I Love Lucy" show the biggest success in television. She specialized in slapstick pantomime and played everything from a ballerina to a Hindu maharanee, from a toothless hillbilly to Tallulah Bankhead. But she had never been cast in a political role before.

The news of Lucille's political contretemps had leaked out belatedly through a blind item on Walter Winchell's radio broadcast. It seemed that earlier that month, Lucille had been secretly questioned by an investigator of the House of Representatives Committee on Un-American Activities and admitted that, when she was a struggling Hollywood actress in 1936, she had registered as a Communist voter in the Los Angeles primary election. However, she declared, she had never actually voted.

After the news about her secret testimony broke, Congressman Donald Jackson, a member of the committee, came to Lucille's defense, possibly spurred on by her television network and sponsors and by her movie studio. Jackson called a news conference in Los Angeles and, before batteries of movie, television and still cameras, stated that there was no evidence that America's beloved Lucy "is or ever was a member of the Communist party." Jackson added that the Un-American Activities Committee had had the information about Lucille for several years but had not thought it fair to divulge it, and that he was now taking the extraordinary step of a press conference because spreading rumors were threatening "irreparable damage" to Lucille.

The following day, Jackson made public a full transcript of the statements given by Lucille and members of her family earlier to a committee investigator in Hollywood. In the testimony, Ball blamed the entire mess on her dear, dead grandpa.

"It was our grandfather, Fred Hunt," she testified. "He wanted us to [register on the Communist ticket] and we just did something to please him. I didn't intend to vote that way. As I recall, I didn't." Lucille averred that Grandpa had been a well-meaning but misguided humanitarian. "All through his life," she said, "he had been a Socialist, as far back as Eugene V. Debs, and he was in sympathy with the working man as long as I have known."

According to Lucille, she and her twenty-one-year-old brother, Freddie, and her mother registered as Communists to do Grandpa "a favor" and "make him happy." She added that Grandpa had "had a couple of strokes" and nobody wanted to get him "overly excited." But, she declared, "I at no time intended to vote that way."

Then, more like the real television Lucy, she also testified that her grandpa's politics constantly disrupted the household. "We were never able to keep a maid," she said, "although we paid the highest prices we could afford or they were getting at that time. My grandfather would walk out into the kitchen and see a maid and would say, 'Well, what is your name? How much are you getting?' 'Oh, twenty or twenty-five dollars a week,' or whatever they were being paid. And he would say, 'That is not a working wage. What are you doing here?' And after a few times of that, you know, they would leave. That is just one instance."

Headlines promptly proclaimed: " 'LUCY NO RED,' SAYS JACKSON.

FANS LOVE HER, DESI TOO." Said Desi: "There's no doll more patriotic than this one. I've been married to this doll for thirteen years and I know she's not a Communist. . . . There's nothing red about that girl except her hair. And even that isn't legitimate."

The next day, Lucille and Desi had an informal press conference at their five-acre ranch at Chatsworth in the San Fernando Valley. The press came in full cry. There was a table sagging with beer, soft drinks and ham and cheese sandwiches, near the free-form swimming pool back of the house. Desi, in slacks and sport shirt, was dishing out drinks and grub to the reporters and photographers. Finally, Lucille herself came out. She was wearing pink slacks, a white blouse with "Lucille" embroidered on it and a pink ribbon in her red hair. She and Desi sat down in poolside blue-and-white canvas chairs with "Desilu" lettered on them. There were four watchful press agents present, one representing Philip Morris (Lucille's TV sponsor), one M-G-M (for whom Lucille and Desi had just made a movie), one Desilu Productions, and one CBS, which had, in 1952, paid Lucille and Desi $8,000,000 for a thirty-month contract. While flashbulbs popped, the reporters popped questions. One reporter asked how Winchell had come to have the news story about her. Lucille, not quite in comedy character, managed a slight gag: "I don't think it is difficult for Mr. Winchell to have access to anything. He told me I was pregnant before I knew it."

Desi commented on Grandpa—"a wonderful guy, a lovable guy—he died three years later—the kind of guy who wanted everybody in the world to be happy and have more money. Everybody tried to please Grandpa. . . . In 1936 it was a kind of joke, a kind of very light thing. If Grandpa was alive today, we might have to lock him in a back room."

But Grandpa, fortunately, was not alive today. And so it ended rosily, like a "Lucy" show. Everyone loved Lucy more than ever when it was all over. As the reporters and photographers trooped out, one of them asked Desi, "Do you think this whole thing would make a good story line in the show?" Replied Desi: "It sounds like a darn good 'Lucy' script." So it did.

All in all, it was a triumph for Americanism, press-agentry and Lucille, the pratfall comedienne, and Desi, the ex-conga drummer, who went on to become among the biggest and most glamorous tycoons in Hollywood, controlling more studio space, for their television empire, than even Louis B. Mayer had in his capitalistic heyday. (They have since gotten divorced.)

There was an interesting postscript in the New York *Times* by Jack Gould:

> Lucille Ball is an extremely fortunate woman. . . . [She] has received all the breaks. Every effort was made to obtain her version of events before the damaging innuendo was spread from coast to coast. Once this was known, relative calmness and reason prevailed.
>
> But in the radio and television industry last week one question was widely heard: what if the person involved had been plain Lizzie Glutz, an unknown actress with no hold on the affections of the millions of viewers and not the star of video's top-ranking comedy series in which there was an investment of millions of dollars? And the answer was unanimous: Lizzie Glutz never would have been heard from again. She would have been finished in radio and TV, a woman bearing the fatal brand of "controversial."

What with political and other complications, much of the fun has gone out of Hollywood in recent years. I can remember some years ago at Warner Brothers when Ida Lupino and Olivia de Havilland, a couple of madcap actresses, were making a movie entitled *Devotion*, about the Brontë sisters. But their behavior on the set was far from devotive. Both actresses liked to while away the long waits between scenes with liquid refreshments. This occasionally delayed production and the studio front office finally issued a firm edict that, under no circumstances, was there to be any fire water in the dressing rooms. However, the girls managed to have their nips anyway. They showed me how one day. They brought their libations to their dressing rooms in a handsome leather case that contained a test-tube rack. Should anyone have inquired about the liquid in the test tubes, they would have gravely explained that these were medical specimens.

Two of the subjects I most enjoyed writing about were James Dean and Greta Garbo for the simple reason that I did not have to meet them personally. Dean was dead at the time I did a piece about him for *Life* Magazine in 1956, and Garbo was traditionally incommunicado to the press when I worked on a story about her for *Collier's* in 1952. In both cases, absence undoubtedly made the journalistic heart grow fonder. Actually, meeting one's subjects is often a reportorial liability. A person will never tell you too much about himself, whether he wants to or not. You can usually find out more by indirection, mainly by talking to other people.

Dean, when I set out on the story about him, was already the object of a morbid posthumous craze. He was described as "the livest dead actor in the movies." He had died September 30, 1955, at the age of twenty-four, when he cracked up in a Porsche sport car across the rear of which he had lettered in red "The Little Bastard." At the time of his death, he had been seen in only one movie, *East of Eden*, and had completed two more, *Rebel Without a Cause* and *Giant*.

The Dean legend quickly mushroomed to spectacular, macabre proportions. It was foreshadowed in the funeral eulogy delivered by the Reverend Xen Harvey in Dean's home town of Fairmount, Indiana, on October 8, 1955. Entitled "The Life of James Dean—a Drama in Three Acts," it ended with "The career of James Dean has not ended. It has just begun. And remember, God himself is directing the production."

As an actor, Dean had been described as being "as instinctive as a cat." "I'm a serious-minded and intense little devil," he once said, "terribly gauche and so tense I don't see how people stay in the same room with me. I know I wouldn't tolerate myself." He said that "I act for the same reason most actors act, to express the fantasies in which I have involved myself."

Dean was a mixed-up kid running around with a wild and unsavory bunch of pre-beatniks. He lived in a small apartment which he referred to as a "wastebasket with walls." He was moody and melancholy. Among his interests were bullfighting and bongo drums. He was described as "a Greek tragedy on a motorcycle." He liked to snake his motorcycle down Sunset Boulevard in the headlights of a speeding car behind him. His customary attire was a black leather jacket, blue jeans and riding boots. He usually entered the Villa Capri, his favorite restaurant, through the kitchen.

Dean's on- and off-screen personality struck a tremendously responsive chord of identification in many youthful moviegoers. Even dead, he was the most popular actor in Hollywood. He was getting up to 8,000 fan letters monthly, more than any living profile. A special fan-mail agency had to deal with this deluge of mail. Most of the letters asked for photographs, but some requested anything that belonged to Dean, from a lock of his hair to a piece of his smashed car.

Many of the letter writers refused to admit that Dean was dead, and spoke of "immortality," "reincarnation" and "resurrection." A widely held theory had it that Dean did not really die in the auto crash but was so badly hurt that he was living out the rest of his life in a sanitarium. Fans wrote him letters as if he were still alive. "Jimmy, darling," one letter read, "I know you are not dead. I know you are just hiding because your face has been disfigured in the crash. Don't hide, Jimmy. Come back. It won't matter to us."

This necrophilic attitude was reflected in fan-magazine articles with titles like " 'Don't Say He's Dead!' Cry Millions of Fans" and "James Dean Is Immortal." There were special magazines devoted entirely to Dean: "Jimmy Dean Returns! Read His Own Words from the Beyond"; "James Dean Album—the Strange Mystery Lives On."

Actress Mercedes McCambridge, who appeared with Dean in *Giant*, said: "If there is such a thing as reincarnation, I would like to come back as James Dean."

Naturally, a Beverly Hills psychoanalyst (a live one, too) was commandeered to interpret all these doings. This particular pundit saw in this need to recreate and perpetuate Dean and excessively mourn him an expression of what he termed the unconscious guilt feelings of his fans. According to this Freudian theory, combined with the love and adoration his followers had for Dean was a deeply rooted hostility toward their idol. Although his fans admired his successful flouting of social convention and rebellion against authority, opined the psychoanalyst, they also resented his non-conformism because he was getting away with things for which they themselves would have been punished.

"Now that he is gone," explained the analyst, "it is as if his fans were saying, 'I wish I had been better to the one I loved.' It is a love and hate conflict. His fans need to bring him back to handle again their feelings about him and principally the unconscious hostile feelings about him. This is one way they have of punishing themselves for the anger they felt not knowingly toward the loved one who died—by continuing to think of the dead person, by keeping his memory alive, by keeping painful feelings alive."

A less weighty reaction to the resurrected Dean was expressed by one Hollywood old-timer: "The story that Dean is not dead is in the same class with other Hollywood falsehoods, like the gossip that once insisted Shirley Temple was a midget."

In Dean's corporeal absence, his fans consoled themselves with mementoes of their idol. Alleged pieces of the Porsche in which he had cracked up were sold as souvenirs. There was a rumor that the body and serial-number plates of the Porsche were stolen soon after the accident and that the thief, armed with these proofs of ownership, was profitably peddling any old pieces of Porsche aluminum to fans as real Dean auto souvenirs.

One Los Angeles firm was doing a land-office business with three-inch-high cast stone heads of Dean. Another concern was marketing a life-size head of the actor finished in Miracleflesh, a plastiflex material that looked and felt like human flesh, so that his fans could even fondle Dean if they so desired.

A barrage of mail came in to most anyone who had ever had as much as a nodding acquaintance with Dean. Julie Harris, who appeared with him in *East of Eden*, got letters asking her "what it felt like to be kissed by Jimmy Dean." George Stevens received missives rather ominously advising him not to cut out as much as one single frame of film of Dean from *Giant*. "It's absolutely weird fan mail," said Stevens, "the most uncomfortable stuff I've ever read."

Sal Mineo and Nick Adams, who acted with Dean in *Rebel Without a Cause*, got more fan mail about Dean than about themselves. "They're such pleading letters," Adams said. "They ask me for anything Jimmy had, anything he came in contact with. They say, 'Send me anything Jimmy touched. If he touched a wall, send a piece of the wallpaper.'" Dean fans would go to the Villa Capri, ask to sit at his favorite table and order his favorite dishes.

A bizarre death motif ran through the Dean legend. "Boy Meets Ghoul," cracked one Hollywoodite. According to some of his fans, Dean had had a mystic premonition of his death. He once posed for a photographer lying in a coffin in an undertaking parlor as a gag. He liked to make a noose out of a lariat and stick his head into it. He had a noose hanging in his living room. One of his cronies was a dark-haired, bony-faced actress, Maila Nurmi, who under the name of Vampira played Charles Addams-like characters on television. "We have the same neuroses," she had said of their friendship. Vampira declared, deadpan, that she was in frequent communication with Dean "through the veil. Mostly he comes to me through the radio." After the Dean story appeared in *Life*, Vampira, who was displeased with it, cast a hex on me via Western Union. It was possible to get Hollywood spiritualists to put you in touch with the ectoplasmic Dean at a séance for a couple of dollars.

George Stevens, who had directed Dean in *Giant* and had had differences with him in the course of production, decried all this as "morbid nonsense. Jimmy had no will to die. He was very much planning for the future. They're trying to make a Bridey Murphy out of him. While he was living, he provoked a little of it. He was a boy with a wonderful sense of the theater. All this encourages other young people, particularly young actors, to behave eccentrically. They saw it paid off for Jimmy. It leads young actors to believe they have spectral as well as earthy qualities."

Stevens added: "Here was a boy just on the rise. He'd hardly broken water, flashing into the air like a trout. A few more films and the fans wouldn't have been so bereft. He shortly would have dimmed his luster. This first bright phase would have become an ordinary light and not produced this kind of thing."

Lew Bracker, a twenty-seven-year-old insurance man who was one of Dean's closest friends, said, "If Jimmy were here and saw what was going on, he'd die all over again without the accident. It's mass hysteria. Somebody has paralyzed the whole country. It's a creepy, almost a sick thing. It's something in Jimmy the teen-agers saw, maybe themselves. Everybody mirrored themselves in Jimmy's fame and Jimmy's death. Have you ever thought if you were dead how many people would mourn you? Jimmy's death was their death. They related it to themselves."

What would Dean himself have made of all this hullabaloo? A wary, suspicious loner, he was markedly averse to publicity during his lifetime. "He ran from fame," said a Hollywood publicist. "He was embarrassed by fame. He really wanted to be left alone." A good friend of his said, "Here Jimmy was so lonely and uncared for during his life. It's strange that so many people want to be his friends today."

Humphrey Bogart summed it all up with "He died at just the right time. He left behind a legend. If he lived, he'd never have been able to live up to his publicity."

Garbo, even *in absentia*, was a fascinating subject. She was a mystery to even her closest friends. Clarence Brown, who directed her in many movies, was once asked what Garbo was thinking of in those great, evocative screen closeups. "Absolutely nothing," he said. But in some strange, magical way, the movie camera made that nothing come alive on the screen.

I talked to many of Garbo's professional and personal acquaintances. They all testified that her well-known desire to be alone was an authentic one. She would even have screens set up around her while making a movie so that she would not be distracted by the presence of the cast and crew. Clarence Brown explained her shyness with "She was always that way, from the very beginning. She didn't like people to watch her. She had folding black flats set up around her set. There was an evolution in the way she used those flats. In the silent days, we had hard lights or arc lights, a lot of them. She couldn't see beyond the lights and she couldn't see the cameraman, electricians, prop men and others watching her. But with the sound film, we developed fast film for which we used incandescent lighting, not much more light than you'd use in a drawing room. With that light, Garbo could see the set and it kept her from concentrating on her acting. She would catch someone's eye. The flats really started with sound."

Garbo's sets were always closed to outsiders and she seemed to have a knack of knowing when a stranger was present. A Hollywood newspaperman once arrived on a Garbo set with Clarence Brown's press agent to speak to the director. "We came on the set the back way between shots," he recalled. "It was an elaborate ballroom set. Garbo was at the top of a grand staircase. She immediately spotted me among 400 people at a tremendous distance in the back and would not continue with the picture until the press agent and I had left the set."

When Garbo was at M-G-M, Billy Grady, the casting director, had a ground-floor office near the studio east gate. To avoid people, Garbo would often climb through the window to see Grady.

Once Garbo thought she heard a burglar at her Beverly Hills home and reportedly slid down the drainpipe in her nightgown. The M-G-M police threw an armed guard around her house. There was no sign of a burglar.

On another occasion, when visitors arrived at her home one night unexpectedly, she became so frightened that she is said to have climbed a tree near the house. When the visitors kept knocking on the front door, Garbo supposedly hollered from the tree, "Not in!"

Reporters, naturally, were anathema to her. Edmund Goulding, one of her directors, said that she had retired from movies partly because "she is not too fond of journalists. If she and the press made up together, she'd make ten pictures tomorrow. One of the reasons for the abortion of her career is that so many things have been said about her and she is afraid of publicity. If the press would lay off her personal life, she and the press could make up. The thing she balks at is people going into her bedroom."

One of her closest friends was Harry Crocker, the columnist. "But," he said, "I never mentioned her name once in my column. I've known her since she arrived in Hollywood. I've been going out with her for eleven years. She stayed at my house once for four months. She is intensely shy. She's never been anything else but shy. There's great integrity in her shyness. It is a sincere and honest thing."

Crocker said that "only a few people call her Greta. I call her Miss Garbo."

According to Crocker, "There's a conspiracy of silence among Garbo's friends about her that is wonderful. Everybody who knows her has such a love for her and a belief in her integrity and in keeping silence. Garbo works with her friends much on the theory of the underground—one cell doesn't know the next cell. She never talks to her friends about any of her other friends.

"For the better part of ten years," said Crocker, "I kept track of all clippings from newspapers and magazines about Garbo. She didn't know anything about it. I had a clipping service send them all to me. I was amazed at the number of clippings that came in. I did this to try to clear up any mistaken ideas about her, such as the criticisms of her lack of war work, and wrote to her critics explaining the facts. The clips came in by the thousands. Every move she made was copy.

"People write entire columns about *not* interviewing her. Earl Wilson once rode up in an elevator with her and wrote a column about it.

"She's been off the screen for ten years and gets more publicity than Academy Award winners. She attracts more attention in obscurity than people in the heyday of their fame."

None of her many friends had an answer to the Garbo riddle (perhaps *Time* should have done this story and called in an assemblage of psychiatrists to help solve it). Pointing up the Garbo enigma, Alice Glazer, one of her cronies, told this story: "Her house in Beverly Hills had only two rooms in it that were furnished, the bedroom and drawing room. Outside of that the house was empty—an empty living room, an empty dining room. . . . She's insecure. She wasn't sure she was going to stay in the house. That's why she didn't furnish it."

And Glazer added that she once asked Garbo what she did when she was in New York. "Sometimes I put on my coat and go out at ten A.M. and follow people," Garbo replied. "I just go where they're going. I mill around." "That way," Glazer explained, "she's with people and she's not alone, but doesn't have to do anything about it."

Garbo was unique among film folk in her avoidance of publicity. But most profiles will go to any lengths for promotional purposes. One Hollywood star who travels abroad extensively on supposedly uplifting missions has garnered much favorable publicity for his work in this field. But I heard an interesting story about this performer when I was in Bangkok recently. The actor had arrived there under the aegis of an influential international organization. The King of Thailand held a reception for him. The Thai representative of the Hollywood company to which the star was under contract arranged all the details.

The actor had also indicated that he was most avid to meet some of the young Thai girls—Bangkok is famed for its fleshpots. It appeared that the profile might be interested in local citizens in ways other than he was representing himself to be. In the middle of the royal reception the star's henchman buttonholed the Thai representative and admonished him: "Look, pal, if you don't have the dames lined up for us as soon as this shindig is over, I'll get you canned." The Thailander was outraged—after all, this was his country and his king who was giving the reception. The Thai people are eminently easygoing and affable, but the Thai representative in this instance told the profile's emissary to go to blazes. True to form, the star did try to get the Thai representative fired when he returned to Hollywood, but the man had such a good job record that he was able to hold onto his position.

Publicity in Hollywood is the equivalent of fame and fortune. Performers on the way up are always anxious for publicity. When they reach the top, they may play it cooler. And when they are headed downhill again, as often happens, they start soliciting publicity once more. I had the unusual opportunity of observing the effect of publicity on one show-business personality while he was in the immediate state of transition between being a relative unknown and a celebrity. Comic George Gobel had just come into the television limelight in 1954 and his press agents were industriously soliciting *Time* Magazine for a story about him. The magazine finally decided to document Gobel. I interviewed him and filed a story to New York. That week, in addition to the upcoming *Time* story, Gobel's journalistic star was also in the ascendant with a number of other leading publications scheduling stories about him. He was suddenly shooting upward in the publicistic and journalistic spheres. As was customary with *Time*'s operation, I asked Gobel's manager at the end of the week for the comic's home phone number in case I had to check anything with him over the weekend (*Time* then went to press on Sunday nights and it was often necessary to reach people when business offices were closed). Gobel's manager coolly informed me that Gobel was not giving out his home phone number to reporters. In effect he was saying that Gobel was already too important by now for his private phone number to be handed out to a mere journalist from *Time* Magazine. Of course, what had helped make Gobel that important was the very fact that he was about to be written up in *Time*. I had caught Gobel in that revealing and fascinating moment between nonentity and fame, between

Dr. Jekyll and Mr. Hyde, so to speak. In due course, when Gobel's publicity dropped off, as it was inevitably bound to, his emissaries were again on the phone soliciting *Time* for another story. And there was no trouble this time about obtaining Gobel's home phone number, had **any**one wanted it.

CHAPTER VIII

The Little People

ONE OF THE MOST NOTABLE FEATS of Hollywood magic I ever witnessed occurred one night during World War II at a party given by Warner Brothers for some top military brass. At this celebration, which took place on a giant sound stage at the Warner studio, a lavish dinner was served to a gathering of several thousand motion-picture people and press and it was followed by a show featuring all the Warner luminaries, from Errol Flynn and Humphrey Bogart to Bette Davis.

The highlight of the show, however, was not any of these stellar names, but a gentleman named Ben Kalmenson. Kalmenson was sales manager of Warner Brothers. He was a short, dark, stocky individual who was in no way competition to Errol Flynn or any of the other handsome profiles. To his complete surprise, Kalmenson was summoned to the stage and a group of Warner technicians went to work on him, converting him from an unglamorous business executive into a ravishing glamour girl. A hairdresser crowned him with a long, silken wig; a make-up man deftly applied make-up; and a dress designer expertly draped him in a beautiful gown (padded with grapefruits). In a matter of minutes and in full view of the rapt audience on a bare, brightly lit stage, the embarrassed Kalmenson was transformed into a glittering glamour girl who looked more alluring than most of the real glamour girls present. It was a fascinating demonstration of Hollywood know-how. And it was said that the amorous Errol Flynn was so smitten with the "new" Kalmenson that he even offered to escort him home that night.

This social spoof was an indirect but eloquent tribute to the Hollywood technicians, the little people of moviedom. The unsung screen specialists do not get much publicity, but they are the craftsmen who are vital to the making of a movie. Their behind-the-scenes ministrations often save the celluloid when the profiles fall flat on their profiles, and when even the directors, writers and producers miss the mark. One rarely hears of them. Most of them are strongly unionized, have job security and just go about doing their work—and doing it well—without any publicistic fanfare. They do not need the publicity and have no special desire for it.

The Hollywood technicians do better work, as a rule, than those who designate themselves as creative artists. The mechanics of Hollywood moviemaking are almost always more refined and perfected than the writing, acting and direction of a movie. The technical side of the screen long ago outstripped the aesthetic elements. This is so partly because there is less front-office interference in the mechanical than in the human aspects of a motion picture, for the simple reason that the studio executives do not know much about the mechanics and do not presume to meddle in them as much.

One of these indispensable specialists without whom many movies would never have gotten made was the late B. Reeves Eason, Hollywood's leading action expert. Eason, who was known as "Breezy," did not get the publicity that a George Stevens or a William Wyler did (for one thing, he did not have personal press agents operating overtime for him, as the aforementioned film-makers do), but he was often as important to a movie as the more famous directors with whom he worked. And I dare say that he contributed more to the art of movies than Walter Wanger, Dore Schary and Stanley Kramer combined, without getting one per cent of the ballyhoo they did.

Action is the touchstone of most Hollywood movies, and Eason was the acknowledged master of his craft. Within the trade he was highly esteemed. But his screen credits were not conspicuous and sometimes he was not even credited on a picture. Eason was what is known as a second-unit director, and second-unit directors rarely receive screen credit because that might detract from the glory of the director. The Directors Guild of America has no contractual stipulation with the studios about credit for second-unit directors because the Guild is primarily interested in promoting credit for the director and not for any of his helpers, no matter how important their contribution to a movie. Although assistant directors today get screen credit, by Directors Guild of America fiat (they did not in years past), the assistant director is essentially a sort of errand boy for the director who does not perform any creative function, and so his screen credit does not reflect on the director's accomplishment, whereas the second-unit director is a creative moviemaker in his own right. Ideally, of course, it is the director himself who should be in charge of the "action" in a movie, but this does not hold true in Hollywood's departmentalized moviemaking.

As a result, Eason was not particularly known outside of Hollywood. Even most of the "students" of the movies were uninformed about him. In his book *The Lion's Share*, a history of M-G-M, Bosley Crowther conspicuously and strangely fails to mention Eason at all, although Eason directed the outstanding scenes in two of the most successful M-G-M pictures of all time, the silent *Ben-Hur* and *Gone with the Wind*.

In 1947 I sought out Eason on his little ranch in North Hollywood, with its smokehouse and all kinds of animals, to have a talk with him about his work. He seemed a little surprised that anyone should be sufficiently interested in his moviemaking to want to discuss it with him. He was a sturdy, reddish-haired man in his late fifties, with a weather-beaten face and a habit of lighting matches by striking them on his teeth. He was a typical old-time Hollywood type, a bit of a roustabout and rather inarticulate, but an expert with the camera. He talked at some length of his moviemaking methods and ideas in his gruff, slow-spoken way.

Born in Fryors Point, Mississippi, in 1891, Eason broke into show business as part of a vaudeville song-and-dance act. But he was also a sure shot with a gun and an expert horseman, and in 1913 he joined Thomas Ricketts' American Film Company in Santa Barbara, a horse-opera outfit, as a sort of jack of all trades. He was writer, actor, stunt man, property man and custodian of the kitchen rolled into one. Later, as a full-fledged director, he made hundreds of modestly budgeted and thoroughly unpretentious westerns and action thrillers with titles like *Lariat Kid*, *Trigger Tricks*, *Roarin' Ranch* and *Call of the Yukon*. But his best work was reserved for the big-budget epics on which he served as second-unit director.

Among his achievements in havoc and holocaust, stampede of man and beast and cataclysm of fire and storm were such outstanding scenes as the chariot race in the original *Ben-Hur*, the burning of Atlanta in *Gone with the Wind*, the land rush in *Cimarron*, the battle footage in *Sergeant York*, the joust episodes in *The Adventures of Robin Hood*, the stallion fighting sequence in *Duel in the Sun*, and the charge in *The Charge of the Light Brigade*.

These were the high points of these pictures. Eason was usually credited, when credit was doled out to him, with the deceptively modest line "Second unit directed by B. Reeves Eason." On *The Adventures of Robin Hood*, he was credited as "joust scenes director." On *The Charge of the Light Brigade*, he was listed as "director of horse action." On *Ben-Hur*, he was "directorial associate" to director Fred Niblo. But frequently Eason had at least as much to do with the picture as the director himself. He had mammoth budgets on *Gone with the Wind* and *Duel in the Sun* for contriving high-priced movie mayhem, and he worked on the chariot races of *Ben-Hur* for four months.

Eason's work was difficult, time-consuming and expensive. A good train- or shipwreck, for instance, was likely to run into sizable sums, even some years ago. Once Eason received his budget for his special work, he was in complete charge of the shooting, with his own crew and cameramen. The director rarely had a hand in these sequences. The script might indicate briefly that an action interlude was required. Eason would develop this skeletal instruction into pictorial continuity by visualizing it in the form of hundreds of camera setups and in terms of angle, distance and movement. The Atlanta fire in *Gone with the Wind* took eight pages of final camera continuity. The train wreck in *Duel in the Sun* was expanded from one page in the screenplay to a fifteen-page shooting document in Eason's hands. In effect, Eason wrote his own sequences. He thought that there was overwriting in pictures and that in movies, particularly, actions spoke louder than words. He disliked static speeches on the screen. "They're just as flat as a sidewalk," he said simply.

Typical of Eason's technique in making movies move is the way he shot the chariot races in the 1926 *Ben-Hur*. These were filmed in a Roman coliseum, assertedly larger than the original Circus Maximus, that M-G-M had constructed in Culver City, California. First, the entire action, with a crowd of thousands of spectators, was filmed in long shots that established the over-all setting. Eason then broke down the scene into its component parts to extract the visual essence from it. In a movie, Eason argued, the sum of the parts equals more than the whole. He pointed up the action with closeups—of chariot wheels, horses' hoofs and nostrils, drivers' faces, straining leashes and individual crowd reactions as twelve teams of four horses raced seven laps around the giant arena, taking spills and making breakneck turns. The result was a high point in Hollywood screen spectacle.

"You can have a small army of people charging across the screen," Eason explained, "and it won't matter much to the audience. But if you show details of the action, like guns going off, individual men fighting or a fist hitting someone in the eye, then you will have more feeling of action than if all the extras in Hollywood are running about. That is why real catastrophes often look tame in newsreels. You need detail work and close shots in a movie. Only then does it come to life."

In M-G-M's new version of *Ben-Hur*, the chariot race, like the rest of the picture, emerged as turgid, theatrical-style spectacle with little cinematic vigor. The new chariot sequence was nowhere near what Eason had accomplished. It lacked the hard, knock-down detail of the original. Eason had broken down the chariot race into crucial bits and pieces of film—in order to build it up dramatically. The new chariot race, which supposedly took three months to film and was directed by action experts Andrew Marton and Yakima Canutt, had few of the telling closeups that Eason had; the new, big screen did not lend itself to closeups. There was a startling near absence of effective, low-angle pit shots, of shots to and from the spectator stands, of shots from the chariots to the racing horses fore and aft, of the camera moving parallel with the moving lines of horses. There was mainly a hopped-up sound track and a lot of spurious commotion on the screen. But the chariot sequence, like the movie as a whole, was without real filmic motion. And *Ben-Hur*, now as then, stands or falls on those chariot scenes. Dilys Powell summed it up in the London Sunday *Times* with the observation that the picture lacked "imaginative size to match its physical size."

In engineering conflagrations, crashes and slugfests, Eason made a fine art of combining trickery, thrills and camera technique. He said that the whole thing was primarily a matter of preparation. He worked closely with most of Hollywood's stunt men. In former years stunting was a rather lethal livelihood. For *Ben-Hur*, Eason dressed cowboys from stunt westerns in togas and offered a prize of $300 to the first man across the line in a chariot. There were some violent shakeups en route. Screen stunting in recent years has largely become a business of carefully planned setups, of brain rather than brawn. Eason prided himself on the fact that, although he had staged many screen battles, he never killed a man or a horse. Stunt men liked to work with him because he understood their problems and did not ask the impossible.

Eason called upon many tricks of the trade for his work. He liked to film a fracas from low-angle shots, with the camera shooting up from a pit in the ground, or from high-angle shots. By intercutting these shots and punctuating them with close shots, such as full-screen heads with fists coming up, he built what he called "action tempo." In film fights the trickery lay in the camera angle. Stunt men might miss one another's jaws by several inches, but this was not apparent on the screen when the camera was strategically placed.

Eason used pit shots a great deal to make the action loom more dramatically. For *The Charge of the Light Brigade*, he placed a camera truck on tracks in a 600-foot-long trench and shot upward as he followed the spectacular action of thirty-eight horses and riders falling in the midst of explosions. He constructed a pit clear across a battlefield for *Sergeant York* to accommodate a truck with four cameras. Two of the cameras were on the floor shooting up at sharp angles, one shot at normal eye level, and one very high-up camera shot down as Gary Cooper, portraying Sergeant York, advanced across the battlefield with explosives dropping all about him. Several cameras often had to be used simultaneously because the action was too dangerous and expensive to be restaged.

Eason did not pretend to be a deep thinker, but in his own blunt, practical way he knew more about moviemaking than most of the renowned directors for whom he worked. He had seen many of the outstanding films, both domestic and foreign, and knew and respected the work of the best moviemakers. He also had a basic grounding in the editing of film that he applied to his action work.

"You get pace in a movie," Eason said, echoing the theories of Griffith and the great Russian moviemakers, "from the way you put the different shots together in the cutting room. The pace doesn't come from movement in a shot or from how much is happening in a shot, but from the combination of all the shots. They can all be static and yet you will think that all hell is breaking loose when they are put together the right way. Shots can be made to clash on the screen and give the effect of conflict just by having one shot heading, say, toward the left, followed by another shot heading toward the right.

"The eye sees differently from the camera. You see things in three dimensions and color with your eye. Your eye also moves about, picking out what it wants to see. It is up to the director to make the camera work like an eye, by having it pick out the highlights of what is happening."

Unfortunately, all these detailed camera setups, this "mosaic" of shots, take time and money to accomplish. The rise of production costs in recent years has caused moviemakers to cut down on such expensive action sequences. The syntax of the screen has become more and more prohibitive financially. As a result, most movies take the easy—and economical—way out and talk about things instead of showing them dramatically.

Before he died in 1956 Eason had moved over to television and was doing the action work for the "Lone Ranger" TV series. No one has ever quite replaced him as an expert in cutting to the chase. His credits, when he was credited, were in rather small type on the screen. But he was responsible for some of the biggest and most actionful moments in American movies.

Slavko Vorkapich is a rather exotic name and the word "montage" seems to be on the esoteric side. But Vorkapich, the former M-G-M montage expert, is a forthright, down-to-earth fellow who talks good, plain common sense about the movies. Montage in Hollywood has a special meaning. When the Yugoslavian, sharp-profiled Vorkapich was working for M-G-M, he devised vivid montages for numerous pictures, mainly to get a point across economically or to bridge a time lapse. In a matter of moments, with images cascading across the screen, he was able to show Jeanette MacDonald's rise to fame as an opera star in *Maytime*, the outbreak of the revolution in *Viva Villa*, the famine and exodus in *The Good Earth*, and the plague in *Romeo and Juliet*.

But the theory behind montage, says Vorkapich, paraphrasing the Russian moviemakers, particularly Eisenstein, has wider applications than mere photographic effects and can be used to tell an entire screen story, not just an isolated moment in it. This theory is the familiar one that motion pictures are a visual medium and that the camera is the means with which the screen creator expresses himself. Although this theory has been set forth frequently, it has too rarely been put into effect. Most movies today, Vorkapich contends, are advisedly "photoplays"—extensions of the stage or novel—rather than real movies. They are based on a theatrical use of talk, with the camera passively "recording" the proceedings instead of participating "creatively" in them. The recent Samuel Goldwyn production of *Porgy and Bess*, which has been described as "a photographed opera," is an extreme instance of this.

As an exponent of the classic theory of movie movement, Vorkapich points out that motion pictures were originally devised to document movement—whether of horses, trains or custard-pie wielders—and that the word "movie" is indicative of the nature of the medium. Vorkapich's theory is that movement arouses an involuntary visceral reaction in the spectator and that different movements can evoke different types of response. An upward movement, for instance, he explains, usually represents aspiration or exaltation. A descending movement is symbolic of heaviness or danger. A circular, revolving movement is emblematic of a cheerful mood. A pendulum movement conveys monotony and relentlessness. And a diagonal, dynamic movement stands for the overcoming of obstacles.

Since he started making movies in 1928, Vorkapich says, he experimented with these various physiological theories, as promulgated by the behaviorist school of psychology, and found them to be true. (Earlier, the leading Russian directors, particularly Eisenstein and Pudovkin, had stated that they based their theories of film montage on behavioristic principles.) Vorkapich wanted to make it clear that he did not believe in motion for its own sake. He held that too many directors used dolly and boom shots simply to have so-called movement in a movie. Vorkapich said that there had to be a reason for each movement, arising out of the subject matter. In the pioneer days of the screen, slapstick comedies and westerns made use of a crude form of this technique. Vorkapich argued that he would like to see it applied to more complex ends in order to convey subtleties of mood and motivation, action and reaction, as the Russians did.

In 1934, Vorkapich devised two montages for Ben Hecht's and Charles MacArthur's *Crime Without Passion*, made at the Astoria studio in New York. One of these, dealing with the symbolic unleashing of the Furies, might be cited as a sort of rapid-fire index to the grammar of the film, of what can be accomplished with visual screen technique.

The sequence, in its original form, ran to only 300 feet, but it encompassed a good many of the things that can be done with a camera and film. The scene opened with Claude Rains shooting Margo. The initial shot was a full-screen closeup of one of Margo's eyes as she stared into the gun. Vorkapich shot this closeup as a still picture in order to make for the reverse of movement, with the resultant feeling of holding one's breath. According to Vorkapich, the absence of movement can be as important to a moviemaker as movement itself: all life is composed of contrasts. From this static closeup he dissolved to a closeup of the muzzle of the gun in an exact overlap that found the revolver in the same place on the screen as the eye had been. He cut back to the eye, this time showing a slight twitch. The next shot was again of the barrel of the gun. The shot of the gun was expressed visually by a number of quick flashes, an all-black frame alternating with a white one. Each of these shots was held on the screen for only two frames. In this way, the rapid, volatile effect Vorkapich wanted was achieved visually.

Vorkapich added that the sound of the gun firing was on the sound track, but the result was all the more effective for being a welding of the visual and aural. He observed that the creative use of sound is important to a motion picture. Sound on the contemporary screen is used mostly to reproduce dialogue or obvious sound effects, but it can be an additional tool to tell a story if handled imaginatively. Some examples come to mind. When Harry Baur starts going deaf in the French film *The Life and Loves of Beethoven*, the sound track becomes totally silent, with occasional snatches of blurred sound fading in and fading out. The grating noise of a metal-works factory in the epileptic-doctor episode of *Un Carnet de Bal* lent added power to that sequence. The same device of hammering noise was used in the opening scene of the German film *Dr. Mabuse* to establish a strenuous, discordant mood. In *M*, the child murderer whistled several bars of "In the Hall of the Mountain King" whenever he was about to commit a crime.

The next shot in the *Crime Without Passion* montage was of Margo's eyes wincing in sudden pain. This was followed by an out-of-focus shot of smoke leaving the gun and of the man behind the gun. Vorkapich explained that in such a shot the spectator's eyes strain to bring the picture into focus and that this effort physically almost forces tears into the viewer's eyes. Then there was a shot of Margo falling to the ground, in slow motion, to prolong the feeling of agony. One of the things a movie can do, Vorkapich pointed out in primer fashion, is to expand time or contract it for dramatic purposes. The famous sequence of the czarist military marching down the Odessa steps in *Potemkin* took a good ten minutes to run on the screen. Actually, such a march might have taken much less in real life. But director Sergei Eisenstein purposely prolonged the action in order to wring the last film foot of suspense out of it.

Before Margo was shown hitting the ground in *Crime Without Passion*, Vorkapich cut to a closeup of a drop of blood striking the ground. Then out of the blood of the victim, the symbolic Furies were depicted rising and flying over the city. Vorkapich shot this scene with the Furies stationary and the camera shooting from above and passing them as it headed down. Since all space on the screen is relative, the Furies seemed to be in motion. Years ago, when I was at the Astoria studio where *Crime Without Passion* was shot, I saw some of the sets from the picture stored away in one corner of a sound stage. The sets were flimsy and incomplete. Hecht and MacArthur, and cameraman Lee Garmes, had no use for fancy, cumbersome sets. They knew exactly what effects they wanted and they were able to obtain them easily and inexpensively by using their ingenuity and by building only the portions of the sets that would actually be seen on the screen.

I cite this montage from *Crime Without Passion* in detail not because it is a world-beater but because it represents a creative approach to moviemaking that has either been relegated to the background or been completely forgotten in recent years. There are other classic instances of this filmic creativeness as opposed to merely presenting a photographic representation of events. Critic Paul Rotha has mentioned, in his *The Film Till Now*, as an example of "how the film assembles the elements of reality to build from them a new reality proper to itself," a scene of an explosion in the Russian silent film *The End of St. Petersburg*. "Director V. I. Pudovkin," wrote Rotha, "photographed a real explosion in its entirety, but it lacked impact on the screen. So he built an explosion out of bits of film by taking separate shots of clouds of smoke and of a magnesium flare and welding them into a rhythmic pattern of light and dark. Into this series of images, he cut a shot of a river that he had taken some time before, which was appropriate owing to its tones of light and shade. When he assembled these shots on the screen they were vividly effective, but they had been achieved without using a shot of the real explosion."

Another example, cited by Rotha, is from Pudovkin's great silent movie, *Mother*. "A scene," wrote Rotha, "showed the son in prison receiving a note telling him he would be freed the next day. Pudovkin wanted to depict his reacting with joy, but he did not just photograph his face lighting up. First, he showed the nervous play of his hands, then a big closeup of the lower half of his face, the lips faintly twisting into a smile. He cut in shots of a brook swollen in springtime, sunlight playing on the water, birds splashing in a pond, and a laughing child. The result of the assembly of these parts was more effective than the whole would have been."

Rotha added that although these sequences were from silent films, the talking picture can be even more effective by adding to this creative visual approach a creative use of sound.

Movies, it has been said, are in their ideal form closer to ballet than to the stage. Vorkapich contends that the world of color is the domain of painting, the world of tone is the province of music, and the world of movement is characteristic of film. The full range of movie movement, he holds—by means of cutting, dissolving, moving shots, pan shots, slow motion, reverse action and the many other camera devices—can be used to probe the most complex and subtle moods and situations. Movement, he maintains, does not have to deal only with physical movement. It can deal also with action within people. One of the most movement-full movies ever made was Jean-Pierre Melville's version of Jean Cocteau's *Les Enfants Terribles* in which most of the "action" was psychological in nature and took place in a "turtle's shell" of a Montmartre apartment and in a few other confined interiors. But there was more movement in this picture than in most outdoor horse operas. In this strange story about the affection of a brother and sister for each other, the camera roved freely and fluently through the limited space and presented great grappling closeups and odd, feverish screen compositions. The result was a baroque, grotesque, always fascinating camera excursion into a dark-bright dream world, cinematically achieved. But Hollywood's infrequent forays into this realm, such as the recent *The Nun's Story*, directed by Fred Zinnemann, which was described as "an adventure of the mind," have largely failed through lack of cinematic know-how.

Vorkapich says that the trouble with motion-picture scripts today is that they are mostly written in terms of theatrical dialogue. Movies, he argues, are suffocated by a bottleneck of words. He contends that talk is only one ingredient in a movie and that silence can be just as important as dialogue. He says he would like to see a scenario written in two sections. On one side of the page would be the dialogue, and on the other would be a detailed résumé of the action and camera manipulations. He holds that if the action did not speak for itself, then there was something lacking in the script. Such a scenario technique would require that the writer be thoroughly trained in the ABCs of motion-picture production before he sat down at a typewriter. It would mean that the writer would think visually instead of from a literary standpoint and would practically write his story with the camera.

"If dialogue interferes with the visual effect," says Vorkapich, "it doesn't belong. Film itself is so powerful that it can express things not possible through other mediums." He cites as an example of film's expressiveness the experiment made by a Russian director whereby, through strategic editing of pieces of film, a variety of different effects were obtained. Between closeups of a man sitting and thinking were sandwiched first a shot of a pretty girl, then a shot of a big steak and finally a shot of a dead body. The effect was entirely different in each case. In the first instance, the man looked sensuous. In the second he looked hungry and in the third he looked like a criminal, all depending upon the way the film was edited.

Another requirement Vorkapich makes of a movie is "rhythm," not a musical or regular rhythm, but "rhythm" arising from the juxtaposition of the different shots in the over-all editing. "A good movie," he says, "is one that has rhythmic action when run upside down without sound."

"Montage," Vorkapich concludes, "is French for any kind of mounting, assembling, putting together. Like many other words it has a general and a special meaning. Thus, the making of a complete picture (assembling individual strips of film) is montage in its general meaning. Although the Russians have developed montage, the possibilities of the method have hardly been touched upon in Hollywood. Practically, it has proven to be a valuable economic device in regular Hollywood productions. Artistically, it could become a true filmic form of expression. Montage ideally is not just a jumble of camera tricks. They are tricks only when they are used for their own sake and not as a most graphic means of expressing something. Montage is in reality a film style of its own, and a very elastic one at that, which uses purely visual means, including all the possibilities of the camera, of movement, of rhythm and of cutting to express feeling and thoughts to tell stories."

According to Vorkapich, finally, montage should not be limited to an "expert," but should rightfully be at the root of the director's initial, over-all conception of a film. Here, too, Hollywood's damaging departmentalization has been a stumbling block to any development of this technique.

Vorkapich long ago left M-G-M. And today, in a Hollywood where movies are literally talking themselves to death with stereophonic sound from overinflated screens, he unfortunately has little opportunity to put into effect these unique moviemaking ideas.

The name of the late William Cameron Menzies, listed as production designer on a motion picture, was just another unknown quantity as far as the average cash customer was concerned. In the movie industry, however, Menzies was a great name. He was a motion-picture designer for almost thirty-five years and literally left his mark on such movies as *Gone With the Wind, Our Town, The Devil and Miss Jones, Pride of the Yankees, King's Row, For Whom the Bell Tolls, Foreign Correspondent* and *Around the World in 80 Days.*

A chunky, ruddy man with thinning gray hair, Menzies was concerned with the cinema as a graphic art. Long before a picture went into production, he was at work "pre-staging" it in terms of pictorial effects that encompassed camera angles, positions of the actors and types of sets. Menzies looked at a script visually and it was said that nature endowed him with a two-inch lens instead of eyes. He held that there was a spot between the scenario and the direction that an artist, trained in film fundamentals, could usefully fill. His production designs were, in that sense, an intermediate stage between the written word and its realization on the screen, although this too should rightfully be the domain of the director instead of being delegated to a specialist.

Before becoming Hollywood's first and foremost production designer, Menzies was an illustrator of children's books. Director George Fitzmaurice became interested in his work and asked him to create a palm grove on a tropic isle for a motion picture. Menzies solved it in the most elementary way, by taking two big palm-leaf fans and projecting their shadows on a background. As a result, he got a job with Fitzmaurice and was embarked on a fruitful career as a motion-picture designer.

Menzies served as art director for Douglas Fairbanks' *The Thief of Bagdad* and *The Iron Mask* and he won an Academy Award for his art direction of *The Tempest*. With *Bulldog Drummond* in 1929, he put into effect the technique of making a complete sketch of every camera setup, which he continued to practice from then on. He directed pictures like *Alice in Wonderland* and *Things to Come*, always doing production-design continuities, and functioned as production designer for *Nothing Sacred*, *The Adventures of Tom Sawyer*, *Intermezzo*, *Pride of the Yankees* and many other movies.

For the average picture, Menzies made between 1,200 and 1,400 different sketches. *Gone with the Wind* ran to 2,500 drawings. There was a sketch for every individual camera setup that was seen in the finished film. Working from the script, he first drew numerous thumbnail sketches that indicated the general lighting and pattern of a scene broken down into its component elements. For key scenes he did a big sketch in detail. If these sketches could have been skimmed rapidly before the eye, they would have added up to a sort of preview of the picture in question.

Menzies had definite ideas about the visual aspects of a motion picture. He liked to compose with the camera frame instead of inside it. In other words, Menzies' sketches reached to the borders of the screen instead of falling within the frame. He did not believe in composition purely as composition. Each shot had to have a purpose and contribute to the story that was being told. He particularly disliked wasting space and he liked to keep his people and backgrounds clarified. Normally, he kept his action close to the camera. He used long shots for mood or violent action. Closeups were for emphasizing a face or character. He believed in cutting and not in the moving camera, for he held that the latter wasted film footage, that the cameraman had less control of composition and that the audience was disturbed by it. He liked pan or follow shots because he considered them physically and psychologically natural.

Menzies used the low camera a good deal, but he seldom placed a camera under table or desk height. He found that, with a low camera, the background usually evolved into plain surfaces like sky or walls and the people stood out more clearly. In Menzies' opinion, people were primary in a picture and he preferred to emphasize them. He held that the face was the all-important part of a person, unless there was a special reason to shift the camera's attention elsewhere. In facial closeups, he said, the eyes, nose and mouth were all that mattered. Sometimes Menzies showed no chin or hair in his facial closeups. A cameraman once said to him, "Let's pull back to a long shot now and show the chin and hair."

Menzies liked to use the wide-angle lens for deep-focus shots. He pointed out that this amounted to a long shot and a closeup simultaneously. In *Our Town*, a striking shot was set in a graveyard, with the mother's head in the immediate foreground and the daughter's full figure in a white dress in the background. Actually, this shot had to be done with a split screen by cameraman Bert Glennon because no lens could carry so deep a focus. In *King's Row*, working with cameraman James Wong Howe, Menzies played a whole scene in lightning, alternating between intense blackness and flashes of light. After each lightning flash, the characters moved closer together. In this case, the lightning amounted to cuts. In *North Star*, again with Howe, the camera angles stressed the low horizons to emphasize the flatness of the Russian plains.

Menzies preferred to work in color because, he said, it offered greater possibilities than black and white. His use of color for dramatic effect in *Gone with the Wind*, such as the childbirth scene, with the woman's black silhouette against a torrid orange background, again won him an Academy Award.

Menzies said his drawings were only shorthand sketches for entrances, first groupings and effective finishes for a scene. He explained that it was impossible to plan everything on paper and that the sketches were amplified in actual execution on the set. Menzies often collaborated with the cameraman during the production-designing stage. He said that he became a producer and director chiefly to protect his interests as a production designer.

Menzies aimed at the utmost fluidity in designing a motion picture. To achieve this, he resorted to all sorts of devices. He might fade out on a big closeup of a head and fade in on a tiny head in the same position. If the preceding composition dovetailed into the following shot, he said, there was an imperceptible blending that was easy on the eye.

Menzies' moviemaking theories harked back to the classic achievements of the silent screen in his stress on cutting and pertinent camera setups. He said that the director who influenced him most was F. W. Murnau, creator of *The Last Laugh* and *Sunrise*. He also cited the visual power of the German *Variety* and the pictures of the leading Russian directors.

For a man who was preoccupied with theory and technique, Menzies was also aware of the sterile pitfalls into which they could lead. He espoused the cause of movie mechanics but only insofar as they made for a more effective depiction of the human element on the screen. He believed that his contribution to a picture was good if it helped the story, acting and direction. "The whole secret of motion-picture making is in preparation," he said. "What comes after that is hard work."

George Amy, a reserved, monolithic, highly competent craftsman, cut the films of that dialectic director, Michael Curtiz, at Warners, for fifteen years. Amy was responsible for many a profile on the cutting-room floor. He spent a year and a half editing *Life with Father*, a movie which Curtiz, Amy and Warners have been trying to forget ever since. He also cut such pictures as *The Green Pastures*, *Captain Blood*, *Yankee Doodle Dandy* and *The Charge of the Light Brigade*. The charge in the latter was one of the most spectacular pieces of up-and-at-'em action that Hollywood ever contrived. Amy finally edited that one sequence down from endless reels of film that were pouring in from Breezy Eason and two other units shooting all over the map.

After a while this footage, "this mess of film, this celluloid spaghetti hanging everywhere," became so immense that Amy went to the producer and told him that he could no longer make positive or negative of it.

"You make yourself Lord Tennyson and cut the picture from the poem," this genius told him.

Since the poem said little besides "Into the valley of Death rode the six hundred," Amy was still in something of a quandary.

"I just took my damn good time," said Amy. "I knew nobody knew what I was doing and I didn't know what I was doing. When Mike [Curtiz] saw the picture afterwards, he said, 'When did I shoot that?'"

Amy, naturally, is of the opinion that editing is vital to the tempo and distinctiveness of a movie. He observes that too few directors in Hollywood get to edit their own movies today.

Amy himself was a director at Warners for a stretch.

"When I became a director," he said, "I wanted to cut my own pictures, but they wouldn't let me. They told me that it was beneath me now that I was a director." He added, somewhat sadly, "So somebody else did it."

Over the years I have interviewed many movie cameramen. As a group, they have probably been around longer than any other technicians and they may have more lore about the movies to impart than most anyone else in Hollywood. However, most movie cameramen, as George Stevens, himself a former cameraman, once said, "are strangely inarticulate, perhaps because they have tried to create something artistic without use of words and have expressed themselves visually."

Not many cameramen, oddly, have become directors. Stevens observed of this that "inarticulation interferes with their making it known they'd want to be a director. I think more cameramen could be directors. But," he hazarded, "maybe good cameramen are too scarce to make directors of them."

Stevens observed that "to be a director, the door is open today. A cameraman, not. Now on account of the union has protected so many so well, it has eliminated new blood, the fresh viewpoint among cameramen."

When Stevens started out in movies in 1921, as an assistant cameraman to Karl Struss, Sol Polito and Floyd Jackman, "advancement was rapid then and I became a full-fledged cameraman at the age of twenty. You couldn't do it now to save your life if you are a young man."

Stevens added: "I still pay dues in the I.A.T.S.E., the cameraman's union, as a director of photography. If I wanted to, I could shoot a picture. I'm proud of that."

Photography, it has been observed, is one of the few things that Hollywood usually handles with skill and often with appreciable artistry. One of the experts at movie photography is James Wong Howe, a small, pug-nosed, Chinese-American lensman. Howe broke into the movies in the silent era and, as a fledgling photographer, shot Gloria Swanson and other glamour girls of the time. In those early Hollywood days, when he missed the streetcar going downtown, he would sometimes stay over at the studio at night, sleeping on a boudoir set in Miss Swanson's plush and perfumed cinematic bed.

Howe helps make the profiles look the way movie heroes and heroines are supposed to look, even though they may be afflicted with bags under the eyes, twin chins, vanishing hairlines or the after-effects of excessive conviviality. In his time, as an expert in low-key, glamour photography, Howe has lensed many of Hollywood's most exotic actresses, from Pola Negri to Hedy Lamarr, but he has also done some rather free-wheeling, realistic photography in pictures like *Viva Villa*, *Air Force* and *Objective, Burma!*

In former years, particularly, says Howe, most everything had to be glamorous. When he photographed *Whipsaw* at M-G-M in 1936, one scene required Myrna Loy to wake up in the morning looking tired after a late night out. Howe suggested that she be filmed with her hair a little mussed and not looking as if she had just emerged from a beauty salon. This was a rather revolutionary idea in that period at M-G-M, but Miss Loy went along with it. Howe shot the scene that way and after the film was developed and shown with the day's rushes, he was called into the office of one of the studio high command, Edward Mannix. Mannix was irate. "What do you mean by shooting that kind of stuff of Loy?" he yelled at Howe (this is an approximate quote; it may have had even less grammar in it than the foregoing). "Here we've spent a couple of million bucks building her up as a glamour girl and you knock the whole thing for a loop with one shot."

Howe tried to explain that this was what the script called for and that Loy and the director had agreed to her being photographed that way. But Mannix would have none of it, and so Howe reshot the scene with the actress looking immaculately groomed, flawlessly made up and thoroughly glamorous after her all-night toot.

But Howe is more than just a glamour lensman. He is also a fairly creative cameraman who has given some thought to the movies and moviemaking and who is among the few photographers who are reasonably articulate about their work. The camera, says Howe, can often be more expressive than the writer or performer. Some of his shots, in movies like *The Power and the Glory*, *Transatlantic*, *Yankee Doodle Dandy*, *The Hard Way* and *The Brave Bulls*, bear out this theory. In one of his movies, *Body and Soul*, he shot the boxing scenes with Eyemos, hand-held cameras which wind like clocks and which have often been used for combat photography. Howe trained three Eyemos on John Garfield and his opponent under the harsh, overhead lights of the boxing ring, and he wielded one camera himself as he was pushed around the ring on roller skates to capture smashing closeups of the prize fighters in action. The result ranked among the best fight footage ever filmed.

"Too many movies today," says Howe, echoing Eason, Menzies, Vorkapich et al., "are photographed stage plays. They don't take advantage of the camera. A movie should be plotted out with the camera in mind. The camera used imaginatively can tell so many things."

The late Joseph August, a cameraman since 1911, shot more than 200 movies, from primitive westerns to overproduced David Selznick films like *Portrait of Jennie*. In the old days a cameraman used to load the film in the camera, crank the machine and poke around in the developing lab afterward. Today, a Hollywood cameraman is called "the director of Cinematography" and has a crew of four assistants.

"Moviemaking," August, a sturdy, gray-haired man, told me in 1947, "is getting more complicated all the time. Shooting a picture was a lot more informal, a lot more fun—and a lot more dangerous in earlier years."

August would shoot silent-screen cowboy William S. Hart in action on a horse by riding alongside him on another horse with his camera propped in his lap. For a John Ford picture, *Men Without Women*, August shot a scene in which a crew was shown entering a submarine and closing down the hatch, with the ship then submerging, all in one continuous shot. August rigged up the camera in a lightweight copper underwater box and fastened it on a tripod to the submarine's bow. He was outfitted in a regular diver's uniform and stood at the camera on the submarine's nose, shooting the sequence above water and then finally underwater as the ship gradually descended.

Rudolph Mate was once one of Hollywood's most successful movie cameramen; he took a salary cut to become a director. Before he came to Hollywood he photographed *The Passion of Joan of Arc* and *Vampire* for director Carl Dreyer in France. Both pictures were shot with primitive equipment but were photographically advanced. In the silent *Passion of Joan of Arc*, the French actress Falconetti, in the title role, wore no make-up whatsoever. A monumental, epic effect was achieved through low-angle shots of Falconetti and the other performers against masonry and sky. Conversely, many of the shots were from high angles shooting downward. Interiors were filmed in an empty garage near Paris. Much of the movie was done in close shots to accentuate the stark drama.

Vampire, one of the more horrific of all horror movies, was shot in and around an actual old castle. Mate used weird slow-motion shots and crazy angles as he maneuvered the camera around the corners of the castle and through its dark corridors. At one point the camera, representing the body of the vampire, was placed in a coffin, and the effect was startling, to say the least.

"The silent pictures," said Mate, a mild-mannered, rather soft-spoken man, "forced the director and the cameraman to develop original and imaginative ideas. There was no speech then, and so the moviemakers had to devise visual methods of getting across their points. Now it is so much easier to talk about something than to show it. The screen has lost some of its individual qualities and taken over many of the aspects of the stage. We are not showing enough today and we are talking too much about things."

The assistant director is the individual who can usually be heard on a movie set shouting "Quiet, please, ready, we're rolling!" just before a scene is shot. But he does not just say "Ready!" He helps get everything ready for the camera and this covers an assortment of duties that require him to be trouble-shooter, whipping boy, father confessor and, in general, the unacknowledged hero who holds down one of Hollywood's most difficult and demanding jobs. John Huston, while directing *The Red Badge of Courage*, told me, "Assistants do all the work and the director gets all the glory." His assistant, Reggie Callow, was too busy at the time to hear the compliment.

An assistant director is, of necessity, a combination top sergeant, wet nurse and amateur psychologist. Practically nothing is supposed to escape his eagle eye. If a distinguished thespian has to retire to the rest room while a movie is in the works, it is the assistant's job to keep track of his whereabouts for possible filmic emergencies. One profile had a fondness for garlic. This caused many a leading lady distress during romantic scenes. So it was the job of the assistant director to see to it that, whenever a love scene was scheduled to follow lunch, the aforesaid artist abstained from his beloved garlic.

When Bette Davis and Miriam Hopkins were making *Old Acquaintance* at Warners, they were at odds with each other. Finally, Davis refused to continue with the picture because, she contended, favoritism was being shown Hopkins since her dressing room was slightly closer to the set than Davis' was. To settle this dispute, the assistant director, a patient and long-suffering fellow, carefully measured the distance between both dressing rooms and the set, made some minor shifts so that they were precisely equidistant from the base of operations, and shooting was resumed with everyone more or less content for the moment.

Erich von Stroheim, a pioneer Hollywood individualist, regularly taxed the resources of his assistant directors. When von Stroheim was directing the silent *Greed* in San Francisco, his bosses in Hollywood became impatient with his protracted absence from the cinema city, which was approaching the year mark. Von Stroheim finally was ordered to return to Hollywood immediately or else.

The director replied that he was packed and ready to come home, but that he had one last mop-up shot to make. A day, two and three went by and there was still no sign of von Stroheim. It seemed that the director, who was a stickler for realism, was filming a scene with one of his characters standing at a high office window overlooking San Francisco. Von Stroheim had previously shot a different angle of this scene and he was now matching up the new "take" with the old one.

The way von Stroheim insisted on it, the weather, the cloud formations in the sky and the traffic in the streets below had to be identical in both shots. To achieve this admirable consistency, Von Stroheim had a small army of assistant directors out regulating San Francisco traffic to conform to the type and density in the preceding "take." As for the weather and cloud formations, he could not very well ask the assistant directors to do anything about them. He just had to bide his time.

Von Stroheim ultimately did get back to Hollywood—approximately a week later.

In 1949 I did a story about Billy Grady, M-G-M's colorful casting director, on assignment for the *Saturday Evening Post*. The story did not appear in the magazine. It was killed through the intercession of the M-G-M publicity and advertising department. At M-G-M, it seems, there was a strict rule that the credit for the discovery of any profile went to studio head Louis B. Mayer and no one else. Even though Grady had unearthed many a movie star, from James Stewart to Van Johnson, M-G-M's policy was that only Mayer was to be credited. And so the studio put pressure, advertising and otherwise, on the *Saturday Evening Post*, and the completed story never saw print.

Grady, a profane, dapper fellow who described himself as a "hustler," was for many years talent head and casting director at M-G-M. Grady had the nickname of "square deal," although W. C. Fields, one of Grady's clients when he was a Broadway agent, claimed that Grady was "as square as an egg." At M-G-M Grady was called upon to cast most anything in a movie, from a Chinese water buffalo (for *The Good Earth*) to a boy with six toes (for *The Devil Is a Sissy*). Before he came to Hollywood, Grady was an actor, and this experience stood him in good stead when he covered plays, night clubs and vaudeville shows in his constant quest for new film finds. Grady's talent reports to the studio were quite uninhibited. Sample Gradyisms: "The leading lady had six friends out front she couldn't forget or keep her eyes off, but otherwise okeh"; "A comedian, so his letterhead says. We see them hanging on hooks in markets"; "If we added three barrels of cabbage to the cast, there would be enough ham and cabbage to feed all the poor of New York."

Grady had a powerful aversion to the designation "talent scout." "It's a darn misnomer," he said in his rich Irish brogue. "I always hated the name. It reminds me of Daniel Boone in a fur cap, swinging on a grapevine, hoping he'd land on an actor. A talent scout doesn't discover people, he just recognizes their talents."

The door to Grady's office at M-G-M was always wide open and he was one of the most accessible tycoons at the studio. But Grady could also give an actor or actress the fastest brush-off in Hollywood. He has been known to look at an aspiring Duse and tell her point-blank that her legs were on upside down or that her hair looked like an old mop. "I don't want actors to think I'm a soft touch," said Grady. "I want them to have respect."

Looks, according to Grady, are not the prime consideration in judging screen talent. Louis B. Mayer used to say that "motion pictures are nothing more than beautiful photographs that move." Grady said that he subscribed to that "but after that I say any good actress can make you believe whatever it is she's portraying. Take Rosalind Russell, Bette Davis, Garbo, Greer Garson. They are not beautiful, beautiful women in the accepted sense. They're not Rita Hayworths or Elizabeth Taylors, but they make you believe they are." Men, Grady avowed, must have "honesty" on the screen and women "larceny." "It's parallel with the old adage," he elaborated, "that a man never runs after a streetcar once he's caught it. A woman has to be unpredictable."

When Grady was at M-G-M, approximately 5,000 people were auditioned annually as possible talent. Fewer than one per cent were given tests after suitable coaching. Of those tested, an average of two were signed. If one of the two went on to reach screen stardom, the studio considered itself fortunate. Grady estimated that a minimum of $150,000 was invested in a star by M-G-M before a return came in and that a star was worth at least $2,500,000 to the studio.

"Many are called, few are chosen," he said. "Hell, everybody can act. Even fleas can act. Did you ever see the flea circus? But there has to be an elimination of fleas to get one that is just right. There's room for everybody in pictures at least once. It's what they do with that once that counts." A framed quotation from Emerson above Grady's desk put it this way: "What we are born is God's gift to us. What we become is our gift to God."

Grady was a great ribber. "I am prone for a joke," he said. "An Irishman's sense of humor is broad, very broad. With me, if you have no sense of humor, you're dead. Well, goddam it, I love to tell stories."

Grady reserved some of his most creative work for the Hollywood gag. Louis B. Mayer, whom Grady described as "a soul-serious man," was frequently offended by Grady's bawdy ribs. Grady liked to relieve the monotony of casting pictures with an occasional foray into tongue-in-camera casting. Once Grady arranged for a couple of Chinese extras to pose as visiting celebrities from abroad and personal friends of Nicholas Schenck, chairman of the board of Loew's, Inc., parent company of M-G-M. The Oriental extras were lavishly feted by the studio brass and taken on a grand tour of the lot by a delegation of geniuses. At the end of the day the tycoon in charge of the proceedings inquired of the supposed dignitaries if there was anything else M-G-M could do for them. "Yes," replied the extras as they extended their Central Casting vouchers for the day, just as Grady had instructed them to do, "where do we cash these?"

As a result of this spoof and "a couple of other things like that," Grady was fired by Mayer one day. According to legend, two studio cops threw him out bodily on Washington Boulevard. Grady went to work as casting director at RKO, but he was unhappy there. "RKO," he said, "is the Sears Roebuck, Metro the Tiffany of the movie business." After six months away from the studio, a truce was negotiated and Grady returned to M-G-M.

Grady, an actor at heart, was described as the most flamboyant performer at M-G-M. But he deferred to Louis B. Mayer in that respect. "Mayer," he said, "is the greatest ham at the studio. He's always 'on.' If I were casting someone as the head of a studio, I'd cast Mayer." (This statement, made before Dore Schary was appointed head of M-G-M, is a stirring testimonial to Grady's casting ability, even if it is from his own mouth.)

One of Grady's chief hates was child actors. "I'd like to give all kids up to six years old a kick in the behind," he said. "Kids shouldn't be in pictures as a career. Give them their youth."

In a philosophical mood, Grady would say, "Actors are ungrateful sons of bitches. When they're on the way up, they adapt themselves to your way. When they've arrived, you've got to adapt yourself to their ways. It never fails."

In the past, Grady had up-and-coming actors sign a gag form contract in which they promised, once they were rolling in swimming pools and convertibles, never to question their roles, never to ask for time off, never to complain about what dressing rooms they were assigned and never to argue about billings and wardrobe calls.

"None of them has lived up to it," said Grady sadly.

Over a bourbon and soda, Grady liked to indulge in one of his favorite pastimes: off-casting. Off-casting, in Hollywood terms, is when there is the role of an Italian father in a picture and J. Carrol Naish is *not* cast for the part. "I'd like to cast Cary Grant as a killer, Ethel Barrymore as a heavy who kicks kids in the teeth and Peter Lorre as the head of an orphanage who loves children," Grady said contemplatively.

When it comes to casting, Willis O'Brien has no problem making his actors adapt themselves to his way. He has one of the largest and oldest stables of actors in Hollywood, but they evince no temperament and show no signs of diminishing in box-office appeal after more than forty years before the cameras.

O'Brien's performers are movie monsters, ranging from the brontosaurus and allosaurus to the triceratops and saber-toothed tiger. They have done their stuff in movies like *The Lost World*, *King Kong* and *Mighty Joe Young*. The latter won O'Brien an Academy Award in 1950 for his camera magic in animating a super-gorilla that is transplanted from the jungle to a Hollywood night club.

O'Brien, a white-haired, bespectacled, soft-spoken gentleman, has been in the movie-monster business since 1918, before the movies even learned to grunt. His first monster movie was *The Dinosaur and the Missing Link*, a prehistoric comedy which ran five minutes on the screen and took two months to make. The dinosaur and the cave men in the movie were constructed of modeling clay over wooden joints, and chunks of granite were used for a Mesozoic background. The stop-motion photography animation was jerky, but the picture was a success.

For his more recent movies, O'Brien constructed monsters on an average of one half to one-and-one-half-inch scale to the foot and about the size of a baby's doll. They were built to precise measurement, with movable arms, legs, eyes and mouths and realistically shaggy skins. Mighty Joe Young, a lineal descendant of King Kong, who towered so menacingly on the screen, actually stood sixteen inches high and consisted of a metal frame padded with sponge and covered with rubber skin. Through hocus-focus, Joe loomed ten feet high on the screen.

It took O'Brien and a crew of twenty-five three years to complete *Mighty Joe Young*. Set against an appropriate background, Joe and the other monster models were moved from a quarter of an inch to more than an inch at a time to achieve the illusion of animation. After each move, the film was exposed and the camera stopped. The model was then moved another portion of an inch and again photographed. When these individual action segments were run together on the screen they gave the impression of movement. One of Joe's steps might have necessitated a dozen separate shifts and camera setups. Later, live actors were combined with the miniature monsters by means of camera trickery.

There have been refinements in O'Brien's technique down the years, but this is substantially the same method he used in his first monster movies. It is a technique requiring time, patience and great skill. Twenty-five feet of film per day is a good output, even though that footage speeds by on the screen in about thirty seconds.

O'Brien is happy with his dinosaurs, pterodactyls, brontosauruses, stegosauruses, plesiosaurs, ichthyosaurs and archaeopteryxes. Not only is there no problem with the performers, but the plots are pretty much the same. There is usually a beast which is transplanted from some primitive setting to captivity in the big city. This monster is unmanageable by anyone but a comely young girl for whom he develops a futile infatuation. In civilized surroundings, the monster always breaks loose, wrecking buildings and terrorizing the citizenry until he is killed off in time for the fadeout.

O'Brien, not an overly talkative fellow, will tell you, when pressed, that pictures of this sort never go out of style. In his opinion they appeal to the adventurous streak in all of us and constitute an imaginative escape from a world of reality populated by too many human monsters. After all these years in the business of devising movie monsters, O'Brien is still at it. Among his recent creations have been *The Black Scorpion*, a 100-foot long animated specimen, and *The Giant Behemoth*, about a prehistoric marine monster activated by atomic propulsion that sets out to destroy London. Latterly, O'Brien even did some work on a remake of *The Lost World*—but this one had live lizards and iguanas doubling for the prehistoric monsters. O'Brien was not too happy about it. "The story is completely changed," he said. "You wouldn't recognize it. They claim that the live technique looks smoother, that animation is jerky. I don't think so. I'd like to see them use a copy of real dinosaurs with animation. But I guess it's all a matter of taste. They felt it would take too long to animate. I don't agree with them. It takes quite a crew with these reptiles. With the big screens, you can't carry focus with CinemaScope and you have to be farther than five feet away." He added sadly: "It makes for complications."

One of the most specialized movie specialists I encountered was a young lady named Fern Barry, an attractive ash blonde, who made a career of portraying the arms and legs of movie stars in closeups. The feet and hands that launched a thousand insert shots in motion pictures were hers.

Most movie stars are too busy to devote hours to closeups of this kind and often their arms and legs are not sufficiently photogenic. As a result, Barry was called in to substitute for Bette Davis, Ann Sheridan, Ida Lupino, Olivia de Havilland and others. It can be reported, in the line of journalistic duty, that her legs are exceedingly shapely and that her hands are the soft, white, romantic type that one loves to touch.

Before she went into the arm-and-leg business, Fern Barry was an actress in her own right. Her first job in the movies was as stand-in and double for Helen Hayes in *A Farewell to Arms*. One of her prized possessions is a photograph of Hayes inscribed to "My Other Self."

Later, she did many bit parts in pictures. She was seen as a secretary, nurse, telephone operator, receptionist and saleswoman. She also portrayed dead bodies and people in an unconscious state who were crammed into the rumble seats of automobiles, fell out of closets and whose faces were not generally visible. Gradually, her feet and hands came to be used in closeups. She estimated that she had done such shots for several hundred films.

Fern Barry adapted her hands to whatever screen characterization was required. She sometimes had to cut her nails and make her hands look old and ugly for a particular role, or have them appear sleek and well groomed for another assignment. Her legs were substantially the same in each role.

At first, she was not particularly happy about the anonymity of her work. Then she gradually began to get a kick out of it. "It's a lot of fun," she said, "being someone else for a little while. Whenever I go to see a picture, I see my hands and feet on the screen and I get a thrill out of it."

Fern Barry still occasionally practices her highly specialized craft today. It can safely be said that she made more of an impression with her arms and legs than a good many movie actresses do with their entire personalities.

Another unique screen specialist is Marguerite Lamkin, an attractive Southern belle with large, limpid eyes and a honey-butter accent who hailed from Monroe, Louisiana. When Lamkin first came to Hollywood, she had aspirations to become a movie actress, but her pronounced Southern accent was an obstacle to her screen career. So she went to a drama coach for many months to eradicate her accent, without much success.

One day Elia Kazan and Tennessee Williams, impressed with her cornpone style of speaking, brought her to New York to coach Barbara Bel Geddes in the role of the Southern belle in *Cat on a Hot Tin Roof*. Before long Lamkin found that her speech was a help and not a hindrance in getting ahead in show business. In due course she became the sole and acknowledged expert on Southern accents. "I had no competition," she said. She was hired, at an appreciable salary, to repeat her speech-coaching job for the movie version of *Cat on a Hot Tin Roof* with Elizabeth Taylor. She also worked in the same capacity on *Raintree County*, *Baby Doll* and *The Long, Hot Summer*.

On a movie set she would confound the film folk with such admonitions as "This accent is Alabama. We need northern Mississippi." After some time she visited her family in Monroe, Louisiana, again, partly to polish her Southern accent, which was by now vital to her Hollywood livelihood. "That trip was tax-deductible," she said.

Studio police are essential to the operation of a movie plant, from shooing away all sorts of supplicants who keep trying to break into the premises, to hushing up or "fixing" scandals in which the profiles become involved. In 1949 I did a story along these lines, entitled "Hollywood Cop," for *Collier's* about W. P. (Whitey) Hendry, chief of police at M-G-M. After the story was turned in to the editors, they okayed it and even shot color photographs for it. But at the last minute they got cold journalistic feet and decided not to run the piece. The subject was too hot for them.

Hendry was one of the veteran studio policemen. A tall, bronzed man with steel-gray hair and mustache, he looked more like a banker than a cop. He started out to be a dentist and switched from fillings to felonies when he became a policeman in Culver City, where M-G-M is located. He went to work for the studio in 1924 and was promoted to police chief a few years later.

Since M-G-M in its prime was the largest of the movie studios, with the longest contract list of profiles, Hendry had his work cut out for him. When the studio came into existence in 1924 it had a police force of twelve men. This department later grew to eighty-seven police, four captains, two plainclothesmen and an inspector. This staff was appreciably larger than the police department of Culver City, where M-G-M was a sort of city within a city.

Part of Hendry's job was to prevent gate-crashing. Some of the crashers went to rather extreme lengths. Several years ago a large crate labeled "statue" arrived at M-G-M addressed to the studio. Such a crate would ordinarily not have attracted much notice since the studio was accustomed to receiving everything from goldfish to pieces of European castles. This particular package, however, tapered to a sharp point at each end and, when it was moved, strange sounds came from inside.

Hendry and two of his men cautiously pried open the mysterious box. Out rolled an aspiring actor who had unsuccessfully been trying to crash the M-G-M gates. In desperation, he explained, he had finally hit upon what he figured would be a foolproof way to get in. He mailed himself to the studio from Chicago, along with food, water and make-up. The pointed ends were to keep the crate and him on their sides. Despite this precaution, he arrived in California in pretty bad shape.

Hendry and his men have never been quite able to figure out why anybody should want to get into a studio in the first place. M-G-M, with its great gray sound-stage bastions, is forbiddingly drab, and it could easily stand the ministrations of some of the studio's smart set designers. One of the M-G-M cops told me, "I don't get it. You'd think there was something hot inside the studio, like a million dollars or an oil gusher. All there is is a lot of big barns coated with plaster and dozens of guys and dames standing around doing practically nothing all day. There's nothing to see because that's how they make movies. It takes eight hours to get a shot of a guy lighting a cigarette or taking his hat off. Most of the time is spent in fixing lights and mikes and shoving things around. For my money, I'd rather watch a guy excavating a hole in the ground."

A cop who was in charge of one of the gates at Warner Brothers once told me that he had no trouble in keeping tabs on the several thousand studio employees, ranging from stars and directors to grips and electricians, who passed by him daily. He had gotten so that he could recognize each of their faces and, even if he did not, he was still able to spot any crashers.

"In Montana, where I come from," he said, "there are guys who handle 3,000 head of cattle at a clip and can pick out any particular cow in two seconds. It's a sort of feeling you get for the thing."

He did not intend to be particularly cynical when he said this.

Occasionally, though, it did happen that a star went unrecognized by the cops at the gate. This is known among Hollywood reporters as the Mistaken Identity story and is good for an appearance in the press about once a month. Garbo was actually barred by the M-G-M police once. She had left her limousine a few blocks from the studio and arrived at the entrance wearing an old, floppy hat, dark glasses and blue slacks. The cop thought she was an extra until she threw her accent at him.

Usually, actors, actresses and executives went very much recognized at M-G-M. As part of their six-week training period, the police had to familiarize themselves with photographs of all personnel under contract to the studio. They also kept up with stars' changes of hair color and other portions of the physiognomy. "Some stars don't look as hot off screen as they do on," said Hendry. "It's all phony glamour." Years ago, regulations required the studio police to salute every time a profile or producer passed by, but this edict was withdrawn after World War II, with the triumph of democracy throughout the world, even in Culver City.

In addition to guarding the gates at M-G-M, Hendry and his men provided for the protection of visiting celebrities, thwarted thefts, exposed fake talent scouts, patrolled premieres, parties, weddings and funerals and watched out for everything from mayhem to murder at the studio. When Clark Gable was under contract to M-G-M he received much ardent fan mail. A young female fan in London sent Gable a photograph of her shapely legs with the message "If this interests you, let me know and I will send along the rest of me." In case she should ever show up in person, Hendry filed this letter for possible future reference in a thick Gable folder next to a photograph of a lady nudist from Florida with the inscription, "Let's go, hon!"

Hendry's biggest job, though, was to keep an eye on the conduct of the numerous big and little profiles under contract to the studio. Today, with studio contract lists on the slim side, this is not much of a problem. But in former years when M-G-M employed a vast assortment of personalities, from Clark Gable to Ava Gardner and from Greer Garson to Lassie (who was sometimes referred to as "Greer Garson with fur"), Hendry's job was not a placid one.

As a studio cop he had to work with the light touch rather than strong-arm tactics. Much of Hendry's work was of a delicate public-relations nature. He conducted confidential investigations and saw to it that cases involving M-G-M people were handled, wherever possible, without reaching the attention of the regular police and the press. Whenever a Metro personality became involved in anything from a hangover to homicide, Hendry wheeled into action. He had cultivated contacts with police officials just about everywhere and regularly entertained visiting cops in Hollywood and presented them with honorary police badges. "I have enough connections in police departments to get tipped off when Metro is in trouble," he boasted.

At night, Hendry slept with a telephone beside his bed in his Santa Monica apartment. "When it rings," he said, "cold chills run up and down my spine. I am like a fireman with my shoes always on." M-G-M had set up an effective tip-off system. When a Metro player got into a jam, as many of them did, Hendry was promptly alerted, by an informant in the police department or by some other tipster, and he sped to the scene of the disaster. Hendry often arrived there before the cops. Ralph Wheelwright, of the publicity department, was informed at the same time and likewise headed for the scene of the crime. While Hendry handled the police angle, Wheelwright took care of the press. This cover-up system, which was described as "the big fix," worked very well most of the time.

"Years ago," Hendry said, "you could square most anything involving the studio. Now every newspaper car has a police radio hookup and those guys get there even before the cops." Also, Hendry might have added, the waning power of the major movie studios, including M-G-M, has made for a less effective "fix" in recent years.

One instance of Hendry's fast footwork was at the suicide of Paul Bern, an M-G-M producer, in 1932. Two months after his marriage to Metro's platinum-blond star, Jean Harlow, Bern shot himself at his rustic mountain home in Benedict Canyon. Bern, a sensitive, introverted man, left a cryptic note to his wife: "Dearest, dear. Unfortunately this is the only way to make good the frightful wrong I have done you and to wipe out my abject humiliation." It was signed "Paul." To this he added: "You understand last night was only a farce."

Bern's butler found the nude body of the dead producer in a dressing closet, a bullet hole in his right temple and a .38-caliber revolver beside him, and alerted the studio. Louis B. Mayer, Irving Thalberg, Hendry and other aides were at the death scene before the cops. In fact, two full hours elapsed before the police were notified. The press later had a hard time digging up the facts and much was made at the coroner's inquest of the delay in informing the authorities. Bern was labeled a suicide, however, and the case was closed. The enigma of the suicide note and the elapsed two hours have not been clarified to this day.

Hendry is sometimes inclined to think that actors are problem children who do not want to be helped. In 1927 John Gilbert, one of the early Metro profiles, turned up at the police station in Beverly Hills at 3:00 A.M. alcoholically demanding to be thrown into jail. The cops obliged and Gilbert spent the night behind bars. Later he was sentenced to ten days for disturbing the peace and using abusive language. Through Hendry's intervention, he was released from jail after only one day.

"If the stars would only keep their mouths shut when they're arrested," sighed Hendry, "everything would be okay. But hell, by the time you get there they've got everybody in the police department so hot you have to wear an asbestos suit."

Sitting in his plain office near the studio's publicity entrance, Hendry philosophized about the many crises in which he has been involved.

"I know the stars in a different light from anyone else in the business," he said. "It's a confidential relationship. They tell me things even their families don't know. They have to tell me the truth to get my help.

"The trouble with stars is they're people the studio has built up from nobodies. They've become Frankensteins to us. They mess us up. They squawk like hell and get panic-stricken when they're recognized and they squawk more when nobody recognizes them."

Hendry has been technical adviser on many a movie about cops. He thought Hollywood had recently done much to improve the type of police officer—"mostly half-wits and bums"—usually seen in pictures.

Directors sometimes asked Hendry if they could put some of his good-looking cops before the cameras.

"No soap," said Hendry. "If I ever thought one of those s.o.b.'s wanted to be an actor, I'd never let him put on a uniform. He'd be no good to me."

There are all sorts of people on the fringes of filmdom who are indispensable to the movie community in their own special ways. The still photographers are among these essential cinema citizens. In a town living by and for the motion picture, the king of the still pictures was the late Hymie Fink. Fink had been recording the camera antics of the screen elite from the earliest days of Hollywood, and his photographic album ran the glamour gamut from Theda Bara and Rudolph Valentino to Frank Sinatra and Elizabeth Taylor.

For many years Fink documented the doings of the profiles with his camera for *Photoplay* Magazine. For a man who had seen probably as much glamour in its off moments as anyone in the business, Fink was a rather simple and unaffected soul. He was a confirmed film fan and his "big loves" were Joan Crawford, Marlene Dietrich and Sonja Henie. After several decades of looking at Hollywood through a camera finder, Fink had not lost his enthusiasm for the movie metropolis.

Although Fink had been in Hollywood practically from scratch, not much of what he had seen and heard had rubbed off on him. When I was trying to put together his reminiscences for *Photoplay* Magazine, he had a hard time remembering some of the many colorful incidents of the past. In Fink's case, as in the case of so many other film folk, very little had actually stayed with him. It had all unreeled and faded away like an old movie.

Fink was of the definite opinion, though, that there was more excitement and glamour to the movie business in former years. "The big shots didn't take themselves so seriously," he said. "There was more mystery about the movies. More was left to the imagination."

The movie stars were fond of Fink because, as he put it, "I play ball with them and they play ball with me." Fink never shot balding profiles like Charles Boyer minus their toupees. He saw to it that poor features like a prominent proboscis or a receding chin were not emphasized in his photographs, that husbands were not lensed with women who were not their wives and that alcohol was not conspicuous on night-club tables.

"The great majority of movie people are wonderful," Fink said with conviction. Some of the stars, though, were not too co-operative. Bing Crosby had a habit of posing for a shot after much urging and then walking away just as the cameraman was about to snap the picture. Clark Gable never allowed photographs to be taken in his home.

Among Fink's favorite shots were one of the elusive Garbo taken when she was not aware of the camera; Bing Crosby standing on his head and eating an ice-cream cone; and Phil Harris and Jean Harlow, then a romantic duo, reading a newspaper at the Coconut Grove during the peak of an earthquake.

According to Fink, there was no such thing as a candid picture. He argued that every good photograph required composition and preparation. He used certain stratagems when shooting celebrities. He usually wisecracked while taking a picture in order to relax the subject. He advised the person he was photographing to smile and not to talk so as to appear more attractive. When photographing a group of celebrities, Fink spotted the less important people at the outside so that they could easily be cut out of the picture later if necessary.

Joan Crawford arranged a fancy wedding for Fink in 1939. She outfitted Fink's bride with an expensive wedding gown and took over the chapel room at the Victor Hugo café for the occasion. Rumors began to spread in screen circles that Crawford herself was about to get married. Most of the photographers in Hollywood showed up at the Victor Hugo only to find that one of their compatriots was being wed. Fink observed, with some satisfaction, that his was one of the best lensed marriages in moviedom.

Harry Drucker, a dark, natty individual, has given the Hollywood profiles some of their best parts. Drucker is not a motion-picture producer. He is barber extraordinary to the film folk. To his tonsorial parlor in Beverly Hills have repaired such customers as Clark Gable, Bing Crosby, Gregory Peck, Orson Welles and Robert Taylor. They come to get Drucker's "invisible haircut," a specialty of the house.

"Actors," said Drucker, "want to look the same every day. They can't act one day with long hair and show up for the next scene with their bare neck hanging out."

The thespian visits Drucker on the average of once a week and is given a haircut that does not look like a haircut. This is accomplished by abbreviating a few hairs in strategic spots. When the client steps out of Drucker's, it is practically impossible to tell that he has been in a barbershop.

Since Drucker's customers are not ordinary folk, some of the incidents that have occurred in his establishment would curdle the lather in a shaving cup. Norman Krasna, the writer and producer, was once sitting in a chair at Drucker's, conversing on the telephone—if you did not have a telephone plugged in at your chair, the other customers were likely to look down on you. Krasna closed a mammoth movie deal on the phone, one that would net him many thousands of dollars. He hung up, turned to the barber and said, "Okay, now I can afford a facial."

When Dore Schary resigned as boss at RKO and prior to his becoming production chief at M-G-M, he came into Drucker's for his standing weekly appointment. "Well, Harry," Schary said to Drucker, "is my credit still good?"

"Not only is it good," replied Drucker magnanimously, "but do you need any money?"

A number of sizable movie deals have been consummated at Drucker's. As Drucker said, "You get a few unscrupulous agents and writers who come in to see producers here. They can't get in to see the producers in their offices and so they bring scripts with them when they come to get a haircut. They force the issue with the producer while he is lying helpless in a chair."

Seating arrangements at Drucker's are juggled so that competitive movie producers are not in adjoining chairs. Drucker prefers to book feuding film folk at different times. He peruses the Hollywood trade papers and gossip columns to keep up on all the latest internecine developments.

Drucker is frequently invited to parties and previews by his celebrated clientele, but he rarely accepts. "I like to keep a boundary line in this business," he has said.

Drucker dreads going to motion-picture previews. He knows that the next day one of his customers, who was probably connected with the picture in some way, will ask him how he liked it.

"I pray to God that the pictures will be good," says Drucker, "so that I won't have to give false flattery."

Drucker lives in Beverly Hills and drives a big car. However, he does not have a swimming pool.

"If word ever got around that a barber in Los Angeles had a swimming pool," he has said, "every barber in the world would put his chair on his back and rush here. I can live without a swimming pool."

Recently, Drucker opened an even bigger and fancier barbershop with a club room, a bar and a steam room. But he still does not have a swimming pool.

"It's flabbergasting," says Drucker of his new tonsorial parlor, "and yet it's real masculine." He adds: "Hollywood is changing. It's all hustle and bustle, with people trying for just one thing—to make money. There are so many psychiatrists in Beverly Hills. This is better than psychiatry. They come in here and really relax and they get a few phony stories too."

Terry Hunt, a gentle, one-time fighter, lives off the fat of the land in Hollywood. He is moviedom's foremost body builder. At his glamorous "healthatorium" with its romantic, green, low-key lights in the steam room, he has helped condition all kinds of customers, from Ben Hecht and Johnny Weissmuller to Marlene Dietrich and Louella Parsons. Among his extensive clientele of picture people have been such assorted physical (and psychical) specimens as Rita Hayworth, George Raft, Mary Pickford, Claudette Colbert, Ingrid Bergman, Paul Muni, Gene Tierney and Hedda Hopper.

Hunt's sweatshop is ironically located on La Cienega Boulevard, which is known as Restaurant Row. But his specialty is taking weight off the stars' stomachs and putting it on their chests, a system that has its points both for Tarzan and the languorous ladies of the screen.

Hunt's headquarters are like no other muscle factory. It is not uncommon to find more screen stars at Hunt's than at Romanoff's. Autographed pictures of the profiles hang everywhere. The Hollywood moguls sit around in the steam room sweating it out both physically and artistically as they peruse copies of the trade papers.

"We sometimes have $100,000,000 worth of talent in the steam room at one time," Hunt says proudly.

When Hunt first opened up for business he had a telephone in the steam room, but he soon found that his customers were spending more time chewing the fat with their studio stooges than shedding it from their torsos, so he pulled out the instrument.

The arrival of the Hollywood elite is a matter of no great moment at Hunt's. Betty Grable and Marlene Dietrich used to walk in minus make-up and in slacks and sweatshirts for setting-up sessions. Hunt has become so inured to seeing the glamour girls without their glamour that he sometimes fails to recognize some of his own clients when he runs into them socially with their faces and clothes on.

The movie stars are generally in better shape than the average person. "They have to be," says Hunt. "It's their livelihood. They work harder at it. You can't fool the camera. Some of the stars aren't getting any younger either. It's not easy for a man of forty-five to play the part of a juvenile of twenty-six. He can't afford to backslide physically."

Actors are inclined to be more streamlined than those engaged in the more cerebral screen crafts. But some paunch-drunk stars have been known to eat themselves out of movies. To accentuate suppleness and poise for thespians, Hunt emphasizes handstands and hanging from bars. For producers, directors and writers, he stresses abdominal work.

"Nearly all writers," Hunt observes, "are extremely nervous. They're under high tension. We get about eight or nine big-name writers in here every day. The writers are more dependable than any other group. They keep coming here year in and year out. I guess it's because they're intelligent and realize they need it."

A Hollywood tycoon once complimented Hunt with "Terry Hunt should get screen credit on more than half the pictures made in Hollywood for his work in superbly conditioning the stars who are featured in them."

Even the pets of the movie stars get specialized attention. The late Dr. Stanley Cooper, a Los Angeles veterinarian, much of whose practice consisted of the pooches and pusses of the profiles, once told me that the prevalent anxiety neuroses of the movie people were reflected in their four-legged pets. Dr. Cooper should have known, because among his patients were the pets of Zsa Zsa Gabor, Samuel Goldwyn, Bing Crosby, Alan Ladd, Jerry Lewis, Joan Crawford, Danny Kaye, James Mason, Jose Ferrer and Edward G. Robinson, and his office was, appropriately, located near the Academy of Motion Picture Arts and Sciences.

"You can tell these days just from looking at a dog," said Dr. Cooper, "whether his master is on the analyst's couch. If the master is neurotic, so is the dog. You definitely see more of it these days. It is part of the times and in Hollywood probably has to do with all the problems of the motion-picture business, such as the competition of television and the business strains of the movie industry."

In other words, Hollywood and its dogs have been going to the dogs together.

Dr. Cooper, a kindly, bespectacled man, said that he noticed "a lot of unemployment among Hollywood writers. When they are unemployed for a while and get to the hysteria stage, the dogs will often start vomiting in the morning like their owners. But as soon as a writer get a good assignment, the problem always straightens itself out. For unemployed owners, I often give the dogs phenobarbital to keep them quiet. The owner is also taking phenobarbital for the same condition, and then both the dog and the master calm down at the same time. But a job is better than pills.

"There are a lot of high-strung people in the movie industry. The effect on their dogs is tremendous. The dogs become real nervous and high-strung. I often suggest a vacation for the dogs, that they be separated from their owners two or three times a year. It helps them tremendously."

Dr. Cooper told me that Jack Benny's female poodle, Topsy, "became ill with bronchitis because Benny had a respiratory infection." Actor Joseph Schildkraut's chihuahuas, Boychik and Bambi, "develop severe gas retention when Schildkraut does the same because of anxiety."

Dr. Cooper applied some simple psychiatric principles to his patients, such as not hospitalizing pets so as to avoid "the grief element." If possible, the pet went home for the night. Dr. Cooper would also call in consulting specialists, registered nurses, and baby or rather pet-sitters whenever necessary. Music was played all day at his veterinarian headquarters to soothe his patients. When Bing Crosby's poodle, Topsy—apparently all Hollywood poodles are named Topsy—heard her master's voice coming over the airwaves at Dr. Cooper's emporium, she went into a dither.

Some of the things that go on in the rarefied reaches of dogdom would make a flea's blood run cold. Many of the motion-picture pooches are afflicted with conjunctivitis, an eye inflammation, caused by looking at television screens. Joan Bennett's poodle, Bambi, received quite a bit of publicity a few years ago, when television was in its formative years, and Bambi came down with conjunctivitis from watching Milton Berle.

Zsa Zsa Gabor had a poodle named Farouk. Perhaps Farouk was looking at too many pictures of the two-legged Farouk, but, said Dr. Cooper, he acquired "a severe bloat. I gave him a colonic and advised the proper diet. It seems he had been eating debris."

On New Year's Day, many dogs would be rushed to Dr. Cooper "so that we can pump the liquor out of them. People just get tight and give their dogs liquor."

Joan Crawford, according to Dr. Cooper, "names her kids and pets with the initial 'C.' She's a little superstitious." Crawford had a parakeet named "Crazy Crawford." She also had a poodle, Cliquot, who fell into her swimming pool one day and ran a high temperature. On another occasion, Cliquot nibbled on a carpet at Republic studio, where Crawford was working, and got sick. His mistress explained it to me this way:

"Cliquot was always happy when I was at the glamorous studios, like M-G-M and Warner Brothers. But when I went to Republic [which was the home of the horse opera and definitely not a glamorous studio], he got into trouble. Cliquot is miserable when I'm not working. When we go to a studio, he is very happy."

When she was at Columbia, Crawford elucidated, "people fed him very much and he gained too much weight. Cliquot usually eats white meat of chicken, ground sirloin, ice cream and ginger ale. He wears custom-made jackets, from Hammacher, Schlemmer. They are red with black velvet collars with 'CC' on them. They have heart-shaped pockets with Kleenex in them in case he has to blow his nose. Cliquot and I wear matching costumes. He wears his red jacket when I wear red slacks and sweater. When I wear green, he wears green. And he has a rhinestone collar for evening."

Marie Wilson's tiny Yorkshire terrier, Hobbs, was the subject of a divorce battle when the actress separated from Alan Nixon. Dr. Cooper said that they both "share time with Hobbs." Hobbs went everywhere with his mistress, including plays and movies, and he even "eats regularly at the Brown Derby." When Hobbs traveled by plane, he was given airsickness pills. Marie Wilson was once quoted as saying, "I won't let a dog in any hotel that isn't air-conditioned." Dr. Cooper had a long, nine-card file listing all the calamities that had befallen Hobbs in recent years. One time a lamp fell on him. "He's so small. And when Marie Wilson is under stress, he starts getting hysterical and starts eating his own hair with the result that he gets intestinal gastritis and we have to give him a colonic."

The James Masons were mad for pets. At various times they have had a wild possum, a hawk, a rabbit and "as many as thirty cats at one time." Dr. Cooper said that the Masons once "announced that they were giving away all their cats. A lot of Hollywood people grabbed at the cats and almost forty cats were given away. You still hear many of the movie people boasting that they have one of the Mason cats. But it was all a big hoax. June Havoc and the Masons thought it up together. The cats were all from the pound and the Masons and June Havoc were trying to find homes for them."

The Masons at one time even had a skunk, deodorized, for a pet. "Mason," said Dr. Cooper, "told everybody the skunk was his agent."

The best is none too good for Hollywood pets. When Bing Crosby's poodle Topsy appeared to have become pregnant some years ago, the late Dixie Lee Crosby "ordered a fancy crib and covers from Saks Fifth Avenue. The Crosbys were very disappointed when it turned out to be a pseudo-pregnancy."

Many of the pets arrived at Dr. Cooper's in imported sports cars or in chauffeured limousines with a butler. In San Fernando Valley there is the famed Pet Cemetery where some of the monuments cost many thousands of dollars. There are dog beauty parlors where poodles can be trimmed and dyed—the color of their mistresses' hair. There is a "cat motel" which boards cats, and a local dude ranch—the Double E—for dogs, with a swimming pool and canopied miniature cabanas with adjoining fire hydrants.

Dr. Cooper said that he frequently consulted psychiatrists about the problems of his patients. And, in turn, "psychiatrists will call me asking me what symptoms an animal has in order to cast light on the problems of the owner.

"You can often go better by an animal than by the owner. An upset person will often give you imaginary symptoms. But a dog can't talk and so can't tell you of imaginary symptoms. With a dog you simply observe and diagnose.

"Some of these Hollywood animals," Dr. Cooper commented reflectively, "are like the Hollywood people. They are so used to being given tablets and vitamins all the time that, unless they get them, they think something is wrong."

Sometimes an intrepid pet will even revolt against the Hollywood system—usually with tragic results. Dr. Herbert Kalmus, head of Technicolor, had a German shepherd dog. But the dog preferred the company of the hired help to that of Kalmus. "This got Kalmus furious," Dr. Cooper said, "and he gave the dog away."

CHAPTER IX

The Snows of Yesteryear

I HAVE SPENT MUCH TIME with the old-timers of Hollywood, the screen stars whose luster has dimmed, the once great who have had a mighty fall in moviedom. It is always a dramatic and sometimes a saddening story—and a frequent one, for in Hollywood fame and fortune can be even less permanent than the film strips on which the shadow plays are imprinted. In the movies, riches and repute often fade away for no particularly valid reason. In Hollywood, it is not always the fittest for their jobs who survive, but rather those who fit themselves into the artistic pigeonholes set up by the glorified filing clerks who are in control of what has aptly been described as the movie "business."

Some of the wealthy and worshiped at least held onto their money. These are in a minority. Most of the old-timers have economic problems as well as the problems of adjusting themseves to a world where they had once been overpaid and overpraised and now have to scramble for a paycheck and a paragraph in print. Those who have fallen on lean days are mostly stoical. They do not complain and they gladly feed on crumbs where once they dined lavishly on the finest spreads.

Many of the old-timers, to be sure, were slobs. They pushed people around—and, when they were no longer in power, they got pushed around, too. Even D. W. Griffith was a lush, an egomaniac and a pretty unpalatable customer personally all around. But at least some of them made some movies that were good, and occasionally perhaps even great. What is of the essence is what they put on the screen, not what they did or how they behaved away from their screen activities. This is the only thing that matters to the moviegoer in the theater. The current movie crop of connivers and pushers don't even have the saving grace of occasionally making good films to go with their bad manners.

Sometimes it seems, in Hollywood, as if just about everybody is dead or dying off. So many people are "late." Or they get "lost" and disappear. So many of them have heart conditions, ulcers and other afflictions. They hobble, they stutter, they stammer, they wear smoked glasses, they have sickly little wry, sly, serious smiles. Nothing really is so sad as the old-timers of the movies and as the old-time mementoes of the movies. Everything fades so fast and furiously, becomes so sadly shabby so quickly. Just riffle through an old almanac of the movies—twenty or thirty years ago. It seems like a couple of hundred. "Only yesterday" in Hollywood is in the far-off past. A year seems like a decade, a couple of years like a century, and the fifty years of the community's progress—or decline—like an entire cycle of lifetimes.

Were they really the good old days? Buddy Adler, the late production chief of Twentieth Century-Fox, spoke piously of Hollywood's current "rejuvenation" and said that the movie metropolis was looking ahead to what he called "the good new days." Do we tend to glamorize the past? One movie columnist says, "Ten years from now we'll say that everyone went broke in Hollywood, and it was funny but there were strikes and the studios were closed. You look back and say 'Ten years ago it seemed great.'" Sidney Skolsky put it this way: "I look back—and not in anger—at Hollywood of some twenty-odd years ago and this is my strangest recollection: being told repeatedly that Hollywood isn't what it used to be; I should have been around in the good old days. Now I hear people speak about these same old abused years as the good old days. Time puts a halo on a lot of things, doesn't it? . . . The present is always the good old days. Wait and see."

Hollywood's sense of the past and feeling for tradition is largely limited to remaking its profitable old pictures, like *Ben-Hur*, in the hope of turning another fast buck today. "If you're thinking further back than what happened today in the motion-picture industry," says one moviemaker, "you're living in the past." Hollywood is afflicted with total amnesia, a complete group blackout and loss of recall when it comes to anything that happened more than twenty-four hours ago. And when somebody occasionally tries to remember something, he remembers it vaguely and wrongly. Hollywood simply does not want to remember what happened. The past is in the past. It is dead and hopefully forgotten.

The movie colony's infrequent ventures into nostalgia are ignominious and depressing. In 1960 a mass statue commemorating eight "top film figures of the past" was unveiled in Beverly Hills. Those honored were Mary Pickford, Harold Lloyd, Tom Mix, Rudolph Valentino, Will Rogers, Douglas Fairbanks, Sr., Conrad Nagel and Fred Niblo. Pickford, Lloyd and Nagel, the only ones surviving, attended the fancy dedication. Griffith and Chaplin, to mention only two, didn't even rate inclusion in this so-called commemorative event.

Under the aegis of the Hollywood Chamber of Commerce, the cinema city is undergoing what is called a "Hollywood Improvement Program," part of which will find coral terrazzo stars, with the names of 1529 show-business personalities, imbedded in the sidewalks as a "Walk of Fame." The name of Charlie Chaplin is not among them; Chaplin is in disfavor in Hollywood for his political views. One of those memorialized will be Fatty Arbuckle, the late silent-screen star, who was involved in one of the most notorious Hollywood rape-murder cases in the Twenties. As one Hollywood observer put it: "It's apparently all right to rape and murder, but it's not all right to be 'pinko.'"

At a recent meeting of the "Hollywood Improvement Program" committee there was a big fuss made over the fact that trees would be planted on Hollywood Boulevard. After listening to the to-do for some time, one Hollywood journalist, who was born in Los Angeles and remembers it from "the good old days," inquired blandly: "Why did you ever tear them down?"

There has been a good deal of publicity for the past several years about a Hollywood Motion Picture and Television Museum, or movie "waxworks," as it has been dubbed, to be sponsored by the Los Angeles County Board of Supervisors, which is planned to house displays, exhibitions, theater showings, a film library and so on. Sol Lesser, who is renowned mostly as the producer of Tarzan movies, was appointed chairman of what is grandiloquently described as "a film industry organizing committee." There have been innumerable press releases, "surveys" and "schematics," and all sorts of backing and filling, but as of this time ground has not even been broken for the project.

There has been little worthwhile and accurate documentation of the old-time pioneers and profiles of the movies. As a result, many of the oldsters have already passed away with their stories untold, and the few who have been chronicled—like Mack Sennett—have been the subjects of rather bogus biographies. In recent years there has been a spate of books about the movies—there sometimes seem to be more books being written than movies being made. As Hollywood becomes "historical," it is a time for reminiscence and remembrance of things past. Most of the reminiscences are faulty, ghostwritten and slick cover-up jobs. Now, as the movies get on in years, more and more of the pioneers are fading from the scene and with them vanishes the best opportunity of unearthing firsthand material about the rise and development—and decline—of the American film.

And the old-timers are most certainly worth chronicling. The aged in the Hollywood have some good and colorful stories to tell and mostly they tell them well and frankly without the perversions and evasions of the present-day film folk. The oldsters have been through the movie mill and have had most of the ego knocked out of them and they are easier to get along with. As someone wisely once said, it is the "outcasts" who are the best sources of material—and perhaps the only real sources—about Hollywood. Even the great and outspoken Griffith had to be seventy-two years old, drunk and washed up in the movie business, so that he could proudly make the claim that he didn't care what he said and what I printed about Hollywood. All in all, almost all the old-timers I talked to were grateful to a journalist for seeking them out, and they afforded me some of the best and most revealing glimpses I have had into Hollywood and its works.

The most venerable of the film figures I interviewed was Edwin S. Porter, one of the original pioneers of the movies, who started out in the business as a mechanic-cameraman and assistant to Thomas Edison in his West Orange, New Jersey, laboratories. In those days, the movies consisted mostly of short, documentary-style films, running a couple of minutes on the screen. They were photographed largely outdoors and dealt with incidents like a parade, a train roaring down the tracks or a scene in the park.

Porter helped appreciably to expand the horizons of the screen both in terms of story and storytelling and is often referred to as the father of the story film. The Pittsburgh-born Porter, who had been an early projection-machine operator, joined Edison in the late Nineties, assisting him in his camera experiments and also functioning as the one-man producer-director-writer of many movies made at Edison's studio. The most famous of these was *The Great Train Robbery* in 1903, which had the mammoth running time of almost ten minutes and told a primitive but dramatic story about bandits holding up a train.

Porter told me that the newsreel-type films of the period were at first popular as "the public flocked to see this novelty, but the appeal soon wore off, and many of the vaudeville houses and theaters where pictures were being shown as addenda to the regular bills began to drop these programs. I felt that there was nothing wrong with the screen itself, but that the public was becoming tired of the short, single-scene type of newsreel films that predominated then." Porter said that he had seen "some of the popular story films of the French pioneer director, Méliès"—trick pictures like *A Trip to the Moon*—and that these led him to the "conclusion that pictures telling a story in continuity form might draw the customers back to the theaters" and so he "set to work in that direction." Porter's *Dreams of a Rarebit Fiend*, which he made in 1906, was a trick film that was obviously inspired by the Méliès movies.

In 1902 Porter produced *The Life of an American Fireman*, which ran the better part of ten minutes and told a thumbnail tale of a fireman's hazardous activities, climaxing in the rescue of a mother and child from a burning building. This film also had what was undoubtedly the first movie closeup, a full-screen shot of a firebox. *The Life of an American Fireman* was followed a year later by *The Great Train Robbery*, shot near Dover, New Jersey, in authentic outdoor settings. This picture also had a rare, early-screen closeup. It came at the very end of the film and was a rather startling full-screen shot of a bandit firing his gun point-blank at the audience. Both of these primitive classics, as they have been called, were tremendously popular. They had color, action and suspense. *The Great Train Robbery*, particularly, was shown time and again by the operators of nickelodeons, which were just then coming into vogue.

In addition to being perhaps the first "story" films of the American screen, these Porter pictures also had a rudimentary but effective editing technique that was revolutionary for the time. They told their stories essentially through a combination of individual, separate shots. This vital editing principle, peculiar to the motion-picture medium, was later developed by Griffith and others into the touchstone of moviemaking.

Griffith's entry into movies was as an actor in a Porter picture. Porter recalled it this way: "I was making a short film for Edison, *Rescued from an Eagle's Nest*, about a mountaineer who retrieves a helpless infant from the clutches of an eagle. That was in 1907. An unknown actor and writer, who identified himself as David Wark Griffith, came to me one day with an adaptation of a French play which he thought had movie possibilities. After a hasty reading of the script, I had no other recourse but to turn it down. But Griffith was so persistent in his desire to do studio work that I finally gave him the role of a mountaineer in the picture. 'You're a little on the slim side,' I told him, for I was make-up man then, too, 'so we'll have to pad out your shoulders and put lifts in your shoes to get you in character.' Griffith took direction from me very well."

Actually, when Griffith presented himself at the Edison studio he submitted an adaptation of the opera *La Tosca* to Porter. He then went by the name of Lawrence Griffith instead of David Wark Griffith. He used the former name because, as an aspiring poet, playwright and stage performer, he wanted to disguise his identity when working in movies, which were then a not exactly fashionable profession.

After being in charge of the Edison studio for more than a decade, Porter left to form his own company, Rex, in 1909, and to become one of the leaders of the independent producers. He purchased the American rights to Sarah Bernhardt's three-reel *Queen Elizabeth* and went into partnership with Adolph Zukor, a former exhibitor, in the formation of Famous Players Company. Subsequently, he drifted away from movie production and, in 1917, became affiliated with a company that manufactured the Simplex projection machines, supplying many of the world's movie theaters. He also was active in some early experiments with sound-on-film and color photography. Latterly, he had worked on a popular 16 mm. camera and projector and what he described as a revolutionary type of still camera.

When I interviewed Porter for the New York *Times* in 1940, he was a white-haired, ailing old man living in a midtown Manhattan hotel room, quite forgotten by the industry in which he had once been a trail-blazer. Swathed in a black silk gown, he lay stretched out on a day bed and spoke haltingly about the past. "I rarely see pictures any more," he said. He added that he had lost most of his interest in films, and he felt that, though pictures had certainly made great strides forward since his time, much of the initiative and excitement had gone out of moviemaking. The film-maker's work, he said, was now cut out for him, what with various experts and front-office operatives handling each and every phase of the separate technical, artistic and business departments. It was otherwise in his day.

Outside his hotel window a spectacular Broadway sign proclaimed *Gone with the Wind*. Porter died the following year, in 1941, at the age of seventy-one.

Gilbert M. (Bronco Billy) Anderson got his screen start in Porter's *The Great Train Robbery* and then went on to become the original movie cowboy and the daddy of all horse-opera heroes. Today, in his late seventies, long retired from the screen and "in mothballs," as he puts it, Anderson lives alone and modestly in a small apartment in a faded part of downtown Los Angeles not far from where movies were once made in the distant past. In 1958 he briefly came out of retirement to accept a special honorary Academy Award bestowed on him as the first movie cowboy and for "his contribution to the development of motion-picture entertainment."

When I interviewed him for the New York Times in 1948, Anderson, a bluff and still sturdy gent, said that he maintained an interest in motion pictures and saw some of them from time to time. But, he added, he did not like to see westerns. "They're just like I used to make," he said in his gruff voice, "except they talk a little. Most of them are mediocre. They all have the same formula —two guns, bullets, 'pardner,' a boy with a crooning voice, horses and a sheriff. It's one big stew out of the same stewpot."

In Anderson's estimation, the manufacturers of movie westerns cannot miss on them. "They cater to the low mentality that wants nothing but excitement and doesn't care why the stagecoach goes over the cliff as long as it goes over," he said. "You can kill six Indians with one bullet, as long as you shoot them dead. The more impossible and incongruous westerns are, the more the audiences like them."

Anderson set a pattern for the horse opera from which it has scarcely deviated since. In the 375 two-reel Bronco Billy epics he ground out at the rate of one a week from 1908 to 1915, Bronco was a good-bad man, a sort of Robin Hood on horseback. He never changed the stolid expression on his face or the costume he sported—corduroy pants and boots, a huge Stetson, an open shirt with a bandanna and two guns. He rode a pinto horse and rescued young ladies, but never kissed them. "We never played our pictures for the physical," he said. "We played them for laughs or action."

Anderson was not particularly suited for the role of the movies' first chaps-and-spurs hero. When he made his movie debut, he could not ride a horse or shoot a gun. He hailed from Little Rock, Arkansas, where he was born Max Aronson in 1882. After a spell as a traveling salesman, he went to New York to crash the theater, found acting assignments few and far between and became a model for illustrators. One day, in 1902, he wandered into the Edison studio on Twenty-third Street to apply for a movie job—stage thespians shunned the "flickers" then—and was immediately hired by Edwin S. Porter as a leading man at fifty cents an hour. Anderson's first opus was entitled *The Messenger Boy's Mistake*. It dealt with a young fellow who quarreled with his sweetheart and attempted to mollify her with flowers and an enclosed card: "If you forgive me, wear these next time I call." The messenger delivered a pair of pajamas by mistake and when the swain arrived to call on his girl, her brothers gave him a sound drubbing.

In *The Great Train Robbery*, Anderson played, as he said, "everything but the camera. I rode a horse. I was a passenger on the train who was killed and I was also the bandit who shot him. I even doubled as a fireman who fought with the bandit in the caboose."

The first day of shooting, Anderson was thrown by a horse and never reached location from a livery stable in West Orange, New Jersey. Later, when he came to make westerns, he mastered the art of sitting on a steed and also aiming artillery. "But I was never anything more than a competent rider," he admitted, "and I used doubles for the sensational stunts. And as for marksmanship—heck, in those movies a blank used to turn a corner and kill a man."

After six months with Porter, Anderson left to become a director and producer as well as actor for other movie companies. In 1906 he joined forces with George K. Spoor, a screen-equipment distributor. They called their company Essanay, derived from their initials, and adopted as a trade-mark the Indian head borrowed from the copper cent piece. As half of Essanay, Anderson went thataway to California in 1907 with a cameraman and Ben Turpin, a cross-eyed comic recruited from vaudeville. In those days Hollywood was a quiet country town. The sight of a movie camera astonished the natives. The three-man unit settled in a downtown Los Angeles hotel and utilized the city as an outdoor studio. Their first picture, *Ben Gets a Duck and Is Ducked*, was shot off the camera cuff in Westlake Park. Turpin, portraying a hungry indigent, dived into the lake after a duck. A real cop dived in after Turpin, with the camera turning all the while. After the situation was explained to the policeman, Turpin was let off, and the movie unit had a completed comedy.

Anderson's next stop was Niles Canyon, near San Francisco, where he went to shoot westerns because of the impressive scenery. The success of *The Great Train Robbery* had prompted him to venture further into the cinematic wide-open spaces. He built a small studio at Niles and produced his initial two-reel horse opera, *The Bandit Makes Good*, in 1908. This film featured a character named Bronco Billy (it was spelled Broncho Billy then), played by Anderson, who robbed a bank and was apprehended by the sheriff. The guardian of the law and his prisoner stopped off at a hotel, where the sheriff lost the bank money at the gaming tables. Bronco Billy saved the day by holding up the gamblers, retrieving the loot and returning it to the sheriff.

The fadeout found Bronco Billy pardoned and appointed a deputy sheriff in his own right.

After several of these pictures, fan mail began to deluge Niles addressed to Bronco Billy, and Anderson decided to change the titles to Bronco Billy. "I directed, wrote and acted in 375 of those dang things in seven years," he recalled. "There was *Bronco Billy's Love Affair, Oath, Bible, Mexican Wife, Leap, Christian Spirit* and *Redemption*, to name a few. I did one every seven days, shooting from a brief outline."

Bronco Billy was invariably an outlaw with a heart of gold. The Essanay blurb for *Bronco Billy's Redemption* (1910), for instance, read: "Bronco Billy, a cattle thief wanted by the law, risks arrest when he drives a girl and her sick father into town for medical aid and is allowed to go free as a reward for his heroism." *The Outlaw and the Child* (1911) was synopsized in this fashion: "A western outlaw sacrifices his life to return the sheriff's lost child. Filmed in Mojave Desert. 1,000 feet."

Each Bronco Billy film was budgeted at $800 and grossed as much as $50,000, according to Anderson. The success of the films was phenomenal. Bronco Billy became world-famous. "Visitors to Los Angeles expected to see cowboys on Main Street," said Anderson. Before long, Essanay was riding high and Anderson was earning $125,000 a year. However, he decided to retire Bronco Billy for more artistic ventures. "That was a big mistake," he said, with the wisdom that comes of hindsight. In 1915 Essanay signed Charlie Chaplin at the then astronomical screen salary of $1,250 per week. Chaplin made twelve comedies for Anderson, most of them at Niles, including *A Night Out, Give and Take* and *The Pugilist*. Chaplin also starred in the first five-reel comedy, *Carmen*, for Essanay in Chicago.

When Chaplin was lured away by Mutual for $10,000 per week, Anderson sold out his interest in Essanay to Spoor and produced several plays. In 1919 he attempted to revive Bronco Billy, but by then William S. Hart and other western stars had supplanted him. Anderson produced some comedies with Stan Laurel and, after 1920, gradually drifted away from the movie business.

"The movies?" said Anderson. "They're still what they were—the maximum amount of entertainment for the minimum amount of price. Today's westerns are no improvement on the early ones. They got the recipes from those pictures and they juggle the ingredients upwards, backwards, forwards and sideways." He did admit a liking, however, for the glorified westerns as represented by the films of a director like John Ford. But Anderson was contemptuous of the singing western. "Music doesn't belong in a cowboy picture," he said. "I never heard of a cowboy who could play a guitar. Those drugstore cowboys —none of them were cowboys, no more than I was."

Until last year you could see the late Mack Sennett, the purveyor of pie in the eye and the kingpin of the Keystone Kops, taking his constitutional around Hollywood most any day. At the age of eighty, Sennett was a white-haired, robust and jaunty figure of a man. He lived for a long time in the heart of Hollywood in the old-fashioned Garden Court apartments. On a window sill stood an Oscar he was awarded by the Academy of Motion Picture Arts and Sciences in 1938 for "lasting contributions to comedy on the screen." The movie industry may not do anything much for its old-timers, but at least it gives some of them gold-plated statuettes.

Although he had been largely inactive in pictures for more than two decades, Sennett's name keeps cropping up constantly. The high spot of the Broadway musical *High Button Shoes* was a hilarious ten-minute Mack Sennett ballet, complete with period bathing beauties, Keystone Kops, mad kiddies and a gorilla. A biography entitled *Mack Sennett, King of Comedy*, about his pie-slinging histrionics of the silent screen, appeared recently; it was originally titled *Custard's Last Stand*. Some years back, Eagle-Lion studio brought out *Down Memory Lane*, in which choice clips from old Sennett movies were incorporated into a present-day television story line. Sennett's silent reels, critics concurred, were much superior to the modern TV sequences in the picture. And Paramount studio has had on its production agenda for some time *The Mack Sennett Story*, a feature-length film biography.

Sennett himself kept busy. He had been working on and off for years, he said, on a modern adaptation of *Molly-O*, an old-time movie hit starring one of his madcap stars, Mabel Normand. He had also, for some time, been polishing a tome, *The Quince*, which he described as "a Mack Sennett comedy in novelized form, dealing with the predatory capers of those who pursue." The cast of this opus, said Sennett, consisted of "J. Wallace Twist, a romantic and likable show-off; Jack Ransome, a suave and shrewd bogus genealogist; Charlie Wellington, young and personable, but predatory; Mary, a co-ed, whose heart beats only for Johnny, a young aviation cadet; and a friendly police dog, a singing crow, an ornery black cat and a heroic bullfrog."

Sennett, a chipper fellow with a hearty voice and a deep laugh, was a bachelor of long standing. For his age he was quite spry and looked as if he could still heave a custard pie with the best of them. As he strolled along Hollywood Boulevard everybody, from newsboys to show-business folk, addressed him deferentially as "Mr. Sennett."

This is a rather starchy appellation for a man who specialized in pratfalls. Sennett's era as the satrap of silent-screen comedy lasted from 1911 to 1922 at its dizzy pinnacle. During that time he perfected the fast-pitched pastries, the rapidly propelled patrolmen and the comely but uncultured bathing beauties that became his composite trademark.

Among the stars who were on his payroll were enough volatile characters to populate a score of comic strips. The baggy-trousered Charlie Chaplin; the bespectacled Harold Lloyd; the cross-eyed Ben Turpin; the childlike Harry Langdon; the rotund Fatty Arbuckle; Ford Sterling, the smirking cavalier; the nincompoop Hank Mann; and the lowering Mack Swain were only a few. In his early talkies, Sennett brought to the screen W. C. Fields and Bing Crosby. Such directors as Frank Capra, Wesley Ruggles, Lloyd Bacon, George Marshall and Roy Del Ruth learned their cinematic ABCs with Sennett.

Sennett's specialty was the screen boffola, the swift kick in the bottom and the burlesque pursuit. His pictures reveled in a low humor that paid off in high laughter. The Sennett movies were really *moving* pictures.

Sennett deplored the passing of this nimble nonsense. "You know," he said, "the art of screen slapstick has been mostly lost. Yet people love slapstick. The lowering of dignity is always funny. There is a great deal of humor in the combination of surprise and violence. I myself like to laugh and I enjoy comedy and that's why I like slapstick. Any little success I have had was because I was one of the mob and catered to the mob.

"The best comedy is a combination of action and line. There is too much of gag lines just being read today. The eye is so much faster than the ear and more important, too. I think the best and timeliest kind of screen comedy today would be the broad belly laugh toned down for modern audiences."

The basis of Sennett's belly laughs was several well-defined slapstick staples. One of these was the Keystone Kops. The cops came into being when, as Sennett related, "our company, including Ford Sterling, Fred Mace, Mabel Normand and a cameraman, got off the train from New York in 1911 and walked square into a Shriners' parade in downtown Los Angeles.

"We decided to move the camera right into the proceedings. We didn't work from carefully prepared scripts in those days and anything that came along that we could use, we used."

Mabel Normand, an impish-eyed siren who could take a fall and play moonlight love scenes without changing her expression, was promptly dispatched into the parade with a dummy infant while Sennett's cameraman set up his equipment in a jalopy labeled "Press." Mabel, clutching the bogus baby, confronted a dignified-looking man in the parade, proclaiming to all the world that he was the father of the tyke. The cops (bona fide ones) started to entangle the ensuing melee while the camera kept grinding. Sennett and his troupe finally beat a hasty retreat, but not until they had what they wanted on film.

The next day, Sennett had a movie with authentic cops. "They were natural comedians," he said. "They were better than our own comics. They looked stout and funny. Anything that has to do with the downfall of dignity does."

Before long, Sennett was masterminding a troupe of maniacal movie cops under the Keystone banner, which was the name of his studio in Edendale, not far from Hollywood. As a rule, new Sennett employees were put to work as cops at three dollars per day and, if they made good at this strenuous pursuit, they were promoted to less arduous activities.

The Keystone Kops were the most improbable policemen in the world. They sported luxurious handlebar mustachios, oversized or undersized uniforms, and they were constantly hell bent for somewhere in a wheezing flivver, piling out of the conveyance in riotous dozens as they went about their futile forays with miscreants.

The cops plowed nonchalantly through telephone poles, houses and fences and drove underwater and over cliffs. They inevitably stalled in front of oncoming express trains and ran head on into dynamite wagons. The Keystone-cop car came completely equipped with a removable steering wheel and was chauffeured by experts who could stop the automobile on a camera frame. To accentuate the velocity of the vehicle, the road was often liberally smeared with soap and, as if this were not enough, the scenes were photographed with a low-speed camera. When projected on the screen, the action appeared twice as fast.

For the train-vs.-automobile encounters, Sennett would sit around with a car full of cops waiting for a real train to come along and then run the flivver right under its nose, perceptibly aging the engineer. Occasionally he would make arrangements with an engineer for the train to go through Pasadena at ten miles per hour and scoot the car past the locomotive while the low-speed camera pepped up the result.

During inclement weather or when the streets of Edendale were being repaired, Sennett utilized his own chase scenery inside the studio. This was something called a Cyclopanorama, or a giant merry-go-round contraption with a treadmill effect on which two automobiles or a dozen cops could proceed abreast. The Cyclopanorama could be speeded up to twenty-five or thirty miles per hour, could rotate clockwise or counter-clockwise, and the scenery behind it could be altered at the drop of a scenario.

The pies, averred Sennett, originated in 1913 when a Keystone megaphoner, Harry Edwards, and comedian Ben Turpin were arguing in front of the camera one day as to whether a certain bit of business was funny or not. "Whaddya want me to do," inquired the cross-eyed comic indignantly, "straighten my eyes perchance?"

At this point, the way Sennett recalled it, Mabel Normand, who happened to be standing behind the camera, decided to inject some humor of her own into the proceedings. She appropriated a pie that a couple of carpenters were conveniently about to eat for lunch and slung it clear across the camera into the profile's profile. The cameraman meanwhile kept grinding away, for Sennett's standing order was that the photographer was never to miss any improvised bit of business.

There was a commotion and one of Sennett's aides was commandeered to soothe the bespattered ham. The arbitrator wanted to know what precisely had happened, and Mabel Normand obliged. To illustrate her point, she picked up another pie (the Sennett studio seems to have been bulging with pies that day) and threw it into the peacemaker's face.

When Sennett saw the rushes of the scene the next day, he got a hearty guffaw out of it. "That stays in," he ordered. From then on, pies were standard equipment at Keystone. The studio bought them from a grocer named Greenberg down the street. In time, Greenberg's Keystone trade became so lucrative that he switched from regular, or eating, pies to custard, or throwing, pies.

"Those were a special kind of pie," explained Sennett. "They were full of a sort of paste and sticky stuff so that when they hit, they didn't splatter too much, but dripped nice and gooey."

The pies were wielded by anyone and everyone. But for difficult scenes, where there could be no retakes, Del Lord, a chase director who doubled as a pie-slinging expert, stepped in for the custard kill.

Lord, said Sennett, never missed. He was one of the most valued talents at the studio.

Sennett had only one rule when it came to pies: "Never hit Mother in the face with a pie. Give it to the mother-in-law, but not Mother."

The bathing beauties were developed two years later as a publicity project. "I saw that I could never get a picture of one of my comedians in the press," said Sennett. "They were so sloppy-looking. But stills with girls the editors always ran. Why, any little waitress in a courtroom, as long as she held her skirt above her knees, got a front-page break, while famous politicians or diplomats were buried on an inside page."

So Sennett photographed his pratfall artists together with shapely young ladies and the pictures were plastered all over the newspapers. From there it was an inevitable step to incorporating the girls into his movies. Soon he had a troupe of temptresses, including Gloria Swanson, Phyllis Haver, Marie Prevost, Carole Lombard, Louise Fazenda and Polly Moran. The most decorative of the girls were given bit parts and ultimately elevated to leading roles.

"Each girl," said Sennett, "received individual treatment. There was no regimented line of girls. The camera focused on a girl's best parts." Sennett particularly liked to have the girls indulge in pastimes like softball games on the beach while they were photographed in slow motion to accentuate their good points.

As bathing beauties, the lasses naturally wore beach attire. At first, this consisted of Victorian-type pantaloons, mammoth hats and bathing shoes and socks that left little of the anatomy exposed. Gradually Sennett stripped this garb away, thereby incurring the wrath of the bluenoses. "The more they squawked, the more I figured it was all right," said Sennett, "and went ahead with peeling off clothes."

To round out the police, the pies and the pulchritude, Sennett threw in four-legged performers. One of these animal actors was Pepper, an Angora cat that had grown up at the studio and took everything, from a pie to an explosion, in its stride. Pepper had long and expressive ears which got a giggle per wriggle. There was also Teddy, a Great Dane, who could drive a locomotive, rescue a tot from a whirlpool and do most anything but talk (those were silent picture days, anyway). Sennett himself was once photographed with a lion on his desk for a scene depicting a quiet day at the studio.

Integral to Sennett's screen lexicon were tricky props like rosin beer bottles, cloth bricks, breakaway police clubs and expanding rubber boilers. He made regular use of a suction pump to cause a comic's hair to stand on end. Improvisation figured in every Sennett film. "We were always looking for new tools to work with," he said. The studio brain trust regularly scanned the newspapers to see what real-life happenings would lend themselves to reel ones. When a 125-foot-high factory chimney was about to be torn down, Sennett quickly contrived a comedy around it, planted a comedian atop the chimney and got him off just prior to the demolition. "We couldn't have afforded to blow up a 125-foot chimney," said Sennett, "and, after seeing the picture, audiences marveled at the lengths we went to for a laugh."

On another occasion, when a lake in the Los Angeles area was to be drained, Sennett placed a hero and heroine in the water in one rowboat and a villain in a second craft. As per the screenplay, the villain was to pull a plug from the bottom of the pond and maroon the lovers. When the lake was drained by municipal mandate, Sennett had his climactic scene ready-made, once more mystifying moviegoers.

Sennett's name was originally Michael Sinnott. He was born in Quebec, Canada, and was a boilermaker before he got into the movies. He worked in burlesque briefly and was hired by D. W. Griffith as an actor at the old Biograph Studio on 14th Street in New York City.

"I always wanted to direct," recalled Sennett, "and the studio finally gave me a chance to do so. The first picture I shot was in Fort Lee, New Jersey, in 1910. A gentleman by the name of Ishnuff, a Russian and a prototype of the late Czar, down to the imperial beard, was the cameraman. He was a former laboratory man and this was his first try at the camera. We had a skinny bankroll and were filming all of our scenes outdoors.

"I sales-talked a Fort Lee housewife into letting us use her front lawn by promising her a Rembrandt-like still picture of herself and her family. Ishnuff cranked the camera very slowly in order to save film, which cost four cents a foot. Neither Ishnuff nor I knew that if you cranked slowly, the film would be speeded up on the screen. When we finally developed the film and showed it in a projection room, there was a blur of jerky figures whizzing across the screen as if shot out of a cannon. I lost my bankroll of $2,500 and had to pawn a $3,500 diamond ring for $800 to start all over again."

In 1911, Sennett and his company of comics migrated to California and opened their picture plant in Edendale. Sennett had acquired the name Keystone for his company from a railroad train. "Such names as Elite, Royal and Crown were already in use," he said. "One day I saw a Pennsylvania train with its keystone trademark going by and I figured if it was good enough for the railroad, it was good enough for me."

The atmosphere at the Sennett studio was informal. "We all worked as a team," said Sennett. "Nobody gave a damn about me at the studio. I was just the big boss." Sennett often ran operations while sitting in a commodious bathtub built into the top floor of a tower in the middle of the studio and he liked to conduct story and business conferences with the water running.

There were a dozen or so rather ramshackle stages, with a swimming pool and volley-ball court for the entertainment of the employees. Gusto instead of glamour was the Sennett credo. Pictures were ground out by the dozen at a rapid clip, with platoons of gag men and directors functioning all over the premises.

Sennett's forte was the one- and two-reel slapstick spoofs he carried off with such verve. In 1914 he took a flyer into a six-reel comedy that ran approximately one hour. It was entitled *Tillie's Punctured Romance*, took fourteen weeks to produce, starred Mabel Normand, Marie Dressler and Charlie Chaplin, and was a hit.

Sennett recalled how he came to hire Chaplin, who was an English music-hall performer in Manhattan. "My big star at Keystone was Ford Sterling, whom I was paying $250 per week," he said. "When his contract expired, I offered him $750 per week to continue. Sterling threw his hat into the air with glee. 'You'll stay then?' I asked him. 'Oh, no,' replied Sterling. 'Then why did you throw your hat into the air when I told you that I was willing to pay you $750 per week?' I asked. 'Because I realized how good I am,' Sterling answered as he walked off the lot."

In desperation, Sennett hired Chaplin for $125 a week. During the year Chaplin worked for him he appeared in several dozen comedies in which he developed his distinctive combination of pathos and pratfalls.

Sennett had Harold Lloyd under contract, too, for a week or so when the comedian was just a newcomer to the movie business. One day Sennett was looking at rushes and said to his assistant, "Who's the guy running around with the glasses?" "Harold Lloyd is his name" was the reply. "He isn't funny to me," said Sennett. "What are we paying him?" "Fifty dollars a week," the aide answered. "Fire him," commanded Sennett.

Not long afterward, Lloyd became one of the leading comedy attractions of the screen.

"Heck," said Sennett, "that just goes to prove that even the great

Mack Sennett can be wrong." He and Lloyd remained the best of friends and Sennett enjoyed telling this story at social occasions in Lloyd's presence.

Sennett ventured outside the realm of the belly laugh only once. He decided to make a serious drama, a triangle story with all the trimmings. It was entitled *Heartbalm*. When the picture was flashed on the screen at its first showing in Los Angeles and the audience read the name Mack Sennett on the credit titles, laughter swept the theater. It continued through the entire film.

Sennett was heartbroken, but finally gave in to the inevitable. He changed the title of the picture to *Crossroads of New York*, added gag subtitles and released it as a comedy. It was a great success. "They laughed with us instead of at us then," said Sennett, somewhat sadly.

Sennett later moved his studio from Edendale to San Fernando Valley on the subsequent site of Republic Pictures, where horse operas supplanted horseplay. When sound pictures faded in, Sennett began to fade out, and in 1935 he relinquished his studio. Three years later he directed his last film, a forgotten item which brought comedienne Joan Davis to the screen.

How did it feel to be an ex-Hollywood tycoon? At one of his last interviews Sennett said: "Everybody goes through that stage in this business, of having their name so big. I have no desire for publicity. I never seek it. I'll tell you how it feels. It's a relief not to wake up in the morning and have to worry about box-office returns, investments, banks, payrolls and whether a picture will click or not. Those are some of the things you don't have to worry about any more."

As Sennett sauntered down Hollywood Boulevard, he was a contented citizen, for had not time been kind to the man and his works? Some years ago several hundred of his one-time employees, from the girl who handled the switchboard at his studio to director Frank Capra, tendered him a dinner at the California Country Club. It was a sincere and heart-felt tribute to a movie master by the people who not only worked for him but liked him and respected him.

Sennett kept up with the latest movies. "Too many pictures today are just plain gabby and have become effete," he said one day when we were out walking on Hollywood Boulevard.

"Look," said Sennett, pointing to the front of Grauman's Chinese Theater, where a current Hollywood comedy was playing. "It's too thin: it doesn't have enough belly laughs to it. You need brevity and controlled pandemonium in a picture. One of the best sources of comedy is violence and sudden surprise.

"But the chief basis of comedy, as in drama, is cause and effect. You can't get a laugh, which is the effect, without having a good cause. Now, supposing I was to push you off this curb. That would be a violent action, but it would not be funny in itself unless there was a good cause for doing so. Too many moviemakers forget that. Cause and effect are what count. Cause and effect."

Boisterous, congested Hollywood Boulevard shimmered in the noonday heat. For a moment—or was it only an hallucination?—the automobiles seemed to be whizzing more rapidly than ever past the white-haired, jaunty Sennett, and the policeman pacing by was a mustachioed, grotesque, hopping figure.

Sid Grauman was renowned as "the master showman." He was a pioneer theater tycoon and the "dean" of West Coast movie exhibitors. He built four of Los Angeles' most lavish movie palaces, among them the Egyptian and the more famous Grauman's Chinese Theater, and he helped develop the premiere-type of opening with klieg lights, movie stars and crowds.

Before his death in 1950, the seventy-year-old Grauman got off a few pointed remarks about what was wrong with the movies and movie exhibition. Sitting in his old-fashioned office overlooking the cement footprints of film stars in the forecourt of his theater one night, the bushy-haired, gaudy impresario said: "People are being weaned away from going to the movies. The novelty of talking pictures is wearing off. It's like the days when silent pictures faded out and made way for sound. If you put a fifty-piece orchestra in every theater pit, you couldn't have brought the customers back with silent movies."

The silver-maned Grauman, Mack Sennett and I had dropped in at the Chinese theater that evening in the course of strolling along Hollywood Boulevard. Grauman was then retired. In his heyday he was known as the showman par excellence. He specialized in gala premieres and spectacular stage prologues before each picture and leaned heavily on high-powered promotion. For the opening of Howard Hughes's aviation epic, *Hell's Angels*, in 1930, he had Hollywood Boulevard roped off for ten blocks, streetcars detoured and 250 searchlights picking out thirty airplanes in the sky, while the Hollywood hills in the background were lit up with Hughes's name.

"I don't think they'll ever kill talkies," Grauman continued, "even with television, but the situation today is a serious one. Actually, it's a miracle that talking pictures have lasted as long as they have. It's only natural that the producers have run out of ideas. There are only so many ideas you can do.

"I'd like to see the men in the studios reach up and pull down an idea. Ideas are all showmen have to work with. The public will still try a good picture. The solution is for studios to make fewer pictures and greater ones, taking more time and more care. They'll get the customers back that way."

Grauman said that he no longer had much faith in ballyhoo. "Showmanship plays a great part," he said, "but you can't fool the people. You can't bring the customers in with superlative phraseology, uniformed ushers, Brussels carpets up to the ankles and twenty-dollar gold pieces and not have a good picture on the screen. The picture is the thing. Today you have to deliver the goods."

As for double bills, Grauman became indignant. "The customers have talking-picture indigestion," he said. "Hollywood has given audiences too much movie and has tired them. A person doesn't want to go to a restaurant and get a tenderloin steak and then have another. One good picture with a stage show and a newsreel and short is the ideal bill of film fare and I think that we will see this soon at all first-run houses."

On the subject of popcorn and candy, Grauman waxed even more wrathful. "What you get is a Coney Island atmosphere," he said, "no matter how much gold leaf you have on the candy stands. All the popcorn does is offset the loss a theater suffers with mediocre movies. The theaters brought in that stuff when business fell off. Some theaters take in five hundred dollars a week just with soft drinks, and that pays their overhead and rent and taxes.

"It's been said that the theaters don't want good movies because they attract class audiences who don't go for the popcorn and candy. I don't know if popcorn makes for low-brow pictures exactly, but there's no doubt that with it the exhibitors are catering to the masses, not the classes."

As Grauman left his Chinese theater, passing through the baroque lobby, he looked—a little pensively—in the direction of the candy stand and soft-drink machine that were competing with the double bill on the screen inside.

At an auction of Grauman's effects after his death, I purchased his personal copy of *Motion Picture Theater Management* by Harold B. Franklin, a standard book about movie exhibition. The volume was elegantly bound in green, gold-tooled leather. But most of the pages had never been cut. I guess Grauman did not need to read the book.

I first encountered Elmo Lincoln (real name Otto Elmo Linkenhelt), the original Tarzan of the early silent screen, when he was ironically cast in a small part in *Tarzan and the Magic Fountain* in 1949. The jungle man in that movie was portrayed by Lex Barker.

Lincoln created the role of Tarzan on the screen in 1918 in *Tarzan of the Apes*. Afterward he starred in *The Romance of Tarzan* and in an eight-episode serial, *The Adventures of Tarzan*. Three decades later, in *Tarzan and the Magic Fountain*, he was playing a jungle fisherman who briefly crossed Tarzan's path.

When I met him Lincoln was still a barrel-chested fellow who looked as if he could swing through the trees with the greatest of ease. He lived alone in a small furnished apartment near the Paramount studio, where he did occasional screen stints, and he occupied his spare time with amateur handiwork.

Lincoln did not think much of the Tarzans who followed him, such as Johnny Weissmuller and Buster Crabbe. "They're sissified," he said in his booming voice. "They've refined Tarzan down today. He doesn't run through trees any more or tangle with lions. They seem to put him in water more now. When Johnny Weissmuller did him, he was a water man. I did water stuff, too—I once dived in among alligators—but it was just accidental.

"When I played Tarzan I was up in the tree tops most of the time. I also tangled with a lion. We had no doubles in those days. The producers bought an old, sick lion from the Griffith Park zoo. His claws were fixed so he couldn't scratch, and he was given a shot of dope. Then I jumped the lion, stabbed him and stepped on him to give the Tarzan yell. As my foot pressed down on him, the air that was left in his lungs escaped with a loud whoosh. You should have seen me jump! That lion wound up as a lobby display when the picture opened at the Broadway Theater in New York."

It was Lincoln's physique that got him into the movies. "I evidently was born with the foundation of it," he said. "I built it up by boxing, baseball and football. I just brought it along with me to Hollywood, I guess." D. W. Griffith took one look at Lincoln's barrel chest and cast him in *The Birth of a Nation* and then as the "Two Sword Man" in *Intolerance*.

Lincoln recalled that he began his career as Tarzan when several actors dropped out of the role. "The Tarzan company was shooting on location in Louisiana," he said. "They had two or three Tarzans, but none of them could go through with the part. The fellow I replaced was from Chicago. He was a ukulele player. He got up a tree, fell out, sprained his ankle and quit. So they called on me.

"I swung around in the trees eight feet above ground. There's nothing to it, providing you hold on and let go at the right time. I was insured for $150,000. When the insurance man saw me running around overhead, he said, 'We'll have to cancel your policy.' But I got through the picture with nothing more than a few bruises, and I was typecast from then on as a tree-swinger."

Of Lex Barker, who was a graduate of Phillips Exeter Academy and Princeton, Lincoln said, "He's a nice kid" and "as good a Tarzan as any." But he bemoaned the fact that "Tarzan is no longer what he was." "The Tarzan stories," he said, "are not the Tarzan as we made them. They seem to have changed character. In the old days I used to beat my chest like the apes. Now Tarzan yells with his hand cupped to his mouth. I wore my hair bobbed and shoulder-length. Now Tarzan has a modern haircut. I played Tarzan barefooted. Barker wears moccasins. Today Tarzan doesn't have a great deal to do with animals outside of a chimpanzee.

"The old Tarzan was an action character. He spoke very little, and when he did he spoke ape talk. Now Tarzan gabs too much. Why, I understand Barker is fighting for more dialogue in his picture."

I once accompanied Lincoln to a "salute" to the stars of the silent era at the Academy Award theater in conjunction with the showing of Universal-International's *Hollywood Story*. There were a number of silent screen personalities on hand, including Francis X. Bushman, Helen Gibson and Hank Mann. Lincoln and they had all been cast in the movie in bit parts as themselves.

There was a good deal of hoopla at the Academy Award theater as the Hollywood Chamber of Commerce and the studio grandiosely saluted "the Hollywood greats who reigned before the days of the Oscar and founded the great industry which brings entertainment and education to millions all over the world . . . the silent-film headliners whose glamour gave the film community its worldwide fame . . . these great stars of the past . . . to show that Hollywood remembers and acknowledges their contribution to its establishment." The entire event had been arranged by Universal-International's publicity department. In fact, the whole thing was nothing more or less than a high-toned publicity stunt.

After the showing I had a talk with Lincoln about the predicament, economic and otherwise, of the onetime "Hollywood greats." Lincoln did not mince words.

"We were all stars one day," he said. "We had the material and the personalities to become stars. We're still remembered by former fans throughout the world.

"The thought that I have is why, since we have had and still have some box-office value, don't the producers use us in pictures when they're making their productions instead of running in people from New York, England and everywhere else?

"Why is it that we can sit here with picture after picture being made where we can play a character part? Why is it that they don't call on us?

"Every time they want to exploit something, like *Hollywood Story*, they call on us.

"The first letter I received from the Hollywood Chamber of Commerce stated they were giving this 'salute' in honor of the old-time troupers who were responsible for Hollywood being what it is today.

"Naturally, I accepted. There was no mention of *Hollywood Story* in the letter.

"In the second letter I got from the Hollywood Chamber of Commerce, they said they were glad I'd be there. Down at the bottom they added that this would be a preview of *Hollywood Story*. It was in the very last paragraph.

"We're not getting any money out of this. There's nothing in it for us outside of the honor of being old-time troupers. That doesn't pay for the groceries.

"All of us who worked in *Hollywood Story* got $15.56 a day—the minimum extra rate—for one day's work. The principals, like Helen Gibson and Francis X. Bushman, who had dialogue, got $55 for their day's work.

"They paid us $15.56 for that one day and they've gotten $15,000 worth of publicity out of it.

"If I had the opportunity, I'd stand right there on that stage tonight and say, 'Why don't we get work? We're still mentally and physically capable and still have a following.'

"I'm not bitter. I don't want to be a star. I just want to have sufficient work to live like a human being.

"I've done so much for Hollywood. Why doesn't Hollywood do something for me?

"I'm not looking for charity. I just want to have a chance to work, which I'm plenty capable of doing.

"Last summer I was out with the Seal Brothers circus for two months in Nevada, Utah, Washington, Oregon, Montana, Dakota. I did the original Tarzan in my Tarzan costume and rode an elephant. My fans were kids.

"Now, because of that and as a result of being on Art Linkletter's radio and TV shows in February, I think I'm going to Dallas to appear in a chain of theaters as the original Tarzan.

"But the motion-picture industry is the most unappreciative, selfish business in America today. There's no industry in America that does not take care of its people after they've served it for years."

Several days later Lincoln received an honorary plaque from the Hollywood Chamber of Commerce inscribed: "In grateful acknowledgment for your outstanding contribution to the motion-picture art, and for your help in making Hollywood the world's film capital." But he never did hear from Universal-International's casting office.

Lincoln died in 1952 at the age of sixty-three. He did not leave any estate behind him.

Paul Panzer was one of the veteran performers of the screen and the onetime villain of the Pearl White serials. Panzer was the suave heavy who chased the intrepid Pearl in *The Perils of Pauline*, *The Clutching Hand*, *The House of Hate* and *Exploits of Elaine*.

When I met Panzer in 1943, he was seventy years old and working as a stock player at Warner Brothers, doing minor character roles in pictures like *The Adventures of Mark Twain*, *Casablanca* and *Action in the North Atlantic*. Panzer was one of a small group of old-timers that the studio kept on the payroll and made extensive use of in bit parts in an assortment of pictures. They more than earned their modest salaries.

Although he was seventy, Panzer did not look fifty and was just about as spry and agile as when he did hair-raising stunts without a double in the serial days. He had black hair, a mustache and a sharp profile. Panzer had been a stage actor with Augustin Daly when he began to make movies for the Vitagraph Company in 1904. Those were the primeval days of motion pictures. His first film was *Stolen by Gypsies*, which ran for half a reel. He played a French cook in it and much of the action was shot on the roof of the Morton Building at 116 Nassau Street in New York. The Vitagraph Company had its office on the second floor of the building and the studio was on the uncovered roof. When a stiff lower-Manhattan breeze hit the roof, the painted canvas sets would start waving. In 1914 Panzer became a serial star in *The Perils of Pauline*. He had been with Warner Brothers since 1934, working for a small salary.

As a studio publicist, I had had some dealings with Panzer because of my special interest in Hollywood's old-timers. Early in 1943 Panzer came into my office all distraught. Together with the rest of the old-time stock players he had been laid off by the studio. Now, in Hollywood, you must understand, when a studio divests itself of its help in its periodic so-called economy moves, it is not some big, fat, overpaid slob in the front office who is let go, but minor employees such as stenographers and bit players. As movie tycoon Joe Schenck, who ought to know, once told me: "In the wave of economy that studios generally have when they get desperate, they drop a few hundred-dollar-a-week employees and then hire a four-thousand-dollar-a-week executive."

That year the studio ax had fallen on the little company of old-time stock players whose aggregate salaries probably would not have kept Jack Warner in pocket money. All this, mind you, at a time when the studio, like all movie studios then, was making inordinate profits, because most any movie that was released during those plush World War II years was a celluloid gold mine.

Panzer cried in my office and his tears were no glycerine ones. He did not know what to do, he said. He needed the money. There was nothing I could say to console him. And so Panzer, at the age of seventy, went to work in the carpenter shop at the studio in order to meet his bills.

After some weeks, the old-timers were all put back on salary as stock players. That was the way those things went at Warner Brothers.

Panzer died in 1958 at the age of eighty-five. If you look at old Warner movies on television today, you can see him in many of them, an expert, inconspicuous character actor, portraying waiters, porters, cab drivers, policemen and other bit parts. He had once been a big star in Hollywood.

The late Erich von Stroheim, one of the great directorial talents of the American film, was run out of Hollywood and came back only briefly years later as a sort of freak performer. I had a long talk with von Stroheim in 1949 when he was in the cinema city to play the part of a silent-screen director in *Sunset Boulevard*, a modern talking picture about the movies. Ironically, in the picture von Stroheim was seen directing Gloria Swanson, whom he actually directed in 1928, when both were eminent film figures.

Von Stroheim is still remembered for his portrayal of evil Huns in World War I movies. He was then known as "the man you love to hate" and people used to throw rolls at him when he entered a Hollywood restaurant. During World War II von Stroheim was still playing hateful Prussians on the screen in pictures like *North Star* and *Five Graves to Cairo*. In the latter, he was cast as Field Marshal Erwin Rommel, whom he portrayed as a poseur and publicity seeker surrounded by a crowd of sycophantic adjutants—"practically like a Hollywood motion-picture director." Von Stroheim observed then that things had changed, however, and although he was still playing Huns, horror had become a commonplace commodity and most moviegoers took it for granted. Von Stroheim pointed out that the most cruel screen depiction of the Nazis did not even begin to measure up to their actual deeds. He spoke from experience. He had a brother who was in Dachau and he said that many friends had told him firsthand stories about the Nazis that he termed "almost unbelievable."

For all his striking screen characterizations, however, von Stroheim has already gone down in movie annals as a director rather than as an actor. He directed some of Hollywood's most significant and sophisticated silent films, such as *Greed, Foolish Wives* and *The Wedding March,* and he ranks with Griffith and Chaplin as one of the big three in the golden age of the American screen. Von Stroheim fought with censors and producers and is sometimes said to have dropped out of Hollywood as a director because of his high-handed and profligate tactics. The last Hollywood picture he directed was *Walking Down Broadway,* with Zasu Pitts, in 1932. After that he worked in France as an actor—his best remembered role of that period was in *Grand Illusion*—and made intermittent appearances in Hollywood movies.

His role in *Sunset Boulevard* found von Stroheim as Max von Mayerling, the ex-director and ex-husband turned butler of faded film star Norma Desmond (Gloria Swanson). In the course of the melodramatic unfolding of the plot, Desmond kills a Hollywood writer and is confronted by police, photographers and newsreel cameras. Max "directs" her final appearance before the cameras for the benefit of the newsreel photographers.

When I interviewed von Stroheim on the set of *Sunset Boulevard* at Paramount, the ex-director who was playing an ex-director in the picture was attired in footman's livery—a black-and-yellow jacket, green apron with gold chain, black bow tie and white gloves. He had just finished a scene with Swanson in the rococo living room of a "1920 Beverly Hills" mansion groaning with ornate mirrors, a gilt-edged piano, candelabra, marble arches, a velvet-framed movie screen and an organ.

"My outfit," said the bullet-headed, bull-necked von Stroheim in his measured speech, "is the correct one for morning-schedule housework. I designed it myself. I work well with Billy Wilder [the director]. He takes suggestions. Some directors I have worked with in the past do not take suggestions from a director of thirty years ago. It's heartbreaking. I just suffered in silence.

"What is it like to take direction from someone else? Let me put it this way: in order to be a good general, you have to be a good private. In order to be able to give orders, you have to be able to take orders.

"I was in Paris feeling good and doing well when Wilder's offer came. The script wasn't finished yet. I've never asked for a script. I wanted to be in the picture.

"It's a terrible thing to have been on the very top, on the pinnacle, and to be reduced, not in the financial sense—in the picture, Gloria's a millionaire, for instance—but not doing anything. They say today that I was extravagant when I made my movies. Now, they say, a director does a picture in seven weeks. But he is part of a big machinery that does everything for him. I not only wrote the original story and continuity and designed the costumes and sets, but cast my pictures, directed them, played the star parts in them and cut them. That took time. Today it is agreed that the longer you take, the better the picture. I knew it then.

"When I finish this picture, I am going back to France, where I will direct *The Fires of St. John*, an original story, a tragedy, and also appear in it. In Hollywood, you're only as good as your last picture. If you haven't got a last picture, you're no good. That's why I live in France. In France, if you write a great book, paint a great painting or direct a great picture, fifty years later you're a master and the young men take their hats off to you. Here the young ones don't know or care even about D. W. Griffith, the greatest of them all. I am proud to say I once worked for D.W."

Billy Wilder deferred to von Stroheim. "When I was a schoolboy," said Wilder, "Von was one of my movie idols." Wilder directed von Stroheim for the first time in *Five Graves to Cairo* in 1943. He told him then: "It is an honor to direct you. You were ten years ahead of your time."

"No," replied von Stroheim, who was not given to false modesty, "twenty years."

Since Hollywood is inclined to be forgetful about its own children, it was not surprising that only a couple of blocks from the center of the cinema city there quietly lived for many years a man who once contributed appreciably to the movies. Probably not many of the film folk knew that he was around.

His contribution to the screen was both a financial and an artistic one—a combination rare at any time. His name was Herbert Brenon.

He was seventy-one years old at the time I interviewed him in 1950 and resided with his wife in a plain home off Cahuenga Boulevard. He had been away from the movies for two decades.

In his day Brenon was one of Hollywood's top directors. He was often listed among the leading megaphoners in the "best" inventories. In 1927 he won *Photoplay*'s Gold Medal award for his *Beau Geste*.

When I saw him he was busying himself writing. He had completed his autobiography, *The Stormy Petrel*, and had authored a suspense story, *Terror at Midnight*.

I talked with Brenon in his old-fashioned living room, the walls of which were decorated with inscribed photographs of Hollywood personalities. He was a Puckish, cultivated man with a bald, white-fringed head who wore horn-rimmed glasses and pinched snuff out of a little box.

Dublin-born Brenon came to the United States when he was sixteen, was a stage actor and director and, after selling two scenarios for twenty-five dollars apiece to the Vitagraph Company, was hired by Carl Laemmle as scenario editor of IMP, the parent company of Universal. Shortly afterward he got an opportunity to direct. His first big success was the 1913 *Neptune's Daughter*, a film fantasy in which Annette Kellerman played a mermaid who had the gift of turning into a human being. Miss Kellerman wore a mermaid's tail, skintight bathing suits and was entirely nude in some scenes. The picture was a great success.

Afterward, Brenon made *Daughter of the Gods*, a follow-up to *Neptune's Daughter*, again with Kellerman as a mermaid. The picture, filmed in Jamaica, took a year to shoot and cost about $700,000, a whopping sum for that day. The studio advertised it as the first million-dollar movie and it was also a smash hit.

Among Brenon's other silent-screen successes were *War Brides* with Alla Nazimova; *Peter Pan* and *A Kiss for Cinderella*, both with Betty Bronson; *Beau Geste* with Ronald Colman, Ralph Forbes and Neil Hamilton; and *Sorrell and Son*.

When talkies came in, Brenon said in his British accent, "I had attributes for the new medium, having been an actor and stage director, but I had no heart in it, principally because I had seen silent pictures develop from a five-cent admission—more or less tripe—and had helped with some others to develop it into what I felt was an art secondary only to painting and sculpture and the other great arts.

"We had reached the stage where our films, I think I can say, were things of artistic beauty, of beautiful composition where one could sit in a theater relaxed and see these silent pictures accompanied by beautiful music. Now it had all turned around and reverted to the stage from which we had through the years completely cut apart and differed.

"I never was in sympathy with the talkies. In the early stages of talkies, all that we had developed in using as little of dialogue and the printed word as possible—to me the great picture was one that told itself with as little dialogue as possible—all that was gone."

After directing several talking pictures, Brenon bowed out of the movies in the Thirties.

"I'd been fortunate enough," he said, "to accumulate a little and decided to retire. I had to face the fact that I had to take a back seat, that younger men were coming up.

"I realized the years were catching up with me and I also saw every one of my colleagues had disappeared or had passed on and I decided I'd spend the evening of my life in retirement.

"The desire to go on in the field in which I had been more or less a creative factor died completely. I had always been at the complete head of my own unit. The director in my time had a studio manager but no producer over him. His imagination ran completely free. As long as he did good work and the money came in, no one interfered with him. But in the new era, the director was surrounded by overseers. The whole thing became a machine.

"I had always worked as a writer on my own pictures with the writers. I like to write now. You can write when you feel like it. In other words, I'm leading a life of leisure and a very happy one. And now that I'm seventy-one, you can't blame me for taking it easy.

"I keep up with the movies, only the very best. I admire among directors Frank Capra, Carol Reed, Frank Borzage. And, of course, there's Cecil DeMille, the perennial Cecil. Cecil has an extremely commercial mind, but far from an artistic mind, to my thinking.

"As the movies reached a peak in the days of *The Covered Wagon*, and I think I can include *Beau Geste* and you can think of others, we had farther to go. But now they have already reached their peak.

"There's no bitterness here. Thank God, I went as far as I did and have so much to be grateful for. I'm only looking at things as they are. Movies today are machine-made. I don't think there's any question that the motion-picture industry is on the decline."

The Hollywood traffic roared by on Cahuenga Boulevard in the early evening. Brenon took a pinch of snuff as he dredged up the past.

"I'm satisfied with my peaceful, happy life," he said, "relieved of the terrible strain I had for thirty-five years. I am positive that those splendid men, like Victor Fleming and others, cracked under that strain. I am so grateful that I did come to the decision to retire and have a peaceful, undisturbed evening of my life."

Brenon died in 1958. He was seventy-eight years old.

Not all tycoons took as gracious an exit as Brenon. In 1949 B. P. Schulberg, one of the early-ish movie moguls, starred in a real-life, riches-to-rags drama with as many sobs and throbs as any picture he had ever produced.

Schulberg, who helped form United Artists in 1918 and was production head of Paramount Pictures from 1925 to 1932, announced that he was out of a job and could not get work in Hollywood. Desperate—and publicity-wise—Schulberg (he had once been a movie press agent) took full-page ads in the Hollywood trade papers of October 25, 1949 (cost: approximately $400). They were addressed "To the top executives of the motion-picture industry." "As most of you know," the ads read in part, "I have devoted a third of a century to our industry. . . . Yet, at this time . . . seems I can't get a job.

"Some of my friends who are *not* top executives tell me that doors are closed because I have in my time talked back to some of the big boys. But I cannot believe that men as narrow and narcissistic as this can undertake to entertain and instruct the world." (This foregoing paragraph was cut out of the ad in the *Hollywood Reporter*, but ran in *Daily Variety*.)

"Sure, I have made some mistakes—as who hasn't?—but I think it will be granted that these have hurt nobody but myself. And what is the juridical code of the industry? Life imprisonment for a misdemeanor and execution for violating a parking law?

"This is the only business I know. I am able to work as hard as anyone in it, and as proficiently as most. . . .

"Must we always wait until a productive pioneer is found dead in some 'obscure Hollywood hotel room' before you reflect upon an 'indifferent and forgetful' industry?"

I talked with fifty-seven-year-old Schulberg as he sat by the telephone in his modest, five-room North Hollywood home waiting for results.

"I wrote the ad myself," said the chipper, white-haired ex-tycoon. "The purpose of this move is to force certain men to open the doors.

"There are only a half dozen men who run this business. Some of them once worked for me. David Selznick was my assistant at Paramount. William Goetz [then head of Universal-International] was an assistant director at Paramount.

"I think they're gonna wonder what I plan from this point on."

Schulberg said that if he got no results from the ad, he planned to write a book about Hollywood. His son, Budd Schulberg, was the author of *What Makes Sammy Run?* a stinging novel about the rise of a conniving Hollywood producer. Schulberg said he was not depicted in the novel in any way.

"But I could write a book about this town that could top *What Makes Sammy Run?* easily," he said.

Budd Schulberg was then in Pennsylvania completing a new novel. B. P. Schulberg said he wrote his son telling him about his move "so he won't be surprised when he reads the ads."

Schulberg thought that Hollywood treated its pioneers "pathetically." He cited D. W. Griffith, who had died the year before that.

"Why did Griffith go from door to door?" asked Schulberg. "He was a man of great sagacity and great picture knowledge. He could have been useful.

"He died of a broken heart. Why do they always wait until they die and then lament them?"

Shortly before this, Schulberg had worked as an advertising and publicity man for an independent Hollywood production company. "I don't want to be retired," he said. "I have a lot of things to do yet." Among them were a projected movie about the life of Goya, to be made in Italy, and a remake of *White Gold*, a silent-screen hit. "I've been trying to sell them for more than a year without success," said Schulberg. "I decided to go back to work at a studio. I was encouraged at two different places until suddenly the curtain came down.

"Someone in power and control must have said, 'I don't like him.' That's enough reason."

Schulberg sat and waited for the phone to ring and for one of the men who had once worked for him to give him a job. But the phone never rang. "No offers," he reported later.

He died in 1957, at the age of sixty-five, in Miami Beach, Florida.

Of the many former film stars I encountered in my journalistic peregrinations, some were bitter about their vanished glory, some philosophical. On the whole, though, they were more interesting and shaped up a good deal better than the current crop of profiles, perhaps because they had already had their little moment in the spotlight and were now no longer frantically jostling to be "on stage."

Nita Naldi, one of the leading "vamps" of the silent screen, was appearing in a "Silver Screen" revue at the Diamond Horseshoe, a Broadway night club, when I caught up with her in 1942. An ample, still exotic woman, her provocative conversation was liberally leavened with a fine irony.

"My contribution to this show," she said, "finds me coming out in a deep-blue spotlight and reciting Kipling's 'A Fool There Was' against a background of males in evening dress. This is all very exotic, but a lot of customers these days seem to have the idea that Kipling is a sort of herring."

Born in the United States of Italian parentage and educated abroad, Nita Naldi appeared as a temptress in such pictures as *Sainted Devil, Cobra, Blood and Sand* and *Dr. Jekyll and Mr. Hyde*. Her last picture was the silent *The Ten Commandments*, in which she played "a moral and physical leper. Churches fell where I walked and I typified all the fallen women in the world." She married and lived mostly abroad during the following years.

"In the silents," she said, "the business of being a vamp was all pictorial pantomime, ebony bathtubs and allure in repose. Even in those days the whole thing was ridiculous. It was difficult to convince an audience that you were such a *femme fatale* that you could lure a man from his work and his woman merely by raising and lowering your eyelashes. The women in the audience hated you for it and the men resented it. As soon as I used to flash on the screen, the customers knew right away the hero would part with his farm.

"Today, with the benefit of screen dialogue, vamping is much more natural. Now an actress can put over a vamp scene in a tweed coat and a hat pulled over her eyes. The entire art of vamping consists in developing the characterization slowly and allowing it to creep up on the audience. The ideal vamp, I think, is a blonde, because blondes are subtle and have more control over their emotions. A Southern accent is of immense help, too," the brunette ex-vamp observed in her pronounced British accent.

In 1955 Nita Naldi was again heard from as she made one of her infrequent forays into show business. Speaking of the passionate and evil sirens of the silent screen, she said, "We were all blind as bats. Theda Bara couldn't see a foot ahead of her and poor Rudy [Valentino] groped his way through many a love scene and I really mean groped. They all used big reflectors to get extra light from the sun—that's how we acquired that interesting Oriental look."

She added: "We didn't have any censors in those days, but we did have our own bosoms and our own eyelashes. . . . And we never took ourselves seriously."

Ramon Novarro, one of the legendary Lotharios of early-day Hollywood (*Ben-Hur, The Prisoner of Zenda, Scaramouche*), had devoted himself to real estate since the advent of talking pictures. Occasionally he dabbled in acting. In 1949, somewhat stouter than he once was, the still handsome Novarro appeared in character roles in several pictures.

"When I was a leading man," Novarro told me at the time, "every part was the same. I was always the hero—with no vices—reciting practically the same lines to the leading lady. The only difference in my roles were my costumes and my leading women. The stories were the same—boy meets girl, boy gets in trouble, boy triumphs over trouble, boy gets girl. But these character roles now have some real meat for an actor."

Novarro was of the opinion that silent pictures had it all over the talking variety because they could "say it with props. It is true that you can say so much with a little something—the raising of an eyebrow or just a look. What you can put in without words!"

But in one respect, at least, Novarro found contemporary movies superior to old-time pictures. "The current crop of movie heroes," he said, "are less handicapped than the old ones. They are more human. The leading men of silent films were always Adonises and Apollos—no one really is, of course. The camera angle had to be just so in each shot and every movement was calculated and precise.

"Today the hero can even take a poke at the leading lady. In my time, a hero who hit the girl just once would have been out. Sometimes, though, I think today's leading men get a little too rough in their treatment of the ladies."

Sitting in the RKO studio commissary, Novarro dug into a large portion of apple pie that the waitress set before him. "And, ah," he said, "in the old days I couldn't eat much dessert. I had to watch my figure. Is it not better to be a character actor?"

A critic once commented of Jackie Coogan, the former child star of the silent screen: "The persistent survival of Jackie Coogan, as a middle-aged man, with a divorce and thinning hair, incidentally, often has an unnerving effect on lady cinema patrons, though they are only vaguely aware of him as a symbol of their own continuity."

Coogan, the famous "Kid" of the silent screen, is today a glib, round-faced man who has been putting on weight and putting off hair. But the image of him as a pathetic tyke in tatters and an oversized, askew cap endures from the celluloid of yesteryear.

Coogan made his movie debut in 1916 at the age of sixteen months in *Skinner's Baby*. Subsequently he made thirty-three pictures, among them the famous *The Kid* with Charlie Chaplin, and earned several million dollars, of which he retained very little.

When I spoke to Coogan in 1950 he was temporarily taking a flyer as a businessman (he is again acting in movies and television today). He said then that he had decided to quit the movies because there was no business in show business.

"I just found out it isn't lasting after being in it for thirty-one years," the onetime Kid said.

Some of the old-timers wound up with wealth as well as with time on their hands. Mary Pickford, who was once known as "America's Sweetheart," is a shrewd businesswoman who has also been called "The Bank of America's Sweetheart." In 1956 she threw a lavish garden party at her elegant hilltop mansion, Pickfair, for more than 200 old-time movie stars. The guest list ranged from Edwin August (once known as "The Biograph Boy"; Mary Pickford was originally known as "The Biograph Girl") to Clara Kimball Young. It was estimated that there was more than $1,000,000,000 worth of talent on the premises at the time. Mary Pickford was photographed reminiscently bussing Edwin August. And there were all sorts of sage and seasoned observations made by the assembled motion-picture profiles of yore.

"I fooled Hollywood," said Eddie Polo, the ex-star. "I went to Europe and made good. I'm just on a vacation. I'm going abroad again and make some more films."

"I was a talkie victim," said Eileen Percy, who had been one of Douglas Fairbanks' leading ladies in silent films. "I got smart, married and settled down."

Pat O'Malley, who was an Edison star in 1907, said he was still working—when he could find a job. "But I get very little work from Hollywood films," he said. "Thank the Lord for television. I pay my grocery bills with TV checks."

In 1949 Cecil B. DeMille and fifty or so other Hollywood old-timers got together for a party in a Hollywood bank. The event took place at the corner of Selma and Vine, where DeMille made *The Squaw Man*, the first feature-length film shot in the movie metropolis. Now, thirty-five years later, a branch of the California Bank had opened on the site, and DeMille and the other screen oldsters showed up for the occasion, which was in the nature of a promotional stunt for the bank's unveiling. There was even a gun lying in close proximity to the money vaults, but nobody gave it a second look. It was a relic from *The Squaw Man*.

The merrymakers foregathered in the bank's basement. A small orchestra played while the stars and starmakers of yesteryear drank punch, sized each other up and were interviewed and photographed. Among those present were such picture pioneers as Jesse Lasky, Mack Sennett, Francis X. Bushman, Elmo Lincoln, William Farnum and Ramon Novarro. The feminine contingent included Blanche Sweet, Arline Pretty, Mae Murray and Theda Bara. The girls all looked quite glamorous, particularly blond Winifred Kingston, leading lady of *The Squaw Man*, who was happily married, living in Hollywood and had long since retired from the screen. Other *Squaw Man* veterans, besides DeMille, were Dick L'Estrange, Arthur Flavin, Tex Driscoll and Wilfred MacDonald, all of them still connected with show business.

Theda Bara, famous vampire of the silent screen, was a rather shy, matronly figure at the party. She was married to Charles Brabin, a former movie director, and was a staid resident of Beverly Hills.

"What are you doing now?" I asked her.

"I'm keeping a very—I hope—happy home. Goodbye," the ex-vamp replied as she scooted away.

DeMille observed that he never thought that there would one day be an imposing bank where he had once shot movies on an open-air stage in the midst of orange and lemon trees. "I was even in doubt then if there'd be a bank in Hollywood," he said. "We used to cash our checks in those days at Hall's grocery store on Hollywood Boulevard. You might say that the California Bank has replaced Hall's grocery store."

The proceedings were not entirely festive. Some of the old-timers were not doing quite as well as DeMille and could have used some ready cash from the bank.

"How are things?" one former screen star was asked.

"Not one hundred per cent," he answered. "But there's nothing wrong that a job wouldn't cure." (But DeMille didn't offer him one.)

Among the old-timers who have done well is Charles Farrell, the onetime star with Janet Gaynor in *Seventh Heaven*. I interviewed him some years ago when he was mayor of Palm Springs, California, and also proprietor of the plush Racquet Club in that desert community. Farrell had quit the movies in 1938 and had later taken a fling at television in "My Little Margie," a TV series produced by Racquet Club member Hal Roach.

Farrell still looked better than most movie juveniles. He had a profile, wavy white hair and a bronzed complexion. He told me that he was "glad to have been in the movies but, to be perfectly frank with you, I don't think I could stand the Hollywood gaff again. Here you're your own boss. Also, this is not an unlucrative business. When I was in the movies, actors used to get pushed around by the studios. It's less true today, but they still get pushed around."

Farrell said that "I love picture people and I love being close to Hollywood. Here I get in on the best part of Hollywood without any of the woe attached to it. I take an awful beating running this business, but if I work until three in the morning, I don't have to get up at the crack of dawn if I don't want to. A movie actor does. I guess I'm getting to that age when I want to sleep a little."

Farrell observed that "my movie experience has helped me in running the club. I can handle picture people on a little different basis. Having worked with a lot of big stars, I meet them on just a little more equal basis than just being a saloon keeper. If Jane Russell walks in I give her a big kiss. If I hadn't the Hollywood experience I did, I'd say, 'How do you do, Miss Russell.' "

Farrell looked around at his elegant club. "I've got sixty-five guys working here," he said. "If I want them to get me a cup of coffee, they get it for me. Hell, Clark Gable only has five guys working for him."

Rod La Rocque and Vilma Banky! What memories those names evoke of a bygone Hollywood! La Rocque was the gay, dashing leading man in a series of pictures with such titles as *Captain Swagger*, *The Love Pirate* and *Hold 'Em Yale*—all made during the carefree Twenties. Vilma Banky was Samuel Goldwyn's blond, beautiful Hungarian siren, appearing opposite Rudolph Valentino in a number of movies. Their marriage in 1927 at the Church of the Good Shepherd in Beverly Hills has become something of a Hollywood legend. Samuel Goldwyn "produced" the fabulous event and there was a small army of police on hand to keep the newsmen, the fans and the top-hatted and be-jeweled movietown elite under control.

Almost a quarter of a century later, in 1950, I found La Rocque and Miss Banky still happily married. They were living in an unostentatious, old-fashioned home, minus swimming pool, on genteel Foothill Road in Beverly Hills. La Rocque was then a real-estate broker specializing in ranch properties. He and his wife had left the motion-picture business far behind them, although La Rocque had "quite a few dealings with the movie people" as a realtor.

At the age of fifty-two, La Rocque still gave evidence of the debonair charm that had made him a Hollywood heart-throb. He wore spectacles and his black hair close-cropped, but he stood an erect six feet three inches, had a hearty speaking voice and the urbane manner that once fluttered many a female filmgoer's heart.

La Rocque said that he and his wife did not miss the studios at all. "As far as the mechanics of moviemaking are concerned," he said, "I can live without them very well. I rarely visit the studios. Not long ago I went to the studio to see Frank Capra on business. When I saw all those old-timers playing extra and bit roles, I got sick. And all of them such sports about it!

"We used to have so much fun making pictures. There was a hail-fellow-well-met, a camaraderie, a gregariousness about it. Now it breaks my heart to hear the things they talk about. Vilma and I look at each other and say, 'What has happened to the business?'"

Although they had been out of the movies since the mid-Thirties, La Rocque's and Miss Banky's names kept popping up in print periodically. "With all those old movies being released for television," said La Rocque, "I suppose sometimes people say, 'I wonder what the devil happened to him?'" There was a reference to La Rocque and Miss Banky in *Sunset Boulevard*. In that picture William Holden looked out at Gloria Swanson's deserted swimming pool and said, "Vilma Banky and Rod La Rocque must have swum in that pool a thousand midnights ago."

"The studio came to me for clearance to use our names," said La Rocque, "and I was glad to give them permission. But Vilma got a big laugh out of it. You see, she doesn't swim a stroke and never has."

La Rocque recalled how he wooed and won Miss Banky. "I was with DeMille in 1927," he said, "and Vilma was a Goldwyn star when I met her and fell in love with her. She spoke very little English. We met through Victor Varconi, a Hungarian actor. He taught me to say 'I love you' in Hungarian. Vilma and I used to have dinner at Marcel's restaurant in Altadena. One night we drove out there through the orange groves. I ordered wine. The music was soft. I looked Vilma straight in the eye and said with all the ham and corn in me, 'I love you,' in Hungarian. She almost collapsed. That Varconi had taught me to say 'Go to hell' in Hungarian."

Miss Banky and La Rocque decided to have a simple wedding at the Santa Barbara Mission, but Samuel Goldwyn took over and the result, at the Church of the Good Shepherd, was far from simple. "DeMille was the best man," recollected La Rocque. "Goldwyn gave the bride away. The ushers included Ronald Colman, Harold Lloyd, Donald Crisp, George Fitzmaurice and Victor Varconi. Tom Mix drew up to the church in a coach and four. I just remember my collar kept wilting.

"After the wedding, a reception was held at the Beverly Hills Hotel —Sam just took over the hotel. There was a buffet, a magnificent spread. Some wag said it was composed partly of papier-mâché turkeys just for display. The reception was so gargantuan, I guess the thought suggested itself. There was no papier mâché, believe me. It was certainly memorable. It was so funny—we thought we'd be married quietly at Santa Barbara.

"That's twenty-four years ago. Gee whiz, it's a long time. A lot has happened," said La Rocque, the real-estate man, somewhat nostalgically, sitting there in his serene, old-fashioned living room on Foothill Road.

William Haines, once a leading movie actor, is today a leading interior decorator. Among his clients have been Joan Crawford, Constance Bennett and Leila Hyams, with whom he appeared in pictures several decades ago. When I profiled him in 1949, Haines, in his late forties, was as personable and impeccably turned out as in the days when he played romantic leads. "I've never been divorced from show business," he told me. "Many of my friends are my clients. I feel part of them. I'm still an actor who's hanging some curtains."

Haines specialized in true-blue, wisecracking characters in movies like *Brown of Harvard*, *Sally, Irene and Mary*, *Tell It to the Marines* and *Slide, Kelly, Slide*. "I became the oldest college boy in North America," he said. "Charlie Farrell became the oldest choir boy. We outgrew our roles, like Shirley Temple."

Haines gave up acting in the early Thirties. Today he runs a sizable firm that has decorated hundreds of homes in the motion-picture-potentate areas. Haines said that there are special problems in designing a residence for the film folk, such as the placement of motion-picture-projection rooms. The movie people, it seems, like to hide their movie equipment, possibly for guilt reasons. Producer William Goetz's projection machines are concealed behind the collection of paintings in his drawing room. An array of dummy books hides Nunnally Johnson's movie projectors. Jack Warner's eighteenth-century English library, which can be converted into a ballroom, also does triple-threat duty as a projection room.

Movie actors, Haines had found, "are much vainer than women. When doing an actor's home, if I can give him plenty of mirrors quietly and never mention it, it is a happy solution."

Haines, who was residing in a fairly modest, "contemporary modified" FHA home in West Los Angeles, had recently completed an autobiography in novel form, *The Silents Were Golden*, dealing with "an actor's rise and fall." He said that he had no intention of making a movie comeback. "I'm content with my work," he said. "It's clean, no mascara on the face. It's a rather pleasant feeling of being away from pictures and being part of them because all my friends are. I can see the nice side of them without seeing the ugly side of the studios."

Today, according to Haines, "ninety-five per cent of our business is out of show business and also out of the state of California. Our work takes us to a national and international field. I attribute it to the changing times. The motion-picture queen is dead. The present run of stars don't have the knowledge and interest in homes that the older ones had. They're a beatnik group of actors with no interest in it at all."

Not only the profiles and picturemakers but the celluloid strips with which they work are perishable. In the last half century, many old movies have either been lost or destroyed, and a good deal of the nitrate stock on which old films were printed has disintegrated. The maximum life of the celluloid base of a picture is thirty years, and, as a result, all the great pictures made up to 1930 are rapidly going the way of old celluloid.

Old movies do not just die, they fade away. Jack Reilly, then head film librarian at M-G-M, told me in 1953 that even some old pictures kept under the best available studio-storage conditions "had gone to pot." When the film cans were opened, they had "a terrific stench." The film had turned to jelly or brown powder and had to be thrown away. Reilly said that "there's no answer to the problem of preserving film. With film that has been given the same development, treatment and storage conditions, some remains fine and some not so fine. You can't tell."

Old films at M-G-M are kept in concrete ventilated vaults with wooden racks, sprinkler systems and raised floors to eliminate the danger of flooding. Films are inspected and rewound annually. "But some," said Reilly, "go bad and some don't. Even Eastman doesn't know why." At intervals, new prints are made of films that are deteriorating.

Reilly estimated that between twenty and thirty per cent of M-G-M silents have deteriorated in spite of the studio's best efforts to preserve them.

But more durable paper prints of movies produced before 1912 have outlasted many of the early films and are today useful records of some of these primitive pictures. Before 1912, movies were not covered by the copyright law although there was a copyright provision for photographs. Some movie producers, therefore, protected their pictures by making paper contact prints from 35 mm. film and depositing them in the Library of Congress copyright office. This practice was pursued until 1912, when the copyright law was amended to include movies.

There are two million feet of paper rolls in the Library of Congress. In 1942 the Academy of Motion Picture Arts and Sciences in Hollywood began to experiment with methods of transferring these old paper prints to modern film and, in 1948, borrowed a selection of the Library's paper rolls and continued the experiments in Hollywood. In 1953 it was decided that the best way to transfer the old paper prints to film was in 16 mm. A firm called Renovare Productions accomplished this, in the words of the Academy's then president, Charles Brackett, with "a lens from a Norden bombsight, bits and pieces from a pinball machine and a helping hand from a can opener." The old, crooked, discolored and faded paper prints had to be laboriously photographed frame by frame, with optical adjustments from one frame to the next. Renovare Productions is today carrying on with this work, which may, in the long run, cast more credit on the Academy of Motion Picture Arts and Sciences, as instigator of the project, than its more ballyhooed, but less worthwhile, Academy Awards.

The Academy described this enterprise as "a significant contribution to the archives of the nation on behalf of the motion-picture industry." I recently looked at some of these old movies that were being transferred from paper to celluloid. They were flickery, grainy and scratched, but in their own rudimentary way they were some of the first attempts to tell a story on the screen and they help trace the first faltering steps in the evolution of screen syntax.

Among them were a 1903 Biograph picture entitled *The Corset Model*, a one-minute epic in which a pleasingly plump lady models the item of apparel referred to in the title; *Gatling Gun Crew in Action*, an Edison release photographed in West Point in 1897; *The Ex-Convict*, a 1904 Edison film about an ex-con who "finds it impossible to get or keep a job because of his criminal record" until he saves a little girl from being run down by an automobile and "is saved by the same little girl whom he had rescued"; *An Englishman's Trip to Paris from London* (Biograph, 1904); *The Great Baltimore Fire* (Biograph, 1904), an early example of on-the-spot camera reporting; *Latina, Contortionist* (Biograph, 1905), starring the hefty Latina; and *International Contest for the Heavyweight Championship, Squires*

Versus Burns (Miles Bros., 1907), photographed at Ocean View, California.

Other intriguing titles were *Flossie's New Peach-Basket Hat* (Lubin, 1909); *A Fatal Flirtation* (Lubin, 1909); *For Her Sweetheart's Sake* (Vitagraph, 1909); *The Cowboy and the Lady* (American Mutoscope and Biograph Co., 1903); *The Duke's Jester or a Fool's Revenge* (Vitagraph, 1909); and *The Little Train Robbery* (Edison, 1905).

Was this an omen—*The Great Train Robbery* in 1903 and *The Little Train Robbery* in 1905? Even in those early years the art of the movies was already undergoing a diminution.

CHAPTER X

The Night Life

of the Gods

IN SPITE OF THE VENERABLE SAYING about Hollywood—"No matter how hot it gets during the day, there's nothing to do at night"— I have found, as a journalist, that there is often more doing after hours away from the camera than during the working day in front of it. And though these after-hours doings are mostly frivolous, they can often be more revealing about the community than a stack of double-dome tomes authored by psychiatrists, anthropologists and sociologists on grants from the Rockefeller, Guggenheim and Ford foundations and sponsored by the Museum of Modern Art Film Library and the Academy of Motion Picture Arts and Sciences combined.

It may well be that Hollywood is ultimately not susceptible to authenticated, final documentation, that everything is elusive, apocryphal and in the domain of the gossip columns. If that is so, then it may also well be that some anecdotal incident, some minor, off-the-cuff nipup, caught on the fly and set to paper, can be more indicative of moviedom and its works than the most ambitious, three-ply research project.

The doodads of the Hollywoodites are essentially not the issue as far as moviemaking is concerned. The picture is—or should be—the thing. But the off-screen peccadilloes of the film folk loom so large precisely because their on-screen achievements are so puny. Beneath the dizziness and the dazzle, as Seymour Stern has pointed out, it is all really very gloomy. "Because underneath it all," he says, "is a tragedy —that this is what has become of the thing Griffith created."

Perhaps some of the melodramatic sensationalism that has constantly surrounded Hollywood was foreshadowed in the life of Eadweard Muybridge, one of the very original precursors of movies. Muybridge, born Edward James Muggeridge in England, was described as "an adventurer." In 1874 he shot and killed a U. S. Army major who had eloped with his wife. After a gamy trial, he was acquitted in 1875 at Napa, California. Muybridge may have bequeathed a legacy of some sort to the moviemakers who followed him.

In its formative years Hollywood's excesses were legendary. The film folk played as hard as, if not harder than, they worked. Rudolph Valentino sported a Voisin tourer with a cobra design on the radiator cap, had a hilltop hacienda known as Falcon's Lair with a canary-and-black bedroom and a living room with a black marble floor and cerise hangings. Gloria Swanson regularly immersed herself in a golden bathtub in a black marble bathroom. Comic Charles Ray had solid-gold doorknobs (he died broke). Clara Bow, the "It" girl of the Twenties, zipped down the movietown boulevards in a Kissel convertible with seven red chow dogs to match her hair. She boasted to an interviewer: "You'd have to look hard to see which was Clara and which were the dogs."

Profile Wallace Reid, who died at thirty of dope, Louella Parsons has recalled, drove a low-slung, robin's-egg-blue car with a horn that played "Yankee-Doodle Dandy," and movie cowboy Tom Mix had a dining room with a fountain that sprayed water alternately blue, pink, green and red. According to Lloyd Morris in *Not So Long Ago*, John Barrymore had a home with three swimming pools, a bowling green, a skeet range, English taproom and lodgings for twelve servants, and actress Lilyan Tashman had an all-white drawing room with all-white piano; the piano was festooned with a blue satin ribbon. Morris also reports that Dolores Del Rio traveled abroad with a menagerie consisting of a Russian wolfhound, a German dachshund, an English pointer, an Irish setter and a Saint Bernard. In a Hearst Sunday supplement, Adela Rogers St. Johns once chronicled that Lupe Velez committed suicide with sleeping pills in an all-white room with thick white carpets, sweeping white satin draperies, mirrored walls with carved white statues reflected in them and a crystal bar with hundreds of bottles of exotic perfumes. Her long black hair, enormous black eyes and dark olive skin made a startling contrast on the white satin bed on which she lay dead in her gleaming white gown.

Lloyd Morris has also dutifully noted that Marion Davies resided in a baronial, ninety-room pillared Georgian mansion on the Santa Monica ocean front (it has since been torn down). The estate had two swimming pools, one filled with salt water and traversed by a marble bridge imported from Italy. Inside were three dining rooms, two bars, an immense drawing room with a ceiling covered in 14-carat gold leaf, and a private movie theater. Davies once threw a circus party with a merry-go-round on the tennis courts. Vamp Theda Bara (an anagram of "Arab" and "Death") was, according to her press agents, born on the Sahara Desert, the offspring of a French artist and his Arabian amour (her real name was Theodosia Goodman and she was the daughter of a Cincinnati tailor). Dressed in indigo outfits to accentuate her deathly pallor, she posed for photographers in the midst of skeletons, skulls and crystal balls.

The fun and games of the latter-day motion-picture profiles—even Liberace with his piano-shaped swimming pool—may not have been quite as baroque as these. The inroads of income taxes and industrialism left their inhibiting marks on moviedom. But Hollywood was still a far cry from Cobb's Corner, Idaho, and was not precisely the cracker-barrel community that its slick apologists in the Association of Motion Picture Producers tried to make out it was. And as television competition increased and movie audiences decreased, Hollywood began to turn more and more to bizarre distractions to take its collective mind off these disasters. Bread and circuses—or rather cake and circuses—were the order of the celluloid day.

As one goggle-eyed tourist commented after gandering at Forest Lawn, known as "the happy cemetery" and "the graveyard with glamour," whose platoons of press agents boasted that one could get christened, married and buried on the premises: "You people sure know how to live out here."

For a while the craze in Hollywood was the fur-covered toilet seat. This was the specialty of furrier Al Teitelbaum. "What do you give somebody who already has everything?" Teitelbaum eloquently asked. "Naturally, you give a fur-covered toilet seat," he logically replied. Teitelbaum covered toilet seats in a range of furs, from rabbit to ermine, the latter at $200 apiece (the customer supplied his own toilet seat). Bing Crosby, no slob he, had an ermine toilet seat covered on *both* sides (cost: $400). "Bing Crosby has one," observed Teitelbaum. "What do you give Crosby?" One motion-picture personality had his ermine-covered toilet seat hanging on the wall of his bar. When the ermine-covered lid was lifted, there was a picture of the owner's wife. "That's where he'd like to have her," explained

Teitelbaum. "Naturally, she's not living with him any more," he added.

During the days when Hollywood was up in arms against television, Teitelbaum covered a TV set in skunk for a moviemaker. When things became a little cozier between TV and the movies, he began to cover television sets in mink. "Naturally, I leave the screen uncovered," he said.

One cinema citizen, Hal Hayes, an erstwhile publicity-minded construction man who hung out with the screen set, became one of the most talked-about hosts in Hollywood with his surrealistic hillside home that had a swimming pool running through it and faucets in the kitchen that gushed forth Scotch, bourbon and champagne, as well as beer for the peasants. Hayes explained that to build this abode, "I cut a hole in the mountain and covered it with glass, concrete and steel." The entrance to the house was through a tunnel. The pool was half inside, half outside the house. A twenty-foot glass wall could be rolled back in warm weather to put the indoor part of the pool outdoors. There was a television set built into a tree trunk. A heavy green rug in the living room ran up a window seat and, when a button was pressed, the rug rolled up the window like a blind in reverse. "This is an effective thing in case of an atomic explosion," said Hayes. "At Hiroshima and Nagasaki, windows blew out and lots of people were killed by glass, which acted like flying shrapnel. There is no way to be safer than to eliminate glass or catch it. This rug window blind catches glass like a net. Since the rug is heavy, it stops gamma rays and neutrons."

Hayes also had a custom-built Cadillac with a record player and a dictaphone, and a resplendent bar, including refrigeration and running water, built into the trunk compartment. Of the bar in his car, Hayes said: "I do a lot of construction work in outlying areas where they don't have bars and there is no other way of getting a drink. It's not good around town, but awful nice out in the desert." Shoe tycoon Harry ("There's no business like shoe business") Karl, former husband of screen actress Marie MacDonald and recent "romance" of Debbie Reynolds, went Hayes one better. He had a gold-plated, $52,000 custom built Cadillac that not only had a bar and a telephone in it but also a TV set and a hi-fi—and even a motor.

In Palm Springs a motor tycoon named Robert McCulloch liked to entertain Bing Crosby and other film folk at his mechanized home. This abode featured a bar where liquor bottles popped up one after another through apertures as they were automatically raised by small elevators. As one bottle was emptied and disposed of, the next bottle materialized by mechanical means, so that the bartender did not have to exert himself unduly by reaching for it. There was also a motorized sun wheel, which revolved slowly so that the outdoor types could obtain an even, over-all suntan—a sort of human spit, so to speak.

At the modernistic, Richard Neutra-designed Holiday House at Malibu, owner (and former movie director) Dudley Murphy at one time announced that he was installing a co-educational steam room. Murphy declared that this innovation was long overdue, that the standard steam baths limited to one sex only were stuffy and passé, and that the Holiday House steam bath would be available to couples interested in the hygienic benefits of steam. "It's an intimate, modernistic Finnish rock bath with an adjacent massage room," Murphy said. "A man and wife can book it as a private deal." He added: "Any couple registered in a hotel is supposed to be man and wife. If they can take a room, they can certainly take a bath."

At the Las Tunas Isle Motel, overlooking the Pacific several miles south of Holiday House, each of the thirteen rooms was decorated in a different, flamboyant motif. There were, for instance, the Jungle Room, featuring a palm tree with a stuffed monkey climbing up it, a fishnet ceiling and a bamboo bar; the Leopard Room, with leopard-skin chairs and bedspread and a black marble fireplace; the Satin Room, with walls covered with black satin studded with gold buttons, and with velvet-covered chairs. The Las Tunas Isle Motel was usually heavily booked in advance, mostly by movietown customers.

One profile, Zachary Scott, who usually played heavies and tough guys on the screen, was sashaying around Hollywood sporting a gold earring in his left earlobe. Six-foot-one Scott said he had his ear pierced and acquired the earring in 1948 on a fishing trip off Acapulco during which the ship's captain had his ear pierced and wore an earring, with the result that the rest of the fishermen followed suit. Scott wore his earring, a plain gold ring, all the time except when he was in front of the camera. According to Mrs. Scott, who was not jealous: "There has never been the slightest unpleasantness about the earring. Of course, it attracts attention, particularly from the ladies. Everybody seems to enjoy the fact he has an earring in his ear."

Other actors were not to be outdone. Movie cowboy Dale Robertson had a $7,500 hand-hammered and carved solid-silver saddle. Said Robertson: "I never use it in movies. I use it in parades. I ride with the sheriff's posse in Los Angeles." The silver saddle, which had two-toned beige and dark maroon cowhide, was kept locked in a vault when not in use.

One Hollywood playboy had flying from the radio aerial on his Jaguar not a squirrel tail but a mink tail. Other furry developments: mink earrings, mink cuff links.

As Hollywood was increasingly bedeviled by present-day headaches, it retreated into the past. The moviemakers were industriously remaking—or rather rehashing—their old movie hits (e.g., *Cimarron*, *The Blue Angel*, *The Four Horsemen of the Apocalypse*). They reminisced inaccurately in literary vein about the old days (e.g., the remembrances of things past by Adolph Zukor, King Vidor, Jesse Lasky, etc.). And there were other withdrawal symptoms.

In suburban Reseda, where a good many of the screen aristocracy live, dinners were at one time being served in the private Roman Room of a restaurant named Sasha's Palate in Roman style—i.e., with the customers reclining on couches. Some of the diners even brought their own togas. The Roman Room, according to proprietor Atanas Katchamakoff, could accommodate as many as "sixteen to eighteen people. But," he advised, "that is too crowded. Twelve is just right." The Roman Room's menu included partridge, pheasant, buffalo steak, suckling lamb, pig or baby goat. Among the restaurant's clientele were Ray Milland, Robert Cummings and Billy Wilder.

In the gold-draped, candlelit Roman Room, epicures ate at a high, L-shaped table covered with red silk damask and groaning with exotic dishes served by waitresses in silky pantaloons and boleros, which may not have been authentically Roman but were decidedly decorative. After dining, one could stretch out on a mauve, upholstered, five-foot-wide divan festooned with pillows which ran along two walls. On the facing wall was a movie screen on which was projected a loop of film depicting a Roman garden and fountain. Proprietor Katchamakoff told me: "The Roman Room gives people a chance to be aristocratic, be elemental, to enjoy themselves like before the last days of Pompeii."

If there were not exactly lions in the streets, there were at least Jaguar convertibles. And Ciro's night club opened up a Pompeii Room featuring a Vesuvius cocktail. The management announced plans for installing a miniature volcano. There were bonfires in the hills where the villas of the Hollywood neo-pagans perched, and smog erupted over the film capital. Some incipient archaeologist dubbed it a Pompeii with palm trees.

Then there was the Bohemia Club, a group of show-business folk dedicated to the feudal life. The forty-odd members, known as knights, squires and pages, met weekly in what is loosely referred to as the heart of Hollywood. The proceedings at these conclaves, I was informed by officers of the club, were patterned after King Arthur's Round Table. Their symbol (of wisdom) was the great horned owl. They wore helmets (of cloth). They carried swords and emblematic shields. They engaged in combat and challenge. They clashed tankards and yowled.

The idea, I was told by Arno Frey, the Supreme Ruling Knight or Imperial Sovereign, was "to completely forget all the outside world, all the troubles and mundane worries and relax in a dreamland one day a week." Since most of the members of the Bohemia Club were actors, musicians and writers (and since many of the actors, musicians and writers in Hollywood were unemployed at the time), this was not a bad idea at all. Frey, who described himself as "an actor by profession," said that "right now, due to the fact that the motion-picture business is shot, I am mostly in television."

According to Frey, "the Bohemian year starts in December and is dated the year of the great horned owl one thousand, for the year 1935 when the club was started. The newcomer to Bohemia is a pilgrim for the first three visits. He then fills in an application for entry to become a burgher or probationary member. Afterwards, he becomes a page and then a squire. After one year he becomes a full-fledged knight.

"We have combat by challenge and there is a choice of weapons. There are mental weapons [writing a literary theme], musical weapons [composing music] and material combat [drinking beer in tankards—no hard liquor was allowed in Bohemia].

"Three things are taboo in Bohemia—talk about religion, politics or business. This leaves all friction out."

Frey told me that the Bohemia Club was planning to build its own headquarters, complete to a moat and drawbridge, and was assembling "a castle fund" for this purpose. Meanwhile, the club met in a cellar room in the Padre Hotel in Hollywood. The walls of the room were decorated to simulate rocks and stones. There were stained-glass windows. There were also elevated thrones for the three ruling knights (Frey and his two liege lords). The knights sat around a long table. They got matters under way by rising and bowing to the great horned owl near the throne. Then they gave the opening yowl (or song). The Bohemians used archaic words, like "gnaw" for eat, "flagon" for glass or stein, "Lucifer" for waiter and "torch" for cigar.

Each knight's by-name was bestowed upon him according to his profession. A radio writer was Knight Static. A movie actor was Knight Pancro (for Panchromatic). And so on.

Another Hollywood group dedicated to the past was the Vikings, a glorified drinking society that met every two weeks at the Scandia Restaurant on the Sunset Strip. The setting was the wooden-beamed Scandia bar, and the society's motto, lifted loosely from Oscar Wilde and emblazoned on the wall, was "Work is the ruin of the drinking classes." Another motto: "The Vikings always have one more." Among the members were such show-business folk as Errol Flynn, John Charles Thomas, Lauritz Melchior, Victor Borge, Carl Brisson, Everett, Larry and Bob Crosby and Michael Wilding. Among their activities were wearing horned Viking helmets and bearlike robes and blowing an ancient Bavarian mountain horn on auspicious occasions. Each Viking had his own glass with either his real name or nickname on it. Jean Hersholt's glass, for instance, had a Band-aid monogrammed on it (Hersholt was the famed Dr. Christian of the entertainment world). The Vikings had their own kind of Valhalla, a top shelf on which reposed the glasses of those Vikings who had passed on. There were approximately fifty members in the organization. One of the leading members was Lud, the Scandia bartender, who was the chief horn blower and who has been described as "the world's worst bugler." The Vikings made news print some years ago when one of the group's members was sued for divorce and his wife offered as court evidence against him a picture of her husband wearing a Viking helmet at Scandia. Incidentally, the chief of the Vikings at one time was, appropriately, Russ Stewart, a vodka salesman.

In Hollywood, ham naturally gravitates to ham, and so a good deal of the social doings took place at restaurants. A popular eatery was The Cock'n Bull, which someone once described as being Hollywood "in a nutshell." One of the leading movietown beaneries was Romanoff's, a place where, as George Jessel once said reverently, "a man can take his family and have a lovely seven-course dinner for $3,400."

Prince Michael Romanoff, who was born Harry Gerguson, the son of a Brooklyn tailor, had a royal record of check bouncing before he went legitimate with his Beverly Hills hashhouse. The bogus prince is highly regarded in screen circles. In a community of pretenders, he is the great pretender. He has been called a prince among fellows, and also a fellow among princes. He was once dubbed "Hollywood's only honest phony."

The shrewd Romanoff has said that he is "a snob of the first order, but not an occupation or possession snob. The mere possession of wealth or name without achievement leaves me uninterested. I call myself a saloonkeeper and I call this a joint." The royal Romanoff crest once consisted of a cocktail glass crossed with a swizzle stick. Latterly, it became a gold-leafed double R, back to back, surmounted by a crown. Romanoff explained that this signified not Romanoff Rex, but Romanoff's Restaurant.

When it comes to high-toned doings in Hollywood, Romanoff is not easily excelled. His backers include Rockefellers and Whitneys as well as mere motion-picture potentates. As he parades through his gastronomic domain, trailed by a retinue of flunkies, and hands out his royal blessing to his little flock, he is a solemnly dignified, even an imperial figure, with his close-cropped, graying hair and bulbous nose. He summons his aides with an alligator riding crop ("I carry it around because I catch cold without it"). He is magnificently tailored. He once informed me that he air-expressed his pongee shirts to Sulka in Manhattan every week to be laundered. Romanoff, naturally, would never stoop to having his linen laundered in the Wild West.

Before moving to his present quarters in 1951, Romanoff was located several blocks away on the same street. In his former sandwich shop he had seven booths in the bar. These were usually reserved for the very cream of the motion-picture industry. If some great name of the screen failed to be seated in one of these cubicles, his celluloid stock could have shot down abysmally. This kind of social setback might conceivably have lost a guy his job and then he might even have been unable to frequent Romanoff's—a nasty thought.

This booth setup, however, led to complications. "At my old restaurant," Romanoff told me, "Alfred Hitchcock always had the first booth. It was a mistake originally by the headwaiter to have given him that booth. Hitchcock was away two years. He came back and was given a booth in the side room. He's never been here since."

His present restaurant, which is done in "early Romanoff" décor, was craftily designed to bypass the previous booth arrangement. The dining room is now composed almost entirely of booths, twenty-four of them, so that everybody can be happy. "This restaurant seats one hundred and twenty-eight," Romanoff explains, "thirty people less than before. I deliberately made it smaller so that all the seats are good. Before, we had select booths. Now every seat is equal and the customers love it.

"In order for a restaurant to be intimate, it has to be smaller. Unless it is intimate, certain tables are undesirable. There is no use having tables people don't want to sit at.

"The arrangement in the old restaurant created a good deal of ill will. Now everyone is satisfied. In my new place the average customers get the same seat as a celebrity. Darryl Zanuck is the equal of anyone else here."

Or so Romanoff said anyway.

"We never give a celebrity the same seat from one day to the next," Romanoff elaborated. "We change the seating around all the time. No side of the room is allowed to become better than the other. We shift people from one side to the other—today here, tomorrow there."

Humphrey Bogart, however, took a liking to the second booth from the left off the entryway and occupied it daily. Romanoff observed that this was "indicative of his occupational neurosis. I tried to give him a different booth each time, but he insisted on the same one." As a result, this booth, by unspoken understanding, gradually took on the status of the number-one table in the restaurant, thereby again setting up a sort of insidious caste seating system.

As one of the ranking arbiters of filmdom's social life, Romanoff sounded a sour note about the advent of television in Hollywood. He deplores television thespians as being mostly of the "dirty shirt" school and prone to dine at a hamburger stand instead of at a class beanery such as Romanoff's.

"The TV actors can afford to eat here," Romanoff says with a pained expression, "but they still think in terms of the drugstore, both artistically and physically." He disdainfully compares the television profiles to a genteel movie actor like Cary Grant. "The television performers," he has said, "think differently, behave differently, live differently. I don't approve of their deliberate snobbery of the dirty shirt—it's a form of snobbery, you know." Romanoff adds: "We do get some television executives here, but very few of the actors."

In general, Romanoff observes, today's youth has "a lack of taste. They don't want to eat in a good restaurant. The old ones eat less and go out less and drink less. They are also inclined to be hypochondriacs."

Another leading Hollywood beanery is Chasen's. Dave Chasen, a onetime stooge for comedian Joe Cook, went on to specialize in the care and feeding of profiles. In the old vaudeville days, Chasen used to get hit over the head with a hammer and a variety of bizarre mechanical devices as part of the Joe Cook routine, and he has observed that this was an excellent training for his present job.

The nurturing of notables requires showmanship as well as a knowledge of calories. "We run this place like a theater," Chasen has said, "with a big cast and a new script every night. Everyone on our staff has to know his or her cues. Our employees have to know just what to do and how to do it at the right time and keep in mind what the customer does or does not like. Actors have to watch their diets and that is only one of the things we have to be up on."

Orson Welles, for instance, is a big eater who likes double steaks and double orders of roast beef. Welles also likes to have a telephone plugged into his booth so that he can make calls while dining. George Raft is "a meat and potato man," says Chasen. "That's all he eats." Howard Hughes dines rather simply—a triple glass of tomato juice, salad, a thin butterfly steak and coffee. He eats the same thing all the time and, like many of the Hollywood gourmets, is on the telephone constantly.

Chasen went from Joe Cook to cooking out of necessity when he found himself out of a job in Hollywood concurrently with the demise of vaudeville. In his Broadway days he had won some renown not only as a professional foil for Cook's shenanigans but also as an amateur chef. After Chasen went to Hollywood and appeared in several pictures, he came to the conclusion that acting was an impermanent profession. "I saw former vaudeville stars looking for handouts at the Hollywood Brown Derby," he said, "and I got worried." Harold Ross, the late editor of *The New Yorker* and one of those who had enjoyed Chasen's barbecued ribs and chili sauce in the East, advised him to get out of show business and into the chow business. Another of Chasen's initial supporters was Frank Capra. "If this place can stand for some of the pictures we make, their stomachs can stand anything," said Capra. At his restaurant, Chasen featured olive oil from Capra's ranch.

At the start, Chasen's consisted of only six tables, a lunch counter and a bar, and Chasen did all the cooking himself. Today Chasen's seats several hundred customers, employs a staff of 94 and is valued at close to a million dollars, including John Decker's portrait of W. C. Fields as Queen Victoria which hangs near the entrance.

From the start, Chasen barred autograph hounds, photographers and roving gossip columnists from the premises. This and the culinary attractions lured the motion-picture profiles. W. C. Fields and director Gregory La Cava liked to play ping-pong in the back yard while James Cagney, Ed McNamara, Pat O'Brien and Frank McHugh harmonized in a corner booth. One night Nunnally Johnson, Charles MacArthur and Joel Sayre were celebrating till the small hours. At 4:00 A.M., Chasen informed the revelers that he was about to close the restaurant, so they threw him out and locked him outside in the rain. After the regular customers left, there were often impromptu shows, with Bert Lahr reciting his woodman number, Ray Bolger hoofing and Frank Morgan doing a strip-tease.

The restaurant flourished. Chasen installed a men's lounge which he premiered in Hollywood style with arc lights and flowers. James Thurber, in an inspired moment, decorated the walls of the lounge with some of his drawings. Chasen was overjoyed with this free artistic acquisition. The next day, when he arrived at the restaurant, he found that a conscientious cleaning man had scrubbed the drawings off the walls in the belief that they were the scribblings of a drunk. Among Chasen's customers were Greta Garbo and a gourmet identified as the Baron Wrangell. The baron sometimes electrified the Chasen customers when he tested the temperature of wine by plunging a gold thermometer into a wine bottle.

Chasen presides over all this in his red silk-lined jacket, a sartorial carry-over from his vaudeville days. He says that he does not miss grease paint in the least. The celebrated names of stage and screen regularly frequent his restaurant and he is able to hobnob and reminisce with them. Several years ago Chasen, giving in to new trends, added a television room to his establishment. It replaced the area where there had once been a steam room that was popular with Chasen's convivial customers.

"There is no more action," Chasen complains. "Everyone has left town and gone to Europe; Bogart got sick, and Flynn—he lived in the steam room. Milly Milestone, the director, and Sy Bartlett—they all went to Europe.

"As the people grow older, they are more concerned with their diet. There's a lot of low-cholesterol diets. They want a substitute salt and no sauces and they won't have anything fried—it has to be broiled."

Chasen adds: "If anybody is in trouble, I take care of 'em—for years. And I seldom lose. They pay off, after eight, nine years."

As the small television screens gave the movie business a large headache, and as movie production fell off, many actors found themselves out of work. As a result, some unusual typecasting job situations arose. Johnny Weissmuller, for instance, went into the swimming-pool business. At one point Gino Corrado, a movie character actor who specialized in headwaiter roles, forsook films, temporarily at least, to become a headwaiter in real life.

When I interviewed him some years ago, Corrado was maître d' at a Beverly Hills restaurant frequented by a number of profiles with whom he had worked in pictures. Now he was waiting on them in reality. Corrado told me that he took the job because "things are very quiet around the studios. The owner of the restaurant asked me if I would accept a position as headwaiter and I agreed. He said to me, 'You have done so much headwaiting in pictures, why don't you do some for me?' I am not ashamed to be doing this kind of work. I took the job with the understanding that if anything came along in the way of a movie role, I'd have the privilege of taking it."

Corrado, a plump, curly-haired man with a small mustache and a suave manner, said that the movies "have stopped building big restaurant and night-club sets in order to economize. And if there are no restaurants and night clubs, how can there be headwaiters?"

A native of Florence, Italy, Corrado had been in pictures since 1921. He played one of the title roles in Douglas Fairbanks' *The Three Musketeers* and was seen in the silent *The Ten Commandments* and *La Boheme*. He became a movie headwaiter in 1933 in *Hallelujah, I'm a Bum*, in which he waited on Al Jolson. He thinks that he may have been cast for the role because he had played heavies prior to that—"some people seem to consider headwaiters heavies"—and because his manner and appearance were suited to the part.

"Since then I have played hundreds of headwaiters, waiters and maître d's, more than anyone in the movies," he said. "I used to get letters from maître d's." So identified did Corrado become with such roles that he had to turn down other parts which required him to shave his distinctive mustache.

Among the pictures in which Corrado appeared were *Top Hat*, as a headwaiter; *Gone with the Wind*, as a waiter serving Clark Gable and Vivien Leigh; *Casablanca*, as a waiter; *An Innocent Affair*, as a headwaiter; *My Wild Irish Rose*, as a café owner who booted out Dennis Morgan for not paying the bill; and *The Stratton Story*, in which he served up oysters to James Stewart. He had a related role, as a chef, in *Pride of the Yankees*, and he once stood in for Charles Coburn in a movie in order to carve a duck. Only his hands and arms were seen on the screen in that film.

"I played those roles to perfection," said Corrado in a thoroughly detached way. "In the movies, you know, everything has to be just so for the value of the camera. I have observed the best maître d's at work in Hollywood and elsewhere. I go to restaurants and talk to headwaiters and watch their mannerisms, how to bow, lead to the table, seat a party and so on. I have studied up on the subject and know everything there is to know about it. I also learned recipes—I am an epicure —and I have my own herb garden at home."

Accordingly, when it came to being a headwaiter in real life, Corrado felt that he was well equipped for the job. He said that he was happy with his work at the restaurant. A good many customers, who recognized him on sight, asked him for his autograph—"sometimes thirty to fifty a day, inscribed on menus," he said.

When I asked him how being a headwaiter compared with being an actor, Corrado replied, "This is also acting. It's all showmanship, down to the serving of the crepes Suzette," as he dashed off to another part of the restaurant to usher in a party.

Corrado's becoming a headwaiter led to some provocative casting conjectures. If this sort of thing were to develop into a trend, the filmtown philosophers speculated, Gary Cooper could then become a cowpoke, Yul Brynner an Oriental potentate and Ernest Borgnine a butcher.

Shortly after Corrado blazed this thespianic trail, another movie actor, Leonid Kinskey, took a similar step. Kinskey, who had also played restaurant proprietors, headwaiters and bartenders in pictures like *Casablanca* for some years, became the host for a while at the Bublichki Restaurant on the Sunset Strip.

"I've had a small financial interest in this restaurant for some time," Kinskey asserted. "When things in the movie industry dropped, I asked myself, 'Where does the money come from?' So I decided to go to work at the Bublichki. But I haven't given up my movie work and if something comes along in pictures, I'm free to take it."

Kinskey, a tall, undernourished-looking fellow with tousled hair, a mustache and glasses that had a habit of sliding down his nose, frequently got double-takes from diners-out who thought they recognized him. But it was only because they had seen him on the screen.

Kinskey said that playing to a restaurant audience was easier than playing to a movie audience. "In the movies," he said, "everything has to be just perfect. Here you can be more human and relaxed."

Gordon Douglas, who directed Kinskey in several pictures, dropped in at the Bublichki one evening. Douglas watched Kinskey bustle about with a fine display of showmanship, and finally got up from his table and shouted, "Cut!"

An even more interesting case was that of George Dolenz. Dolenz, a rather dashing sort of chap, was a maître d' at Ciro's night club some years ago when he caught the eye of movie tycoon Howard Hughes. Hughes took him out of Ciro's and made him a movie star in swashbuckling-type roles. Then, when the recession hit Hollywood and when even Hughes gave up the movies to concentrate on his tool and aviation interests, Dolenz also reverted to his former calling. "Even actors have to eat," he said. He took over a well-known Hollywood restaurant, the Marquis, and could be seen nightly at the door greeting movie profiles and producers—including, at times, even Howard Hughes.

But, of course, it took a real McCoy maître d', one who did not dabble in silly sidelines like acting, to be the maître d' *par excellence*. Such a one was André Dusel, who was maître d' for many years at the Mocambo and other flossy filmtown establishments. André looked and acted like every yokel's idea of a maître d'. He was even better at the job than Gino Corrado, Leonid Kinskey and George Dolenz.

Still recollected with awe in Hollywood is the time, during the World War II meat-shortage years, that André became maître d' at an elegant restaurant known as Somerset House. One night Philip J. Raffin, a meat packer and the owner of Somerset House, came in to his own restaurant and ordered a filet. As André later related: "I explained we were all out of steaks and finally it got to the point where I asked him, in effect, 'Don't you know there's a war on?' He slugged me." André complained to the cops and Raffin was booked on assault and battery. A local newspaper ran the story as "Restaurant owner has to beat up his own manager to get a steak." In due course André left Somerset House and went on elsewhere, and not long afterward Somerset House went out of existence.

Sometimes the ham of Hollywood literally extends to the Hollywood ham. Louis B. Mayer had a special—and excellent—chicken soup that was served at M-G-M named after him. One of the most delectable dishes at the late Lucey's restaurant, a movietown hangout, was Chicken Hash Rachmil, named after producer Lewis J. Rachmil. After a while the Chicken Hash Rachmil became more renowned than Rachmil himself. Unfortunately, even the Chicken Hash finally faded away when Lucey's went out of business.

At the Paramount studio, one of the commissary specialties was boss Y. Frank Freeman's bread, little squares of corn bread that were prominently featured at all the lunch tables. During the course of a chat with Pauline Kessinger, who had been head of the Paramount restaurant for more than twenty years, I found out that profiles like to have dishes named after them. If you do not have a dish named after you in Hollywood, it appeared, you might as well put your head in the oven. Kessinger claimed that William Holden was the sole exception to the rule. She held that this was because Holden was "an unassuming sort of guy. He's rather shy. He has never allowed us to name a dish after him. No one at this studio ever turned down a dish to be named after them before. The various stars even ask us to name dishes after them."

According to Kessinger, a brisk, efficient woman, this trend toward platters named after profiles at Paramount started some years ago with "Turkey and Eggs à la Crosby," one of Bing Crosby's favorite dishes, which was still on the menu at the time at $1.50 (served with toast). Kessinger said that this dish was "Crosby's idea."

On the Paramount menu then were such delicacies as the Bob Hope cocktail (tomato juice and yogurt with a dash of Lea and Perrins, price twenty-five cents); English kippers and eggs à la Danny Kaye, $1.25; Strawberries Heston (named after Charlton Heston), consisting of fresh strawberries with sour cream, honey and cinnamon; tenderloin steak sandwich à la Dmytryk (director Edward Dmytryk), $1.50; Spanish omelette à la Alan Ladd, $1.25; Dorothy Lamour salad (fresh pineapple, sliced bananas and strawberries, with cream cheese bar le duc, $1.25). This was about all that was left of Dorothy Lamour at Paramount.

Also on the Paramount menu was something called Cuddlesburger, price $1.00, with the following note: "This is for real." A description of the Cuddlesburger, composed by comic Jerry Lewis, read: "Fashioned from an old Martin and Lewisonian recipe of prize-winning, whitefaced cow cow burgie. We won't steer you wrong. A chip off the old beef. Inspired by Cuddles, the 1,800-pound dramatic star of Paramount's *Pardners*—the one performer who carries more weight around the studio than Dean and Jerry." *Pardners*, of course, was a Dean Martin–Jerry Lewis movie.

Other tidbits from the Paramount menu: "Martin and Lewis Special (stewed toads, broiled birds, with woodchucks on Ry-Krisp, $33.00); Martin and Lewis special high-calorie diet (egg foo fish, almond crisp plateau salmon with egg shell—to be eaten in the isolation booth only—$64.00)."

Talent scout Billy Grady not only had a salad named after him at Chasen's, but had his own private table there. Chasen, a chum of Grady's from Broadway, had a special booth for Grady built near the bar—at Grady's expense. Grady could be found there most every night, but when he was away, the booth was given to other favored customers. Above the table was a framed photograph of Grady and a small plaque reading "You are using this booth through the courtesy of Billy (Square Deal) Grady. P.S. But strictly on your own."

The Billy Grady salad, featured on the Chasen menu, was composed, symbolically for a casting director, of mixed greens and shredded ham.

Among the few points of resemblance between Hollywood and the average American community is that one of the social centers of the movie metropolis is a corner drugstore. It is known as Schwab's, and in it movie small fry and bigwigs who may have brushed them off earlier that day rub shoulders on a fairly democratic basis.

Schwab's had the movie-type drugstore business pretty much to itself for many years until the Beverly Wilshire Hotel drugstore began giving Schwab's a run for its ice-cream sodas and Miltowns. As a result, the competition between the two pill palaces developed into a regular battle of the drugstores, and even *Time* Magazine saw fit to cover the story.

I reported to the editors in New York that "the Beverly Wilshire drugstore is making a play for the movie mob with any number of attractions," among them staying open twenty-four hours a day, selling $500 hairbrushes and $250 shaving brushes, providing, for a time, plug-in telephones at the soda fountain and even having a press agent. The drugstore, designed in colorful modernistic style by an eminent architect, Paul Williams, also put out a monthly magazine, entitled *Chatter*, which chronicled, in Parsons and Hopper fashion, the doings of its customers. Samples: "Never noticed before what beautiful blue eyes Peter Lawford has" . . . "Betty Grable snacking and poring over a racing form" . . . "Overheard George Raft telling friends that the cherry burgundy ice cream is the best in the world" . . . "That fascinatin' Jack Palance stands the place on its ears when he comes in" . . . "Marilyn Monroe in a pastel dress looked like a picture" . . . "And sitting at the next table Sylvia and Bunny Plotkin spending the evening with the Morrie Coopers." (The Plotkins and the Coopers were helpfully identified by the drugstore management as "nobody in particular. Everybody that's a patron of our store has some importance to us.")

Chatter carried New York and overseas social columns, as well as movie reviews, beauty hints and signed columns by the soda jerks, the pharmacists, the cashiers and the kitchen help, all testifying to the glories of serving the drugstore's celebrated clientele. Sample, by Bing Lee, the drugstore's Chinese chef: "I've been a chef for years at top spots. I've cooked for crowned heads and always enjoyed it. But cooking for you here is a special pleasure and a satisfaction such as I've never known before. We have so many regulars who like our atmosphere, service and food. . . . And once in a while when I get a few moments to peek out of my kitchen it's fun to say hello to you."

Since a good many of the profiles were at liberty at the time, they had little to do but hang around Schwab's and the Beverly Wilshire drugstore. Rock Hudson used to get mail and phone calls at the Beverly Wilshire. Hudson even penned a personal tribute to the drugstore for an issue of Chatter. He wrote: "The first time I walked in, I felt at home. Of course, my favorite home-town drugstore in Winnetka, Illinois, is smaller and much less pretentious. But the feeling is the same. After a tough grind at the studios all day I love to drop in here for a soda and yak with my friends. . . . And besides, no one (outside of Winnetka) can make a chocolate soda like George."

Songwriter Jimmy McHugh wrote a jingle dedicated to the Beverly Wilshire drugstore: "My friend, here's a bit of advice, here is a drugstore that's nice, drop in for a snack, ten to one you'll be back, it's tops in my book, ain't that nice?"

Owner Milton Kreis told me that the Beverly Wilshire drugstore "has now become almost like a country club on a special night. The women wear the best outfits here on a Saturday night because they know they will be seen in this drugstore. . . . Almost everyone gets here sooner or later.

"Easterners marvel at a drugstore with two hostesses in attendance all the time. We deliver our sandwiches and prescriptions in a black delivery truck with gold-leaf lettering that looks like it might belong to a jewelry store. We just forget about the expense and give our customers the finest merchandise."

In Kreis's opinion, Hollywood was such a drugstore-dedicated community "because out here night clubs are not the same as in the East. Night clubs do not thrive here. Maybe it's because of the casualness of living or because people retire at an earlier hour and the home becomes the focal point. People's interests are more homey. If I leave for the corner drugstore, there is no concern whether I stay out too late or drink too much. The type of environments that are homey are the type of environments that appeal here. The trend out here is sort of back to the old general-store idea of meeting rather than go to a night club and have to pick up big bills and drink liquor."

Alert to the importance of the press, Kreis was attempting to lure the Hollywood columnists to his premises. Sheilah Graham was a regular customer ("Sheilah Graham quietly dining with friends, never missing a trick," noted Chatter). Kreis was even trying to carry off a columnar coup by getting Sidney Skolsky, who had made his headquarters at Schwab's for years and who was almost synonymous with Schwab's, to shift his base of operations to the Beverly Wilshire drugstore. Itemed Chatter seductively: "Sid Skolsky in again, and what a sweet guy that is." Kreis added: "Skolsky was originally a Schwab man, but he goes where the trend is."

Soon the battle of the Hollywood drugstores flared into the open. Schwab's announced that it had snagged three comely young Italian actresses—Elsa Martinelli, Luisa Cerasoli and Iris Branchi, who were in Hollywood to promote an Italian movie entitled *Three Girls from Rome*—to be guests at Schwab's and be photographed there drinking ice-cream sodas.

The Beverly Wilshire drugstore retaliated with the pronouncement that the Ritz brothers were throwing a party at booth number one Saturday in the form of a midnight snack for a group of friends arriving from New York. Said Kreis: "The Ritzes are meeting their friends at the airport and coming direct to the drugstore with them. They have prevailed upon us to hold the table for them for a midnight snack and shindig. This is the table where the formation of the RKO-Stolkin deal was practically concluded some time ago."

Kreis added: "We know the Schwab boys. They have an interesting and colorful store and a very fine operation. But this store is regarded as a rich man's Schwab's. Our clientele is different from the Schwab's clientele. Their clientele is in the Ford category. Our clientele is in the Cadillac category. Not that any man's dollar isn't worth 100 cents.

"We don't consider Schwab's competitors at all. We're friendly."

Leon Schwab, one of the four Schwab brothers, said of the Beverly Wilshire drugstore: "They're just an imitation. They're getting our overflow. We wish them the best of luck." He pointed out that Schwab's was going as strong as ever, but that it stayed open only until midnight. The Beverly Wilshire drugstore, which was open round the clock, got a large after-midnight trade.

Sidney Skolsky, the Boswell of Schwab's, was called in as spokesman for the four Schwab brothers. Skolsky practically grew up at Schwab's, got his mail and telephone calls there, and had a drawer, labeled Sidney Skolsky, in the back of the store where the prescriptions were made up. As a matter of fact, it had been asserted that Skolsky's fingernail parings wound up in some of the Schwab prescriptions.

"Offhand," said Skolsky after some rumination, "the big difference between the two drugstores is that Schwab's, like Topsy, just grew. The Beverly Wilshire is a typically Hollywood operation in the fact that it's got a press agent and goes out for quotes. It's a pumped-up, created job.

"Schwab's is the only drugstore where you can pick up a magazine—the part of the store where the magazine stand is is called the reading room—and read it while eating or drinking a Coke and then put it back on the rack. It is thought odd and queer if a Schwab regular buys a magazine. That's only for strangers. However, if you get a coffee stain on the magazine, you are supposed to buy it.

"Schwab's doesn't seek publicity. It still wants to be a little drugstore. The Schwab brothers now have four drugstores. But they don't publicize the fact that they have four.

"After closing, a lot of shows go on in Schwab's. The other night Keefe Brasselle [who appeared in the title role of Skolsky's movie production, *The Eddie Cantor Story*] dropped in and did the night-club act that he will do at the Flamingo Hotel in Las Vegas in December. Shelley Winters did her whole future Las Vegas night-club act at Schwab's one night, too.

"After the premiere of *The Jolson Story* [also a Skolsky production] we had a big party at Schwab's. Not at Romanoff's, but Schwab's. We gave out lollipops, ice-cream sodas and bubble gum to all the celebrities.

"Schwab's doesn't mind the Coke-stretchers. That's the guy who takes a Coke and stretches it to drinking it for an hour. Schwab's likes to keep the personal touch. In Schwab's, the customers don't come in dressed up fancy but as they are. Not long ago, some people there were looking around for celebrities. There was Shelley Winters sitting at the fountain, her hair in curlers and wearing a bandanna and no make-up. 'There are no celebrities here,' they said, not recognizing her. I've been at Schwab's with Lana Turner when she picked up a fan magazine looking at a picture of herself and looking nothing like it.

"Marilyn Monroe was coming in all the time, reading fan magazines, two and one half to three years ago, and she'd say to me, 'Do you ever think I'll get my picture in one of these magazines?'

"I started coming to Schwab's because I liked the people. It was a good news source. People met me there. Letters came for me there. It grew. Today the New York *Post* [which runs Skolsky's syndicated column] will often phone me at Schwab's.

"I call it the Schwabadero. I named it after the Trocadero [a long-shuttered night club on the Sunset Strip nearby]. I wanted it to be swanky. The Schwabadero has outlasted the Trocadero.

"Years ago, when Dick Powell was married to Joan Blondell, they lived up in the Canyon near Schwab's, and they asked their son Norman what he wanted for a Christmas present. He said he wanted to sweep the floor and wait behind the counter at Schwab's. They let him do it for Christmas.

"I'm still faithful to Schwab's. I go to the Beverly Wilshire drugstore only occasionally after Schwab's closes and I'm in the Beverly Hills district and need a ride home.

"Whenever I walk into the Beverly Wilshire drugstore, everybody says to me, 'What are you doing, cheating?'"

These pharmaceutical findings were weighed and compounded by *Time*'s editors and came out in typical *Time* style—i.e., improperly blended. However, the Schwab brothers were pleased with the resultant journalistic prescription and sent me a bottle of whiskey in gratitude. But Milton Kreis was rather put out about the story, which he thought had done the Beverly Wilshire drugstore wrong and was a bitter pill for him to swallow. For a while he let it be known that I was not exactly welcome at his establishment. This was the first time I had been barred by a drugstore—I had previously been banned by movie studios, theaters, night clubs and restaurants—and I was rather proud of it. But then, as time healed the wounds inflicted by *Time*, I was again welcomed back at the Beverly Wilshire drugstore and was free once more to mingle with Peter Lawford, Betty Grable, George Raft and Sylvia and Bunny Plotkin and the Morrie Coopers.

Recently there was even a rumor that the Schwab brothers were opening drugstores in London, Paris and Rome, "evidence that the motion-picture business has become decentralized," as one Hollywood columnist noted. However, Skolsky, as spokesman for Schwab's, denied it. Schwab's, at least, is still faithful to Hollywood.

There was still a third Hollywood drugstore, Turner's, on the Sunset Strip, that went Schwab's and the Beverly Wilshire drugstores one better in at least one respect. Turner's would deliver money, as well as pills and potions, by messenger. At one time I resided in a flossy Sunset Strip apartment house where most of the tenants had charge accounts at the nearby Turner's. It was possible to phone Turner's, order beer or booze, aspirin or toothpaste and also ask for fifty or one hundred dollars in cash to be sent up via the delivery boy. The money, of course, was charged to the customer's account. But it was nice having money delivered by messenger when you wanted it, merely by picking up the telephone.

The Sunset Strip always had more than its share of characters. For a time some years back there was a market near Schwab's drugstore, on the Strip, that was unique among markets. To the casual eye it appeared to be a regulation market. But, on closer inspection, it turned out to have a rather meager stock of supplies. The help, furthermore, did not seem overly interested in selling anything and spent most of the time chinning with some of the film folk who hung out there regularly.

After a while the market was exposed for what it really was—a front for narcotics. But by that time the proprietor had amassed a small fortune and retired. Today part of the expanded Schwab's is on the premises.

And, speaking of narcotics, there was one well-known movie profile who was, for a time, involved in a good deal of publicity about his addiction to marijuana. Since he did not dare keep any dope on his person, on his home premises or in his automobile, he and a friend evolved a most original and daring plan. Believe it or not, the duo stashed reefers in palm trees along Sunset Boulevard. Whenever they wanted a smoke, they would cruise around until they made sure they were not being followed, stop and discreetly pluck a "weed" from a tree.

Premieres and motion-picture festivities were always good for Hollywood high jinks. I once reported on a movie premiere from the lobby of a theater without ever seeing the movie inside (it worked out just fine that way). I documented the premiere of a television show while flying in an airplane over Los Angeles (that was the high spot of the program). I even mingled with the autograph hounds outside the Mocambo night club one night to see how the glamour boys and girls looked from this vantage point (they did not look any better than from any other vantage point).

When it comes to Hollywood hoopla, the annual Academy Awards —or Oscars—are the most publicized of moviedom's extracurricular events. However, the Academy Awards are no more genuine than the gold-plated Oscars themselves. They are part promotion, part politics and part theatrics. Quantitatively, the Academy Awards are suspect, since they are computed by the vote of only 2,000-odd members of the Academy of Motion Picture Arts and Sciences, who constitute only a fraction of the more than 20,000 salaried employees in the motion-picture industry.

Qualitatively, the Academy Awards are even more spurious, since they usually reflect not the best picture but the best publicized picture, and studio lobbying and ballyhoo rather than sober, considered balloting. A major studio, by controlling large blocks of votes, can often steamroller a picture into the winning spot. In that sense, the Oscars, although they are not actually rigged, can be, in effect, rigged promotionally. Furthermore, as has been pointed out, Academy members will often automatically vote for the best-known picture that has registered on their minds. For example, in 1960 Ben-Hur won a record-breaking twelve Oscars in a variety of categories, undoubtedly because it was the most heavily publicized picture of the year and carried over as a winner into the various prize-winning divisions.

The Academy Awards have sometimes been described as Hollywood's "moment of truth." They have also been called Hollywood's "ignoble" prize. The Oscars have been indicted by critics as "a publicity gimmick designed to sell movies" and as being "a little too much of a matter of the motion-picture industry applauding itself in public, a sort of admiration of the film industry's own navel." The Academy Awards are usually a cloying spectacle of Hollywood patting itself on the head. The film folk whip themselves up into a lather over the awards, with the result, as Bob Hope put it, that some of the best acting performances of the year go on right in the audience during the event.

The Oscars are handed out by the self-styled, so-called Academy of Motion Picture Arts and Sciences, which has little science and less art. The Academy was founded in 1927 by Louis B. Mayer, Irving Thalberg, Douglas Fairbanks and a group of other movie people for the avowed purpose of "encouraging the arts and sciences of the profession" through "award of merit for distinctive achievement." The Academy is actually a private organization that has been described as a "genteel company union." It is maintained by a levy of one fourth of one per cent on the gross income of each of the major studios, which comes to about $100,000 per company annually. All of the studios, except Universal-International (which is largely devoted to television), belong to the Academy. The rest of the Academy's financing comes from the sponsorship of the annual Oscar telecast. Academy members are chosen from among those who have "attained some form of status in the motion-picture industry," according to an Academy spokesman. An Academy applicant must be "sponsored" by two members of the movie branch to which he belongs, then okayed by that branch and finally by the Academy board of governors. Although the Academy has a fancy-sounding front, it is nothing more than an aggregation of supernumeraries, and it functions, via its Oscars, as a gilt-edged publicity mouthpiece for the movie business.

The Academy and the Academy Awards have some shameful blots on them. Neither Garbo nor Charlie Chaplin, for instance, has ever received a regular, full-fledged Oscar. They have, it is true, been doled out minor "honorary" Oscars—the same Oscars that have also been given to such great Hollywood talents as Louis B. Mayer, Harry Warner, Joseph Schenck, and even the late B. B. Kahane, vice-president of Columbia Pictures and president of the Academy.

At the 1960 Academy Awards, the Oscars reached a new low when

Shelley Winters, in accepting an Academy Award for her supporting performance in *The Diary of Anne Frank*, was good enough to bestow her gratitude on the late Anne Frank and, in the selfsame breath, on her agent from the Music Corporation of America. As an indication of how preposterous the Oscars can get, *The Diary of Anne Frank* was awarded an Academy Award for set decoration and was up for an Academy Award in the costume design category(!).

If the Oscars are rather unrewarding artistically, they are even more cut-and-dried journalistically, particularly in recent years when the Academy Awards have been staged at the Pantages Theater for the split-second-timed television cameras. The Oscars are held on Mondays, a slow theater night, so as not to hurt movie box office too much. The last Academy Award dinner was at the Coconut Grove in 1943 and it is still remembered as the event where Greer Garson, who was chosen the best actress of the year for *Mrs. Miniver*, thanked practically everyone but her manicurist in a marathon acceptance speech. For television purposes, acceptance speeches have been held down to the bare minimum. The winners rattle off phrases like "great honor," "thrilling experience," "I am gratified," or they just stand there and stammer and swallow. Once in a great while someone steps out of line, like composer Dimitri Tiomkin, who, in accepting an Oscar for a movie score he did, thanked Beethoven, Bach and Brahms. The Oscars have become so dull and suspenseless that most of the motion-picture people prefer to sit at home on Academy Award night and watch the Oscar festivities on their television screens without having to brave the crowds and the traffic congestion. About the only movie personalities who show up at the event are those who are in the running for an Oscar or who are participating in the television show.

In 1951 I decided to try a new tack in reporting the Academy Awards for the Los Angeles *Daily News*. What with 437 reporters and photographers documenting this particular event—a crew large enough to cover the Normandy invasion—I figured it was futile to try to compete with this exhaustive (and exhausting) inside coverage, and so I arranged to write about the proceedings from the bleachers where the fans sat outside the Pantages Theater.

I got to the bleacher stands a good several hours before Academy Award time and, with the help of a couple of cops, managed to snag a seat for myself. I found that, although the fans may not have been nourished much artistically that night, they were doing all right in keeping the inner man fed with staples like peanut-butter sandwiches and jelly apples. As the screen celebrities drew up in front of the

Pantages in their bedizened conveyances, the bleacher spectators invariably oohed and ahed at their favorite profiles and greeted the tycoons and the lesser stars with apathy. The most telling remark of the evening was when, in the crush of film folk, a big black car disgorged two elegantly attired young ladies. "Who are they?" said one bleacher fan. "Awww—just people!" replied another disappointedly.

I never got to see the Academy Awards that night, either on the Pantages stage or on television, but it was one of the most satisfactory Oscar events I ever covered. And the story made colorful, banner-lined copy for the *Daily News*.

If the Oscars are Hollywood's biggest award, they are far from the only one. There are dozens and dozens of awards. Almost all the different guilds hand out awards. Awards are named after Irving Thalberg, Cecil B. DeMille and Jesse Lasky. Even the movie animals get awards, known as PATSYS (Picture Animal Top Star of the Year). There had originally been a plan to name these the Film Annual Royal Trophy, but it was quickly scotched. The PATSY awards today follow the Oscar so as not to compete with the two-legged actors. If you don't get some kind of award in Hollywood, you are a bum. I once gave myself an award. It was while I was engaged in journalistic activity in Hollywood. I got an old-fashioned china flush handle, with the word PRESS on it, off a toilet and had it elegantly mounted on a trophy base inscribed to myself as a distinguished member of the Hollywood press. And so even I had an award.

Ben Crisler, years ago, in compiling some Hollywood-type definitions in the New York *Times*, under the title "Out of a Blue Funk & Webster's," had this one for "Plaque": "An award given annually by the New York Film Critics for the best picture of the year; hence, an epidemic, a scourge, as 'the seven plaques of Egypt.'"

Perhaps the most noteworthy development in the entire history of Hollywood awards occurred on January 24, 1960, when some 700 "industry notables" foregathered at the Beverly Hilton Hotel to attend a Screen Producers Guild annual Milestone Awards dinner for Jack L. Warner. Warner was getting the wreath of honor for his "historic contribution to the American motion picture" (if all the people who supposedly made "historic" contributions to the American film, judging from Hollywood awards, were rounded up, they would overflow the Hollywood Bowl). Things were going along at the customary dull clip when Jack Benny got up to introduce Eva Marie Saint, an actress who had long been typed as a sweet, colorless sort on the screen. She was to bestow the Jesse L. Lasky Intercollegiate film award on a student from Yale University. Benny delivered a long, flowery, tongue-in-cheek introduction. When Saint finally got up to the microphone, she unburdened herself of the following words: "All I can say after that is 'Oh, shit!' " Hollywood was rocked to its very honorary foundations.

There was no end of comment, both in print and otherwise. As someone observed: "It just came out of her, that's all." Saint herself explained that she just got "carried away." Commented Mike Connolly: "Eva Marie Saint isn't quite as saintly after that shame-shame-double-shame four-letter word she bombshelled from the dais at the Screen Producers Guild banquet. Even so, Eva is in great demand for picture parts—particularly since the incident fits in perfectly with her campaign to quit playing the goody-goody roles. Director Peter Glenville, for one, is goading her to play Desdemona in his swingin' modern version of Shakespeare's *Othello*. Proving, as Shakespeare himself once said, 'Sweet are the uses of adversity.' "

Naturally, Louella Parsons sounded off too in an "Open Letter" to Eva Marie Saint:

If you think I'm on a soap box to lecture you about that headlined "word" you used at the Producer's Dinner, you are mistaken. I've known you ever since you came to Hollywood and I know you to be a fine mother, wife and actress—and a very "nice" person as well, as much as you hate being called "nice."

But, my dear, never be afraid to say "I'm sorry."

So far, you've said everything else.

When I talked with you over the phone the following morning, you said: "You've known me well enough to know I don't ordinarily use such language.

"I had expected Jack Benny to say just a few words introducing me —instead he made such a flowery speech, including how George Jessel would have said it, that I didn't think I could reply with a mere 'thank you.'

"It was a closed party—that is, no TV or radio—and I thought I was among friends. I guess I wanted to 'top' Mr. Benny, a dramatic impulse of an actress—and, well, it just popped out!

"But with all the important things happening all over the world— they've sure made a big fuss about me on the front pages."

And you are right, there was a lot of comment—some being indulgent and excusing you, others having the proverbial "fit" gasping, "Eva Marie Saint, of all people!" Well, so much for the unfortunate slip itself—and the ensuing reaction.

But afterward, there were some stories printed that you woke up in the middle of the night laughing about it, and there were other stories insinuating that you didn't really care about saying that word.
I don't believe it. But I do think that if you ever get in a spot like this again (heaven forbid) it would be so easy—and so like the real Eva Marie Saint—to say that one little phrase, "I'm sorry."

All in all, it was truly a Milestone event.

Probably the most distinctive premiere I ever witnessed was one that took place on a streetcar. It was the idea of Leonard Levinson, impresario of a minor animated-cartoon company known as Impossible Pictures (slogan: "If it's a good picture, it's Impossible"). Economy-minded Levinson unveiled four of his "Jerky Journeys" movie travelogues aboard a Los Angeles streetcar, complete with popcorn, motion-picture projectionists, arc lights and movie celebrities.

"Jerky Journeys," subtitled "Little Known Visits to Lesser Known Countries by Completely Unknown People," were made by Levinson with a maximum of ingenuity and a minimum of cash. The premiere was staged in similar style. A number of Hollywood press and personalities assembled at the Brown Derby for refreshments, which were limited to short-order desserts and coffee, in keeping with Levinson's short-subject type of entertainment.

From the Derby the group was transported by bus to Melrose Avenue, near the RKO and Paramount studios, where a spanking-new streetcar of the Los Angeles transit lines was about to set out on its journey. The streetcar bore the name Impossible lettered on its side. Inside were placards proclaiming: "This is the first time a movie has ever been shown in a streetcar."

The guests, clutching bags of popcorn, boarded the vehicle in the glare of arc lights while a television camera was trained on them and several hundred local citizens, normally inured to the doings of the film folk, looked on in amazement.

"This premiere," said Levinson, "harks back to the turn of the century when one of the first popular types of screen showings was 'Hale's Tours' in a theater designed like a railroad car, with the screen where the observation platform was. Tonight's showing will set back the art of movie exhibition to where it began. Now we can get a fresh start, and this time we should do better."

For the Levinson premiere, a movie screen had been set up at the front end of the streetcar, while two operators supervised the projection of the animated cartoons with 16 mm. equipment connected to the vehicle's generator. The lights in the trolley darkened, a bell clanged, and, escorted by police cars fore and aft, the omnibus set out on its predetermined course through downtown Los Angeles while the films were unreeled.

There were, in order of progression, *Beyond Civilization to Texas*, narrated by Senator Claghorn; *Romantic Rumbolia*, an imaginary travelogue through a non-existing South American country; *Bungle in the Jungle*, starring an explorer-hero named Dr. Livingstone I. Presume; and *The Three Minnies: Sota, Tonka and Ha-Ha*, a take-off on "Hiawatha."

There was a good deal of consternation on the part of pedestrians, automobile drivers and apartment-house dwellers as the blacked-out trolley car rambled along with the films showing on the screen in color and the sound track amplified. Whenever the streetcar stopped for a traffic light, passers-by crowded about to see what this latest development in Hollywoodiana was. The showing went off without a hitch, however, and, approximately an hour later, the streetcar named Impossible was back where it had started on its improbable odyssey.

It is too bad that Levinson, a bulky, bespectacled former gag writer, is no longer operating Impossible Pictures because it was one of the most original movie developments since the invention of the sprocket hole. Although he produced a number of better-than-average animated cartoons, Levinson said that he gave his pictures the imprimatur of Impossible in order to beat the critics to the punch. The company was housed in a tiny office. Levinson's part-time secretary answered incoming calls with the singsong phrase "This is Impossible." Many local citizens phoned in just to hear her say that.

Levinson's coat of arms was a cuckoo rampant on a sun dial, defying the world. He said that he founded Impossible Pictures after a number of movie executives turned down his animated-cartoon ideas with the criticism that they would not work out—in short, were impossible. To pare his budgets, Levinson called on some clever ideas. In *Bungle in the Jungle*, an African travelogue, he cut his costs by not using animation at all. He explained this to the audience on the grounds that the cameraman and his equipment were swallowed by a lion and Levinson therefore had to carry on with a still camera.

Another economy measure was verbal wit, or what Levinson called "picture puns." The explorer-hero of *Bungle in the Jungle*, Dr. Livingstone I. Presume, was described as having "a raft of friends." The intrepid doctor was shown floating downstream on a raft of humans. In *Romantic Rumbolia*, one scene depicted the South American natives taking their daily siesta. "A fiesta has sapped their strength," the commentator observed, "and siesta is putting the strength back into the saps."

When Levinson was not producing animated cartoons, he liked to rib Hollywood. He sent out publicity stories satirizing the usual motion-picture press-agent handout. One such story read: "Leonard L. Levinson, president of Impossible Pictures, Inc., is making preparations *not* to go to Dallas for the premiere of his new cartoon, *Beyond Civilization to Texas.*"

Another publicity release was to this effect: "Following completion of the cartoon *Bungle in the Jungle*, Impossible Pictures, Inc., had its office redecorated . . . new lining was put in the producer's hat."

To qualify one of his cartoons for an Academy Award nomination, Levinson booked it into a Hollywood theater. He issued press passes good for eight minutes, the running time of the opus. "Can you imagine," Levinson complained, "people have to sit through a full-length picture in order to see my cartoon."

When one Hollywood journalist heard of Impossible Pictures he commented, "Sounds like a merger of the whole damned business." And the late Fred Allen wrote Levinson: "I'm glad you are president of Impossible Pictures. So many pictures I have seen recently have been impossible, you must be producing all of the product coming from Hollywood at this time."

In his spare time Levinson authored a book about food, *The Brown Derby Cook Book.* He inscribed a copy to me: "In a town where dog eats dog—this shows you how."

Another novel movie company was Mono-Grant, consisting of still photographers Allan Grant and his brother, writer Ralph Goodman—two guys with a camera, a typewriter, a few thousand feet of film and no conscience. Their first production was *Six O'Clock Low*, a satire on the aviation movie *Twelve O'Clock High. Six O'Clock Low* was a compendium of just about every flight-film cliché on record. The movie's production notes read as follows:

The Story—A veteran of sixty missions over Schweinhunt, General Max Effort (photographer John Florea), vacationing in England, revisits the graveyard of his old command only to find it alive with memories of Darryl Zanuck and Twelve O'Clock High. Six O'Clock Low is an original idea by Ralph Goodman . . . who got the original idea while watching Twelve O'Clock High.

The Cast—Mono-Grant was fortunate in acquiring the services of

Mr. John Florea (who just happened to be between pictures) to play the difficult lead. In addition to Mr. Florea, the cast includes such forgettable names as Bernard Murphy, Schuyler Crail, Richard Carter, Frank Friedrichsen and John Zimmerman. Also assisting were William Holden and Buster Keaton, signed immediately by Mono-Grant after seeing their bits in the recent Paramount musical, Sunset Boulevard. It has long been the policy of Mono-Grant studios to help young hopefuls along the road to success.

Music—The outstanding musical score was made possible by the combined efforts of Max Steiner, Miklos Rozsa, Daniele Amfitheatrof and a long-playing needle.

The Budget—Six O'Clock Low has brought in exactly $999,902.41 under its original budget of $1,000,000. As a matter of fact, the entire cost of this mammoth production was exactly $97.59 (tax included).

Special Effects—To help keep costs down, many special effects were used. The English countryside was cleverly duplicated by photographing Pasadena through a monocle. In those scenes involving Nazi aircraft, a German lens was used.

Running time: 25 minutes. Running time if film breaks: 35 minutes.

In Hollywood, it is customary for movies to be sneak-previewed in the hope that advance audience reaction will give the producers some idea of whether the picture is good or bad. This procedure hardly ever works because the producers, who do not really want an honest reaction at all, hold almost all previews—for self-protection—in communities and theaters where the moviegoers are preview-conditioned through long exposure to advance screen showings. In addition, the audience reactions, as expressed on the preview cards, are mostly a mess of vague, meaningless verbiage. After a "sneak preview" of Six O'Clock Low in Allan Grant's living room, these perky preview cards were distributed to the select onlookers:

How would you classify this picture?
    Excellent.... Wonderful.... Terrific....
Would you recommend it to your friends? Good God, yes!....
Who are your friends?
    Blonde.... (Phone).... Brunette.... (Phone)....
Remarks..
Your age group: 12–18.... 18–35.... Serutan....
Male.... Female.... Really?....

When things got a little dull in Hollywood, the Holmby Hills Rat Pack could be counted upon to provide some local color. Since Bogart's death, Frank Sinatra has, more or less, taken over.

The Rat Pack is noted for its playfulness. On one occasion Bogart tried to push Irving Lazar, a truncated Hollywood agent, into a swimming pool fully dressed (no Hollywood pool is complete without a fully clothed occupant). Lazar, as the Hollywood press gleefully reported, then threw Bogart's watch into a martini, flung it into a fire to dry it and finally into the pool to cool it off. Several days later, Bogart received a beautifully wrapped package from Lazar at Romanoff's and opened it to find a new watch which cost one dollar.

Bogart once explained to me the noble aims of the Holmby Hills Rat Pack. "Frank Sinatra," he said, "is the president of the rats. Judy Garland is vice-president. Miss [Lauren] Bacall is the den mother. I am the rat in charge of public relations. Irving Lazar is the treasurer. But we have no money. That's probably the reason why he's treasurer.

"Sinatra had dinner with a leading colyumist the other night and he might have to be dropped out of the rat pack as a result. We don't approve of colyumists. I'm not naming the colyumist because I'm a rat.

"Claudette Colbert's name was brought up and suggested for membership in the rats. Miss Bacall said, 'She's a very nice person, but she's not a rat.'

"What is a rat? We have no constitution, charter or by-laws yet, but we know a rat when we see one. There are very few rats in this town. David Niven is a rat. Jimmy Van Heusen is a rat. Mike Romanoff is a rat. He's a Russian rat, a foreign rat.

"Rats are extremely well behaved. We elected Noel Coward an honorary rat. He's our representative in Jamaica.

"You might say that rats are for staying up late and drinking lots of booze. We're against squares and being bored and for lots of fun and being real rats, which very few people are, but if you're a real rat, boy!"

Bogart informed me that a coat of arms had been drawn up for the rat pack. "There's a lamp representing late nights and a bottle and glass representing convivial imbibing. In one corner there's a dagger in a hand and in another corner a woman's breast floating on a cloud. There's a slogan underneath: 'Never rat on a rat.' We're also going to make up a pin showing an angry rat with a human arm in its mouth."

Bogart concluded with "To be a rat, you've got to have talent. Don't you think that Mike Romanoff has talent? And don't you think Judy Garland and David Niven and Jimmy Van Heusen have talent? And, old boy, don't you think Miss Bacall and I have talent? We are all very talented.

"One of our first principles is that we don't care who likes us as long as we like each other. We like each other very much."

Recently the Rat Pack, or the "clan," as it is also known, was repudiated by none other than its spiritual leader, Frank Sinatra. In a rather stuffy statement issued by his public-relations counselors he claimed that the clan didn't really exist, that it was just "a figment of someone's imagination" and that he and his friends, including Peter Lawford, Dean Martin and Sammy Davis, Jr., did "not gather together in childish fraternities." Bogart must have been revolving underground.

Though never a member of the Holmby Hills Rat Pack, Darryl Zanuck contributed more than his share of after-hours excitement to Hollywood at Ciro's night club on the night of January 18, 1954. The mustached, buck-toothed Zanuck, then vice-president in charge of production of the powerful Twentieth Century-Fox studio, threw a party that evening at Ciro's for his daughter Susan and studio starlet Terry Moore. Ciro's described the event as "the first of a series of parties for international personalities." The festivities started off, in the words of one celebrant, "simply enough, with a small group of us dining on octopus and sake."

There was also some entertainment. One of the acts was the Goofers, trapeze artists. After they finished their performance, Zanuck decided to get into the show himself. Stripped to the waist, he tried to do a one-arm pull-up on the trapeze. He tried three times, but couldn't make it. Zanuck's act was later labeled "The Darryl Old Man on the Flying Trapeze."

Actually there was nothing particularly playful or festive about the incident. Zanuck, who had been partying for several hours, was in an odd, exuberant mood. Among the edgy spectators to this extraordinary display were Zanuck's wife, Virginia, who tried desperately to stop him, and Bella Darvi, originally Bella Wegier from Sosnoviec, Poland, a green-eyed French "actress" whom Zanuck had put under contract at Fox. Zanuck, Mrs. Zanuck and Bella Darvi were an almost inseparable threesome. Darvi, whose name was a combination of Darryl and Virginia, lived with the Zanucks for a long time, accompanied them to many social functions and traveled abroad with them.

As the illustrious Zanuck suddenly leaped to the trapeze and chinned himself with gusto, quite oblivious to the goggle-eyed spectators, a hush fell over the crowded night club. There were a few reporters and photographers on hand. Operating on the unwritten rule of Hollywood, almost all the photographers desisted from shooting pictures. Several intrepid lensmen, among them one from *Holiday* and one from *Life*, snapped away. They were almost mobbed by frantic Zanuckites, bent on protecting their boss, who tried to stop them. *Life's* Loomis Dean dashed out of Ciro's, locked his camera in the trunk compartment of his car and sped away.

The next day the Zanuck trapeze act was the talk of the town. It was as if the august head of General Motors or U. S. Steel had put on an acrobatic display publicly. The story, unavoidably, broke in all the newspapers. But Fox publicity chief Harry Brand did his best to kill it off and tone it down wherever he could, including at *Time* and *Life*, where he was largely successful because of Zanuck's personal friendship with Henry Luce. Virginia Zanuck sent thank-you notes to the photographers at Ciro's who had kept their cameras down when Zanuck was trying to get his chin up on the trapeze.

There were, naturally, all sorts of theories and explanations for Zanuck's behavior proffered after the event. One observer commented, "Zanuck has created so many stars and now he wants to get into the act himself. It's fascinating for a psychiatrist." A movie director opined, "Zanuck was suffering from battle fatigue. He has been working like a madman in recent months putting across CinemaScope with the exhibitors and the public."

Zanuck told one gossip columnist, "In one way or another I've been on a trapeze or the equivalent all my life and I intend to stay on one both mentally and physically as long as I live, although next time it won't be at Ciro's."

Naturally, the Hollywood wits rose to the occasion. One columnist chronicled: "DFZ, since Monday night, was chinning with Spyros Skouras about future product and has been burning the midnight oil at 20th, not in the gym, but in the cutting room." Another columnist noted: "We hear Sol Lesser has contacted Zanuck about starring in his next Tarzan picture. . . . Well, whatever they say, they've gotta admit Zanuck's a trailblazer: the same guy who came out with CinemaScope and brought millions of payees back to the boxoffice came out swinging Monday night and brought the producers back into the limelight."

There was some speculation that, what with Zanuck stealing the show from the personalities who worked for him, other movie executives might follow suit. It was suggested that Harry Cohn, who once played a piano in silent-movie houses, might go in for thumping the keyboard again; that Samuel Goldwyn could go on television with his Goldwynisms; and that the elusive and mysterious Howard Hughes could always get a job being a rubber-sneakered menace in horror movies.

Don Hartman, late production chief at Paramount, observed, "It seems to be the fashion for studio executives to entertain audiences, and I hope we'll have as good a crowd when I swim to Catalina and back next Tuesday morning."

One columnist pontificated, "This story could only be topped if Louis B. Mayer climbed into the bird cage at the Mocambo. The act established a very important point. Before this, he [Zanuck] has always been a vague power far removed from the public. Now, possibly for the first time, it has been proven that he is a human being as well. He swung from the trapeze. And I have a brand-new, profound respect for him. Somewhere deep in every man's heart is a smoldering desire to swing from a trapeze and say the hell with everything."

James Byron, then press agent for Ciro's, took out an ad in the Hollywood trade papers reading "Thank you, Darryl Zanuck. James Byron, promotion, BR2–1684 or CR4–6211."

And the final comment was made by one columnist who wrote, "Things-are-looking-up department: For a long time the movie industry was hanging by a thread. Now it's hanging by a trapeze."

The advent of Nikita Khrushchev in Hollywood on September 19, 1959, jolted the community out of its social doldrums. The Soviet premier, temporarily, eclipsed Jerry Wald and Tuesday Weld and, even without a Hollywood press agent, managed to crack all the movie-town columns.

The Khrushchev visit, or "Khrushchev caper" as it was called in Hollywood, lost most of its more complex manifestations in the cinema city and became just another show-business act. *Daily Variety* covered it in a "review" as if it were another Hollywood production, rating the standing-room-only movie luncheon for Khrushchev at Twentieth Century-Fox as "the greatest spectacle ever staged in a motion picture studio. . . . The guest star was, of course, Russia's aging but vigorous and multi-faceted character actor, Nikita Khrushchev." *Daily Variety* complimented Khrushchev—"the Communist world's top banana in Hollywoodland"—as being "a consummate actor" in this "four-hour comedy-drama." There was general agreement on Khrushchev's qualities as a performer. Eric Johnston, head of the Motion Picture Association of America, solemnly avowed that Khrushchev was "a great actor." Army Archerd of *Daily Variety* observed that "Scribes who covered the tour said his Hollywood performance was the best they'd seen." Mike Connolly noted that "no one has staged a performance like his around here since Buck Jones's hoss curled his lips and stamped his hoofs when Buck got the gal.... We're convinced K has studied the Method. Maybe our politicos should too."

At the luncheon, which was emceed by Frank Sinatra, Khrushchev got into what was described as "a sparring session" with Spyros Skouras (or "Comrade Greek"), president of Twentieth Century-Fox, and "clobbered" him. Skouras, one of the original movie mastodons, emerged as a lamb compared to Khrushchev and gave a good many film folk food for thought as to whether the old movie moguls were really as tough as they were cracked up to be. One local citizen commented that "twentieth century fox visits Twentieth Century-Fox."

At one point during Khrushchev's speech, when Skouras wanted to get up and reply, or to "upstage him," as one trade paper phrased it, shouts of "No, No" came from the assembled guests, forcing Skouras to sit down and prompting the *Hollywood Reporter* to exclaim: "It probably was the first time in his life Skouras ever was told on the 20th lot to shut up and sit down."

After the luncheon, Khrushchev watched a dance number, with Shirley MacLaine, being shot for the movie *Can-Can* on one of the Fox sound stages. Later he termed both the movie and the Fox luncheon as "very tasteless." The *Hollywood Reporter*, thoroughly aroused, blasted away at this "payoff line" with "... by any yardstick of measurement he came closer to biting the hand that fed him than had any tourist ever shown the courtesy of a tour of a film studio." The *Reporter* headlined its story "Mr. K's 'Tasteless' Crack at 20th Could Apply to His Own Act."

The terpsichorean issue seemed to be a touchy one all around. Archerd itemed that "the crowd bristled audibly when Khrushchev claimed his country's ballet topped anything we have." Connolly came through with "Shirley MacLaine, leading the *Can-Can* corps de ballet, gave the lie right back to K's Big Lie that Russian ballerinas are The Best."

In a general vein of Hollywood-social-notes-from-all-over, it was chronicled that "the new focus on Hollywood was the most intense in its history" with "Western Union clocking out 400,000 words" in one day from the 573 newsmen of all categories and with the wire services "operating photo transmission units from the studio still lab." The 300 or so Hollywood luminaries on hand were reportedly themselves "star-struck" trying to get to see the guest of honor. According to Archerd, "the Hollywood crowd got its biggest laugh outta the fact Marilyn Monroe and Liz Taylor were the first to arrive, the first time in years either has been on time." Archerd also observed that "Liz

Taylor (with Eddie Fisher) was seated to the left of the Chairman's table, Debbie Reynolds to the right—but the girls could see each other across the crowded room." Billy Wilder was quoted as saying that "in order to have Marilyn Monroe show up on time at 20th for *Let's Make Love*, Khrushchev should direct the pic."

More comments: From Don Quinn: "Pfui on Khrui—doesn't he know Disney's been conducting trips to the moon daily at Disneyland for years?" From Maurice Chevalier (referring to Khrushchev's long speech): "He didn't know when to get off. Well, that's show business." From Connolly: "Go home, Gospodin—tell 'em how you invented Marilyn Monroe." From George Stevens (getting in a plug for his next picture, *The Greatest Story Ever Told*): "After atheist Khrushchev's performance, I hope there still is religion around in two years—or this will be just a film biography." From Archerd: "After luncheon, when Khrushchev met Kim Novak, he was heard to say, 'I wish I had a daughter like you.' Mr. K can't be all bad!"

Sidney Skolsky remarked that in the old days "it was unthinkable for a notable to enter and leave Hollywood without attending a dinner party at Pickfair. Only yesterday Nikita Khrushchev visited Hollywood and was honored with a chicken and green peas luncheon at the Twentieth Century-Fox commissary. Hollywood's greatest hostess, Mary Pickford, wasn't even on the guest list."

It was all a sort of Hollywood's-eye-view of Khrushchev in America. *Daily Variety* concluded sadly: "One thing is certain, Hollywood has never been the origin of a production of such spectacular proportions and, chances are, never will get a chance to do a remake."

Almost all Hollywood parties are thrown for promotional and publicity purposes. Rarely is a motion-picture gathering held just for the simple fun of it. There is usually something bought or sold. And rarely do the partygoers care what the purpose of the party is. They are primarily interested in eating, drinking and devoting themselves, to the best of their abilities, to damaging the premises. One experienced Hollywood partygoer liked to hand out the following printed forms to his guests:

Social Form Letter. Sign name on the dotted line................. regrets exceedingly his deplorable conduct while a guest at your party last evening and humbly craves your pardon for the breach of etiquette checked in column at left:

Striking hostess with bottle; spanking hostess or female guests; riding to hounds in drawing room; riding to hounds in ballroom; continuous noisy speech; excessive screaming; dumping drinks in piano; frequent absence from party; protracted absence from party; extreme inebriation; excessive destruction of furniture; complete loss of equilibrium; throwing glass; quarreling with guests; insulting guests; indiscreet petting; nausea.

One of the most fantastic breaches of social etiquette in the checkered history of Hollywood took place at a top-level party thrown at the Warner Brothers studio some years ago. At that event, Errol Flynn, noted for his bawdy ribs, pulled the most conspicuously outrageous practical joke of his career. During the serving of the lavish dinner, Flynn had one of his fun-loving cronies come out in a white jacket, dressed as a waiter, and bearing a platter of cold cuts to the table where the eminent guests of honor were seated. On the beautiful silver tray that Flynn's sidekick was carrying reposed an attractively garnished segment of wurst. Only it was not delicatessen. It was part of the party in question. The festivities almost blew up before they quite got under way. The bogus waiter was ejected from the studio, and Flynn himself did not dare show up for several days.

Hollywood, of course, has to contend with the fact that it has not been around very long and has not had the opportunity to acquire much of a social tradition. This is pointed up in the matchbooks which are distributed at the King's Arms Restaurant in San Fernando Valley near the Warner Brothers studio. Proudly emblazoned on the matchbooks is this legend: "Since 1954."

And still the film folk can be suave on occasion. Producer Arthur Hornblow, Jr., who was more famed for the finesse of his social functions than of his films, once threw a sumptuous dinner party for a gathering of Hollywood notables. The late Herman Mankiewicz, writer and wit, tippled a little too much at the affair, with the result that he became ill in the midst of the repast and committed the unpardonable social error of losing his food at the beautifully set table. A deadly hush descended over the assembled guests. Finally Mankiewicz broke the silence himself. Not too sick to get off a good line, he managed to say to his host, "It's all right, Arthur, the white wine came up with the fish."

Some of the more interesting studio plots were hatched not during the working day but after hours. One neophyte female writer, imported to Hollywood from the East, was bothered by her wolfish producer. This authoress, a robust young lady, could have handled the producer easily enough simply by throwing him out of his office window, but she wanted to make good in Hollywood and was therefore in something of a predicament. The producer was persistent and she did not know what to do. Finally, a girl friend of hers, who had been a press agent in New York and who had come to Hollywood for a visit, came up with a suggestion. She had evolved a plan that not only would help the writer get rid of the producer but would also advance her own aspirations to become a Hollywood agent.

Everything went off according to this ingenious blueprint. The next time the producer made a pass at the authoress, she gave him the come-on and asked him to drop by at her apartment at the end of the day. The producer showed up at her door, panting, and with his jacket already stripped off. The young lady, attired in a seductive dressing gown, had some trouble holding off the amorous moviemaker. In the ensuing tussling she purposely planted a great deal of lipstick on his face and shirt front. Then, as preplanned, the girl press agent walked in just at the strategic moment. The producer was no fool. He had been around Hollywood long enough to know a plant when he saw one and realize when he was outpointed. He sized up the situation immediately and took it all in his Hollywood stride. He got up, adjusted his tie and said casually, "Okay, girls, what's the game? What do you want?" The press agent said that all she wanted was a firm introduction to the production boss at the studio. Sure enough, she got it the next day. It helped her get started on a lucrative career as an agent. And the authoress was never again bothered by the producer.

Another real-life Hollywood tale that beggared fiction had to do with a charming, titian-tressed young lady who was being financially sponsored by three Hollywood producers simultaneously. This was quite a feat in itself, and it was all the more impressive because the three producers worked at the same studio, Twentieth Century-Fox. Since they were all married men, they had fixed nights of the week when they visited their red-haired charge, and so everything went off smoothly for a while without any of the three tycoons knowing anything about each other. But then, as was sooner or later bound to happen, a hitch occurred in these Hollywood proceedings when one producer accidentally got off schedule and ran into one of the other moguls at the young lady's apartment. In short order all three producers were filled in on the full ramifications of the romantic combine. They were most indignant. They got together and held a big war conference. The young lady, realizing that she had flouted a hallowed Hollywood tradition, just packed up and took it on the lam.

She went East, went straight and married a businessman who had several million dollars. In due course the newly married couple arrived in Hollywood and checked in at an expensive bungalow at the Beverly Hills Hotel. Through mutual connections I was asked to call upon the newlyweds to see if there was anything I could do for them. "Yes," the redheaded bride said, "we'd like to take a studio tour." I suggested —what else?—Twentieth Century-Fox. A deluxe, super-duper tour was set up for them and the redhead must have relished every minute of it. And so they left Hollywood happily ever after.

CHAPTER XI

Fade-out

I FIRST CAME TO THE MOVIES youthfully fired by their magic, excitement and glory and the intimations of far-off horizons. The symphonic Odessa steps sequence of *Potemkin*, the final, shattering cavalry charge of *Mother*, the great, gray close-ups of Mae Marsh in the strike-breaking episode of *Intolerance* spoke with a thundering eloquence from the silent screen. The soft-focus lyricism of *Broken Blossoms*, the grave, insidious distortions of the madman's world of *The Cabinet of Dr. Caligari*, the political poetry of *The Crowd* were accomplishments known about, written about, read about. There seemed to be literally nothing that the movies and their talented, pioneer creators—the Eisensteins, the Pudovkins, Griffiths and Vidors —could not achieve.

I read about the movies—and collected a vast library on the subject. I went to see all the old and new movies I could. I tried to meet as many of the moviemakers as possible. I wrote about the movies myself. I guess I was a movie fan, in the better sense of the word.

Later, when I became a movie publicist and then a reporter and critic, some disillusionment crept in. Most of the silent-screen pioneers whose work I admired were gone—or had been cast off by the movie business. The silents had been golden. Now the silver screen had found a tongue, but had lost much of its eloquence. Critic Richard Watts, speaking of the "retrogressive effect of sound," claimed that the talking film would result merely in a hybrid reflection of the stage. He turned out to be right. In place of the talented directors of the silent screen there had risen a generation of highly touted makers of talking pictures, most of whom were little more than hacks and hustlers with a talent for publicity.

When I came to Hollywood the studios and their works were endlessly fascinating to me. The making of movies was an engrossing mechanical process and the prosaic, plaster studios a kind of wonderland. Christopher Isherwood summed it up vividly in his *Prater Violet*, which is probably the best novel ever written about the movies:

> Within the great barnlike sound-stage, with its high bare padded walls, big enough to enclose an airship, there is neither day nor night: only irregular alternations of activity and silence. Beneath a firmament of girders and catwalks, out of which the cowled lamps shine coldly down like planets, stands the inconsequent, half-dismantled architecture of the sets; archways, sections of houses, wood and canvas hills, huge photographic backdrops, the frontages of streets; a kind of Pompeii, but more desolate, more uncanny, because this is, literally, a half-world, a limbo of mirror-images, a town which has lost its third dimension. Only the tangle of heavy power cables is solid, and apt to trip you as you cross the floor. Your footsteps sound unnaturally loud; you find yourself walking on tiptoe.
>
> In one corner, amidst these ruins, there is life. A single set is brilliantly illuminated. From the distance, it looks like a shrine, and the figures standing around it might be worshippers. But it is merely the living room of Toni's home. . . .

All this, of course, had little to do with the finished product and was like watching a show in rehearsal. The lights, the sets, the props, the technical crews and the complex paraphernalia of motion-picture production were usually much more interesting than the film itself. I remember how amazed I was, as a Warner Brothers publicist, that one of the long-time press agents at the studio rarely bothered to leave his office to go out on the lot. The movies and the moviemakers bored him and he found the process of film-making tedious, as it undeniably was. He simply invented stories to write about them, undoubtedly on the theory that fiction was more colorful than fact.

When I tried to talk to gifted moviemakers like Michael Curtiz, I was unable to extract from them much in the way of an enlightening explanation about their material and methods. Sometimes it almost seemed as if I knew more about their work—and was more interested in it—than they themselves were. Curtiz, for instance, was somewhat taken aback as I rattled off sequences that I admired in his past pictures. I came to the unavoidable conclusion that any primer student of the movies knew more about the movies—and the work of these moviemakers—than these highly publicized and supposedly talented picture people did.

In time I learned that knowledge of the movies and enthusiasm about them marked me as a kind of freak in Hollywood. The fact that I collected books about the movies occasioned a good many amusedly raised eyebrows, somewhat as if I had lost my intellectual trousers. To my knowledge, there is not one moviemaker of repute in Hollywood who has a library on the subject. I learned that it was wiser and easier simply not to say much about my interest in the movies.

In lieu of the essential all-important creative scene, the social scene in Hollywood then proved a diverting substitute. A good many of the film folk were colorful characters away from the cameras. They threw unusual parties and engaged in odd after-hours activities. They sometimes said witty and quotable things. From a journalistic standpoint these high jinks were often more rewarding than an investigation of the mostly non-existent art of the movies. It was easier to document John Huston's practical jokes and Billy Wilder's bitter wisecracks than to write about their art—and exactly what art was there really to write about? The crucial thing, of course, was what these people did on, not off, the screen, but there simply was almost nothing on the screen to think about—and write about. There was no content or craftsmanship, no theme or technique. Taking critical issue with this lack of creativity was equivalent to beating an artistic dead horse.

Almost anything was possible in Hollywood. There had been, according to legend, a press agent named Bragg, and there was a producer named Dull. There were kidney-shaped swimming pools and pool-shaped kidneys. And so I sought out the colorful movie people, the oddballs, the bright talkers. They were happy to oblige with material. Many of them were bored with what they themselves were doing and liked to make quips about it. They welcomed me ardently. They were delighted to talk to a journalist who would listen—and then, of course, write, spelling the name correctly. They sometimes expended more energy, time and talent on their talk than on their moviemaking. I let them talk and talk—and they literally talked themselves to death, journalistically speaking.

But, after some time, even Hollywood's waggeries seemed increasingly less amusing and entertaining. Perhaps that was because there was a sense of desperation about them, like the drolleries of a condemned man, and also because they were not backed up by anything tangible, solid and creative on the screen. I didn't object to the personal didoes of the film folk—but to their professional doings. It was one thing for the talented Erich von Stroheim to play the sardonic wit, which he did so well—he had the authority of a vast body of his own rich, identifiable, serious work behind him. It was something else for Billy Wilder, who confessedly modeled himself after von Stroheim, to do the identical thing; Wilder was just a wise guy and a lightweight moviemaker shooting off his yap for publicity. The repartee of these Hollywood characters also developed a repetitive flavor as the local wits ran out of material and started borrowing from each other—and from themselves.

I remembered Wilson Mizner's line: "Hollywood is a carnival—where there are no concessions."

Beneath its sleek make-up, I began to see the movie metropolis for what it really was—a tough, ruthless town where much was at stake financially and where the citizens would go to almost any lengths not to get caught short. Hollywood's egotism, exhibitionism and narcissism gradually palled on me. As John Barrymore once observed of Hollywood: "Isn't it extraordinary how one can earn a living by puking?"

And as someone else put it: "You visit the zoo—but you don't live in it."

A friend of mine, a veteran of the Hollywood wars, summed it up: "What a bunch—what a collection—the psychotic peacocks of the jungle! How can any product come out of a crew like that? These are the characters of the town. The place is swarming with them. Were they that way before they came to the film or did the film make them that way? That could be a subject for a separate analysis."

He continued: "What a town—what a place—the hate, the intrigue! This is what wears you down—there is no joy, no exuberance. It is very depressing. There is no end objective.

"In the old days in Hollywood, the longest day was too short—now the shortest day is too long."

And so, as time went by and as I began to find the movies neither edifying nor educational, neither amusing nor meaningful, I found myself writing less and less about the nipups of the movie people, too. I even started interviewing other members of the press in desperation. Could it be that I was simply growing up, somewhat belatedly? It even occurred to me—heretical thought—that there might just possibly be things in the world more interesting and important than the movies. But then the question arose: once I stopped writing about the pranks and the pleasantries of the famous film folk, what was there left to write about?

Assuredly not about the newcomers to Hollywood, the so-called new talents. As a rule they knew little about the movies today and less about the movies of yesterday. Carl Foreman, who was supposed to be one of the more able contemporary screen writers, told me that silent movies were no good because they did not talk. He had little comprehension of the essential nature of motion pictures and of the value of silence on the screen. He was one of those many movie writers whom words, you might say, have failed.

Foreman was a homegrown Hollywood talent. Director Elia Kazan came from the stage. After completing his movie version of *A Streetcar Named Desire*, Kazan modestly announced that the picture was "a landmark" and bypassed "all that old rot the motion-picture industry is built on." Actually, *A Streetcar Named Desire* was far from a motion-picture landmark. And, although Hollywood has certainly had more than its share of celluloid "rot," it has also had fine films, some of which were true landmarks. I will not mention any titles here, but merely refer Kazan to any elementary history of the movies.

There were a few promising directorial newcomers. But Robert Rossen, after some vigorous movies like *Body and Soul* and *All the King's Men*, got hoisted on the un-American petard and left Hollywood. After recanting politically, he made a comeback with such lethargic films as *Alexander the Great* and *They Came to Cordura*. Anthony Mann, who started out with muscular action movies, ended up making muscle-bound box-office pictures like *Anna Lucasta*.

The alleged talent that Hollywood has thus far borrowed from television—the movie business is always borrowing, from the stage, from literature and even from itself—is of no particular help. It is a callow talent mostly, epitomized in the person of John Frankenheimer, a self-publicized, thirty-one-year-old TV director who also makes movies. I once had occasion to interview Frankenheimer, who is a rather opinionated young man. He told me glibly that, in his firm opinion, *Shane* was the greatest movie ever made at any time, anywhere. He did not mention *The Passion of Joan of Arc*, *Open City*, *Umberto D.*, *Rashomon*, *Intolerance*, *Mother*, *Arsenal*, *The Gold Rush* and—you fill in the rest of the list. Personally, I doubt if he knew about those movies. He mentioned *Shane*, because *Shane* was a recent picture that had been highly publicized and of which he was aware.

Of the relative newcomers who managed to get a camera-hold in Hollywood, some were politically blacklisted by the industry overlords as known or suspected Communists. As a result a certain amount of talent was sacrificed to politics. Actually, it was most debatable if anything un-American—or pro-American, for that matter—ever crept into Hollywood movies through the high density, front-office filters. But if it was doubtful that the movies were un-American, it was overwhelmingly certain that they were un-cinematic and inhuman. The movies had nothing subversive about them. In fact, they simply had nothing—subversive or the obverse.

Some of those barred from working under their own names in movies for political reasons sold scripts under assumed names. Conspicuous among these was "Robert Rich," who won an Academy Award in 1957 as author of the best original story for The Brave One. However, there was no "Robert Rich." It turned out to be a pseudonym for Dalton Trumbo, a talented—but blacklisted—writer. In 1959 there was a similar case when the co-author of The Defiant Ones, Nathan E. Douglas, after winning an Academy Award for the best original story and screenplay with Harold Jacob Smith, was revealed to be Nedrick Young, another blacklisted writer.

As the omnipresent Billy Wilder said: "Blacklist, schmacklist, as long as they're all working." And he added: ". . . of the Unfriendly Ten only two have talent—the other eight are just unfriendly."

Since then, some of the blacklisted writers have increasingly been coming out into the open. With great publicity fanfare Otto Preminger announced that he had hired Dalton Trumbo to write Exodus, and Stanley Kramer broadcast it that Nedrick Young had authored the screenplay of Inherit the Wind. There was sometimes doubt as to whether it was promotion or principle precisely that motivated these moves. Where, for instance, was Kramer when Carl Foreman was being pilloried politically some years ago? The answer is that Kramer was nowhere in evidence at the time and allowed Foreman to be drummed out of Hollywood. It was, of all people, Gary Cooper, who was then starring in Kramer's High Noon, which Foreman had written, who came to Foreman's defense. It was not fashionable at the time to side with the blacklistees—but it is much more fashionable, and much easier, to do so today.

Undoubtedly spurred on by the fact that actor Kirk Douglas had had Dalton Trumbo write the screenplay of his ultra-capitalistically budgeted independent production of Spartacus, Frank Sinatra, in 1960, announced that he had hired Albert Maltz, one of the original "Hollywood Ten," to write his independent production of The Execution of Private Slovik. There was a barrage of press criticism. Sinatra took out trade-paper ads proclaiming that he had hired Maltz because he was "the best man to do the job" and adding that "I am prepared to stand on my principles." But Sinatra's principles were apparently too shaky. Although Sinatra has always violently maintained that he doesn't give a damn about the press and what it writes, he quickly did an ungracious about-face and dropped Maltz. In another batch of trade-paper ads he said that "in view of the reaction of my family, my friends and the American public, I have instructed my attorneys to make a settlement with Albert Maltz and to inform him that he will not write the screenplay for *The Execution of Private Slovik*." He added that he was accepting the "majority opinion" of "the American public"—as if anyone had ever taken a poll.

It is noteworthy that the one great remaining original talent of the American screen—Charlie Chaplin—lives and works abroad today, a refugee from America and from Hollywood. And that the distinctive talents of the screen—an Akira Kurosawa, a Roberto Rossellini, a Vittorio De Sica, a Federico Fellini—are products of other countries who have not let themselves be lured to Hollywood, which has been the artistic graveyard of so many foreign moviemakers.

Assuredly there is not much to write about Hollywood's own relationship to the world at large—for instance the stand it has taken on the vital issue of censorship. Hollywood likes to sound off in high-flown phrases—through such hollow spokesmen as Eric Johnston, head of the Motion Picture Association of America—about the evils of censorship and other restrictive controls. But Hollywood never had the character and conviction to fight for freedom of the screen. It was less troublesome to make deals, to back water, to compromise, to censor itself, to do anything not to endanger the box-office bonanza that Hollywood had almost all to itself until television came along.

There are two forms of Hollywood screen censorship. One is the self-censoring Production Code, set up by the motion-picture industry in 1930 to placate repeated protests against "vile and unwholesome" films by the Catholic Legion of Decency and other religious, fraternal and educational groups. The Code, which was implemented in 1934, sets forth "correct standards of life," ranging from sex to religion, and is couched in vague generalities. All pictures playing theater circuits affiliated with the major Hollywood studios were required to carry a Code certificate of approval. This was supposed to be "voluntary" censorship exercised at the source by the Hollywood producers.

The other form of censorship is externally imposed and is assertedly opposed by Hollywood. This exists today in New York, Pennsylvania, Virginia, Maryland and Kansas. There are also municipal censors in approximately fifty major cities like Chicago, Atlanta, Detroit and Memphis.

The Production Code has been a convenient smokescreen for Hollywood. The story is told that a foreign director, visiting Hollywood for the first time, perused the Code with its clauses covering crime, sex, obscenity, profanity, vulgarity, indecent exposure and other interesting taboos that are supposed to take the sin out of cinema and remarked, "What a marvelous scenario!"

Recently the Production Code was eased up, perhaps to help movies compete more comfortably with television. Now allowed in pictures are such previously prohibited words as "hell," "damn," "fanny," "hold your hat," "nerts" and "tom cat," and movies can deal with smuggling, branding of people or animals and miscegenation and are even permitted to tell traveling-salesman and farmer's-daughter jokes.

Not all moviemakers, however, welcomed this relinquishing of restrictions. Censorship has a definite publicity value which is reflected at the box office in the perverse attention of moviegoers that automatically defeats the censor's avowed purpose. Many moviemakers capitalized on censorship. As director-writer Claude Binyon has said: "Hollywood must never permit censorship to collapse—it's far too good for the box office!"

The Production Code has been a powerful handicap to honest Hollywood movies. In commenting on these taboos imposed on movies "by organized pressure groups or else by unorganized but highly vocal minorities with a taste for outsize fig leaves," Wolcott Gibbs observed: "This makes it impracticable to name political philosophies or explain what they stand for, to discuss religion in any terms conceivably startling to the inmates of a parochial school or a Baptist seminary, to speak disparagingly of any specific business, except, perhaps, dope-running or the white-slave trade, or to deal with sex in any way that might indicate that minor irregularities are not necessarily punishable by a lifetime of social ostracism and a lonely and untended grave."

The censorship rules regularly required that good triumph in movies. In an unusually forthright interview, the late movie producer and journalist Mark Hellinger told me in 1948, "Hollywood is gutless. You can't make an honest, forceful picture here. Hollywood is the whipping boy, the natural target for all kinds of pressure groups, and the movie industry does not stand up to them. Hollywood is to blame for everything that has happened to it. There is fear out here. There is a lot of easy money in this business and easy money makes for attacks from people who want to get in on it.

"The moviemakers have never been able to stand together because they don't get along with each other. They got together only once to form the Hays Office, and that was in desperation. The individual producer in Hollywood is powerless to resist attacks. No matter what you do in movies, you're wrong. *Going My Way* got squawks from the Protestants. *The Best Years of Our Lives* was attacked for its presentation of bankers. You can't win when you make a picture. If you make a movie with punch, you are sure to get protests. If you make a movie that is all sweetness and light, nobody comes to the box office."

Hellinger said that "the code under which we now operate is highly restrictive. *Open City*, about which many people are shouting, could never have been made here under any circumstances. You can't show dope on the screen or suicide. Cain killed Abel in the testament and yet the Bible is not suppressed. *The Killers*, which was a Hemingway classic in book form, never met with any opposition, but the movie version [a Hellinger production] was criticized for those very things that highlighted the Hemingway original. The trouble with *Brute Force* [another Hellinger film] was that it was not brutal enough. At the time the picture was released and being made the subject of all sorts of criticism, the papers carried headlines about sixteen Negro prisoners being killed for talking back to a warden. Not long ago the headlines screamed about a Chicago slaying. If I put that stuff in a picture tomorrow what would happen?

"We can do films as well as anywhere in the world, if we will give ourselves a chance to do them. I bought *Knock on Any Door* for picture purposes. The book is a best-seller and has been serialized in the Hearst papers and abridged in *Look* and *Omnibook*. Millions of people are familiar with it. And yet I will be lucky to get some semblance of it on the screen. Eighty million people will be after my scalp if I make a faithful picturization of the book.

"No one suggests newspapers omit crime news. You can do much more on the radio than you can on the screen. Hollywood should stand up and fight for its freedom of speech and expression."

But Hollywood was the last to take up the cudgels for itself. Many an outside voice was raised against the evils of nonsensorship. "Motion pictures have ruined a lot more evenings than they have morals," one commentator observed. It was argued that movies were entitled to the constitutional guarantees of a free press. Champions of a liberated Hollywood screen contended that the province of censorship is propriety, not truth, and that censorship is not concerned with art or even with sociology. Censors, their critics maintained, are nearsighted and inconsistent—they believe that morality can be legislated into people and that police power is a substitute for physical or psychological fact. Heywood Broun wrote that "the censor believes that he can hold back the mighty traffic of life with a tin whistle and a raised right hand. For, after all, it is life with which he quarrels." The censor was indicted as operating on the theory that what you do not know will not hurt you—although there was precious little illusion the moviegoer brought with him to the theater any longer.

Since Hollywood has always scared very easily when confronted by pressure groups, it gave in readily on the censorship issue. And so all sorts of preposterous shackles were imposed on it, by political groups, theological groups and by aggregations of suburban dilettantes functioning under a variety of highfalutin names. Most everyone had a say about the movies except the artists who made them.

It took a strange and brave little hunchbacked man named Joseph Burstyn to fight—and win—the censorship battle for the movies. Burstyn, a former press agent for Jewish theaters, was an astute and successful foreign-film importer and distributor. He brought Roberto Rossellini's great movies, *Open City*, *Paisan* and *The Flowers of St. Francis*, among other outstanding films, to the United States. At his own expense, and without any backing or encouragement from the fat motion-picture industry, he carried the case against screen censorship clear to the Supreme Court and won a resounding victory.

Burstyn started his fight in 1951 when Rossellini's *The Miracle* was banned in New York State on the grounds that it was "sacrilegious." He told me then that he was waging the battle not only as a businessman.

"Sure, I am a businessman," he said. "But freedom is the life blood of business. The movies, I think, are in such bad shape because they allowed themselves to be stifled in their freedom of expression.

"This case involving *Ways of Love* [an Italian trilogy of which *The Miracle* was one part] goes far beyond one picture. It has to do with censorship of the screen. The screen has let itself speak only to immature people. If the movie industry wants to sleep comfortably, let it. It will wake up one day to find there is no business left.

"I have won four New York film critics' awards with *Open City*, *Paisan*, *Bicycle Thief* and *Ways of Love*. I had to fight for each of these pictures. I insist on presenting films as freely as a writer writes a book or a painter paints a picture.

"I feel that, in pressing this case, the outcome also can help Hollywood, more than Hollywood can help itself. The movie industry has given in to pressure groups for years and it is almost impossible for it to jump into the battle and change overnight."

In 1952 the Supreme Court, in a momentous decision, backed up Burstyn and guaranteed free speech to the movies. This ruling overturned a position the court had held for thirty-seven years. In 1915 the court had ruled in an Ohio case that the exhibition of movies was a "business pure and simple" and not to be included in the constitutional guarantees. In its new ruling, the court announced that "we conclude that expression by means of motion pictures is included within the free speech and free press guaranty of the First and Fourteenth Amendments. To the extent that language in the opinion [the Ohio case] is out of harmony with the views here set forth, we no longer adhere to it."

I was functioning as *Time*'s movie critic in New York when the Supreme Court decision was announced, and I distinctly recall the magazine's New York office querying the Beverly Hills bureau—or Bevedit—to get statements from the movie bigwigs commenting on Burstyn's historic censorship victory—a victory that meant more for Hollywood than for Burstyn himself. A cross-section of studio executives was queried by a *Time* correspondent. But they were either so afraid that they refused to give out a statement, or they made meaningless, innocuous remarks. Even after Burstyn had won the battle for them, the Hollywood tycoons were still fearful of speaking up against censorship. Burstyn, unfortunately, is dead today. He knew more about the movies—both as art and commerce—and he had more guts than all the Hollywood naboobs combined.

In 1959 another historic judgment in the battle against censorship was handed down by the Supreme Court when it upset the New York State ban on the French film *Lady Chatterley's Lover* as being unconstitutional. Like *The Miracle*, this case was argued by Ephraim London, one of the country's leading censorship attorneys, in this instance on behalf of Kingsley International Pictures, the distributor.

Even the *Hollywood Reporter* was moved to comment at the time that both of the Supreme Court cases were "prosecuted by a distributor of foreign films, without the MPAA even offering amicus curiae support." The trade paper added that "the film industry—specifically Eric Johnston's MPAA—never has had the intestinal fortitude nor the wisdom to challenge the fallacious philosophy of censorship."

As a result of the Supreme Court judgments, state and civic censorship has suffered some bad blows. The *Hollywood Reporter* pointed out in 1959 that four states (New York, Kansas, Maryland, Virginia) "now are rewriting their censorship statutes to 'stay in business.'" Ohio and Massachusetts have abolished censorship. Pennsylvania, whose former censorship law was held unconstitutional by the Pennsylvania Supreme Court on the basis of prior U. S. Supreme Court rulings, in 1959 pushed through a bill re-establishing censorship. But, according to Ephraim London, this bill is so patently unconstitutional and "badly drawn" that it can easily be challenged. London says that the state and city censors are on the defensive today and that censorship has "eased up tremendously." He foresees that "ultimately all state censorship boards will go and that it is even more true of municipal laws."

Bolstered by these battles that were fought and won by individuals outside of Hollywood, the movie industry has become somewhat braver than it was before. The liberalizing of its own self-censoring Production Code is a step in the right direction. Recently some moviemakers have been flouting the Code entirely and releasing their pictures without a Code seal. But, although Hollywood's press agents and publicity-minded producers and directors speak sententiously today of "adult" themes, it is doubtful whether they are really tackling them. The use of the words "hell" and "damn" in a movie does not necessarily make it more realistic. And, furthermore, "adult" themes can easily be vitiated by immature moviemaking.

Recently there has been a rash of movies dealing with most everything from abortion to prostitution. As Bob Hope cracked in 1960, "Our big pictures this year have had some intriguing themes—sex, perversion, adultery and cannibalism. We'll get those kids away from their TV sets yet." Sometimes these pictures with their sensationalism seem to be aimed at the box office rather than at the brave new world. Producer-writer Robert Buckner put the issue in these words some years ago: "Studios today sense that the public is tired of hackneyed themes, but they are afraid to explore new ground. They feel very big and brave whenever they make a film about insanity or alcoholism or racial prejudice. But what was in any of these pictures with which anybody could take serious issue? They were fairly safe bets, like mother love or marriage. Their only faults were usually dullness.

"Every time the boys get a little out of line, they are so proud of themselves. But they usually wind up hedging on controversial subjects. They lose their guts halfway through a picture.

"They realize the box office is jaded and they want to give it a boost. But they are torn between what is a controversial subject and what is too controversial and they wind up in true and tried style."

Or, as another moviemaker said of a recent picture: "It's very frank. They say 'sex relations' six times."

There has been some talk recently of establishing a "Classification" system for Hollywood movies, like the one in effect in England, whereby pictures would be graded for adults, youngsters, etc. But this classification idea has met with opposition in the industry because it would be damaging to box-office receipts, since about half of U.S. moviegoers are in the teen-age classification. Hollywood movies no longer have any particular appeal to adults today, and the teen-agers grow out of the moviegoing habit as they grow up.

Assuredly there is not much to say about Hollywood's relationship to the strange new world of television that has come along to plague it so powerfully. At first the movie business dealt with the phenomenon of television mainly by its time-honored, ostrichlike tactic of trying to pretend it was not there. Finally, when the movies were forcibly backed into the hard fact of television, they tried to combat it with bigger screens, louder sound and fatter budgets—in fact, everything but better movies.

Hollywood has traditionally opposed innovation. When the Warner Brothers premiered *Don Juan*, the first movie with sound accompaniment, in 1927, they were not particularly keen about talking pictures. They were toying with sound as a novelty that might help them avoid bankruptcy. All the other studios, with the exception of Fox, pooh-poohed sound. There were such industry criticisms as from "fad to worse," "came the din" and "all-talking, all-singing, all-nothing." Ultimately, the public's enthusiasm for the new process could no longer be disregarded and Hollywood found itself in a critical situation.

Warners itself had initially intended sound as what has been described as "an adjunct to the silent film" and "to supplant expensive, live orchestras with a more economical, recorded musical accompaniment." Warners even wanted to do away with the name "talking pictures" and to concentrate solely on musical orchestration.

As a result, according to William deMille in *Hollywood Saga*, the sound revolution in 1928 was sweeping and devastating and found the industry as a whole utterly unprepared to cope with it. DeMille noted: "If the motion picture industry as a whole had had the power to decide this vital question [of the advent of sound] the chances are that talkies would still be in their infancy, or, if perfected at all, would be held back from popular consumption in order to prevent wrecking the business as it was in 1928."

And Benjamin Hampton, in *A History of the Movies*, observed: "Years before, the autocrats of General Film had rejected feature pictures because of their conviction that the masses could not assimilate them; the autocrats of 1925–1926 rejected talkies because of their conviction that talkies were not good enough to satisfy the masses. Blinded by their own vast empire, by the bricks and mortar of their temple-theaters, by the power of wealth and the adulation of sycophants, the pioneers of yesterday had grown cautious, fearful of endangering the solid position they so comfortably enjoyed. And thus they missed their opportunity and the screen went through still another of the mad gyrations that had made its history the most romantic and unpredictable of all American industrial endeavours. . . . The overlords of the screen were proven to have lost their sensitivity to the unspoken desires of the mass of ticket buyers."

This lack of sound judgment—so to speak—was repeated with the advent of television. Today television, of course, has literally taken over Hollywood—and its audiences. TV producers are occupying most of the available studio space, from the stages where Charlie Chaplin and Mack Sennett made their movies to the studio where *The Jazz Singer* was shot. Several big movie lots—like RKO and Universal-International—have been bought by television interests. Many Hollywood directors, writers and technicians are employed in television—otherwise they would be jobless. And television has influenced the movies in other ways. One movie director I know, a specialist in horse operas, sits in front of his television set for hours, industriously scanning TV westerns for cinematic inspiration. Three good television oater episodes combined, he said, add up to a good feature-length horse opera. This is ironic because the makers of TV westerns get most of their ideas from old Hollywood horse operas.

Television, with its streamlined studios and split-second production techniques, has also proved what many moviemakers themselves have long been saying—that the movie studios and their molasses-slow methods of production are archaic and have long been outdated. Hollywood was simply muddling along on the supposition that what was good enough at the very beginning of movies was still good enough—as long as the money kept coming in. No serious, concerted attempt was made at researching and planning a program of technical development and improvement.

The movie business has studiously never investigated its audiences, its marketing methods and its manufacturing techniques. It has had no long-range program, as most industries have, for perfecting its production tools. The studios in which movies are made today are substantially the same big barns that they were in the days of early silent films, except that they were padded for soundproofing when talking pictures came along. There has been little development in production methods from the days of D. W. Griffith. Cameras are still cumbersome instruments and it still takes hours to set up the lighting for a shot. There has, for instance, been no real effort to explore the possibilities of rapid, maneuverable 16 mm. filming, which, cameramen will tell you, is entirely feasible. Nor has there been any attempt to set up a proper training program for young moviemaking talent.

Today, at the end of an era, Hollywood is sitting tight and hoping for pay television so that movies can be commercially marketed overnight on TV for vast sums. The only salvation for the movies, many film folk contend, is if pay TV pays off for Hollywood. "Movies and TV," said one observer, "hope to be married, after which the happy bride and groom plan to raise a large family of slot machines." Meanwhile, Hollywood's sales pitch is that television is inferior to motion pictures because of its small screens, that the new, big, swollen movie screens offer more to the spectator. That is equivalent to saying that mass is synonymous with merit, that quantity is identical with quality.

Actually, television is only a transmission medium. It is not an art. It still consists of images on a screen—the same images that stem from the magic lantern. It is still, in Athanasius Kircher's words of 1671, the great art of light and shadow that was later developed by Marey, Muybridge, Edison and others into moving images on a screen.

Frank Capra, who has directed both movies and television shows, told me, "Working in television is the same as working in movies. In TV, I'm just making films. It's not much different from what I've been doing. It's still on film. About the only concession I've made to TV is getting the image a little more in the center so they don't cut it off like they do in TV. Television to me is the same as a movie. TV is simply a private theater in every home as far as I'm concerned."

Ultimately all movies will probably be shown on television screens—convenience alone will dictate it—and, if the engineers and technicians have half the know-how they have evidenced thus far, TV screens will inevitably be much larger, too. The result, as Capra says, will be truly a movie theater in the home. And who says a movie has to be shown in a theater? After all, it is indubitably better to read a book in one's living room than in the public library.

TV and the movies are intrinsically both the same medium—the medium of motion pictures. And down the centuries the progress of the motion picture, from the magic lantern to television, has been marked by certain constant factors. All the various phases of the motion-picture medium have had much in common. The history—

and the pre-history—of movies prove that there is nothing particularly new in this area anyway. It was all prefigured and pretold hundreds of years ago. As I skim through the books in my library, it is evident that the same pressures and problems that confront the movies today were confronting the ancestors of movies before the movies were even invented.

It appears that the movies were being attacked even before there were any movies. Among my books on the pre-history of movies—the days of magic lanterns, stereopticons, revolving disks, stereo-fantascopes, zoetropes, praxinoscopes and other devices dating back to as early as 1660—are a number of antique folios revealing that the critics were already pouncing on the screen in its pre-movie phase.

It is interesting to see how these problems and ideas of several hundred years ago parallel the problems and ideas of today. Almost 250 years ago the people who made those primitive shows were accused of producing only horror pictures. The critics then argued that those devices should be used for instructive and educational purposes. This, of course, is a standard complaint today as articulated by a variety of do-gooders. William Molyneux, an Irish teacher and scientist who was the first man to write about the magic lanthorn (magic lantern to you) in English, observed in his *Dioptricks:* "This is usually some ludicrous or frightfull representation, the more to divert the spectators."

A few years later there was a blast from a German devotee, Creiling by name, who pilloried the kind of program usually shown then and urged that the magic lantern be utilized for noble and uplifting purposes.

Also during that period Johann Zahn, another German student of the pre-cinema, urged the educational application of the magic lantern. Zahn suggested that honey be smeared on a lantern slide and that a fly then be put into the ointment. The slide could then be projected on a wall and the fly's movements studied. But this was probably turned down by some early eighteenth-century producer of lantern slides who figured that there was not sufficient love interest in the plot.

Naturally, the primeval horror films continued to flourish. In 1770 in Germany, for instance, a projection room was described as being full of "mysteriously smelling smokes," with the spectators placed in a magic circle during the showing of these primitive spine-chillers. It is pertinent to note that the customers were not allowed to eat anything during the performances then so as not to detract from the austerity of the event. This must have put quite a crimp in the candy and popcorn concessions.

After the French revolution an entrepreneur named Etienne Gaspard Robertson put on what he called Phantasmagoric shows by means of a magic lantern mounted on a wheel that gave the illusions of ghosts on a screen of smoke. The more horrible these shows were, the better the patrons liked them.

A Teutonic horror-film impresario named Philipsthal put on shows said to "have terrific effects" upon audiences. These exhibitions, staged in complete darkness, featured skeletons and other frightening figures viewed through an invisible gauze screen. To the accompaniment of lightning and thunder, these spectral figures were alternately magnified and shrunken, and they appeared and disappeared with horrific results.

As if this were not bad enough, the sponsors of such magic-lantern divertisements were also branded as money-grubbing wretches interested solely in filthy lucre.

In *Ars Magna Lucis et Umbrae* (The Great Art of Light and Shadow), one of the earliest works on the magic lantern, author Athanasius Kircher took a crack at the commercialism of those magic-lantern operators who were accused of earning a fortune by showing their slides "to Italian noblemen." The author apparently held that money was the root of all evil when it came to magic lanterns.

Which simply goes to show that history, particularly in regard to the movies, repeats itself.

In former film days the plots and personalities were pretty much the same as they are today. Some movie titles of a half century or so ago were *Jim West, Gambler, Her Happiness, A Shriek in the Night, The Battle of Elderbush Gulch* and *The Curious Case of Meredith Stanhope.* One of the hits of that time was *The Call of the Traumerei,* described by the producers as "the story of a bewitching French actress who fails to hold her artist lover when he hears his old sweetheart playing."

Hollywood's advertising in its romper era was as inflated and flamboyant as it still is today. Mutual Movies then ballyhooed its product as follows: "The most thrilling pictures from the great West. Exciting dramas that make the heart throb. Side-splitting comedies that lighten dull care. Mystery plays that fascinate and thrill. Romances of love that melt the heart. Great feature plays remembered for a lifetime. Sweet childhood stories that mothers love."

To point up the fact that there is nothing really new in movies, it is interesting to compare Hollywood's occasional latter-day ventures into subjects of "significance" with the identical subjects that were treated —and sometimes better—in the earlier days of the movies.

In recent years Hollywood has released, with much fanfare, some movies, like *Broken Arrow*, that sympathetically depicted the American Indian. It was claimed that these were brave innovations. Actually there have been many movies of this type. In 1934 Warners made *Massacre*, with Richard Barthelmess as a college-educated Indian who returned to the reservation to champion the rights of his people. In 1926 *Braveheart* starred Rod La Rocque in the role of a redskin who had the benefit of a higher education and became a spokesman for his race. That picture also had a romantic sub-theme between the Indian and a white girl. Even in the earliest days of the silent screen there were pictures such as *The Red Man and the Child*, *The Seminole's Trust*, *Indian Land Grab* and *Lo, the Poor Indian* which espoused the Indian cause.

When you come right down to it, just about every one of Hollywood's recent and much publicized attempts at themes of so-called social significance was essayed before.

The Negro problem was touched on in *The Emperor Jones*, *Hallelujah* and such earlier pictures as *A Persistent Suitor* and *Judge's Story*. The Jew came in for his share of celluloid attention in *The Jazz Singer*, *Humoresque* and films like *Child of the Ghetto* and *The Patriarch*, the latter two made around 1910 and portraying the Jew as a character of relative dignity, intelligence and understanding. Irish, Italian, Mexican and Oriental minorities were also subjects of reasonably sympathetic screen treatment.

The movies have only recently recaptured some of the outspokenness and forthrightness they had when they were younger and before censorship and hidebound commercialism began to make them pussyfoot about almost everything. Here, for instance, is a random sampling of pictures made not long past the turn of the century, shortly after movies had come into existence: *A Trip to the Moon* (early science fiction); *The White Caps*, about the evils of liquor; *The Crooked Banker*, about corruption in the realm of high finance; *A Desperate Encounter*, about the economic causes of crime; and *The Great Train Robbery*, the progenitor of thousands of westerns. In those early film days movies covered practically every theme under the sun, from social injustice (*The Eviction*) to parole (*The Ex-Convict*). They treated, without excessive fuss, subjects such as prize fighting, bullfighting, narcotics, white slavery, capital and labor, the Dreyfus case, and what have you.

Later, in the films of D. W. Griffith, Erich von Stroheim and others, the screen really came to grips with social themes. Griffith's epic *Intolerance*, in its modern strike sequence, presented a harrowingly realistic picture of a cross-section of contemporary society. Von Stroheim's *Greed* was a corrosive analysis of the money motive in the world we live in. There were, more recently, many other movies—from King Vidor's *The Crowd*, a compassionate study of a young married couple struggling to make their way, to William Wellman's *Wild Boys of the Road*, a drama of the depression years—which spoke their pieces boldly.

This sketchy inventory indicates that the movies have been brave enough in the past. To the extent that they are occasionally brave once more today—that is all to the good. But it should not be forgotten that just about every one of the current themes was treated long ago, with less press-agentry and perhaps more artistry than today. And it might be instructive and a little humbling for some of the present-day self-glorifying moviemakers to acquaint themselves with a few elementary facts out of screen annals.

These facts will reveal that, since the days of D. W. Griffith and the original pioneers, there has been no appreciable advance in the making of motion pictures in this country. True, there have been some minor improvements and developments in movie mechanics—such as photography, sound recording, film processing and the creation of special effects—as differentiated from cinematic technique. But in one other essential factor of the movie industry has there been no particular improvement—and that is in the story department.

In the nickelodeon days most motion pictures were the filmic counterparts of pulp fiction. They catered to the childish imagination of the customers by feeding them elementary tales of boy-meets-girl, of virtue triumphing over villainy and of cowboys and Indians. Essentially, the Hollywood movie still adheres to these formulas.

Perhaps that is because the written word and the idea are held in relative contempt in Hollywood, compared to the complex and often hard-to-comprehend activities of the mechanical departments. Perhaps it is because, as the film industry became a more corporate enterprise, the financial interests in Hollywood were reluctant to seek out experimental paths.

But this wariness on the part of the producers resulted in quite the opposite effect from what they had intended. By sticking to well-worn ruts they managed not to keep enticing their audiences but gradually to alienate them. Once the great novelty of motion pictures began to wear off in the Twenties, the box office began to suffer. No longer intrigued by the newness of motion pictures in general, the cash customers began to assess motion pictures in particular and find many of them lacking in both theme and entertainment.

Fortunately, just at that juncture, the sound film came along to revive the declining box office. But sound could not keep attracting the customers forever. Since it was not implemented by anything more significant, its effect began to wane. Before long Hollywood found itself in the same predicament as before. It tried everything, from Banko and Bingo to Dish Night and Double Features, without much success.

Fortunately again—for Hollywood's purpose—World War II came along. The war brought with it boom times, increased prosperity for the average consumer and a high-tension atmosphere that demanded alleviation through entertainment at any cost. And so Hollywood prospered once more. But this prosperity was an illusory and transient one, too. It was merely another fortunate phase in the fifty-odd-year history of the screen. That history has been a record of the appeal generated by the novelty of motion pictures, by new mechanical developments, by colorful personalities in the performing ranks and by external crises. It was not a prosperity that had ever arisen from really supplying the public with a solid celluloid staple—namely, stories and screenplays that were realistic, relevant and had some relationship to the world we live in.

Since then Hollywood has had the greatest reversals in its history. There has been divorcement of the cozy arrangement whereby the movie companies produced pictures, distributed them themselves and played them in their own theaters. The government's trust-busters broke up this monopoly, forcing separation of the comfortable, airtight production-distribution-exhibition setup. It was an historic blow against Hollywood.

On my bookshelves I have a specially bound legal pamphlet as a commemoration of this event. Its frontispiece reads "In the District Court of the United States of America, Petitioners v. Paramount Pictures, Inc., et al., Defendants—Petition—Filed July 20, 1938." It also lists Loew's, R-K-O, Warner Bros., Twentieth Century-Fox, Columbia, Universal and United Artists. In the anti-trust suit, the eight major movie companies were accused by the Department of Justice of combining and conspiring to restrain trade in the production, distribution and exhibition of motion pictures and with attempting successfully to monopolize such trade in violation of the Sherman Act.

The avowed purpose of the suit was to have movies divorce their production and distribution activities from their theater operations.

The trust-busters charged in a 119-page complaint that because of the monopolistic setup, moviegoers were getting no opportunity to exercise choice as to the type of picture they wanted to see and that every week eighty-five to ninety million people were taking what was dished out to them by the defendants. The day the story broke on the front page of the New York *Times*, that newspaper carried ads for the following movies: Mickey Rooney and Judy Garland in *Love Finds Andy Hardy*, Shirley Temple in *Little Miss Broadway*, Harold Lloyd in *Professor Beware* and Rudy Vallee and Hugh Herbert in *Gold Diggers in Paris*—eloquent corroborative evidence of the government's charges.

Hard on the heels of the suit, Douglas Churchill reported in the New York *Times* that the movie industry had made desperate attempts to quash the anti-trust suit without success. According to Churchill, the movie people had even gone direct to the President in the hope of having the charges called off. It was typical of Hollywood's time-honored tactics.

It was the beginning of the end for Hollywood. After World War II, movie business declined. Then along came television and Hollywood could see the writing of the antennae on the rooftops. In 1950 the movies embarked on a high-pressure promotion campaign to recapture audiences. There were all sorts of brave slogans like "Movies Are Better Than Ever! Tell It! Yell It! Sell It!" The sale of popcorn and candy kept many a movie theater going ("Movies are butter than ever," cracked one moviegoer). Most movie theaters became little more than mammoth candy stands with, incidentally, some half-baked cinematic confections on the screen.

Unhappily, saying or even yelling that movies were better than ever did not make them so. It brought to mind Herman Mankiewicz's suggestion for luring audiences back into the picture palaces: "Let's show the movies in the street and drive the people into the theaters."

But the theaters kept closing. In 1960, when New York's Roxy Theater was about to be torn down, Bosley Crowther wrote in the New York *Times:* "The news that the Roxy Theatre has finally been sold to a large realty firm that apparently intends to demolish it and use the property for extending an adjacent hotel is one more indication of the dilemma of the famous movie palaces along Broadway. These days there simply are more people who will pay money to sleep in hotels than will pay money to sleep in theatres."

The Roxy Theater site was to be used for an extension of the adjoining Taft Hotel, where I had once interviewed Edwin S. Porter, the maker of The Great Train Robbery, shortly before his death.

Hollywood's narrow minds came up with a panacea—wide screens. Since television screens were small, movie screens would get larger. There was CinemaScope, VistaVision—everything but artistic scope. But what Hollywood desperately needed was not larger screens but greater vision. When CinemaScope made its debut with The Robe in 1953, a critic pointedly said, "In this initial test of CinemaScope, it was more of a new kind of crutch than a fresh kind of wing." There were the usual wisecracks. Said a moviegoer after seeing a picture on one of the new panoramic screens: "There was quite a lot of action at my end—what happened over on your side?"

But some moviemakers were concerned. The late Don Hartman, then Paramount's production chief, said in 1954 that movies should get back to "the principle of picture making—not picture framing." George Stevens, objecting to CinemaScope's ribbonlike form, observed: "After all these years of technical developments in motion pictures, we finally come up with a medium more suitable to the photographing of snakes than men!" (But the way Hollywood pressures operate, even the supposedly independent Stevens ended up shooting—of all pictures—the claustrophobic The Diary of Anne Frank on the rambling CinemaScope screen, thereby appreciably detracting from the drama of the film.)

The new wide screens narrowed down and flattened out the film's dramatic field of vision. Their static, panoramic viewpoints and lack of cutting took much of the motivity and motive out of motion pictures. There was no room any longer, among the Technicolored, mammoth-screen movies, for the simple, incisive, "small" black-and-white film. Director Clarence Brown pointed out that "the big screen is completely out of proportion for any artistic composition. If you put a closeup of a face on it, you've got forty feet of nothing all around. The big screen destroys intimacy." Critic Bela Balazs had written in his book, Theory of the Film: "The closeup has not only widened our vision of life, it has also deepened it." Hollywood's new wide screen assuredly brought no new depth to the motion picture.

There were other shots in the Hollywood arm. A horror picture, The Tingler, had theater seats wired to shock the customer electrically. The gimmick was called Percepto. Another thriller, The House on Haunted Hill, featured something known as the Emergo process, whereby an illuminated skeleton mounted on trolley wires moved out from the side of the screen over the heads of the audience. Movie reviewers complained that their jobs were becoming physically as well as psychologically hazardous. "The next step in that direction," observed one Hollywoodite, "will be a live murder." For a horror epic entitled *Macabre*, the producers took out a $1,000 insurance policy covering patrons "in case of heart attack." But one critic noted that the picture "couldn't cure a child's hiccups."

There were all sorts of trick screens and photographic techniques. Moviemaking became a matter of anamorphic devices, prisms, mirrors, depth of focus, image definition, wide angles. The screens kept getting bigger and bigger. There was even a 360-degree screen.

The movies were busting out all over. One picture, *4D Man*, was a horror film about a scientist who could penetrate solid matter. There was Smell-o-Vision, or "smellies" for short, devised to lend additional odor to a fusty little thriller, *Scent of Mystery*, by means of perfumes wafted through the theater. In 1929 M-G-M's musical *Hollywood Revue* had featured a finale, "Orange Blossom Time," with Charles King and the Albertina Rasch ballet, in which an aroma of oranges was wafted through the theater. Smell-o-Vision brought fifty scents, from garlic to shoe polish, tied in with the action on the screen, via a tube system to each individual spectator. "Glorious Smell-o-Vision" was advertised as "the process to end all processes" and was ballyhooed with this legend: "First They Moved (1893)—Then They Talked (1927) —Now They Smell (1959)." A good many critics concurred. Who knew what the future would bring—"feelies" perhaps, as Aldous Huxley had once fictionally envisioned them in his *Brave New World*?

When the studios could not strike moviemaking oil, one way or another, they struck oil literally. The two main landmarks in Hollywood were the television aerials and the oil wells sticking up out of the movie lots. Those movie studios that were not gobbled up by the television monster parceled out some of their real estate for housing and commercial developments. A 500 million-dollar super-business and housing "city" was planned to go up on the back lot of Twentieth Century-Fox.

It was the demise of the major studios. "Majors Worth More Dead Than Alive," headlined *Daily Variety*. The movie business became decentralized. The old, top-heavy assembly-line operations were being replaced by aggregations of smaller, independent units functioning, more or less autonomously, within the studios. The studios became little more than rental plants.

This was the way the movies had begun a half century ago—with small, independent, individual production companies. But most of the new producers were far from being individual artistically and they were still dependent on old-hat movie themes and moviemaking techniques. Many of these producers were profiles turned moviemakers. The overpaid profiles—and their grasping agents—had got a stranglehold on Hollywood and were calling the camera turn. It started a decade ago when the major studios, in a false economy move, decided to rid themselves of their expensive contract lists. The agents then moved in for the kill and set up almost impossible financial barriers between the makers of movies and the few top free-lance stars they wanted for their films.

As representatives of the much-in-demand stars, the big agencies, such as Music Corporation of America, William Morris and Famous Artists, wielded tremendous power and practically took over control of the movie business. For instance, when Twentieth Century-Fox was casting *The Young Lions*, the studio announced Marlon Brando, Montgomery Clift and Tony Randall for the leading roles. Shooting was about to begin when MCA, which represented Brando and Clift, stepped in and told the studio that the agency wanted Dean Martin, another of its clients, in the Randall role. The studio had no recourse but to accede to MCA's wishes or the agency might have pulled Brando and Clift out of the picture. Randall was dropped and replaced by Dean Martin. In effect, MCA and not Twentieth Century-Fox was casting *The Young Lions*.

The top stars were in the ascendant more than ever and their agents helped jack up their salaries to astronomic levels. A Gary Cooper, James Stewart or Cary Grant could write his own ticket, appropriate the major profit percentage of a film and have approval rights on just about everything from script to director. Stars like William Holden and John Wayne received as much as $750,000 straight salary, aside from a percentage, for one picture. Elizabeth Taylor was paid $1,000,000 to play Cleopatra. But percentage and not salary was the accepted thing. Gary Cooper was reported to have earned about $1,000,000 from his share in one hit movie, *Vera Cruz*, and about $600,000 from *High Noon*. Marlon Brando even got 100 per cent of the net profits for one picture. The studio with which he made the deal was content to settle for its percentage as distributor of the movie, which still added up to a tidy sum. There seemed to be a percentage in the movies for everybody but the moviegoer.

The lunatics, seemingly, had taken over the asylum. It was a world of flesh and flesh peddlers. And, since the studios had not taken the trouble to build up many new stars, much of the flesh was superannuated: many of the actors playing romantic roles were grandfathers in real life, making for what one trade paper termed a "lack of identification" with youthful moviegoers. But it all added up to spanking profits for the profile-producers, even if it did not add up to good movies. The star-suzerains made a mess of most movies and dimmed the luster of the screen and themselves even more.

And so, in the final years of the 1950s, the Hollywood dream factory became a nightmare. The plush, lush old days had gone forever. The palmy, balmy Hollywood was as passé as the once fashionable frankfurter stands in the shape of hot dogs and the restaurants in the shape of derby hats. The movie moguls were as extinct as their Oriental counterparts. It was truly, as the fade-out titles on many a movie had proclaimed, The End of Hollywood.

Hollywood's own astigmatism and insularity have kept it from much of the realization and awareness necessary to cope with its problems. It is, in many respects, a never-never land. Hollywood has, significantly, been characterized as "Bagdad on the Pacific," "Poughkeepsie with Palms" and "the warm Siberia." But perhaps the most telling description is Carey McWilliams', which he applied to greater Southern California, as "an island on the land."

Hanging on my living-room wall is an ancient Dutch map, circa 1662, in which California is prophetically depicted as an island off the main body of the United States. Shaped like a lopsided cornucopia, with the wide end in the north, this huge and top-heavy California island is the outstanding feature of the American continent. This island was reported to be barren and craggy and literally strewn with gold and precious jewels. Upon it supposedly dwelt an amazing race of Amazons of whom the fairest and strongest was their queen, Califia.

This cartographic legend of California as an island lasted more than 100 years. The Dutch cartographers of the time did not know any better—or, perhaps, they really were foresightedly aware of what they were up to. They might very well not change their minds—and their maps—if they were around to survey the present-day topographical and cultural scene.

Hollywood, in its narcissistic self-absorption, is insulated and isolated and indeed "an island on the land." It has been said that in Hollywood "most of the people who make movies only know what they see in other movies and that is why so many screen stereotypes are perpetuated." Functioning in Hollywood is something like partaking of the communal life of an institution for the mentally deficient. At first you may believe that you are reasonable and that the others are deranged, but after a while you are no longer certain. The majority is against you and you are shut off from a reassuring corroboration of your own sanity.

Hollywood, with its insularity, ignorance, arrogance and avarice, with its colossal vulgarity and bad taste, is bad not only for the rest of America and the world but for Hollywood itself. It needs a breath of fresh air from the outside. It needs a cosmopolitan measuring rod that has more scope than its own rube rule of thumb. It needs to let the world in, to be de-Hollywoodized.

Often, when Hollywood's self-aggrandizement becomes overpowering, I like to take a reassuring look at a small, simply framed theater program that hangs above my desk. I bought it, for a couple of dollars, at the auction of Sid Grauman's effects in 1950. It is dated 1903— the year of *The Great Train Robbery*, when the movies were just getting started—and is from Grauman's Theater, which Sid's father, D. J. Grauman, was managing for the Pacific Coast Vaudeville Co., Props., in San Francisco at the time. The faded brown leaflet lists the "Programme, Week Commencing Monday, June 29, 1903. Evening Performance 8:15 Sharp, Matinees 2:15 Sharp: Waddell, King of Clubs; R. Clinton Montgomery, Will Render 'Only a Soldier Boy'; Nusa la Var, Singing and Dancing Comedienne; Bros. Waldron, Dutch Comedians; Medley Selection—'Down on the Farm,' Von Tilzer; Marsh Craig, Sensational Novelty Acrobat; McIntyre & Primrose, Something New; Little Anna Gillman, Juvenile Entertainer; Les Incroyables, Europe's Foremost Pantomimists; The Bioscope With a New Series of Moving Pictures."

The vaudeville acts, of course, were the stellar attractions of the Grauman bill. The Bioscope, bringing up the rear, consisted of the brief little movie scenes of that era which were so crude that they were usually used as a chaser to drive the customers out of the theater so that there would be a solid turnover before the next vaudeville show got under way.

And motion-picture history, as I have said, does repeat itself. Now the movies, which finally killed off vaudeville, are again in the position of playing second fiddle, or chaser, to television, which is the vaudeville of today.

The fifty or more intervening years since the bouncy young Bioscope have seen Hollywood and its works grow bigger and fatter—and tireder. It is hard to envision the fresh little sylvan community that was once Hollywood in the grim, grimy, rundown tank town that is today part of the loosely strung together conglomeration of suburban communities that constitute so-called greater Los Angeles.

Sometimes, as I strolled along Hollywood Boulevard with the late Mack Sennett, he reminisced about the old, golden Hollywood. One night Sennett, that prince of pratfalls, that sultan of slapstick, was promenading down the boulevard. The lights were blazing and the traffic was churning.

"You'd meet Abraham Lincoln and General Grant in makeup coming home from work in the old days," said Sennett, pausing near Vine Street. "Everyone was historical then."

Sennett was talking of the time when the movies were young and Hollywood was a hamlet, more than forty years ago.

"Here, where this theater is, was a lemon grove. The boulevard was a semi-dirt street with a little pavement in the center and a one-track trolley. When it rained it was muddy. You had to put chains on your tires.

"I had a Stanley and a Fiat. I had a close call in my 120 horsepower racing Fiat. I was driving with Mabel Normand. We were all kids, for Godsakes! I haven't driven since.

"I used to live at Westmoreland Park, almost an hour's drive from the boulevard. It took a full hour to get out to Hollywood from Los Angeles. It was like going out to the country, into the wilds." (Today it sometimes takes longer.)

Sennett lit a cigar. "A trolley ride was a nickel then and a nickel was a nickel. Five cents—that was gold, pure gold.

"A helluva good lunch could be had for forty-five or fifty cents at the Hollywood Hotel. The price scale for a big-name actor was around a hundred dollars a week. Gloria Swanson got sixty-five a week when she started with me. Wally Beery got fifty.

"Land was worth nothing except for the valuable orange-grove trees. The Hollywood Hills were nothing but a lot of vacant land. Maybe a thousand dollars could have bought the Broadway-Hollywood department-store corner.

"On Vine Street, they grew grapes. The street got its name from the grapes. We'd shoot movies right around Cahuenga. Named after the Cahuenga Indians. You know—the Cahuenga tribe. Look up your history books.

"Mr. and Mrs. Wilcox lived on Wilcox Street. On Wilcox Ranch. Very famous for its lemons. That Warner Theater—it was a riding academy with horses.

"When we made movies, we took charge of the boulevard in those days. We could ask the citizens to move aside and give us the street. There was a friendly attitude toward the movies in that era—oh, absolutely! They let us use houses, lawns. You'd say, 'Can I borrow your dining-room table for a movie?' Certainly.

"We'd have a story conference right on the boulevard. You kinda knew everybody. There was a hospitality then—came down from the old Spaniards.

"They had only a few little stores, grocery stores and a couple of things like that. It was a little village then. A little, typical village. It wasn't glamorous. Glamour? No.

"They had no searchlights then. Oh, God, no searchlights! Women didn't wear slacks on the boulevard—no, oh, no!

"No gossip columnists. I had my own newspaper. Harry Carr was editor; 15,000 to 16,000 copies went to exhibitors, barbershops and dentist and doctor offices.

"We brought box lunches with us and picked oranges right off the trees. No orange-juice stands. You could pick oranges right off the trees—oranges—oh, sure!

"We had more fun then. We were younger and had more pep and didn't take things so seriously. We were more friendly. You didn't have to go through a lot of secretaries just to get anyone on the telephone."

Sennett paused at noisy, jazzy Las Palmas. "Probably a tree on this corner. Probably some goats, too."

The traffic roared across Highland, past the faded façade of the Hollywood Hotel.

"The Hollywood Hotel. They gave dances, they gave dinner parties then. The nicest people in Hollywood went there. The stars lived there. It was a lovely place to live, a country home. That was a barley field over there."

Sennett stopped in front of the majestic old Garden Court apartments where he lived. He looked, a little sadly, at the gas station that had replaced the tennis court near the once elegant edifice.

"Progress, eh?" said Mack Sennett.

As I sometimes walk around Hollywood—and it is possible with great strength of character to walk in this land of the freeways—I can see some of the physical changes that have taken place in the once small country town whose name is synonymous with movies. Where the famous old Hollywood Hotel stood now towers a modern bank and office building.

The Hollywood Hotel was the oldest landmark in the plaster city until it was torn down several years ago. Built in 1902, when nothing but barley fields and orange groves flourished in the area, it epitomized the entire growth of the movie metropolis. In its latter years it was a faded, rambling structure with streetcars clattering by. But it still contained mementoes of its heyday when it was the social center for screen celebrities. On the ceiling of the old-fashioned dining room were the gold-starred names of luminaries, among them Rudolph Valentino, Douglas Fairbanks, William Farnum, Norma Shearer and Alla Nazimova, who had supped there regularly.

Valentino's bed was reputed still to be in the hotel. Whenever a lady guest complained that she did not sleep comfortably, the manager told her, "You probably slept in Valentino's bed."

When the Hollywood Hotel originally opened as a real-estate development project, it had thirty-three rooms and two baths. Later it grew to one hundred rooms and sixty-six baths. Hollywood, at the turn of the century, was a lonely and distant suburb of Los Angeles, connected with the city by a single-track car line. The hotel had its own power and ice plants and was a completely self-contained unit in the rural wilderness.

From 1902 to 1912 the Hollywood Hotel was a country resort. From 1912 to 1925, when the leading men of the movies supplanted the oranges, it became the focal point for the glamour children of the silent screen. The Who's Who of the movie capital lived there. Louis B. Mayer and Irving Thalberg shared a suite. Other registered guests were Jack Warner, Jesse Lasky, Carl Laemmle, Wallace Reid, Hobart Bosworth, Gloria Swanson, Lon Chaney and Pola Negri. The film folk would meet on the front porch every evening. On Thursday nights the rugs in the lobby were rolled back and the profiles made merry, dancing to "Alexander's Ragtime Band" and "Kiss Me Again."

Life was quite uncomplicated then. One profile leaped into the room of his leading lady from the garden. The next day the manager ordered cactus planted in front of all the ground-floor apartments. When this did not stop the traffic, the ground-floor windows were nailed shut.

Valentino and Jean Acker, both celluloid stars, lived at the hotel. One evening in November 1919 Valentino requested the key to Miss Acker's suite. The room clerk refused to let him have it. Valentino informed him that Miss Acker and he had been married that day and intended to occupy the same apartment. The hotel management was not convinced and the great lover of the screen almost did not get to spend his wedding night with his wife.

Unorthodox living was already a hallmark of Hollywood. The walls of three suites were torn out to make room for William Farnum, a $10,-000-a-week star, and his retinue of seventeen. Greta Garbo registered incognito.

When sound came to the screen and newer hotels were constructed, the Hollywood Hotel gradually lost its movie clientele. In 1937 the hotel figured in a picture called *Hollywood Hotel*, but the picture had little to do with the real Hollywood Hotel.

In its time the Hollywood Hotel witnessed the birth, growth and glamour of Hollywood, but its guests did not think of themselves as particularly glamorous at the time. Alla Nazimova once told Joe McLellan, manager of the hotel, "We were too busy then to think about glamour. We simply worked hard and played hard."

Shortly before the hotel was torn down I talked to some of the residents. A few of them had been there for as long as thirty-five years and were concerned about their accommodations when the hotel would be dismantled. One old lady, rocking away on the shabby front porch, overlooking the streetcars and the crowds on garish Hollywood Boulevard, said, "I don't want to go to heaven. I want to stay here."

At the corner of Sunset Boulevard and La Brea Avenue was the quaint, Old English-style Charlie Chaplin studio. In front of it, in the midst of a lemon grove, stood a stately white house that had once been occupied by Chaplin's brother, Sydney. Today the residence has been replaced by a supermarket. And the studio, where Chaplin produced *The Gold Rush*, *City Lights* and *Modern Times*, is no longer turning out super pictures but cinematic canned goods, mostly for television.

The Chaplin studio was a small, neat, compact movie plant built in 1918 when La Brea was nothing but a dirt road running through the ubiquitous orange and lemon groves. The first picture Chaplin shot there was *A Dog's Life*, a two-reeler. He also made *The Kid*, *Shoulder Arms*, *The Circus*, *The Great Dictator* and all his other great movies there.

In 1951 Roland Totheroh, who had been Chaplin's cameraman for more than thirty-five years, took me on a tour of the studio. There were only two sound stages on the premises. Totheroh showed me the street that was built for *City Lights*, the little courtyard used in *The Great Dictator*, the open-air sky backing constructed for a sidewalk-café scene in *Monsieur Verdoux*. He pointed out where sets had been covered with artificial snow for *The Gold Rush* and the big, wooden gears from *Modern Times* stored in the prop shed.

We looked into the little bungalow, once a stable, where Chaplin worked. It was furnished with a settee and chairs and had a kitchen and dinette. Chaplin kept a cook around to prepare his meals. He would pore over the stories and scripts of his pictures there.

Chaplin, who made no more than one picture every four years, would keep his key people, about twenty of them, on the payroll between productions.

Totheroh led me to the old-fashioned corner dressing room that was "always reserved for the leading lady." The first to occupy it was Edna Purviance, then Lita Grey, Georgia Hale, Virginia Cherrill, Paulette Goddard and Martha Raye.

He showed me footprints in the sidewalk near the cement shop signed "Charlie Chaplin, Jan. 21, 1918," the date when the cement was originally laid. We looked at an old pine tree, more than forty feet high, "that was my height when I first came here."

The studio, not being used by Chaplin at the time, was already being rented out, for the production of religious movies and television films. Totheroh told me: "There's little activity now. Chaplin finally consented to rent the studio out so it wouldn't become dilapidated. Of course, you know, television—they're in one day and gone the next. Chaplin takes his time and works on his pictures until he has them just right."

Near the studio entrance Totheroh showed me a little doghouse and fire plug that were once the studio mascot's. "He's gone now. Boots, a black cat, has been living there for five years. Chaplin is crazy about cats," Totheroh said.

We stood outside the modest, antiquated studio, which was little more than a collection of ramshackle buildings that the genius of Chaplin had fired in the making of his great movies.

In the sunny afternoon the traffic roared past Sunset and La Brea, where a used-car lot, gas station and drive-in restaurant faced the old, slightly faded, yet majestic studio.

One of the few oases in the Hollywood desert is the little Movie Theater on Fairfax Avenue where silent pictures are shown exclusively. As far as I know, it is the only theater of its kind not only in Los Angeles but in the entire United States. The Movie does not have a flashy front, uniformed ushers, double features or popcorn. For an admission price of five cents for the youngsters and sixty cents for the older customers who are young in heart, it dispenses every day but Sunday at 7:00 and 9:00 P.M. a silent feature film together with selected cartoons, comedy shorts and cliffhangers, or serials.

The Movie Theater is the creation of John and Dorothy Hampton, who hail from Oklahoma City. They built the Movie in 1941 and it was opened to the public in February 1942. Although it is no motion-picture palazzo, the Movie is sound both architecturally and aesthetically. It has full staggered seating, a bowl-shaped floor, excellent acoustical design and a pleasing monochrome brown color scheme.

John runs the projection machines and synchronizes records to the films, while his wife handles the box office. The front is plain and minus supercolossals. There are carefully assembled displays of stills and informative material about the program playing within and a neatly lettered sign dedicating the Movie Theater "to those who cherish the movies as the living history-record of our changing styles, manners and social customs."

The Movie is the only theater in Hollywood devoted to the art of the silent film. Lettered in a frame near the box office is this paragraph from William deMille's fine book, *Hollywood Saga*: "The highest function of motion picture art is to express the people to themselves. The voice of the screen is the voice of common humanity trying to put into living words its thoughts and emotions, its ideals and its dreams."

The Movie fulfills these aims to the best of its ability. Its admission prices and its surroundings are geared to the majority. It provides an hour or two of retrospection for older people and a glimpse into another world for the younger folk. It revives the pantomimic genius of Chaplin, the naïveté of Pickford, the clean-cut comedy of Lloyd, the spectacle of Griffith, the eternal adventure of Fairbanks, the indigenous wit of Rogers, the romantic appeal of Valentino.

The good movies of the past deserve to be seen. They should be as accessible as the good books of the past. But the few old movies that are revived from time to time around the country are usually oohed and ahed over by long-hairs or cackled at by bird brains. At the Movie, old films are revived soberly and sensibly without pretension or oleo atmosphere. The Hamptons conscientiously and unostentatiously present old pictures without fuss, fanfare or snobbery, unlike the pretentious Museum of Modern Art Film Library in New York, the weak-wrist, cultish Coronet Theater in Los Angeles and other self-appointed custodians of celluloid. The Movie takes old movies away from the aesthetes and the promoters and gives them back to the public, to whom they rightfully belong.

Among its patrons, who seem to prefer the better old-time pictures to most of Hollywood's present-day product, are young people who never saw a silent film and are curious about the early "flickers," college students who take their movies somewhat more seriously, and actors, directors and technicians from the Hollywood studios who want to re-examine some of the original epics of the screen. Some of the current stars, as well as the old profiles themselves, show up on occasion.

"Television hurt us at first," says John Hampton, "but business gradually came back. Interest is now more intense in old movies. Silent movies have become a sort of specialized thing, like symphony or opera or ballet. But silent pictures could be more popular and universal in their appeal than talking pictures. Now we have a whole generation to whom silents are a different language. They have to read a little, but they don't like to read."

Within the twilight premises of the Movie there flourishes a convivial spirit. An infrequent celebrant may want to know why those blokes on the screen do not talk. And those customers who can lip read can sometimes derive added amusement from some of the scenes. At a recent showing of an ancient opus, an actor, in a silent deathbed sequence, said sadly by way of bidding his tearful wife farewell: "I'll die and no mistake if they shoot this scene again."

A typical program might consist of *The Sea Lion*, a 1921 drama of whaling ships, adventure and retribution, with Hobart Bosworth and Bessie Love; Houdini, the handcuff king, in *The Master Mystery* serial; Koko the Kangaroo in an early animated cartoon; and Mack Sennett's *All Night Long* with Harry Langdon.

Come in and see gnarled, grizzled Captain Bosworth rescue his long-lost daughter, wide-eyed Bessie Love, from the raging sea. See the ship's crew battling officers with belaying pins. See the wonderful happenings aboard the ship of a half-mad captain who sails the seas from the Arctic to the tropics. And see Koko the Kangaroo flying to the North Pole in a surrealistic zeppelin; sad-eyed Harry Langdon making with the slapstick; and Houdini, as Operative Locke of the Department of Justice, embroiled in a hair-raising plot involving a giant automaton, a temptress named Deluxe Dora, and the Madagascar Madness in episode five of *The Master Mystery* serial (1918).

The images float across the screen, larger than life, with that strange, disembodied poetry of the silent film, unencumbered by earthbound dialogue, existing in their own symphonic, ballet world which the sound film, at its best, has never yet fully recaptured.

Here are pratfalls and passion, unabashed emotion and a kind of primitive grandeur; the clean, rangy sharpness of pre-panchromatic photography; the sense of voyaging and discovery of those pioneering, halcyon days of Hollywood.

The lights go on and the show is over. The next one goes on in a few minutes at 9:00 P.M. when the captain, the kangaroo, the comic and the handcuff king will do their stuff again through the magic of the movies.

Next week: Elmo Lincoln in the original *Tarzan of the Apes* with Enid Markey; Charley Chase and Oliver Hardy in *Be Your Age*; and episode six of *The Master Mystery*. Bring the kiddies.

And, sitting in the Movie Theater, one naturally philosophizes about the movies and speculates about their past and their future. What is it that once attracted untold millions all over the world to see these giant moving images on a screen? Was it some bright, vividly remembered childhood dream, illuminated in the warm, womblike dark? Was it an escape from a less glamorous and more cruel world outside? Was it a neurotic and juvenile withdrawal from reality and the easy entry into a fairyland where wars, death and disaster were only make-believe?

Perhaps as the fast-moving world, as you and I, mature—and as Hollywood has failed to keep pace with us and the world around us—we have now begun to see more clearly than ever the movies' lack of maturity. Whatever it is that once attracted audiences to the movies and whatever it is that has lessened this attraction, the urge to see movies still exists in good measure—as the few good films prove. But today most movies are not good and audiences have flocked to television instead. Television is cheaper, more easily accessible and offers more variety—including some of the better old movies that Hollywood made.

TV is a wonderful way to reassess the old movies in the privacy and comfort of one's home. You can see some of the best—as well as the worst—of the old movies on television. And the good Hollywood movies, mostly those made up to the latish Thirties, are better than ever, particularly when viewed without distraction on TV. If you are interested, you will note that the credits on the best of these older movies are usually brief (unlike today's preposterously long credits—or rather discredits) and that there are often no producers, only directors, writers and technicians, listed. As I have contended at some length earlier, it is the directors who make the movies and who will one day again have to make them if Hollywood is to try to regain the great, ardent audiences it once had—on a television screen or off.

In the past decade or so Hollywood's production, box-office receipts and attendance have been approximately halved. Today about 50 per cent of Hollywood's audience is not in the United States, where moviegoers are shopping carefully for entertainment, but abroad, where housing is generally substandard and people like to get out as much as they can and where television has not yet taken hold. But housing in those areas will inevitably improve and television will inevitably take hold. And where will that leave Hollywood then? Even now the movie studios are surviving largely on the sale of their old movies to TV—and on income derived from sale of their real estate and from drilling for oil on studio property. And many movie studios have been belatedly forced into television production themselves.

But, in some form or other, whether on a television screen or not, and whether made in Hollywood studios or not, movies will assuredly still continue to enchant and enthrall many millions. And who will inherit this great and exciting medium of the movies? Not the pimps and panderers, the fags and the flesh peddlers, the press agents and promoters. No, not the hucksters and hustlers, the stooges and sycophants, the poseurs and pranksters, the shysters and shoddy merchants, the bully boys and the money boys. No, movies, to continue to exist and draw audiences, will have to be made by the artists, by the Kurosawas, the Fellinis, the Rossellinis. Hollywood will have to decide whether it favors art or industry—indicatively, it has always referred to itself as "the industry"—and, if it is to be the former, it will have to reaffirm the role of the creative moviemaker. For the mighty movie industry of multimillion-dollar investments is founded on the fragile dreams of a few artists, on small pictures with big ideas. The names and the reputations and the movie money and manipulations fade almost as fast as the celluloid on which they are reared. Where are the snows—and the stars and starmakers—of yesteryear? All that remains is not the production edifice, the profile or the publicity, but the screen accomplishment, the elusive, evanescent idea embodied on film, the intent, the imagination. That is all that really matters and all that is at the base of this vast pyramid of studios, theaters, actors, actresses, technical experts and others that constitute the motion-picture "industry." It is easy to forget this. You realize this when you skim through the pages of moviedom's past.

And there is no rule that says the movies will have to be made in Hollywood. The movies originally went west for the sunshine and the California topography. Today, the sunshine has been smogged over and, what is worse, the intellectual climate has become hazy, too. And movies no longer need Hollywood's sound stages. Today all the world's a stage—movies can be filmed anywhere under any conditions with advanced technical equipment. And, when the movies get out of Smogville on the Pacific, the results are usually the better for it. As one old-time moviemaker told me: "The people who make movies don't go out and find the lives of people any more. I think they ought to burn up the big studios and go out into the world and make movies. It's folly to build sets. The real thing is better."

And there is no rule either that says the movies have to remain in the familiar mold they have been in for these many years. Thomas Edison, who can rightfully be called the founder of the American film, had some relevant thoughts on the subject. In a dinner given him in 1924 by more than 600 representatives of the motion-picture industry on his seventy-seventh birthday, he said: "I believe as I have always believed that you control the most powerful instrument in the world for good or evil. Whatever part I have played in its development was mainly along mechanical lines. The far more important development of the motion picture as a medium for artistic efforts and as an educational factor is in your hands. Because I was working before most of you were born, I am going to bore you with a little advice. Remember that you are servants of the public, and never let a desire for money or power prevent you from giving to the public the best work of which you are capable. It is not the quantity of riches that counts; it's the quality which produces happiness, where that is possible. I thank you for your kindness in remembering me, and wish you a prosperous, useful and honorable future."

And, in *The Diary and Sundry Observations of Thomas A. Edison*, Edison had this further to say: "It may seem curious, but the money end of the movies never hit me the hardest. The feature that did appeal to me about the whole thing was the educational possibilities I thought I could see. I had some glowing dreams about what the camera could be made to do and ought to do in teaching the world things it needed to know—teaching it in a more vivid, direct way.

"I figured that after the novelty wore off the camera would either be taken up by the big educators and pushed as a new agency in the schools—or that it would be developed mostly along straight amusement lines for entertainment and commercial purposes. I guess up to date the entertainment and commercial purposes have won."

And he added: "I do not believe that any other single agency of progress has the possibilities for a great and permanent good to humanity that I can see in the motion picture. And those possibilities are only beginning to be touched."

Edison wrote those words in the Twenties. They are still pertinent and timely in today's television era. And they bring up the question of how many Hollywood movies have anything to do with life or, as one critic put it, deal with "some recognizable fragment of our common experience." To what use has Hollywood put the tools of its trade, both mechanical and human? In a world wracked by vast, epic events, Hollywood is still peddling its piddling shadow plays and "the strut and trade of charms on the ivory stages." Where, in a time "of crisis and dismay," as the dangerous flood of history rises, is the strict and adult cinematic pen that, as W. H. Auden wrote, "can warn us from the colours and the consolations, the showy arid works, reveal the squalid shadow of academy and garden, make action urgent and its nature clear" and give us that "nearer insight to resist the expanding fear, the savaging disaster"? How can Hollywood find its way back, "by almost obliterated tracks," from decades of easy box-office celluloid to the more difficult and remunerative work of art that, in the words of Dylan Thomas, pays "no praise or wages" but labors, on behalf of moviegoers, for "the common wages of their most secret heart."

Perhaps these were some of the things intimated in the best of the screen's achievements to date. I am reminded of that monumental scene in the epic Russian silent film *Arsenal*, where the mad horses tear over the icebound steppes bearing the body of their master to his grave. As they fly like wraiths over the snowy expanse, they are depicted, in a surrealistic passage of sheer, overwhelming screen poetry, singing a song of praise to their dead master.

And there is the opening of another film by the same director, Alexander Dovjhenko, who may well be the most fiery talent that the film has yet nurtured. It was called *Shors* and was made in 1939. The film faded in on a vast, somnolent field of verdant sunflowers which suddenly and stunningly came alive with clashing sabers and the deadly sounds of war.

There was, too, the sordid sweetness of *La Maternelle*; the wrenching, elegaic voyage into the past of *Un Carnet de Bal*; the classic, stripped-clean comedy of Buster Keaton's *The Navigator*; the luminous pathos of *City Lights*; the high-wire melodrama of *Variety*; the massive, methodical realism of *Greed*. These will not soon be forgotten.

These were all the works of individual, unfettered artists—most of them outside of Hollywood—who rose above the mechanics and the market places of the movies to achieve the personal, pinpointed, uncontaminated screen statement. As a confirmed moviegoer—and one who still loves the medium of movies if not the tedium of most movies—I can only reaffirm this belief in a personal screen expression as my filmic credo.

As Hollywood completes its half-century cycle and the founders of the movie industry—the DeMilles and Laskys and Mayers—die off, some with trumpeting and testimonials and others, like the pioneer director J. Searle Dawley, anonymously and unsung, at the Motion Picture Country House for needy film folk—they are taking the movie edifice they built with them. They have seen to it that the movie business, as we know it, should decline and fall with them. And perhaps that is all for the best.

It is fashionable to speak well of the dead; the funerals of the movie moguls are awash in crocodile tears and such fine phrases as "great contributions to the motion-picture industry," "the motion picture has lost a great and forceful leader," "he gave greatly of himself" and "he will be missed and mourned for many years to come." But the plain, harsh fact of the matter is that almost all of these tycoons were arrogant, evil, avaricious old men. Much of the best that was accomplished in Hollywood under them was achieved in spite of them, not because of them. They preached of the good, noble and beautiful, and they themselves fostered in their lives and works the evil, the ignoble, the ugly. The moguls championed love of mother and family in their films and did not use "damn" or "hell" on the screen the while they debauched, debased and defiled the individual and the idea in real life. They kept their young mistresses—and discarded the old masters. In their hands the movies were not an art, not even, as Harry Cohn, one of them, had said, a business—but a racket. They built an empire on lies, distortion and drivel; on the fast buck and also—as it turned out—on quicksand.

In Hollywood there is no one as pathetic as an ex-tycoon. The late Louis B. Mayer, in his day the mightiest and most feared Hollywood mogul of them all, having been booted out of M-G-M by an even bigger tycoon, his New York boss, Nicholas Schenck (who was, in turn, later booted out by *his* bosses, the bankers), spent his last days a rather lonely and thoroughly inconsequential cinema citizen, just like many a lesser panjandrum whom he had jettisoned in his time. At one point Mayer even hired a press agent to solicit publicity for him, although at M-G-M he had been as unapproachable to reporters as the Grand Lama.

After his departure from M-G-M in 1951 Mayer maintained a fairly modest office in Beverly Hills. With his uniformed chauffeur tagging along, he would shop for meat at the Farmer's Market and he liked to go into the butcher's locker where the sides hung to select prime cuts. He did a good deal of walking in Bel Air, trailed by his limousine. And nobody feared him or even cared about him any more. "The old gray Mayer," the Hollywood saying went, "he ain't what he used to be."

Already Mayer is remembered by a good many people not so much for the mostly thin and tasteless movies he made at M-G-M but for the rich and appetizing chicken soup that bore his name at the studio. Too many cooks may have spoiled Mayer's movie broths, but Mayer's chicken soup was unexcelled. The soup, with fat, succulent, nourishing pieces of chicken afloat in it, was a meal in itself. At first it was served only in Mayer's private dining room, but, as its fame spread, it was featured on the regular restaurant menu, where it long remained one of the most popular dishes at the studio.

"It was his special chicken soup," says Howard Strickling, his long-time press agent and front-runner (who is today press agent and front-runner for the mogul who succeeded Mayer at M-G-M). "He was a great lover of soup. It originated at his home. When he took over the studio, he took the commissary chef to his home, where he learned how to make it. It was his special chicken soup. There were pieces of chicken in it, good old Jewish style, with rice or matzo balls or noodles. It could be served any way at M-G-M. It is still served at the studio. It was thirty-five cents for a bowl. It's still the same price."

And so, as an ex-Hollywood chronicler, I beg leave to take this occasion to say goodbye, not to Louis B. Mayer, but to Louis B. Mayer's chicken soup.

INDEX

Abbott, George, 175
Abraham Lincoln, 3
Academy Awards, 2, 14, 28–29, 49, 68, 169, 174, 176, 182, 205, 210, 309, 310, 319, 341, 344, 355, 373, 396–99, 403, 419
Academy of Motion Picture Arts and Sciences, 14, 150, 252, 331, 344, 373, 396, 397; *see also* Academy Awards
Ace in the Hole, 201
Acker, Jean, 442
Across the Pacific, 203, 269
Action in the North Atlantic, 269, 357
Actors Studio, 224, 232, 237; *see also* Strasberg, Lee
Adamic, Louis, 151
Adams, Mark, 84–85
Adams, Nick, 291
Adamson, Harold, 28
Adler, E. Maurice (Buddy), 185, 197, 198, 235, 336
Adventures of Mark Twain, The, 357
Adventures of Robin Hood, The, 181, 211, 299, 300
Adventures of Tarzan, The, 354
Adventures of Tom Sawyer, The, 309
After Hours Poetry, 58
Agar, John, 25
Agee, James, 153–54, 157
Air Force, 313
Alamo, The, 81
Albert, Katherine, 91–94
Alexander, Roy, 147, 148
"Alexander's Ragtime Band," 442
Alexander's Ragtime Band, 208
Alexander the Great, 418
Alice in Wonderland, 309
All About Eve, 223–24
Allen, Fred, 403
Allenberg, Bert, 275
All Night Long, 446
All the King's Men, 418

Allyson, June, 22, 83
Aly Khan, 24, 224
Ameche, Don, 136, 137
American Cinema Editors, 163
American Cinematographer, 150
American Film Co., 299
American Mercury, 13, 74, 123
American Mutoscope and Biograph Co., 374
American Society of Cinematographers, 163
American Tragedy, An, 207
Ames, Stephen, 67
Amfitheatrof, Daniele, 404
Amy, George, 211, 311–12
Anderson, Gilbert M. (Bronco Billy), 340–44
Anderson, Lindsay, 179
Anderson, Sherwood, 186
Andrews, Dana, 165
animal actors, 69, 284, 348, 399
Anna Karenina, 47
Anna Lucasta, 418
anti-trust suits, 433–34
Arbuckle, Fatty, 337, 345
Archerd, Army, 19, 29, 408–10
Arnaz, Desi, 285, 286
Arnow, Max, 277–80
Around the World in 80 Days, 53, 96, 194–98, 308
Arsenal, 418, 450
Ars Magna Lucis et Umbrae (The Great Art of Light and Shadow), 430
Asher, Jerry, 108
Asphalt Jungle, The, 223, 228
assistant directors, 315–16
Associated Press, 26
Association of Motion Picture Producers, 36, 42, 77, 100–1, 377
Astaire, Fred, 189
Atlantic Monthly magazine, 158
Auden, W. H., 450
August, Edwin, 367

August, Joseph, 314
Austin, Jerry, 244

Baby Doll, 322
Bacall, Lauren, 150, 235, 257, 260, 265, 266, 268, 405–6
Background to Danger, 204
Back Street, 25
Bacon, Lloyd, 345
Baker, Gladys, 221–22, 225–26
Balázs, Béla, 435
Ball, Lucille, 285–88
Bandit Makes Good, The, 342
Bankhead, Tallulah, 285
Bank of America, 14, 171
Banky, Vilma, 369–71
Bara, Theda, 327, 365, 368, 377
Barker, Lex, 354–57
Barney's Beanery, 29
Barry, Fern, 321
Barrymore, Ethel, 319
Barrymore, John, 6, 376, 417
Barrymore, Lionel, 6, 10
Barthelmess, Richard, 208, 431
Bartlett, Hall, 149
Bartlett, Sy, 386
Baruch, Bernard M., 178
Battleground, 148, 210
Battle of Elderbush Gulch, The, 430
Baur, Harry, 305
Bautzer, Greg, 60
Beau Geste, 361, 362
Beckley, Paul V., 140
Bee, Molly, 91
Beebe, Lucius, 17
Beery, Noah, 131, 132
Beery, Wallace, 440
Behind the Screen, 178
Bel Geddes, Barbara, 322
Bell, Alexander Graham, 136
Bell, Book and Candle, 279
Belmont Theater, 128–30
Beloved Infidel, 33
Benchley, Robert, 258
Bengal Tiger, 182
Ben Gets a Drink and Is Ducked, 342

453

Ben-Hur, 69–70, 133–34, 152, 299–301, 336, 366, 396
Bennett, Constance, 34, 128, 371
Bennett, Joan, 32, 186, 332
Benny, Jack, 69, 270–71, 331, 399–400
Bergman, Ingrid, 244, 270, 271, 330
Berle, Milton, 332
Bern, Paul, 325–26
Bernhardt, Sarah, 122, 340
Best, Barbara, 60
Best Years of Our Lives, The, 10, 165, 422
Beverly Hills, Calif., 217, 326, 337, 369
Beverly Hills Hotel, 22, 96, 150, 371, 413
Beverly Hilton Hotel, 399–400
Beverly Wilshire Hotel, 205, 391–95
Beymer, Stan, 58
Beyond Civilization to Texas, 402–3
Be Your Age, 447
Bible, 422
Bicycle Thief, 423
Binyon, Claude, 421
Bioff, Willie, 59–60
Biograph studio, 9, 349, 367, 373, 374
Bioscope, 439
Birth of a Nation, The, 1, 2, 6, 7, 9, 10, 13–15, 354
Black Fury, 211
Black Scorpion, The, 320
Blanke, Henry, 110, 181–82, 203
Blaustein, Julian, 61
Blondell, Joan, 394
Blood and Sand, 365
Blowitz, Bill, 257
Blue Angel, The, 380
Blue Light, The, 8
Body and Soul, 313, 418
Bogart, Humphrey, 51, 181, 182, 203, 204, 217, 246, 252, 256–71, 281, 292, 297, 384, 386, 405–6
Bohemia Club, 380–81
Bolender, Albert and Ida, 225, 226, 240
Bolger, Ray, 386
Booth, Edwin, 269
Borge, Victor, 382
Borzage, Frank, 362
Bosworth, Hobart, 442, 446
Bourgin, Simon, 42
Boyer, Charles, 150, 327
Boy with Green Hair, The, 67
Bow, Clara, 376
Bowdon, Dorris, 23
B Pictures, 182
Brabin, Charles, 368
Bracker, Lew, 292
Brackett, Charles, 14, 373

Branchi, Iris, 393
Brand, Harry, 29, 42, 96, 146, 234, 407
Brando, Marlon, 94, 164, 189, 235–36, 437
Brasselle, Keefe, 394
Brave Bulls, The, 313
Braveheart, 431
Brave New World, 436
Brave One, The, 419
Breen office, 263
Brennan, Walter, 125
Brenon, Herbert, 360–63
Bright, John, 109
Brinkman, Paul, 107
Brisson, Carl, 382
Broadway Rose, 103
Broadway Theater, 354
Broken Arrow, 431
Broken Blossoms, 1, 2, 8, 13, 14, 414
Bromfield, Louis, 258
Bronco Billy, *see* Anderson, Gilbert M.
Bronson, Betty, 361
Brontë sisters, 288
Brooks, Richard, 31, 262, 267
Broun, Heywood, 423
Brown, Clarence, 173–74, 292, 293, 435
Brown Derby, 29, 385, 401
Brown Derby Cook Book, 403
Browning, Robert, 11
Brown of Harvard, 371
Brute Force, 422
Brynner, Yul, 388
Bublichki Restaurant, 388
Buck, Pearl, 151
Buckner, Robert, 425
Bulldog Drummond, 309
Bundle of Joy, 86
Bungle in the Jungle, 402, 403
Burns, Fritz B., 14
Burns, George, 27
Burns, Lillian, 175
Burrows, Abe, 179
Burstyn, Joseph, 423–24
Bushman, Francis X., 355, 356, 368
Bus Stop, 220, 221, 223, 231, 235, 237, 239, 241
Butler, Nicholas Murray, 103
Butterfield 8, 86
Butterworth, Charlie, 258
Byron, James, 408

Cabinet of Dr. Caligari, The, 414
Cagney, James, 46, 256, 263, 385
Caine Mutiny, The, 264
Calhoun, Rory, 52, 281
California, legend of, 438
California Bank, 367–68
California Country Club, 351
California Racquet Club, 22

Call of the Traumerei, The, 430
Call of the Yukon, 299
Callow, Reggie, 315
cameramen, 312–15
Cameron, Kate, 152
Campbell, Jo-Ann, 80
Can-Can, 409
Cantor, Eddie, 27
Canutt, Yakima, 301
Capra, Frank, 2, 9, 10, 161–62, 178, 188, 199, 205, 345, 351, 362, 370, 385, 428
Captain Blood, 311
Captain Swagger, 369
Carmen, 343
Carnegie Hall, 124, 126
Carnovsky, Morris, 108
Carol, Martine, 195–96
Caron, Leslie, 270
Carr, Harry, 441
Carroll, Harrison, 29, 115–16
Carroll, Madeleine, 133
Carter, Richard, 404
Casablanca, 165, 211, 357, 387, 388
Cassell, Jeff, 262
casting director, 316–19
Cathay, 199
Cat on a Hot Tin Roof, 322
CBS, 287
censorship, motion picture, 6–7, 11, 15, 76, 264, 269, 420–26, 431; taboos, 7, 264, 421, 425
censorship, press, 11, 41–46, 76–78, 123–33, 135–38, 147, 316; *see also* press
Cerasoli, Luisa, 393
Champion, 187
Chandler, Jeff, 275
Chandler, Norman, 276
Chandler, Raymond, ix, 239
Chaney, Lon, 442
Chaplin, Charlie, 13, 14, 98, 147, 337, 343, 345, 350, 359, 367, 397, 420, 427, 443–45
Chaplin, Sydney, 443
Charge of the Light Brigade, The, 211, 299, 300, 302, 311
Charlie Bow-Tie Proceeds, 107
Chase, Borden, 65
Chase, Charley, 447
Chasen, Dave, 17, 257, 258, 261, 384–86, 390
Chasen's restaurant, 18, 47, 220, 261, 384–86, 390
Chatter magazine, 391–92
Chayefsky, Paddy, 242
Chekhov, Michael, 232
Cherrill, Virginia, 444
Chevalier, Maurice, 410
Child of the Ghetto, 431
Churchill, Douglas, ix, 45–46, 434
Church of the Good Shepherd, 369–71

Cimarron, 299, 380
Cinderfella, 95
CinemaScope, 232, 321, 407, 435
Circus, The, 98, 443
Ciro's night club, 18, 112, 113, 380, 388, 406–8
Citizen Kane, 10, 228
City Lights, 98, 443, 450
Clark, Dane, 109
Clash by Night, 230
Clift, Montgomery, 437
Clifton, Elmer, 4
Clock, The, 158
Clurman, Harold, 281
Clutching Hand, The, 357
Cobra, 365
Coburn, Bob, 280–82
Coburn, Charles, 387
Cock'n Bull restaurant, 382
Coconut Grove, 27, 174, 327, 398
Cocteau, Jean, 307
Cohan, George M., 6
Cohen, John S., 154
Cohen, Mickey, 17
Cohn, Ben, 105
Cohn, Harry, 44, 52, 57–58, 62, 115, 175–78, 188, 191, 207, 238, 246, 275, 277–80, 285, 407, 451
Colbert, Claudette, 330, 405
Collier's magazine, 220, 288, 322
Collins, Joan, 22
Colman, Ronald, 361, 370
Columbia Pictures, 52, 57–58, 62, 114, 115, 175, 177, 188, 189, 191, 207, 223, 235, 245–46, 275, 277–81, 283, 397, 433
Columbia University, 103
columnists, 16–17, 21–40, 46–47, 98–99
Common Council for American Unity, 151
Common Ground, 151
Communism and Communists, 10, 62–63, 148, 285–86, 418–19
Compton, Walter, 61
Confidential magazine, 40, 50–53, 78–79, 81, 116, 238
Confidential Agent, 150
Connolly, Mike, 21, 58, 400, 408, 410
Coogan, Jackie, 366–67
Cook, Joe, 384, 385
Cooper, Gary, 244, 256, 264, 269, 280, 302, 388, 419, 437
Cooper, Dr. Stanley, 331–34
Coote, Bob, 261
Coronet magazine, 12, 183
Coronet Theater, 445
Corrado, Gino, 386–89
Corset Model, The, 373
Country Girl, The, 271
Covered Wagon, The, 362

Coward, Noel, 196, 405
Cowboy and the Lady, The, 374
Cowles, Fleur, 236
Crabbe, Buster, 354
Craft, Roy, 220–21, 232–33, 235
Crail, Schuyler, 404
Crane, Lionel, 40
Crawford, Joan, 82, 90–94, 98, 269, 327, 328, 331, 332, 371
Crime Without Passion, 304–6
Crisler, Benjamin R., 123–25, 127–35, 140, 399
Crisp, Donald, 13, 14, 370
Cristal, Linda, 80–81
Crocker, Harry, 98–99, 293–94
Cromwell, Richard, 132
Crooked Banker, The, 431
Crosby, Bing, 73, 100, 247, 327, 328, 331–33, 345, 377, 378, 390
Crosby, Bob, 382
Crosby, Dixie Lee, 333
Crosby, Everett, 382
Crosby, Larry, 382
Crossroads of New York, 351
Crowd, The, 188, 414, 432
Crowley, Arthur, 40
Crowther, Bosley, 53, 123–30, 140, 141, 156, 299, 434
Croy, Homer, 13
Cry of the Werewolf, The, 115
Cry Terror!, 215
Cue magazine, 144
Cukor, George, 17
Culver City, Calif., 172, 300, 322–23
Cummings, Jack, 173
Cummings, Robert, 380
Curious Case of Meredith Stanhope, The, 430
Curtis, Tony, 78, 89
Curtiz, Michael, 107, 165, 168, 211–12, 260–61, 311, 415
Custard's Last Stand, 344
Custer's Last Stand, 15
Cyclopanorama, 347

Daily Variety, 19, 25, 38, 53–57, 59–71, 119, 152, 153, 363, 408, 410, 436
Daily Worker, 62
Daly, Augustin, 357
Darin, Bobby, 80
Darrach, Henry, 147
Darvi, Bella, 406
Daughter of the Gods, 361
Davies, Marion, 99, 376–77
Davis, Bette, 82, 115, 297, 315, 317, 321
Davis, Joan, 351
Davis, Sammy, Jr., 53, 406
Dawley, J. Searle, 451
Day, Doris, 80

Dead End, 127, 180
Dean, James, 82, 288–92
Dean, Loomis, 407
Decker, John, 385
Dee, Sandra, 25
Defiant Ones, The, 419
de Havilland, Olivia, 288, 321
Delaney, Frank, 238
Del Rio, Dolores, 376
Del Ruth, Roy, 345
DeMille, Cecil B., 13, 66–67, 199–201, 210, 217, 362, 367–68, 370, 399, 451
deMille, William C., ix, 200, 426, 445
Dempster, Carol, 9
De Sica, Vittorio, 150, 160, 420
Desilu Productions, 287
Des Moines Tribune, 156
Desperate Encounter, A, 431
Devil and Miss Jones, The, 308
Devil Is a Sissy, The, 316
Devotion, 288
de Wilde, Brandon, 207
Diamond Horseshoe, 364
Diary of Anne Frank, The, 102, 165–66, 207, 398, 435
Dienes, André de, 229
Dietrich, Marlene, 46, 47, 194, 197, 233–34, 327, 329, 330
Dietz, Howard, 133, 147
Dietz, Jorgen, 92–93
DiMaggio, Joe, 224
Dinosaur and the Missing Link, The, 319
Dinosaurus, 56
Dioptricks, 429
directors, 1, 2, 9, 10, 160–70, 177, 199–216, 298–308, 312, 314–16, 358–62
Directors Guild of America, 163, 207, 298
Disney, Walt, 151, 183–85, 217
Dmytryk, Edward, 390
Dr. Jekyll and Mr. Hyde, 365
Dr. Mabuse, 305
Dodge City, 105
Dodsworth, 127
Dog's Life, A, 443
Dolenz, George, 388–89
Donahue, Troy, 95
Don Juan, 426
Dostoevsky, Fëdor, 238
Double Indemnity, 68, 201
Dougherty, Jim, 222, 227–28, 238
Douglas, Gordon, 388
Douglas, Kirk, 419
Douglas, Melvyn, 7
Douglas, Nathan E., 419
Douglas, Robert, 131
Dovjhenko, Alexander, 450
Dowell, Mary, 106
Downes, Olin, 127–28
Down Memory Lane, 344
Drake, Betsy, 73

455

Dreams of a Rarebit Fiend, 339
Dream Street, 4, 8
Dreiser, Theodore, 207
Dressler, Marie, 350
Dreyer, Carl, 314
Dreyfus case, 431
Driscoll, Tex, 368
Drucker, Harry, 328–29
Duel in the Sun, 10, 68, 299, 300
Duke's Jester, The, or a Fool's Revenge, 374
Dunne, Irene, 75–76
Dupont, E. A., 2
Duse, Eleonora, 122
Dusel, André, 389
Dwan, Allan, 161
Dyer, Peter John, 2–3

Eagle, S. P., see Spiegel, Sam
Eagle-Lion studio, 344
Eason, B. Reeves, 211, 298–303, 311, 314
East of Eden, 289, 291
Eddie Cantor Story, The, 394
Eddy Duchin Story, The, 276
Edendale, Calif., 346–47, 349, 351
Edge of Darkness, 108
Edison, Thomas A., 338, 339, 428, 449
Edison studio, 340, 341, 367, 373, 374
Editor & Publisher, 45, 135
Edwards, Harry, 347
Egg and I, The, 110
Einfeld, Charles, 105, 106, 140, 141
Eisenhower, Dwight D., 44, 251
Eisenstein, Sergei, 8, 166, 303–5
Ekberg, Anita, 229
Elliott, Denholm, 70
El Morocco night club, 104
Emergo process, 435
Emerson, Ralph Waldo, 318
Emperor Jones, The, 431
End of St. Petersburg, The, 306
English, Richard, 23
Englishman's Trip to Paris from London, An, 373
Epstein, Dave, 118–20
Epstein, Julius, 191
Epstein, Milton, 66–67
Epstein, Philip, 191
Escape, The, 8
Esquire magazine, 133–34, 158, 186–87, 190, 210
Essanay studios, 342–43
Ettinger, Margaret, 24
Evans, Joan, 82
Every Girl Should Be Married, 67
Eviction, The, 431

Ex-Convict, The, 373, 431
Execution of Private Slovik, The, 419–20
Exodus, 166, 167, 419
Exploits of Elaine, 357

Fairbanks, Douglas, 309, 337, 367, 397, 442, 445
Fairbanks, Douglas, Jr., 91–94
Falconetti, 314
Famous Artists agency, 224, 230, 235, 437
Famous Players Co., 340
fan magazines, 24, 43, 45, 53, 72–96, 267
Farber, Manny, 148
Farewell to Arms, A, 162, 321
Farmer's Market, 219, 451
Farnum, William, 368, 442, 443
Farrell, Charles, 368–69, 371
Farrington, Ned, 118–19
Fatal Flirtation, 374
Faulkner, William, 105–6
Faye, Alice, 128
Fazenda, Louise, 348
Feldman, Charles, 224, 230, 238, 241
Fellini, Federico, 160, 420, 448
Fernandel, 195–96
Ferrer, Jose, 331
Fervent Years, 281
Field, Betty, 235
Fields, W. C., 316, 345, 385
55th Street Playhouse, 61, 142
film editor, 311–12
Films in Review, 153
Film Till Now, The, 306
Fink, Hymie, 326–28
Fires of St. John, The, 360
Fisher, Eddie, 82–89, 410
Fitzgerald, F. Scott, 33, 170, 188
Fitzmaurice, George, 309, 370
Five Graves to Cairo, 358, 360
5000 Fingers of Dr. T., The, 147, 189
Flaherty, Robert, 164
Flavin, Arthur, 368
Fleming, Victor, 206, 363
Florea, John, 403–4
Flossie's New Peach-Basket Hat, 374
Flowers of St. Francis, The, 423
Flynn, Errol, 34, 67, 107–8, 211, 269, 297, 382, 386, 411
Foolish Wives, 359
Forbes, Ralph, 361
Ford, Glenn, 83, 87–89
Ford, John, 140, 205, 209, 210, 314, 344
Foreign Correspondent, 308
Foreman, Carl, 187, 189, 418, 419
Forest Lawn Cemetery, 184, 377

For Her Sweetheart's Sake, 374
Fortune magazine, 277
42nd Street, 105
For Whom the Bell Tolls, 308
4D Man, 436
Four Horsemen of the Apocalypse, The, 380
Fourposter, The, 189
Fowler, Gene, 119
Fox, William, 135–38
Fox Films, 135, 426
Fox West Coast movie theater chain, 146, 174
Foy, Bryan, 182
Francis, Connie, 80, 95
Franco, Francisco, 128
Frank, Anne, 102, 166, 207, 398
Frank, Melvin, 148
Frankenheimer, John, 418
Franklin, Harold B., 353
Freeman, Dore, 117
Freeman, Y. Frank, 29, 207, 254, 389
French, Hugh, 235
Fresnay, Choteau, 119, 120
Freud, Sigmund, 248
Frey, Arno, 381
Friedrichsen, Frank, 404
Friendly Persuasion, 150
From Under My Hat, 32
Funicello, Annette, 79, 91
Furry, Elda, see Hopper, Hedda

Gable, Clark, 27, 235, 269, 272, 324, 327, 328, 369, 387
Gabor, Zsa Zsa, 218, 331, 332
Gallico, Paul, 158–59
Gang, Martin, 65
gangster pictures, 263–64
Garbo, Greta, 47, 98, 220, 265, 271, 272, 288, 292–94, 317, 324, 327, 386, 397, 443
Gardner, Ava, 39, 73, 80, 116–17, 189, 190, 324
Garfield, John, 62, 108–9, 251, 263, 313
Garland, Judy, 247, 257, 405, 434
Garmes, Lee, 305
Garrett, Betty, 28
Garson, Greer, 317, 324, 398
Gatling Gun Crews in Action, 373
Gay Illiterate, The, 23, 47, 93–94
Gaynor, Janet, 76–77, 210, 262, 368
General Film, 426
General Motors, 197, 269
German films, 8, 10, 311
Geronimi, Gerry, 184
Gershwin, George, 158, 179
Giant, 165, 207, 289–91
Giant Behemoth, The, 320

456

Gibbons, Cedric, 2
Gibbs, Wolcott, 122, 155, 421
Gibson, Helen, 355, 356
Gilbert, John, 170, 326
Gilbert, Justin, 141
Gilman, Lawrence, 124
Girl Was Young, The, 213
Gish, Dorothy, 1, 9
Gish, Lillian, 1, 3, 9
Give and Take, 343
Glad, Gladys, 279
Glass, George, 147, 148, 187, 189, 190
Glass Key, The, 46
Glazer, Alice, 294
Glennon, Bert, 310
Glenville, Peter, 400
Globe Theater, 131
Gobel, George, 295-96
Goddard, "Doc" Ervin Sillaman, 227
Goddard, Grace McKee, 222, 226, 227, 230
Goddard, Paulette, 444
Goddess, The, 242
Goebbels, Joseph, 8
Goetz, Edith Mayer, 174
Goetz, William, 174, 183, 192, 203, 363, 371
Going My Way, 422
Gold Diggers in Paris, 434
Golden Boy, 252
Golden Globe Awards, 49-50
Golding, David, 193
Gold Rush, The, 418, 443
Goldwyn, Samuel, ix, 13, 22, 123-128, 151, 178-80, 192, 200, 211, 217, 246, 303, 331, 369-71, 407
Gone with the Wind, 10, 38, 174, 299, 300, 308-10, 340, 387
Good Earth, The, 303, 316
Goodman, Ralph, 403
Goodrich, Frances, 166
Goofers, the, 406
Gottlieb, Alex, 176-77
Gould, Jack, 288
Goulding, Edmund, 293
Goya, Francisco, José de, 364
Grable, Betty, 234, 235, 330, 391
Grady, Billy, 293, 316-19, 390
Graham, Sheilah, 21-22, 33-34, 95, 392
Grand Illusion, 163, 359
Grant, Allan, 403-4
Grant, Cary, 27, 39-41, 82, 90, 319, 384, 437
Grapes of Wrath, The, 137
Grauman, D. J., 439
Grauman, Sid, 352-53, 439
Grauman's Chinese Theater, 228, 351-53
Grauman's Egyptian Theater, 352

Grauman's Theater (old), 439
Graves, Ralph, 9
Grayson, Charles, 203
Great Art of Light and Shadow, The, 430
Great Baltimore Fire, The, 373
Great Dictator, The, 443
Greatest Story Ever Told, The, 166, 410
Great Goldwyn, The, 178
Great Moment, The, 158
Great Train Robbery, The, 8, 160, 338-40, 342, 374, 431, 439
Greed, 160, 316, 359, 432, 450
Greene, Graham, 150
Greene, Milton, 221, 224, 230-31, 234, 238, 239, 241
Green Pastures, The, 311
Greenstreet, Sidney, 203
Grey, Lita, 444
Griffith, David Wark, 1-15, 20, 160, 164, 166, 207, 302, 335, 337-40, 349, 354, 359, 360, 364, 375, 428, 432, 445
Griffith, D. W., Award, 9, 207
Griffith, D. W., Junior High School, 15
Griffith Index, The, 7
Gris, Henry, 49
Grunwald, Henry Anatole, 116-17
Guernsey, Otis, 140
Guild, Leo, 103-4
Gunfighter, The, 165, 208
Guys and Dolls, 179
Gwynn, Edith, 25, 58-59

Habit, 168
Hackett, Albert, 166
Haines, William, 371-72
Hale, Georgia, 444
Hall, Frederick Mordaunt, 135, 136, 140
Hallelujah, 431
Hallelujah, I'm a Bum, 387
Hamilton, Neil, 361
Hamilton, Sara, 87, 89, 95
Hammerstein, Oscar II, 23
Hampton, Benjamin, 426-27
Hampton, Hope, 56
Hampton, John and Dorothy, 444-46
Hanley, Dick, 67
Happy Time, The, 189
Hard, Fast and Beautiful, 35
Hard Way, The, 313
Hardy, Oliver, 206, 447
Harlow, Jean, 46, 77, 230, 325
Harper's magazine, 12
Harris, Jack H., 56
Harris, Julie, 291
Harris, Phil, 327
Harrison, Judge Ben, 177
Harrison, Robert, 53
Hart, William S., 314, 343
Hartman, Don, 67, 408, 435

Harvey, Rev. Xen, 289
Hathaway, Henry, 235
Haver, June, 222-23
Haver, Phyllis, 348
Havoc, June, 333
Hawks, Howard, 210, 232
Hawthorne, Calif., 225, 226, 239
Hayes, Hal, 378
Hayes, Helen, 321
Hays, Will, 13
Hays Office, 7, 77, 158, 422
Hayward, Louis, 109
Hayworth, Rita, 24, 73, 194, 246, 275, 277, 278, 317, 330
Hearst, William Randolph, 22, 26, 98, 99
Hearst, William Randolph, Jr., 141
Hearst newspapers, 141, 422
Heartbalm, 351
Heaven Can Wait, 3-4
Hecht, Ben, 161, 176, 243, 304, 305, 329
Hecht, Harold, 192-94
Hecht-Hill-Lancaster, 192-94
Hedison, Al, 95
Heiftz, Jascha, 123-28
Hellinger, Mark, 258, 261-62, 421-22
Hellman, Lillian, 180
Hell's Angels, 352
Hemingway, Ernest, 17, 422
Henaghan, Jim, 59, 119-20, 232, 235
Hendry, W. P. (Whitey), 322-26
Henie, Sonja, 327
Henriettas, *see* Golden Globe Awards
Hepburn, Audrey, 217, 265, 270-71, 272, 278
Hepburn, Katharine, 271, 273
Herbert, F. Hugh, 170-71, 434
Her Happiness, 430
Hersholt, Jean, 382
Heston, Charlton, 69, 390
Heyn, Ernest V., 92
Higgins, Andrew J., 33
High Button Shoes, 344
High Noon, 189, 419, 437
High Sierra, 264
Hill, George, 206
Hill, James, 192-94
Hilton, Conrad, 32
History of the Movies, A, 426-27
Hitchcock, Alfred, 10, 199, 210, 212-14, 272, 279, 383
Hitler, Adolf, 8
Hoffman, Irving, 102
Hold 'Em Yale, 369
Holden, William, 201, 202, 217, 230, 251-56, 265, 370, 389, 404, 437
Holiday magazine, 407
Holiday House, Malibu, 379

457

Holliday, Judy, 284
Hollywood, community, 3, 16–22, 27–28, 33, 53–54, 155, 159, 329–34, 375–413, 415–20, 444–52; early days, 342, 440–44
Hollywood, 19
Hollywood Boulevard, 337, 345, 351, 352, 368, 440, 443
Hollywood Chamber of Commerce, 337, 355–57
Hollywood Close-Up magazine, 41
Hollywood Foreign Press Association, 49
Hollywood Hotel, 440–43
Hollywood Hotel, 443
Hollywood Improvement Program, 337
Hollywood Motion Picture and Television Museum (proposed), 337
Hollywood Night Life magazine, 245
Hollywood Rajah, 53
Hollywood Reporter, 21, 53, 56–63, 65–67, 70–71, 77, 119, 152, 172, 173, 363, 409, 424
Hollywood Revue, 436
Hollywood Roosevelt Hotel, 3, 4
Hollywood Saga, ix, 426, 445
Hollywood Screen Parade magazine, 80, 85, 87–88
Hollywood Story, 355, 356
Hollywood Studio Club, 223
Hollywood Ten, the, 28, 418–20
Hollywood, the Dream Factory, 19
Holmby Hills, 185, 238
Holmby Hills Rat Pack, 252–53, 405–6
Home of the Brave, 187
Hope, Bob, 22, 26, 141, 171, 172, 200, 390, 397, 425
Hopkins, Miram, 76, 315
Hopper, Hedda, 16, 21, 24–27, 31–34, 37, 50, 58, 83, 87, 94, 95, 174, 330
Hornblow, Arthur, Jr., 23, 118, 411
Horne, Lena, 43
Horns of the Devil, 230
Horwits, Al, 145, 175
Houdini, Harry, 446
House of Hate, The, 357
House on Haunted Hill, The, 435
House Un-American Activities Committee, 10, 30, 189, 285–87, 418–19
Hover, Herman, 113
Howard, Sidney, 162
Howe, James Wong, 150, 310, 312–14

How to Marry a Millionaire, 233
Hubley, John, 185
Hudson, Rock, 79, 265, 281, 392
Hughes, Howard, 35, 191, 352, 385, 388–89, 407
Hughes, Rupert, 76
Humberstone, H. Bruce (Lucky), 118
Humoresque, 431
Huneker, James, G., 124, 134
Hunt, Fred, 286
Hunt, Terry, 281, 329–31
Hunter, Ross, 25
Hunter, Tab, 88, 281
Hunters, The, 141
Huston, John, 39, 62, 162, 166, 181, 182, 202–5, 210, 211, 217, 223, 241, 248, 257, 266, 315, 416
Huston, Walter, 3, 205
Huxley, Aldous, 169, 436
Hyams, Joe, 39–41
Hyams, Leila, 371
Hyde, Johnny, 223, 224, 241

I Am a Fugitive from a Chain Gang, 180, 215
I.A.T.S.E., 312
"I Love Lucy," 285
I'm No Angel, 115
IMP, 361
Impossible Pictures, 401–3
Indian Land Grab, 431
Indians (American), 431
Informer, The, 183, 209
Ingram, Margaret, 226–27
Inherit the Wind, 419
Innocent Affair, An, 387
In Old Chicago, 208
Intermezzo, 309
International Contest for the Heavyweight Championship, Squires Versus Burns, 373–74
International Pictures, 174, 183
Intolerance, 1, 2, 4, 6–9, 14, 160, 354, 414, 418, 432
Iron Mask, The, 309
Ireland, John, 91, 95
Isherwood, Christopher, 415
Isn't Life Wonderful, 8
Israel, 166
It Ain't No Sin, 114–15
It Happened One Night, 188
It's a Wonderful Life, 10
Ivens, Joris, 130
Iwerks, Ub, 184

Jackman, Floyd, 312
Jackson, Donald, 286
James, Harry, 247
James, Nat, 99
Jazz Singer, The, 4, 427, 431
Jean Harlow Story, The, 230

Jeanne Eagels, 274, 275
"Jerky Journeys," 401
Jesse L. Lasky Intercollegiate film award, 399–400
Jessel, George, 29, 60, 67, 382
Jet Pilot, 163
Jim West, Gambler, 430
Johnson, Erskine, 26
Johnson, Nunnally, 22–23, 138, 233, 258, 264, 265, 371, 385
Johnson, Van, 316
Johnston, Alva, 178
Johnston, Eric, 408, 420, 424
Jolson, Al, 387
Jolson Story, The, 46, 394
Jones, Buck, 409
Jones, Jennifer, 62
Juarez, 105
Judge's Story, 431
Juggler, The, 189
Julie, 215
Jungle Jim series, 69

Kafka, Franz, 188
Kahane, B. B., 397
Kalmenson, Ben, 297
Kalmus, Dr. Herbert, 334
Kanter, Hal, 19
Karl, Harry, 83–84, 94, 378
Kashfi, Anna, 94
Katchamakoff, Atanas, 380
Katz, Sam, 189
Kaye, Danny, 331, 390
Kazan, Elia, 56, 210, 281, 322, 418
Keaton, Buster, 404, 450
Keats, John, 11
Keller, Jack, 29, 247
Kellerman, Annette, 361
Kelley, Tom, 223, 238
Kellum process (recorded sound), 4, 7–8
Kelly, Grace, 271–72
Kelly, Nancy, 128
Kennedy, King, 32
Kessinger, Pauline, 389–90
Keystone Kops, 344–46
Keystone studio, 346, 347, 349–50
Khrushchev, Nikita, 44, 408–10
Kid, The, 367, 443
Kid Galahad, 211
Killers, The, 422
Killiam Co. of New York, 14
King, Charles, 436
King, Henry, 2, 165, 208–9
King, Vance, 119
King Brothers, 15
King Kong, 319
King's Arms Restaurant, 411
Kingsley, Grace, 149
Kingsley, Sidney, 180
Kingsley International Pictures, 424
King's Row, 308, 310
Kingston, Winifred, 368

Kinskey, Leonid, 388, 389
Kipling, Rudyard, 365
Kircher, Athanasius, 428, 430
Kiss for Cinderella, A, 361
"Kiss Me Again," 442
Knickerbocker Hotel, 3, 9–10, 13
Knock on Any Door, 422
Kohlmar, Fred, 284
Koko the Kangaroo, 446
Kramer, Stanley, 60–61, 147–49, 187–90, 264, 298, 419
Kramer Company, 189
Krasna, Norman, 191, 328
Kreis, Milton, 392, 395
Krim, Mac, 274, 282
Kubrick, Stanley, 58
Kurosawa, Akira, 160, 420, 448

La Barba, Fidel, 168
La Boheme, 387
La Cava, Gregory, 2, 385
Ladd, Alan, 73, 82, 83, 253, 271, 331, 390
Ladies Courageous, 150
Lady Chatterley's Lover, 424
Lady Vanishes, The, 213
Laemmle, Carl, 169, 361, 442
Lahr, Bert, 386
Lait, George, 281–83
Lamarr, Hedy, 313
La Maternelle, 450
Lamkin, Marguerite, 322
Lamour, Dorothy, 390
Lancaster, Burt, 192–94
Lang, Fritz, 235
Lang, Jennings, 186
Lang, Otto, 168
Lang, Walter, 235
Langdon, Harry, 345, 446
Lange, Hope, 223
Lariat Kid, 229
La Rocque, Rod, 369–71, 431
Lasky, Jesse L., 13, 200, 368, 380, 399, 442, 451
Lasky, Jesse L., Jr., 200
Lasky Feature Play Company, 200
Lassie, 324
Last Laugh, The, 311
Last Tycoon, The, 33, 170
Last Voyage, The, 215
Latina, Contortionist, 373
La Tosca, 340
Laughton, Charles, 46
Laurel, Stan, 206, 343
Lawford, Peter, 391, 406
Lawrance, Jody, 227
Lazar, Irving, 405
Leaf, Earl, 235, 280
LeBaron, William, 118
Lederer, Charles, 259, 266
Lee, Bing, 391
Leeds, Andrea, 125
Legion of Decency, 64, 420
Lehman, Ernest, 193
Leigh, Janet, 78, 89

Leigh, Vivien, 387
Lejeune, C. A., 189
Lenin, Nikolai, 7–8
Lerner, Max, 86
Leroy, Mervyn, 215–16
Les Enfants Terribles, 307
Les Miserables, 46
Lesser, Sol, 337, 407
L'Estrange, Dick, 368
Let's Make Love, 242, 410
Letters of Edna St. Vincent Millay, The, 225
Letters to a Young Poet, 229
Let There Be Light, 204–5
Levant, Oscar, 249
Levee, Michael, 92
Levinson, Leonard, 401–3
Lewis, Jerry, 29, 94–95, 145, 331, 390
Liberace, Wladziu, 377
Library, The, 60–61
Library of Congress, 373
Life and Loves of Beethoven, The, 305
Life magazine, 33, 101, 196–97, 280, 288, 291, 407
Life of an American Fireman, The, 339
Life of Emile Zola, The, 110, 181
Life with Father, 311
Limelight, 147
Lincoln, Abraham, 3
Lincoln, Elmo, 53–55, 368, 447
Lindbergh, Charles, 202
Linkletter, Art, 356
Lin Yutang, 151
Lion's Share, The, 299
Lipton, Harry, 222, 223, 234
Little Caesar, 180, 215
Little Miss Broadway, 434
Little Old New York, 137
Little Train Robbery, The, 374
Lloyd, Harold, 337, 345, 350–51, 370, 434, 445
Lockwood, Margaret, 213
Loesser, Frank, 179
Loew's Inc., 152, 174, 318, 433
Logan, Joshua, 220, 223, 235, 238, 239, 278, 279
Loke Wan Tho, 199
Lombard, Carole, 253, 348
London, Ephraim, 424, 425
London, 320
London *Daily Mirror*, 40
London *Evening Standard*, 156
London *Observer*, 189
London *Times*, 301
Lonelyhearts, 186–87
"Lone Ranger" (TV series), 303
Longfellow, Henry Wadsworth, 122
Long, Hot Summer, The, 322
Longstreet, Stephen, 160
Look magazine, 40, 116, 167, 230, 422

Lord, Del, 347–48
Lorre, Peter, 70, 203, 257–61, 268, 319
Los Angeles, 44, 144, 252, 342, 343, 352, 401–2, 442
Los Angeles County Board of Supervisors, 337
Los Angeles *Daily News*, 25, 28, 145, 146, 148, 153, 187, 191, 219, 249, 398, 399
Los Angeles Dept. of Charities, 222
Los Angeles *Examiner*, 23–25, 27, 98–99
Los Angeles General Hospital, 221
Los Angeles *Herald-Express*, 39, 115
Los Angeles *Independent*, 24
Los Angeles *Mirror-News*, 18, 25, 145
Los Angeles Orphans' Home Society, 222, 226, 240
Los Angeles *Times*, 7, 27, 31, 32, 40, 49, 97, 115, 144, 145, 149, 173, 220, 276
Lost Weekend, The, 1
Lost World, The, 319, 320
Lo, the Poor Indian, 431
Lourau, Georges, 195
Love, Bessie, 446
Love Finds Andy Hardy, 434
Love Is a Many Splendored Thing, 152
Love Pirate, The, 369
Lower, Ana, 222, 226
Lower Depths, The, 163
Low Man on a Totem Pole, 103
Loy, Myrna, 313
Lubitsch, Ernst, 4, 50, 136
Luce, Henry, 147, 407
Lucey's restaurant, 389
Luck of the Irish, 103
Lumberjack, 182
Luna, Barbara, 94
Lunt, Alfred, 258
Lupino, Ida, 109, 203, 288, 321
Lupino, Stanley, 109
Luske, Ham, 184
Lux Radio Theater, 70–71
Lytess, Natasha, 223, 229–30, 238, 241

M, 305
Macabre, 436
Macao, 159
MacArthur, Charles, 304, 305, 385
MacArthur, Gen. Douglas, 259
Macaulay, Richard, 191
MacDonald, Dwight, 133–34, 186–87, 190, 243
MacDonald, Jeanette, 303
MacDonald, Marie, 378
MacDonald, Wilfred, 368

459

Mace, Fred, 345
Mack Sennett, King of Comedy, 344
Mack Sennett Story, The, 344
MacLaine, Shirley, 90, 409
Maeterlinck, Maurice, 127
magic lantern, 429–30
Make-Up Artists and Hair Stylists, 163
Maltese Falcon, The, 110, 181
Maltz, Albert, 419–20
Mamoulian, Rouben, 179
Mankiewicz, Herman, 411, 434
Mann, Anthony, 418
Mann, Hank, 345, 355
Mann, May, 95
Mann, Thomas, 151
Mannix, Edward, 313
Mansfield, Jayne, 44, 272–73, 283, 284
Mantle, Burns, 76
Mantz, Paul, 239
Man Who Knew Too Much, The, 213
Marcel's restaurant, Altadena, 370
March, Fredric, 46, 210, 262–63
Marey, E. J., 428
Margo, 304, 305
Marie Antoinette, 133, 172
Marilyn Monroe Productions, Inc., 239
Markey, Enid, 447
Mark Hellinger Story, The, 279
Marquis, Don, 233
Marquis restaurant, 389
Marsh, Mae, 15, 414
Marshall, Brenda, 251
Marshall, George, 345
Martin, Dean, 29, 145, 390, 406, 437
Martin, Dr. Harry W. (Docky), 22, 24, 28
Martin, Pete, 97, 272
Martinelli, Elsa, 393
Marton, Andrew
Marty, 192
Marx, Groucho, 186, 235
Mason, James, 10, 331, 333
Mason General Hospital, 204
Masonic Temple, 13
Masquers Club, 27
Massacre, 431
Massacre, The, 15
Massey, Raymond, 269
Master Mystery, The, 446, 447
Mate, Rudolph, 206, 314–15
Matthews, T. S., 147
Mayer, Arthur, 123, 143, 151
Mayer, Louis B., 53, 67, 113, 158, 161, 171–74, 179, 186, 317, 318, 325, 389, 397, 408, 442, 451–52; relations with press, 31, 44, 96, 97, 133, 175, 188, 316
Maytime, 303
McBain, Diane, 95
McCambridge, Mercedes, 290
McCarey, Leo, 2, 10, 118, 206
McCarthy, Ed. 13
McClory, Kevin, 195–96
McCombe, Leonard, 280
McCrea, Joel, 125, 158
McCulloch, Frank, 251
McCulloch, Robert, 378
McHugh, Frank, 385
McHugh, Jimmy, 22, 28, 392
McLellan, Joe, 443
McNamara, Ed, 385
McWilliams, Carey, 438
Meade, Fred and Marjorie, 52
Melchior, Lauritz, 382
Méliès, Georges, 339
Melville, Jean-Pierre, 307
Men, The, 164, 187
Mender of Nets, The, 9
Menninger Clinic, 18
Men Without Women, 314
Menzies, William Cameron, 308–11, 314
Meremblum, Peter, 127
Merry Widow, The, 170
Messenger Boy's Mistake, The, 341
Methot, Mayo, 258–59
M-G-M, 42, 47, 56, 86, 158, 161, 169, 186, 218, 272, 287, 293, 299–301, 313, 322–25, 372, 389, 436, 451, 452; formation of, 179; press relations, 26, 31, 78, 96, 116–17, 133–34, 147–48, 156, 316–18
Michael, Dolores, 79
Mickey Awards, 28–30, 113
Mickey Mouse, 184–85
Midsummer Night's Dream, A, 181
Mighty Joe Young, 319–20
Miles Bros., 374
Milestone, Lewis, 262, 386, 399, 401
Milestone Awards, 399–400
Milland, Ray, 380
Miller, Arthur, 236, 241
Miller, Colin, 70–71
Miller, Marilyn, 223
Miller, Wade, 33
Million and One Nights, A, ix, 76
Mills, Hillis, 148–49
Mineo, Sal, 291
minority groups, 431
Miracle, The, 423, 424
Miracle of Morgan's Creek, The, 10
Miserable, 114
Misfits, The, 241
Miss Cheesecake of 1951, 220
Mission to Moscow, 106
Miss Lonelyhearts, 186
Mitchum, Robert, 233
Mix, Tom, 337, 370, 376
Mizner, Wilson, 417
Mocambo, 59, 389, 396, 408
Modern Screen magazine, 73, 80, 83–84, 91–95
Modern Times, 443
Mogambo, 272
Molly-O, 344
Molyneux, William, 429
Mono-Grant, 403–4
Monroe, Marilyn, 47, 52, 217–42, 272–73, 280, 283, 284, 391, 394, 409–10
Monsieur Verdoux, 443
montages, 303–8
Montgomery, George, 250, 251
Montgomery, Robert, 78
Moore, Grace, 133
Moore, Terry, 218, 406
Moran, Jim, 110–14
Moran, Polly, 348
Moran Awards, 113
Mordkin, Michael, Jr., 103–4
Morgan, Dennis, 387
Morgan, Frank, 386
Morris, Lloyd, 13, 376
Morris, Nan, 95
Moses, Grandma, 101, 188
Moskowitz, Joe, 137, 138
Mother, 306, 414, 418
Motion Picture magazine, 73, 78, 79, 83, 87, 94–96
Motion Picture Association of America, 42, 408, 420, 424
Motion Picture Center studio, 187
Motion Picture Country House, 451
Motion Picture Herald, 142
motion picture industry, 2, 21, 27–28, 41–42, 77, 101, 155, 159, 160–216, 297–326, 419–52; early history, 335–74; 428–30, 440–44
Motion Picture Theater Management, 353
Mouse That Roared, The, 114
Movieland and TV Time magazine, 84
Movie Life magazine, 85–86, 94
Movie Mirror magazine, 86, 87
movie monsters, 319–21
movie reviewers, 121–59
Movies Illustrated magazine, 80, 87, 89
Movie Stars TV Close-Ups magazine, 87–89
Movie Theater, Los Angeles, 444–47
Mrs. Miniver, 2, 3, 157, 398
Muir, Florabel, 17–18, 25
Muni, Paul, 263, 267, 330
Muntz, Madman, 111
Murnau, F. W., 311

Murphy, Bernard, 404
Murphy, Dudley, 379
Murray, Mae, 170, 368
Museum of Modern Art Film Library, 445
Music Corp. of America, 224, 239, 398, 457
Mussolini Speaks, 176
Mutual Movies, 343, 430
Muybridge, Eadweard, x, 376, 428
My Darling Clementine, 10
My Friend Flicka, 3
My Man Godfrey, 2
My Wild Irish Rose, 387

Nabokov, Vladimir, 80
Nagel, Conrad, 337
Naish, J. Carrol, 319
Naldi, Nita, 364–65
narcotics, 395–96
Narrow Margin, 152
Nathan, Robert, 158
Nation, The, magazine, 106, 143, 153, 157
National Velvet, 154
Navigator, The, 450
Nazimova, Alla, 361, 442, 443
Neal, Robert, 84
Negri, Pola, 313, 442
Negroes, 431
Negulesco, Jean, 235
Nelson, Ricky, 82, 90
Neptune's Daughter, 361
Neutra, Richard, 379
New Republic magazine, 143
Newspaper Enterprise Association, 26
Newsweek magazine, 38, 42, 101
New York *Daily Mirror,* 141, 152
New York *Daily News,* 17–18, 32, 143, 152, 156
New Yorker, The, magazine, 39, 155, 157
New York Film Critics Circle, 141, 152, 399, 423
New York *Graphic,* 190–91
New York *Herald Tribune,* 39–40, 140, 141, 152, 154, 220
New York *Morning Telegraph,* 43
New York *Post,* 140, 142, 143, 394
New York *State,* 420, 423, 424
New York State Legislature, 103
New York *Sun,* 154
New York *Times,* 12, 45, 53, 60, 118, 123–38, 140, 152, 154, 159, 161, 178, 187, 288, 340, 341, 434
New York University, 115

Next Voice You Hear, The, 210
Niblo, Fred, 300, 337
Nichols, George, 116–17, 148, 186
Night Holds Terror, The, 214–15
Night Out, A, 243
Nights of Cabiria, The, 160
Niven, David, 197, 405
Nixon, Alan, 333
Noah's Ark, 168
Normand, Mabel, 9, 169, 344–47, 350, 440
North Star, 310, 358
Norton, Mildred, 145, 146
Nothing Sacred, 209, 309
Not So Long Ago, 13, 376
Novak, Kim, 52, 80, 95, 175, 176, 217, 245–46, 250, 272–85, 410
Novarro, Ramon, 365–66, 368
Nugent, Frank, 131–33, 136–40
Nun's Story, The, 69, 307
Nurmi, Maila ("Vampira"), 291
Nurse Edith Cavell, 131
Nuyen, France, 94

Oakie, Jack, 76
Objective, Burma!, 313
Oblath, George, 68
O'Brien, Pat, 39, 67, 267, 385
O'Brien, Willis, 319–21
Ochs, Adolph S., 133, 135
O'Connell, Arthur, 235
O'Hara, John, 258
Oklahoma!, 23
Old Acquaintance, 315
old-timers, 335–74
Olivier, Sir Laurence, 153, 193, 238, 241
O'Malley, Pat, 367
Omnibook, 422
One Third of a Nation, 128–29
On the Beach, 189–90
Open City, 418, 422, 423
"Open End" TV program, 148
Orphans of the Storm, 1
Oscars, *see* Academy Awards
Othello, 400
Our Town, 308, 310
Outlaw and the Child, The, 343
Over 21, 23
Ox-Bow Incident, The, 183, 209–10

Paar, Jack, 88
Paisan, 423
Pal, George, 150
Palance, Jack, 256, 391
Paliwada, Amby, 184
Pal Joey, 245–46, 274, 277
Palm Springs, Calif., 368
Palo Alto, Calif., x

Panama, Norman, 148
Pantages Theater, 398–99
Panzer, Paul, 357, 358
Paramount Pictures, 14, 29, 68, 103, 106, 114, 128, 133, 141, 207, 252–54, 271, 279, 344, 354, 359, 363, 389–90, 404, 408, 433, 435
Pardners, 390
Parsons, Louella, 21–29, 31–34, 36–37, 47, 50, 58, 83, 93–95, 98, 112, 329, 376, 400–1
Partisan Review, 157
Pasadena, Calif., 255, 256
Pasadena Playhouse, 98, 252
Passage to Marseilles, 259, 260
Passion of Joan of Arc, The, 314, 418
Patriarch, The, 431
Patrick, Lee, 23
PATSY (Picture Animal Top Star of the Year) Award, 69, 284, 399
Paul, Elliott, 158
Pauling, Dr. Linus, 189
Payne, Lee, 20, 145
Peasants in Ermine, ix
Peck, Gregory, 190, 208, 264, 328
Peer, Robert, 80–81
Percepto, 435
Percy, Eileen, 367
Percy, Esme, 131
Perils of Pauline, The, 357
Perkins, Millie, 102
Perlberg, William, 272
Persistent Suitor, A, 431
Personal Column, 117
Peter Pan, 361
pets, 331–34, 376
Philip Morris, 287
Photoplay magazine, 22, 75, 76, 78, 79, 84, 87, 89, 94, 95, 227, 327, 361
Pickford, Mary, 60–61, 99, 273, 330, 337, 367, 410, 445
Picnic, 278, 279
Picon, Molly, 4
Pink Tights, 224
Pippa Passes, 11
Pitts, Zasu, 359
Place in the Sun, A, 207
Playboy magazine, 81
PM, 13
Polito, Sol, 312
Pollock, Lou, 118
Polo, Eddie, 367
Popular Screen magazine, 87, 95
Porgy and Bess, 179, 303
Porter, Edwin S., 8, 160, 338–42, 435
Portrait of Jennie, 314
Potemkin, 8, 305, 414
Powdermaker, Hortense, 19
Powell, Dick, 394

461

Powell, Dilys, 301
Powell, Eleanor, 88, 89
Power, Tyrone, 133, 136, 137, 276, 277
Power and the Glory, The, 313
Prater Violet, 415
Preminger, Otto, 166, 167, 419
Presley, Elvis, 82, 91
press, 15, 16–99, 245, 247, 253, 267–68; "accreditation" at studios, 42; advertising pressure on, 20, 45, 62, 66, 123, 128, 137, 140–44, 146, 156, 316; foreign representatives, 48–50; gifts and hospitality to, 18, 34–38, 96; *see also* censorship, press; fan magazines; movie reviewers; scandal sheets; trade papers
press agents, 18, 20, 26, 41, 42, 53, 78, 97, 100–20, 167, 186, 282–84
Pretty, Arline, 368
Prevost, Marie, 348
Pride of the Yankees, 308, 309, 387
Prince and the Showgirl, The, 241
Prisoner of Zenda, The, 366
Proctor, Jack, 33
producers, 160–216
Production Code, 7, 420, 421, 425
production designers, 308–11
Professor Beware, 434
Protestant churches, 422
Proud and the Profane, The, 255
Pryor, Thomas, 60
psychoanalysts, 17, 247–50, 272–74, 290
Public Enemy, The, 180, 188, 209
Pudovkin, V. I., 304, 306
Pugilist, The, 343
Purviance, Edna, 444
Pushover, 274, 279, 283–84

Quarterly of Film, Radio and Television, 48–49
Queen Elizabeth, 340
Quince, The, 344
Quine, Richard, 279, 283–84
Quinn, Don, 410
Quinn, Frank, 152
Quirk, James R., 76

Rachmil, Lewis J., 389
Racquet Club, Palm Springs, 368–69
Raffin, Philip J., 389
Raft, George, 204, 263, 264, 330, 385, 391
Rains, Claude, 304
Raintree County, 322
Ramsaye, Terry, ix, 76
Randall, Tony, 437

Rapper, Irving, 107
Rasch, Albertina, 436
Rashomon, 160, 418
Rave magazine, 52
Ray, Charles, 376
Raye, Martha, 444
Reader's Digest, 241
Reagan, Ronald, 73
Rebel Without a Cause, 289, 291
Reckless, 46
Red Badge of Courage, The, 39, 315
Redgrave, Michael, 213
Red Man and the Child, The, 431
Reed, Carol, 199, 362
Reid, Wallace, 376, 442
Reid, Ogden, family, 141
Reilly, Jack, 372
Reinhardt, Max, 181
Remick, Lee, 31
Renna, Mme, 235
Renoir, Jean, 153, 162–63
Renovare Productions, 373
Reporter magazine, 188
Report from the Aleutians, 204
Republic Pictures, 38, 332, 351
Rescued from an Eagle's Nest, 339
Reseda, Calif, 380
Rettig, Tommy, 90
Reventlow, Lance, 95
Rex Pictures, 340
Reynolds, Debbie, 82–90, 94, 378, 410
Reynolds, Gene, 125, 126
Rhapsody in Blue, 158
Rich, Robert, 419
Ricketts, Thomas, 299
Riefenstahl, Leni, 8
Rigler, Ruth, 95
Rilke, Rainer Maria, 229, 238
Rin Tin Tin, 167
Rise and Fall of Free Speech in America, The, 10
Ritz Brothers, 136, 393
River, The, 153
River of No Return, 233
Rivoli Theater, 123, 124, 126–27, 129
RKO, 35, 67, 152, 159, 215–16, 279, 318, 366, 427, 433
Roach, Hal, 368
Roaring Twenties, The, 263
Roarin' Ranch, 299
Roark, Aidan, 168
Robe, The, 215–16, 435
Robertson, Dale, 379
Robertson, Etienne Gaspard, 430
Robinson, Edward G., 182, 256, 263, 331
Robson, Mark, 164
Rochlen, Kendis, 245
Rodgers, Richard, 23

Rogers, Will, 337, 445
Rogers and Cowan, 78
Rogues' Gallery, 263
Roman Catholic Church, 132, 420
Romance of Tarzan, The, 354
Roman Holiday, 270
Romanoff, "Prince" Michael, 258, 261, 265, 268, 382–84, 405
Romanoff's restaurant, 31, 257, 261, 265, 267, 268, 382–84, 405
Romantic Rumbolia, 402
Romeo and Juliet, 303
Rommel, Field Marshal Erwin, 358
Romola, 208
Rooney, Mickey, 434
Roots of Heaven, The, 202
Rosenstein, Jaik, 41
Ross, Harold, 385
Ross, Lillian, 39
Rossellini, Roberto, 420, 423, 448
Rossen, Robert, 418
Rosten, Leo, 19
Rosten, Norman, 238
Rotha, Paul, 306
Roxy Theater, 128, 137, 142, 434–35
Rozsa, Miklos, 404
Ruggles, Wesley, 345
Russell, Gail, 10
Russell, Jane, 159, 220, 235, 369
Russell, Joe, 21
Russell, Rosalind, 273, 317
Russian films, 1, 7–8, 320–8, 311, 450
Ruttenberg, Joseph, 2
Ryman, Lucille, 234

Sabotage, 212–14
Sabrina, 265–66, 271
Sadick, Aly and Amad, 49
Saint, Eva Marie, 232, 399–401
Sainted Devil, 365
St. John, Jill, 95
St. Johns, Adela Rogers, 75–76, 376
Sakall, S. Z., ix
Sally, Irene and Mary, 371
Samson and Delilah, 200, 201
"Samuel Goldwyn Presents," 179
Sanctuary, 31
Sands, Tommy, 91
San Fernando Valley, 14, 333, 351
San Francisco, 35, 316, 342
Sanicola, Hank, 245
San Pietro, 204
Saratoga Trunk, 244
Saroyan, William, 235
Sasha's Palate, 380

Saturday Evening Post, 22–23, 97, 272, 277, 316
Saturday Review of Literature, 155
Saud El Saud, 112
Sayre, Joel, 385
scandal sheets, 41, 50–53, 78–79, 245
Scandia Restaurant, 382
Scaramouche, 366
Scent of Mystery, 436
Schallert, Edwin, 97–98, 115
Scharper, Al, 65
Schary, Dore, 54–56, 67–69, 117, 147–48, 173, 186–88, 210, 298, 318, 328
Schazman, Capt. William, 190
Schenck, Joseph, 42, 58, 60, 168, 174, 223, 234, 238, 358, 397
Schenck, Nicholas, 42, 171–74, 318, 451
Scheuer, Philip K., 7, 27, 144–45
Schildkraut, Joseph, 1, 331
Schneider, Benno, 281
Schoenfeld, Joe, 60–61, 153
Schreiber, Lew, 235
Schroeder, Carl, 43
Schulberg, B. P., 363–64
Schulberg, Budd, 191, 364
Schwab's drugstore, 29, 46–47, 51, 193, 219, 230, 238, 391–96
Scott, Lizabeth, 73
Scott, Stormy Lee, 220, 221
Scott, Zachary, 379
Screen Actors Guild, 252
Screen Directors Guild, 8, 27, 163
Screenland Plus TV-Land, 80
Screen Producers Guild, 163, 167, 168, 399–400
Screen Stars magazine, 91
Screen Stories magazine, 84, 86
Screen World and TV, 86–87
Screen Writer magazine, 123
Screen Writers Guild, 62–66
Script magazine, 150
Scudda Hoo, Scudda Hay, 222
Sea Hawk, The, 211
Seal Brothers circus, 356
Sea Lion, The, 446
Seaton, George, 64, 66
second-unit directors, 298–302
Seen Any Good Movies Lately?, 140
Seitz, John, 202
Selwyn, Arch and Edgar, 179
Selznick, David O., 38, 68, 162, 167, 174, 314, 363
Selznick International Pictures, 174
Seminole's Trust, The, 431
Sennett, Mack, 13, 20, 337,
344–52, 368, 427, 440–41, 446
Sennwald, André, 154
Sequoia, 46
Sergeant York, 299, 302
Seventeen, 103
Seventh Heaven, 368
Seventh Veil, The, 10
Seven Year Itch, 231
Shades of Gray, 204
Shakespeare, William, 9, 170, 181, 400
Shamroy, Leon, 235
Shane, 207, 418
Shaw, George Bernard, 10, 127
Shaw, Runme and Run Run, 198–99
Shaw, Sam, 194
Shearer, Douglas, 173
Shearer, Norma, 78, 133, 169, 173, 243, 442
Shepley, James, 250
Sheridan, Ann, 22, 321
Sherman, Vincent, 203–4
Sherwood, Robert E., 76, 169, 258
Shore, Dinah, 19, 250–51
Shors, 450
Shoulder Arms, 443
Showdown, 107
Shriek in the Night, A, 430
Shulman, Milton, 156
Shumlin, Herman, 150
Shurr, Louis, 280, 282, 283
Sidney, George, 175, 207, 225, 246, 284
Sidney, Sylvia, 129
Siegel, Sol, 117
Sight and Sound, 2
Silents Were Golden, The, 372
Silverman, Sime, 59
Silver Screen magazine, 95
Silver Spurs Award, 208
Simmons, Jean, 270
Simplex projection machines, 340
Sinatra, Frank, 194, 217, 218, 244–47, 257, 267, 276, 277, 327, 405–6, 409, 419–20
Singapore, 198–99
Sitwell, Edith, 238
Six O'Clock Low, 403
Skinner's Baby, 366
Skolsky, Sidney, 3, 46–48, 112, 219, 220, 230, 238, 241, 336, 392–95, 410
Skouras, Charles, 146, 174
Skouras, George, 174
Skouras, Spyros, 146, 168, 174, 198, 407, 409
Sleeping Prince, The, 237
Slide, Kelly, Slide, 371
Smell-o-Vision, 70, 436
Smith, Darr, 146
Smith, H. Allen, 103
Smith, Harold Jacob, 419
Smith, John, 281
Smith, Robert L., 146
Snively, Emmeline, 228–29
Sokolsky, George, 86
Some Like It Hot, 201, 231, 242
Somerset House, 389
Song of Bernadette, The, 208
Sophocles the Hyena, 114
Sorrell and Son, 361
So This Is New York, 187
Spain Fights On, 128–30, 132
Spanish Earth, The, 130
Spartacus, 419
Sperling, Milton, 175
Spiegel, Sam, 281
Spirit of St. Louis, The, 201
Splendor in the Grass, 56
Spoor, George K., 342, 343
Squaw Man, The, 201, 367, 368
Stafford, Jo, 247
Stage Door, 2
Stalag 17, 68, 201
Star Is Born, A, 209, 210, 262
Star Maker, 13
Starr, Jimmy, 39
Stein, Irving, 238
Stein, Ronald, 56
Steiner, Max, 404
Stella Dallas, 208
Sterling, Ford, 345, 350
Stern, Seymour, 3–5, 7, 12, 13, 15, 375
Sternberg, Josef von, 159, 163
Sterne, Herb, 115, 150–51
Stevens, George, 2, 44, 102, 165–66, 205–8, 210–12, 230, 291–92, 298, 312, 410, 435
Stewart, James, 256, 264, 279, 316, 387, 437
Stewart, Russ, 382
still photography, 326–28
Stolen by the Gypsies, 357
Stone, Andrew and Virginia, 214–15
Stork Club, 104
Storm, Gale, 80
Stormy Petrel, The, 361
Story of Alexander Graham Bell, The, 136–37
Story of Cuddles, The, ix
Story of Louis Pasteur, The, 181
Strand Theater, 103
Strasberg, Lee, 220, 224, 232, 233, 241
Strasberg, Paula, 220, 231, 233, 238
Strasberg, Susan, 231
Stratton Story, The, 387
Strauss, Robert, 68–69
Strauss, Theodore, 97, 123, 149, 154, 156
Streetcar Named Desire, A, 418
Strickling, Howard, 42, 147–48, 452

463

Stroheim, Erich von, 2, 4, 117–18, 160, 170, 266, 316, 358–60, 417, 432
Struggle, The, 1–2
Struss, Karl, 312
studio police, 322–26
studio technicians and specialists, 297–328
Sturges, Preston, 2, 3, 10, 261
Sturies, Susan, 84
Stuttering Sam (Mary Dowell), 106
Sudan, 155–56
Suddenly, Last Summer, 85, 89
Sullivan, Ed, 32–33
Sulzberger, Arthur Hays, 123–25, 133, 138, 178
Summer Place, A, 25
Sunrise, 311
Sunrise at Campobello, 69
Sunset Boulevard, 14, 200–2, 253, 358, 359, 370, 404
Sun Valley, Idaho, 221, 231, 239
Swain, Mack, 345
Swanson, Gloria, 202, 312, 348, 358–60, 376, 440, 442
Sweet, Blanche, 15, 368
Sweet Smell of Success, The, 193
Swisher, Viola, 60–61

Tail Spin, 128
Taplinger, Robert, 191
Tarantino, Jimmie, 245
Tarzan and the Magic Fountain, 354
Tarzan of the Apes, 354, 447
Tarzan pictures, 353–57, 447
Tashman, Lilyan, 376
Tatiana, 119
Taub, Billy, 56
Taylor, Elizabeth, 18, 82–89, 154, 317, 322, 327, 409–10, 437
Taylor, Robert, 269, 328
Teitelbaum, Al, 377–78
Telephone Girl, The, 167
television, x, 17, 22, 32, 175, 285, 303, 367, 378, 384, 397, 418, 425–28, 434, 447, 448
Tell It to the Marines, 371
Tempest, The, 309
Temple, Shirley, 25–26, 47, 136, 234, 290, 371, 434
Ten Commandments, The, 66–67, 199–200, 365, 387
Terror at Midnight, 361
Tetzlaff, Ted, 206
Thailand, King, of, 294, 295
Thalberg, Irving, 29, 161, 169–71, 173, 325, 397, 399, 442
That Certain Feeling, 141
That's My Boy, 145
Theisen, Earl, 235

Theory of the Film, 435
They Came to Cordura, 418
They Drive by Night, 263
They Shall Have Music, 123–28, 132
They Won't Forget, 180, 215
Thief of Bagdad, The, 309
Things to Come, 309
Thirer, Irene, 143
39 Steps, The, 213
This Week magazine, 220
Thomas, Dylan, 450
Thomas, John Charles, 382
Three Girls from Rome, 393
Three Minnies, The, 402
Three Musketeers, The, 387
Thurber, James, 386
Tierney, Gene, 330
Tiger Shark, 182
Tillie's Punctured Romance, 350
Time magazine, 21, 24, 26, 31, 53, 66, 96, 101, 116–17, 134, 140, 294–96, 391, 395, 407, 424; cover stories, 175, 184, 217–20, 224, 236–41, 245, 247, 248, 250–51, 256–58, 267, 268, 270, 272–73, 276; movie reviews, 146–53, 156, 172
Tingler, The, 435
Tiomkin, Dimitri, 398
Tirman, Jack, 104–105
Tobelmann, Toby, 184
Tobias, George, 109
Todd, Mike, 53, 67, 85–86, 96, 194–98, 235
Todd, Mike, Jr., 70
Todd, Sarah, 70
Todd-AO, 198
Tol'able David, 165, 208
Tone, Franchot, 18
Top Hat, 387
Torpedoed, 131, 132
Torrance, Calif., 240
Totheroh, Roland, 443–44
Tracy, Spencer, 10, 269
trade papers, 19, 43, 45, 53–72, 151–53; *see also Daily Variety; Hollywood Reporter*
"Trades, The," 54–56
Transatlantic, 313
Trapeze, 140
Treadmill, The, 11
Treasure of Sierra Madre, The, 110, 181, 205
Tree Is a Tree, A, 169
Trigger Tricks, 299
Trip to the Moon, A, 339, 431
Triumph of the Will, 8
True Confession magazine, 81
Trumbo, Dalton, 28, 419
Trussell, Jake, 58
Tufts, Sonny, 67
Turner, Lana, 57, 283, 394
Turner's drugstore, 395

Turpin, Ben, 342, 345, 347, Tusher, William, 79
TV and Movie Screen magazine, 84, 86
Twelve O'Clock High, 208, 403
Twentieth Century-Fox, 128, 168, 174, 183, 185, 197–98, 208, 210, 249, 406, 412–13, 433, 436, 437; Khrushchev visit, 408–10; Marilyn Monroe promotion, 219–24, 229, 230, 232, 235, 237, 240; press relations, 24, 29, 42, 48, 52, 96, 136–41, 146, 220, 407
"21" restaurant, 104, 258, 261, 265

Umberto D., 150, 160, 418
Un Carnet de Bal, 305, 450
Ungar, Arthur, 59–60, 71
Unger, Bertil and Gustav, 49
United Artists, 81, 140, 174, 363, 433
United Nations, 18, 100
United Press International, 26, 49, 117
United Productions of America, 185
U. S. Army, 106
U. S. Army Signal Corps, 204
U. S. Dept. of Justice, 433
United States Pictures, 175
U. S. Supreme Court, 423–25
Universal-International Pictures, 25, 52, 56, 145, 174, 235, 355, 357, 363, 397, 427
Universal Pictures, 169, 361, 433

Valentino, Rudolph, 20, 273, 327, 337, 365, 369, 376, 442, 445
Vallee, Rudy, 434
"Vampira," 291
Vampire, 314–15
Van Doren, Mamie, 235
Van Dyke, W. S., 4
Van Heusen, Jimmy, 405
Van Nuys, Calif., 227, 240
Van Orden, Robert, 281
Varconi, Victor, 370
Variety (film), 2, 311, 450
Variety (trade paper), 59–63, 71, 135, 137
Velez, Lupe, 376
Vera Cruz, 437
Verdon, Gwen, 59, 217
Verdugo, Calif., 240
Vertigo, 279
Victor, Henry, 131
Victor Hugo Café, 328
Vidor, Charles, 177
Vidor, King, 162, 169, 188, 209, 380, 432
Vikings (club), 381–82

Villa Capri restaurant, 289, 291
Virginia City, 105
VistaVision, 435
Vitagraph Co., 357, 361, 374
Viva Villa, 303, 313
Vogel, Joseph, 152, 173
Vorkapich, Slavko, 303–8, 314

Wald, Connie, 191
Wald, Jerry, 12, 41, 110, 175, 190–92, 224, 255, 263, 264, 283, 284, 408
Wales, Clarke (Duke), 42
Walking Down Broadway, 359
Walk of Fame, 337
Wallis, Hal, 102, 145
Walsh, Raoul, 264
Wanger, Walter, 150–51, 185–88, 298
War Brides, 361
Warner, Albert, 181
Warner, Harry, 136, 175, 180, 181, 203, 397
Warner, Jack L., 25, 69, 105–7, 110, 113, 167, 168, 175, 180–2, 188, 191, 259–60, 358, 371, 399–400, 442
Warner Brothers, 25, 56, 102, 103, 105–10, 115, 116, 136, 140, 167, 175, 181, 182, 188, 192, 203, 204, 211, 259–60, 263, 267, 288, 297, 311, 312, 315, 323, 332, 357–58, 411, 415, 426, 431, 433
Wasserman, Lew, 238
Watts, Richard, Jr., 154-55, 414
Way Down East, 1, 10, 14
Wayne, John, 90, 230, 235, 437
Ways of Love, 423
Webb, Clifton, 262, 264
Wedding March, The, 359
Weingarten, Lawrence, 173
Weissmuller, Johnny, 69, 329, 354, 386
Weld, Tuesday, 44, 58, 79, 90, 91, 95, 243, 408
Welles, Orson, 10, 328, 385
Wellman, William, 188, 209–10, 432

West, Mae, 7, 114
West, Nathanael, 186–87
Western Costume Co., 112
We Were Strangers, 62
What Makes Sammy Run?, 187, 191, 364
Wheelwright, Ralph, 325
Whipsaw, 313
White, Pearl, 357
White Caps, The, 431
White Gold, 364
White Sister, The, 208
White Zombie, 123
Whitney, Dwight, 24, 27
Whitty, Dame May, 213
Who Killed Cock Robin? 214
wide screen, x, 4, 198, 435, 436
Widmark, Richard, 256
Wilcox, Herbert, 131–32
Wilcoxon, Henry, 200
Wild Boys of the Road, 432
Wilde, Oscar, 382
Wilder, Billy, 68, 148, 166, 200–2, 210, 211, 231–32, 253–56, 265–66, 271, 359, 360, 380, 410, 416, 417, 419
Wilder, W. Lee, 166
Wilding, Michael, 382
Wiles, Buster, 108
Wilkerson, W. R. (Billy), 57–59, 71, 172
Wilkie, Jane, 79
Wilkinson, Lupton, 186
William Morris talent agency, 223, 224, 275, 437
Williams, Paul, 391
Williams, Tennessee, 239, 322
Willson, Henry, 281
Wilson, Carey, 170, 173
Wilson, Earl, 294
Wilson, Marie, 333
Wilson, Woodrow, 142
Wilson, 139, 142
Winchell, Walter, 19, 22, 37, 128, 191, 240, 285–87
Windsor, Marie, 95–96
Wing, Toby, 220
Wings, 209
Winsten, Archer, 140–44
Winters, Shelley, 73, 394, 398

Woman Alone, The, 212
Wood, Natalie, 56, 89, 102
Wood, Sam, 118, 119
Wood, Thomas, 22–24
World War I movies, 358
World War II, 105, 106, 131–32, 148, 180–81, 203–5, 297, 324, 358, 389, 433, 434
Wotjkiewicz, Wojciechowicz Stanislaus (Bow Wow), 21
Wrangell, Baron, 386
Wright, Cobina, 22
Wright, Frank Lloyd, 175
Wright, Loyd, 230
Writers Guild of America, 163
Wuthering Heights, 127
Wyler, William, 44, 69–70, 134, 149–50, 165, 166, 180, 205, 210, 211, 298
Wyman, Jane, 73

X-M (eyeglass defogger), 113

Yale University, 400
Yankee Doodle Dandy, 211, 311, 313
Young, Clara Kimball, 367
Young, Collier, 203
Young, Gig, 109–10
Young, Loretta, 95–96, 137
Young, Nedrick, 419
Young and Innocent, 213
Young Lions, The, 437

Zahn, Johann, 429
Zanuck, Darryl, 17, 28, 29, 31–32, 48, 122, 136–39, 142, 167–69, 183, 198, 210, 236, 249, 281, 384, 406–8
Zanuck, Susan, 406
Zanuck, Virginia, 406, 407
Zimbalist, Efrem, 25
Zimmerman, John, 404
Zinnemann, Fred, 161, 164, 166, 178, 307
Zinsser, William, 140, 141, 143–44, 152
Zugsmith, Albert, 148
Zukor, Adolph, 340, 380
Zunser, Jesse, 144, 155–56

ABOUT THE AUTHOR

EZRA GOODMAN was born and educated in New York City. In the past twenty years he has worked as publicity and advertising director of the 55th Street Playhouse, New York, as publicist for Warner Brothers studio, Hollywood, as Hollywood columnist for the New York Morning Telegraph, and as Hollywood columnist and motion-picture critic for the Los Angeles Daily News. In the early 1950s he became cinema critic for Time Magazine in New York, then Hollywood correspondent for the same publication. He has written feature articles on the movies for many other newspapers and magazines. In 1958 Mr. Goodman took a six-month trip around the world. His subsequent time has been spent writing this book, which is his first. He is now writing a novel set in Los Angeles.

DATE DUE

28 DAY

OCT 2 9 2002	
DEC 3 1 2003	
FEB 1 7 2004	
SEP 0 1 2006	
MAY 5 2007	
DEC 0 8 2010	

BRODART Cat. No. 23-221

791.4 G65
Goodman, Ezra/The fifty-year decline and dewey

3 1750 00045 2709

1855

MECHANICS' INSTITUTE LIBRARY
57 POST ST., SAN FRANCISCO, CALIFORNIA 94104
PHONE 421-1750